Fodor's

Seventh New Edition

Austria

"When it comes to information on regional history, what to see and do, and shopping, these guides are exhaustive."

—*USAir Magazine*

"Usable, sophisticated restaurant coverage, with an emphasis on good value."

—Andy Birsh, *Gourmet Magazine* columnist

"Valuable because of their comprehensiveness."

—*Minneapolis Star-Tribune*

"Fodor's always delivers high quality...thoughtfully presented...thorough."

—*Houston Post*

"An excellent choice for those who want everything under one cover."

—*Washington Post*

Fodor's Travel Publications, Inc.
New York • Toronto • London • Sydney • Auckland
http://www.fodors.com/

Fodor's Austria

Editor: Robert I.C. Fisher

Area Editor: George W. Hamilton

Contributors: Robert Andrews, Alan Levy, Willibald Picard, Mary Ellen Schultz, M.T. Schwartzman (Gold Guide editor), Linda K. Schmidt, Dinah Spritzer, Earl Steinbicker, George Sullivan, Charlotte van der Reyden, Angela Walker

Creative Director: Fabrizio La Rocca

Cartographer: David Lindroth, Eureka Cartography

Cover Photograph: Uniphoto Picture Agency

Text Design: Between the Covers

Copyright

Seventh Edition

ISBN 0-679-03173-1

Special Sales

Fodor's Travel Publications are available at special discounts for bulk purchases for sales promotions or premiums. Special editions, including personalized covers, excerpts of existing guides, and corporate imprints, can be created in large quantities for special needs. For more information, contact your local bookseller or write to Special Markets, Fodor's Travel Publications, 201 East 50th Street, New York, NY 10022. Inquiries from Canada should be directed to your local Canadian bookseller or sent to Random House of Canada, Ltd., Marketing Department, 1265 Aerowood Drive, Mississauga, Ontario L4W 1B9. Inquiries from the United Kingdom should be sent to Fodor's Travel Publications, 20 Vauxhall Bridge Road, London, England SW1V 2SA.

PRINTED IN THE UNITED STATES OF AMERICA

10 9 8 7 6 5 4 3 2 1

CONTENTS

Maps

ON THE ROAD WITH FODOR'S

WE'RE ALWAYS THRILLED to get letters from readers, especially one like this:

It took us an hour to decide what book to buy and we now know we picked the best one. Your book was wonderful, easy to follow, very accurate, and good on pointing out eating places, informal as well as formal. When we saw other people using your book, we would look at each other and smile.

Our editors and writers are deeply committed to making every Fodor's guide "the best one"—not only accurate but always charming, brimming with sound recommendations and solid ideas, right on the mark in describing restaurants and hotels, and full of fascinating facts that make you view what you've traveled to see in a rich new light.

About Our Writers

Our success in achieving our goals—and in helping to make your trip the best of all possible vacations—is a credit to the hard work of our extraordinary writers and editors.

Even before **George W. Hamilton** first arrived in Vienna in 1960, his heart would beat in three-quarter time whenever he heard the intoxicating waltzes of Johann Strauss. Falling in love with the Austrian captial, George found a handy excuse to become a resident: he settled in as manager of the recording studio of the Vienna Symphony Orchestra. Along the way, our longtime area editor has helped found the orchestra's renowned Johann Strauss Ensemble and even discovered unrecorded waltzes. Among his favorite times in Austria are those brilliant spring days when the not-so-blue Danube manages to turn the proper Straussian shade. Music is not the only Austrian specialty George appreciates. His direct experience as hotelier and restaurateur served as the basis for the critical evaluations found in this guide's dining and lodging sections. "Whenever I pick up a cookbook on Austrian cuisine, I first check the recipe for goulash," he chuckles. "If it says anything other than equal parts onion and meat, the book is bogus." Today, as a reporter for the *Economist* and the *Financial Times* research units specializing in travel and economics, he loves to dine out with guests at the Vier Jahreszeiten or—for a more *gemütlich* evening—at the atmospheric Ofenloch.

"To the age, its art; To art, its freedom" was the motto of the famous Vienna Secession group, and **George Sullivan** firmly believes in this maxim, as any reader of our Vienna tours can vouch. The history, art, and architecture of European cities have been his favorite subject since he spent a college summer in London many years ago. A native of Virginia, he gets to Europe as often as he can (he's also written about Florence for Fodor's) and is currently working on an architectural guide to Rome. Austria—the country that gave us "Silent Night, Holy Night"—is never too far from his thoughts: in addition to his writing assignments, he helps run his family's Christmas-tree farm.

Like a true Viennese, **Willibald Picard** believes that coffee drinking is a life's work. Updating our Vienna chapter, he rarely could resist stopping into his favorite coffeehouses, the Frauenhuber and the Haag, for a Mazagran—a glass of iced mocha topped with a maraschino cherry—and, of course, for the latest city news and gossip. A free-lance writer and art historian, Willibald also assisted our area editor in tackling the Eastern Austria and Danube Valley chapters. Considering the number of mountains he hiked up and down, he feels writing for Fodor's should be considered an Olympic track event.

When **Charlotte van der Reyden** first explored the beautiful district of the Salzkammergut, she thought the color of the lakes out-sapphired the gems at Tiffany's back home in New York City. Updater of the Salzberg and Salzkammergut chapters, she particularly loves Alt-Aussee, which many people-in-the-know—in years past, these have included Brahms, Freud, and the Counts of Hohenlohe—consider the most idyllic forgetaway in Austria. A highpoint of her Salzberg stay was attending a performance of *The Marriage of Figaro,* then walking through the Mirabell gardens which once delighted Mozart afterward.

One of **Angela Walker**'s most memorable moments living in Vienna was the night she spent at the Lawyer's Ball at the Hofburg palace, whirling around the dance floor in the same ballroom where Elisabeth—the legendary Habsburg empress—once waltzed. Most of her evenings, however, were spent at the Opera House, listening to the likes of José Carreras and Jessye Norman. She left Vienna far behind, however, while revamping our Vorarlberg, Carinthia, Tirol, and Eastern Alps chapters. A native of Maryland, she spends part of each year in Europe and has been a reporter for the *Washington Post* and *Associated Press.*

Robert I.C. Fisher—editor of *Austria '96,* art history buff, and Mozart-worshipper—toasts the Austria team with a hearty *"Prosit"* (cheers). Robert comes to Austria via the legends of Hollywood—such films as Disney's *Miracle of the White Stallions* (the famed Lippizaners) and *Almost Angels* (on the Vienna Boys Choir), and, of course, *The Sound of Music.* He urges readers to discover the perfect antidote for the high sugar content of the Rodgers and Hammerstein musical: the inspiring book, written by Baroness von Trapp—the real Maria—that served as the basis for the film. The *Story of the Trapp Family Singers* is filled with great good nature and wit, and for travelers, there could be no better introduction to the endearing qualities of the Austrian people.

Danke, vielen Dank (Many thanks) to the directors of the Austrian National Tourist Offices in Vienna and in New York—especially Tony Winkler and Gabriele Wolf—and the individual tourist offices for each of the provinces for their generous and considerable assistance in preparing this new edition. Frau Altendorfer of the Salzberg Tourist Office and Roswitha von Baltz of the Salzkammergut Tourist Office were particularly helpful.

New This Year

This year we've reformatted our guides to make them easier to use. Each chapter of *Austria* begins with brand-new recommended itineraries to help you decide what to see in the time you have; a section called When to Tour points out the optimal time of day, day of the week, and season for your journey. You may also notice our fresh graphics, new in 1996. More readable and more helpful than ever? We think so—and we hope you do, too.

Like an intricate painting, Vienna takes careful study to fully appreciate its myriad wonders. To help you do that, we've dramatically expanded our Vienna chapter to uncover the city in a new way—from its broad, rough strokes down to the tiniest details that will capture the most demanding traveler's interest. We begin with an introduction that lets you in on the big picture, then introduce each neighborhood section and suggest—in A Good Walk—a wonderful way to discover it. Finally, we present all the neighborhood sights alphabetically. To allow you the delights of free-form touring, this helps you design your own personalized itinerary and also allows you to find your list of must-sees in a snap.

We've also subdivided the section on side trips from Vienna into a brand new chapter; with its seductive excursions to Baden, the Wine Country, Mayerling, and the Vienna Woods, it's a true day tripper's delight. In addition, we've refocused our coverage on the Voralberg. Even though it's the smallest of Austria's federal states (with the exception of Vienna), it's so packed with pleasures and treasures—Lake Constance, the Bregenz Music Festival, the Bregenzerwald, Züürs, the Schubertiade, and Lech—the region demands expanded coverage and a chapter all to itself.

Also check out Fodor's Web site (http://www.fodors.com/), where you'll find travel information on major destinations around the world and an ever-changing array of travel-savvy interactive features.

How to Use this Book

Organization

Up front is the **Gold Guide.** Its first section, **Important Contacts A to Z,** gives addresses and telephone numbers of organizations and companies that offer destination-related services and detailed information and publications. **Smart Travel Tips A to Z,** the Gold Guide's second section, gives specific information on how to accomplish what you need to in Austria as well as tips on savvy traveling. Both sections are in alphabetical order by topic.

The Vienna and Salzberg chapters are subdivided by neighborhood; each subsection recommends a walking tour and lists sights in alphabetical order. Each regional chapter is divided by geographical area; within each area, towns are covered in logical geographical order, and attractive stretches of road and minor points of interest between them are indicated by the designation *En Route*. Throughout, Off the Beaten Path sights appear after the places from which they are most easily accessible. And within town sections, all restaurants and lodgings are grouped together. Each chapter covers exploring, then highlights regional topics such as shopping, outdoor activities and sports, dining and lodging, and nightlife and the arts.

To help you decide what to visit in the time you have, all chapters begin with recommended itineraries; you can mix and match those from several chapters to create a complete vacation. The **A to Z section** that ends all chapters covers getting there, getting around, and helpful contacts and resources.

Icons and Symbols

- ★ Our special recommendations
- ✕ Restaurant
- 🏨 Lodging establishment
- ✕🏨 Lodging establishment whose restaurant warrants a detour
- Good for kids (rubber duckie)
- ☞ Sends you to another section of the guide for more information
- ✉ Address
- ☎ Telephone number
- ⏲ Opening and closing times
- Admission prices (those we give apply only to adults; substantially reduced fees are almost always available for children, students, and senior citizens)

Numbers in white and black circles—② and ❷, for example—that appear on the maps, in the margins, and within the tours correspond to one another.

Dining and Lodging

The restaurants and lodgings we list are the cream of the crop in each price range: $$$$ Very Expensive; $$$ Expensive; $$ Moderate; $ Inexpensive. Price charts appear in the Pleasures and Pastimes section that follows each chapter introduction.

In all restaurant price charts, costs are per person for a three-course meal, with house wine, and usually including sales tax and service (but leaving an additional 5%–7% is customary). Meals in the top price categories usually include a dessert or cheese and coffee. In hotel price charts, rates are for standard double rooms, with city and state sales taxes, and service charges where applicable, during peak season (where applicable).

Hotel Facilities and Reservations

We always list the facilities that are available—but we don't specify whether they cost extra: When pricing accommodations, always ask what's included.

Today, many travelers make hotel reservations by telephone and follow-up fax. For those who decide to write, note that you will often come across hotels in this guide—generally based in smaller towns and villages—that use only postal codes (for example, A–3478) or have, in certain instances, *no* official street address at all. In such cases, simply post your letter with the hotel name, town, and Austrian province. **At all times, be sure to include the town's name when using addresses listed in the hotel reviews of this guide**—the postal code alone will not guarantee delivery. Assume that hotels operate on the **European Plan** (EP, with no meals) unless we note that they use a **full- or partial-board** plan (with some or all meals); other hotels operate on the **Continental Plan,** with a Continental breakfast daily. For complete information, inquire when booking.

A Note About Austrian Addresses

In many cases, they don't exist—to put it simply. Throughout this guide, you will find numerous churches, museums, castles, and other attractions with no discernable street address. As with hotels and restaurants, these sights often don't have definite addresses other than the postal code and town name. This is most often the case in smaller towns and villages, but this can also occur in cities. So when there is no street address listed, consult this book's map or just ask a passerby—the magic phrase is "*Entschuldigen Sie. Wo ist...?* (Excuse me. Where is...?).

Restaurant Reservations and Dress Codes

Reservations are always a good idea; we note only when they're essential or when they are not accepted. Book as far ahead as you can, and reconfirm when you get to town. Unless otherwise noted, the restaurants listed are open daily for lunch and dinner. We mention dress only when men are required to wear a jacket or a jacket and tie. Look for an overview of local habits under Dining in Smart Travel Tips A to Z and in the Pleasures and Pastimes section that follows each chapter introduction.

Credit Cards

The following abbreviations are used: **AE,** American Express; **DC,** Diners Club; **MC,** MasterCard; and **V,** Visa. Discover is not accepted outside the United States.

Don't Forget to Write

You can use this book in the confidence that all prices and opening times are based on information supplied to us at press time; Fodor's cannot accept responsibility for any errors. Time inevitably brings changes, so always confirm information when it matters—especially if you're making a detour to visit a specific place. In addition, when making reservations be sure to mention if you have a disability or are traveling with children, if you prefer a private bath or a certain type of bed, or if you have specific dietary needs or any other concerns.

Were the restaurants we recommended as described? Did our hotel picks exceed your expectations? Did you find a museum we recommended a waste of time? If you have complaints, we'll look into them and revise our entries when the facts warrant it. If you've discovered a special place that we haven't included, we'll pass the information along to our correspondents and have them check it out. So send your feedback, positive *and* negative, to the *Austria* editor at 201 East 50th Street, New York, New York 10022—and have a wonderful trip!

Karen Cure
Editorial Director

Austria

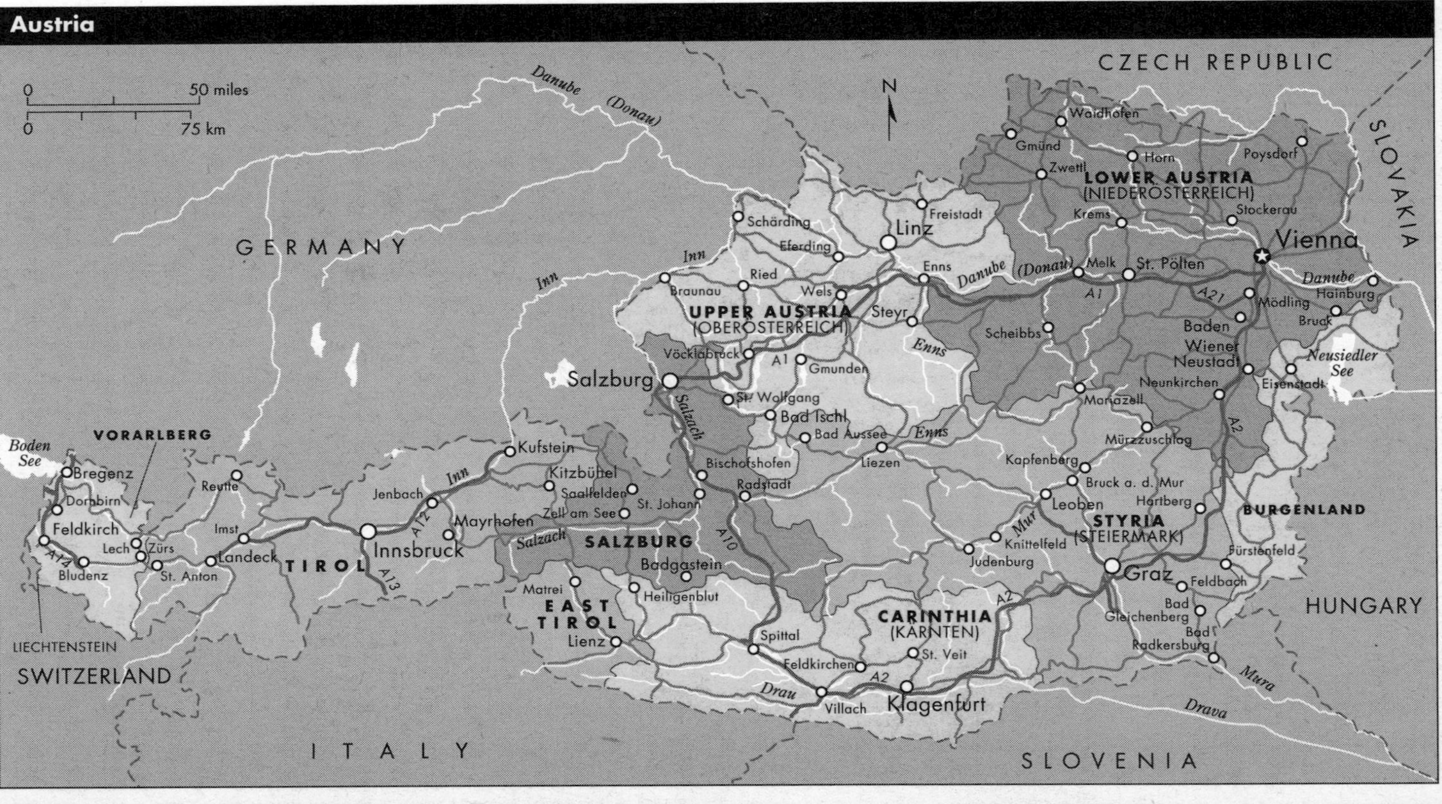
0
50 miles
0
75 km
N
CZECH REPUBLIC
SLOVAKIA
GERMANY
HUNGARY
SLOVENIA
ITALY
SWITZERLAND
LIECHTENSTEIN
LOWER AUSTRIA
(NIEDERÖSTERREICH)
UPPER AUSTRIA
(OBERÖSTERREICH)
STYRIA
(STEIERMARK)
CARINTHIA
(KÄRNTEN)
SALZBURG
TIROL
EAST
TIROL
VORARLBERG
BURGENLAND
Danube
(Donau)
Inn
Enns
Salzach
Mur
Mura
Drau
Drava
Boden
See
Neusiedler
See
Vienna
Waidhofen
Gmünd
Horn
Zwettl
Poysdorf
Krems
Stockerau
Linz
Freistadt
Schärding
Eferding
Ried
Braunau
Wels
Enns
Melk
St. Pölten
Mödling
Hainburg
Bruck
Baden
Wiener
Neustadt
Eisenstadt
Neunkirchen
Steyr
Scheibbs
Vöcklabruck
Gmunden
Salzburg
St. Wolfgang
Bad Ischl
Bad Aussee
Liezen
Mariazell
Mürzzuschlag
Kapfenberg
Bruck a. d. Mur
Leoben
Hartberg
Knittelfeld
Judenburg
Fürstenfeld
Graz
Feldbach
Bad
Gleichenberg
Bad
Radkersburg
Bischofshofen
Radstadt
St. Johann
Kufstein
Kitzbühel
Saalfelden
Zell am See
Jenbach
Mayrhofen
Innsbruck
Badgastein
Heiligenblut
Matrei
Lienz
Spittal
Feldkirchen
St. Veit
Villach
Klagenfurt
Bregenz
Dornbirn
Feldkirch
Bludenz
Lech
Zürs
St. Anton
Reutte
Imst
Landeck
A1
A2
A10
A12
A13
A14
A21

Ski Areas

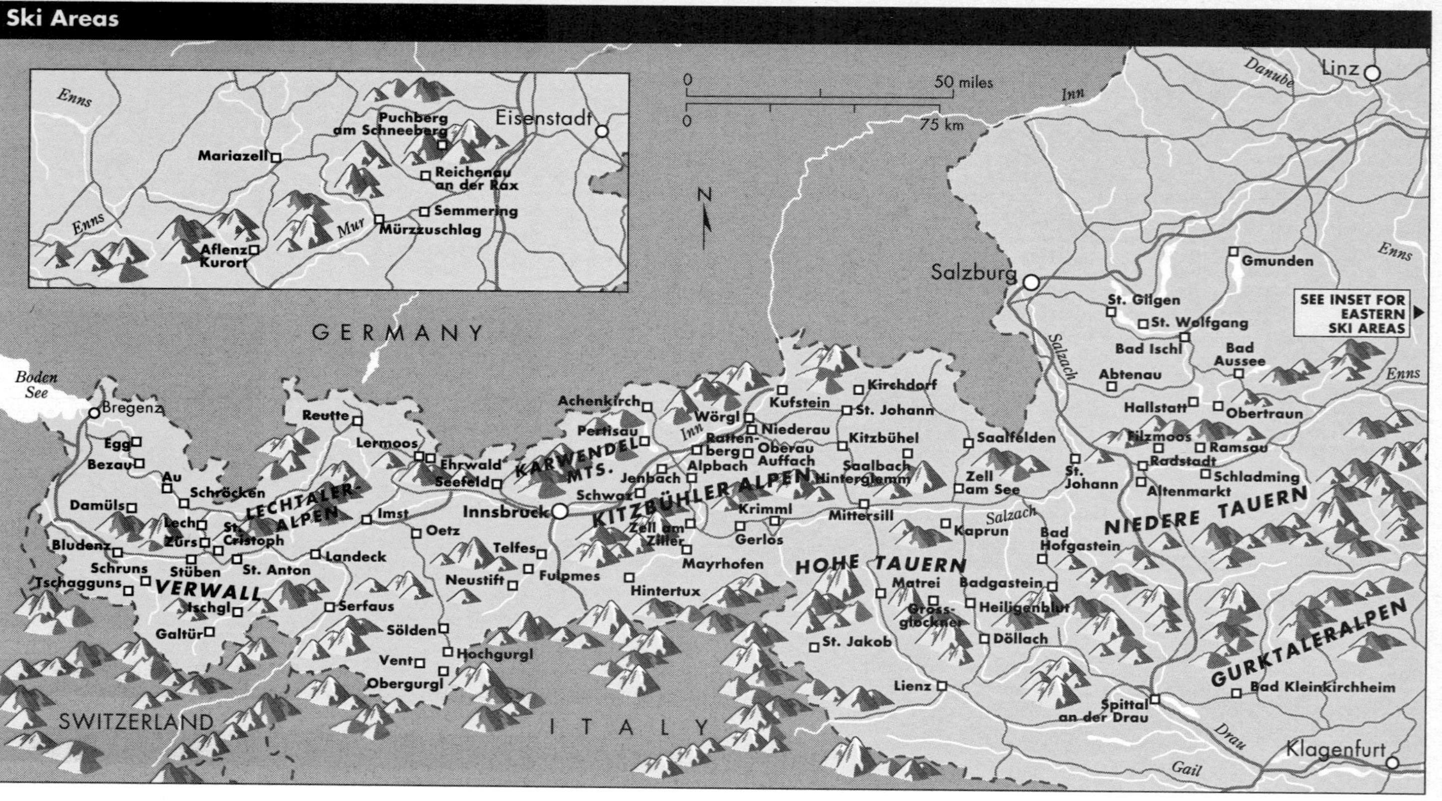
Enns
Puchberg am Schneeberg
Eisenstadt
Mariazell
Reichenau an der Rax
Semmering
Mur
Mürzzuschlag
Aflenz Kurort
0
50 miles
0
75 km
N
Danube
Linz
Inn
Salzburg
Gmunden
St. Gilgen
St. Wolfgang
Bad Ischl
Bad Aussee
SEE INSET FOR EASTERN SKI AREAS
GERMANY
Boden See
Bregenz
Egg
Bezau
Au
Schröcken
Damüls
Lech
Zürs
St. Cristoph
Bludenz
Schruns
Stüben
St. Anton
Tschagguns
VERWALL
Ischgl
Galtür
LECHTALER-ALPEN
Reutte
Lermoos
Ehrwald
Seefeld
Imst
Landeck
Oetz
Serfaus
Sölden
Vent
Hochgurgl
Obergurgl
Innsbruck
Telfes
Fulpmes
Neustift
KARWENDEL MTS.
Achenkirch
Pertisau
Jenbach
Schwaz
Wörgl
Rattenberg
Alpbach
Niederau
Oberau
Auffach
Kufstein
Kirchdorf
St. Johann
Kitzbühel
Saalbach
Hinterglemm
KITZBÜHLER ALPEN
Zell am Ziller
Mayrhofen
Hintertux
Krimml
Gerlos
Mittersill
HOHE TAUERN
Matrei
Grossglockner
St. Jakob
Lienz
Saalfelden
Zell am See
Kaprun
Salzach
Bad Hofgastein
Badgastein
Heiligenblut
Döllach
Abtenau
Hallstatt
Obertraun
Filzmoos
Radstadt
Ramsau
Schladming
Altenmarkt
St. Johann
NIEDERE TAUERN
GURKTALERALPEN
Bad Kleinkirchheim
Spittal an der Drau
Drau
Gail
Klagenfurt
SWITZERLAND
ITALY

IMPORTANT CONTACTS A TO Z

An Alphabetical Listing of Publications, Organizations, and Companies that Will Help You Before, During, and After Your Trip

Half the fun of traveling is looking forward to your trip—but when you look forward, don't just daydream. There are plans to be made, things to learn about, serious work to be done. The following organizations, books, and brochures will supplement the information in this guide book. For related information, including both basic tips on visiting Austria and background information on many of the topics below, study Smart Travel Tips A to Z, the section that follows Important Contacts A to Z. The main information numbers for the national tourist agency offices in the United States, Canada, and the United Kingdom are found under Visitor Information in Smart Travel Tips A to Z. For information on the national tourist offices in Austria itself, see the Essentials section that ends each regional chapter in this guide.

A

AIR TRAVEL

The major gateway to Austria is Vienna's Schwechat airport (☎ 011–43/1–71110), about 12 miles southeast of the city.

FLYING TIME

Flying time is 8 hours from New York, 11 hours from Chicago, and 13 hours from Los Angeles.

CARRIERS

Carriers that directly serve Austria include **Austrian Airlines** (☎ 800/843–0002), **Delta** (☎ 800/221–1212), **Lauda Air** (☎ 800/325–2832), and **Air Canada** (☎ 416/925–2311 or 800/268–7240). Many major American air carriers—such as TWA, American, and United—do not service Vienna directly; they fly passengers to major European hubs, such as London or Zurich for transfers to flights with other airlines.

FROM THE U.K.➢ **British Airways** (☎ 0181/897–4000 or 0345/222–111 outside London), **Austrian Airlines** (☎ 0171/434–7300) and **Lauda Air** (☎ 0171/630-5924) have nonstop service from London to Vienna.

COMPLAINTS

To register complaints about charter and scheduled airlines, contact the U.S. Department of Transportation's **Aviation Consumer Protection Division** (✉ C-75, Washington, DC 20590, ☎ 202/366–2220). Complaints about lost baggage or ticketing problems and safety concerns may also be logged with the **Federal Aviation Administration (FAA) Consumer Hotline** (☎ 800/322–7873).

CONSOLIDATORS

For the names of reputable air-ticket consolidators, contact the **United States Air Consolidators Association** (925 L St., Suite 220, Sacramento, CA 95814, ☎ 916/441–4166, FAX 916/441–3520). For discount air-ticketing agencies, *see* Discounts & Deals, *below*.

PUBLICATIONS

For general information about charter carriers, ask for the Department of Transportation's free brochure **"Plane Talk: Public Charter Flights"** (✉ Aviation Consumer Protection Division, C-75, Washington, DC 20590, ☎ 202/366–2220). The Department of Transportation also publishes a 58-page booklet, **"Fly Rights,"** available from the Consumer Information Center (✉ Supt. of Documents, Dept. 136C, Pueblo, CO 81009; $1.75).

For other tips and hints, consult the Consumers Union's monthly **"Consumer Reports Travel Letter"** (✉ Box 53629, Boulder, CO 80322, ☎ 800/234–1970; $39 1st year).

WITHIN AUSTRIA

Austrian carriers include **Austrian Airlines** (☎ 0222/7007-0; main Austrian office at Kärtner Ring 18, 1010

Vienna) and its subsidiary, **Austrian Air Services,** which offer service from Vienna to Linz; **Tyrolean** (another AA subsidiary) flies between Vienna and Innsbruck and to points outside Austria; and **Rheintalflug,** with service between Vienna and Altenrhein (Switzerland, near Bregenz), with bus connections for points in Vorarlberg. Winter schedules on all domestic lines depend on snow conditions.

B

BOAT TRAVEL

For current fares and schedules for boat travel on the Danube, contact your travel agent or, in Austria, the **Blue Danube Navigation** (☒ Handelskai 265, A–1020 Vienna, ☏ 0222/727–50–540). Fares vary according to the type of accommodation.

BUS TRAVEL

Austria features an extensive national network of post-office and railroad buses. In addition, some of the leading private companies in Austria are **Bundesbus** (☏ 0222/71101), **Austrobus** (☏ 022/534–11–0), **Blaguss Reisen** (☏ 022/501–80–0), and **Dr. Richard** (☏ 0222/331–00–0).

C

CAR RENTAL

The major car-rental companies represented in Austria are **Alamo** (☏ 800/327–9633; in the U.K., 0800/272–2000), **Avis** (☏ 800/331–1084; in Canada, 800/879–2847), **Budget** (☏ 800/527–0700; in the U.K., 0800/181181), **Dollar** (☏ 800/800–4000; in the U.K., 0990/565656, where it is known as Eurodollar), **Hertz** (☏ 800/654–3001; in Canada, 800/263–0600; in the U.K., 0345/555888), and **National InterRent** (sometimes known as Europcar InterRent outside North America; ☏ 800/227–3876; in the U.K., 01345/222–525). Rates in Austria begin at AS856 (about $80) a day and AS3712 (about $347) a week for an economy car with unlimited mileage. This does not include tax on car rentals, which is 20% plus a 1% contract tax. If you rent at the airport, you'll also pay a 9% surcharge. If you rent and pay before you arrive, you'll save a considerable amount of money (☞ Renting a Car *in* Smart Travel Tips A to Z, *below*).

One of the cheapest local rental firms is **Autoverleih Buchbinder** (☒ Schlachthausgasse 38, A–1030 Vienna, ☏ 0222/717–50–0, FAX 0222/717–5022, with offices throughout Austria).

RENTAL WHOLESALERS

Contact **Auto Europe** (☏ 207/828–2525 or 800/223–5555), **Europe by Car** (☏ 800/223–1516; in CA, 800/252–9401), or the **Kemwel Group** (☏ 914/835–5555 or 800/678–0678).

RVS

For RV rental, try **Gebetsroither** (☒ Brunnerstr. Industriegelände, A–2201 Hagenbrunn, ☏ 02246/4150, FAX 02246/4711) or **Sun Cruiser** (☒ Hintere Ortstr. 65, A–2325 Himberg, ☏ 02235/87550, FAX 02235/87550–83). Compare prices and be sure to reserve early.

CHILDREN & TRAVEL

BABY-SITTING

In Vienna, you can call on the baby-sitters of the **Austrian Academic Guest Service** (☒ Operngasse 24, A–1040, ☏ 0222/587–3525).

KNOW-HOW

Family Travel Times, published quarterly by Travel with Your Children (☒ TWYCH, 40 5th Ave., New York, NY 10011, ☏ 212/477–5524; $40 per year), covers destinations, types of vacations, and modes of travel.

LODGING

There's a whole town in Carinthia—it began with Austria's First Baby Hotel (☒ Trebesing Bad 1, A–9852 Trebesing, ☏ 04732/2350–0, FAX 04732/2263)—where parents accompany the babies instead of the other way around; services for the babies are incredible.

CUSTOMS

IN THE U.S.

The U.S. Customs Service (☒ Box 7407, Washington, DC 20044, ☏ 202/927–6724) can answer questions on duty-free limits and publishes a helpful brochure, "Know Before You Go." For information on registering foreign-made articles call 202/927–0540 or write U.S.

Customs Service, Resource Management, 1301 Constitution Ave. NW, Washington DC, 20229.

COMPLAINTS➤ Note the inspector's badge number and write to the commissioner's office (✉ 1301 Constitution Ave. NW, Washington, DC 20229).

CANADIANS

Contact Revenue Canada (✉ 2265 St. Laurent Blvd. S, Ottawa, Ontario K1G 4K3, ☎ 613/993–0534) for a copy of the free brochure "I Declare/Je Déclare" and for details on duty-free limits. For recorded information (within Canada only), call 800/461–9999.

U.K. CITIZENS

HM Customs and Excise (✉ Dorset House, Stamford St., London SE1 9NG, ☎ 0171/202–4227) can answer questions about U.K. customs regulations and publishes a free pamphlet, "A Guide for Travellers," detailing standard procedures and import rules.

D

DISABILITIES & ACCESSIBILITY

LOCAL INFORMATION

The Austrian National Tourist Office (☞ Visitor Information, *below*) can provide a guide to accessible Austrian hotels.

Once in Austria, check with the Österreichischer Zivilinvalidenverband (✉ Brigittenauer Lände 42, A–1200 Vienna, ☎ 0222/330–6189) for more information. The Sozialamt der Stadt Wien (✉ Gonzagagasse 23, A–1010, ☎ 0222/531–14–0) and the Vienna Tourist Office (✉ Obere Augartenstr. 40, A–1025, ☎ 0222/211–14–0) also have a booklet on Vienna hotels and a city guide for travelers with disabilities.

TRAVEL AGENCIES & TOUR OPERATORS

The Americans with Disabilities Act requires that all travel firms serve the needs of all travelers. That said, you should note that some agencies and operators specialize in making travel arrangements for individuals and groups with disabilities, among them Access Adventures (✉ 206 Chestnut Ridge Rd., Rochester, NY 14624, ☎ 716/889–9096), run by a former physical-rehab counselor.

TRAVELERS WITH MOBILITY PROBLEMS➤ Contact Flying Wheels Travel (✉ 143 W. Bridge St., Box 382, Owatonna, MN 55060, ☎ 507/451–5005 or 800/535–6790), a travel agency specializing in European cruises and tours; Hinsdale Travel Service (✉ 201 E. Ogden Ave., Suite 100, Hinsdale, IL 60521, ☎ 708/325–1335), a travel agency that benefits from the advice of wheelchair traveler Janice Perkins; and Wheelchair Journeys (✉ 16979 Redmond Way, Redmond, WA 98052, ☎ 206/885–2210 or 800/313–4751), which can handle arrangements worldwide.

TRAVELERS WITH DEVELOPMENTAL DISABILITIES➤ Contact the nonprofit New Directions (✉ 5276 Hollister Ave., Suite 207, Santa Barbara, CA 93111, ☎ 805/967–2841).

DISCOUNTS & DEALS

AIRFARES

For the lowest airfares to Austria, call 800/FLY–4–LESS.

CLUBS

Contact Entertainment Travel Editions (✉ Box 1068, Trumbull, CT 06611, ☎ 800/445–4137; $28–$53, depending on destination), Great American Traveler (✉ Box 27965, Salt Lake City, UT 84127, ☎ 800/548–2812; $49.95 per year), Moment's Notice Discount Travel Club (✉ 7301 New Utrecht Ave., Brooklyn, NY 11204, ☎ 718/234–6295; $25 per year, single or family), Privilege Card (✉ 3391 Peachtree Rd. NE, Suite 110, Atlanta, GA 30326, ☎ 404/262–0222 or 800/236–9732; $74.95 per year), Travelers Advantage (✉ CUC Travel Service, 49 Music Sq. W, Nashville, TN 37203, ☎ 800/548–1116 or 800/648–4037; $49 per year, single or family), or Worldwide Discount Travel Club (✉ 1674 Meridian Ave., Miami Beach, FL 33139, ☎ 305/534–2082; $50 per year for family, $40 single).

HOTEL ROOMS

For hotel room rates guaranteed in U.S. dollars, call Steigenberger Reservation Service (☎ 800/223–5652).

PASSES

See Train Travel *in* Smart Travel Tips A to Z, *below.*

STUDENTS

Members of Hostelling International–American Youth Hostels (☞ Students, *below*) are eligible for discounts on car rentals, admissions to attractions, and other selected travel expenses.

PUBLICATIONS

Consult ***The Frugal Globetrotter,*** by Bruce Northam (✉ Fulcrum Publishing, 350 Indiana St., Suite 350, Golden, CO 80401, ☎ 800/992–2908; $16.95 plus $4 shipping). For publications that tell how to find the lowest prices on plane tickets, *see* Air Travel, *above.*

Also see Fodor's ***Affordable Europe*** (available in bookstores, or ☎ 800/533–6478; $18.50).

DRIVING

AUTO CLUBS

Austria has two automobile clubs, ÖAMTC and ARBÖ, both of which operate motorist service patrols. You'll find emergency phones along all the key highways. Otherwise, if you have problems, call ARBÖ (☎ 123) or ÖAMTC (☎ 120) from anywhere in the country. No area or other code is needed for either number. Both clubs charge nonmembers for emergency service.

MAPS

A set of eight excellent, detailed road maps is available from the Austrian Automobile Club/ÖAMTC (Schubertring 1–3, A–1010 Vienna, ☎ 0222/711–99–55), at most service stations, and at many bookstores. The maps supplied without charge by the Austrian National Tourist Office are adequate for most needs, but if you will be covering much territory, the better ÖAMTC maps are a worthwhile investment.

E

EMERGENCIES

Important emergency numbers in Austria are 133 for 24 hour access to the police; 122 for Fire; 144 for Ambulance; 123 for ARBÖ and 120 for ÖAMTC, the two national auto clubs.

F

FERRIES

Several ferries take cars from the United Kingdom to the continent. The Sally Line ferry (☎ 01843/595566, 01843/850503) from Ramsgate takes about 2½ hours to cross to Dunkirk, about 4 to Oostende. Sailings from Felixstowe to Zeebrugge on P&O European Ferries (☎ 0181/575–8555 or 01304/203388, FAX 01304/223464) are about 6 hours; from Dover to Calais, about 1¼ hours. The best arrangement is to take a morning ferry, then stop overnight in Belgium or Germany.

G

GAY & LESBIAN TRAVEL

LOCAL INFORMATION

In Austria, key information sources are Homosexuelle Initiative (✉ Novaragasse 40, A–1020 Vienna, ☎ 0222/216–6604) and Rosa Lila Villa (✉ Linke Wienzeile 102, A–1060 Vienna, ☎ 0222/586–8150). The twice-monthly magazine Xtra! runs a calendar of daily events and addresses.

HEALTH

FINDING A DOCTOR

For its members, the International Association for Medical Assistance to Travellers (✉ IAMAT, membership free; ✉ 417 Center St., Lewiston, NY 14092, ☎ 716/754–4883; ✉ 40 Regal Rd., Guelph, Ontario N1K 1B5, ☎ 519/836–0102; ✉ 1287 St. Clair Ave. W., Toronto, Ontario M6E 1B8, ☎ 416/652–0137; ✉ 57 Voirets, 1212 Grand-Lancy, Geneva, Switzerland, no phone) publishes a worldwide directory of English-speaking physicians meeting IAMAT standards.

I

INSURANCE

IN CANADA

Contact Mutual of Omaha (✉ Travel Division, 500 University Ave., Toronto, Ontario M5G 1V8, ☎ 800/465–0267(in Canada) or 416/598-4083).

IN THE U.S.

Travel insurance covering baggage, health, and trip cancellation or interruptions is available from Access America (✉ 6600 W. Broad St., Richmond, VA 23230, ☎ 804/285–3300 or 800/334–

7525), Carefree Travel Insurance (✉ Box 9366, 100 Garden City Plaza, Garden City, NY 11530, ☎ 516/294–0220 or 800/323–3149), Near Travel Services (✉ Box 1339, Calumet City, IL 60409, ☎ 708/868–6700 or 800/654–6700), Tele-Trip (✉ Mutual of Omaha Plaza, Box 31716, Omaha, NE 68131, ☎ 800/228–9792), Travel Guard International (✉ 1145 Clark St., Stevens Point, WI 54481, ☎ 715/345–0505 or 800/826–1300), Travel Insured International (✉ Box 280568, East Hartford, CT 06128, ☎ 203/528–7663 or 800/243–3174), and Wallach & Company (✉ 107 W. Federal St., Box 480, Middleburg, VA 22117, ☎ 540/687–3166 or 800/237–6615).

IN THE U.K.

The Association of British Insurers (✉ 51 Gresham St., London EC2V 7HQ, ☎ 0171/600–3333) gives advice by phone and publishes the free pamphlet "Holiday Insurance and Motoring Abroad," which sets out typical policy provisions and costs.

L

LODGING

The Austrian National Tourist offices (☞ Visitor Information, *below*) have detailed brochures (in German) on farm and village holidays, on family apartments, and on hotels specializing in families with small children.

For information on hotel consolidators, *see* Discounts, *above.*

APARTMENT & VILLA RENTAL

Among the companies to contact are Europa-Let (✉ 92 N. Main St., Ashland, OR 97520, ☎ 541/482–5806 or 800/462–4486, FAX 541/482–0660), Hometours International (✉ Box 11503, Knoxville, TN 37939, ☎ 423/588–8722 or 800/367–4668), Interhome (✉ 124 Little Falls Rd., Fairfield, NJ 07004, ☎ 201/882–6864, FAX 201/808–1742), Rent-a-Home International (✉ 7200 34th Ave. NW, Seattle, WA 98117, ☎ 206/789–9377 or 800/488–7368, FAX 206/789–9379, rentahome-international@msn.com), and Villas International (✉ 605 Market St., Suite 510, San Francisco, CA 94105, ☎ 415/281–0910 or 800/221–2260, FAX 415/281–0919). Members of the travel club Hideaways International (✉ 767 Islington St., Portsmouth, NH 03801, ☎ 603/430–4433 or 800/843–4433, FAX 603/430–4444, info@hideaways.com; $99 per year) receive two annual guides plus quarterly newsletters and arrange rentals among themselves.

CASTLES

For accommodations in historic castles, get the catalog from Schlosshotels und Herrenhäuser in Österreich (✉ Ferdinand-Hanusch-Pl. 1, A–5020 Salzburg, ☎ 0662/846825–0, FAX 0662/846826).

FARM HOLIDAYS

Contact Farmhouse Holidays in Austria (✉ Hardtgasse 19, A–1190 Vienna, ☎ 0222/368–0111, FAX 0222/368–0111–13).

HOME EXCHANGE

Some of the principal clearinghouses are HomeLink International/Vacation Exchange Club (✉ Box 650, Key West, FL 33041, ☎ 305/294–1448 or 800/638–3841, FAX 305/294–1148; $78 per year), which sends members five annual directories, with a listing in one, plus updates; and Intervac International (✉ Box 590504, San Francisco, CA 94159, ☎ 415/435–3497, FAX 415/435–7440; $65 per year), which publishes four annual directories.

ROMANTIK HOTELS

For the coziest, most personal accommodations in elegant surroundings, some say the best options are the Romantik Hotels & Restaurants found throughout Austria. Among agents who can book are AAA travel agencies as well as Euro-Connection (✉ Box 2397, 1819 207th Place SW, Lynwood, WA 98036, ☎ 206/670–1140 or 800/645–3876), DER Tours (✉ 11933 Wilshire Blvd., Los Angeles, CA 90025, ☎ 310/479–4140 or 800/421–4343), MLT Vacations (✉ 5130 Highway 101, Minnetonka, MN 55345, ☎ 612/474–2540 or 800/362–3520, Romantik Travel and Tours (✉ 16932 Woodinville-Redmond Rd., Suite

A107, Box 1278, Woodinville, WA 98072, ☎ 206/486–9394 or 800/826–0015).

M

MONEY

ATMS

For specific foreign Cirrus locations, call 800/424–7787; for foreign Plus locations, consult the Plus directory at your local bank.

CURRENCY EXCHANGE

If your bank doesn't exchange currency, contact Thomas Cook Currency Services (☎ 800/287–7362 for locations). Ruesch International (☎ 800/424–2923 for locations) can also provide you with foreign banknotes before you leave home and publishes a number of useful brochures, including a "Foreign Currency Guide" and "Foreign Exchange Tips."

WIRING FUNDS

Funds can be wired via MoneyGram[SM] (for locations and information in the U.S. and Canada, ☎ 800/926–9400) or Western Union (for agent locations or to send money using MasterCard or Visa, ☎ 800/325–6000; in Canada, 800/321–2923; in the U.K., 0800/833833; or visit the Western Union office at the nearest major post office).

P

PASSPORTS & VISAS

IN THE U.S.

For fees, documentation requirements, and other information, call the State Department's Office of Passport Services information line (☎ 202/647–0518).

CANADIANS

For fees, documentation requirements, and other information, call the Ministry of Foreign Affairs and International Trade's Passport Office (☎ 819/994–3500 or 800/567–6868).

U.K. CITIZENS

For fees, documentation requirements, and to request an emergency passport, call the London Passport Office (☎ 0990/210410).

PHOTO HELP

The Kodak Information Center (☎ 800/242–2424) answers consumer questions about film and photography. The ***Kodak Guide to Shooting Great Travel Pictures*** (available in bookstores; or contact Fodor's Travel Publications, ☎ 800/533–6478; $16.50 plus $4 shipping) explains how to take expert travel photographs.

S

SENIOR CITIZENS

EDUCATIONAL TRAVEL

The nonprofit Elderhostel (✉ 75 Federal St., 3rd Floor, Boston, MA 02110, ☎ 617/426–7788), for people 55 and older, has offered inexpensive study programs since 1975. Courses cover everything from marine science to Greek mythology and cowboy poetry. Costs for two- to three-week international trips—including room, board, and transportation from the United States—range from $1,800 to $4,500.

Interhostel (✉ University of New Hampshire, 6 Garrison Ave., Durham, NH 03824, ☎ 603/862–1147 or 800/733–9753), for travelers 50 and older, has two- to three-week trips; most last two weeks and cost $2,000–$3,500, including airfare.

ORGANIZATIONS

Contact the American Association of Retired Persons (✉ AARP, 601 E St. NW, Washington, DC 20049, ☎ 202/434–2277; annual dues $8 per person or couple). Its Purchase Privilege Program secures discounts for members on lodging, car rentals, and sightseeing.

Additional sources for discounts on lodgings, car rentals, and other travel expenses, as well as helpful magazines and newsletters, are the National Council of Senior Citizens (✉ 1331 F St. NW, Washington, DC 20004, ☎ 202/347–8800; annual membership $12) and Sears's Mature Outlook (✉ Box 10448, Des Moines, IA 50306, ☎ 800/336–6330; annual membership $14.95).

SPORTS

Here's a quick-and-easy rundown on associations that can help you learn more about the most popular sports activities in Austria. For a complete picture on recreation in the great Austrian outdoors, *see* Sports and the Outdoors *in* Smart Travel Tips, *below,* and the section on skiing in

Pleasures & Pastimes in Chapter 1.

BALLOONING

Filzmoos in the Tirol is one of several ballooning centers. Contact the Austrian Ballooning Club (✉ Endresstr. 79/4, A–1230 Vienna, ☎ 0222/889–8222); Austrian Aero-Club (✉ Prinz Eugen-Str. 12, A–1040 Vienna, ☎ 0222/505–1028, FAX 0222/505–7923) or the Balloon Sportclub Vienna (✉ Mariahilfer Str. 41–43, A–1060 Vienna, ☎ 0222/587–8139–20).

BICYCLING

Tourist Offices have details (in German), including maps and hints for trip planning and mealtime and overnight stops. Ask for the booklet Radtouren in Österreich, or contact Austria Radreisen (✉ Fritz–Holzingerstr. 546, A–4780 Schärding, ☎ 07712/5511–0, FAX 07712/4811), which organizes cycling tours. There's also a brochure in English: "Biking Austria—On the Trail of Mozart" that provides details in English on the cycle route through the High Tauern mountains in Salzburg Province.

BOATING AND SAILING

Contact the Österreichischer Segel-Verband, the Austrian Yachting Club (✉ Grosse Neugasse 8, A–1040 Vienna, ☎ 0222/587–8688, FAX 0222/586–6171).

CAMPING

For details, check with the tourist offices of the individual Austrian provinces and with the Österreichischer Camping Club (✉ Schubertring 1–3, A–1010 Vienna, ☎ 0222/71199–1272, FAX 0222/71199–1498).

GLIDING

Contact the Austrian Aero Club (✉ Prinz Eugen-Str. 12, A–1040 Vienna, ☎ 0222/505–1028–74, FAX 0222/505–7923).

GOLF

Austrian National Tourist Offices have golfing brochures, or you can contact the Österreichischer Golfverband (✉ Prinz Eugen-Str. 12, A–1040 Vienna, ☎ 0222/505–3245–0, FAX 0222/505–4962) or Golf Green Austria (✉ Bräuhausstr. 1a, A–5020 Salzburg, ☎ 0662/827852, FAX 0662/822098).

HIKING AND CLIMBING

Tourist offices have details on hiking holidays; serious climbers can write directly to Österreichischer Alpenverein/ÖAV (✉ Austrian Alpine Club, Wilhelm-Greil-Str. 15, A–6020 Innsbruck, ☎ 0512/595470, FAX 0512/575528) for more information. Membership in the club (AS460, about $43) will give you a 50% reduction from the regular fees for overnights in the 275 mountain refuges it operates. Senior memberships have a reduced price.

British mountaineers can get details via a branch of the ÖAV (✉ 13 Longcroft House, Fretherne Rd., Welwyn Garden City, Hertfordshire AL8 6PQ, ☎ 01707/324835).

SKIING

To determine which destination, holiday plan, or ski itinerary might be best for your skills, schedule, and interest, contact the Austrian National Tourist Office or the Oesterreichischer Skiverband, or Austrian Ski Federation (✉ Olympiastr. 10, A–6020 Innsbruck, ☎ 0512/33501–22, FAX 0512/361998), which is open weekdays 8:15–noon and 1–5.

STUDENTS

HOSTELING

In the United States, contact Hostelling International–American Youth Hostels (✉ 733 15th St. NW, Suite 840, Washington, DC 20005, ☎ 202/783–6161, FAX 202/783–6171); in Canada, Hostelling International–Canada (✉ 205 Catherine St., Suite 400, Ottawa, Ontario K2P 1C3, ☎ 613/237–7884); and in the United Kingdom, the Youth Hostel Association of England and Wales (✉ Trevelyan House, 8 St. Stephen's Hill, St. Albans, Hertfordshire AL1 2DY, ☎ 01727/855215 or 01727/845047). Membership (in the U.S., $25; in Canada, C$26.75; in the U.K., £9.30) gives you access to 5,000 hostels in 77 countries that charge $5–$40 per person per night.

ORGANIZATIONS

A major contact is the Council on International Educational Exchange (Mail orders only; ✉ CIEE, 205 E. 42nd St., 16th floor,

New York, NY 10017, ☎ 212/822–2600). The Educational Travel Centre (✉ 438 N. Frances St., Madison, WI 53703, ☎ 608/256–5551 or 800/747–5551, FAX 608/256–2042) offers rail passes and low-cost airline tickets, mostly for flights that depart from Chicago.

In Canada, also contact Travel Cuts (✉ 187 College St., Toronto, Ontario M5T 1P7, ☎ 416/979–2406 or 800/667–2887).

PUBLICATIONS

Check out the ***Berkeley Guide to Germany & Austria*** (available in bookstores; or contact Fodor's Travel Publications, ☎ 800/533–6478; $19.50 plus $4 shipping).

T

TELEPHONES

The country code for Austria is 43. In Austria, the AT&T access number for the United States is 022/903–011; for MCI, 022/903–012; and for Sprint, 022/903–014. To learn about international service, including the codes you need to dial a number in Austria, contact, AT&T USADirect (☎ 800/874–4000 or 412/553–7458), MCI Call USA (☎ 800/444–4444), or Sprint Express (☎ 800/793–1153). For complete information on using phones in Austria, *see* Telephones *in* Smart Travel Tips A to Z, *below.*

TOUR OPERATORS

Among the companies that sell tours and packages to Austria, the following are nationally known, have a proven reputation, and offer plenty of options.

GROUP TOURS

SUPER-DELUXE➢ **Abercrombie & Kent** (✉ 1520 Kensington Rd., Oak Brook, IL 60521-2141, ☎ 708/954–2944 or 800/323–7308, FAX 708/954–3324), and **Travcoa** (✉ Box 2630, 2350 S.E. Bristol St., Newport Beach, CA 92660, ☎ 714/476–2800 or 800/992–2003, FAX 714/476–2538).

DELUXE➢ **Globus** (✉ 5301 S. Federal Circle, Littleton, CO 80123, ☎ 303/797–2800 or 800/221–0090, FAX 303/795–0962), **Maupintour** (✉ Box 807, 1515 St. Andrews Dr., Lawrence, KS 66047, ☎ 913/843–1211 or 800/255–4266, FAX 913/843–8351), and **Tauck Tours** (✉ Box 5027, 276 Post Rd. W, Westport, CT 06881, ☎ 203/226–6911 or 800/468–2825, FAX 203/221–6828).

FIRST-CLASS➢ **Brendan Tours** (✉ 15137 Califa St., Van Nuys, CA 91411, ☎ 818/785–9696 or 800/421–8446, FAX 818/902–9876), **Caravan Tours** (✉ 401 N. Michigan Ave., Chicago, IL 60611, ☎ 312/321–9800 or 800/227–2826), **Central Holidays** (✉ 206 Central Ave., Jersey City, NJ 07307, ☎ 201/798–5777 or 800/935–5000), **Collette Tours** (✉ 162 Middle St., Pawtucket, RI 02860, ☎ 401/728–3805 or 800/832–4656, FAX 401/728–1380), **Delta Dream Vacations** (☎ 800/872–7786), **DER Tours** (✉ 11933 Wilshire Blvd., Los Angeles, CA 90025, ☎ 310/479–4411 or 800/782–2424), **General Tours** (✉ 53 Summer St., Keene, NH 03431, ☎ 603/357–5033 or 800/221–2216, FAX 603/357–4548), **Insight International Tours** (✉ 745 Atlantic Ave., Boston MA 02111, ☎ 617/482-2000 or 800/582–8380), and **Trafalgar Tours** (✉ 11 E. 26th St., New York, NY 10010, ☎ 212/689–8977 or 800/854–0103, FAX 800/457–6644).

BUDGET➢ **Cosmos** (☞ Globus, *above*) and **Trafalgar Tours** (☞ *above*).

PACKAGES

Independent vacation packages are available from major airlines and tour operators. Contact **Austrian Airlines** (☞ Central Holidays, *above*) and **Delta Dream Vacations** (☎ 800/872–7786). Also try the companies listed under Group Tours, *above.*

FROM THE U.K.➢ Contact **First Choice** (✉ First Choice House, Peel Cross House, Peel Cross Rd., Salford, Manchester M5 2AN, ☎ 0161/745–7000) for the lakes, mountains, and cities, **Crystal Holidays** (✉ Crystal House, Arlington Rd., Surbiton, Surrey KT6 6BW), or **Thomson Holidays** (✉ Greater London House, Hampstead Rd., London NW1 7SD, ☎ 0171/707–9000) for package and activity holidays including rafting.

THEME TRIPS

Travel Contacts (✉ Box 173, Camberley, GU15 1YE, England,

☎ 127667–7217, FAX 12766–3477), which represents 150 tour operators, can satisfy travelers who have virtually any special interest.

ADVENTURE➢ For hiking, biking, skiing, and more, contact **Wilderness Travel** (✉ 801 Allston Way, Berkeley, CA 94710, ☎ 510/548–0420 or 800/368–2794, FAX 510/548–0347, info@wildernesstravel.com).

BALLOONING➢ **Buddy Bombard European Balloon Adventures** (✉ 855 Donald Ross Rd., Juno Beach, FL 33408, ☎ 407/775–0039 or 800/862–8537, FAX 407/775–7008) takes you up and away over Alpine foothills. Trips include first-class accommodations and gourmet dining.

BARGE/RIVER CRUISES➢ For cruises on the Danube and the Rhine, contact **Abercrombie & Kent** (☞ Group Tours, *above*). **KD River Cruises of Europe** (✉ 2500 Westchester Ave., Purchase, NY 10577, ☎ 914/696–3600 or 800/346–6525, FAX 914/696–0833) is another good source for trips that enable you to barge through Austria.

BICYCLING➢ For bike tours of Austria, contact **Backroads** (✉ 1516 5th St., Berkeley, CA 94710-1740, ☎ 510/577–1555 or 800/462–2848, FAX 510/527–1444, goactive@Backroads.com), **Butterfield & Robinson** (✉ 70 Bond St., Toronto, Ontario, Canada M5B 1X3, ☎ 416/864–1354 or 800/678–1147, FAX 416/864–0541), **Classic Adventures** (✉ Box 153, Hamlin, NY 14464-0153, ☎ 716/964–8488 or 800/777–8090, FAX 716/964-7297), **Euro-Bike Tours** (✉ Box 990, De Kalb, IL 60115, ☎ 800/321–6060, FAX 815/758–8851), **Himalayan Travel** (✉ 112 Prospect St., Stamford, CT 06901, ☎ 203/359–3711 or 800/225–2380, FAX 203/359–3669), and **Uniquely Europe** (✉ 2819 1st Ave., #280, Seattle, WA 98121-1113, ☎ 206/441–8682 or 800/426–3615, FAX 206/441–8862).

CHRISTMAS/NEW YEAR'S➢ Contact the **Annemarie Victory Organization** (✉ 136 E. 64th St., N.Y., N.Y. 10021, ☎ 212/486–0353) for their spectacular "New Year's Eve Ball in Vienna" excursion. This highly respected organization has been selling out this tour—which includes deluxe rooms at the Bristol, the Imperial Palace Ball, and a Konzerthaus New Year's Day concert—for ten years running. In 1996, Annemarie Victory premiered a "Christmas in Salzburg" trip, with rooms at the Goldener Hirsch and a side trip to the Silent Night Chapel in Oberndorf. **Smolka Tours** (✉ 82 Riveredge Rd., Tinton Falls, NJ 07724, ☎ 908/576–8813 or 800/722–0057) also conducts festive holiday-season tours that include concerts and gala balls.

FOOD AND WINE➢ **Herzerl Tours** (✉ 355 Lexington Ave., New York, NY 10017, ☎ 212/867–4830 or 800/684–8488, FAX 212/986–0717) specializes in Austria and offers trips focused on cooking, gardens, art, wine, and history. **I.S.T. Cultural Tours** (✉ 225 W. 34th St., #913, New York, NY 10122-0994, ☎ 212/563–1202 or 800/833–2111, FAX 212/594–6953) has study tours that explore the subtleties of Austrian culture and cuisine.

HIKING➢ **Himalayan Travel** (✉ 112 Prospect St., Stamford, CT 06901, ☎ 203/359–3711 or 800/225–2380, FAX 203/359–3669).

HISTORY AND ART➢ For tours that highlight Austria's artistic treasures, contact **Five Star Touring** (✉ 60 E. 42nd St., #612, New York, NY 10165, ☎ 212/818–9140 or 800/792–7827, FAX 212/818–9142), **I.S.T. Cultural Tours** (☞ Food and Wine, *above*), or **Smolka Tours** (☞ Christmas/New Year's, *above*). **Herzerl Tours** (☞ Food and Wine, *above*) offers tours that examine the art of Vienna in depth, and **Smithsonian Study Tours and Seminars** (✉ 1100 Jefferson Dr. SW, Room 3045, MRC 702, Washington, DC 20560, ☎ 202/357–4700, FAX 202/633–9250) often has itineraries with an Austrian emphasis.

HORSEBACK RIDING➢ **FITS Equestrian** (✉ 685 Lateen Rd., Solvang, CA 93463, ☎ 805/688–9494 or 800/666–3487, FAX 805/688–2943) leads riders through the beautiful, historical countrysides of Austria and the Czech Republic.

MOTORCYCLING➢ **Beach's Motorcycle Adventures** (✉ 2763 W. River Pkwy., Grand

Island, NY 14072-2053, ☎ 716/773–4960, FAX 716/773–5227, robbeach@buffnet.net) takes you on Alpine adventures via scenic Austrian byways.

MOUNTAIN CLIMBING➢ For climbing in the Austrian Alps, contact **Mountain Travel-Sobek** (✉ 6420 Fairmount Ave., El Cerrito, CA 94530, ☎ 510/527–8100 or 800/227–2384, FAX 510/525–7710, Info@MTSobek.com, http://www.MTSobek.com).

MUSIC➢ **Dailey-Thorp Travel** (✉ 330 W. 58th St., #610, New York, NY 10019-1817, ☎ 212/307–1555 or 800/998–4677, FAX 212/974–1420) specializes in classical music and opera programs. **I.S.T. Cultural Tours** (☞ Food and Wine, *above*) visits the cities and homes of the great classical composers and also features performances and seminars. Performing arts tickets and packages in Vienna and Salzburg are also available from **Smolka Tours** (☞ Christmas/New Year's, *above*).

TRAIN TOURS➢ **Abercrombie & Kent** (☞ Group Tours, *above*) is the American agent for the transcontinental Venice-Simplon Orient Express, which journeys through Austria. The company also offers travel (accompanied by a bellhop so that you don't have to lug your own bags) by regularly scheduled trains, with stays in first-class and deluxe hotels. For a special treat, hire your own private rail car once used by kings and heads of state. For details, contact **Le Majestic Nostalgie-Reisen** (✉ Franziskanerpl. 4, A-1010 Vienna, ☎ 0222/512–1062).

SKIING➢ For trips down the slopes contact **Value Holidays** (✉ 10224 N. Port Washington Rd., Mequon, WI 53092-5755, ☎ 414/241–6373 or 800/241–5329).

WALKING➢ Leisurely strolls through the Alps and other scenic regions are the province of **Alphorn Tours** (✉ Box 356, 5788 Rte. 202, Lahaska, PA 18931, ☎ 215/794–2577 or 800/257–4676), **Herzerl Tours** (☞ Food and Wine, *above*), and **Wilderness Travel** (☞ Adventure, *above*).

TRAIN TRAVEL

When in Austria, obtain railway information from a travel agent (or National Tourist Office) or at the rail station. For handy railway phone numbers for each region, *see* By Train *in* each chapter's Essentials section throughout this guide. For a complete rundown on the many rail passes available, and on traveling by train in Austria, *see* Train Travel *in* Smart Travel Tips A to Z, *below.*

For ticket information and reservations made in the United States, apply through your travel agent, or Rail Europe (✉ 226-230 Westchester Ave., White Plains, NY 10604, ☎ 800/848–7245 nationwide, FAX 800/432–1329; or 2087 Dundas E, Suite 105, Mississauga, Ontario L4X 1M2, ☎ 416/602–4195), DER Tours (✉ Box 1606, Des Plaines, IL 60017, ☎ 800/782–2424, FAX 800/282–7474), or CIT Tours Corp. (✉ 342 Madison Ave., Suite 207, New York, NY 10173, ☎ 212/697–2100 or 800/248–8687, FAX 212/697–1394; ☎ 310/670–4269 or 800/248–7245 in western U.S.).

FROM THE U.K.

For rail travel from the United Kingdom, contact Eurotrain (✉ 52 Grosvenor Gardens, London SW1W OAG, ☎ 0171/730–3402), which offers excellent deals for those under 26, or British Rail Travel Centers (☎ 0171/834–2345). For additional information, call DER Travel Service (☎ 0171/408–0111) or the Austrian National Tourist Office (☞ Visitor Information, *below*).

TRAVEL AGENCIES

For names of reputable agencies in your area, contact the American Society of Travel Agents (✉ ASTA, 1101 King St., Suite 200, Alexandria, VA 22314, ☎ 703/739–2782), the Association of Canadian Travel Agents (✉ Suite 201, 1729 Bank St., Ottawa, Ontario K1V 7Z5, ☎ 613/521–0474, FAX 613/521–0805) or the Association of British Travel Agents (✉ 55-57 Newman St., London W1P 4AH, ☎ 0171/637–2444, FAX 0171/637–0713).

V

VISITOR INFORMATION

Contact the **Austrian National Tourist Office.**

IN THE U.S.

✉ 500 5th Ave., 20th floor, New York, NY 10110, ☎ 212/944–6880, FAX 212/730–4568, or write to Box 1142, New York, NY 10108; ✉ 11601 Wilshire Blvd., Suite 2480, Los Angeles, CA 90025, ☎ ~~310/477–3332,~~ FAX 310/477–5141, or write to Box 491938, Los Angeles, CA 90049; ✉ 500 N. Michigan Ave., Suite 1950, Chicago, IL 60611, ☎ 312/644–8029, FAX 312/644–6526; ✉ 1300 Post Oak Blvd., Suite 1700, Houston, TX 77056, ☎ 713/850–8888, FAX 713/850–7857; ✉ 1350 Connecticut Ave. NW, Suite 501, Washington DC 20036, ☎ 202/835–8962, FAX 202/835–8960.

IN CANADA

✉ 2 Bloor St. E, Suite 3330, Toronto, Ontario M4W 1A8, ☎ 416/967–3381, FAX 416/967–4101; ✉ 1010 Sherbrooke St. W, Suite 1410, Montréal, Québec H3A 2R7, ☎ 514/849–3709, FAX 514/849–9577; ✉ 200 Granville St., Suite 1380, Granville Sq., Vancouver, British Columbia V6C 1S4, ☎ 604/683–5808 or 604/683–8695, FAX 604/662–8528.

IN THE U.K.

Austrian National Tourist Office (✉ 30 St. George St., London W1R 0AL, ☎ 0171/629–0461).

W

WEATHER

For current conditions and forecasts, plus the local time and helpful travel tips, call the Weather Channel Connection (☎ 900/932–8437; 95¢ per minute) from a Touch-Tone phone.

SMART TRAVEL TIPS A TO Z

Basic Information on Traveling in Austria and Savvy Tips to Make Your Trip a Breeze

A

AIR TRAVEL

If time is an issue, **always look for nonstop flights,** which require no change of plane. If possible, **avoid connecting flights,** which stop at least once and can involve a change of plane, even though the flight number remains the same; if the first leg is late, the second waits.

For better service, fly smaller or regional carriers, which often have higher passenger satisfaction ratings. Sometimes they have such in-flight amenities as leather seats or greater legroom, and they often have better food.

CUTTING COSTS

The Sunday travel section of most newspapers is a good place to look for deals.

MAJOR AIRLINES➢ The least-expensive airfares from the major airlines are priced for round-trip travel and are subject to restrictions. Usually you must **book in advance and buy the ticket within 24 hours** to get cheaper fares, and you may have to **stay over a Saturday night.** The lowest fare is subject to availability, and only a small percentage of the plane's total seats is sold at that price. It's smart to **call a number of airlines, and when you are quoted a good price, book it on the spot**—the same fare may not be available on the same flight the next day. Airlines generally allow you to change your return date for a $25 to $50 fee. If you don't use your ticket, you can apply the cost toward the purchase of a new ticket, again for a small charge. However, most low-fare tickets are nonrefundable. To get the lowest airfare, check different routings. If your destination has more than one gateway, compare prices to different airports.

FROM THE U.K.➢ To save money on flights, look into an APEX or Super-Pex ticket. APEX tickets must be booked in advance and have certain restrictions. Super-PEX tickets can be purchased right at the airport.

CONSOLIDATORS➢ Consolidators buy tickets for scheduled flights at reduced rates from the airlines, then sell them at prices below the lowest available from the airlines directly—usually without advance restrictions. Sometimes you can even get your money back if you need to return the ticket. Carefully read the fine print detailing penalties for changes and cancellations. If you doubt the reliability of a consolidator, **confirm your reservation with the airline.**

B

BOAT TRAVEL

For leisurely travel between Vienna and Linz or eastward across the border into Slovakia or Hungary, consider taking a Danube boat. More than 300 kilometers (187 miles) of Austria's most beautiful scenery awaits you, as you glide past castles and ruins, medieval monasteries and abbeys, and lush vineyards. One of the lovelier sections, particularly in spring, is the Wachau valley near Vienna.

Most of the immaculate white-painted craft carry about 1,000 passengers each on their three decks. As soon as you get on board, give the steward a good tip for a deck chair and ask him to place it where you will get the best views. Be sure to book cabins in advance. Day trips are also possible on the Danube, and in the Wachau you can use the boats to move from one riverside community to the next. The Eurailpass includes the DDSG network (☞ Boat Travel *in* Important Contacts A to Z), although this might change following reorganization of DDSG last year.

Hydrofoils run daily from Vienna to Bratislava in Slovakia and to Budapest in Hungary. You can travel via the Danube to the

Black Sea and back on river passenger ships.

BUS TRAVEL

Where Austrian trains don't go, buses do, and you will find the railroad and post-office buses (bright yellow for easy recognition) in the remotest regions carrying passengers as well as the mail. You can get tickets on the bus, and in the off-season there is no problem getting a seat, but on routes to favored ski areas and during holiday periods reservations are essential. Bookings can be handled at the ticket office (there's one in most towns with bus service) or by travel agents. In most communities, bus routes begin and end at or near the railroad station, making transfers easy. Increasingly, coordination of bus service with railroads means that many of the discounts and special tickets available for trains apply to buses as well.

BUSINESS HOURS

Banks in most cities are open weekdays 8–3, Thursday until 5:30 PM. Smaller bank offices close from 12:30 to 1:30. All are closed on Saturday, but you can change money at various locations (such as American Express offices on Saturday morning and major railroad stations around the clock).

Museum hours vary from city to city and museum to museum; if there's a closing day, it is usually Monday. Few Austrian museums are open at night.

In general, you'll find **shops** open weekdays from 8:30 or 9 until 6, with a lunchtime closing from noon to 1 or 1:30. In smaller villages, the midday break may run until 3. Many food stores, bakeries, and small grocery shops open at 7 or 7:30 and, aside from the noontime break, stay open until 6 or 6:30. Shops in large city centers take no noon break. On Saturday, shops stay open until noon or 1, except on the first Saturday of the month, when (except for food stores) they stay open until 5, a few until 6. Barbers and hairdressers traditionally take Monday off, but there are exceptions.

NATIONAL HOLIDAYS

All banks and shops are closed on national holidays: Jan. 1, New Year's Day; Jan. 6, Epiphany; Mar. 30–31, Easter Sunday and Monday; May 1, May Day; May 8, Ascension Day; May 18–19, Pentecost Sunday and Monday; May 29, Corpus Christi; Aug. 15, Assumption; Oct. 26, National Holiday; Nov. 1, All Saints' Day; Dec. 8, Immaculate Conception; Dec. 25–26, Christmas. Museums are open on most holidays and closed on Good Friday and Dec. 24. Banks and offices are closed on Dec. 8, but most shops are open.

C

CAR RENTAL

CUTTING COSTS

To get the best deal, **book through a travel agent who is willing to shop around.** Ask your agent to look for fly-drive packages, which also save you money, and ask if local taxes are included in the rental or fly-drive price. These can be as high as 20% in some destinations. Don't forget to find out about required deposits, cancellation penalties, drop-off charges, and the cost of any required insurance coverage.

Also **ask your travel agent about a company's customer-service record.** How has it responded to late plane arrivals and vehicle mishaps? Are there often lines at the rental counter, and—if you're traveling during a holiday period—does a confirmed reservation guarantee you a car?

Always **find out what equipment is standard** at your destination before specifying what you want; automatic transmission and air-conditioning are usually optional—and very expensive.

Be sure to **look into wholesalers**—companies that do not own their own fleets but rent in bulk from those that do and often offer better rates than traditional car-rental operations. Prices are best during off-peak periods; rentals booked through wholesalers must be paid for before you leave the United States.

INSURANCE

When driving a rented car, you are generally responsible for any damage to or loss of the rental vehicle. Before you rent, **see what coverage you already have** under the terms of your personal auto insurance policy and credit cards.

If you do not have auto insurance or an umbrella insurance policy that covers damage to third parties, purchasing CDW or LDW is highly recommended.

Collision policies that car-rental companies sell for European rentals typically do not cover stolen vehicles. Before you buy additional coverage for theft, find out if your credit card or personal auto insurance will cover the loss.

LICENSE REQUIREMENTS

In Austria your own driver's license is acceptable. An International Driver's Permit is a good idea; it's available from the American or Canadian automobile associations, or, in the United Kingdom, from the AA or RAC.

SURCHARGES

Before you pick up a car in one city and leave it in another, **ask about drop-off charges or one-way service fees,** which can be substantial. Note, too, that some rental agencies charge extra if you return the car before the time specified on your contract. To avoid a hefty refueling fee, **fill the tank just before you turn in the car**—but be aware that gas stations near the rental outlet may overcharge.

CHILDREN & TRAVEL

When traveling with children, plan ahead and **involve your youngsters as you outline your trip.** When packing, include a supply of things to keep them busy en route (☞ Children & Travel *in* Important Contacts A to Z). On sightseeing days, try to schedule activities of special interest to your children, like a trip to a zoo or a playground. If you plan your itinerary around seasonal festivals, you'll never lack for things to do. In addition, check local newspapers for special events mounted by public libraries, museums, and parks.

BABY-SITTING

For recommended local sitters, **check with your hotel desk.**

DRIVING

Car seats are required for small children. If you are renting a car, don't forget to arrange for one when you reserve. Sometimes they're free.

FLYING

As a general rule, infants under two not occupying a seat fly at greatly reduced fares and occasionally for free. If your children are two or older **ask about special children's fares.** Age limits for these fares vary among carriers. Rules also vary regarding unaccompanied minors, so again, check with your airline.

SAFETY SEATS➢ According to the FAA, it's a good idea to **use safety seats aloft** for children weighing less than 40 pounds. Airline policies vary.

FACILITIES➢ When making your reservation, **request children's meals or freestanding bassinets if you need them**; the latter are available only to those seated at the bulkhead, where there's enough legroom. If you don't need a bassinet, **think twice before requesting bulkhead seats**—the only storage space for in-flight necessities is in inconveniently distant overhead bins.

LODGING

Most hotels allow children under a certain age to stay in their parents' room at no extra charge; others charge them as extra adults. Be sure to **ask about the cutoff age.**

CUSTOMS & DUTIES

To speed your clearance through customs, keep receipts for all your purchases abroad and be ready to show the inspector what you've bought. If you feel that you've been incorrectly or unfairly charged a duty, you can appeal assessments in dispute. First ask to see a supervisor. If you are still unsatisfied, write to the port director at your point of entry, sending your customs receipt and any other appropriate documentation. The address will be listed on your receipt. If you still don't get satisfaction, you can take your case to customs headquarters in Washington.

IN AUSTRIA

Travelers over 17 coming from European countries—regardless of citizenship—may bring in duty-free 200 cigarettes or 50 cigars or 250 grams of tobacco, 2 liters of wine and 1 liter of spirits, one bottle of toilet water (approximately 300 milliliters), and 50 milliliters of perfume. These limits may be liberalized or eliminated under terms of the European Union agreement. Travelers from all other countries (such as those coming directly from the United States or Canada) may bring in twice these amounts. All visitors may bring gifts or other purchases valued at up to AS2,500 (about $235), although in practice you'll seldom be asked.

IN THE U.S.

You may bring home $400 worth of foreign goods duty-free if you've been out of the country for at least 48 hours and haven't already used the $400 allowance, or any part of it, in the past 30 days.

Travelers 21 or older may bring back 1 liter of alcohol duty-free, provided the beverage laws of the state through which they reenter the United States allow it. In addition, regardless of their age, they are allowed 100 non-Cuban cigars and 200 cigarettes. Antiques, which the U.S. Customs Service defines as objects more than 100 years old, are duty-free. Original works of art done entirely by hand are also duty-free. These include, but are not limited to, paintings, drawings, and sculptures.

Duty-free, travelers may mail packages valued at up to $200 to themselves and up to $100 to others, with a limit of one parcel per addressee per day (and no alcohol or tobacco products or perfume valued at more than $5); on the outside, the package must be labeled as being either for personal use or an unsolicited gift, and a list of its contents and their retail value must be attached. Mailed items do not affect your duty-free allowance on your return.

IN CANADA

If you've been out of Canada for at least seven days, you may bring in C$500 worth of goods duty-free. If you've been away for fewer than seven days but for more than 48 hours, the duty-free allowance drops to C$200; if your trip lasts between 24 and 48 hours, the allowance is C$50. You cannot pool allowances with family members. Goods claimed under the C$500 exemption may follow you by mail; those claimed under the lesser exemptions must accompany you.

Alcohol and tobacco products may be included in the seven-day and 48-hour exemptions but not in the 24-hour exemption. If you meet the age requirements of the province or territory through which you reenter Canada, you may bring in, duty-free, 1.14 liters (40 imperial ounces) of wine or liquor or 24 12-ounce cans or bottles of beer or ale. If you are 16 or older, you may bring in, duty-free, 200 cigarettes, 50 cigars or cigarillos, and 400 tobacco sticks or 400 grams of manufactured tobacco. Alcohol and tobacco must accompany you on your return.

An unlimited number of gifts with a value of up to C$60 each may be mailed to Canada duty-free. These do not affect your duty-free allowance on your return. Label the package "Unsolicited Gift—Value Under $60." Alcohol and tobacco are excluded.

IN THE U.K.

If your journey was wholly within European Union (EU) countries, you no longer need to pass through customs when you return to the United Kingdom. If you plan to bring back large quantities of alcohol or tobacco, check in advance on EU limits.

D

DINING

Austrians often eat up to five meals a day: a very early Continental breakfast of rolls and coffee; *Gabelfrühstück,* a slightly more substantial breakfast with eggs or cold meat—possibly even a small goulash—at mid-morning (understood to be 9, sharp); a main meal, usually served between noon and 2; afternoon *Jause* (coffee with cake) at teatime; and, unless dining out, a light supper to end the day, between 6 and 9, tending toward the later hour. Many restaurant kitchens close in the afternoon, but some post a notice saying DURCHGEHEND WARME KÜCHE, meaning that hot food is available even between regular mealtimes.

When dining out, you'll get the best value at simpler restaurants. Most post menus with prices outside. If you begin with the *Würstelstand* (sausage vendor) on the street, the next category would be the *Imbiss-Stube*, for simple, quick snacks. Many meat stores serve soups and a daily special at noon; a blackboard menu will be posted outside. A number of cafés also offer lunch, but watch the prices; some can turn out to be more expensive than restaurants. *Gasthäuser* are simple restaurants or country inns. Austrian hotels have some of the best restaurants in the country, often with outstanding chefs.

WHAT TO WEAR

If you plan to spend much time in cities or the better resorts and go to top-notch places, you will find Austrians more formal, on the whole, than Americans and Britons. While a jacket and tie are generally advised for restaurants only in the top price categories, many dining establishments smile on gentlemen in jackets and invariably seat them at better tables. For lower priced restaurants, casual-smart resort wear is fine, although in Vienna jacket and tie are preferred in the higher price–category restaurants at dinner. **When in doubt, it's best to look spiffy.** Remember that if you are going to investigate any high altitudes (and it's pretty hard not to in Austria), you will find evenings chilly even in midsummer, so carry a warm sweater.

DISABILITIES & ACCESSIBILITY

The Austria National Tourist Office in New York has a guide to Vienna for people with disabilities and a special map of the city's accessible sights. The Hilton, InterContinental, and Marriott chain hotels plus a number of smaller ones are accessible. The railroads are both understanding and helpful. If prior arrangements have been made, taxis and private vehicles are allowed to drive right to the train platform; railway personnel will help with boarding and leaving trains; and with three days' notice, a special wheelchair can be provided for getting around train corridors. If you're traveling by air, ask in advance for assistance or a wheelchair at your destination. A number of stations in the Vienna subway system have only stairs or escalators, but elevators are being added at major stations.

When discussing accessibility with an operator or reservationist, **ask detailed questions.** Are there any stairs, inside or out? Are there grab bars next to the toilet and in the shower/tub? How wide is the doorway to the room? To the bathroom? For the most extensive facilities that meet the latest legal specifications, **opt for newer accommodations,** which more often have been designed with access in mind. Older properties or ships must usually be retrofitted and may offer more limited facilities as a result. Be sure to discuss your needs before booking.

DISCOUNTS & DEALS

You shouldn't have to pay for a discount. In fact, you may already be eligible for all kinds of savings. Here are some time-honored strategies for getting the best deal.

LOOK IN YOUR WALLET

When you use your credit card to make travel purchases, you may get free travel-accident insurance, collision damage insurance, medical or legal assistance, depending on the card and bank that issued it. Visa and MasterCard provide one or more of these services, so **get a copy of your card's travel benefits.** If you are a member of the AAA or an oil-company-sponsored road-assistance plan, always ask hotel or car-rental reservationists for auto-club discounts. Some clubs offer additional discounts on tours, cruises, or admission to attractions. And don't forget that auto-club membership entitles you to free maps and trip-planning services.

SENIORS CITIZENS & STUDENTS

As a senior-citizen traveler, you may be eligible for special rates, but you should mention your senior-citizen status up front. Students or those under 26 can also get discounts, especially if you have an official ID card (☞ Senior-Citizen Discounts *and* Students on the Road, *below*).

DIAL FOR DOLLARS

To save money, **look into "1-800" discount reservations services,** which often have lower rates. These services use their buying power to get a better price on hotels, airline tickets, and sometimes even car rentals. When booking a room, **always call the hotel's local toll-free number (if one is available) rather than the central reservations number**—you'll often get a better price. Ask the reservationist about special packages or corporate rates, which are usually available even if you're not traveling on business.

GET A GUARANTEE

When shopping for the best deal on hotels and car rentals, look for guaranteed exchange rates, which protect you against a falling dollar. With your rate locked in, you won't pay more even if the price goes up in the local currency.

DRIVING

The Austrian highway network is excellent, and roads are well maintained and well marked. Secondary roads may be narrow and winding. The main through routes (autobahns) are packed during both Austrian and German school holidays, as well as on weekends in summer. As a nod to the environment, less salt is being used on highways in winter, but few drivers seem to take heed of the greater hazard. **Remember that in winter you will need snow tires and often chains,** even on well-traveled roads. Austrians are aggressive drivers and are inclined to take chances; drive defensively.

RULES OF THE ROAD

Tourists from EU countries may bring their cars to Austria with no documentation other than the normal registration papers and their regular driver's license. A Green Card, the international certificate of insurance, is recommended for EU drivers and compulsory for others. All cars must carry a first-aid kit and a red warning triangle (obtainable at border crossings or from the Automobile Club; ☞ Driving *in* Important Contacts A to Z) to use in case of accident or breakdown.

The minimum driving age in Austria is 18, and children under 12 years must ride in the back seat; smaller children require a restraining seat. **Note that passengers in the front seats must use seat belts.** Vehicles coming from the right have the right of way, except that at unregulated intersections streetcars coming from either direction have the right of way. No turns are allowed on red.

Unless otherwise marked, the speed limit on autobahns is 130 kph (80 mph), although this is not strictly enforced. On other highways and roads, the limit is 100 kph (62 mph), 80 kph (49 mph) for RVs or cars pulling a trailer weighing more than 750 kilos (about 1,650 lbs). In built-up areas, a 50 kph (31 mph) limit applies and is likely to be taken seriously.

GASOLINE

Gasoline is readily available, but on Sunday rural stations may be closed. Stations carry only unleaded (bleifrei) gas, both regular and premium (super). Diesel fuel may not be easy to find off the beaten path. Gasoline prices are the same throughout the country, slightly lower at discount and self-service stations. Expect to pay about AS11 per liter for regular, AS12.50 for premium. Oil in Austria is expensive, retailing at AS50–AS80 per liter.

FROM THE U.K.

The best way to reach Austria by car from England is to take a North Sea/Cross Channel ferries to Oostende or Zeebrugge in Belgium or Dunkirk in northern France. An alternative is the Channel Tunnel; motoring clubs can give you the best routing to tie into the continental motorway network. Then take the toll-free Belgian motorway (E5) to Aachen, and head via Stuttgart to Innsbruck and the Tirol (A61, A67, A5, E11, A7) or east by way of Nürnberg and Munich, crossing into Austria at Walserberg and then on to Salzburg and Vienna. Total distance to Innsbruck is about 1,100 kilometers (650 miles); to Vienna, about 1,600 kilometers (1,000 miles). The most direct way to Vienna is virtually all on the autobahn via Nürnberg, Regensburg, and Passau, entering Austria at Schärding. In summer, border delays are much shorter at Schärding than at Salzburg. The trip to Innsbruck via this route will take 2–3 days.

If this seems like too much driving, in summer you can put the car on a train in s'Hertogenbosch in central southern Netherlands on Thursday, or in Schaerbeek (Brussels) on Friday, for an overnight trip, arriving in Salzburg early the following morning and in Villach three hours later. DER Travel Service (✉ 18 Conduit St., London W1R 9TD, ☎ 0171/290–0111, FAX 0171/629–7442) has details of fares and schedules.

H

HEALTH

No special shots are required before visiting Austria, but if you will be cycling or hiking through the eastern or southeastern parts of the country, **get inoculated against encephalitis**; it can be carried by ticks.

I

INSURANCE

Travel insurance can protect your monetary investment, replace your luggage and its contents, or provide for medical coverage should you fall ill during your trip. Most tour operators, travel agents, and insurance agents sell specialized health-and-accident, flight, trip-cancellation, and luggage insurance as well as comprehensive policies with some or all of these coverages. Comprehensive policies may also reimburse you for delays due to weather—an important consideration if you're traveling during the winter months. Some health-insurance policies do not cover preexisting conditions, but waivers may be available in specific cases. Coverage is sold by the companies listed in Important Contacts A to Z, *above*; these companies act as the policy's administrators. The actual insurance is usually underwritten by a well-known name, such as The Travelers or Continental Insurance.

Before you make any purchase, review your existing health and homeowner's policies to find out whether they cover expenses incurred while traveling.

BAGGAGE

Airline liability for baggage is limited to $1,250 per person on domestic flights. On international flights, it amounts to $9.07 per pound or $20 per kilogram for checked baggage (roughly $640 per 70-pound bag) and $400 per passenger for unchecked baggage. Insurance for losses exceeding the terms of your airline ticket can be bought directly from the airline at check-in for about $10 per $1,000 of coverage; note that it excludes a rather extensive list of items, shown on your airline ticket.

COMPREHENSIVE

Comprehensive insurance policies include all the coverages described above plus some that may not be available in more specific policies. If you have purchased an expensive vacation, especially one that involves travel abroad, comprehensive insurance is a must; **look for policies that include trip delay insurance,** which will protect you in the event that weather problems cause you to miss your flight, tour, or cruise. A few insurers will also sell you a waiver for preexisting medical conditions. Some of the companies that offer both these features are Access America, Carefree Travel, Travel Insured International, and TravelGuard (☞ Insurance *in* Important Contacts A to Z).

FLIGHT

You should **think twice before buying flight insurance.** Often purchased as a last-minute impulse at the airport, it pays a lump sum when a plane crashes, either to a beneficiary if the insured dies or sometimes to a surviving passenger who loses his or her eyesight or a limb. Supplementing the airlines' coverage described in the limits-of-liability paragraphs on your ticket, it's expensive and basically unnecessary. Charging an airline ticket to a major credit card often automatically provides you with coverage that may also extend to travel by bus, train, and ship.

U.K. TRAVELERS

You can buy an annual travel insurance policy valid for most vacations during the year in which it's purchased. If you are pregnant or have a preexisting medical condition make sure you're covered before buying such a policy.

TRIP

Without insurance, you will lose all or most of your money if you cancel your trip regardless of the reason. Especially if your airline ticket, cruise, or package tour is nonrefundable and cannot be changed, it's essential that you buy **trip-cancellation-and-interruption insurance.** When considering how much coverage you need, look for a policy that will cover the cost of your trip plus the nondiscounted price of a one-way airline ticket should you need to return home early. Read the fine print carefully, especially sections that define "family member" and "preexisting medical conditions." Also **consider default or bankruptcy insurance,** which protects you against a supplier's failure to deliver. Be aware, however, that if you buy such a policy from a travel agency, tour operator, airline, or cruise line, it may not cover default by the firm in question.

L

LANGUAGE

German is the official national language in Austria. In larger cities and in most resort areas, you will usually have no problem finding people who speak English; hotel staffs in particular speak it reasonably well, and many young Austrians speak it at least passably. However, travelers do report that they often find themselves in stores, restaurants, and railway and bus stations where it's hard to find someone who speaks English—so **it's best to have some native phrases up your sleeve** (*see* the vocabulary section in the back of this book). **Note that all public announcements on trains and buses are in German,** so if you have any questions, try to get answers before boarding.

LODGING

You can live like a king in a real castle in Austria or get by on a modest budget. Starting at the lower end, you can find a room in a private house or on a farm, or dormitory space in a youth hostel. Next up the line come the simpler pensions, many of them identified as *Frühstückspension,* meaning bed-and-breakfast. Then come the *Gasthäuser,* the simpler country inns. The fancier pensions in the cities can often cost as much as hotels; the difference lies in the services they offer. Most pensions, for example, do not staff the front desk around the clock. Among the hotels, you can find accommodations ranging from the most modest, with a shower and toilet down the hall, to the most elegant, with every possible amenity.

Austria has few very expensive ($$$$) hotels outside Vienna, Salzburg, and the major resorts, but has numerous expensive ($$$) ones, usually with swimming pools—sometimes indoor and outdoor—saunas, fitness rooms, and other amenities. The moderate ($$) accommodations in country areas or smaller cities and towns are generally more than adequate: Food, service, and cleanliness are of high standards. The newer inexpensive ($) seasonal hotels have private showers. *See* Lodging *in* individual chapters for prices, which vary widely among large cities, resorts, and small country towns, as well as in peak season and in low. Outside of the largest cities, Austria remains a country of smaller innkeepers, often family operations. This fact opens the way for a warm relationship with owners and staff, adding to the pleasures of a vacation.

Assume that hotels operate on the European Plan (EP, with no meals) unless we note differently. Most hotels—except the most expensive options—include a free breakfast. In rural and resort areas, however, some hotels opt for half-board basis (breakfast and one meal a day must be taken), particularly in the Western Alps region—we note if this is the case in our reviews. Top resort hotels throughout the country can insist on half or even full board in peak season; at other times, you can set your own terms.

All hotel prices include service charges (usually 10% but occasionally higher) and federal and local taxes—and in a few places, a small local tourism tax is added later. Some country hotels may add a heating supplement in winter.

APARTMENT & CHALET RENTAL

If you want a home base that's roomy enough for a family and comes with cooking facilities, **consider taking a furnished rental.** This can also save you money, but not always—some rentals are luxury properties (economical only when your party is large). Home-exchange directories list rentals—often second homes owned by prospective house swappers—and some services search for a house or apartment for you (even a castle if that's your fancy) and handle the paperwork. Some send an illustrated catalog; others send photographs only of specific properties, sometimes at a charge; up-front registration fees may apply.

M

MAIL

Within Europe, all mail goes by air, so there's no supplement on letters or postcards. A letter of up to 20 grams (about ¾ ounce) takes AS7, a postcard AS6. To the United States or Canada, a letter of up to 20 grams takes AS10 minimum, plus AS1.50 per 5 grams for airmail. If in doubt, mail your letters from a post office and have the weight checked. The Austrian post office also adheres strictly to a size standard; if your letter or card is outside the norm, you'll have to pay a surcharge. Postcards via airmail to the United States or Canada need AS8.50. Post offices have air-letter (aerogram) forms for AS12 to any overseas destination.

RECEIVING MAIL

When you don't know where you'll be staying, American Express mail service is a great convenience, with no charge to anyone either holding an American Express credit card or carrying American Express traveler's checks. Offices are at ✉ Kärntner Str. 21–23, A–1015 Vienna, ☎ 0222/515–40–0; ✉ Mozartpl. 5, A–5020 Salzburg, ☎ 0662/8080–0; ✉ Brixner Str. 3, A–6020 Innsbruck, ☎ 0512/582491–0; and ✉ Bürgerstr. 14, A–4021 Linz, ☎ 0732/669013. You can also have mail held at any Austrian post office; letters should be marked Poste Restante or Postlagernd. You will be asked for identification when you collect mail. In Vienna, if not addressed to a specific district post office, this service is handled through the main post office (✉ Fleischmarkt 19, A–1010 Vienna, ☎ 0222/515–09–0).

MEDICAL ASSISTANCE

No one plans to get sick while traveling, but it happens, so **consider signing up with a medical assistance company.** These outfits provide referrals, emergency evacuation or repatriation, 24-hour telephone hot lines for medical consultation, cash for emergencies, and other personal and legal assistance. They also dispatch medical personnel and arrange for the relay of medical records.

MONEY

The Austrian unit of currency is the schilling (AS), subdivided into 100 groschen. At press time (spring 1996), the exchange rate was about AS10.4 to the dollar, AS15.9 to the pound sterling. These rates can and will vary. The schilling is pegged to the German mark at a constant 7-to-1 ratio.

There are Austrian coins for 5, 10, and 50 groschen and for 1, 5, 10, and 20 schillings. The paper notes have AS20, AS50, AS100, AS500, AS1,000, and AS5,000 face value. There is little visible difference between the 100- and 500-schilling notes; **be careful, since confusion could be expensive!** Legally, foreign exchange is limited to licensed offices (banks and exchange offices); in practice, the rule is universally ignored.

ATMS

CASH ADVANCES➢ Before leaving home, **make sure that your credit cards have been programmed for ATM use in Austria.** Note that Discover is usually not accepted in Austria. Local bank cards often do not work overseas either; ask your bank about a Visa debit card, which works like a bank card but can be used at any ATM displaying a Visa logo. In Europe, travelers report that cash cards often only access checking, and not savings, accounts back home.

TRANSACTION FEES➢ Although fees charged for ATM transactions may be higher abroad than at home, Cirrus and Plus exchange rates are excellent, because they are based on wholesale rates offered only by major banks.

COSTS

A cup of coffee in a café will cost about AS25; a half-liter of draft beer, AS27–40; a glass of wine, AS35; a Coca-Cola, AS25; an open-face sandwich, AS25; a mid-range theater ticket AS200; a concert ticket AS250–500; an opera ticket AS600 upwards; a 1-mile taxi ride, AS35. Outside the hotels, laundering a shirt costs about AS30; dry cleaning a suit costs around AS130–140; a dress, AS100–120. A shampoo and set for a woman will cost around AS350–450, a manicure about AS150–180; a man's haircut (without shampoo) will cost about AS200–250.

CREDIT CARDS

Credit cards are only slowly coming into widespread use, so figure on generally using travelers checks and having some cash available. Most Austrian travel agencies still take only Diner's Club cards, if any, the standard exception being American Express's own travel offices. Of the major credit cards, the most widely accepted are Visa, MasterCard, and American Express. Some establishments may refuse cards for small amounts; others may accept cards grudgingly.

EXCHANGING CURRENCY

For the most favorable rates, **change money at post offices or banks.** You won't do as well at exchange booths in airports or rail and bus stations, in hotels, in restaurants, or in stores, although you may find their hours more convenient. To avoid lines at airport exchange booths, **get a small amount of the local currency before you leave home.**

TRAVELER'S CHECKS

Whether or not to buy traveler's checks depends on where you are headed; **take cash to rural areas and small towns, traveler's checks to cities.** The most widely recognized checks are issued by American Express, Citicorp, Thomas Cook, and Visa. These are sold by major commercial banks for 1%–3% of the checks' face value—it pays to shop around. Both American Express and Thomas Cook issue checks that can be countersigned and used by either you or your traveling companion. So you won't be left with excess foreign currency, **buy a few checks in small denominations** to cash toward the end of your trip. Before leaving home, contact your issuer for information on where to cash your checks without incurring a transaction fee. Record the numbers of all your checks, and keep this listing in a separate place, crossing off the numbers of checks you have cashed.

WIRING MONEY

For a fee of 3%–10%, depending on the amount of the transaction, you can have money sent to you from home through MoneyGram[SM] or Western Union (☞ Money Matters *in* Important Contacts A to Z). The transferred funds and the service fee can be charged to a MasterCard or Visa account.

P

PACKING FOR AUSTRIA

Austrians dress conservatively; slacks on women are as rare as loud sport shirts are on men. That noted, jeans are ubiquitous in Austria as everywhere, but are considered inappropriate at concerts (other than pop) or formal restaurants. For concerts and opera, women may want a skirt or dress, and men a jacket; even in summer, gala performances at small festivals tend to be dressy. And since an evening outside at a *Heuriger* (wine garden) may be on your agenda, be sure to take a sweater or light wrap. Unless you're staying in an expensive hotel or will be in one place for more than a day or two, **take hand-washables;** laundry service gets complicated. Austria is a walking country, in cities and mountains alike. So **pack sturdy, comfortable shoes.** You'll need flat heels to cope with the cobblestones.

Mountainous areas are bright, so **bring sunscreen lotion,** even in winter. Consider packing a small folding umbrella; Salzburg, especially, is noted for its brief but sudden deluges. Bring an extra pair of eyeglasses or contact lenses in your carry-on luggage, and if you have a health problem, **pack enough medication** to last the trip or have your doctor write you a prescription using the drug's generic name, because brand names vary from country to country (you'll then need a duplicate prescription from a local doctor). It's important that you **don't put prescription drugs or valuables in luggage to be checked,** for it could go astray. To avoid problems with customs officials, carry medications in the original packaging. Also, don't forget the addresses of offices that handle refunds of lost traveler's checks.

ELECTRICITY

To use your U.S.–purchased electric-powered equipment, **bring a converter and an adapter.** The electrical current in Austria is 220 volts, 50 cycles alternating current (AC); wall outlets take continental-type plugs, with two round prongs.

If your appliances are dual-voltage, you'll need only an adapter. Hotels sometimes have 110-volt outlets for low-wattage appliances near the sink, marked FOR SHAVERS ONLY; don't use them for high-wattage appliances like blow-dryers. If your laptop computer is older, carry a converter; new laptops operate equally well on 110 and 220 volts, so you need only an adapter.

PASSPORTS & VISAS

If you don't already have one, get a passport. It is advisable that you leave one photocopy of your passport's data page with someone at home and keep another with you, separated from your passport, while traveling. If you lose your passport, promptly call the nearest embassy or consulate and the local police; having the data page information can speed replacement.

IN THE U.S.

All U.S. citizens, even infants, need only a valid passport to enter Austria for stays of up to three months. Application forms for both first-time and renewal passports are available at any of the 13 U.S. Passport Agency offices and at some post offices and courthouses. Passports are usually mailed within four weeks; allow five weeks or more in spring and summer.

CANADIANS

You need only a valid passport to enter Austria for stays of up to three months. Passport application forms are available at 28 regional passport offices, as well as post offices and travel agencies. Whether for a first or a renewal passport, you must apply in person. Children under 16 may be included on a parent's passport but must have their own to travel alone. Passports are valid for five years and are usually mailed within two to three weeks of application.

U.K. CITIZENS

Citizens of the United Kingdom need only a valid passport or EU identity card with photograph to enter Austria. Applications for new and renewal passports are available from main post offices and at the passport offices in Belfast, Glasgow, Liverpool, London, Newport, and Peterborough. You may apply in person at all passport offices, or by mail to all except the London office. Children under 16 may travel on an accompanying parent's passport. All passports are valid for 10 years. Allow a month for processing.

S

SENIOR-CITIZEN DISCOUNTS

Austria has so many senior citizens that facilities almost everywhere cater to the needs of older travelers, with discounts for rail travel and museum entry. Check with the Austrian National Tourist Office to find what form of identification is required, but generally if you're 65 or over (women 62), once you're in Austria the railroads will issue you a Seniorenpass (you'll need a passport photo and passport or other proof of age) entitling you to the senior citizen discounts regardless of nationality.

To qualify for age-related discounts, **mention your senior-citizen status up front** when booking hotel reservations, not when checking out, and before you're seated in restaurants, not when paying the bill. Note that discounts may be limited to certain menus, days, or hours. When renting a car, **ask about promotional car-rental discounts**—they can net even lower costs than your senior-citizen discount.

SPORTS AND THE OUTDOORS

The Austrians are great sports lovers and go in en masse for a greater variety of sports than any other European nation. At a snowflake's notice, half the population will take to their skis; in summer, water sports are just as popular. The reason is simple: the scenic splendor of Austria makes her an ideal country in which to live an outdoor life. Unrivaled Alpine scenery, hundreds of lakes, mountain streams and dense woodlands—for the most part off the beaten track and yet easily accessible by train and bus—offer a myriad selection of alfresco sports activities. In a country celebrated for being Europe's largest reserve of unpolluted air, travelers will delight in many sports, ranging from bicycling to mountain climbing to sailing. In the summer you'll find Austrians hiking, canoeing, swimming, gliding, and playing soccer. In the wintertime, of course, skiing is the main attraction, and every Austrian, young and old, may be seen getting about with astonishing speed and skill on his Brettl. For an introductory overview on this Austrian pastime, **read the section on skiing in Pleasures and Pastimes** in Chapter 1.

In addition to skiing, skating and tobogganing are two sports that help transform Austria into a Winter Wunderland for all-out active-types, and these sports can be indulged in nearly everywhere in Austria. To top off an active day in snow country, don't forget to try a sleigh ride, a delightfully romantic option at some of the chicer resorts. This can be great fun on a moonlit evening after dinner. The winter sports season starts in December and lasts until the end of April.

The water-sports season, obviously, has its peak in July and August when the beaches of the Carinthian lakes and Lake Constance are positively swarming with swimmers. The waters of the beautiful Salzkammergut lakes are cooler, but they have just as much sailing and boating. **Remember that reservations are a must in the main summer and winter resorts during the peak seasons.**

New sports attractions are appearing; golf, for example, is becoming more common, and snowboarding is sweeping the winter slopes. National Tourist Offices have information on many specific sports; for specific sports organizations, *see* Sports *in* Important Contacts A to Z, *above*.

BICYCLING

Cyclists couldn't ask for much more than the new cycle track that runs the length of the Danube or the many cycling routes that crisscross the country, major cities included. You can rent a bicycle for AS100 per day (AS50, if you have a rail ticket in your hand) at any of about 100 railroad stations throughout the country and return it to another. With an all-day ticket (AS30), you can take your bike on the train with you anywhere in the country.

BOATING AND SAILING

Small boats can be rented on all the lakes of the Salzkammergut region and on the large lakes in Carinthia. You can rent a rowboat on almost all of Austria's lakes and on the side arms of the Danube (Alte Donau and the Donauinsel) in Vienna.

Windsurfing (Windsegeln) is extremely popular, particularly on the Neusiedler See in Burgenland, the Attersee in Upper Austria, and on the side arms of the Danube in Vienna. There are schools at all these locations with lessons and rentals.

CAMPING

If your idea of a good holiday is the "great outdoors" and if you purse is a slender one, a camping holiday may be just the thing for you. Austrians love the idea and there are practically as many tourists under canvas as in the hotels and Gasthäuser. You'll find more than 450 campsites throughout the country, usually run by regional organizations, a few private. Most have full facilities, often including swimming pools and snack bars or grocery shops. Charges average about AS200 per day for a family of three, depending on the location and the range and quality of services offered. Many campsites have a fixed basic fee for three adults and one child, parking included. Camping is not restricted to the summer season; some sites are open year-round, with about 155 specifically set up for winter camping.

FISHING

Among Austria's well-stocked lakes are the Traunsee, Attersee, Hallstätter See, and Mondsee in Upper Austria; the Danube, Steyr, Traun, Enns, Krems, and Alm rivers also provide good fishing. Tirol is another good region; try the Achensee, Traualpsee, Walchsee, Plansee, and nearby streams. Also try the Inn and Drau in East Tirol and the Ziller in the Zillertal. Styria provides some of the best trout fishing in Austria, as do the lakes in the Styrian Salzkammergut. Carinthian lakes and the streams in Lower Austria also abound in fish. Ask the Austrian National Tourist Office for the guidebook "Austrian Fishing Waters"; it includes licensing details. The separate provinces also have detailed brochures on waters and licensing. Unfortunately, the rights along many of the best streams have been given, meaning that no additional licenses will be issued, but ask at the local tourist office. Some hotels have fishing rights; we note these throughout the book.

GLIDING

From May to September you can glide solo or learn to glide at one of Austria's schools, at Zell am See (Salzburg province); Niederöblarn and Graz-Thalerhof (Styria); in Wiener Neustadt and Spitzberg bei Hainberg (Lower Austria). In Zell am See and at Wien-Donauwiese (Vienna) there are two-seater gliders, for instructor and passenger; at the other airfields you're on your own.

GOLF

Austria now has more than 50 courses. Most are private, but for a greens fee you can arrange a temporary membership. Many courses are associated with hotels, so package arrangements can be made.

HIKING AND CLIMBING

With more than 50,000 kilometers (about 35,000 miles) of well-maintained mountain paths through Europe's largest reserve of unspoiled landscape, the country is a hiker's paradise. Three long-distance routes traverse Austria: E-4, the Pyrenees–Jura–Neusiedler See route, ending in Burgenland on the Hungarian border; E-5 from Lake Constance in Vorarlberg to the Adriatic; and E-6 from the Baltic, cutting across mid-Austria via the Wachau Valley region of the Danube and on to the Adriatic. Wherever you are in Austria, you will find shorter hiking trails requiring varying degrees of ability. Routes are well marked, and maps are readily available from bookstores, the Österreichischer Alpenverein/ÖAV (☞ Hiking *in* Important Contacts A to Z), and the automobile clubs.

Of the more than 700 refuges in Austria, about a quarter are at altitudes of between 8,200 and 9,800 feet. Mountain guides typically charge AS2,200 a day for glacier tours and easy-to-moderate climbs, with the guides responsible for their own food. For more strenuous climbing and longer periods, you can arrange a fixed fee in advance. A tip is usual at the end of the climb.

If you're a newcomer to mountain climbing or want to improve your skill, schools in Tirol, Carinthia, Styria, and Salzburg province will take you on. Ask the ÖAV for addresses. All organize courses and guided tours for beginners and more advanced climbers.

HORSEBACK RIDING

Whether you want to head off cross-country

or just canter around a paddock, Austria offers many kinds of equestrian holidays, and some hotels have their own riding schools. Ask for the booklet "Riding Arena Austria" from the tourist office. The provinces of Styria, Burgenland, and Upper and Lower Austria are particularly popular with riders.

SNOWBOARDING

The latest winter sports craze has hit with enthusiasm. Snowboarders will find halfpipes and ample challenges in all major winter resorts. You can rent boards and take lessons in many Salzburg province, Tirol, Carinthia, and Vorarlberg ski areas.

SKIING

Skiing is without doubt the queen of winter sports, and Austria is one of the finest places—if not the finest—in which to learn or practice the far from gentle art of skiing. If you are already an expert skier, it is sufficient to state that literally anywhere in the Tyrol, Vorarlberg, and most parts of Carinthia, Salzburg, Western Styria, and Lower Austria, you will find skiing slopes of every type you could wish for. Other visitors, who have perhaps just emerged from the Skihaserl, or novice stage, can also find hundreds of places to accommodate their level. Whatever your degree of skill (or lack of it) there's a perfect spot for you in Austria—to help find it, read the complete section on skiing in Pleasures and Pastimes in Chapter 1.

WATER SPORTS AND SWIMMING

Waterskiing and sail skiing are popular on the Wörther See (where there's also spectacular night waterskiing with torches) and Millstätter See in Carinthia; on the Traunsee, Attersee, and Wolfgangsee in Salzkammergut; in Zell am See in Salzburg Province; and on the Bodensee (Lake Constance) in Vorarlberg. Waterskiing is not permitted on many of the smaller Austrian lakes, so check first. There are hundreds of places to swim throughout Austria, and with very few exceptions, the water is unpolluted. All the lakes in the Salzkammergut, Carinthia, and Tirol have excellent swimming, but are crowded in the peak season. In the Vienna area, the Alte Donau and Donauinsel arms of the Danube are accessible by public transportation and are suitable for families. It's best to go early to avoid the crowds on hot summer weekends. The Alte Donau beaches have changing rooms and checkrooms. Swimming in the Neusiedler See in Burgenland is an experience; you can touch bottom at virtually any place in this vast brackish lake.

SPECTATOR SPORTS

Soccer is a national favorite. Every town has at least one team, and rivalries are fierce; matches are held regularly in Vienna and Innsbruck. When Austrians aren't skiing, they like to watch the national sport; downhill and slalom races are held regularly in Innsbruck, Kitzbühel, Seefeld, and St. Anton. There's horse racing with pari-mutuel betting at the track in the Prater in Vienna. Tennis matches are held in Vienna, Linz, and Innsbruck.

STUDENTS ON THE ROAD

To save money, **look into deals available through student-oriented travel agencies.** To qualify, you'll need to have a bona fide student ID card. Members of international student groups are also eligible (☞ Students *in* Important Contacts A to Z).

T

TELEPHONES

Austria's telephone service is in a state of change as the country converts to a digital system. We make every effort to keep numbers up to date, but do recheck the number—particularly in Innsbruck, Linz, and Vienna—if you have problems getting the connection you want (a sharp tone indicates no connection or that the number has been changed). All numbers given in this guide include the city or town area code; if you are calling within that city or town, dial the local number only. Note that if you're calling Vienna from within Austria the city area code is 0222;

if you call from outside Austria, it's 01.

Basic telephone numbers in Austria are three to seven digits; longer numbers are the basic number plus a direct-dial extension of two to five digits.

LONG-DISTANCE

You can dial direct to almost any point on the globe from Austria. However, it costs more to telephone from Austria than it does to telephone to Austria. Calls from post offices are always the least expensive and you can get helpful assistance in placing a long-distance call; In large cities, these centers at main post offices are open around the clock.

The long-distance services of AT&T, MCI, and Sprint make calling home relatively convenient, but in many hotels you may find it impossible to dial the access number. The hotel operator may also refuse to make the connection. Instead, the hotel will charge you a premium rate—as much as 400% more than a calling card—for calls placed from your hotel room. To avoid such price gouging, **travel with more than one company's long-distance calling card**—a hotel may block Sprint but not MCI. If the hotel operator claims that you cannot use any phone card, ask to be connected to an international operator, who will help you to access your phone card. You can also dial the international operator yourself. If none of this works, try calling your phone company collect in the United States. If collect calls are also blocked, call from a pay phone in the hotel lobby. Before you go, find out the local access codes for your destinations.

To make a collect call—you can't do this from pay phones—dial the operator and ask for an *R-Gespräch* (pronounced air-ga-shprayk). Most operators speak English; if yours doesn't, you'll be passed to one who does.

The international access code for the United States and Canada is 001, followed by the area code and number. For Great Britain, first dial 0044, then the city code without the usual "0" (171 or 181 for London), and the number. Other country and many city codes are given in the front of telephone books (in Vienna, in the A-H book).

When placing a long-distance call to a destination within Austria, you'll need to **know the local area codes,** which can often be found by consulting the telephone numbers that are listed in this guide's regional chapters. The following are area codes for Austria's major cities: Vienna, 0222; Graz, 0316; Salzburg, 0662; Innsbruck, 0512; Linz, 0732. When dialing from outside Austria, the 0 should be left out. Note that calls within Austria are one-third cheaper between 6 PM and 8 AM on weekdays and from 1 PM on Saturday to 8 AM on Monday.

OPERATORS AND INFORMATION

For information on local calls, dial 1611 or 08; for assistance with long-distance service, dial 1616 or 09; and for information on direct dialing out of Austria, call 08 or 1613.

PAY PHONES

Coin-operated pay telephones are numerous and take AS1, 5, 10, and 20 coins. A three-minute local call costs AS1. Drop in the one-schilling piece, pick up the receiver and dial; when the party answers, push the indicated button and the connection will be made. If there is no response, your coin will be returned into the bin to the lower left. Most pay phones have instructions in English on them. Add AS1 when time is up to continue the connection.

If you plan to make many calls from pay phones, a *Wertkarte* is a convenience. You can buy this electronic credit card at any post office for AS190, AS95, or AS48, which allows AS200, AS100, or AS50 worth of calls from any *Wertkartentelephon.* You simply insert the card and dial; the cost of the call is automatically deducted from the card. A few public phones in the cities also take American Express, Diners, Mastercard, and Visa credit cards.

TIPPING

Although virtually all hotels and restaurants include service charges in their rates, tipping is still customary, but at a level lower than in the

United States. Tip the hotel doorman AS10 per bag, and the porter who brings your bags to the room another AS10 per bag. In very small country inns, such tips are not expected but are appreciated. In family–run establishments, tips are generally not given to immediate family members, only to employees. Tip the hotel concierge only for special services or in response to special requests. Room service gets AS10–AS20 for snacks or ice, AS20 for full meals. Maids normally get no tip unless your stay is a week or more or service has been special.

In restaurants, round up the bill by AS5 to AS50 or 5%–7%, depending on the size of the check and the class of the restaurant. Big tips are not usual in Austrian restaurants, since 10% has already been included in the prices. Hat-check attendants get AS7–AS15, depending on the locale. Washroom attendants get about AS2–AS5. Wandering musicians and the piano player get AS20, AS50 if they've filled a number of requests.

Round up taxi fares to the next AS5 or AS10; a minimum AS5 tip is customary. If the driver offers (or you ask for) special assistance, such as carrying your bags beyond the curb, an added tip of AS5–AS10 is in order.

TOUR OPERATORS

A package or tour to Austria can make your vacation less expensive and more hassle-free. Firms that sell tours and packages reserve airline seats, hotel rooms, and rental cars in bulk and pass some of the savings on to you. In addition, the best operators have local representatives available to help you at your destination.

A GOOD DEAL?

The more your package or tour includes, the better you can predict the ultimate cost of your vacation. Make sure you know exactly what is covered, and **beware of hidden costs.** Are taxes, tips, and service charges included? Transfers and baggage handling? Entertainment and excursions? These can add up. Also, **make sure your travel agent knows the accommodations and other services.**

BUYER BEWARE

Each year a number of consumers are stranded or lose their money when operators—even very large ones with excellent reputations—go out of business. To avoid becoming one of them, take the time to **check out the operator**—find out how long the company has been in business and ask several agents about its reputation. Next, **don't book unless the firm has a consumer-protection program.** Members of the USTOA and the NTA are required to set aside funds for the sole purpose of covering your payments and travel arrangements in case of default. Note: When it comes to tour operators, **don't trust escrow accounts.** Although there are laws governing those of charter-flight operators, no governmental body prevents tour operators from raiding the till.

Next, contact your local Better Business Bureau and the attorney general's offices in both your own state and the operator's; have any complaints been filed? Finally, **pay with a major credit card.** Then you can cancel payment, provided that you can document your complaint. Always **consider trip-cancellation insurance** (☞ Insurance, *above*).

USING AN AGENT

Travel agents are excellent resources. In fact, large operators accept bookings made only through travel agents. But it's good to **collect brochures from several agencies** because some agents' suggestions may be skewed by promotional relationships with tour and package firms that reward them for volume sales. If you have a special interest, **find an agent with expertise in that area;** ASTA can provide leads in the United States. (Don't rely solely on your agent, though; agents may be unaware of small-niche operators, and some special-interest travel companies only sell direct.)

TRAIN TRAVEL

WITHIN AUSTRIA

Austrian train service is excellent: It's fast and, for Western Europe, relatively inexpensive, particularly if you take advantage of the discount fares. Trains on the mountainous routes are slow, but driving is no faster, and the scenery is gorgeous! Many of the remote rail routes will give you a look at traditional Austria, complete with Alpine cabins tacked onto mountainsides and a backdrop of snow-capped peaks.

For train schedules, ask at your hotel or stop in at the train station and look for large posters labeled Abfahrt (departures) and Ankunft (arrivals). In the Abfahrt listing you'll find the departure time in the main left-hand block of the listing and, under the train name, details of where it stops en route and the time of each arrival. There is also information about connecting trains and buses, with departure details.

Austrian Federal Railways trains are identifiable by the letters that precede the train number on the timetables and posters. The IC (InterCity), EC (EuroCity), EN (EuroNight), and SC (SuperCity) trains are fastest, but a supplement of AS50 is included in the price of the ticket. All tickets are valid without supplement on D (express) and E (Eilzug; semi-fast) and local trains. Seat reservations are required on some trains; on most others you can reserve for AS30 up until a few hours before departure. Be sure to do this on the major trains at peak holiday times.

The difference between first and second class on Austrian trains is mainly a matter of space. First- and second-class sleepers, and couchettes (six to a compartment), are available on international runs, as well as on long trips within Austria. If you're driving and would rather watch the scenery than the traffic, you can put your car on a train in Vienna and take it to Salzburg, Innsbruck, Feldkirch, or Villach. You relax in a compartment or sleeper for the trip, and the car is unloaded when you arrive.

Railroad enthusiasts and those with plenty of time can treat themselves to rides on narrow-gauge lines found all over Austria that amble through Alpine meadows; some even make flower-picking stops in season. A few lines still run under steam power, and steam excursions are increasingly easy to find. Local stations have descriptive brochures with dates, points of origin, and fares.

RAIL PASSES

To save money, **look into rail passes** (for addresses and telephone numbers, *see* Important Contacts A to Z, *above*). But be aware that if you don't plan to cover many miles, you may come out ahead by buying individual tickets.

Many travelers assume that rail passes guarantee them seats on the trains they wish to ride. Not so. You need to **book seats ahead** even if you are using a rail pass; seat reservations are required on some European trains, particularly high-speed trains, and are a good idea on trains that may be crowded—particularly in summer on popular routes. You will also need a reservation if you purchase overnight sleeping accommodations.

WITHIN AUSTRIA➢ Depending on the length of their stay, travelers can save money on one of the discount rail fares—even if they'll be in the country for only a short time. Discount arrangements and prices are likely to be changed in 1997 but were correct at press time.

Check on availability of the **Euro Domino Card** and **Domino Junior Card.** You've a choice of unlimited rail travel on three, five or ten days, first or second class regular, second class junior, within a month period. At press time, prices for the second class passes were 3-day, AS1,460; 5-day, AS1,630; and 10-day, AS2,920.

A ***Bundesnetzkarte*** (full-network pass) gives you unlimited travel for a month (AS5,400 for first class, AS3,600 second class). The ticket is also good on the suburban rail system (*S-Bahn*) around Vienna and ships on the Wolfgangsee. Apply at any large rail station. You will need a passport photo. With a ***Familien-Pass*** (Family Pass), two parents travel at half price and any number of their children under 15 travel free. You'll need a passport photo of one of the adults. The pass costs AS170 for rail and bus, is good for a year, and is the key to getting the reduction on regular tickets.

For AS260 and a passport photo, women over 60 and men over 65 can obtain a ***Seniorenpass,*** which carries discounts up to 50% on rail tickets. The pass also has a host of other benefits, including reduced-price entry into museums. Most rail stations can give you information.

Travelers under 26 should inquire about discount fares under the Billet International Jeune (BIJ). The special one-trip tickets are sold by **Eurotrain International,** travel agents, and youth-travel specialists, and at rail stations.

FOR EUROPE AND AUSTRIA➢ Austria is one of 17 countries in which you can use **EurailPasses,** which provide unlimited first-class rail travel during their period of validity. Standard passes are available for 15 days ($522), 21 days ($678), one month ($838), two months ($1,148), and three months ($1,468). **Eurail Saverpasses** valid for 15 days cost $452 per person, for 21 days $578, for one month $712 per person; you must do all your traveling with at least one companion (two companions from April through September). **Eurail Youthpasses,** which cover second-class travel, cost $598 for one month, $798 for two; you must be under 26 on the first day you travel. **Eurail Flexipasses** allow you to travel first class for 10 ($616) or 15 ($812) days within any two-month period. **Eurail Youth Flexipasses,** available to those under 26 on their first travel day, allow you to travel second class for 10 ($438) or 15 ($588) days within any two-month period.

Another option is the **Europass,** featuring a minimum of 5 and a maximum of 15 days (within a two-month period) of unlimited rail travel in your choice of three to all five of the participating countries (France, Germany, Italy, Spain, and Switzerland); cost for 5 days is $316 first class (three countries); for 8 days, $442 first class (four countries); and for 11 days, $568 first class (all five countries). Each extra rail day costs $42.

Another option that allows you to discount travel through various countries is the **European East Pass,** good for travel within Austria, Czechoslovakia, Hungary, Poland, and Slovakia: cost is $185 for any 5 days unlimited travel within a 15-day period, and $299 for any 10 days within a month's period; or you can combine renting a car with train travel using the **European East Rail 'N Drive Pass,** which costs between $299 and $675 for any 8 days (5 rail and 3 car), depending on the car size and number of people traveling together. Apply through your travel agent. Note that all the above prices are subject to change.

FROM THE U.K.

There's a choice of rail routes to Austria, but check services first; long-distance passenger service across the Continent is undergoing considerable reduction. There is daily service from London to Vienna via the *Austria Nacht-express.* Check other services such as the *Orient Express.* If you don't mind changing trains, you can travel via Paris, where you change stations to board the overnight *Arlberg Express* via Innsbruck and Salzburg to Vienna. First- and second-class sleepers and second-class couchettes are available as far as Innsbruck.

When you have the time, a strikingly scenic route to Austria is via Cologne and Munich; after an overnight stop in Cologne, you take the EuroCity Express *Johann Strauss* to Vienna.

W

WHEN TO GO

Austria has two main tourist seasons. The weather usually turns glorious around Easter to mark the start of the summer season and holds until about mid-October, often later. Because much of the country remains "undiscovered," you will usually find crowds only in the major cities and resorts. May and early June, September, and October are the pleasantest months for travel; there is less demand for restaurant tables, and hotel prices tend to be lower.

An Italian invasion takes place between

Christmas and New Year's Day and over the long Easter weekend, and hotel rooms in Vienna are at a premium; otherwise July and August and the main festivals (☞ Festivals and Seasonal Events *in* Chapter 1) are the most crowded times.

The winter-sports season starts in December, snow conditions permitting, and runs through April. You can ski as late as mid-June on the high glaciers, at altitudes of 8,000 feet or more. Although reservations are essential in the major ski resorts in season, travelers can frequently find rooms in private houses or small pensions if they're prepared to take a slight detour from the beaten path.

CLIMATE

Austria has four distinct seasons, all fairly mild. But because of altitudes and the Alpine divide, temperatures and dampness vary considerably from one part of the country to another; for example, northern Austria's winter is often overcast and dreary, while the southern half of the country basks in sunshine. In winter it's wise to check with the automobile clubs for weather conditions, since mountain roads are often blocked, and ice and fog are hazards.

The following are average monthly maximum and minimum temperatures for three cities in Austria:

Climate in Austria

VIENNA

Jan.	34F	1C	May	66F	19C	Sept.	68F	20C
	25	− 4		50	10		52	11
Feb.	37F	3C	June	73F	23C	Oct.	57F	14C
	27	− 3		57	14		45	7
Mar.	46F	8C	July	77F	25C	Nov.	45F	7C
	34	1		59	15		37	3
Apr.	59F	15C	Aug.	75F	24C	Dec.	37F	3C
	43	6		59	15		30	− 1

Jan.	36F	2C	May	66F	19C	Sept.	68F	20C
	21	− 6		46	8		50	10
Feb.	39F	4C	June	72F	22C	Oct.	57F	14C
	23	− 5		52	11		41	5
Mar.	48F	9C	July	75F	24C	Nov.	46F	8C
	30	− 1		55	13		32	0
Apr.	57F	14C	Aug.	73F	23C	Dec.	37F	3C
	39	4		55	13		25	− 4

Jan.	34F	1C	May	68F	20C	Sept.	70F	21C
	19	− 7		46	8		50	10
Feb.	39F	4C	June	75F	24C	Oct.	59F	15C
	23	− 5		52	11		41	5
Mar.	52F	11C	July	77F	25C	Nov.	46F	8C
	32	0		55	13		32	0
Apr.	61F	16C	Aug.	75F	24C	Dec.	36F	2C
	39	4		54	12		25	− 4

1 Destination: Austria

BEYOND THE SCHLAG

TODAY'S AUSTRIA—and in particular its capital, Vienna—reminds me of a formerly fat man who is now at least as gaunt as the rest of us, but still allows himself a lot of room and expects doors to open wide when he goes through them. After losing two world wars and surviving amputation, annexation, and occupation, a nation that once ruled Europe now endures as a tourist mecca and a neutralized, somewhat balkanized republic.

It takes any foreign resident in Austria, even a German or Swiss, the whole first year to find out what questions one should be asking. It takes the second year to start getting answers; beginning with the third year, one can sift the merits of the answers. This is why I tell our friends from embassies, agencies, banks, and businesses—people doing two- or three-year stints in Austria—that they need a minimum of five years here to liquidate the investment of effort and utilize the contacts they've made. To tourists, I have just three words of advice: "Don't even try." Were you to succeed in thinking like the Viennese, for example, you would be a prime candidate for Doctor Freud's couch at Berggasse 19; but he and it aren't there anymore—the house is now the Sigmund Freud Museum, and the couch is in London.

Sitting in a loge in the Vienna State Opera in the 1970s, my wife and I gasped with dismay when a young ballerina slipped and fell, but while we applauded the girl's quick recovery, the ancient dowager next to me merely murmured: "In the days of the monarchy, she'd have been taken outside and shot."

I hope it was hyperbole, but she had a point. In a world of tattered glitter and tacky taste, jet-lagged superstars and under-rehearsed choruses, opera and operetta aren't what they used to be (though Viennese ballet has climbed steadily uphill in the decades since that girl's fall).

Still, there are oases of perfection, such as those Sunday mornings from September to June when—if you've reserved months in advance—you can hear (but not see) those "voices from heaven," the Vienna Boys Choir, sing mass in the marble-and-velvet royal chapel of the Hofburg. Lads of 8 to 13 in sailor suits, they peal out angelic notes from the topmost gallery, and you might catch a glimpse of them after mass as you cut across the Renaissance courtyard for the 10:45 performance of the Lippizaner stallions in the Spanish Riding School around the corner. Beneath crystal chandeliers in a lofty white hall, expert riders in brown uniforms with gold buttons and black hats with gold braid put these aristocrats of the equine world through their classic paces.

Just past noon, when the Spanish Riding School lets out, cross the Michaelerplatz and stroll up the Kohlmarkt to No. 14: Demel's, the renowned and lavish pastry shop founded shortly after 1848 by the court confectioner. It was an instant success with those privileged to dine with the emperor, for not only was Franz Josef a notoriously stodgy and paltry eater, but, when he stopped eating, protocol dictated that all others stop, too. Dessert at Demel's became a must for hungry higher-ups. Today's Demel's features a flawless midday buffet offering venison en croûte, chicken in pastry shells, beef Wellington, meat tarts, and frequent warnings to "leave room for the desserts."

Closer to the less costly level of everyday existence, my family and I laid on a welcoming meal for visitors just off plane or train: a freshly baked slab of *Krusti* Brot to be spread with *Liptauer,* a piquant paprika cream cheese, and *Kräuter Gervais,* Austria's answer to cream cheese and chives, all washed down by a youngish white wine. Such simple pleasures as a jug of wine, a loaf of bread, and a spicy cheese or two are what we treasure as Austrian excellence in democratic days. Though our visitors managed to live well back home without Grüner Veltliner and Rheinriesling to drink or Liptauer and Kräuter Gervais to eat, they did find it hard to rejoin the outside world of white bread that wiggles. And if they really carried on about our wine, we could take them on the weekend to the farm it was from, for going to the source is one of the virtues of living in this small, unhomogenized land of 7.5 million people that is modern Austria.

"Is it safe to drink the water?" is still the question I'm asked most by visitors to Vienna. "It's not only safe," I reply, "it's recommended." Sometimes they call back to thank me for the tip. Piped cold and clean via Roman aqueducts from a couple of Alpine springs, the city's water has been rated the best in the world by such connoisseurs and authorities as the Austrian Academy of Sciences and an international association of solid-waste-management engineers. Often on a summer evening, when our guests looked as though a cognac after dinner might be too heavy, I brought out a pitcher of iced tap water, and even our Viennese visitors smacked their lips upon tasting this refreshing novelty. But don't bother to try for it in a tavern; except for a few radical thinkers and the converts I've made, virtually all Viennese drink bottled mineral water, and few waiters will condescend to serve you any other kind.

People say that after two decades in Vienna one must feel very Viennese, and maybe they're right, because here I am chatting about food and drink, which is the principal topic of Viennese conversation. So, before leaving the capital for the provinces, let me call your attention to three major culinary inventions that were all introduced to Western civilization in Vienna in the watershed year of 1683: coffee, the croissant, and the bagel.

That was the year the second Turkish siege of Vienna was at last repelled, when King Jan Sobieski of Poland and Duke Charles of Lorraine rode to the rescue, thereby saving the West for Christianity. The Sultan's armies left behind their silken tents and banners, some 25,000 dead, and hundreds of huge sacks filled with a mysterious brownish bean. The victorious Viennese didn't know what to make of it—whether to bake, boil, or fry it. But one of their spies, Franz George Kolschitzky, a wheeler- dealer merchant who had traveled in Turkey and spoke the language, had sampled in Constantinople the thick black brew of roasted coffee beans that the Turks called *"Kahve."* Though he could have had almost as many sacks of gold, he settled for beans—and opened history's first Viennese coffeehouse. Business was bad, however, until Kolschitzky tinkered with the recipe and experimented with milk, thus inventing the *Mélange:* taste sensation of the 1680s and still the most popular local coffee drink of the 1990s.

While Kolschitzky was roasting his reward, Viennese bakers were celebrating with two new creations that enabled their customers truly to taste victory over the Muslims: a bun curved like a crescent, the emblem of Islam (what Charles of Lorraine might have called *croissant,* Austrians call *Kipferl*), and a roll shaped like Sobieski's stirrup, for which the German word was *Bügel.* The invention of the bagel, however, proved less significant, for it disappeared swiftly and totally, only to resurface in America centuries later, along with Sunday brunch.

THOUGH VIENNA'S is more a wine culture than a beer culture, in its hundreds of *Heurigen* (young-wine taverns identified by a bush over their door) the Viennese male indulges in a beer-garden ritual that I call "airing the paunch." With one or two buttons open, he exposes his belly to sun or moon or just passing admiration. One would be hard put to tell our sometimes smug and self-satified Viennese gentleman that Wien (the German name for the capital) is not the navel of the universe, let alone of Austria, but the person who could tell it to him best would be a Vorarlberger. The 305,600 citizens of Austria's westernmost province live as close to Paris as they do to Vienna, which tries to govern them; their capital, Bregenz, is barely an hour's drive from Zürich, but eight or more from Vienna, and the natives sometimes seem more Swiss than Austrian.

The Kleinwalsertal, a remote valley of Vorarlberg that juts into Bavaria, cannot be reached directly from Austria by car, bus, or train. A few summers ago, I joined some intrepid Austrians on a strenuous and sometimes treacherous two-day up- and downhill climb from Lech am Arlberg to the Kleinwalsertal. Along the way, we saw an eagle, vultures, and marmots—and I wouldn't have traded the trip for a sack of coffee beans; nor would I ever undertake such a venture again. When we tried to buy some coffee, the locals were reluctant to accept our schillings because the Deutschmark is their official currency. While the rest of Austria aspires to enter the European Union, the Kleinwalsertal, through monetary union, has been quietly living in it from its outset.

The northern reaches of Tirol and the western parts of Upper Austria also border on Germany and have a heartier, beerier character than the eastern and southern provinces. (There are nine provinces in all; Vienna, the capital, counts as a state, too, and its mayor is also a governor.) Although the glittering city of Salzburg, capital of rugged Salzburg province, perches right on the German border 16 miles from Berchtesgaden, Austrian traditions, folk customs and costumes, and the music of native son Mozart flourish there as nowhere else in the country—revered and cherished, revived and embroidered. And defended! Once, sitting at sundown in the Café Winkler high up on the Mönchsberg, watching the lights of the city come on below, I heard a man from Munich exclaim in admiration of the same view: "Ah, Salzburg! Still the most beautiful of Bavarian cities." From three sides of the restaurant, three glasses smashed in Austrian hands. The man from Munich hastily paid up and left.

AUSTRIA BORDERS not just on Germany and Switzerland, but also on Liechtenstein, Italy, Slovenia, the Czech Republic, Slovakia, and Hungary. In Austria's greenest province, Styria, one side of the road is sometimes in Slovenia, and you're never far from Hungary or Italy. Styria is so prickly about its independence, even from Austria, that it maintains its own embassies in Vienna and Washington. It is the source of Schilcher, Austria's best rosé wine, which you almost never see in Viennese restaurants. A few years ago, at a farmhouse near Graz, the Styrian capital, I was sipping some Schilcher that went with some wonderful lamb. "Where is this lamb from?" I asked my host.

"Right here," he replied. "Styrian lamb wins all kinds of prizes."

"Then why can't we find it in Vienna?" I wondered. "When we do get lamb, it comes all the way from New Zealand and costs a fortune."

"That's because we don't grow lambs or Schilcher for export," he replied, dead serious.

The influx and tastes of Balkan and Turkish workers have made lamb cheaper and plentiful all over Austria, and now, since the crumbling of the Iron Curtain, Austria is reluctantly becoming even more of a melting pot than it was in the days of the Habsburg empire. The most assimilable province will surely be Burgenland, which used to be part of Hungary. It retains much of its Magyar character in villages where you open a door and find, instead of a courtyard, a whole street full of steep-roofed houses, people, and life. With the dissolution of the Austro-Hungarian empire after World War I, Burgenland was ceded to Austria, pending a plebiscite in 1921. The population voted overwhelmingly to stay Austrian—except for the people of Ödenburg, which was then its capital and is now Sopron in Hungary. Later, but too late, it was discovered that Ödenburg's pro-Hungarians had registered the inhabitants of several cemeteries to achieve a majority. By enlisting their ancestors, they doomed their descendants to two generations behind the Iron Curtain and a difficult job of catching up. Their move also meant, until lately, that to go from one point in Burgenland to another 20 kilometers (12½ miles) away, Westerners sometimes had to detour up to 100 kilometers (62 miles).

Burgenland also boasts a culturally active Croatian minority, while Carinthia, Austria's southernmost province, has a proud Slovenian minority that is still fighting for the legal right not to Germanize the names of its villages.

The ultimate identity problem, however, belonged until recently to the province of Lower Austria, which is neither low nor south but takes its name from the part of the Danube it dominates on the map. Before 1986, Lower Austria had no capital city; its state offices were scattered around Vienna, the metropolis it envelops with forest. Upon its selection as the provincial seat, the small city of St. Pölten, with a core of lovely churches and cloisters that swirl around you like a Barococo ballet, danced onto the map of tourist destinations. Already coming to life as a sightseeing attraction, St. Pölten is starting to thrive as a center of government, though Lower Austria's bureaucrats in Vienna are relocating slowly and grudgingly, if at all; many are contemplating early retirement.

Any day of the year, you can take an express train at Wien's Westbahnhof for an eight-hour, 770-kilometer (480-mile) east–west crossing of most of the country, stopping at five of Austria's nine provincial capitals: St. Pölten; Linz, the Upper Austrian seat; Salzburg; Innsbruck in Tirol; and Bregenz in Vorarlberg. But you would be well rewarded, as the pages that follow will demonstrate, by disembarking at each one and giving it a day or two or more of your life.

—Alan Levy

Now editor-in-chief of the *Prague Post,* Alan Levy lived in Vienna for 20 years.

WHAT'S WHERE

Poised in the very heart of the continent, Austria is as topographically diverse as it is historically wealthy. What it may lack in size (the country is larger than the state of Maine), it makes up for in diversity, for it has some of just about everything: a thousand-year-old recorded history; an Alpine region that—as the setting for *The Sound of Music*—remains one of the most beloved regions in all Europe; Salzburg, a jewel of a city filled with the music-box tinkle of Mozart; and, arguably one of the great cities of the world, Vienna. If you take a Grand Tour of the country, you'll learn there are as many Austrias as there are crystals on a chandelier in a Viennese ballroom. Its Alps rival those of neighboring Switzerland; its vineyards along the Danube match those of the Rhine and Mosel River valleys; its museums and Baroque churches are without peer for old-world splendor. In addition, nowhere else are there such pastry shops!

For most people, Austria is Vienna or Innsbruck or Salzburg or the Tirol region. These places have grandeur, plus all that is superlative in style and scenery. But some half dozen other vacation areas exist from the splendid Vorarlberg to warm Carinthia, and remote Burgenland and Styria, for instance—and there is a good case for spending some time in these areas. You will even find that many of the smaller country towns reproduce in miniature the glories of the great centers. Although it is one of Europe's smallest countries, Austria manages to pack within its border as many mountains, lakes, and picturesque cities as countries five times its size. Here is a quick overview to help you travel civilized roads, both back in time and forward.

Vienna

Think of Vienna and you think of operettas and psychoanalysis, Apfelstrudel and marble staircases, Strauss waltzes and Schubert melodies. Baroque and imperial, it goes without saying that the city (Wien, in German) has an old-world charm—a fact that the natives are both ready to acknowledge and yet hate being reminded of. Today, Vienna is a white-gloved yet modern metropolis, a place where Andrew Lloyd Webber's *Phantom of the Opera* plays in the same theater that premiered Mozart's *Magic Flute.* A walk through the city's neighborhoods—many dotted with masterpieces of Gothic, Baroque, and Secession architecture—offers a fascinating journey thick with history and peopled by the spirits of Empress Maria Theresa, Haydn, Beethoven, Metternich, Mozart, and Klimt.

Most visitors start along the Ring, the grand boulevard that surrounds the inner city; here, you'll find art treasures in the Fine Arts Museum, magnificent spectacles at the Vienna State Opera (one reason why Vienna remains for many the musical capital of the world), and the Hofburg, Vienna's gigantic Imperial Palace, whose chapel showcases the Vienna Boys Choir and whose stables shelter the Lipizzaner stallions (when they aren't prancing at the Spanish Riding School). The city comes alive during the "Merry Season"—the first two months of the year—when raised trumpets and opera capes adorn its great Fasching balls; then more than ever, Vienna moves in three-quarter time. Near the city are the legendary Vienna Woods, with the famous spa of **Baden,** the **Weinviertel** (Wine District), and poetic **Mayerling,** where Crown Prince Rudolf and his lover met a tragic end.

Eastern Austria

A great white stork glides to a landing on the chimney of the hooded roof of an "Old Mother Muchabout" (Mother Goose) house—a timeless image as far from the bustle of civilization as you can imagine, and one common in Austria's easternmost province. For those familiar with other parts of Austria, this region's far-awayness offers the contrast of simple, homely, exceptionally charming pleasures: whitewashed Magyar-style houses, vast stretches of flat prairie-like *puszta,* evenings filled with the haunting sounds of Gypsy music—legacies attesting to the fact that much of Eastern Austria belonged to Hungary before World War I.

A region of castle-capped hills, fields of grain, and vineyards (some of the best Austrian wines, including the regal Trockenbeerenauslesen, are produced here), **Burgenland** has major sights, including **Lake Neusiedl**—so gigantic it's called the "Viennese Sea"—and the old-world town of **Eisenstadt,** site of the exquisite Esterházy Palace where famed composer Josef Haydn worked for many years (don't miss a concert in the palace's Haydn Hall). **Graz,** the capital of Styria—Austria's southeastern province—is the country's second largest city and boasts a historic city center that is as strikingly preserved as any.

The Danube Valley

The scenes along a trip down the Austrian Danube unfold like a picture-book of history. In a parade of sights, Roman ruins, Baroque monsteries with "candle-snuffer" cupolas, and medieval castles-in-air beyond counting dot the length of the river, stoking the imagination with their legends and myths. Here is where Richard the Lion Hearted spent years locked in a dungeon and where the Nibelungs—immortalized by Wagner—caroused at the top of their lungs in battlemented forts. Clearly, the Danube is liquid history, and you can enjoy drifting eight hours downriver in a steamer or—even better—18 hours upriver against the current.

Along the way you discover **the Wachau** Valley—"crown jewel of the Austrian landscape"—the Baroque abbey of **Melk,** and the robber castles of Studen and Werfenstein. A convenient base point is **Linz,** Austria's third-largest city (and its most underrated): its Old Town is filled with architectural treasures, glockenspiel chimes, and pastry shops that offer the best linzertortes around. The town is right on the Danube, which, if you catch it on a bright summer day, takes on the proper shade of Johann Strauss "blau."

Salzkammergut

Remember the first five minutes of *The Sound of Music*? Castles fronting on water, mountains hidden by whipped-cream clouds, verdant forests, and flower-strewn valleys crisped with cool blue lakes: a Hollywoodian Austria in all the splendor of its genre. They were actually filmed here, not far from the very sites where Maria and the von Trapp children "Do-Re-Mied." If Austria were rated on a beauty-measuring gauge, the needle would fly off the scale here in the **Lake District,** known in Austria as the Salzkammergut, the "land of the salt mines." The region stretches into three provinces—from Salzburg through Styria to Upper Austria, and its unofficial capital is **Bad Ischl,** the charming summer resort of Emperor Franz Josef (where, on August 18, his birthday is still celebrated!) and the place where Franz Lehar wrote *The Merry Widow.*

Nearby are the storybook towns of **St. Wolfgang** (whose White Horse Inn inspired a famous operetta) and **Hallstatt,** a relentlessly picturesque village that seems to rise out of Swan Lake itself. The most Valkyrian backdrop of all is the Dachstein massif, with needle-like snow-capped peaks that put Chamonix's Aiguilles to shame: this ne plus ultra of Austrian scenery seems to study its reflection in the mirrored surfaces of the three **Gosau** lakes—a setting so superb it inspired some of Wagner's greatest music. Don't forget to go spelunking through the region's great salt caves (where Hitler once stored stolen art treasures). Throughout the entire Lake District, travelers have always celebrated the simplest of life's pleasures in the greatest style. Many come just to spend blissful days hiking, boating, and swimming.

Salzburg

Mozart, Mozart, Mozart! Birthplace of Wolfgang Amadeus, Salzburg is a world-class music mecca. If Mozart's native city did him little honor in his lifetime, it is making up for it now. His symphonies are heard in the city's churches, castles, palaces, and concert halls; his operas are given enchanting productions by the Salzburg Marionette Theater; Mozartkugeln candies delight countless chocolate lovers; and every August, the Salzburg Music Festival creates Mozartian harmonies at the world's snobbiest music gathering. Austria's rich and famous wear Tirolian Formal to attend events in the Grosses Festspielhaus, and high ticket prices mean you'll hear the sound of money as well.

While Mozart rules over the festival months of July and August, visitors have discovered innumerable other attractions during the rest of the year. Art lovers call Salzburg the **Golden City of High Baroque;** thanks to powerful archbishops of the Habsburg era, few other places offer an equivalent abundance of Baroque architecture. Visitors tour the city to the strains of music from the film that made Salzburg a household name in the United States; From Winkler Terrace to Nonnberg Convent, it's hard to go exploring without hearing someone humming "How Do You Solve a Problem Like Maria?"

Carinthia

Carinthia could be labeled "Extract of Austria" since many travelers feel it contains a greater variety of Austria's charms than any other province. The country's sunniest (and southernmost) province, Carinthia—called Kärnten in German—is the region frazzled Viennese dream of. Here you'll find **the Austrian Riviera,** a happy blend of mountains, valleys, and placid blue-green lakes, that rest serenely between the shoulders of low forested hills and reflect the golden-white light of the rocky faces of the Karawanken and Carnic Alps. Around the shores of the largest lake, the Wörther See, waterside gaiety emanates from **Maria Wörth** and **Velden,** resorts where, thanks to beachscapes that allow travelers to sun and soak, everything goes swimmingly.

Nature's glories are only part of Carinthia's allure, for many of its Alpine towns contain artistic treasures. **Spittal** contains the Schloss Porcia, a renowned Renaissance palace (its arcaded courtyard is the sublime setting for summer concerts and plays); a great Romanesque cathedral broods over Gurk; **St. Veit an der Glan**'s town square is probably the most beautiful in the country; and when you see the 9th-century Fortress Hochosterwitz from afar, high atop a hill, you almost expect a dragon to appear in a puff of smoke or to hear troubadours warbling (the castle was the model for Walt Disney's *Snow White*). **Klagenfurt** is the official capital of Carinthia, but **Villach** has emerged as the "secret" capital, no more so than when the town hosts the most riotous Carnival celebration in Austria.

Eastern Alps

If you want a region that conveniently packages the panoramic, the most gemütlich little towns in Austria, and an all-out array of sports, head for the Eastern Alps, magnificently sited within the regions of East Tirol, Salzburg Province, and West Styria. It's easy to feel on top of the world when you journey here, since you'll probably travel over the longest and most thrilling pass over the Alps, the **Grossglockner High Alpine Highway,** which traverses Austria's highest peak. There's a thrill every hundred yards along this route but your first will be the sighting of **Heiligenblut,** a town commemorated in a thousand postcards. Nowhere else does the spire of a church's steeple seem to find such affirmation amid a setting of soaring peaks. Skiing, mountain climbing, or just gazing at the mouthwatering scenery will whet your appetite for a delicious regional feast of roasted mountain goat and potato pancakes.

Lienz is another town famous for its scenic mountainscape, with the Dolomites providing dramatic backdrop. All through this region you can enjoy breathtaking Alpine vistas, visit castles still inhabited by members of centuries-old noble families, discover ice caves and wild gorges, walk through meadows ablaze with *roses des Alps,* take in top skiing and generally a full refresher course in relaxation. The Eastern Alps year-round can be just the ticket to a suntan or snowtan—but keep in mind the season for Alpine wildflowers is May to June.

Tirol and Innsbruck

Tirol has a great deal, if not everything: the Holy Roman Empire splendors of Innsbruck, Hansel-and-Gretel villages, majestic mountain peaks, masked carnival revelers, and more—much more. The best base for exploration is **Innsbruck,** the only major city in the entire Alpine range of Europe. The "hub of the Alps" has a natural setting that provides an appropriate backdrop for some splendid examples of architecture—including the famous "Golden Roof" mansion—the legacy of the "last knight," Habsburg Emperor Maxmilian I.

Then dust off your dirndl, shine up your best lederhosen, and set out for the **Tirol.** Here, you're more likely to find native folk costumes on the street, not in museums. While your tonsils may not be up for *Jodeln*—Tirolian singing—you'll probably want to shop for some cuckoo clocks, Gothic-style chairs of pine, and some Tirolian knee socks and knickers. After some dreamy castle-hopping, head for the great ski resorts—St. Anton, Kitzbühel (once the Duke of Windsor's favorite *Winter Wunderland*), and St. Johann—where sport *und Spiel* are always in high gear.

Vorarlberg

"What God has put asunder by a mountain, let no man join by a tunnel"—so said the Vorarlbergers of old. Once the Arlberg Tunnel linked Austria's westernmost province to the rest of the country, the secret was out. Vorarlberg—nicknamed the *Ländle,* the "Little Province"—was really Austria's Switzerland: cheaper in some ways, perhaps less efficient in others.

Tops on all visitors' lists are the fresh air and aria-making of the **Bregenz Music Festival** on Lake Constance, the **Bregenerwald**—forests of Wagnerian romanticism—the **Schubert Festival in Hohenems,** and the piste-splattered ski regions. A few years ago, Princess Diana and her two sons could be spotted making snowplows on the well-groomed slopes of **Lech.** Whether you catch the fresh green of spring pastures or the snow white of its winter peaks, each season in the Voralberg has a particular allure.

PLEASURES AND PASTIMES

Mozart Mania

Somewhere, at almost any hour, an orchestra will be playing his music; somewhere, shoulders will be swaying, fingers tapping. It may be at a gala evening concert, an outdoor festival, or an Easter Mass. But chances are the music of Johannes Chrysostomus Theophilus Wolfgang Amadeus Mozart will be traveling through the air when you visit Austria. The most purely inspired of any composer crammed a prodigious amount of composing into his short 35-year life. Today—thanks to Tom Hulce's characterization in the film *Amadeus*—this youthful genius and native son of Salzburg wears the crown of the rock star of the 18th century.

And confirmation of his continuing popularity is renewed each year at the annual Salzburg Music Festival, perhaps the world's most polished and prestigious musical gathering. What Wagner is to Bayreuth, Mozart is to Salzburg. Well, not absolutely—many performances at Salzburg are devoted to other composers—but the true spirit, soul, and style of the magical city are best captured when "Wolfi" takes center stage at the Grosses Festspielhaus. On such nights, platoons of the rich and famous may take in a new production of *Don Giovanni* in one theater, hear the hottest conductor take on the "Linz" Symphony in another, then head over to the Goldener Hirsch for extravagant after-opera meals and diva-watching.

Schnitzels, Strudels, and Sachertortes

Travelers in Austria can be faced with a moveable feast of enticing choices. There are the four-star dining establishments that are proud to feature the latest in *Neue Küche,* or Viennese nouvelle cuisine. Some visitors head first for those Hungarian-themed eateries that specialize in Genghis Khan's Flaming Sword, plum brandy, Turkish coffee, and a Primaś, a gypsy orchestra in which the leading violinist plays your favorite song. Others skip right to dessert and check out a Konditorei—such as Demel's, where you can feast on pastries that are among the gastronomic wonders of Europe. There are gemütlich wine taverns, Heurigen, where you can always get a bite to eat and listen to *Schrammel* music. Then there are those who swear the best meal in Austria is a simple *Frankfurter und Pfefferminz* at the street corner *Wurstelstand* (sausage vendor).

Whatever your pick, restaurant food in Austria ranges from fine (and expensive) offerings at elegant restaurants to simple, inexpensive, and wholesome meals in small country inns. Wherever you go, you will find traditional restaurants, with all the atmosphere typical of such places—good value included. If you crave a Big Mac you can find it, and you can even get a bad meal in Austria, but it will be the exception; the simplest *Gasthaus* takes pride in its cooking, no matter how standard it may be. Some Austrians even believe you have a better chance getting a wonderful meal at a simple neighborhood Beisel than at a *nobel* four-star establishment.

Austrian cuisine is heavily influenced by that of its neighbors. This accounts for the cross-fertilization of tastes and flavors, with Hungarian, Czech, Slovak, Polish, Yugoslav, and Italian cooking all in the mix. The delicious, thick Serbian bean soup came from an area of the former Yugoslavia; the bread dumpling (*Knödel*) that accompanies many standard dishes has its parentage in the former Czechoslovakia; the exquisitely rich (more butter than sugar) *Dobostorte* comes straight from Hungary.

All too often justice is not done to the relatively few Austrian national dishes. You're likely to get a soggy Wiener schnitzel as often as a supreme example, lightly panfried in a dry, crisp breading. Austrian cooking on the whole is more solid than delicate. Try *Tafelspitz* (boiled beef); when properly done it is outstanding in flavor and texture. Reflecting the Italian influence, Austrian cooking also leans heavily on pastas and rice. *Schinkenfleckerl* is a good example: a casserole of confettilike flecks of ham baked with pasta. A standard roast of pork (*Schweinsbraten*) served hot or cold can be exquisite. As for other dishes, here's a list of traditional Austrian favorites: *Leberknödelsuppe,* a meat broth with liver dumplings; *Fischbeuschlsuppe,* a thick, piquant, Viennese soup made from freshwater fish; *Fogosch,* pike, and *Krebs,* succulent little crawfish, all from the lakes and rivers of Austria; the various Schnitzels—*Holsteiner, Pariser, Natur;* pork specialities such as *Schweinscarrée,* a very special cut; *Rehrücken,* or venison; especially pheasant and wild-boar (incidentally, today's nouvelle chefs are serving up sublime prosciuttos of the latter); *Gulyas* (goulash), seasoned with superlative Hungarian paprika; *Backhuhn* or *Backhendl,* young chicken breaded and fried to a golden brown; and *Steirisches Brathuhn,* chicken roasted on a spit. And don't forget those wonderful Austrian sausages.

Austrian vintage wines range from good to outstanding. Don't hesitate to ask waiters for advice, even in the simpler restaurants. The best whites come from the Wachau and Kamptal, Weinviertel (Lower Austria), Styria, and the area around Vienna. Grüner Veltliner, a light dry-to-medium-dry wine that goes well with many foods, is the most popular. The Welschriesling is a slightly heavier, fruitier wine. The favored Austrian reds are those of Burgenland. Blauer Portugieser and Zweigelt tend to be lighter. For a slightly heavier red, select a Blaufränkisch, Blauer Burgunder, or St. Laurent. These are all good value, and there is little difference among the years. Most of these wines can be bought by the glass. Look for labels from vintners Beck in Gols, Bründlmayer in Langenlois, Hirtzberger in Spitz/Donau, Jamek in Joching, Nikolaihof in Mautern, Sonnhof in Langenlois, Dolle in Strass, Wieninger in Vienna, and Freie Weingärtner Wachau in Dürnstein.

Souvenirs, Austrian-Style

Not so long ago, almost any store on Vienna's Kärntnerstrasse could boast that it once created its exquisite jewelry, fine leather goods, or petit-point handbags (as Viennese as St. Stephen's Cathedral) for the imperial Habsburgs. This may no longer be the case, but rest assured, Miss Average Tourist will receive service fully as gracious as that once accorded to Their Imperial Majesties the Emperor and Empress. For the most lasting souvenir, however, visitors might consider a foray into the realm of Austrian arts and crafts. Of great age and agelessness, these objects are often made outside Vienna. For instance, the world-famous firm of Riedel, based in the charming town of Kufstein—between Salzburg and Innsbruck—produces glassware with the thinnest of stems and designs that can be strikingly contemporary (even though the company was founded in 1756). Perhaps you'll agree that wine tastes better in a Riedel glass.

Northeast of Salzburg on the shores of Lake Traum, you'll find Count Hohenberg's Gmundner Keramic, celebrated for its

16th-century green-and-white *Grüngeflammt* pattern ceramics. Choose a sturdy beer stein, or for a splurge, buy a reproduction *Knöde-Schüssel*—a gigantic platter on which a 16th-century family would divvy up the communal Sunday meal. For the best in linen nightwear, dirndls, and lodels, head for Lanz of Austria, the No. 1 choice of chic Salzburgers. Lanz changes its motifs—deer, farmhouse, or flower—from year to year on its skirts and aprons. Part *Trachten* (folk dress), part *Haute Confection* (what Austrians call high-quality fashion), these very designs have been known to inspire Yves Saint Laurent. For furnishings, check out rural antique dealers for a rustic "Empire Peasant" painted wooded chest. Or try to buy the most unique Austrian souvenir of all—one of those colored and mirrored glass orbs, garden ornaments typical of the Biedermeier era, and the Austrians' right-on version of a scarecrow.

Powder-Perfect Skiing

Skiing is without doubt the queen of winter sports, and Austria is one of the finest places—if not the finest—in which to learn or practice the far from gentle art of skiing. If you are already an expert skier, it is sufficent to state that literally anywhere in the Tirol, Vorarlberg, and most parts of Carinthia, Salzburg, Western Styria, and Lower Austria, you will find skiing slopes of every type you could wish for. Other visitors, who have perhaps just emerged from the *Skihaserl,* or snow bunny stage, can also find hundreds of places to accommodate their level. With skiing such a major sport—and industry—in Austria, most natives won't laugh when beginners fall down. For many of them, you are their bread and butter, and the "customer is always right."

Whatever your degree of skill (or lack of it) there's a perfect spot for you in powder-perfect Austria, a nation which seems to have been designed by nature for winter sports. In addition to snow-bowl excitement, there are resorts to satisfy every *après-ski* taste, from the burger-and-beer crowd to the chichi caviar-sandwich set. At the top of everyone's list are Kitzbühel, St. Anton, and Lech-Zürs. "Kitz" is picture-perfect and posh—all medieval cobbled streets, wrought-iron signs, and candles flickering in the windows of charming restaurants. The Hahnenkahm Downhill is the electrifying ski event here for professionals, but everyone can find a thrill on the slopes, including some spectacular floodlit-at-night downhill runs. Lech and Zürs are the co-stars of the Arlberg region, with Lech's well-groomed trails drawing the royal set. Immediately after the Arlberg Pass you come to St. Anton: It was here that Hannes Schneider started the school that was to become the model for modern ski instruction. Perhaps the most popular skiing destination remains Innsbruck, an entire city set magnificently within the Alps, with many ski runs nearby. Wherever skiers head, they've discovered that spas are now offering the perfect cure for ski-fatigued bodies and windblown faces. After a week on the slopes, many opt for plenty of pampering at an Alpine spa retreat.

Skiing is the Austrian national sport, so you'll have plenty of company wherever there's a slope and a snowflake. The season runs from late November to April, depending on snow conditions. The Obertauern region at 5,700 feet in Salzburg province guarantees snow from November to May. But there are enough year-round skiing regions on glaciers at 11,000 feet or more to satisfy even the wildest enthusiast. The well-established winter–summer regions include Kitzsteinhorn (Kaprun) in Salzburg province, Rettenbachferner (Sölden), Stubaier Glacier (Renalt), Wurmkogel (Hochgurgl), Tuxer Ferner (Hintertux), St. Leonhard (Pitztal), Kaunertal Glacier in Tirol, and Dachstein (Ramsau) in Styria.

Special Attractions➢ In many areas, cable cars, chairlifts, and T-bars have been arranged so you can ski all day long on the same ski pass without using the same slope twice and end up in the afternoon exactly where you started that morning. Kitzbühel and Saalbach–Hinterglemm in particular are noted for their "ski circuses," which offer such round-trip possibilities. The Salzburg province Amadé area includes 120 lifts in eight villages on one pass. From Innsbruck, you can ski six separate areas. The Salzburg ski-safari combines seven areas within easy reach of the city. At all centers you will find experienced instructors, and the schools take children beginning at age 3. You can bring your own gear or rent skis, boots, and poles—even clothes in some areas—at the resorts. If you rent, reserve in advance to have a selection and the right sizes.

PACKAGES AND DISCOUNTS➢ You can head for the popular and known resorts, but if a skiing holiday without all the frills (and expense) is what you want, you'll find good facilities and excellent slopes with far lower prices in East Tirol, Styria, Lower Austria, Carinthia, and parts of Salzburg province and Upper Austria. Ski areas offer weekly passes for use on all lifts, cable cars, and usually swimming pools, at 20%–30% reductions. Your hotel or the local tourist office will have details. Many resorts, including several of the more expensive and fashionable towns, offer all-inclusive weekly rates, sometimes including ski schools and lifts. Contact the Austrian National Tourist Office for detailed information on the various packages.

FAVORITE DESTINATIONS➢ A good-sized ski guidebook would be necessary to describe all the leading sites in Austria, but here's a quick run down. For easy reference, see the Ski Areas map that precedes the Gold Guide.

Vorarlberg/Arlberg. In the Vorarlberg, many head for **Schruns** and **Tschagguns** in the Montafon Valley, where the slopes of the Raetikon, Ferwall, and Silvretta Alps offer great downhill runs. In the Arlberg district, a top choice is **Zuers,** one of the country's best known winter sports centers; even at over 5,000 feet, there is plenty of good powder from November to May. One of the best and longest runs, from the Zuersersee lift, takes you down to posh **Lech,** where several first-class hotels draw jet-setters and royalty. By gondola cable car you reach **Ober Lech,** at 5,500 feet, where there is another nest of big hotels and some splendid runs along the top of the Alps.

Immediately after the Arlberg Pass you come to **St. Anton,** at 4,300 feet, one of the most famous winter sports resorts in the world. It was here that Hannes Schneider started the school that was to become the model for modern ski instruction. A short bus ride to the top of the pass brings you to **St. Christoph,** at 5,800 feet. The beginner would do well to stay down at St. Anton where there are better—and gentler—nursery slopes.

Ötz Valley. Head by bus from the Ötztal station to **Soelden,** 4,500 feet, which attracts many because of lower prices. The mountain village of **Obergurgl,** at 6,321 feet, lies at the head of the valley, where you can ski until early summer.

Innsbruck/Tirol. At the far end of the Tirol lies **Kitzbühel,** at 2,500 feet, which vies with St. Anton as the most famous winter sports resort in the Austrian Tirol. "Kitz"—once the most fashionable ski resort in Austria—continues to draw aficionados who like its so-called "ski circus," a system of ski-lifts and trails, some spectacularly floodlit at night, whereby skiers may ski for weeks without going over the same ground or retracing their steps.

Salzburg Area. Zell am See, at 2,470 feet, has some excellent skiing, with many experts drawn to its so-called *Schmittenhöhe Spaziergang* (promenade) starting from the top of the Schmittenhöhe cable car, and then running along the tops of the mountain peaks, at an average height of 6,500 feet. Moving south, you'll find the wealthy spa town of **Badgastein,** at 3,560 feet, which offers a full range of services to revitalize bodies weary of the slopes.

The Great Outdoors

Austria is one of the most participant-sport-minded countries in the world. Babies barely out of diapers practically learn to walk on skis. At a snowflake's notice, half the population takes to the slopes; in summer, water sports are just as popular. New attractions are appearing; golf and snowboarding are sweeping the country. One "sport"—an activity we are all experts at—is an Austrian passion: walking. Austria is a walker's El Dorado, and its sights—once you're off the Autobahn—are amazing: valleys that inspired Anton Bruckner's symphonies; alleés of linden trees immortalized in Klimt's paintings; gorgeous medieval villages such as Steyr; and Sound-of-Music meadows that make you want to spread your arms and whirl around. Because Austrians so love *das Wandern* (as they refer to walking and hiking), you can be sure there will be complete information about the country's many trails—including the famous "Romantic Road" running from Salzburg through the Salzkammergut to the Danube Region—from National Tourist Offices.

NEW AND NOTEWORTHY

The music never stops in Vienna. The 1997 year opens with a burst, with the annual New Year's Day concert by the Vienna Philharmonic, conducted by Riccardo Muti, and a performance of Beethoven's Ninth Symphony by the Vienna Symphony under Roger Norrington promises to be an oustanding if possibly controversial experience. Both concerts are scheduled for New Year's Eve and repeated on the morning of New Year's Day. The Vienna State Opera, the Volksoper, and opera houses in other cities mount Strauss' comic opera, *Die Fledermaus,* on New Year's Eve. Other cities have followed Vienna's lead and also offer New Year's concerts.

After the round of New Year's events come the Mozart weeks (actually a little over a week) in Salzburg at the end of January; this year will be marked by the **performances of Mozart's seldom-heard opera *Mitridate, Re do Ponto*** under Roger Norrington's direction. The fate of Salzburg's Easter Festival is being debated, but performances seem certain this year, with the same caveat applying to the Whitsun (Pfingsten) concerts at the end of May. The **Vienna Festival this year moves into the historic Konzerthaus.** This year marks the 200th anniversary of the birth of Franz Schubert, meaning that the festival will be overflowing with his works. The Salzburg Festival in midsummer remains one of the world's great musical experiences, with prices as stratospheric as ever.

The festival on the lake at Mörbisch in Burgenland will float Offenbach's spicy *Pariser Leben,* can-can dancers and all. Opera is also featured in a festival at the opposite end of the country, on the lake at Bregenz. At the Vienna opera, new productions include two rarities, Richard Strauss's *Die Schweigsame Frau* and Boito's *Mephistophles,* with Samuel Ramey in the title role. Ballet under director Renato Zanella will present a "Viennese Evening," complete with Balanchine's *La Valse.*

Highlights of the ball season in Vienna will include the Philharmonic Ball on January 16 in the Musikverein and the Opera Ball on February 6, which takes place in the elegantly decorated Opera House. The main ball season runs through *Fasching,* the carnival period, which ends on Ash Wednesday. As always, the Imperial Ball in the Hofburg wraps up the year in style on December 31.

The main musical event of 1997 is the **200th anniversary of the birth of Franz Schubert.** The Biedermeier-era composer was born in 1797 and died tragically (from typhoid) at the age of 31 in 1828. Schubert's music reflects the soul of Vienna as Mozart's does that of Salzburg, so the capital, fittingly, will lead the festivities with its annual **Schubertiade,** along with a major Schubert show in the Historical Museum of the City of Vienna, an international choral competition in November, and special concerts at both the Festwochen (mid-May–late-June) and the Klangbogen/Musikalischer Sommer (July–September)—the city's two major summer music festivals. Other focal points for special commemorative concerts (small, given the spaces involved) will be his birthplace in Nudorfer Strasse and his brother's house, where he died, in Kettenbruckengasse. In the Vorarlberg, the annual Schubertiade held in Feldkirch and Hohenens will convene with stellar artists in May, June, and September.

The **Vienna Card** is proving to be a popular success. It includes unlimited travel on public transportation for 72 hours, reduced museum entrance fees, shopping discounts, and a number of other attractions, all for AS180. It inspired the new **Salzburg Card,** which allows unlimited rides on all of Salzburg's transit lines (except Bus 80) and the Untersberg aerial tram, admission to the top sightseeing attractions and Casino, and various discounts on cash purchases. The card comes in three versions, ranging from one to three days (AS180–350).

Driving still remains one of the best ways to see the countryside, but **highways are showing signs of heavy congestion** of late, particularly on weekends and holidays and on the major north–south routes that carry transit traffic between Germany and Italy. **More towns and cities are adding pedestrian zones,** so check on access and parking possibilities with your hotel before you arrive. Cars have been almost totally banned from such resorts as Zürs and Lech; parking in the center of Vienna is restricted, with whole squares cleared of cars. Where you're forced to walk—in the inner cities of Vienna, Salzburg, Innsbruck, and Graz, for example—remember that this is really the best way to capture the feeling and flavor of those places anyway.

This year, skiers are being looked after in even better fashion, as **more ski areas join to form associations** in which general lift passes are valid. This means you get more for your lift investment and can try more slopes and snows. Cities, too, are onto the skiing concept; Salzburg has a new scheme that combines the culture and variety of the city with skiing the surrounding mountain areas, to which access is made easy. Snowboarding enthusiasts are being treated to new and challenging half-tube runs in most major ski-resort areas.

Also, **cycling is increasingly the way to go.** Bikers are supported by maps, repair shops, friendly overnight lodging possibilities, and transport of heavier, bulkier bags between destinations. Routes will take you along the Danube—in most places, you've a choice of north or south bank—or to other more challenging parts of Austria. **Hiking, too, has become more organized;** see, for example, the new self-guided hiking tours out of Saalfelden or those around the Salzkammergut area. Be sure to book your hiking tour well in advance, as the popularity of the new packages has meant that the more remote accommodations are quickly filled up before the start of the peak season.

Austria's membership in the European Union is taking longer to be digested than most officials in Vienna had hoped. The public had been promised instantly lower prices which have not materialized—a fact travelers will notice at every turn. A recent austerity budget extends into 1997 and has served to hold the government together and, at least, kept the lid on inflation. Austria remains one of Europe's most expensive countries, with some travelers reporting prices as high as the Mönchsberg peak that perches over Salzburg. However, the good news is that the exchange rate is looking slightly more favorable for the dollar (at press time). Already, CNN Travel News has reported Austria could be one of Europe's three hottest destinations for the coming year.

FODOR'S CHOICE

No two people agree on what makes a perfect vacation, but it's fun and helpful to known what others think. Here's a compendium from the must-see lists of hundreds of Austrian travelers. For detailed information about these memories-in-the-making, refer to the appropriate chapters in this book.

Quintessential Austria

★ **New Year's Day concert in Vienna's Musikverein.** You've seen it on television, but now you're *here* in the Golden Hall—its gilt bare-breasted ladies supporting the balconies, the walls festooned with floral displays—sharing in the excitement of a Vienna Philharmonic concert seen and heard by millions around the world.

★ **Waltzing around the clock at a Fasching ball.** Whether you go to the Opera Ball or the Zuckerbäckerball (sponsored by pastry cooks), remember that gala etiquette states a gentleman can kiss only a lady's hand.

★ **Boating on Lake Neusiedl at sunset.** The red globe of the sun disappears behind the hills to the west, its shimmering mirror image slowly fading from the lake's surface; evening birds rustle in the lakeshore reeds as an occasional stork wings back to its chimneytop nest in a nearby town.

★ **Opening night at the Salzburg Music Festival.** Chances are the performance will be extraordinary, but what could be more exciting than watching the entire town square break into applause when concertgoers catch sight of diva Jessye Norman after the show?

★ **Making the Eisbar scene at Lech.** Here in a resort where the seeing is just as important as the skiing, check out the Eisbars—beverage counters sculpted of snow and ice—set up near the slopes. Chances are you'll be enjoying your mug of Pfefferminz Tee with the the royal offspring of Monte Carlo, Denmark, Norway, and the Netherlands.

★ **High Mass on Sunday in the Augustinerkirche in Vienna.** Particularly if it's a mass by Mozart or Haydn, the soaring music and the church architecture elevate the event to a soulful experience as you focus on the great altar and the pomp of the ceremony.

★**The most festive Christmas delights.** In Vienna, head for Demel's pastry shrine to try the *Mohr im Hemd*—a heavenly hot chocolate and whipped cream pudding called "Moor in a Shirt"; in Salzburg, attend the Christmas Eve candlelight chamber music recital of Mozart and Haydn in the rose Marble Hall of the Mirabell Palace; and in most every town, check out the outdoor *Christkindlmarkt,* or gift market.

★**The Lippizaner stallions at the Spanish Riding School.** Where else can you see horses dance a minuet to Mozart? For sheer elegance, the combination of the chestnut-colored riding habits of the trainers and the pure white of the horses' coats can't be beat.

Top Art

★**Brueghel's *Hunters in the Snow.*** The confrontation alone is dramatic: You've seen this painting, and most of the other Brueghels that are hung in Vienna's Kunsthistorisches Museum, reproduced a thousand times over. It's incredible detail could keep you fascinated for hours, even if you're not an art aficionado.

★**Klimt's *The Kiss.*** Arguably Austria's greatest painter, Gustav Klimt fuses high romanticism with eye-knocking pattern to create one of his—and the 20th century's—most memorable images, on view in the Österreichische Galerie of Vienna's Belvedere Palace.

★**The Michael Pacher winged altar in St. Wolfgang.** This great 15th-century 33-foot-high masterpiece, a brilliant combination of woodcarving, painting, lighting, and perspective brings a dramatic third dimension to scenes from the life of Christ.

Sights to Remember

★**Gosau am Dachstein.** In a vista that many consider one of the most beautiful in Austria, the Dachstein massif seems to pose for the tourist's camera. The mountain's ermine mantle of snow is mirrored in the Gosau lakes below—a vision so breathtaking it inspired some of Wagner's greatest music.

★**The view up Maria Theresien-Strasse in Innsbruck.** This classic postcard view sets the Anna column in the forefront of a dramatic backdrop of sheltering snow-capped mountains behind, looking close enough to reach out and touch.

★**Salzburg from the Kapuzinerberg after the first snow.** A mantle of white softens the somber gray of the city and brings buildings and squares to life; you'll see features you'd overlooked before, with the solid Festung watching patiently over the Christmas-card scene.

★**Hallstatt on a misty morning.** At "the world's prettiest lakeside village," the surrounding mountains often disappear into the mist, leaving the unforgettable shadowy outline of the church and town buildings hugging the lakeshore.

Unforgettable Drives

★**The Wachau when its apricot trees are in blossom.** In spring, the narrow Danube Valley becomes a riot of fruit trees in delicate pastel blossom sweeping up hillsides from the very river banks.

★**Grossglockner Highway between East Tirol and Salzburg Province.** This engineering masterpiece challenges the driver but brings, one after another, glorious panoramas of snowswept Alpine horizons and lush meadows. Take the side route up to the vast glacier whose runoff feeds the many mountain streams.

★**Route 145 along the Traunsee.** Meander from Gmunden south along the picturebook coastline of the Traunsee with peaks reflected in the deep blue waters; the inspiring view ahead looks up into the salt-filled mountains of the Salzkammergut.

Taste Treats

★**Sampling wine at a romantic *Heuriger* in Rust.** The Burgenland red wines taste their best when enjoyed outdoors at wooden tables accompanied by chunks of country bread and spicy *Liptauer* cheese spread, fresh radishes, and slivers of bell peppers; the vintner will set you up with a memorable picnic.

★***Bosner Wurst* (hot dog with Balkan spice) in the arcaded passageway between the Getreidegasse and Universitätsplatz.** A "Bosner" is one of Salzburg's enduring snack treats, and although others have tried to copy it, the original remains the one and only, for which the hungry willingly cue up.

★***Stollen* (cake) with coffee at the Café Zauner in Bad Ischl.** A favorite of Emperor

Franz Josef—both the café and its pastries—is still very popular today, enhanced by outdoor tables directly overlooking the river; this is a pilgrimage regularly made by Austrians as well as tourists.

Great Hotels

★ **Bristol, Vienna.** The Bristol is a classic that has moved with the times; service is impeccable and at no time will a guest feel anything but the luxury of old-world traditions tempered by contemporary comforts. *$$$$*

★ **Goldener Adler, Innsbruck.** Over the second-floor doors of this historic hostelry appear the names of those with whom you will have shared, in spirit, a room: The list of royal and famous as well as infamous personages is impressive. The house exudes the accumulated warmth of past centuries. *$$$$*

★ **Elefant, Salzburg.** An atmosphere conducive to comfort pervades this hotel on the edge of the pedestrian zone in the Old City center. No wonder: The building itself dates back 500 years and amenities such as modern plumbing have been tucked in wherever possible, giving individual character to each of the rooms. *$$*

Memorable Restaurants

★ **Hedrich, Vienna.** When owner-chef Richard Hedrich cooks, for his own as well as his guests' pleasure, the results are outstanding in a city of fine dining establishments. The plainness of the single, smallish room allows better concentration on the creations emanating from the kitchen. *$$$$*

★ **Landhaus Bacher, Mautern.** Understatement is the rule here, where frills and decoration never get in the way of the superb food quality. Whether inside or outside in the shaded garden, the atmosphere is relaxed and service exemplary, making the excursion into the countryside all the more worthwhile. While other top chefs have skyrocketed only to burn out quickly, Lisl Bacher-Wagner maintains her talent for innovation with a steady keel. *$$$$*

★ **Tiroler Stuben, Innsbruck.** Friedrich Wolf concentrates on ingredients in this comfortable, relaxed restaurant, bringing in fresh fish and lamb from France several times weekly. Treatments vary, but dishes are imaginative without being superficial, adding up to very fine dining indeed. *$$$*

★ **Zum Eulenspiegel, Salzburg.** Ignore the Salzburgers who turn up their noses at the mention of this charming restaurant, and go both for the food and the unique setting. The house is hundreds of years old and full of wonderful nooks and crannies reached by odd staircases. This isn't kitsch; it's genuine Old-World authentic. The evening candlelit atmosphere probably enhances the food, but the latter, if not the city's top, is good anyway. *$$$*

Historic Towns/ Picturesque Squares

★ **Hauptplatz, Linz.** The spacious main square of the Upper Austrian capital has been handsomely restored; church spires rather than skyscrapers shape the skyline. The square is the site for local markets just as it was centuries ago, with many of the same buildings gracing the scene.

★ **Old City, Graz.** Narrow winding streets tucked below the city's "mountain" invite exploration. The old quarter exudes charm and has attracted a host of boutiques and tiny restaurants, all wedged willy-nilly into odd corners. This is one of Austria's better-kept secrets.

★ **Steyr, Upper Austria.** Wonderfully colorful decorative facades address the main square, brooded over by the castle above. Tiny, half-concealed stairways lead upward to the castle area, other stone steps take you down the opposite side to the riverbank. The setting is an ensemble worthy of Hollywood; in this case, it's all charmingly real.

Classic Cafés

★ **Hawelka, Vienna.** No visit to Vienna is complete without a stop at this famous landmark, virtually unchanged since Herr Hawelka got it running again in 1945. This remains the artists' stylishly shabby, smoky hangout in name if not always in fact.

★ **Schwarzenberg, Vienna.** This winner among the city's hundreds of cafés, with its brass-topped tables, is a favorite meeting place or the spot for an after-work wine at the tables outside facing the Ring. Piano music at cocktail hour lends a classic Viennese touch.

★**Tomaselli, Salzburg.** An almost reverent atmosphere pervades this enduring temple to café culture, but you'll find the usual accoutrements, such as a stack of newspapers to accompany your coffee and dessert.

Churches and Abbeys

★**Melk, Lower Austria.** Probably the most impressive of Europe's abbeys, Melk perches like a magnificent yellow-frosted wedding cake overlooking the Danube, its ornate library holding rows of priceless treasures. If you can visit only one abbey in all of Europe, Melk should be among the top contenders.

★**St. Florian, Upper Austria.** This abbey, where composer Anton Bruckner was organist, is impressive for its sheer size alone. Add to the symmetrical structure the glorious church and the representational rooms, and you have one of Austria's religious highlights.

★**St. Stephen's Cathedral, Vienna.** The country's spiritual life centers on St. Stephen's, rebuilt after disastrous ruin in the last days of World War II. Today known as the "skyscraper," the church has witnessed many notable events, including the marriage of Mozart. Inside, the penumbral light means that the nave's sweeping heights are felt but seldom seen.

Parks and Gardens

★**Kaiserpark, Bad Ischl.** It's not hard to imagine Emperor Franz Josef, hands clasped behind his back, strolling through these cultivated gardens; the Empress Elisabeth was less happy, knowing that his majesty was keeping his favorite mistresses in villas around the town. Her own petite castle in the park is still occupied by a Habsburg descendant.

★**Mirabell Garden, Salzburg.** For an idyllic picture-postcard view, look up through the formal garden to the castle (Festung) dominating the city, but don't miss the droll Baroque side garden with its amusing stone dwarfs.

★**Schönbrunn, Vienna.** Was the palace an excuse for the gardens, or vice versa? The manicured trees, the symmetrical walkways, the discoveries at various intersections, all add to the pleasure of exploration here. Climb to the Gloriette for a sweeping perspective of the gardens and the city beyond.

FESTIVALS AND SEASONAL EVENTS

WINTER

JAN. 1➢ The **New Year** opens in Vienna with the world-famous concert by the Vienna Philharmonic Orchestra, this year under the direction of Riccardo Muti (✉ Vienna Philharmonic, Musikverein, Bösendorferstr. 12, A–1010 Vienna, ☎ 0222/505–6525; write a year—or more—in advance). Those who can't get into the Philharmonic concert can try for one of the performances of the Johann Strauss operetta *Die Fledermaus* in the State Opera and Volksoper (✉ Bundestheaterverband, Goethegasse 1, A–1010 Vienna, ☎ 0222/513–1513) or for Beethoven's Ninth (Choral) Symphony by the Vienna Symphony Orchestra with the controversial conductor Roger Norrington (✉ Konzerthaus, Lothringerstr. 20, A–1030 Vienna, ☎ 0222/712–1211). Those who want to dance their way into the new year can do so at the Kaiserball in the elegant rooms of the Hofburg (✉ WKV, Hofburg, Heldenplatz, A–1014 Vienna, ☎ 0222/587–3666–14).

JAN. 24–FEB. 2➢ **Mozart Week** in Salzburg features choral and orchestral works. Performers this year include the Amsterdam Concertgebouw Orchestra under Nikolaus Harnoncourt; the Vienna Philharmonic under John Eliot Gardiner, Horst Stein, and Neville Marriner and Academy of Ancient Music under Christopher Hogwood. The opera highlight will be Mozart's **Mitridate,** with Roger Norrington conducting (✉ Mozarteum, Schwarzstr. 26, A–5020 Salzburg, ☎ 0622/872996).

FEB. 13➢ The Opera House in Vienna is transformed into the world's most elegant ballroom for the annual **Opera Ball.**

SPRING

LATE-MAR.–EARLY APR.➢ **Easter Festival,** Salzburg's "other" major music festival, offers opera and concerts of the highest quality, with ticket prices to match (✉ Hofstallgasse 1, A–5020 Salzburg, ☎ 0662/8045–361).

MID-MAY–MID-JUNE➢ The **Wiener Festwochen** takes place in Vienna—a festival of theater, music, films, and exhibitions (✉ Lehargasse 11, A–1060 Vienna, ☎ 0222/582–2222).

SUMMER

JUNE 2➢ The religious holiday **Corpus Christi** is celebrated throughout Austria with colorful processions and parades. In the Lungau region of Land Salzburg, villagers dress up in local costumes. Equally colorful are the processions of gaily decorated boats and barges on the Traun and Hallstätter lakes.

MID-JUNE➢ A **Schubert Festival** with top international artists is held in Feldkirch in Vorarlberg.

JUNE 21➢ **Midsummer Night** is ablaze with bonfires throughout the country, with the liveliest celebrations taking place in the mountains of Tirol and in the Wachau region along the Danube in Lower Austria.

JULY–AUG.➢ **Carinthian Summer** combines concerts, opera, and literature in the modern Congress House in Villach and the exquisite monastary and baroque chapel in Ossiach (✉ Carinthischer Sommer, Gumpendorfer Str., A–1060 Vienna, ☎ 0222/596–8198 or 0222/597–9492 through May; ✉ Stift Ossiach, A–9570 Ossiach, ☎ 04243/2510 June–Aug.).

Musical Summer/Klangbogen in Vienna has nightly recitals in one of the city's many palaces or orchestral concerts in the courtyard of the city hall (✉ Klangbogen Wien, Laudongasse 29, A–1080 Vienna, ☎ 0222/4000–8410).

The **Bregenz Festival** increases in prestige from year to year and has become one of Europe's outstanding music festivals, noted particularly for its opera performances on the lake (✉ Bregenzer Festspiele, Box 311, A–6901 Bregenz, ☎ 05574/4920-223).

The **Salzburg Festival** brings together the world's greatest musical artists for a citywide celebration. Write several months in advance (✉ Salzburger Festspiele, Postfach 140, A–5010 Salzburg, ☎ 0662/8045–322).

AUTUMN

SEPT. 1➢ This date marks the start of the **theater and music season** in Vienna (✉ Wiener Fremdenverkehrsverband, Obere Augartenstr. 40, A–1020 Vienna, ☎ 0222/211–140–14–0).

EARLY SEPT.➢ A series of **trade fairs** packs Vienna during the first weeks of the month; the most interesting is the Hit consumer electronics show, where new products are showcased.

The **Haydn Festival** takes place in Eisenstadt in Burgenland (✉ Burgenländische Haydn Festspiele, Schloss Esterházy, A–7000 Eisenstadt, ☎ 02682/618660).

The **International Bruckner Festival** makes Linz come alive: Theater, concerts, fireworks, and art exhibits extend to the St. Florian monastery, where the composer Anton Bruckner worked and is buried (✉ Untere Donaulände 7, A–4010 Linz, ☎ 0732/775230).

MID-OCT.➢ **Viennale** in Vienna shows films ranging from the avant-garde to retrospectives (✉ Wiener Filmfestwochen Viennale, Stiftsgasse 6, A–1070 Vienna, ☎ 0222/526–5947).

NOV. 11➢ **St. Martin's Day** is as good as a holiday; restaurants throughout the country serve traditional roast goose and red cabbage in honor of the patron saint of publicans and innkeepers. Called *Martinigansl* or *Ganslessen* ("Martin's goose" or "goose eating"), it's much more than a feast of goose; people celebrate with parties and processions, church services, and village parades. The most enthusiastic celebrations take place in Burgenland, of which Martin is the patron saint.

DEC. 6➢ On **St. Nicholas's Day** the patron saint of children is honored at *Christkindl* (Christchild) festivals, open-air markets throughout the country selling toys, favors, decorations, and food. The town of Christkindl in Styria comes into its glory each year at this time.

DEC. 24➢ The **Christmas Eve** service in the tiny memorial chapel at Oberndorf, north of Salzburg, features the singing of *Silent Night,* which Franz Gruber wrote when he was an organist here in the early 19th century. **Christmas Eve midnight mass** at St. Stephen's cathedral in Vienna is an impressive, if crowded, event; get an entrance pass at the cathedral in advance.

2 Vienna

Magnificent, magnetic, and magical, Vienna beguiles one and all with old-world charm and courtly grace. It is a place where head waiters still bow as if saluting a Habsburg prince, where Lipizzaner stallions dance minuets to Mozart—a city that waltzes and works in three-quarter time. Like a well-bred grande dame, Vienna doesn't hurry and neither should you. Saunter through its stately streets—peopled by the spirits of Beethoven and Strauss, Metternich, and Freud—marvel at its Baroque palaces, and dream an afternoon away at a cozy Kaffeehaus.

By George H. Sullivan

Revised and updated by Willibald Picard

THE CITIZENS OF VIENNA, it has been said, properly waltz only from the waist down, whirling around the crowded dance floor while holding their upper bodies motionless and ramrod straight. The sight can be breathtaking in its sweep and splendor, and its elegant coupling of freewheeling exuberance and rigid formality—of license and constraint—is quintessentially Viennese.

Architecture is frozen music, said the German poet Goethe, and the closest that European architecture ever came to embodying the Viennese waltz, appropriately enough, is the Viennese town palace. Built mostly during the 18th century, these Baroque mansions can be found all over the inner city, and they present in stone and stucco the same artful synthesis of license and constraint as the dance that was so often performed inside them. They make Vienna a Baroque city that is, at its best, an architectural waltz.

Today, visitors who tour Vienna can easily feel they're doing so in three-quarter time. As they explore its churches filled with statues of golden saints and pink-cheeked cherubs, wander through its treasure-packed museums, or while away the afternoon in those multitudinous meccas of mocha (those inevitable cafés) they can begin to feel lapped in lashings of rich, delicious, whipped cream—the beloved *Schlagobers* that garnishes most Viennese pastries. The ambience of the city is predominantly ornate and fluffy: white horses dancing to elegant music; snow frosting the opulent draperies of Empress Maria Theresa's monument, set in the formal patterns of "her" lovely square; a gilded Johann Strauss, playing gracefully among a grove of green trees; rich decorations, secretly filling the interior courtyards of town houses that present a severe face to the outside world; the transformation of grim Greek legends by the voluptuous music of Richard Strauss; the tangible, geometric impasto of Klimt's paintings; the stately pavane of a mechanical clock. All these will create in the visitor the sensation of a metropolis that likes to be visited and admired—and which indeed is well worth admiring and visiting.

For many centuries, this has been the case. One of the great capitals of Europe, Vienna was for centuries home to the Habsburg rulers of the Austro-Hungarian Empire. Today the empire is long gone, but many reminders of the city's imperial heyday remain, carefully preserved by the tradition-loving Viennese. When it comes to the arts, the glories of the past are particularly evergreen, thanks to the cultural legacy created by the many artistic geniuses nourished here.

From the late 18th century on, Vienna's culture—particularly its musical forte—was famous throughout Europe. Haydn, Mozart, Beethoven, Schubert, Brahms, Strauss, Mahler, and Bruckner all lived in the city, producing music that is still played in concert halls all over the world. And at the tail end of the 19th century the city's artists and architects—Gustav Klimt, Egon Schiele, Oskar Kokoschka, Josef Hoffmann, Otto Wagner, and Adolf Loos among them—brought about an unprecedented artistic revolution, a revolution that swept away the past and set the stage for the radically experimental art of the 20th century.

At the close of World War I the Austro-Hungarian Empire was dismembered, and Vienna lost its cherished status as the seat of imperial power. Its influence was much reduced, and (unlike most of Europe's other great cities) its population began to decline, from around 2 million to the current 1.7 million. Today, however, the city's future looks brighter, for with the collapse of the Iron Curtain, Vienna may at long last regain its traditional status as the hub of central Europe.

For many first-time visitors, the city's one major disappointment concerns the Danube River. The inner city, it turns out, lies not on the river's main stream but on one of its narrow offshoots, known as the Danube Canal. As a result, the sweeping river views expected by most newcomers fail to materialize.

The Romans are to blame, for when Vienna was founded as a Roman military encampment around AD 100, the walled garrison was built not on the Danube's main stream but rather on the largest of the river's eastern branches, where it could be bordered by water on three sides. The wide, present-day Danube did not take shape until the late 19th century, when its various branches were rerouted and merged to prevent flooding.

The Romans maintained their camp for some 300 years (the emperor Marcus Aurelius is thought to have died in Vindobona, as it was called, in AD 180) and finally abandoned the site around AD 400. The settlement survived the Roman withdrawal, however, and by the 13th century growth was sufficient to require new city walls to the south. According to legend, the walls were financed by the English: In 1192 the local duke kidnapped King Richard I the Lionhearted, en route from the Third Crusade, and held him prisoner in Dürnstein, upriver, for two years until he was expensively ransomed.

Vienna's third set of walls dates from 1544, when the existing walls were improved and extended. The new fortifications were built by the Habsburg dynasty, which ruled the Austro-Hungarian Empire for an astonishing 640 years, beginning with Rudolf I in 1273 and ending with Karl I in 1918. The walls stood until 1857, when Emperor Francis Joseph finally decreed that they be demolished and replaced by the famous tree-lined Ringstrasse (Ring Street).

During medieval times the city's growth was relatively slow, and its heyday as a European capital did not begin until 1683, after a huge force of invading Turks laid siege to the city for two months, to be finally routed by an army of Habsburg allies. Among the supplies that the fleeing Turks left behind were sacks filled with coffee beans. It was these beans, so the story goes, that gave a local entrepreneur the idea of opening the first public coffeehouse; they remain a Viennese institution to this day.

The passing of the Turkish threat produced a Viennese building boom, and the Baroque style was the architectural order of the day. Flamboyant, triumphant, joyous, and extravagantly ostentatious, the new art form—imported from Italy—transformed the city into a vast theater in the 17th and 18th centuries. Life became a dream—the gorgeous dream of the Baroque, with its gilded madonnas and cherubs, its soaring, twisted columns, its painted heavens on the ceilings, its sumptuous domes. In the 19th century, a reaction set in—the Biedermeier epoch, when middle-class industriousness and sober family values set a new style. Then came the Strauss era—that lighthearted period that conjures up imperial balls, "Wine, Women, and Song," heel-clicking, and hand-kissing. Today, visitors will find that all these eras have left their mark on Vienna, making it a city possessed of a special grace. It is this grace that gives Vienna the distinctive architectural character that sets the city so memorably apart from its great rivals—London, Paris, and Rome.

Pleasures and Pastimes

Café Society

They used to say that there were more cafés and coffeehouses in Vienna than there were banks in Switzerland. Whether or not this can still be claimed, you can't savor the true flavor of Vienna without visiting some of its Meccas of Mocha. Every afternoon at 4, the coffee-and-pastry ritual of *Kaffeejause* takes place from one end of the city to the other. Regulars take their *Stammtisch* (usual table) and sit until they go home for dinner. They come to gossip, read the papers, negotiate business, play cards, meet a spouse (or someone else's), or—who knows?—just have a cup of coffee. Whatever the reason, Viennese use cafés and coffeehouses as club, pub, bistro, and even a home-away-from-home. (Oldtimers recall the old joke: "Pardon me, would you mind watching my seat for awhile so I can go out for a cup of coffee?")

In fact, to savor the atmosphere of the coffeehouse, you must allow time. There is no need to worry about outstaying one's welcome, even over a single small cup of Mokka—so set aside a morning or afternoon, and take along this book. For historical overtones, head for the Café Central—where Stalin and Trotsky hatched the Russian Revolution; for Old-World charm, check out the opulent Café Landtmann (even it's plush velvet interior is chocolate-colored) or the elegant Café Sacher (famous for its cake); for an art scene, go to the Café Hawelka. Wherever you go, never ask for just a cup of coffee; request, at the very least, a Mocha *mit Obers*—with whipped cream—from the "Herr Ober" or any of the other delightful variations discussed within the Cafés section in the Dining listings below.

The Heurigen

It is a memorable experience to sit at the edge of a vineyard on the Kahlenberg with a tankard of young white wine, and listen to the *Schrammel* quartet playing sentimental Viennese songs. How far-sighted of the Emperor Joseph to decree in 1784 that winegrowers could sell their wines together with cold food to customers whenever they liked. At the same time, the Viennese discovered that it was cheaper to go out to the wine than to bring it inside the city walls where taxes were levied. Mutual interest has thus made an institution of these Heurigen polka-dotting the hills surrounding Vienna.

Today, in such villages as Sievering, Nussdorf, and Grinzing, there seem to be more heurigen than homes. The heuriger owner is supposed to be licensed to served only the produce of his own vineyard, a rule long more honored in the breach than in the observance (it would take a sensitive palate indeed to differentiate among the various vineyards). Head for the taverns that mark their doorways with a green branch, spend a wonderfully relaxing afternoon or evening over a mug or two of wine and you'll truly learning the full Austrian meaning of the German term gemütlichkeit. There are so many of these taverns that it would be frivolous to single any out: everyone in Vienna has his favorite which is also, of course, the best. Beethoven, however, knew a good thing when he lived at his house on the Pfarrplatz in Heiligenstadt for some time. Now belonging to the Mayer family, this noted address houses a Heuriger, the Mayer, which really serves its own wines and has long been a favorite of many famous Viennese. If you go to this region in the fall, try a glass of *Sturm,* a cloudy drink halfway between grape juice and wine, with a delicious yeasty fizz. A word of warning: Heuriger wine tastes like water at first. Newcomers blithely say, "I can drink a barrel of this." Then, after the first liter has gone down, it feels as if a little man comes up from behind and slugs you on the skull.

Jugendstil Jewels

From 1897 to 1907, the Vienna Secession movement gave rise to one of the most spectacular manifestations of the pan-European style known as Art Nouveau. Viennese took to calling the look "Jugenstil," or the "young style." In such dazzling edifices as Otto Wagner's Wienzeile majolica-adorned mansion or Adolf Loos's Looshaus, Jugendstil architects rebelled against the prevailing 19th-century historicism that had created so many imitation Renaissance town houses and faux Grecian temples. Josef Maria Olbrich, Josef Hoffman, and Otto Schönthal took William Morris's Arts and Crafts movement, added dashes of Charles Rennie Mackintosh and flat-surface Germanic geometry, and came up with a luxurious style that shocked turn-of-the-century Viennese (and infuriated Emperor Francis Joseph). Many artists united to form the Vienna Secession—whose most famous member was painter Gustav Klimt—and the Wiener Werkstätte, which transformed the objects of daily life with a sleek modern look. Today, Jugendstil buildings are among the most fascinating structures in Vienna. The shrine of the movement is the world-famous Secession Pavilion—the work of Josef Maria Olbrich—the cynosure of all eyes on the Friedrichstrasse.

Museums and Marvels

You could spend months just perusing Vienna's 90 museums. Subjects range alphabetically from Art to Wine, and in between are found such oddities as bricks and burials, such marvels as carriages and clocks, and such memorials as Mozart and martyrs. If your time is short, the one museum not to be overlooked is the *Kunsthistorisches,* Vienna's famous art museum. Here you'll discover the originals of paintings you've otherwise seen only on calendars or in books. The most famous room of all is, of course, the one given over to masterpieces by Pieter Brueghel the Elder, the famed 16th-century Netherlandish painter, including his *Peasant Wedding, Peasant Dance,* and the unforgettable *Hunters in the Snow.*

Given a little more time, the *Schatzkammer,* or Imperial Treasury, is well worth a visit, for its opulent bounty of crown jewels, regal attire, and other trappings of court. The sparkling new museum of court silver and tableware is fascinating for its "behind the scenes" views of state banquets and other elegant representational affairs. The best-known museums tend to crowd up in late morning and mid-afternoon hours; you can beat the mobs by going earlier or around the noon hour, at least to the larger museums that are open without a noontime break.

The Sound—and Sights—of Music

What closer association to Vienna is there but music? Boasting one of the world's greatest concert halls (Musikverein), two of the world's greatest symphony orchestras (Vienna Philharmonic and Vienna Symphony), and one of the top opera houses (Staatsoper), it's no wonder that music and the related politics are subjects of daily conversation. During July and August—just in time for tourists—the city hosts the Vienna Summer of Music, with numerous special events and concerts.

For the musical tourist who is excited at the prospect of treading in the footprints of the mighty, seeing where masterpieces were committed to paper, or standing where a long-loved work was either praised or damned at its first appearance, Vienna is tops: The city is saturated with musical history. There is the apartment where Mozart wrote his last three symphonies, the house where Schubert was born, and, just a tram ride away, the path that inspired Beethoven's Pastoral Symphony. Just below, you'll find a handy list of these musical landmarks.

Of course, there is also music to delight as well as inspire. The statue of Johann Strauss II in the Stadtpark tells all. To see him, violin tucked under his chin, is to imagine those infectious waltzes, "Wine, Women, and Song," "Voices of Spring," and best of all, the "Emperor." But quite possibly you will not need to imagine them. Chances are, somewhere in the distance, an orchestra will be playing them. Head for the Theatre an der Wien to hear great operetta (*Die Fledermaus* and *The Merry Widow* both premiered here) or to the Volksoper. While the traditional classics are the main fare for the conservative, traditional Viennese, acceptance of modern music is growing, as are the audiences for pop and jazz.

Musicians' residences abound and many are open as museums. The most famous are Mozart's Figarohaus and Beethoven's Pasqualatihaus, which are discussed in the city sections below. Vienna has many other music landmarks scattered over the city—here's a Whitman's Sampler. Schubert—a native of the city, unlike most of Vienna's other famous composers—was born at Nussdorferstrasse 54 (☎ 01/317–3601, U-Bahn (subway) U2/Schottenring then Streetcar 37 or 38 to Canisiusgasse), in the Ninth District, and died in the Fourth District at Kettenbrückengasse 6 (☎ 01/581–6730, U-Bahn U4/Kettenbrückengasse). Joseph Haydn's house, which includes a Brahms memorial room, is at Haydngasse 19 (☎ 01/596–1307, U-Bahn U4/Pilgramgasse or U3/Zieglergasse) in the Sixth District; Beethoven's Heiligenstadt residence, where at age 32 he wrote the "Heiligenstadt Testament," an anguished cry of pain and protest against his ever-increasing deafness, is at Probusgasse 6 in the 19th District (☎ 01/375408, U-Bahn U4/Heiligenstadt then Bus 38A to Wählamt). The home of the most popular composer of all, waltz king Johann Strauss the Younger, can be visited at Praterstrasse 54 (☎ 01/214–0121, U-Bahn U4/Nestroypl.), in the Second District; he lived here when he composed "The Blue Danube Waltz" in 1867. All the above houses contain commemorative museums. *AS25, block of 10 AS25 tickets for city museums AS160. Tues.–Sun. 9–12:15 and 1–4:30.*

One of the most delightful musicians' residences is the Lehár Villa (✉ Hackhofergasse 18, ☎ 01/371–8213), generally open by appointment only. For a wistful experience, phone ahead and arrange to visit the exquisite house where the composer Franz Lehár lived and worked. Parts of the miniature *Schloss* date to the 1600s; from 1802–1812 it belonged to Emanuel Schikaneder, who wrote the libretto for Mozart's *The Magic Flute.* The main sitting room is given over to Lehár memorabilia, including his dreadfully out-of-tune piano. Ask to see the charming front garden and the tiny chapel (in which the singer Richard Tauber was married). To get to the villa, take U2/Schottenring, then Streetcar D to Nussdorferplatz.

Stepping Out in Three-Quarter Time

Ever since the 19th-century Congress of Vienna—when pundits laughed *"Elle danse, mais elle ne marche pas"* (the city "dances, but it never gets anything done")—Viennese extravagance and gaiety have been world famous. Fasching, the season of Prince Carnival, was given over to court balls, opera balls, masked balls, Chambermaids' and Bakers' balls, and a hundred other gatherings, many held within the glittering interiors of Baroque theaters and palaces. Presiding over the dazzling evening gowns and gilt-splashed uniforms, towering headresses, flirtatious fans, *chambres séparées,* "Wine, Women, and Song," *Die Fledermaus,* "Blue Danube," hand-kissing and gay abandon, was the baton of the waltz emperor, Johann Strauss. White-gloved women and men in white tie would glide over marble floors to his heavenly melodies. They still do. Now, as in the days of Francis Joseph, Vienna's old three-quarter-time rhythm strikes up anew each year during Carnival time, from New Year's Eve until Mardi Gras.

During January and February, as many as 40 balls may be held in a single evening, the most exclusive being Prince Willi Thurn und Taxis's Ball der Silbernen Rose and the most famous—some say too famous—being the Opernball. On February 6, this event transforms the Vienna Opera House into the world's most beautiful ballroom (and transfixes all of Austria when shown live on national television). For a price, anyone can attend, but corporate interests often buy up most of the tickets. The invitation to the Opernball reads, "Frack mit Dekorationen," which means that it's time to dust off your Legion of Honor medal and women mustn't wear white (reserved for debutantes). Remember that you must dance the *Linkswalzer*—the counter-clockwise, left-turning waltz that is the only way to dance in Vienna. After your gala evening, finish off the morning with a Kater Frühstuck—a hangover breakfast—of goulash soup. For a run-down on the major balls that the public can attend during the winter season, *see* Nightlife *in* Nightlife and the Arts, *below.*

EXPLORING VIENNA

To the Viennese, the most prestigious address of Vienna's 23 *Bezirke,* or districts, is the First District (the inner city, bounded by the Ringstrasse and the Danube Canal). The Second through Ninth districts surround the inner city (starting with the Second District across the Danube Canal and running clockwise); the 10th through 23rd districts form a second concentric ring of suburbs. The vast majority of sightseeing attractions is to be found in the First District. For hard-core sightseers who wish to supplement the key attractions that follow, the tourist office (☞ Contacts and Resources *in* Vienna A to Z, *below*) has a booklet by the same name, "Vienna from A–Z" (AS60), that gives short descriptions of some 250 sights around the city, all numbered and keyed to a fold-out map at the back, as well as to numbered wall plaques on the buildings themselves. Note that the nearest U-Bahn (subway) stop to most city attractions described below is included at the end of the service information (for a handy map of the Vienna subway system, *see* the map *in* Getting Around *in* Vienna A to Z, *below*). The more important churches have coin-operated (AS10) tape machines that give an excellent commentary in English on the history and architecture of the church.

Vienna is a city to explore and discover on foot. The description of the city on the following pages is divided into seven areas: six that explore the architectural riches of central Vienna, and a seventh that describes Schönbrunn Palace and its gardens. Above all, *look up* as you tour Vienna: Some of the most fascinating architectural and ornamental bits are on upper stories or atop the city's buildings.

Great Itineraries

IF YOU HAVE 1 DAY

Touring Vienna in a single day is a proposition as strenuous as it is unlikely, but those with more ambition than time should first get a quick view of the lay of the city by taking a streetcar ride around the Ringstrasse, the wide boulevard that encloses the heart of the city. Then spend the time until early afternoon exploring the city center, starting at Vienna's cathedral, the **Stephansdom,** and including the neighboring streets. About 2 PM, head for **Schönbrunn Palace** to spend the afternoon touring the magnificent royal residence, then return to the city center to take a quick look at the most famous art treasures in town, the legendary Pieter Brueghel paintings at the **Kunsthistoriches Museum** (who could possibly visit Vienna and not see Brueghel's *Hunters in the Snow*?). After the museum closes at 6 PM, relax over coffee at a café, then spend a musical evening at a concert, opera, or operetta, or a convivial evening at a Heuriger, one of the wine restaurants for which Vienna is also famous.

IF YOU HAVE 3 DAYS

Given more time, day one can be a little less hectic, and in any case, you'll want more time for the city center. Rather than the do-it-yourself streetcar ride around the Ringstrasse, take an organized sightseeing tour, which will describe the highlights. Plan to spend a full afternoon at the **Schönbrunn Palace.** Reserve the second day for art, and tackle the rest of the exciting **Kunsthistoriches Museum** (having taken in the Brueghels on your first day) before lunch and the magnificent collection of Old Master drawings of the **Albertina,** the impressive **Belvedere Palace** for a contrasting step into modern art in the afternoon—don't miss Klimt's legendary *The Kiss.* Do as the Viennese do, and fill in any gaps with stops at cafés, reserving evenings for relaxing over music or wine. On the third day, head for the world famous **Spanish Riding School** and watch the Lipizzaners prance through morning training. While you're in the neighborhood, view the sparkling court jewels in the **Schatzkammer**—the imperial treasury—and the glitzy **Silberkammer,** the museum of court silverware and table settings, and take in one of Vienna's most spectacular Baroque settings, the glorious Grand Hall of the **Hofbibliothek Prunksaal** (National Library). For a total contrast, head out to the **Prater** amusement park in late afternoon for a ride on the giant Ferris wheel and end the day in a wine restaurant on the outskirts, such as Sievering or Nussdorf.

IF YOU HAVE 7 DAYS

Spend your first three days as outlined in the itinerary above. Then begin your fourth day getting better acquainted with the Fourth District—the heart of the city. Treasures here range from Roman ruins to the **residences of Mozart and Beethoven,** and, slightly afield, **Sigmund Freud's apartment** (in the Ninth District) or the oddball **Hunderwasserhaus** (in the Third). Put it all in contemporary perspective with a backstage tour of the magnificent **Staastoper,** the opera house. For a country break on the fifth day, take a tour of the **Vienna Woods** or the Danube Valley, particularly the glorious **Wachau district** where vineyards sweep down to the river's edge. On the sixth day, fill in some of the blanks with a stroll around the **Naschmarkt** food market district, taking in the nearby **Secession Building** with Gustav Klimt's famous Beethoven Frieze. Don't overlook the superb **Jugendstil** buildings on the north side of the market. If you're still game for museums, head for any one of the less usual offerings, such as the Jewish Museum, the Musical Instruments or Ephesos museums in **the Hofburg,** or the city's **Historical Museum;** by now, you'll have acquired a good concept of the city and its background, so the exhibits will make more sense. Cap the day by visiting the **Kaisergruft** in the Kapuzinerkirche to view the serried ranks of Habsburgs responsible for so much of Vienna.

The Inner City: Historic Heart of Vienna

A good way to break the ice on your introduction to Vienna is to get a general picture of its layout as presented to the cruising bird or airplane pilot. There are several beautiful vantage points from which you can look down and over the city—including the terrace of the Upper Belvedere Palace—but the city's preeminent lookout point, offering fine views in all directions, is gained from **Stephansdom** (St. Stephen's

Cathedral) by toiling up the 345 steps of "Alt Steffl" (Old Stephan, its south tower) to the observation platform. The young and agile will make it up in 8 to 10 minutes; the slower-paced will make it in closer to 20. An elevator, and no exertion, will present you with much the same view from the terrace. From atop, you can see that St. Stephen's is the veritable hub of the city's wheel.

Most of Vienna lies roughly within an arc of a circle, with the straight line of the Danube as its chord. Its heart, the *Innere Stadt* (Inner City) or First District—in medieval times, the entire city of Vienna—is bounded by the Ringstrasse (Ring), which forms almost a circle, with a narrow arc cut off by the Danube Canal, diverted from the main river just above Vienna and flowing through the city to rejoin the parent stream just below it. The city spreads out from the Stephansdom, accented by the series of magnificent buildings erected—beginning in the 1870s, when Vienna reached the zenith of its imperial prosperity—around the Ringstrasse: the Opera House, the National Art Gallery and the National Museum of Natural History, the "New Wing" of the Hofburg, the House of Parliament, the Rathaus, the University, and the Votivkirche. For more than eight centuries, the enormous bulk of the cathedral has remained the nucleus around which the city has grown. The bird's-eye view can be left until the last day of your visit when the city's landmarks will be more familiar. First day or last, the vistas are memorable, especially if you catch them as the cathedral's famous "Pummerin" (Boomer) bell is tolling.

Numbers in the text correspond to numbers in the margin and on the Vienna map.

A Good Walk

Stephansplatz, in the heart of the city, is the logical starting point from which to track down Vienna's past and present, as well as any acquaintance (natives believe that if you wait long enough at this intersection of eight streets you'll run into anyone you're searching for). Although it's now in what is mainly a pedestrian zone, **Stephansdom** ①, the mighty cathedral, marks the point from which distances to and from Vienna are measured. Visit the cathedral (it's quite impossible to view all its treasures, so just soak up its reflective Gothic spirit) and consider climbing its 345-step Alt Steffl tower or descending into its Habsburg crypt. Then wander up the Wollzeile, cutting through the narrow Essiggasse and right into the Backerstrasse, to the **Universitätskirche** ② or Jesuitenkirche, a lovely Jesuit church—the pink and green interior is topped by a trompe l'oeil ceiling painted by Andrea Pozzo in 1705—where masses are sung in Latin on many Sunday mornings. Note the contrasting **Academy of Science** diagonally opposite (Beethoven premiered his Battle Symphony in its Ceremonial Hall). Follow the Sonnenfelsgasse, ducking through one of the tiny alleys on the right to reach the Backerstrasse; turn right at Gutenbergplatz into the Köllnerhofgasse, right again into tiny Grashofgasse and through the gate into the surprising **Heiligenkreuzerhof square** ③, a peaceful oasis (unless a a handicrafts market is taking place). Through the square, enter the Schönlaterngasse (Beautiful Lantern Street) to admire the house fronts—film companies at times block this street to make shots in the picturesque atmosphere—on your way to the **Dominikanerkirche** ④, the Dominican church with its marvelous Baroque interior. Following Predigergasse and Falkestrasse, in back of the church is the architectural contrast of the **Post Office Savings Bank** ⑤ and former **War Ministry,** facing each other. Retrace your steps, following Postgasse into **Fleischmarkt** ⑥. Nearby Hoher Markt, reached by taking Rotenturmstrasse west to Lichtensteg or Bauernmarkt, was part of the early Roman encampment, witness the Roman Ruins under **Hoher Markt** ⑦. The extension of Fleischmarkt ends in a set of stairs leading up past the eccentric Kornhäusal Tower. Up the stairs to the right on Ruprechtsplatz is **Ruprechtskirche** ⑧, St. Rupert's Church, allegedly the city's oldest. Take Sterngasse down the steps, turn left into Marc Aurel-Strasse and right into Salvatorgasse to discover the lacework **Maria am Gestade** ⑨, Maria on the Banks, which once sat above a small river, now underground.

TIMING

If you're pressed for time and happy with facades rather than what's behind them, this route could take half a day, but if you love to look inside, stop to ponder and explore the myriad narrow alleys, figure at least a day for this walk. During services, wandering around the churches will be limited, but otherwise, you can tackle this walk about any time at your convenience.

Sights to See

Basilikenhaus (House of the Basilik). One of the most intriguing houses in Vienna is the House of the Basilik, located at Schönlaterngasse (Beautiful Lantern Street)—once part of Vienna's medieval *Quartier Latin* and rapidly becoming so again. Along the street's Baroque houses (note the colorfully painted facades) and chic shops you'll find the house known as the Basiliskenhaus, at No. 7. According to legend, it was first built for a baker; on June 26, 1212, a foul-smelling basilisk (half-rooster, half-toad, with a glance that could kill) took up residence in the courtyard well, poisoning the water. An enterprising apprentice dealt with the problem by climbing down the well armed with a mirror; when the basilisk saw its own reflection it turned to stone. The petrified creature can still be seen in a niche on the building's facade. Today, modern science accounts for the contamination with a more prosaic explanation: natural-gas seepage. Be sure to take a look in the house's miniature courtyard for a trip back to medieval Vienna (the house itself is private). The picturesque street is named for the ornate wrought-iron wall lantern at No. 6. Just a few steps from the Basilikenhaus, take a look into the Baroque courtyard at No. 8—one of the city's prettiest—and at No. 9, you'll find the **Alte Schmiede**, the Old Smithy, a blacksmith workshop that is now a museum.

❹ **Dominikanerkirche** (Dominican Church). The Postgasse, to the east of Schönlaterngasse, introduces an unexpected visitor from Rome: the Dominikanerkirche. Built in the 1630s, some 50 years before the Viennese Baroque building boom, its facade is modeled after any number of Roman churches of the 16th century. The interior illustrates why the Baroque style came to be considered the height of bad taste during the 19th century and still has many detractors today. "Sculpt till you drop" seems to have been the motto here, and the viewer's eye is given no respite. This sort of Roman architectural orgy never really gained a foothold in Vienna, and when the great Viennese architects did pull out all the decorative stops—Hildebrandt's interior at the Belvedere Palace, for instance, they did it in a very different style and with far greater success. ✉ *Postgasse 4,* ☎ *01/512–7460. U-Bahn: U3 Stubentor/Dr. Karl-Lueger-Pl.*

❻ **Fleischmarkt No. 11.** Fleischmarkt and the picturesque tiny Griechengasse just beyond the glittering 19th-century Greek Orthodox church are part of the city's oldest core. This corner of the inner city has a medieval feel that is quite genuine; there has been a tavern at No. 11 for some 500 years. The wooden carving on the facade of the current Griechenbeisl restaurant commemorates Max Augustin—best known today from the song "Ach du lieber Augustin"—an itinerant musician who sang here during the plague of 1679.

NEED A BREAK? Take a pause for coffee at the corner of Fleischmarkt and Wolfengasse, at the **Café Vienne** (✉ Fleischmarkt 20, ☎ 01/512–4457) famous for baking what may be the biggest and most enticing cakes in the city.

6 **Heiligenkreuzerhof.** Tiny side streets and alleys run off of Sonnenfelsgasse, parallel to Bäckerstrasse. Amid the narrow streets is Heiligenkreuzerhof (Holy Cross Court), one of the city's most peaceful backwaters. This complex of buildings dates from the 17th century but got an 18th-century face-lift. Appropriately, the restraint of the architecture—with only here and there a small outburst of Baroque spirit—gives the courtyard a distinct feeling of retreat. The square is a favorite site for seasonal markets at Easter and Christmas, and for occasional outdoor art shows. Just around the bend is **Schönlaterngasse,** one of Vienna's most picturesque streets (☞ Basilikhaus, *above*).

7 **Hoher Markt.** This square was badly damaged during World War II, but the famous Anker Clock at the east end survived the artillery fire. The huge mechanical timepiece took six years (1911–17) to build and still attracts crowds at noon when the full panoply of mechanical figures representing Austrian historical personages parades by. The figures are identified on a plaque to the bottom left of the clock. The graceless buildings erected around the square since 1945 are not aging well and do little to show off the square's lovely Baroque centerpiece, the St. Joseph Fountain (portraying the marriage of Joseph and Mary), designed in 1729 by Joseph Emanuel Fischer von Erlach, son of the great Johann Bernhard Fischer von Erlach.

The Hoher Markt does harbor one wholly unexpected attraction, however: **underground Roman ruins.** This was once the main east–west axis of the Roman encampment of Vindobona, and the foundations of several officers' houses built in the 2nd century have been uncovered. The officers lived well: their houses even had central heating, and you can see the pipes that carried the hot water. The excavations are entered through the sushi snack bar in the passageway at No. 3; a short descriptive pamphlet in English is available at the ticket table. ✉ *Hoher Markt/Fischhof 3,* ☎ *01/535–5606.* 🎫 *AS25.* ⏲ *Tues.–Sun. 9–12:15 and 1–4:30. U-Bahn: U1, U3 Stephansplatz.*

9 **Maria am Gestade** (St. Mary on the Banks). The middle-Gothic, seven-sided tower of Maria am Gestade, crowned by a delicate cupola, is a sheer joy to the eye, and dispels the idea that Gothic must necessarily be autere. Built around 1400 (but much restored in the 17th and 19th centuries), the church incorporated part of the Roman city walls into its foundation; the north wall, as a result, takes a slight but noticeable dogleg to the right halfway down the nave. Like St. Stephen's, Maria am Gestade is rough-hewn Gothic, with a simple but forceful facade. The church is especially beloved, however, because of its unusual details—the pinnacled and saint-bedecked gable that tops the front facade, the stone canopy that hovers protectively over the front door, and (most appealing of all) the intricate openwork lantern atop the south-side bell tower. Appropriately enough in a city famous for its pastry, the lantern lends its tower an engaging suggestion of a sugar caster, while some see an allusion to hands intertwined in prayer. ✉ *Passauer Pl./Salvatorgasse. U-Bahn: U1, U3 Stephansplatz.*

5 **Postsparkasse** (Post Office Savings Bank). The Post Office Savings Bank is one of modern architecture's greatest curiosities. It was designed in 1904 by Otto Wagner, whom many consider the father of 20th-century architecture. In his famous manifesto, *Modern Architecture,* Wagner condemned 19th-century revivalist architecture and pleaded for a modern style that honestly expressed modern building methods. Accordingly, the

Academy of Fine Arts, **43**
Albertina Museum, **41**
Belvedere Palace, **47**
Blutgasse quarter, **37**
Bohemian Court Chancery, **10**
Burgtheater, **32**
Café Central, **17**
Demel's, **24**
Dominikanerkirche, **4**
Figarohaus, **38**
Fleischmarkt No. 11, **6**
Freud's Apartment, **35**
Heiligenkreuzerhof, **3**
Historisches Museum der Stadt Wien, **46**
Hofburg, **25**
Hoher Markt, **7**
Jewish Museum, **20**
Justizpalast, **29**
Kaisergruft, **40**
Karlskirche, **45**
Kinsky Palace, **13**
Kirche Am Hof, **11**
Kohlmarkt, **23**
Kunsthistorisches Museum, **26**
Looshaus, **19**
Maria am Gestade, **9**
Michaelerplatz, **18**
Ministry of Finance, **39**
Minoritenkirche, **16**
Museum Moderner Kunst, **36**
Palais Ferstel, **12**
Parliament, **30**
Pasqualatihaus, **15**
Peterskirche, **22**
Postsparkasse, **5**
Rathaus, **31**
Ruprechtskirche, **8**
Schottenkirche, **14**
Secession Pavilion, **44**
Spittelberg quarter, **27**
Stock-im-Eisen, **21**
St. Stephen's Cathedral, **1**
State Opera House, **42**
Universität, **33**
Universitätskirche, **2**
Volksgarten, **28**
Votivkirche, **34**

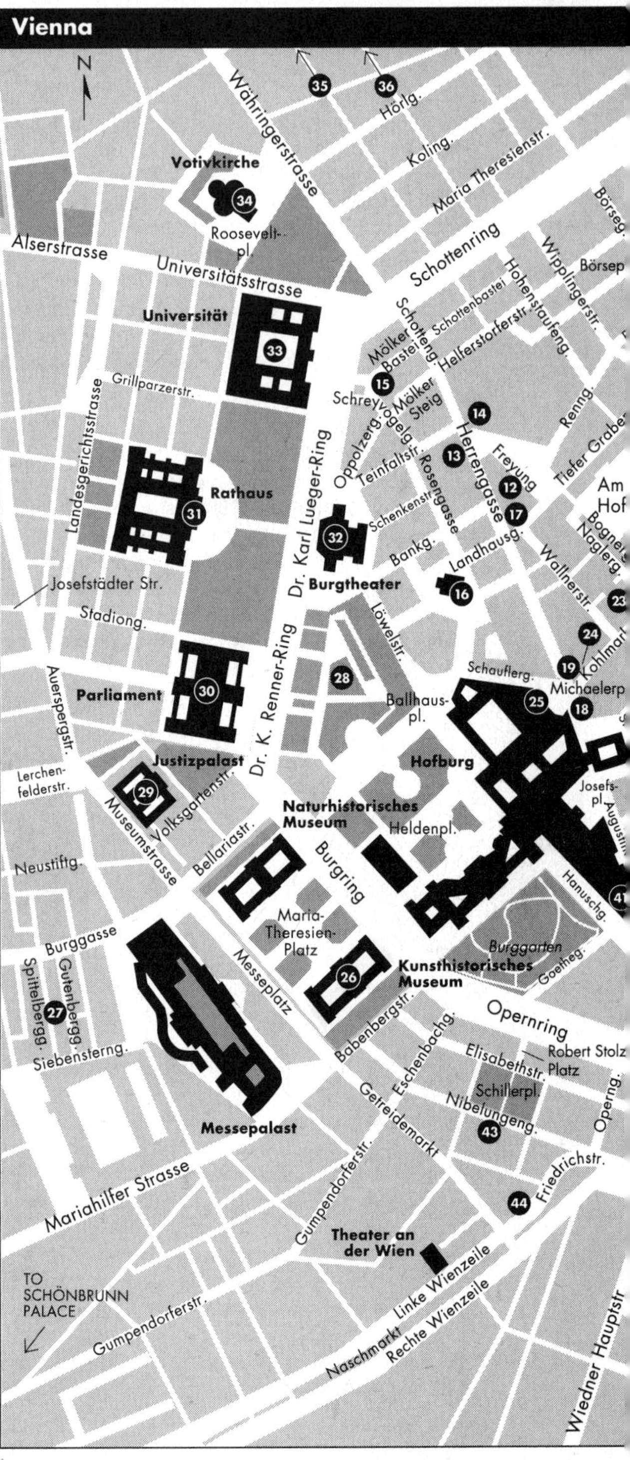

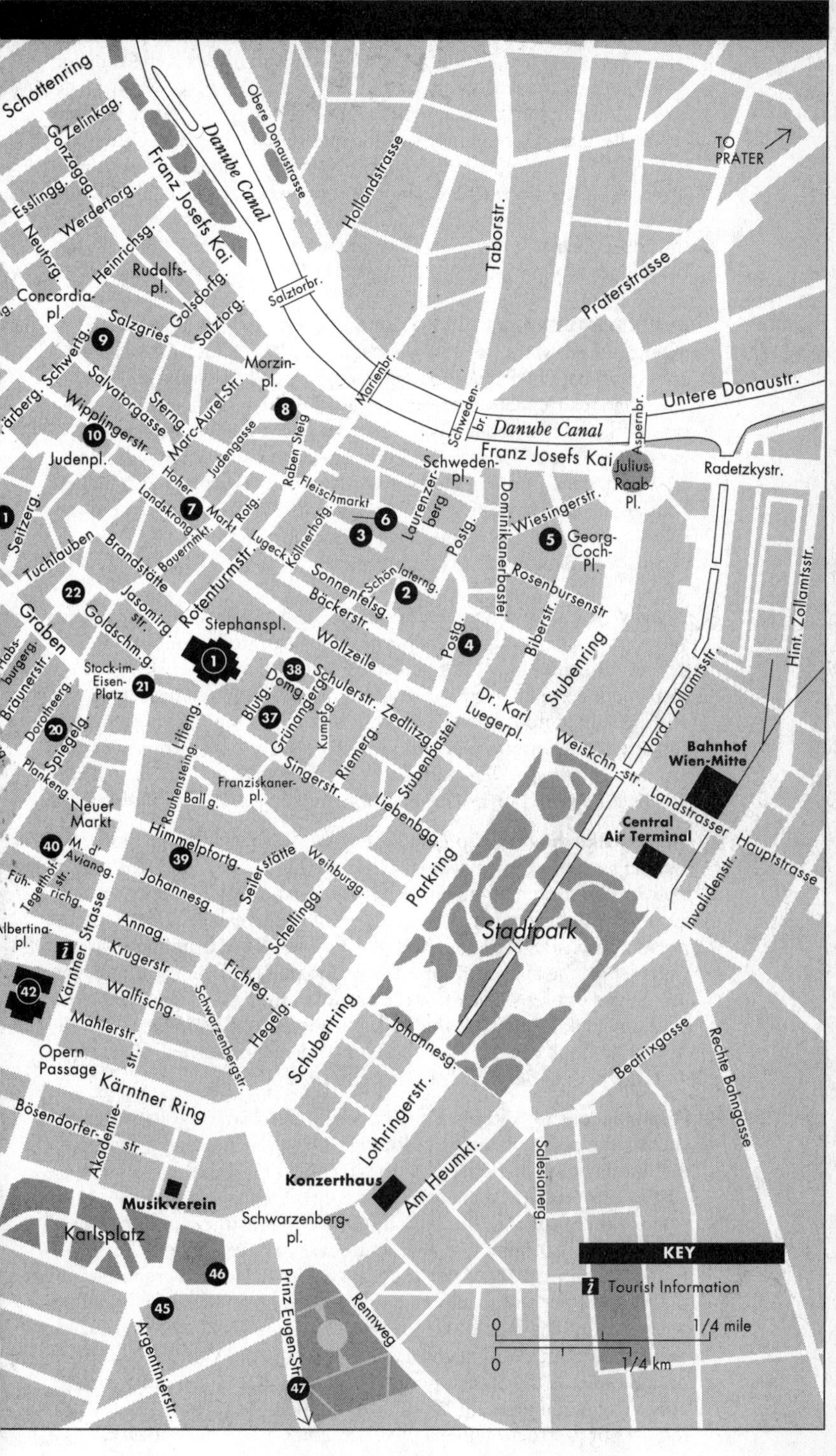

Danube Canal
Franz Josefs Kai
Stadtpark
TO PRATER
Praterstrasse
Untere Donaustr.
Stephanspl.
Karlsplatz
Konzerthaus
Musikverein
Bahnhof Wien-Mitte
Central Air Terminal
Schwarzenberg-pl.
Kärntner Ring
Schubertring
Parkring
Stubenring
KEY
Tourist Information
1/4 mile
1/4 km

exterior walls of the Post Office Savings Bank are mostly flat and undecorated; visual interest is supplied merely by varying the pattern of the bolts that were used to hold the marble slabs in place on the wall surface during construction. Later architects were to embrace Wagner's beliefs wholeheartedly, although they used different, truly modern building materials: glass and concrete rather than marble. The Post Office Savings Bank was indeed a bold leap into the future, but unfortunately the future took a different path and today the whole appears a bit dated. Go inside for a look at the restored and functioning *Kassa-Saal,* or central cashier's hall, to see how Wagner carried his concepts over to interior design. ✉ *Georg-Coch-Pl. 2,* ☎ *01/51400.* ⏲ *Lobby weekdays 8–3.*

OFF THE BEATEN PATH

HUNDERTWASSERHAUS – To see one of Vienna's most amazing buildings, travel eastward from Schwendenplatz or Julius-Raab Platz along Radetzkystrasse to the junction of Kegelgasse and Löwengasse. Here, you'll find the Hundertwasserhaus, a 50-apartment public-housing complex designed by Friedensreich Hundertwasser, Austria's best-known living painter. The structure looks as though it had been decorated by a crew of mischievous circus clowns wielding giant crayons. The building caused a sensation when it was erected in 1985 and still draws crowds of sightseers. ✉ *Löwengasse/Kegelgasse. U-Bahn: U1 or U4/Schwedenpl., then Streetcar N to Hetzgasse.*

Nearby, you'll find another Hundertwasser project, the **KunstHaus Wien** art museum, which mounts outstanding international exhibits in addition to showings of the colorful Hundertwasser works. Like the apartment complex nearby, the building itself is pure Hundertwasser, with irregular floors, windows with trees growing out of them, and sudden architectural surprises, a wholly appropriate setting for modern art. ✉ *Untere Weissgerberstr. 13,* ☎ *01/712–0491–0.* ⏲ *Daily 10–7. U-Bahn: U1 or U4/Schwedenpl., then Streetcar N to Radetzkypl..*

❽ **Ruprechtskirche** (St. Ruprecht's Church). Ruprechtsplatz, another of Vienna's time-warp backwaters, lies to the north of the Kornhäusel Tower. The church in the middle, Ruprechtskirche, is the city's oldest. According to legend it was founded in 740; the oldest part of the present structure (the lower half of the tower) dates from the 11th century. Set on the ancient ramparts overlooking the Danube Canal, it is serene and unpretentious. Try the one door, though it's usually locked. You can look in through the grill, but the lack of windows generally obscures what can be seen of the arcaded, unadorned interior. ✉ *Ruprechtspl. U-Bahn: U1, U4 Schwedenpl.*

❶ **Stephansdom** (St. Stephen's Cathedral). This soaring structure enshrines the heart of Vienna, although it is curious to note that in its earliest days, as the parish church which was built in the years 1144–1147, it stood outside the walls of the city. Vienna can thank a period of hard times for the Mother Church for the distinctive silhouette of the cathedral. Originally the structure was to have had matching 445-foot-high spires, a standard design of the era, but funds ran out, and the north tower to this day remains a happy reminder of what gloriously is not. The lack of symmetry creates an imbalance that makes the cathedral instantly identifiable from its profile alone. The cathedral, as well as the Staastoper and some other major buildings, were very heavily damaged in World War II. Since then, it has risen from the fires of destruction like a phoenix, and as with the phoenix, it is a symbol of regeneration.

It is difficult now, sitting quietly in the shadowed peace, to tell what was original and what parts of the walls and vaults were reconstructed.

No matter: its history-rich atmosphere is dear to all Viennese. That noted, St. Stephen's possesses a fierce presence that is blatantly un-Viennese. It is a stylistic jumble ranging from 13th-century Romanesque to 15th-century Gothic. Like the exterior, St. Stephen's interior lacks the soaring unity of Europe's greatest Gothic cathedrals, with much of its decoration dating from the later Baroque era.

The wealth of decorative sculpture in St. Stephen's can be demoralizing to the nonspecialist, so if you wish to explore the cathedral in detail, you may want to buy the admirably complete English-language description sold in the small room marked *Schriften und Opferkerzen* (Pamphlets and Votive Candles). One particularly masterly work, however, should be seen by everyone: the stone pulpit attached to the second freestanding pier on the left of the central nave, carved by Anton Pilgram around 1510. The delicacy of its decoration would in itself set the pulpit apart, but even more intriguing are its five sculpted figures. Carved around the outside of the pulpit proper are the four Latin Fathers of the Church (from left to right: Saint Augustine, Saint Gregory, Saint Jerome, and Saint Ambrose), and each is given an individual personality so sharply carved as to suggest satire, perhaps of living models. There is no satire suggested by the fifth figure, however; below the pulpit's stairs Pilgram sculpted a fine self-portrait, showing himself peering out a half-open window. Note the toads, lizards, and other creatures climbing the spiral rail alongside the steps up to the pulpit. As you walk among the statues and aisles, remember that many notable events occurred here, including the marriage of Mozart in 1782 and his funeral in December 1791.

St. Stephen's was devastated by fire in the last days of World War II, and the extent of the damage may be seen by leaving the cathedral through the south portal, where a set of prereconstruction photographs commemorates the disaster. Restoration was protracted and difficult, but today the cathedral once again dominates the center of the city. The bird's-eye views from the cathedral's beloved **Alte Steffl** (Old Steven) tower will be a highlight for some. The tower is 450 feet high and was built between 1359 and 1433. The climb or elevator ride up is rewarded with vistas that extend to the rising slopes of the Wienerwald. ✉ *Stephanspl.,* ☎ *01/515–52–526.* 💳 *Each tour AS40, elevator AS40.* ⏲ *Daily 6 AM–10 PM; tour Mon.–Sat. at 10:30 and 3, and Sun. and holidays at 3; evening tour July and Aug., daily at 7; catacombs tour Mon.–Sat. at 10, 11, 11:30, 2, 2:30, 3:30, 4, and 4:30, and Sun. and holidays at 2, 2:30, 3:30, 4, and 4:30; North Tower elevator to "Pummerin" bell Apr.–Sept., daily 9–6, and Oct.–Mar., daily 8–5. U-Bahn: U1, U3 Stephanspl.*

Vienna of the Middle Ages is encapsulated in the streets in back of St. Stephen's cathedral. You could easily spend half a day or more just prowling the narrow streets and passageways—Wollzeile, Bäckerstrasse, Blutgasse—typical remnants of an early era. Café Alt Wien at Bäckerstrasse 9 is a true original and a hangout for artists and students young and old. Other cafés, bars, and small restaurants along the street are equally worth a visit. Don't overlook the amusing, 18th-century cow playing checkers painted on the facade of the house at No. 12.

❷ **Universitätskirche** (Jesuit Church). The east end of Bäckerstrasse is punctuated by Dr.-Ignaz-Seipel-Platz, named for the theology professor who was chancellor of Austria during the 1920s. On the north side is the Universitätskirche, or Jesuitenkirche, built around 1630. Its flamboyant Baroque interior contains a fine trompe l'oeil ceiling fresco by that master of visual trickery, Andrea Pozzo, who was imported from Rome in 1702 for the job. You may hear a Mozart or Haydn mass sung here in Latin on many Sundays. ✉ *Dr. Ignaz-Seipl-Pl.*, ☎ *01/512–5232. U-Bahn: U3 Stubentor/Dr. Karl-Lueger-Pl.*

OFF THE BEATEN PATH

PRATER – Vienna's most famous park and most beloved attraction for children can be found by heading out northeast from the historic city center, across the Danube Canal along Praterstrasse: the famous Prater, or more correctly, Volksprater (or as the Viennese call it, *Wurstelprater*), the city's foremost amusement park. In 1766, to the dismay of the aristocracy, Emperor Joseph II decreed that the vast expanse of imperial parklands known as the Prater would henceforth be open to the public. East of the inner city between the Danube Canal and the Danube proper, the Prater is a public park to this day, notable for its long promenade (the Hauptallee, more than 4½ kilometers, or 3 miles, in length, its sports facilities (a golf course, a stadium, a race track, and a swimming pool, for starters), and the *Wurstelprater* with its giant Ferris wheel (Riesenrad), the traditional, modern amusement-park rides, plus a number of less innocent indoor, sex-oriented attractions, a planetarium, and a small but interesting museum devoted to the Wurstelprater's long history. If you look carefully, you can discover a handful of children's rides dating to the 1920s and 30s which survived the fire that consumed most of the Volksprater in 1945. The best-known attraction is the 200-foot-Ferris wheel that figured so prominently in the 1949 film *The Third Man*. One of three built in Europe at the end of the last century (the others were in England and France, but have long since been dismantled), the wheel was badly damaged during World War II and restored shortly thereafter. Its progress is slow and stately (a revolution takes 10 minutes), the views from its cars magnificent, particularly toward dusk. ☎ *01/729–5430.* *AS45.* ⏲ *Apr., daily 10 AM–11 PM; May–Sept., daily 9 AM–midnight; Oct., daily 10–10; Nov., daily 10–8; Dec., weekends 10–6. U-Bahn: U1/Praterstern.*

Bittersweet Vienna: Baroque Gems and Cozy Cafés

As the city developed and expanded, the core quickly outgrew its early confines. New urban centers sprang up, to be ornamented by government buildings and elegant town residences. Since Vienna was the beating heart of a vast empire, nothing was spared to make the edifices as exuberant as possible, with utility often a secondary consideration. The best architects of the day were commissioned to create impressions as well as buildings, and they did their job well. That so much has survived is a testimony to the solidness both of the designs and of the structures on which the ornamentation has been overlayed.

Those not fortunate enough to afford town palaces were relegated to housing that was often confining and far less than elegant. Rather than suffer the discomfitures of a disruptive household environment, the city's literati and its philosophers and artists took refuge in cafés, which in effect became their combined salons and offices. To this day, cafés remain an important element of Viennese life. Many residents still have their *Stammtisch,* or regular table, at which they appear daily. Talk still prevails—but increasingly so do handy radio telephones and even laptops.

A Good Walk

Start in the Wipplingerstrasse at the upper (west) end of Hohe Markt to find touches of both the imperial and the municipal Vienna. On the east side is the **Altes Rathaus,** which served as the city hall until 1885; on the west, the **Bohemian Court Chancery** ⑩, once diplomatic headquarters for Bohemia's representation to the Habsburg court. Turn south into the short Fütterergasse to reach **Judenplatz,** in the Middle Ages, center of Judaism in Vienna. A clockwatcher's delight is down at the end of Kurrentgasse in the form of the **Uhrenmuseum** (Clock Museum); around the corner through the Parisgasse to Schulhof, a children's delight is the **Puppen- und Spielzeug-Museum** (Doll and Toy Museum). Follow Schulhof into the huge **Am Hof** square, boasting the **Kirche am Hof** ⑪ and what must be the world's most elegant fire station. The square hosts an antiques and collectibles market most of the year on Thursdays and Friday, plus other ad hoc events. Take the miniscule Irisgasse from Am Hof into the Naglergasse, noting the mosaic Jugendstil facade on the pharmacy in the Bognergasse, to your left. Around a bend in the narrow Naglergasse is **Freyung,** an irregular square bounded on the south side by two wonderfully stylish palaces including **Palais Ferstel** ⑫, now a shopping arcade, and the elegantly restored **Palais Harrach** next door, now an outpost of the Kunsthistoriches Museum. Opposite, the privately-run **Kunstforum** art museum mounts varied and outstanding exhibitions. The famous **Kinsky Palace** ⑬ at the beginning of Herrengasse is still partly a private residence. The north side of Freyung is watched over by the **Schottenkirche** ⑭, the Scottish church in fact established by Irish monks. The complex also houses a small but worthwhile museum of the order's treasures. Follow Teinfaltstrasse from opposite the Schottenkirche, turning right into Schreyvogelgasse. Climb the ramp on your right past the so-called Dreimäderlhaus at Schreyvogelgasse 10—note the ornate facade of this pre-Biedermeier patrician house—to reach Molker Bastei, where Beethoven lived in the **Pasqualatihaus** ⑮, now housing a museum memorializing the composer. Follow the ring south to Löwelstrasse, turning left into Bankgasse, then turn right into Abraham-a-Santa Clara-Gasse (our map doesn't show this street by name—for obvious reasons of space!—but it's the tiny street that runs off the Bankgasse) to Minoritenplatz and the **Minoritenkirche** ⑯, the Minorite church with its odd, hat-less tower. Inside is a kitschy mosaic Last Supper. Landhausgasse will bring you to Herrengasse, and diagonally across the street, in the back corner of the Palais Ferstel, is the **Café Central** ⑰, one of Vienna's hangouts for the famous. Going south up the Herrengasse on the left is the odd Hochhaus, a twentieth-century building once noted as Vienna's skyscraper. Opposite are elegant Baroque former town palaces, now used as museum and administration buildings by the province of Lower Austria.

TIMING

The actual distances in this walk are relatively short, and you could cover the route in 1½ hours or so. But if you take time to linger in the museums and sample a Kaffee mit schlag in the Café Central, you'll develop a much better understanding of the contrasts between old and newer in the city. You could easily spend a day following this walk, if you were to take in all of the museums; note that these, like many Viennese museums, are closed on Mondays.

Sights to See

10 **Bohemian Court Chancery.** One of the architectural jewels of the Inner City can be found at No. 7 Wipplingerstrasse, the former Bohemian Court Chancery, built between 1708 and 1714 by Johann Bernhard Fischer von Erlach. Fischer von Erlach and his contemporary, Johann Lukas von Hildebrandt, were the reigning architectural geniuses of Baroque Vienna; they designed their churches and palaces during the building boom that followed the defeat of the Turks in 1683. Both had studied architecture in Rome, and both were deeply impressed by the work of the great Italian architect Francesco Borromini, who had brought to his designs a wealth and freedom of invention that was looked upon with horror by most contemporary Romans. But for Fischer von Erlach and Hildebrandt, Borromini's ideas were a source of triumphant

architectural inspiration, and when they returned to Vienna they produced between them many of the city's most beautiful buildings. Alas, narrow Wipplingerstrasse allows little more than a oblique view of this florid facade. The back side of the building, on Judenplatz, is less elaborate but gives a better idea of the design concept. The building first served as diplomatic and representational offices of Bohemia (now a part of the Czech republic) to the Vienna-based monarchy, and, today, still houses government offices.

Altes Rathaus (Old City Hall). Opposite the Bohemian Chancery (☞ *above*) stands the Altes Rathaus, dating from the 14th century but sporting 18th-century Baroque motifs on its facade. The interior passageways and courtyards, which are open during the day, house a Gothic chapel (open at odd hours), a much-loved, Baroque wall-fountain (Georg Raphael Donner's **Andromeda Fountain** of 1741), and display cases exhibiting maps and photos illustrating the city's history.

Am Hof. Am Hof is one of the city's oldest squares. In the Middle Ages the ruling Babenberg family built their castle on the site of No. 2; hence the name of the square, which means simply "at court" (the grand residence hosted such luminaries as Barbarossa and Walter vonder Vogelweide, the famous Minnesinger who features in Wagner's *Tannhauser*). The Baroque **Column of Our Lady** in the center dates from 1667, marking the Catholic victory over the Swedish Protestants in the Thirty Years' War (1618–48). The onetime **Civic Armory** at the northwest corner has been used as a fire station since 1685 (the high-spirited facade, with its Habsburg eagle, was "Baroqued" in 1731) and today houses the headquarters of Vienna's fire department. The complex includes a firefighting museum (open only on Sunday and holiday mornings). Presiding over the east side of the square is the noted Kirche Am Hof church (☞ *below*). In Bognergasse to the right of the Kirche Am Hof, around the corner from the imposing Bank Austria headquarters building, at No. 9 is the **Engel Pharmacy,** with a Jugendstil mosaic depicting winged women collecting the elixir of life in outstretched chalices. At the turn of the century the inner city was dotted with storefronts decorated in a similar manner; today this is the sole survivor. Around the bend from the Naglergasse is the picturesque Freyung square (☞ Palais Kinsky, *below*).

17 **Café Central.** Part of the Ferstel Palace complex, at the corner of Herrengasse and Strauchgasse, the Café Central is one of Vienna's more famous cafés, its full authenticity blemished only by complete restoration in recent years. In its prime (before World War I), the café was home—in the literal as well as the figurative sense—to some of the most famous literary figures of the day. In that era, housing was one of the city's most intractable problems. As a result, many of Vienna's artists and writers spent as little time as possible in their "homes" and instead ensconced themselves at a favorite café, where they ate, socialized, worked, and even received mail. The denizens of the Central favored political argument; indeed, their heated discussions became so well known that in October 1917, when Austria's foreign secretary was informed of the outbreak of the Russian Revolution, he dismissed the report with a facetious reference to a well-known local Marxist, the chess-loving (and presumably harmless) "Herr Bronstein from the Café Central." The remark was to become famous all over Austria, for Herr Bronstein had disappeared and was about to resurface in Russia bearing a new name: Leon Trotsky. No matter how crowded the café may become, you can linger as long as you like over a single cup of coffee and a newspaper from the huge international selection provided. Across Herrengasse at No. 17 is the Café Central Konditorei, an excellent pastry and confectionery shop associated with the café.

⊠ Herrengasse 14, ☎ 01/5333–3726–26. AE, DC, MC, V. Closed Sun. U-Bahn: U3 Herrengasse.

The Freyung. Naglergasse, at its curved end, flows into Heidenschuss, which in turn leads down a slight incline from Am Hof to one of Vienna's most prominent squares, the Freyung, meaning "freeing." The square was so named because for many centuries the monks at the adjacent Scottish Church (☞ *below*) possessed the privilege of offering sanctuary for three days. In the center of the square stands the allegorical **Austria Fountain** (1845), notable because its Bavarian designer, one Ludwig Schwanthaler, had the statues cast in Munich and then supposedly filled them with cigars to be smuggled into Vienna for black-market sale. Around the sides of the square are some of Vienna's greatest patrician residences, including the Ferstel, Harrach, and Kinsky Palaces (☞ *below*).

Judenplatz. From the 13th to the 15th century, Judenplatz—off Wiplingerstrasse—was the center of Vienna's Jewish ghetto. Today the square's centerpiece is a rectangular block intended as a Holocaust memorial; the architect's concept was a stylized stack of books to recall Jewish strivings toward learning. Nearby is a statue of the 18th-century Jewish playwright Gotthold Ephraim Lessing, erected after World War II; disconcertingly, the statue suggests the underground comics of the American artist R. Crumb.

13 **Kinsky Palace.** Just one of the architectural treasures that comprises the urban set piece of the Freyung, the Palais Kinsky is the square's best-known palace, one of the most sophisticated pieces of Baroque architecture in the city. Located at Freyung 4, it was built between 1713 and 1716 by Hildebrandt. Its only real competition comes a few yards farther on: the Greek temple facade of the Schottenhof (☞ *below*), which is at right angles to the Schottenkirche church, up the street from the Kinsky Palace.

11 **Kirche am Hof** (Church of the Nine Choirs of Angels). The Kirche Am Hof, on the east side of the Am Hof square, is identified by its sprawling Baroque facade, designed by Carlo Carlone in 1662. The somber interior lacks appeal but the checkerboard marble floor may remind you of Dutch churches. ⊠ *Am Hof 1.* U-Bahn: U3 Herrengasse.

16 **Minoritenkirche** (Church of the Minorite Order). The Minoritenplatz is named after its centerpiece, the Minoritenkirche, a Gothic affair with a strange stump of a tower, built mostly in the 14th century. The front is brutally ugly, but the back is a wonderful (if predominantly 19th-century) surprise. The interior contains the city's most imposing piece of kitsch: a large mosaic reproduction of Leonardo da Vinci's *Last Supper,* commissioned by Napoléon in 1806 and later purchased by Emperor Francis I. ⊠ *Minoritenpl. 2a, ☎ 01/533–4162. U-Bahn: U3 Herrengasse.*

12 **Palais Ferstel.** At Freyung 2 stands the recently restored Palais Ferstel, which is not a palace at all but a commercial shop-and-office complex designed in 1856 and named for its architect, Heinrich Ferstel. The facade is Italianate in style, harking back, in its 19th-century way, to the Florentine palazzi of the early Renaissance. The interior is unashamedly eclectic: vaguely Romanesque in feel and Gothic in decoration, with here and there a bit of Renaissance or Baroque sculpted detail thrown in for good measure. Such eclecticism is sometimes dismissed as mindlessly derivative, but here the architectural details are so respectfully and inventively combined that the interior becomes a pleasure to explore. The 19th century stock exchange rooms upstairs are now gloriously restored and used for conferences and concerts.

Next door to the Palais Fersel is the newly renovated **Palais Harrach,** part of which now houses a small but worthwhile gallery of paintings and art objects from the main Kunsthistorisches Museum (which has far more treasures than space in which to display them) as well as special exhibits. ✉ *Freyung 3,* ☎ *01/523–7593.* 🎫 *Combined ticket with Kunsthistorisches Museum AS45.* ⏲ *Wed.–Mon. 10–5.*

The huge gold ball atop the doorway across the Freyung at the corner of Renngasse marks the entrance to the **Kunstforum,** an extensive art gallery run by Bank Austria featuring outstanding temporary exhibitions. ✉ *Freyung 8,* ☎ *01/711–91–5742.* 🎫 *AS90.* ⏲ *Thurs.–Tues. 10–6, Wed. 10–9. U-Bahn: U3 Herrengasse.*

⓯ **Pasqualatihaus.** Beethoven lived in the Pasqualatihaus while he was composing his only opera, *Fidelio,* as well as his Seventh Symphony and Fourth Piano Concerto. Today his apartment houses a small commemorative museum (in distressingly modern taste). After navigating the narrow and twisting stairway, you might well ask how he maintained the jubilant spirit of the works he wrote there. This house is around the corner from the Third Man Portal (☞ *below*). ✉ *8 Mölker Bastei,* ☎ *01/535–8905.* 🎫 *AS25.* ⏲ *Tues.–Sun. 9–12:15 and 1–4:30. U-Bahn: U2 Schottentor.*

Puppen und Spielzeugmuseum (Doll and Toy Museum). As appealing as the clockworks of the Uhrenmuseum located just next door is this doll and toy museum, with its collections of dolls, dollhouses, teddies, and trains. ✉ *Schulhof 4,* ☎ *01/535–6860.* 🎫 *AS60.* ⏲ *Tues.–Sun. 10–6. U-Bahn: U1, U3 Stephansplatz.*

Schottenhof. Found on the Freyung square and designed by Joseph Kornhäusel in a very different style from his Fleischmarkt tower, the Schottenhof facade typifies the change that came over Viennese architecture during the Biedermeier era (1815–48). The Viennese, according to the traditional view, were at the time so relieved to be rid of the upheavals of the Napoléonic Wars that they accepted without protest the ironhanded repression of Prince Metternich, chancellor of Austria, and retreated into a cozy and complacent domesticity. Restraint also ruled in architecture, with Baroque license rejected in favor of a new and historically "correct" style that was far more controlled and reserved. Kornhäusel led the way in Vienna; his Schottenhof facade is all sober organization and frank repetition. But in its marriage of strong and delicate forces it still pulls off the great Viennese-waltz trick of successfully merging seemingly antithetical characteristics. *U-Bahn: U2 Schottentor.*

NEED A BREAK? In summer, **Café Haag** and **Wienerwald** restaurant share the tree-shaded courtyard of the Schottenhof (☞ *above*), ideal for a relaxing coffee or a glass of wine.

⓮ **Schottenkirche.** In 1758–61 the famous Italian painter Canaletto painted the Freyung square looking north toward the Schottenkirche; the pictures hang in the Kunsthistorisches Museum and the similarity to the view you see about 240 years later is arresting. In fact, a church has stood on the site of the Schottenkirche since 1177; the present edifice dates to the mid-1600s when it replaced its predecessor, which had collapsed after the architects of the time had built on weakened foundations. The interior, with its ornate ceiling and a decided surplus of cherubs and angels' faces, is in stark contrast to the plain exterior. The adjacent small **Museum im Schottenstift** includes the best of the monastery's art works, including the celebrated late-Gothic high altar dating to about 1470. The winged altar is fascinating for its portrayal of the Holy Family in flight into Egypt—with Vienna clearly identifiable in the background. ✉ *Freyung 6,* ☎ *01/534–9820; museum, 01/534–9860–0.* 🎟 *AS40.* ⏲ *Thurs.–Sat. 10–5, Sun. noon–5. U-Bahn: U2 Schottentor.*

"Third Man" Portal. The doorway at No. 8 Schreyvogelgasse (up the incline) was made famous in 1949 by the classic film *The Third Man;* it was here that Orson Welles, as the malevolently knowing Harry Lime, stood hiding in the dark, only to have his smiling face illuminated by a sudden light from the upper-story windows of the house across the alley. The film enjoys a renaissance each summer in the Burg Kino and is fascinating for its portrayal of a postwar Vienna still in ruins. To get here from the nearby and noted Schottenkirche (☞ *above*), follow Teinfaltstrasse one block west to Schreyvogelgasse on the right.

Uhrenmuseum (Clock Museum). Kurrentgasse leads south from the east end of Judenplatz; the beautifully restored 18th-century houses on its east side make this one of the most unpretentiously appealing streets in the city. And at the far end of the street is one of Vienna's most appealing museums: the Uhrenmuseum, or Clock Museum (enter to the right on the Schulhof side of the building). The museum's three floors display a splendid array of clocks and watches—more than 3,000 timepieces—dating from the 15th century to the present. The ruckus of bells and chimes on any hour is impressive, but try to be here at noon for the full cacophony. Right next door is the Puppen und Spielzeugmuseum (☞ *above*). ✉ *Schulhof 2,* ☎ *01/533–2265.* 🎟 *AS50.* ⏲ *Tues.–Sun. 9–4:30. U-Bahn: U1, U3 Stephansplatz.*

Vienna's Shop Window: From Michaelerplatz to the Graben

The compact area bounded roughly by the back side of the Hofburg palace complex, the Kohlmarkt, the Graben, and Kärntner Strasse belongs to the oldest core of the city. Remains of the Roman city are just below the present-day surface. This was and still is the commercial heart of the city, with shops and markets for various commodities; today, the Kohlmarkt and Graben in particular offer the choicest luxury shops, overflowing into the Graben end of Kärnter Strasse. The area is marvelous for its visual treats, ranging from the squares and varied architecture to window shopping. The evening view down Kohlmarkt from the Graben is an inspiring classic, with the night-lit gilded dome of Michael's Gate to the palace complex as the glittering backdrop.

A Good Walk

Start your walk through this fascinating quarter at **Michaelerplatz** ⑱, one of Vienna's most evocative squares, where the feel of the imperial city remains very strong; the buildings around the perimeter present a synopsis of the city's entire architectural history: medieval church spire, Renaissance church facade, Baroque palace facade, 19th-century apartment house, and 20th-century bank. Look in on **Michaelerkirche** (St. Michael's Church). Opposite the church is the once-controversial **Looshaus** ⑲, considered a breakthrough in modern architecture (visitors are welcome to view the restored lobby). From Michaelerplatz, take the small passageway to the right of the church; in it on your right is a relief dating to 1480 of Christ on the Mount of Olives. Follow the Stallburggasse through to Dorotheergasse, and turn right to discover the **Dorotheum,** the government-run auction house and the Vienna equivalent of Christie's or Sotheby's. On your right in the Dorotheergasse toward the Graben is the enlarged **Jewish Museum** ⑳, which includes a bookstore and café. On the left is the famous **Café Hawelka,** home to the contemporary art and literature crowd. Turn right in the Graben to come to **Stock-im-Eisen Platz** ㉑; the famous nail-studded tree trunk is encased in the corner of the building with the Bank Austria offices. Opposite and impossible to overlook is the agressive **Neues Haas Haus,** an upmarket restaurant and shopping complex. Wander back through the Graben for the full effect of this harmonious square and, above all, look up to see the ornamentation on the buildings. Pass the **Pestsäule** (Plague Column), which shoots up from the middle of the Graben like a geyser of whipped cream. Just off to the north side is **Peterskirche** ㉒, St. Peter's Church, a Baroque gem almost hidden by its surroundings. At the end of the Graben, turn left into the **Kohlmarkt** ㉓ for the classic view of the domed arch leading to the Hofburg, the imperial palace complex. Even if your feet aren't calling a sit-down strike, finish up at **Demel's** ㉔, at Kohlmarkt 14, with some of the best *patisserie* in the world.

TIMING

Inveterate shoppers, window or otherwise, will want to take time to pause before or in many of the elegant shops during this walk, which then could easily take most of a day or even longer. If you're content with facades and general impressions, the exercise could be done in a bit over an hour, but it would be a shame to bypass the narrow side streets. In any case, look into St. Michael's and consider the fascinating Dorotheum, itself easily worth an hour or more.

Sights to See

Café Hawelka. At No. 6 Dorotheergasse, hidden behind an unprepossessing doorway, the Café Hawelka is one of the few famous inner-city cafés that has survived without major restoration. The Hawelka's air of romantic shabbiness—originally the product of Viennese *Fortwursteln*, or "muddling through," now sacrosanct literally as a national monument—is especially evocative. The smoky room has been home to most of Austria's leading artists and writers since 1945, and the Hawelka family has amassed an enviable art collection by taking paintings in lieu of cash from destitute artists who later became famous. ✉ *Dorotheergasse 6,* ☎ *01/512–8230.* ⊙ *Wed.–Sat., Mon. 8 AM–2 AM. No credit cards. U-Bahn: U1, U3 Stephanspl.*

Dorotheum. The narrow passageway just to the right of St. Michael's, with its large 15th-century relief depicting Christ on the Mount of Olives, leads into the Stallburggasse. The area is dotted with antiques stores, attracted by the presence of the Dorotheum, the famous Viennese auction house that began as a state-controlled pawnshop in 1707 (affectionately known as "Aunt Dorothy" to its patrons). Merchandise coming up for auction is on display at Dorotheergasse 17. The showrooms—packed with everything from carpets and pianos to cameras and jewelry and postage stamps—are well worth a visit. Some wares are not for auction but for immediate sale. ✉ *Dorotheergasse 17,* ☎ *01/515–60–0.* ⊙ *Weekdays 8–6, Sat. 8–noon. U-Bahn: U1, U3 Stephanspl.*

The Graben. One of Vienna's major crossroads, the Graben, leading west from Stock-im-Eisen-Platz, is a street whose unusual width gives it the presence and weight of a city square. Its shape is due to the Romans, who dug the city's southwestern moat here, adjacent to the original city walls. The Graben's centerpiece is the effulgently Baroque **Pestsäule,** or Plague Column, erected by Emperor Leopold I between 1687 and 1693 in thanks to God for delivering the city from a particularly virulent plague. Today the representation looks more like a host of cherubs doing their best to cope with the icing of a wedding cake wilting in the hot sunshine. Staunch Protestants may be shocked to learn that the foul figure of the Pest stands also for the heretic plunging away from the "True Faith" into the depth of hell. But they will have to get used to the fact that the Catholic Church has triumphed over Protestantism in Austria and frequently recalls the fact on stone and on canvas.

20 **Jewish Museum.** The former Eskeles Palace, once an elegant private residence, is now home to the city's Jüdisches Museum der Stadt Wien. New permanent exhibitions tell of the momentous role that Viennese-born Jews played in realms from music to medicine, art to philosophy, both in Vienna—until abruptly halted in 1938—and in the world at large. Changing exhibits add contemporary touches. The museum complex includes a café and bookstore. ✉ *Dorotheergasse 11,* ☎ *01/535–0431.* 💴 *AS70.* ⏲ *Sun.–Fri. 10–6, Thurs. 10–9. U-Bahn: U1, U3 Stephansplatz.*

23 **Kohlmarkt.** The Kohlmarkt, aside from its classic view of the domed entryway to the imperial palace complex of the Hofburg, is best known as Vienna's most elegant shopping street. The shops, not the buildings, are remarkable, although there is an entertainingly ironic odd-couple pairing: No. 11 (early 18th century) and No. 9 (early 20th century). The mixture of architectural styles is similar to that of the Graben, but the general atmosphere is low-key, as if the street were consciously deferring to the showstopper dome at the west end. The composers Haydn and Chopin lived in houses on the street, and indeed, the Kohlmarkt lingers in the memory when flashier streets have faded.

NEED A BREAK?

24 **Demel** (✉ Kohlmarkt 14, ☎ 01/535–1717–0), Vienna's best-known (and priciest) pastry shop, offers a dizzying selection, and if you possess a sweet tooth, a visit will be worth every penny of the extra cost. Chocolate lovers will want to participate in the famous Viennese Sachertorte debate by sampling Demel's version and then comparing it with its rival at the Sacher Café, which is in Hotel Sacher. For considerably less elegance with a touch of the Formica-cool '50s, but excellent coffee and pastries as well as value, go instead to the **Arabia** café (✉ Kohlmarkt 5, ☎ 01/503–0929).

19 **Looshaus.** In 1911, Adolf Loos, one of the founding fathers of 20th-century modern architecture, built the Looshaus on august Michaelerplatz, facing the Imperial Palace entrance. It was considered nothing less than an architectural declaration of war. After two hundred years of Baroque and neo-Baroque exuberance, the first generation of 20th-century architects had had enough. Loos led the revolt against architectural tradition; *Ornament and Crime* was the title of his famous manifesto, in which he inveighed against the conventional architectural wisdom of the 19th century. Instead, he advocated buildings that were plain, honest, and functional. When he built the Looshaus for Goldman and Salatsch (men's clothiers) in 1911, the city was scandalized. Archduke Franz Ferdinand, heir to the throne, was so offended that he vowed never again to use the Michaelerplatz entrance to the Imperial Palace. Today the Looshaus has lost its power to shock, and the facade seems quite innocuous; argument now focuses on the post-modern Neues Haas-Haus (☞ *below*) opposite St. Stephen's cathedral. The recently restored interior of the Looshaus remains a breathtaking surprise; the building now houses a bank and you can go inside to see the stylish chambers and staircase. ✉ *Michaelpl. 3. U-Bahn: U3 Herrengasse.*

18 **Michaelerplatz.** In Michaelerplatz, one of Vienna's most historic squares, the buildings seem to crowd in toward the center of the small plaza as if acceding to the center of the small plaza. Rightly so, for this is now the site of an excavation revealing Roman plus 18th and 19th century layers of the past. The excavations are a latter-day distraction from the

Michaelerplatz's most noted claim to fame—the eloquent entryway to the palace complex of the Hofburg. *U-Bahn: U3 Herrengasse.*

Neues Haas-Haus. Stock-im-Eisen-Platz is home to central Vienna's (for the moment, at least) most controversial piece of architecture: the Neues Haas-Haus designed by Hans Hollein, one of Austria's best-known living architects. Detractors consider its aggressively contemporary style out of place opposite St. Stephen's, seeing the cathedral's style parodied by being stood on its head; advocates consider the contrast enlivening. Whatever the ultimate verdict, the new building has not been the expected commercial success; its restaurants may be thriving, but its boutiques are not. ✉ *Stephanspl. 12.* ⏲ *Shops weekdays 9–6, Sat. 9–noon.*

22 **Peterskirche** (St. Peter's Church). Considered the best example of church Baroque in Vienna—certainly the most theatrical—the Peterskirche was constructed between 1702 and 1708 by Lucas von Hildebrandt. According to legend, the original church on this site was founded in 792 by Charlemagne, a tale immortalized by the relief plaque on the right side of the church. The facade possesses angled towers, graceful towertops (said to have been inspired by the tents of the Turks during the siege of 1683), and an unusually fine entrance portal. Inside the church, the Baroque decoration is elaborate, with some fine touches (particularly the glass-crowned galleries high on the walls to either side of the altar and the amazing tableau of the martyrdom of St. John Nepomuk), but the lack of light and years of accumulated dirt create a prevailing gloom, and the much-praised ceiling frescoes by J. M. Rottmayr are impossible to make out. Just before Christmastime each year, the basement crypt is filled with a display of nativity scenes. The church is shoehorned into tiny Petersplatz, just off the Graben. ✉ *Peterspl. U-Bahn: U1, U3 Stephanspl.*

21 **Stock-im-Eisen.** In the southwest corner of Stock-im-Eisen-Platz, set into the building on the west side of Kärntnerstrasse, is one of the city's odder relics: the Stock-im-Eisen, or the "nail-studded stump." Chronicles first mention the Stock-im-Eisen in 1533, but it is probably far older, and for hundreds of years any apprentice metalsmith who came to Vienna to learn his trade hammered a nail into the tree trunk for good luck. During World War II, when there was talk of moving the relic to a museum in Munich, it mysteriously disappeared; it reappeared, perfectly preserved, after the threat of removal had passed.

An Imperial City: The Hofburg and the Ringstrasse

The Hofburg

A walk through the Imperial Palace, known as the **Hofburg** ㉕, brings you back to the days when Vienna was the capital of a mighty empire in which the sun never set. You can still find in Vienna shops vintage postcards and prints that show the revered and be-whiskered Emperor Francis Joseph starting out on a morning drive from his Hofburg palace in his carriage; Today, at the palace—which faces Kohlmarkt on the opposite side of Michaelerplatz—you can walk in his very footsteps, as well as gaze at the old tin bath the emperor kept under his simple iron bedstead and marvel at his bejeweled christening robe. Let alone, of course, feast your eyes on great works of art, impressive armor, and some of the finest Baroque interiors in Europe along the way.

Until 1918 the Hofburg was the home of the Habsburgs, rulers of the Austro-Hungarian Empire. As a current tourist mecca, it has become a vast smorgasbord of sightseeing attractions: the Imperial Apartments, two Imperial treasuries, *six* museums, the National Library, and the famous Winter Riding School all vie for attention. The entire complex takes a minimum of a full day to explore in detail; if your time is limited (or if you want to save most of the interior sightseeing for a rainy day), you should omit the Imperial Apartments and all the museums mentioned below except the Kunsthistorisches (the Museum of Art History), the new Museum of Court Silver and Tableware, and probably the Schatzkammer (Crown Jewels and Court Treasury). An excellent multilingual, full-color booklet describing the palace in detail is for sale at most ticket counters within the complex; it gives a complete list of attractions and maps out the palace's complicated ground plan and building history wing by wing.

Vienna took its imperial role seriously, as evidenced by the sprawling Hofburg complex, today, as then, the seat of government. But this is generally understated power; while the buildings cover considerable area, the treasures lie inside, not to be flamboyantly flaunted. Certainly under Francis Joseph II, the reign was beneficient—witness the broad Ringstrasse he ordained and the array of museums and public buildings it hosts. With few exceptions (Vienna City Hall and the Votive Church), rooflines are kept to an even level, creating an ensemble effect that helps integrate the palace complex and its parks into the urban landscape without making a domineering statement. Diplomats still bustle in and out of high-level international meetings in the elegant halls. Horse-drawn carriages still traverse the Ring and the roadway that cuts thorugh the complex. Ignore the cars and tour buses and you can easily imagine yourself in a Vienna of a hundred or more years ago.

Architecturally, the Hofburg—like St. Stephen's—is far from refined. It grew up over a period of 700 years (its earliest mention in court documents is 1279, at the very beginning of Habsburg rule), and its spasmodic, haphazard growth kept it from attaining any sort of unified identity. But many of the bits and pieces are fine, and one interior (the National Library) is a tour de force.

After a tour of the Hofburg complex this chapter concludes with an exploration of Vienna's famed Ringstrasse and the major attractions of its environs, including the Kunsthistoriches Museum and Freud's Apartment. The walks found below split up the marvels and museums of this area into two digestible bites.

Numbers in the text correspond to numbers in the margin and on the Hofburg map.

A GOOD WALK

When you begin to explore the Hofburg you realize that the palace complex is like a nest of boxes, courtyards opening off courtyards and wings (*trakts*) spreading far and wide. First tackle **Josefsplatz** ①, the remarkable square that interrupts Augustinerstrasse, ornamented by the equestrian **statue of Josef II** ②—many consider this Vienna's loveliest square. Indeed, the beautifully restored imperial decor adorning the roof of the buildings forming Josefsplatz are one of the few visual demonstrations of Austria's one-time widespread power and influence. On your right to the north is the **Spanische Reitschule** ③, the Spanish Riding School—one part of Vienna known throughout the world—where the famous white horses reign. Across Reitschulgasse under the arches are the **Imperial Stables** ④. To the south stands the **Augustinerkirche** ⑤, St. Augustine's Church, where the Habsburg rulers' hearts are preserved in urns. The grand main hall of the **Hofbibliothek Prunksaal** ⑥, the National Library, is one of the great Baroque treasures of Europe, a sight not to be missed (enter from the southwest corner of Josefsplatz).

Under the Michaelerplatz dome is the entrance to the **Imperial Apartments** ⑦, hardly the elegance you would normally associate with roy-

The Hofburg (Imperial Palace)

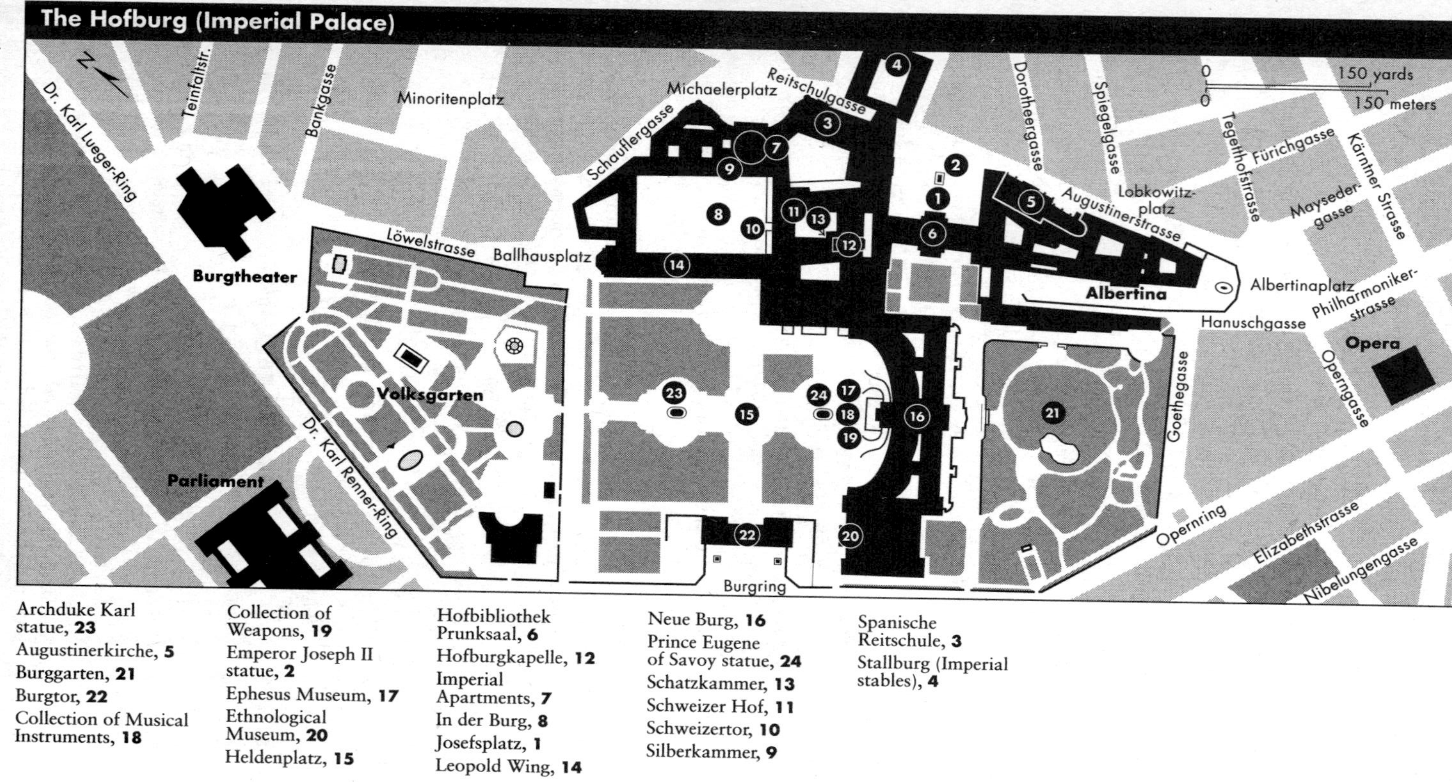

Archduke Karl statue, **23**
Augustinerkirche, **5**
Burggarten, **21**
Burgtor, **22**
Collection of Musical Instruments, **18**
Collection of Weapons, **19**
Emperor Joseph II statue, **2**
Ephesus Museum, **17**
Ethnological Museum, **20**
Heldenplatz, **15**
Hofbibliothek Prunksaal, **6**
Hofburgkapelle, **12**
Imperial Apartments, **7**
In der Burg, **8**
Josefsplatz, **1**
Leopold Wing, **14**
Neue Burg, **16**
Prince Eugene of Savoy statue, **24**
Schatzkammer, **13**
Schweizer Hof, **11**
Schweizertor, **10**
Silberkammer, **9**
Spanische Reitschule, **3**
Stallburg (Imperial stables), **4**

alty, but Francis Joseph II, the residing emperor from 1848 to 1916, was anything but ostentatious in his personal life. For the representational side, however, go through into the **In der Burg courtyard** ⑧ and look in at the elegant **Silberkammer** ⑨ museum of court silver and crystal. Go through the **Schweizertor** ⑩, the Swiss gate, to the south off of In der Burg, to reach the small **Schweizer Hof** ⑪ courtyard with stairs leading to the **Hofburgkapelle** ⑫, the Imperial Chapel where the Vienna Boys Choir makes its regular Sunday appearances. In a back corner of the courtyard is the entrance to the **Schatzkammer** museum ⑬, the Imperial Treasury, overflowing with jewels, robes, and royal trappings. From In der Burg, the roadway leads under the **Leopold Wing** ⑭ of the complex into the vast park known as **Heldenplatz** ⑮, or Hero's Square. The immediately obvious heroes are the equestrian **statues of Archduke Karl** ㉓, toward to the city hall, and closer, the **statue of Prince Eugene of Savoy** ㉔. The Hofburg wing to the south with its concave facade is the **Neue Burg** ⑯, the "new" section of the complex, now housing four specialized museums. Depending on your interests, consider the **Ephesus Museum** ⑰, with Roman antiquities, the **Collection of Musical Instruments** ⑱, where you also hear what you see, the impressive **Weapons Collection** ⑲, with tons of steel armor, or the **Ethnological Museum** ⑳, including Montezuma's headdress. Ahead, the **Burgtor** ㉒ gate separates the Hofburg complex from the Ringstrasse. The quiet oasis in back of the Neue Burg is the **Burggarten** ㉑. Catch your breath and marvel that you've only seen a small part of the Hofburg—a large part of it still houses the offices of the Austrian Government and cannot be visited by the public.

Timing: If you were simply to combine the two walks in this section as one, you'd need over half a day—that's without taking in any of the museums. How much time you will need with museum stops is an individual affair. You could spend a day in the Hofburg complex alone, another half to full day in the Kunsthistoriches Museum (found in the Ringstrasse walk, below). For most of the smaller museums, figure on anything from an hour upward.

SIGHTS TO SEE

5 **Augustinerkirche** (Church of the Augustinian Order). Across Josefsplatz from the Riding School is the entrance to the Augustinerkirche, built during the 14th century and possessing the most unified Gothic interior in the city. But the church is something of a fraud; the interior, it turns out, dates from the late 18th century, not the early 14th. A historical fraud the church may be, but a spiritual fraud it is not. The view from the entrance doorway is stunning: a soaring harmony of vertical piers, ribbed vaults, and hanging chandeliers that makes Vienna's other Gothic interiors look earthbound by comparison. The imposing Baroque organ sounds as fine as it looks, and the Sunday morning high mass—frequently by Mozart or Haydn—sung here can be the highlight of a trip. To the right of the main altar in the small Loreto Chapel stand silver urns in serried ranks; they contain the hearts of Habsburg rulers. This rather morbid sight is viewable after early mass on Sunday, Monday, or by appointment. ✉ *Josefspl.,* ☎ *01/533–7099–0. U-Bahn: U3 Herrengasse.*

21 **Burggarten.** The intimate Burggarten in back of the Neue Burg is a quiet oasis which includes a statue of a contemplative Kaiser Francis Joseph and an elegant statue of Mozart, moved here from the Albertinaplatz after the war, when the city's charred ruins were rebuilt. The former greenhouses under the wall to the Augustine church are being restored into a café complex replete with palms and winter garden setting. ✉

Access from Opernring and Hanuschgasse/Goethegasse. U-Bahn: U2 Babenbergerstr.

6 **Hofbibliothek Prunksaal** (National Library). This is one of the grandest Baroque libraries in the world, in every sense a cathedral of books. Its centerpiece is the spectacular Prunksaal—the Grand Hall of the National Library—which probably contains more book treasures than any comparable collection outside the Vatican. The main entrance to the ornate reading room is in the left corner of Josefsplatz. Designed by Fischer von Erlach the Elder just before his death in 1723 and completed by his son, the Grand Hall is full-blown High Baroque, with trompe l'oeil ceiling frescoes by Daniel Gran. The library may not be to everyone's taste, but in the end it is the books themselves that come to the rescue. They are as lovingly displayed as the gilding and the frescoes, and they give the hall a warmth that the rest of the palace decidedly lacks. On the third floor is an intriguing museum of globes that should not be overlooked. ⊠ *Josefspl. 1, at top of stairs inside; library,* ☎ *01/534–10–397; museum,* ☎ *01/534–10–297.* 🎫 *Library AS20, museum AS10.* ⊙ *Library Nov.–May, Mon.–Sat. 10–noon; June–Oct., Mon.–Sat. 10–4 (hrs vary depending on exhibitions); museum Mon.–Wed. and Fri. 11–noon, Thurs. 2–3. U-Bahn: U3 Herrengasse.*

12 10 **Hofburgkapelle** (Chapel of the Imperial Palace). The ancient **Schweizertor,** or Swiss Gate (dating from 1552 and decorated with some of
the earliest classical motifs in the city), leads from In der Burg through
to the oldest section of the palace, a small courtyard known as the
11 **Schweizer Hof**—named after the Swiss Guards who were once stationed
here. In the southeast corner (at the top of the steps) is the entrance to
12 the **Hofburgkapelle,** or Imperial Chapel, where the **Vienna Boys Choir**
(Wiener Sängerknaben) sings Mass at 9:15 on Sunday, Monday, and
holidays from September to June. Alas, the arrangement is such that
you *hear* the choirboys but don't see them; their soprano and alto voices
peal forth from a gallery behind the seating area. ⊠ *Hofburg, Schweizer
Hof,* ☎ *01/533–9927.*

8 **In der Burg Courtyard.** A prominent courtyard of the Hofburg complex, it features a statue of Francis II and the noted **Schweizertor** gateway—built in 1552 and painted maroon, black, and gold, it gives a fine Renaissance flourish to its building facade. Also note the **clock** on the far upper wall at the north end of the courtyard: it tells time by the sun dial, also gives the time mechanically, and even, above the clock face, indicates the phase of the moon.

1 **Josefsplatz.** Josefsplatz is the most imposing of the Hofburg courtyards, with an **equestrian monument to namesake Emperor Joseph II** (1807) in the center.

7 **Kaiserappartements** (Imperial Apartments). The domed rotunda on Michaelerplatz signals the entrances to two of the Hofburg museums. To the left under the dome is the access to the Kaiserappartements. The long, repetitive suite of conventionally luxurious rooms has a sad and poignant feel. The decoration (19th-century imitation of 18th-century Rococo) tries to look regal, but much like the empire itself in its latter days, it is only going through the motions and ends up looking merely official. Among the few signs of genuine life are Emperor Francis Joseph's spartan, iron field bed, on which he slept every night, and the Empress Elisabeth's wooden gymnastics equipment, on which she exercised every morning. Amid all the tired splendor they look decidedly forlorn. ⊠ *Hofburg, Schweizer Hof,* ☎ *01/587–5554–515.* 🎫 *AS70, combination ticket with Museum of Court Silver AS90, tour AS20 per museum.* ⊙ *Daily 9–5. U-Bahn: U2 Herrengasse.*

16 **Neue Burg.** The Neue Burg stands today as a symbol of architectural overconfidence. Designed for Emperor Francis Joseph in 1869, this "new chateau" was part of a much larger scheme that was meant to make the Hofburg rival the Louvre, if not Versailles. The German architect Gottfried Semper planned a twin of the present Neue Burg on the opposite side of the Heldenplatz, with arches connecting the Neue Burg and its twin with the other pair of twins on the Ringstrasse, the Kunsthistorisches Museum (Museum of Art History) and the Naturhistorisches Museum (Museum of Natural History). But World War I intervened, and with the Empire's collapse the Neue Burg became merely the last in a long series of failed attempts to bring architectural order to the Hofburg. The failure to complete the Hofburg building program left the Heldenplatz without a discernible shape, and today
22 it is amorphous, with the **Burgtor** (the old main palace gate) stranded
in the middle. The space nevertheless is punctuated by two superb eques-
23 24 trian statues of **Archduke Karl** and **Prince Eugene of Savoy.**

14 **Neue Burg Museums.** A long tract of offices known as the **Leopold Wing**
15 separates the In der Burg courtyard from the vast **Heldenplatz.** The older
section on the north includes the offices of the federal president. The long wing with the concave bay on the south is the youngest section of the palace, called the Neue Burg. (From its main balcony, in April, 1938, Adolf Hitler, telling a huge cheering crowd below of his plan for the new German empire, declared that Vienna "is a pearl! I am going to put it into a setting of which it is worthy!") Today, visitors flock to the Neue Burg because it houses no fewer than four specialty muse-
17 ums: the **Ephesus Museum,** containing exceptional Roman antiquities
unearthed by Austrian archaeologists in Turkey at the turn of the cen-
18 tury; the listenable **Collection of Musical Instruments,** including pianos
that belonged to Brahms, Schumann, and Mahler (an acoustic guided
tour allows you to actually hear the various instruments on head-
20 phones as you move from room to room); the **Ethnological Museum**
(Museum für Völkerkunde), devoted to anthropology (Montezuma's
19 feathered headdress is a highlight of its collection); and the **Collection**
of Weapons, rivaling the armory in Graz as one of the most extensive arms-and-armor collections in the world. The first three museums are entered at the triumphal arch set into the middle of the curved portion of the facade; the Ethnological Museum is entered farther along, at the west end pavilion. ✉ *Heldenpl.,* ☎ *01/521–77–0.* 🎫 *Combination ticket for Ephesus, Musical Instrument, and Weapons museums AS30; Ethnological Museum AS30.* 🕓 *Ephesus, Musical Instrument, and Weapons museums Tues.–Sun. 10–6; Ethnological Museum Wed.–Mon. 10–4. U-Bahn: U2 Babenbergerstrasse.*

13 **Schatzkammer** (Imperial Treasury). The entrance to the Schatzkammer, or Imperial Treasury, with its 1,000 years of treasures is tucked away at ground level behind the staircase to the Hofburgkapelle. The elegant display is a welcome antidote to the monotony of the Imperial Apartments, for the entire Treasury was completely renovated in 1983–87, and the crowns and relics and vestments fairly glow in their new surroundings. Here you'll find such marvels as the Holy Lance—reputedly the lance that pierced Jesus's side—the Imperial Crown (a sacred symbol of sovereignty once stolen on Hitler's orders), and the Saber of Charlemagne. Don't miss the Burgundian Treasure, connected with that most romantic of medieval orders of chivalry, the Order of the Golden Fleece. ✉ *Schweizer Hof,* ☎ *01/533–7931.* 🎫 *AS60.* 🕓 *Wed. and Fri.–Mon. 10–6, Thurs. 10–9. U-Bahn: U2 Herrengasse.*

9 **Silberkammer** (Museum of Court Silver and Tableware). The large courtyard on the far side of the Michaelertor rotunda is known as In der

Burg; here on the west side is the entrance to the sparkling new Silberkammer. There's far more than forks and fingerbowls here; stunning decorative pieces vie with glittering silver and gold for attention. Highlights include Francis Joseph's vermeil banqueting service, the Jardinière given to the Empress Elisabeth by Queen Victoria, and gifts from Marie-Antonette to her brother, Josef II. The presentation of full table settings gives an idea of court life both as a daily routine and on festive occasions. ✉ *Hofburg, Michalertrakt,* ☎ *01/533–1044.* 🎫 *AS70, combination ticket with Imperial Apartments AS90.* ⏲ *Daily 9–5.*

★ ❸ **Spanische Reitschule** (Spanish Riding School). Located between Augustinerstrasse and the Josefsplatz is the world famous Spanish Riding School, a favorite for centuries, and no wonder: who can resist the sight of the stark white Lipizzaners going through their masterful paces? For the last 300 years they have been perfecting their *haute école* riding demonstrations to the sound of Baroque music in an ballroom that seems to be a crystal-chandeliered stable. The breed was started in 1580 and proved themselves in battle as well as in the complicated "dances" for which they are famous. The interior of the riding school, the 1735 work of Fischer von Erlach the Younger, is itself an attraction—surely Europe's most elegant sports arena—and if the prancing horses begin to pall, move up to the top balcony and examine the ceiling. The School's popularity is hardly surprising, and tickets to some performances must be ordered in writing many weeks in advance. Information offices have a brochure with the detailed schedule (performances are usually from March through December, with the school on vacation in July and August). Generally the full, 80-minute shows take place Sunday at 10:45 AM plus selected Wednesdays at 7 PM. Check for hour-long morning performances on Saturday at 10; tickets for Saturday shows are only available from ticket and travel agencies (a list of these agencies is included in a free leaflet about the Spanish Riding School available from the Austrian National Tourist Office; the leaflet also includes the full year schedule of performances). Morning training sessions (without music) held Tuesday through Saturday, with a few in February and August on Mondays as well, are usually open to the public. Tickets can *only* be bought at the door for these morning training sessions—in other words, no reservations (the relocated entrance is currently next to the Schweizertor, in the In der Burg courtyard, but might be moved back to Josefsplatz, so check), and the line starts forming between 9 and 9:30 for the opening at 10; most sightseers are unaware that visitors may come and go as they please between 10 and noon. Note, however, there are special training sessions on Saturday mornings that are accompanied by music—these tickets are available only by reservation through ticket agencies. Note that ticket agencies (legally) add a commission of 22%–25% to the face price of the ticket. For Sunday and Wednesday performance ticket orders, write to Spanische Reitschule (✉ Hofburg, A–1010 Vienna). Pick up reserved tickets at the office under the Michaelerplatz rotunda dome. ✉ *Michaelerpl. 1, Hofburg,* ☎ *01/533–9031–0,* FAX *01/535–0186.* 🎫 *Seats AS240–AS800, standing room AS190, Saturday morning training session with music AS240, other morning training session AS100.* ⏲ *Mar.–June and Sept.–mid-Dec.; closed tour wks.*

The Ringstrasse and Its Environs

Along with the Hofburg, the Ringstrasse is Vienna's major urban set piece. This grand series of thoroughfares bounds the heart of Vienna, the Innere Stadt (Inner City) or First District. It follows the lines of what, until an imperial decree ordered their leveling in 1857, were the defenses of the city. By the 1870's, Vienna had reached the zenith of her imperial prosperity, and this found ultimate expression in the series of magnificent buildings erected around the Ringstrasse—the Opera House, the Kunsthistoriches Museum, the Natural History Museum, and the Rathaus, University, and Votivkirche. Here follows the major sights and attractions on and around the Ringstrasse.

Numbers in the text correspond to numbers in the margin and on the Vienna map.

A GOOD WALK

Is there a best way to explore the Ring? You can walk it from one end to the other—from where it begins at the Danube Canal to where it returns to the Canal after its curving flight. Or you can explore it whenever you happen to cross it on other missions (while it is a pleasant sequence of boulevards, seeing its succession of rather pompous buildings all in one walk can be a bit overpowering). Or you can obtain the best of both options by following this suggested itinerary, which leavens the bombast of the Ring with some of Vienna's most fascinating sights. Immediately across the Ringstrasse from the Hofburg are two twin buildings, both museums. To the west is the **Natural History Museum,** to the east, the **Kunsthistorisches Museum** ㉖, the art museum packed with world-famous treasures. Allow ample time for exploration here. Further to the west of the museum square is the compact **Spittelberg Quarter** ㉗ of tiny streets between Burggasse and Sibensterngasse, often site of handicraft and seasonal fairs. The **Volksgarten** ㉘ on the inside of the Ringstrasse to the north of the museum square numbers a café and rose garden among its attractions; look also for the small memorial to Francis Joseph's wife Empress Elisabeth in the back corner. Tackle the Ringstrasse buildings by starting with the **Justizpalast** ㉙, the ministry of justice, moving along to **Parliament** ㉚, the **Rathaus** ㉛, the Vienna city hall, the **Burgtheater** ㉜ opposite on the inside of the Ring, then the **Universität** ㉝, the main building of Vienna's university, beyond, again on the outside of the Ring. Next to the university stands the neo-Gothic **Votivkirche** ㉞. If you've still time and energy, walk farther along the Ring to discover the Börse at the corner of the Ring and Wipplingerstrasse. The outside end of Hohenstaufengasse leads into Liechtensteinstrasse, which will bring you to Berggasse. Turn right to reach No. 19, the **Sigmund Freud Apartment** ㉟, now a museum and research facility. By continuing along Liechtensteinstrasse four blocks or taking the "D" streetcar two stops from the Böre, you will arrive at Fürstengasse, where the **Museum of Modern Art** ㊱ is incongruously housed in the legendary Palais Liechtenstein.

Timing: If you can, plan for Vienna's Louvre—the Kunsthistorisches Museum—early in the day before the crowds arrive, although the size of crowds depends greatly on whatever special shows the museum may be exhibiting. As for the main sights off the Ringstrasse, you could easily lump visits to the Sigmund Freud Apartment and the Museum of Modern Art together, figuring on about a half day for the two combined.

SIGHTS TO SEE

35 **Freud's Apartment.** Not far from the historic Hofburg district, beyond the Votive Church at the Schotterning along the Ringstrasse, you can skip over several centuries and visit that outstanding symbol of 20th-century Vienna: Sigmund Freud's Apartment at Berggasse 19 (Apartment 6, one flight up; ring the bell and push the door simultaneously); this was his residence from 1891 to 1938. The five-room collection of memorabilia is mostly a photographic record of Freud's life, with some documents, publications, and a portion of his collection of antiquities also on display. The waiting room furniture is authentic, but the consulting room and study furniture (including the famous couch)

can be seen only in photographs. ✉ *Berggasse 19,* ☎ *01/319–1596.* 🎟 *AS60.* ⏲ *July–Sept., daily 9–6; Oct.–June, daily 9–4. U-Bahn: U2 Schottentor.*

26 **Kunsthistorisches Museum** (Museum of Fine Art) One of the finest art collections in the world, the Kunsthistorisches Museum is the jewel of Vienna's museums, and lies across the street from the Hofburg's Neue Burg museum complex. The collection was assembled by the ruling Habsburgs over several hundred years, and even a cursory description would run on for pages. Invidious as it might be to try to select from this incredible wealth of pictures, a brief selection might help you to steer around the maze of galleries (the rooms are numbered in two sequences and around two courtyards). One trick to keep in mind: the large rooms have all the big-scale paintings—some of them striking, some merely pompous; the smaller rooms contain most of the jewel-like pictures, also many of the best portraits. So if you suffer from museumitis or are short on time, do the small rooms first! Head of the list, of course, is Room X, where you enter the world of Pieter Brueghel the Elder, one of the greatest painters of all time. Here, in one salon, you'll see more than half of Brueghel's surviving output. Here are the landscapes vividly changing with the seasons (pride of place goes to the winter view, *Hunters in the Snow*) and his panels swarming with throngs of animated 16th-century peasants. In other rooms, most of the great European old masters are represented (although some of the masterpieces are disgracefully dirty). Even the shortest list of highlights must include Rogier van der Weyden's *Crucifixion Triptych,* Raphael's *Madonna in the Meadow,* Holbein's *Portrait of Jane Seymour, Queen of England,* Correggio's *Jupiter Embracing Io,* Parmegianino's *Cupid Cutting a Bow,* Caravaggio's *Madonna of the Rosary,* a fine selection of Rembrandt portraits, Rubens's *Nude of Helene Fourment,* and Vermeer's peerless *Allegory of the Art of Painting.* Benvenuto Cellini's famous gold saltcellar—certainly one of the most sumptuous pieces of tableware ever created—is on display amid the treasures of the applied-arts wing. ✉ *Maria-Theresien-Pl.,* ☎ *01/521–77–0.* 🎟 *AS45 (higher for special exhibits).* ⏲ *Tues.–Sun. 10–6, picture gallery Thurs. 6–9 PM.*

Museum für angewandte Kunst, or MAK (Museum of Applied Arts). This museum contains a large collection of Austrian furniture and art objects; the Jugendstil display devoted to Josef Hoffman and his followers at the Wiener Werkstätte is particularly fine. The museum also features a number of changing exhibitions of contemporary arts and crafts, ranging from Chris Burden to Nam June Paik. ✉ *Stubenring 5,* ☎ *01/711–36–0.* 🎟 *Standing exhibits AS30, special exhibits AS90.* ⏲ *Tues., Wed., and Fri.–Sun. 10–6, Thurs. 10–9. U-Bahn: U3 Stubentor.*

36 **Museum Moderner Kunst** (Museum of Modern Art). Housed in the celebrated **Palais Liechtenstein,** the Museum Moderner Kunst's official address may be at Fürstengasse 1, but Liechtensteinstrasse is the address by which most Viennese know it. The large 18th-century mansion was originally the Liechtenstein Summer Palace; today it houses the national collection of 20th-century art and the outstanding private Ludwig collection, mainly of Austrian artists. Artists from Gustav Klimt to Robert Rauschenberg and Nam June Paik are represented, and a more inappropriate environment for modern art would be hard to imagine. Twentieth-century art and 18th-century architecture here declare war on each other and fight to an uneasy draw. Still, if you can shut out the architecture (or the art, depending on your taste), the museum is well worth a visit. ✉ *Fürstengasse 1,* ☎ *01/317–6900.* 🎟 *AS45.* ⏲ *Tues.–Sun. 10–6. U-Bahn: U2 Schottentor, then Streetcar D to Fürstengasse.*

Naturhistorisches Museum (Natural History Museum). The formal museum complex just outside the Ring has two elements—to the east is the celebrated Kunsthistorisches Museum, to the west is the Naturhistorisches Museum, or Natural History Museum. This is home of, among other artifacts, the famous Venus of Willendorf, a tiny statuette thought to be some 20,000 years old and symbol of the Iron Age Hallstatt civilization. The reconstructed dinosaur skeletons understandably draw the greatest attraction. ✉ *Maria-Theresien-Pl.,* ☎ *01/521–77–0.* 🎟 *AS30.* 🕒 *Wed.–Mon. 9–6; winter, ground floor only, Wed.–Mon. 9–3. U-Bahn: U2, U3 Volkstheater.*

28–34 **Ringstrasse.** The **Volksgarten,** just opposite the Hofburg, is a green oasis with a beautifully planted rose garden, a 19th-century Greek temple, and a rather wistful white marble monument to the Empress Elisabeth—Francis Joseph's Bavarian wife who died of dagger wounds inflicted by a martyr in Geneva in 1898. If not overrun with latter-day hippies, these can offer appropriate spots to sit for a few minutes and consider Vienna's most ambitious piece of 19th-century city planning: the famous Ringstrasse. Late in 1857, Emperor Francis Joseph issued a decree announcing the most ambitious piece of urban redevelopment Vienna had ever seen. The inner city's centuries-old walls were to be torn down, and the *glacis*—the wide expanse of open field that acted as a protective buffer between inner city and outer suburbs—was to be filled in. In their place was to rise a wide, tree-lined boulevard, upon which would stand an imposing collection of new buildings that would reflect Vienna's special status as the political, economic, and cultural heart of the Austro-Hungarian Empire. During the 50 years of building that followed, many factors combined to produce the Ringstrasse as it now stands, but the most important was the gradual rise of liberalism after the failed Revolution of 1848. By the latter half of the Ringstrasse era, support for constitutional government, democracy, and equality—all the concepts that liberalism traditionally equates with progress—was steadily increasing. As the Ringstrasse went up, it became the definitive symbol of this liberal progress; as Carl E. Schorske put it in his *Fin-de-Siècle Vienna,* it celebrated "the triumph of constitutional *Recht* (right) over Imperial *Macht* (might), of secular culture over religious faith. Not palaces, garrisons, and churches, but centers of constitutional government and higher culture dominated the Ring."

But what should these centers of culture look like? The answer was the result of a new passion among the intelligentsia: architectural historicism. Greek temples, it was argued, reminded the viewer of the cradle of democracy; what could be more appropriate than a Parliament building designed in Greek Revival style? Gothic architecture, on the other hand, suggested the church and the rise of the great medieval city-states; the new Votive Church and the new City Hall would therefore be Gothic Revival. And the Renaissance Era, which produced the unprecedented flowering of enlightenment and creativity that put an end to the Middle Ages, was most admired of all; the style of the new centers of high culture—the museums, the theaters, and the university—would be Renaissance Revival. In building after building, architectural style was dictated by historical association, and gradually the Ringstrasse of today took shape.

The highest concentration of public building occurred in the area around the Volksgarten, where are clustered (moving from south to north, from Burgring to Schottenring) the ☞ **Museum of Art History,**
29 the ☞ **Museum of Natural History,** the **Justizpalast** (Palace of Justice),
 30 31 32 the **Parliament** (Parliament), the **Rathaus** (City Hall), the **Burgtheater**
33 34 (National Theater), the **Universität** (University of Vienna), the **Votivkirche,** and slightly farther along, the **Börse** (Stock Exchange) on Schottenring. As an ensemble, the collection is astonishing in its architectural

presumption: it is nothing less than an attempt to assimilate and summarize the entire architectural history of Europe. As critics were quick to notice, however, the complex suffers from a serious organizational flaw: Most of the buildings lack effective context. Rather than being the focal points of an organized overall plan, they are plunked haphazardly down on an avenue that is itself too wide to possess a unified, visually comprehensible character.

To some, the monumentality of it all is overbearing; others however find the architectural panorama exhilarating, and growth of the trees over 100 years has served to put the buildings into different perspective. There is no question but that the tree-lined boulevard with its broad sidewalks gives the city a unique ribbon of green and certainly the distinction that the emperor sought. *U-Bahn for Volksgarten: U2 Lerchenfelder Strasse.*

㉗ **Spittelberg Quarter.** The Spittelberg quarter, one block northwest of Maria-Theresien-Platz off of the Burggasse, offers a fair visual idea of Vienna outside of the city walls a century ago. Most buildings have been replaced, but the engaging 18th-century survivors at Burggasse Nos. 11 and 13 are adorned with religious and secular decorative sculpture, the latter with a niche statue of St. Joseph, the former with cherubic work-and-play bas-reliefs. For several blocks around—walk down Gutenberggasse and back up Spittelberggasse—the 18th-century houses have been beautifully restored. The sequence from No. 5 to No. 19 Spittelberggasse is an especially fine array of Viennese plain and fancy. Around holiday times, particularly Easter and Christmas, the Spittelberg quarter, known for arts and handicrafts, hosts seasonal markets offering unusual and interesting items.

Monarchs and Mozart: From St. Stephen's to the Opera House

The cramped, ancient quarter behind St. Stephen's Cathedral offers a fascinating contrast to the luxurious expanses of the Ringstrasse and more recent parts of Vienna. This was—and still is—concentrated residential territory in the heart of the city. Mozart lived here; later, Prince Eugene and others built elegant town palaces as the smaller buildings were replaced. Here you get a feeling of old and newer Vienna in contrast over the centuries. Streets, now mostly reserved for pedestrians, are narrow and tiny alleysways abound. Facades open into courtyards that once housed the carriages and horses. The west side of the Kärnter Strasse which since time immemorial has formed a north–south axis through the heart of the city, brings you face-to-face with the former monarchs, their remains and their monuments. Musically, you might encounter Mozart again, at the magnificent State Opera House, which shares with St. Stephen's the honor of being one of the city's most familiar and beloved landmarks.

A Good Walk

To pass through these streets is to take a short journey through history and art. In the process—as you visit haunts of Mozart, kings, and emperors—you can be easily impressed with a sense of exactly how Vienna's glittering Habsburg centuries unfolded. Start from St. Stephen's Cathedral by walking down Singerstrasse to Blutgasse and turn left into the **Blutgasse district** ㊲—a neighborhood redolent of the 19th century. At the north end in Domgasse is the so-called **Figarohaus** ㊳, now a memorial museum, the house in which Wolfgang Amadeus Mozart lived when he wrote the opera *The Marriage of Figaro.* Follow Domgasse east to Grünangergasse, which will bring you to Franziskanerplatz and the Gothic-Renaissance Franziskanerkirche (St. Francis Church). Follow the ancient Ballgasse to Rauhensteingasse, turning left onto **Himmelpfortgasse**—"The Gates of Heaven Street." Prince Eugene of Savoy had his town palace here at No. 8, now the **Ministry of Finance** ㊴, living here when he wasn't enjoying his other residence, the Belvedere Palace. Continue down Himmelpfortgasse to Seilerstätte, and turn right into **Annagasse** and its beautiful houses, which brings you back to the main shopping street **Kärnter Strasse,** where you can find everything from Austrian jade to the latest Jill Sander turnouts. Turn left, walking north two blocks and take the short Donnergasse to reach **Neuer Markt** square and the Providence Fountain. At the southwest corner of the square is the **Kaisergruft** ㊵ in the **Kapuzinerkirche,** the burial vault for rows of once-ruling Habsburgs. Tegetthofstrasse south will bring you to Albertinaplatz, the square noted for the obvious war memorial but more for the **Albertina** ㊶, one of the world's great collections of Old Master drawings and prints. The southeast side of the square is bounded by the famous **Staatsoper** ㊷, the State Opera House; check for tour possibilities or, better, book tickets for a great *Der Rosenkavalier.*

TIMING

A simple walk of this route could take you a full half day, assuming you stop occasionally to survey the scene and take it all in. The restyled Figarohaus is worth a visit, but note the odd closing hours and schedule accordingly. The Kaisergruft in the Kapuziner church is impressive for its shadows of past glories, but there are crowds, and you may have to wait to get in; the best times are early morning or around lunchtime. Tours of the State Opera House take place in the afternoons; check the schedule posted outside one of the doors on the arcaded Kärtner Strasse side. Figure about an hour each for the various visits and tours.

Sights to See

41 **Albertina Museum.** On the west side of Albertinaplatz stands the Albertina Museum, an unpretentious affair housing one of the world's finest collections of drawings, engravings, and prints by leading Old Masters. The Albertina is currently undergoing extensive renovations, but some of its most famous works (for example, Albrecht Dürer's *Praying Hands*) are too popular to be hidden away in security archives and are on view. The monthly city information brochure lists Albertina events and times. ✉ *Augustinerstr. 1,* ☎ *01/534–83–0.* ⏲ *Call for hrs during renovation. U-Bahn: U1, U3 Stephansplatz.*

NEED A BREAK?

Take a coffee break at one of the nearby cafés. The **Café Sacher** (✉ Hotel Sacher, ☎ 01/512–1487. ⏲ Daily 6:30 AM–10:30 PM) on Philharmonikerstrasse—the street directly behind the Opera House leading east from the south end of Albertinaplatz—is the most formal of them all (no shorts allowed inside during the summer); its famous Sachertorte can also be purchased at a small Kärntner Strasse shop on the hotel's east side. The **Café Tirolerhof** (✉ Tegetthoffstr. 8, ☎ 01/512–7833. ⏲ Mon.–Sat. 7 AM–9 PM, Sun. 9:30 AM–8 PM), on the north side of Albertinaplatz, is a less upscale (but more typically Viennese) alternative, with good desserts as well.

37 **Blutgasse District.** The small block bounded by Singerstrasse, Grünangergasse, and Blutgasse is known as the Blutgasse District. Nobody knows for certain how the gruesome name—Blut is German for blood—originated, although one legend has it that Knights Templar were slaughtered here when their order was abolished in 1312, although in later years the narrow street was known in those unpaved days as Mud Lane. Today the block is a splendid example of city renovation and restoration, with cafés, small shops and galleries tucked into the corners. You can look inside the courtyards to see the open galleries that connect var-

ious apartments on the upper floors, the finest example being at Blutgasse No. 3. At the corner of Singerstrasse sits the 18th-century **Neupauer-Breuner Palace,** with its monumental entranceway and inventively delicate windows. Opposite at No. 17 is the **Rottal Palace,** attributed to Hildebrandt, with its wealth of classical wall motifs. For a contrast, turn up the narrow Blutgasse, with its simple 18th-century facades.

38 **Figarohaus.** One of Mozart's 11 rented Viennese residences, the Figarohaus has its entrance at No. 5 Domgasse, the tiny alley behind St. Stephen's (although the facade on Schulerstrasse is far more imposing). It was in this house that Mozart wrote *The Marriage of Figaro* and the six quartets dedicated to Joseph Haydn (who once called on Mozart here, saying to Leopold, Mozart's father, ". . . your son is the greatest composer that I know in person or by name."). The apartment he occupied now contains a small commemorative museum—"created," alas, by an architect more interested in graphic blandishment than a sense of history; you'll have to use your imagination to picture how Mozart lived and worked here. ✉ *Domgasse 5,* ☎ *01/513–6294.* 🎫 *AS25.* 🕒 *Tues.–Sun. 10–12:15 and 1–4:30. U-Bahn: U1, U3 Stephansplatz.*

39 **Finanzministerium** (Ministry of Finance). The architectural jewel of Himmelpfortgasse, this imposing abode—designed by Fischer von Erlach in 1697 and later expanded by Hildebrandt—was originally the town palace of Prince Eugene of Savoy. As you study the Finanzministerium, you'll realize its Baroque details are among the most inventively conceived and beautifully executed in the city; all the decorative motifs are so softly carved that they appear to have been freshly squeezed from a pastry tube. The Viennese are lovers of the Baroque in both their architecture and their pastry, and here the two passions seem visibly merged. Such Baroque elegance may seem inappropriate for a finance ministry, but the contrast between place and purpose could hardly be more Viennese. ✉ *8 Himmelpfortgasse 8.*

Himmelpfortgasse. The maze of tiny streets including Ballgasse, Rauhensteingasse, and Himmelpfortgasse (literally, "The Gates of Heaven Street") masterfully conjures up the Vienna of the 19th century. The most impressive house on the street is the Ministry of Finance (☞ *above*). The back side of the Steffl department store on Rauhensteingasse now marks the site of the house in which Mozart died in 1791. There's a commemorative plaque that once identified the streetside site together with a small memorial corner to Mozart on the 5th floor of the store.

40 **Kaisergruft** (Imperial Burial Vault). In the basement of the **Kapuzinerkirche,** or Capucin church (on the southwest corner of the Neuer Markt), is one of the more intriguing sights in Vienna: the Kaisergruft, or Imperial Burial Vault. The crypts contain the partial remains of some 140 Habsburgs (the hearts are in the Augustinerkirche and the entrails in St. Stephen's) plus one non-Habsburg governess ("She was always with us in life," said Maria Theresa, "why not in death?"). Perhaps this is the wrong way to approach the Habsburgs in Vienna, starting with their tombs, but it does give you a chance to get their names in sequence as they lie in their serried ranks, their coffers ranging from the simplest though positive explosions of funerary conceit with decorations of skulls and other morbid symbols to the lovely and distinguished tomb of Maria Theresa and her husband. Designed while the couple still lived, their monument shows the empress in bed with her husband—awaking to the Last Judgment as if it were just another weekday morning, while the remains of her son (the ascetic Josef II) lie in a simple casket at the foot of the bed as if he were the family dog. ✉ *Neuer Markt/Tegetthoffstr. 2,* ☎ *01/512–6853–0.* 🎫 *AS40.* 🕒 *Daily 9:30–4. U-Bahn: U1, U3 Stephansplatz.*

Kärntner Strasse. The Kärntner Strasse remains Vienna's leading central shopping street. These days Kärntner Strasse is much maligned. Too commercial, too crowded, too many tasteless signs, too much gaudy neon—the complaints go on and on. Nevertheless, when the daytime tourist crowds dissolve, the Viennese arrive regularly for their evening promenade, and it is easy to see why. Vulgar the street may be, but it is also alive and vital, possessing an energy that the more tasteful Graben and the impeccable Kohlmarkt lack. For the sightseer beginning to suffer from an excess of art history, classic buildings, and museums, a Kärntner Strasse window-shopping pause will be welcome.

Neuer Markt. The centerpiece in the Neuer Markt square, Georg Raphael Donner's **Providence Fountain,** has not had a happy life. Put up in 1739, it was at the time the very latest word in civic improvement, with elegantly mannered nude statuary meant to personify the Danube and four of its tributaries. The Empress Maria Theresa, however, was offended; she disapproved of nudity in art. The figures were removed and put away and later nearly melted down for munitions. They were finally restored in 1801, but were once again taken away (to be replaced by the present copies) in 1873. The original figures can be studied in quiet at the Lower Belvedere Palace.

42 **Staatsoper** (State Opera House). The famous Vienna Staatsoper on the Ring vies with the cathedral for the honor of marking the emotional heart of the city—it is a focus for Viennese life and one of the chief symbols of resurgence after the cataclysm of World War II. Its directorship is virtually the top job in Austria, almost as important as that of president, and one that comes in for even more public attention. Everyone thinks they could do it just as well and, since the huge salary comes out of the taxes, they feel they have every right to criticize, often and loudly. The first of the Ringstrasse projects to be completed (in 1869), the opera house suffered disastrous bomb damage in the last days of World War II (only the outer walls, the front facade, and the main staircase area behind it survived). The auditorium is plain when compared to the red and gold eruptions of London's Covent Garden or some of the Italian opera houses, but it has an elegant individuality that shows to best advantage when the stage and auditorium are turned into a ballroom for the great Opera Ball.

The construction of the Opera House is the stuff of legend. When the foundation was laid, the plans for the Opernring were not yet complete, and in the end the avenue turned out to be several feet higher than originally planned. As a result, the Opera House lacked the commanding prospect that its architects, Eduard van der Nüll and August Sicard von Sicardsburg, had intended, and even Emperor Francis Joseph pronounced the building a bit low to the ground. For the sensitive van der Nüll (and here the story becomes a bit suspect), failing his beloved emperor was the last straw. In disgrace and despair, he committed suicide. Sicardsburg died of grief shortly thereafter. And the emperor, horrified at the deaths his innocuous remark had caused, limited all his future artistic pronouncements to a single immutable formula: *Es war sehr schön, es hat mich sehr gefreut* ("It was very nice, it pleased me very much").

Rebuilt after the war, it is unable to belie its 1950s look, for the cost of fully restoring the 19th-century interior decor was prohibitive. The original basic design was followed in the 1945–55 reconstruction, meaning that sight lines from some of the front boxes are poor at best. These disappointments hardly detract from the fact that this is one of the world's half dozen greatest opera houses, and experiencing a performance here can be the highlight of a trip to Vienna. Tours of the Opera House are given regularly, but starting times vary according to opera rehearsals; the current schedule is posted at the east side entrance under the arcade on the Kärntner Strasse marked GUIDED TOURS, where the tours begin. Alongside under the arcade is an information office that also sells tickets to the main opera and the Volksoper. ✉ *Opernring 2,* ☎ *01/514–44–0 or 01/51444–2656.* 💴 *Tour AS50.* ⏲ *Weekdays 10–1 hr before performance begins, Sat. 9–2. U-Bahn: U1, U2, U4 Karlsplatz.*

Pomp and Circumstance: South of the Ring to the Belvedere

City planning in the late 1800s and early 1900s clearly was essential to manage the growth of the burgeoning imperial capital. The elegant Ringstrasse alone was not a sufficient showcase, and anyway, it focused on public rather than private buildings. The city fathers as well as private individuals commissioned the architect Otto Wagner to plan and undertake a series of projects. The area around Karlsplatz and the fascinating open food market remains a classic example of unity of design. Not all of Wagner's concept for Karlsplatz was realized, but enough remains to be convincing and to convey the impression of what might have been. The unity concept predates Wagner's time in the former garden setting of Belvedere Palace, one of Europe's greatest architectural triumphs.

A Good Walk

The often overlooked **Academy of Fine Arts** ㊸ is an appropriate starting point for this walk, as it puts into perspective the artistic arguments being raised around the turn of the century. While the Academy represented the conservative viewpoint, a group of modernist revolutionaries broke away and founded the Secessionist movement, with its culimination in the gold-crowned **Secession Building** ㊹. Their achievement, now housing changing exhibits and Gustav Klimt's provocative *Beethoven Frieze,* stands appropriately close by the Academy; from the Academy, take Makartgasse south one block. The famous **Naschmarkt** open food market starts diagonally south from the Secession; follow the rows of stalls southwest. Pay attention to the northwest side of the Linke Wienzeile as you go; at the intersection with Millöckergasse stands the Theater an der Wien, an opera house–theater in which Mozart and Beethoven personally premiered some of their finest works. The Otto Wagner gems on the street are the apartment blocks at No. 38 and 40—the famous "Majolica House"—Jugendstil in fullest bloom. Wagner also designed the stations on what is now the U4 line; a good example is at Kettenbrückengasse; opposite is the market office, another Jugendstil prize. Head back north through the Naschmarkt; at the top end, cross Wiedner Hauptstrasse to your right into the park complex that forms Karlsplatz, creating a setting for the classic **Karlskirche** ㊺, St. Charles's Church. Around the park, note the **Technical University** on the south side, the Otto Wagner subway station buildings on the north. Across Lothringer Strasse on the north side are the **Künstlehaus** art exhibit hall and the **Musikverein,** the superb concert hall from which the New Year's Day concerts are broadcast worldwide. The out-of-place and rather undistinguished modern building to the left of Karlskirche houses the worthwhile **Historisches Museum der Stadt Wien** ㊻, the Museum of the City of Vienna. Cut through Symphonikerstrasse (a passageway through the modern complex) and take Brucknerstrasse to **Schwarzenbergplatz.** The Jugendstil edifice on your left is the **French Embassy**; ahead is the **Russian War Memorial.** On a rise behind the memorial sits **Schwarzenberg Palais,** a jewel of a one-time summer palace and now a luxury hotel. Follow Prinz Eugen-Strasse up to the entrance of the **Belvedere Palace** ㊼ complex on your left. Admire the baroque ornamentation: cake decoration everywhere but without being overdone, held together by the symmetry of the building itself. Here, you'll find the noted entry hall—a Baroque fantasia where huge supporting columns rising out of the stone floors are transformed into muscular giants. Besides the palace itself are other structures and, off to the east side, a remarkable botanical garden. After viewing the palace and the grounds, you can exit the complex from the lower building, Untere Belvedere, into Rennweg, which will steer you back to Schwarzenbergplatz.

TIMING

The first part of this walk, taking in the Academy of Fine Arts and the Secession, plus the Naschmarkt and Karlsplatz, can be accomplished in an easy half day. The Museum of the City of Vienna is good for a couple of hours, more if you understand some German. Give the Belvedere Palace and grounds as much time as you can. Organized tours breeze in and out—without as much as a glance at the outstanding modern art museum—in a half hour or so, not even scratching the surface of this fascinating complex. If you can, budget up to a half day here, but plan to arrive fairly early in the morning or afternoon before the busloads descend. Bus tourists aren't taken to the Lower Belvedere, so you'll have that and the formal gardens to yourself.

Sights to See

㊸ **Academy of Fine Arts.** An outsized statue of the German author Schiller announces the Academy of Fine Arts on Schillerplatz. (Turn around and note his more famous contemporary Goethe, pompously seated in an overstuffed chair, facing him from across the Ring.) The Academy was founded in 1692 but the present Renaissance Revival building dates to the late 19th century. The idea was conservatism and traditional values, even in the face of a growing Arts and Crafts movement that scorned formal rules. It was here in the 1920s that an aspiring Adolf Hitler was refused acceptance on grounds of insufficient talent. The academy includes a museum focusing on Old Masters. The collection is mainly of interest to specialists, but Hieronymus Bosch's famous *Last Judgment* tryptich hangs here, an imaginative if gruesome speculation of the hereafter. ✉ *Schillerpl. 3,* ☎ *01/588–16–225.* 💶 *AS30.* ⏲ *Tues., Thurs., and Fri. 10–2; Wed. 10–1 and 3–6; weekends and holidays 9–1. U-Bahn: U1, U2, U4 Karlsplatz.*

★ ㊼ **Belvedere Palace.** Baroque architect Lucas von Hildebrandt's most important Viennese work is wedged between Rennweg (entry at No. 6A) and Prinz Eugen-Strasse (entry at No. 27): the Belvedere Palace. In fact the Belvedere is two palaces with extensive gardens between. Built outside the city fortifications between 1714 and 1722, the complex originally served as the summer palace of Prince Eugene of Savoy; much later it became the home of Archduke Franz Ferdinand, whose assassination in 1914 precipitated World War I. Though the lower palace is impressive in its own right, it is the much larger upper palace, used for state receptions, banquets, and balls, that is Hildebrandt's acknowledged masterpiece. The usual tourist entrance for the Upper Belvedere is the gate on Prinz-Eugen-Strasse, for the Lower Belvedere, the Rennweg gate—but for the most impressive view of the upper palace, approach it from the south garden closest to the South Rail Station. The upper palace displays a remarkable wealth of architectural invention in its facade, avoiding the main design problem common to all palaces because of their excessive size: monotony on the one hand and pomposity on the other. Hildebrandt's decoration here approaches the Rococo, that final style of the Baroque era when traditional classical motifs all but disappeared in a whirlwind of seductive asymmetric fancy. The main interiors of the palace go even farther: Columns are transformed into muscle-bound giants, pilasters grow torsos, capitals sprout great piles of symbolic Imperial paraphernalia, and the ceilings are set aswirl with ornately molded stucco. The result is the finest Rococo interior in the city.

Today both the upper and lower palaces of the Belvedere are noted museums devoted to Austrian painting. The **Österreichisches Barockmuseum** (Austrian Museum of Baroque Art) in the lower palace at Rennweg 6a displays Austrian art of the 18th century (including the original figures from Georg Raphael Donner's *Providence Fountain* in the Neuer Markt)—and what better building to house it! Next to the Baroque Museum (outside the west end) is the converted Orangerie, devoted to works of the medieval period. The main attraction is the upper palace's **Österreichische Galerie** (Austrian Gallery), the legendary collection of 19th- and 20th-century Austrian paintings, centering on the work of Vienna's three preeminent early 20th-century artists: Gustav Klimt, Egon Schiele, and Oskar Kokoschka. Klimt was the oldest, and by the time he helped found the Secession movement, he had forged a highly idiosyncratic painting style that combined realistic and decorative elements in a way that was completely revolutionary. *The Kiss*—his greatest painting and one of the icons of modern art—is here on display. Schiele and Kokoschka went even farther, rejecting the decorative appeal of Klimt's glittering abstract designs and producing works that completely ignored conventional ideas of beauty. Today they are considered the fathers of modern art in Vienna. Modern music, too, has roots in the Belvedere complex: the composer Anton Bruckner lived and died here in 1896 in a small garden house now marked by a commemorative plaque. ✉ *Upper Belvedere, Prinz-Eugen-Str. 27, Lower Belvedere, Rennweg 6A,* ☎ *01/798–0700.* 🎟 *All Belvedere museums AS60.* ⏲ *Tues.–Sun. 10–5. U-Bahn: U1, U2, U4 Karlsplatz; then for upper Belvedere, Streetcar D to Belvederegasse.*

46 **Historisches Museum der Stadt Wien** (Museum of Viennese History). Housed in an incongrously modern building at the east end of the regal Karlsplatz, this museum possesses a dazzling array of Viennese historical artifacts and treasures: models, maps, documents, photographs, antiquities, stained glass, paintings, sculpture, crafts, and reconstructed rooms. Paintings include Klimts and Schieles, and there's a life-size portrait of the composer Alban Berg painted by his contemporary Arnold Schönberg. Alas, display information and designations in the museum are only in German, and there's no guidebook in English. ✉ *Karlspl.,* ☎ *01/505–8747–0.* 🎟 *AS50.* ⏲ *Tues.–Sun. 9–4:30. U-Bahn: U1, U2, U4 Karlsplatz.*

★ 45 **Karlskirche.** Dominating the Karlsplatz is one of Vienna's greatest buildings, the Karlskirche, dedicated to St. Charles Borromeo. At first glance, the church seems like a fantastic vision—one blink and you half expect the building to vanish. For before you is a giant Baroque church framed by enormous free-standing columns, mates to the famous Trajan's Column of Rome's ancient Forum. These columns may be out of keeping with the building as a whole, but were conceived with at least two functions in mind; one was to portray scenes from the life of the patron saint, carved in imitation of Trajan's triumphs, and thus help to emphasize the Imperial nature of the building; and the other was to symbolize the Pillars of Hercules, suggesting the right of the Habsburgs to their Spanish dominions which the Emperor had been forced to renounce. Whatever the reason, the end result is an architectural tour de force.

The Karlskirche was built in the early 18th century on what was then the bank of the river Wien and is now the southeast corner of the park complex. The church had its beginnings in a disaster. In 1713 Vienna was hit by a brutal plague outbreak, and Emperor Charles VI made a vow: If the plague abated, he would build a church dedicated to his namesake Saint Charles Borromeo, the 16th-century Italian bishop who was famous for his ministrations to Milanese plague victims. In 1715 construction began, using an ambitious design by Johann Bernhard Fischer von Erlach that combined architectural elements from ancient Greece (the columned entrance porch), ancient Rome (the Trajaneseque columns), contemporary Rome (the Baroque dome), and contemporary Vienna (the Baroque towers at either end). When it was finished, the church received a decidedly mixed press. History, incidentally, delivered a negative verdict: In its day the Karlskirche spawned no imitations, and it went on to become one of European architecture's most famous curiosities. Notwithstanding, seen lit at night, the building is magical in its setting.

The main interior of the church utilizes only the area under the dome, and is surprisingly conventional given the unorthodox facade. The space and architectural detailing are typical High Baroque; the fine vault frescoes, by J. M. Rottmayr (1725–30), depict Saint Charles Borromeo imploring the Holy Trinity to end the plague. ✉ *Karlspl.,* ☎ *01/504–61–87.* ⏲ *Weekdays 7:30–7, Sat. 8–7, Sun. 9–7. U-Bahn: U1, U2, U4 Karlspl.*

Karlsplatz. Like the space now occupied by the Naschmarkt, Karlsplatz was formed when the River Wien was covered over at the turn of the century. At the time Wagner expressed his frustration with the result—too large a space for a formal square and too small a space for an informal park—and the awkwardness persists to this day. The buildings surrounding the Karlsplatz, on the other hand, are quite sure of themselves: the area is dominated by the classic **Karlskirche** (☞ *above*), the less dramatic for the unfortunate reflecting pool with its Henry Moore sculpture, wholly out of place, in front. On the south side of the Resselpark, that part of Karlsplatz named for the inventor of the ship's screw propeller, stands the **Technical University** (1816–18). In a house that occupied the space closest to the church, Italian composer Antonio Vivaldi died in 1741; a plaque marks the spot. On the north side across the heavily-traveled roadway are the **Künstlerhaus** (the exhibition hall in which the Secessionists refused to exhibit, built in 1881 and still in use) and the **Musikverein** (☞ Music *in* the Arts, *below*). The latter building, finished in 1869, is now home to the Vienna Philharmonic. The downstairs lobby and the two halls upstairs have been gloriously restored and glow with fresh gilding. The main hall has what may be the world's finest acoustics; this is the site of the annual, globally televised New Year's Day concert.

Some of Otto Wagner's finest Secessionist work can be seen two blocks east on the northern edge of Karlsplatz. In 1893 Wagner was appointed architectural supervisor of the new Vienna City Railway, and the matched **pair of small pavilions** he designed for the Karlsplatz station in 1898 are among the city's most ingratiating buildings. Their structural framework is frankly exposed (in keeping with Wagner's belief in architectural honesty), but they are also lovingly decorated (in keeping with the Viennese fondness for architectural finery). The result is Jugendstil at its very best, melding plain and fancy with grace and insouciance. The pavilion to the southwest is utilized as a small, specialized museum. In the course of redesigning Karlsplatz, it was Wagner, incidentally, who proposed moving the fruit and vegetable market to what is now the Naschmarkt (☞ *below*).

Naschmarkt. The area between Linke and Rechte Wienzeile has for 80 years been home to the Naschmarkt, Vienna's main outdoor produce market, certainly one of Europe's—if not the world's—great open-air markets, where packed rows of polished and stacked fruits and vegetables compete for visual appeal with braces of fresh pheasant in season; the nostrils meanwhile are accosted by spice fragrances redolent of Asia or the Middle East. *U-Bahn: U1, U2, U4 Karlsplatz.*

NEED A BREAK? Who can resist exploring the Naschmarkt without picking up a snack as you go along. The stands marked *Imbiss* (Snack) will sell you a *Hühnerschnitzel-Semmel* (chicken schnitzel inside a Viennese roll); **Heindl & Co. Palatschinkenkuch'l** (pancake kitchen) sells a wide variety of meat and dessert crepes; and the **Naschmarkt Bäckerei** has pastry. You can find a "Stehkaffee" (literally, standup coffee)—limited seats but high tables on which to lean—at the **Anker** pastry and bakery shops.

Otto Wagner Houses. The Ringstrasse-style apartment houses that line the Wienzeile are an attractive if generally somewhat standard lot, but two stand out: **Linke Wienzeile Nos. 38 and 40**—the latter better known as the "Majolica House"—designed (1898–99) by the grand old man of Viennese fin-de-siècle architecture, Otto Wagner, during his Secessionist phase. A good example of what Wagner was rebelling against can be seen next door, at **Linke Wienzeile No. 42,** where decorative enthusiasm has blossomed into Baroque Revival hysteria. Wagner had come to believe that this sort of display was nothing but empty pretense and sham; modern apartment houses, he wrote in his pioneering text *Modern Architecture,* are entirely different from 18th-century town palaces, and architects should not pretend otherwise. Accordingly, he banished classical decoration and introduced a new architectural simplicity, with flat exterior walls and plain, regular window treatments meant to reflect the orderly layout of the apartments behind them. There the simplicity ended. For exterior decoration, he turned to his younger Secessionist cohorts Joseph Olbrich and Koloman Moser, who designed the ornate Jugendstil patterns of red majolica-tile roses (No. 40) and gold stucco medallions (No. 38) that gloriously brighten the facades of the adjacent houses—so much so that their Baroque-period neighbor is ignored. The houses are private.

OFF THE BEATEN PATH **AM STEINHOF CHURCH** – Otto Wagner's most exalted piece of Jugendstil architecture is not in the inner city but in the suburbs to the west: the Am Steinhof Church, designed in 1904 during his Secessionist phase (head out to the church by taking the U4 subway line, which is adjacent to the Wagner houses discussed above). On the grounds of the Vienna City Psychiatric Hospital, Wagner's design unites mundane functional details (rounded edges on the pews to prevent injury to the patients and a slightly sloped tile floor to facilitate cleaning) with a soaring, airy dome and glittering Jugendstil decoration (stained glass by Koloman Moser). The church is open once a week for guided tours (in German). ✉ *Baumgartner Höhe 1,* ☎ *01/910-60-2391.* 🎫 *Free.* ⊙ *Sat. 3–4. U-Bahn: U4/Unter-St.-Veit, then Bus 47A to Psychiatrisches Krankenhaus; or U2/Volkstheater, then Bus 48A.*

Schwarzenbergplatz. A remarkable urban ensemble, the Schwarzenbergplatz comprises some notable sights. The center of the lower square off the Ring is marked by an oversized equestrian Prince Schwarzenberg—he was a 19th century field marshall for the imperial forces. Admire the overall effect of the square and see if you can guess which building is the newest; it's the one on the northeast corner (No. 3) at Lothringer Strasse, an exacting reproduction of a building destroyed by war damage in 1945, and dating only to the 1980s. The military monument occupying the south end of the square behind the fountain is the **Russian War Memorial,** set up at the end of World War II by the Soviets; the Viennese, remembering the Soviet occupation, call its unknown soldier "the unknown plunderer." South of the memorial is the stately **Schwarzenberg Palace,** designed as a summer residence by Johann Lukas von Hildebrandt in 1697, completed by Fischer von Erlach father and son, and now (in part) a luxury hotel (☞ Dining and Lodging, *below*). The delightful formal gardens wedged between Prinz Eugen–Strasse and the Belvedere gardens can be enjoyed from the hotel restaurant's veranda.

OFF THE BEATEN PATH

CENTRAL CEMETERY – Taking a streetcar out of Schwarzenbergplatz, music lovers will want to make a pilgrimage to the **Zentralfriedhof** (Central Cemetery, ✉ 11th District on Simmeringer Hauptstr.), which contains the graves of most of Vienna's great composers: Ludwig van Beethoven, Franz Schubert, Johannes Brahms, the Johann Strausses (father and son), and Arnold Schönberg, among others. The monument to Wolfgang Amadeus Mozart is a memorial only; the approximate location of his unmarked grave can be seen at the now deconsecrated St. Marx-Friedhof at Leberstrasse 6–8. *Streetcar 71 to St. Marxer Friedhof, or on to Zentralfriedhof Haupttor/2.*

★ 44 **Secession Pavilion.** If the Academy of Fine Arts represents the conservative attitude toward the arts in the late 1800s, then its antithesis can be found immediately behind it to the southeast: the Secession Pavilion. Restored in the mid-1980s after years of neglect, the Secession building is one of Vienna's preeminent symbols of artistic rebellion. Rather than looking to the architecture of the past like the revivalist Ringstrasse, it looked to a new anti-historicist future. It was, in its day, a riveting trumpet-blast of a building, and is today considered by many to be Europe's first example of full-blown 20th-century architecture.

The Sezession—to use the German spelling—began in 1897 when 20 dissatisfied Viennese artists, headed by Gustav Klimt, "seceded" from the Künstlerhausgenossenschaft, the conservative artists' society associated with the Academy of Fine Arts. The movement promoted the radically new kind of art known as Jugendstil, which found its inspiration in both the organic, fluid designs of Art Nouveau and the related but more geometric designs of the English Arts and Crafts Movement. (The Secessionists founded an Arts-and-Crafts workshop of their own, the famous Wiener Werkstätte, in an effort to embrace the applied arts.) The Secession building was the movement's exhibition hall, designed by the architect Joseph Olbrich and completed in 1898. The lower story, crowned by the entrance motto *Der Zeit Ihre Kunst, Der Kunst Ihre Freiheit* (To Every Age Its Art, To Art Its Freedom), is classic Jugendstil: The restrained but assured decoration (by Koloman Moser) beautifully complements the facade's pristine flat expanses of cream-color wall. Above the entrance motto sits the building's most famous feature, the gilded openwork dome that the Viennese were quick to christen "the golden cabbage" (Olbrich wanted it to be seen as a dome of laurel, a subtle classical reference meant to celebrate the triumph of art). The plain white interior—"shining and chaste," in Olbrich's words—was also revolutionary; its most unusual feature was movable walls, allowing the galleries to be reshaped and redesigned for every show. One early show, in 1902, was an exhibition devoted to art celebrating the genius of Beethoven; Gustav Klimt's *Beethoven Frieze,* painted for the occasion, has now been restored and is permanently installed in the building's basement. ✉ *Friedrichstr. 12,* ☎ *01/587–5307–0.* 🎫 *AS60.* 🕓 *Tues.–Fri. 10–6, weekends and holidays 10–4. U-Bahn: U1, U2, U4 Karlsplatz.*

Splendors of the Habsburgs: A Visit to Schönbrunn Palace

The glories of Imperial Austria are nowhere brought together more convincingly than in the Schönbrunn Palace (Schloss Schönbrunn) complex. Brilliant "Maria Theresia Yellow"—she, in fact, caused Schöbrunn to be built—is everywhere in evidence. Imperial elegance flows unbroken throughout the grounds and the setting, and the impression even today is interrupted only by ceaseless hiccups of tourists. This, after all, one of Austria's primary tourist sites, although sadly, few stay long enough to discover the real Schönbrunn (including the little maiden with the water jar, after whom the complex is named). While the assorted outbuildings might seem eclectic, they served as centers of entertainment when the court moved to Schönbrunn in the summer, accounting for the zoo, the priceless theater, the fake Roman ruins, the greenhouses, and the walkways. In Schönbrunn, you step back three hundred years into the heart of a powerful and growing empire and follow it through to defeat and demise in 1917.

Numbers in the text correspond to numbers in the margin and on the Schönbrunn Palace and Park map.

A Good Walk

The usual start for exploring the Schönbrunn complex is the main palace. There's nothing wrong with that approach, but as a variation, consider first climbing to the **Gloriette** on the hill overlooking the site, for a bird's-eye view to put the rest in perspective (take the stairs to the Gloriette roof for the ultimate experience). While at the Gloriette, take a few steps west to discover the **Tiroler House** ㊿ and follow the zigzag path downhill to the palace; note the picturebook views of the main building through the woods. Try to take the full tour of the **palace** ㊺ rather than the shorter, truncated version. Check whether the ground floor back rooms (*Berglzimmer*) are open to viewing. After the palace guided tour, take your own walk around the grounds. The "Schöner Brunner," the namesake fountain, is hidden in the woods to the southeast; continue along to discover the convincing (but fake) Roman Ruins. At the other side of the complex to the west are the excellent **Tiergarten** ㊾ (zoo), the **Palmenhaus** ㊽ (tropical greenhouse), and the attached **Schmetterlinghaus** (butterfly house). Closer to the main entrance, both the **Wagenburg** ㊻ (carriage museum) and **Schlosstheater** (palace theater) are frequently overlooked treasures. Before heading back to the city center, visit the **Hofpavillion** ㊼, the private subway station built for Emperor Francis Joseph, located to the west across Schönbrunner Schlossstrasse.

TIMING

If you're really pressed for time, the shorter guided tour will give you a fleeting impression of the palace itself, but try to budget at least half a day to take the full tour and include the extra rooooms and grounds as well. The 20-minute hike up to the Gloriette is a bit strenuous but worthwhile, and there's now a café as reward at the top. The zoo is worth as much as much time as you can spend, and figure on at least a half hour to an hour each for the other museums. Tour buses begin to unload for the main building about mid-morning; start early or utilize the noon lull to avoid the worst crowds. The other museums and buildings in the complex are far less crowded.

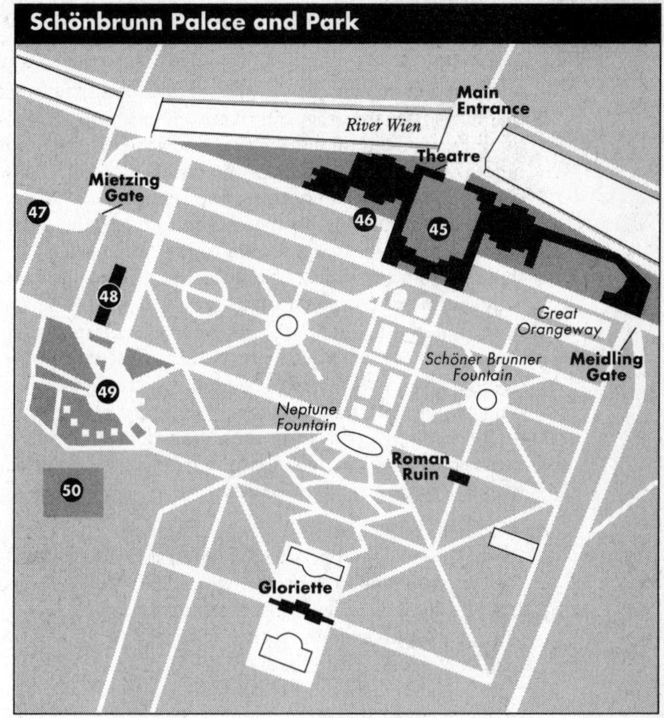

Sights to See

Hofpavillon. The most unusual interior of the palace complex, the restored Imperial subway station known as the Hofpavillon is just outside the palace grounds (at the northwest corner, a few yards east of the Hietzing subway station). Designed by Otto Wagner in conjunction with Joseph Olbrich and Leopold Bauer, the Hofpavillon was built in 1899 for the exclusive use of the Emperor Francis Joseph and his entourage. Exclusive it was: The emperor used the station only once. The exterior, with its proud architectural crown, is Wagner at his best, and the lustrous interior is one of the finest examples of Jugendstil decoration in the city. ✉ *Schönbrunner Schloss-Str., next to Hietzing subway station,* ☎ *01/877–1571.* 🎫 *AS25.* ⏲ *Tues.–Sun. 9–12:15 and 1–4:30. U-Bahn: U4 Hietzing.*

★ 45 **Schönbrunn Palace.** Designed by Johann Bernhard Fischer von Erlach in 1696, Schönbrunn Palace, the huge Habsburg summer residence lies well within the city limits, just a few subway stops west of Karlsplatz on line U4. The vast and elegantly planted gardens are open daily from dawn till dusk, and multilingual guided tours of the palace interior are offered daily. A visit inside the palace is not included in most general city sightseeing tours, which offer either a mercilessly tempting drive past or else an impossibly short half hour or so to explore. The four-hour commercial sightseeing bus tours of Schönbrunn offered by tour operators cost several times what you'd pay if you tackled the easy excursion yourself; their advantage is that they get you there and back with less effort. Go on your own if you want time to wander the magnificent grounds.

The most impressive approach to the palace and its gardens is through the front gate, located on Schönbrunner Schloss-Strasse halfway between the Schönbrunn and Hietzing subway stations. The vast main courtyard is ruled by a formal design of impeccable order and rigorous symmetry: Wing nods at wing, facade mirrors facade, and every part stylistically complements every other. The courtyard, however, turns out to be a mere appetizer; the feast lies beyond. The breathtaking view that unfolds on the other side of the palace is one of the finest set pieces in all Europe and one of the supreme achievements of Baroque planning. Formal *allées* (garden promenades) shoot off diagonally, the one on the right toward the zoo, the one on the left toward a rock-mounted obelisk and a fine false Roman ruin. But these, and the woods beyond, are merely a frame for the astonishing composition in the center: the sculpted fountain, the carefully planted screen of trees behind, the sudden almost vertical rise of the grass-covered hill beyond. At the crest of the hill, topping it all off, sits a Baroque masterstroke: Johann Ferdinand von Hohenberg's incomparable **Gloriette,** now restored to its original splendor. Perfectly scaled for its setting, the Gloriette—a palatial pavilion that once offered royal guests a place to rest and relax on their tours of the palace grounds and that now houses an equally welcome café—holds the whole vast garden composition together, and at the same time crowns the ensemble with a brilliant architectural tiara.

Within the palace, the magisterial state salons are quite up to the splendor of the gardens, but note the contrast between these chambers and the far more modest rooms in which the rulers—particularly Francis Joseph—lived and spent most of their time. Of the 1,400 rooms, 40 are open to the public on the regular tour, and two are of special note: the Hall of Mirrors, where the six-year-old Mozart performed for the Empress Maria Theresa in 1762, and the Grand Gallery, where the Congress of Vienna (1815) danced at night after carving up Napoléon's collapsed empire during the day. Ask about viewing the ground-floor living quarters (*Berglzimmer*), where the walls are fascinatingly painted with palm trees, exotic animals, and tropical views. As you go through the palace, take an occasional glance out the windows; you'll be rewarded by a better impression of the beautiful patterns of the formal gardens, punctuated by hedgerows and fountains. These window vistas were enjoyed by rulers from Maria Theresa and Napoléon to Francis Joseph. ✉ *Schönbrunner Schloss-Str.,* ☎ *01/811–13–239.* 🎫 *Grand tour of palace interior (40 rooms) AS140, self-guided grand tour (40 rooms) AS110, self-guided imperial tour (20 rooms) AS80.* ⏲ *Apr.–Oct., daily 8:30–5; Nov.–Mar., daily 8:30–4:30. U-Bahn: U4 Schönbrunn.*

Schönbrunn Palace Park. The palace grounds boast a bevy of splendid divertissements, including a grand zoo (☞ Tiergarten, *below*) and carriage museum (☞ Wagenburg, *below*). Climb to the Gloriette for a panoramic view out over the city as well as the palace complex. If you're exploring on your own, seek out the intriguing Roman ruin, now used as a backdrop for outdoor summer opera. The marble *"schöner Brunnen"* (beautiful fountain) with the young girl pouring water from an urn is nearby. The fountain gave the name to the palace complex.
50 The charming **Tiroler House** to the west of the Gloriette was a favorite retreat of Empress Elisabeth; it now includes a small restaurant (open according to season and weather). 🎫 *Gloriette roof AS20.* ⏲ *May–Oct., daily 9–5. U-Bahn: U4 Schönbrunn.*

48 On the grounds to the west of Schönbrunn Palace is the **Palmenhaus,** a huge greenhouse filled with exotic trees and plants. ✉ *Nearest entrance Hietzing,* ☎ *01/877–5087–406.* 🎫 *AS40, combination ticket with Schmetterlinghaus AS65.* ⏲ *May–Sept., daily 9:30–6 (last admission 5:30); Oct.–Apr., daily 9:30–5 (last admission 4:30).*

Close by the Palmenhaus is another Schönbrunn Palace favorite, the **Schmetterlinghaus,** given over to hordes of live butterflies, orchids, and other floral displays. ✉ *Nearest entrance Hietzing,* ☎ *01/877–5087–421.* 🎟 *AS40, combination ticket with Palmenhaus AS65.* ⏲ *May–Sept., daily 10–5 (last admission 4:30); Oct.–Apr., daily 10–3:30 (last admission 3).*

49 Claimed to be the world's oldest, the **Tiergarten** (Zoo) has retained its original Baroque decor and, today, has acquired world class recognition under director Helmut Pechlaner. New settings have been created for both animals and public; in one case, the public looks out into a new natural display area from one of the Baroque former animal houses. The zoo is constantly adding new attractions and undergoing renovations, so there's plenty to see. ☎ *01/877–1236–0.* 🎟 *AS90.* ⏲ *Nov.–Jan., daily 9–4:30; Oct. and Feb., daily 9–5; Mar., daily 9–5:30; Apr., daily 9–6; May–Sept., daily 9–6:30. U-Bahn: U4.*

46 Most of the carriages in the **Wagenburg** (Carriage Museum) are still roadworthy and, indeed, Schönbrunn dusted off the gilt-and-black royal funeral carriage that you see here for the burial ceremony of Empress Zita in 1989. ✉ *Wagenburg,* ☎ *01/877–3244.* 🎟 *AS30.* ⏲ *Nov.–Mar., Tues.–Sun. 10–4; Apr.–Oct., daily 9–6. U-Bahn: U4 Schönbrunn.*

DINING

Whether the locale be one of the city's finest or a modest neighborhood *Beisl,* the Viennese take their dining seriously and can tell you to a crumb what they've had to eat for at least the last fortnight. This development is remarkable since, not so long ago, Vienna was a culinary backwater. In recent years, however, Vienna has produced a new generation of chefs willing to slaughter sacred cows and create a New Vienna Cuisine. The movement is well past the "less is more" stage that nouvelle cuisine traditionally demands (and to which most Viennese vociferously objected), relying now on lighter versions of the old standbys and clever combinations of such traditional ingredients as liver pâtés and sour cream.

In a first-class restaurant you will pay as much as in most other major Western European capitals. But you can still find good food at refreshingly low prices in the simpler restaurants, particularly at neighborhood *Gasthäuser* in the suburbs. If you eat your main meal at noon (as the Viennese do), you can take advantage of the luncheon specials.

Vienna's restaurant fare ranges from Arabic to Yugoslav, with strong doses of Chinese, Italian, and Japanese, but assuming you've come for what makes Vienna unique, our listings focus not on the exotic but on places where you'll meet the Viennese and experience Vienna.

Many restaurants are closed one or two days a week (often weekends), and most serve meals only 11:30–2:30 and 6–10. An increasing number now serve after-theater dinners, but reserve in advance. The pocket-sized paperback book *Wien wie es isst* (in German; from almost any bookstore) gives up-to-date information on the restaurant, café, and bar scene. For an overview on the pleasures of Austrian cuisine, *see* "Schnitzels, Strudels, and Sachertortes" *in* Pleasures and Pastimes *in* Chapter 1.

CATEGORY	COST*
$$$$	over AS500
$$$	AS300–AS500
$$	AS150–AS300
$	under AS150

**per person, including a small glass of open house wine or beer, service (usually 10%), sales tax (10%), and additional small tip (5%–7%)*

Restaurants

$$$$ ★ ✕ **Korso.** For many, this is Vienna's top restaurant, in the Bristol Hotel; you're surrounded by subdued dark-paneled and gold elegance; tables are set with fine linen, glassware, and silver. The food matches the setting; chef Reinhard Gerer is one of Austria's great creative cooks; unfortunately the kitchen is occasionally left to the second brigade, hardly a disaster, but not up to the master's achievements. Try such specialties as roast duck with savoy cabbage or *Rehnüsschen,* tiny venison fillets. Ask sommelier Christian Zach to recommend an appropriate wine; the choice is international, although the Austrian list is outstanding. ⊠ *Mahlerstr. 2,* ☏ *01/515–16–546,* FAX *01/515–16–550. Reservations essential. Jacket and tie. AE, DC, MC, V. Closed Aug. No lunch Sat.*

$$$$ ✕ **Palais Schwarzenberg.** This restaurant, in a former private palace, has one of the most impressive settings in Vienna, but be sure to book a table on the glassed-in terrace; you'll be surrounded inside by greenery, with a view out over the formal gardens. The food is a notch or two below Korso's (☞ *above*), but still extremely good, and new top chef Christian Petz gives promise of even better. The service may lag if the restaurant is full, so be prepared to relax and enjoy the setting. You can't go wrong with the fillet of beef in red wine sauce, medallions of lamb, or the delicate pike. ⊠ *Schwarzenbergpl. 9,* ☏ *01/798–4515–600,* FAX *01/798–4714. Reservations essential. Jacket and tie. AE, DC, MC, V.*

$$$$ ★ ✕ **Steirer Eck.** Critics are in agreement that this is Austria's top restaurant. You dine handsomely in classical elegance, among businesspeople at noon, amid politicians and personalities at night. Tables are set with flower arrangements and elegant crystal, with a flair that matches the food. Chef Helmut Österreicher is a genius at combining ideas and tastes; lobster with artichoke is a successful example, venison with leek and mushrooms another, but creations are constantly changing. The fixed-price menu at noon is an outstanding value. The house wine list is overwhelming; you can ask sommelier Adolf Schmid for advice with the assurance that it will be good. ⊠ *Rasumofskygasse 2,* ☏ *01/713–3168,* FAX *01/713–5168–2. Reservations essential. Jacket and tie. AE, DC, MC, V. Closed weekends.*

$$$$ ★ ✕ **Vier Jahreszeiten.** The Inter-Continental's restaurant is an excellent if conservative choice for both the ample noontime buffet and evening dining. The atmosphere is elegant without being overdone. Service, too, is attentive but discreet, the wine list impressive but not overwhelming. The delicate roast lamb is consistently delicious; so is the fillet of beef with raw mushrooms. For dessert, ask for a *Mohr im Hemd,* literally, a moor in a shirt, a chocolate sponge-cake confection with chocolate sauce and whipped cream. ⊠ *Johannesgasse 28,* ☏ *01/711–22–143,* FAX *01/713–4489. Reservations essential. Jacket and tie. AE, DC, MC, V. Closed weekends, 2 wks in Jan., and 3 wks in July.*

$$$$ ✕ **Zu den Drei Husaren.** The Three Hussars is again solidly in the ranks of Vienna's gourmet temples; despite redecoration producing a brighter ambience, the house remains embalmed in its draped green-yellow velvet and gold. If you don't mind the heavy hand (which occasionally carries over to the food and service), you'll probably enjoy this touch of "old" Vienna, evening piano music included. Evenings are enjoyed by celebrities, lunchtime is for business, and both are for tourists. The noontime limited menu offers sufficient choice and is good value. Be warned of the enticing but unpriced evening hors d'oeuvre trolley; a single dip here can double your bill. The Husaren does best with the classic standards: *Leberknödelsuppe* (liver-dumpling soup), Wiener schnitzel, roast beef, and the like. Finish with *Husarenpfannkuchen,* the house crepes. ⊠ *Weihburggasse 4,* ☏ *01/512–1092,* FAX *01/512–*

1092–18. *Reservations essential. Jacket and tie. AE, DC, MC, V. Closed mid-July–mid-Aug.*

$$$ ★ ✕ **Hedrich.** This tiny, unassuming restaurant offers astonishingly fine food. Richard Hedrich, the owner and chef, decided to go into business for himself and cook to his and his guests' pleasure; his wife looks after the tables and the guests, including giving wine recommendations. The menu changes regularly, so ask for recommendations; recent offerings have included a fragrant whipped basil soup and medallions of pork in a cheese dough crust. ✉ *Stubenring 2,* ☎ *01/512–9588. Reservations essential. No credit cards. Closed Fri., weekends, and Aug.*

$$$ ★ ✕ **Imperial Café.** In the Imperial Hotel, the café is much more than just a (very good) meeting spot for coffee or *Torte*; both lunch and after-concert supper are popular and reasonably priced. The rooms are understated by local standards; crystal and velvet are evident but not overdone. The city's politicians, attorneys, and business types gather here for solid Viennese fare, selecting either from the choice daily specialties, which generally include a superb cream soup, or relying on such standards as *Leberknödelsuppe* and *Tafelspitz,* Viennese boiled beef. In summer, the terrace outside is enticing but noisy. ✉ *Kärntner Ring 16,* ☎ *01/501–10–359,* FAX *01/501–10–410. AE, DC, MC, V.*

$$$ ✕ **Plachutta.** In two settings that pleasantly mix traditional and modern, attention focuses on the excellent Tafelspitz, various cuts of beef cooked and served in their own delicious soup, for which you order the "supplement," perhaps thin pancake strips (*Frittaten*) or liver dumpling (*Leberknödel*). Steaks or grilled fish are alternatives. To finish, select a rhubarb strudel or fresh fruit. The traditional accompaniment to Tafelspitz is beer, but the house open wines are excellent. The otherwise top service may lag a bit as the evening comes to a close. ✉ *Wollzeile 38,* ☎ *01/512–1577,* FAX *01/512–1577–20;* ✉ *Heiligenstädter Str. 179,* ☎ *01/374125,* FAX *01/374125–20. Reservations essential. MC, V. Closed last wk of July–mid-Aug.*

$$$ ✕ **Schnattl.** If you're not outdoors in the idyllic courtyard, the setting could be described as cool postmodern: the main room has now acquired a warmer patina but is relatively unadorned, letting you concentrate instead on the attractively set tables and excellent cuisine (which offers occasional surprises such as medallions of mountain ram). Traditional dishes like roast pork are transformed with such touches as a light mustard sauce, lamb with a trace of rosemary, with offerings dependent on season and availability of fresh ingredients. ✉ *Lange Gasse 40,* ☎ *01/405–3400. AE, DC. Closed Sun., 2 wks around Easter, and late Aug.–mid-Sept. No lunch Sat.*

$$$ ✕ **Sirk.** This comfortable restaurant in traditional style is ideal for a light lunch or an evening snack. The glassed-in sidewalk terrace is perfect for afternoon coffee and dessert, but for more privacy, take a table upstairs; those overlooking the Opera House are best, but at noon you'll have to fight Vienna's business establishment for one of them. The daily menu is excellent value, or you might choose the rare roast beef with black-mushroom sauce. The post-opera menu is consistently good. ✉ *Kärntner Str. 53,* ☎ *01/515–16–552,* FAX *01/515–16–550. AE, DC, MC, V.*

$$$ ✕ **Zum Kuckuck.** This intimate, wood-paneled restaurant, in a building many hundreds of years old, draws its clientele from the ministries in the neighborhood at noon. The kitchen does such variations on regional themes as fillet of veal in mushroom sauce and fillet of venison in puff pastry. Try the warm fig cake with rum sauce for dessert. ✉ *Himmelpfortgasse 15,* ☎ *01/512–8470,* FAX *01/523–3818. AE, DC, MC, V. Closed weekends.*

$$ ✕ **Bastei Beisl.** You'll find good basic Viennese cuisine in this unpretentious, friendly, pine-paneled restaurant. Try the *Zwiebelrostbraten,* a rump steak smothered in fried onions. The tables outside in summer add to the plea-

Aida, **31, 46**
Alte Backstübe, **2**
Augustinerkeller, **38**
Bastei Beisl, **33**
Bei Max, **13**
Bräunerhof, **28**
Brezlg'wölb, **18**
Café Central, **12**
Café Hawelka, **26**
Demel, **24**
Demel Vis-à-vis, **25**
Esterházykeller, **15**
Figlmüller, **23**
Frauenhuber, **43**
Gerstner, **35**
Gigerl, **36**
Glacis-Beisl, **6**
Gösser Bierklinik, **16**
Gösser Brau, **48**
Göttweiger Stiftskeller, **29**
Gulaschmuseum, **32**
Haag, **9**
Hedrich, **57**
Heiner, **22, 45**
Imperial Café, **52**
Königsbacher bei der Oper, **47**
Korso (Bristol), **51**
Kurkonditorei Oberlaa, **30**
Landtmann, **8**
Lustig Essen, **20**
Melker Stiftskeller, **10**
Myer's Kaiserwalzer-Bräu, **4**
Museum, **49**
Naschmarkt, **11, 54**
Ofenloch, **17**
Palais Schwarzenberg, **56**
Pantherbräu, **19**
Plachutta, **34**
Reinthaler, **39**
Rosenberger Marktrestaurant, **41**
Schnattl, **1**
Schnitzelhaus, **5**
Schwarzenberg, **53**
Sirk, **50**
Sluka, **7**
Stadtbeisl, **14**
Steirer Eck, **58**
Tirolerhof, **40**
Trzesniewski, **27**
Vier Jahreszeiten, **55**
Zu d. Drei Hacken, **37**
Zu d. Drei Husaren, **42**
Zu ebener Erde und im ersten Stock, **3**
Zum Kuckuck, **44**
Zwölf Apostel-Keller, **21**

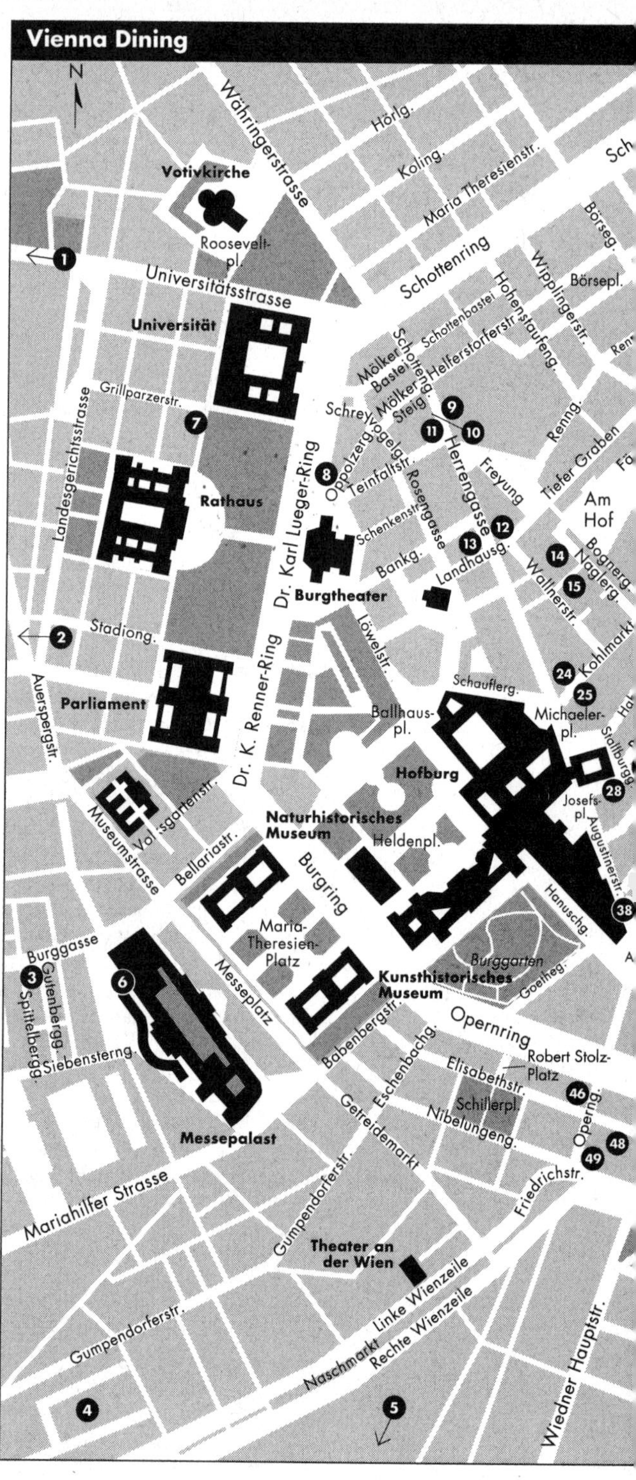

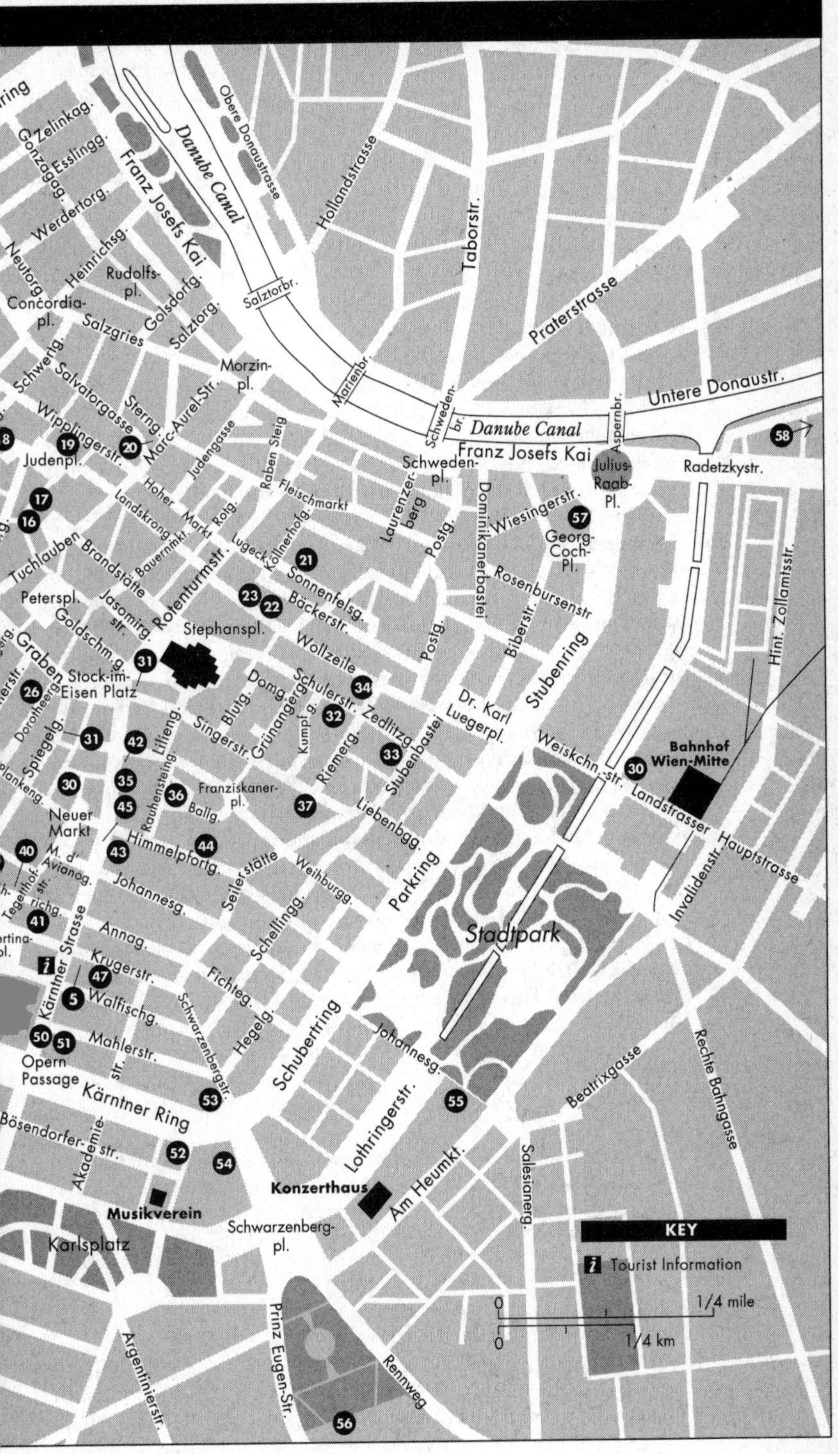
Danube Canal
Franz Josefs Kai
Obere Donaustrasse
Hollandstrasse
Taborstr.
Praterstrasse
Untere Donaustr.
Salztorbr.
Marienbr.
Schwedenbr.
Aspernbr.
Stephanspl.
Stock-im-Eisen Platz
Graben
Rotenturmstr.
Wollzeile
Stubenring
Parkring
Schubertring
Kärntner Ring
Kärntner Strasse
Stadtpark
Bahnhof Wien-Mitte
Landstrasser Hauptstrasse
Konzerthaus
Musikverein
Karlsplatz
Schwarzenberg-pl.
Prinz Eugen-Str.
Rennweg
Lothringerstr.
Am Heumkt.
KEY
Tourist Information
1/4 mile
1/4 km

sure at noon or in the evening. ✉ *Stubenbastei 10,* ☎ *01/512–4319. AE, DC, MC. Closed Sat. July and Aug., Sun., and holidays.*

$$ ✕ **Bei Max.** The decor is somewhat bland, but the tasty Carinthian specialties—the cheese-and-meat-filled ravioli known as *Käsnudeln* and *Fleischnudeln* in particular—pack this friendly restaurant, a favorite with officials from neighboring government offices and with students alike. You'll also find such classic standards as Tafelspitz, as well as outstanding desserts. The *Kletzennudeln,* a form of bread pudding with dried fruit and cinnamon, is a house feature. Both bottled and open wines are good and generally reasonable, and the beer is excellent. ✉ *Landhausgasse 2/Herrengasse,* ☎ *01/533–7359. No credit cards. Closed weekends, last wk of July, and 1st 3 wks of Aug.*

$$ ★ ✕ **Figlmüller.** If you'll accept the style of the house (you sit at a series of benches elbow-to-elbow with the other guests), this is *the* spot for Wiener schnitzel—one that overhangs the plate. (Waiters understand the doggie-bag principle.) Other choices are somewhat limited, and you'll have to take wine or mineral water with your meal because no beer or coffee is served. No desserts are offered; you probably couldn't manage one anyway. But Figlmüller is an experience you'll want to repeat. ✉ *Wollzeile 5,* ☎ *01/512–6177. No credit cards.*

$$ ★ ✕ **Glacis-Beisl.** This restaurant, tucked beneath a section of the old city wall, is no longer the secret it once was, but the charm of the indoor rooms is still appealing, and its garden under grape arbors is unique. Alas, a proposed rebuilding of the Messepalast (dubbed the Museumquartier, a venue used for art exhibits and theater events) into a cultural complex threatens the existence of this fascinating corner of Vienna. The menu is long; ask the waiter for help. You'll find most of the Viennese standards, but the place seems right for grilled chicken (*Brathendl*) and a mug of wine. ✉ *Messepalast (follow signs to rear right corner), Messepl. 1,* ☎ *01/526–6795. Reservations essential. No credit cards. Closed Sun., Jan.–mid-Feb., and holidays.*

$$ ✕ **Gösser Bierklinik.** The rooms go on and on in this upstairs (more formal) and downstairs (preferred) complex that dates back four centuries. The fare is as solid as the house; the Wiener schnitzel here is first class. The salad bar is new. And there's a menu in English. The beer, of course, is Austrian, from the Gösser brewery in Styria. ✉ *Steindlgasse 4,* ☎ *01/535–6897. AE, DC, MC, V. Closed Sun. and holidays.*

$$ ✕ **Gösser Brau.** This vast *Keller* (cellar) with a faux copper brewing vat is a noontime hangout of businesspeople who appreciate the good food and generally prompt service. Go for the game when it's available. *Rehrücken* (rack of venison) is a specialty. The appropriate accompaniment is Gösser beer, of course. ✉ *Elisabethstr. 3,* ☎ *01/587–4750. AE, DC, MC, V.*

$$ ★ ✕ **Königsbacher bei der Oper.** The small, paneled and arched rooms or the tables outside seem just right for Viennese standards such as schnitzel and roast pork. The daily special—this might be ravioli or meat loaf—is an excellent value. Service is friendly, beer is German, and the open wines are good. ✉ *Walfischgasse 5,* ☎ *01/513–1210. No credit cards. Closed Sun. No dinner Sat.*

$$ ✕ **Myer's Kaiserwalzer-Bräu.** Traces of the elegant "old Vienna" atmosphere remain in this former town house with its wood paneled rooms inside and large dining garden out front. The menu is as eclectic as the decor but both are genuine. You'll find standards such as Tafelspitz alongside relative exotica like *Vitello tonnato,* roast veal with a delicate tuna fish and capers sauce. The shorter menu changes weekly according to season. The excellent beer comes from Salzburg, the wines mainly from Austria. ✉ *Esterházygasse 9,* ☎ *01/587–0494,* FAX *01/587–0494. AE, DC, MC, V. No lunch.*

$$ ★ **Ofenloch.** Unique for its turn-of-the-century ambience, this restaurant features waitresses in costume and a menu in miniature newspaper form. The fare is based on original recipes and the offerings change periodically according to what's in season. Garlic fans will find the *Vanillerostbraten,* a rump steak prepared not with vanilla but with garlic, delicious. The misleading name came about because in early days, no one would admit to ordering anything with garlic. Desserts—try the *Palatschinken,* cream-filled crepes ladled with chocolate sauce—are consistently good and utterly seductive. ✉ *Kurrentgasse 8,* ☎ *01/533–8844. Reservations essential. AE, DC, MC, V.*

$$ **Stadtbeisl.** The smallish dark-paneled rooms are packed at noon, as is the summer garden amid the ivy outside. Better say "no" to the waiter's (expensive) offer of a *Schnaps* (liquor) to start. Take the game in season; otherwise try one of the good Viennese standards. ✉ *Naglergasse 21,* ☎ *01/533–3507. V.*

$$ **Zu den Drei Hacken.** This is one of the last of the old *Gasthäuser* in the center of town; Schubert, among other luminaries of the past, is alleged to have dined here. You will find excellent Viennese fare, from schnitzel to Tafelspitz. The outdoor garden is attractive but jammed. ✉ *Singerstr. 28,* ☎ *01/512–5895. AE, DC, MC, V. Closed Sun.*

$$ ★ **Zu ebener Erde und im ersten Stock.** This gem of a historic house has an upstairs/downstairs combination: In the tiny room upstairs, done in Biedermeier old Vienna decor, the cuisine reflects the setting, with Viennese favorites and others such as medallions of lamb or rump steak with bread crust. The selection concentrates on a narrower range of excellently-prepared dishes. There's simpler (and cheaper) fare on the ground floor. ✉ *Burggasse 13,* ☎ *01/523–6254. Reservations essential. AE, V. Closed Sat. afternoon, Sun., Mon., and 1st 3 wks of Aug.*

$ **Brezlg'wölb.** Casual food—soups in mini-tureen portions and salad plates—and a cozy, friendly atmosphere draw the crowds here. If you sit in the quiet courtyard between Am Hof and Judenplatz, you look up at classical facades; inside, small, brick-vaulted rooms offer a comfortable interlude to diners. Downstairs, many come just to enjoy the excellent wine, beer, and coffee in the candle-lit cellar rooms. ✉ *Ledererhof 9,* ☎ *01/533–8811. No credit cards.*

$ ★ **Gigerl.** This charming and original wine restaurant offers a hot and cold buffet, specializing in vegetable and pasta dishes; try the macaroni salad or the *Schinkenfleckerl,* a baked noodle and ham dish. They go remarkably well with the light wines that the costumed waitresses keep pouring into your glass. In winter the rooms can get smoky and stuffy; in summer, the outside tables are delightful. ✉ *Rauhensteingasse 3/Blumenstockgasse 2,* ☎ *01/513–4431. AE, DC, MC, V.*

$ **Göttweiger Stiftskeller.** In this traditional, basic restaurant, look for grilled and fried chicken, schnitzel variants, tasty liver dishes such as Leberknödelsuppe plus occasional surprises like oxtail soup. The food helps compensate for the rather unexciting rooms. The wines, on the other hand, are outstanding. ✉ *Spiegelgasse 9,* ☎ *01/512–7817. No credit cards. Closed weekends.*

$ **Gulaschmuseum.** The original idea behind this modern restaurant is literally dozens of tasty variants on the theme of goulash. They're just right for a between-meal snack, although most of the goulashes served are filling enough for a complete meal. There are alternatives as well. ✉ *Schulerstr. 20,* ☎ *01/512–1017. No credit cards.*

$ **Lustig Essen.** The name means "amusing dining." The concept in these modern rooms involves smaller portions (although generous enough for most) at remarkably reasonable prices, so that you can sample more of the outstanding dishes on the menu. Try the cream of garlic soup, the lamb ragout, or grilled shrimp. ✉ *Salvatorgasse 6,* ☎ *01/533–3037. No credit cards.*

$ ✕ Naschmarkt. In this attractive cafeteria the food is good, of excellent value, and of far more variety than at the next-door McDonald's. Look for the daily specials on the blackboard. You'll also find good soups (gazpacho on hot summer days), sandwiches, a salad bar, and a no-smoking area. ✉ *Schwarzenbergpl. 16,* ☎ *01/505–3115;* ✉ *Schottengasse 1,* ☎ *01/533–5186. No credit cards. No dinner Sun. at Schottengasse.*

$ ✕ Pantherbräu. This neighborhood *Gasthaus* is packed at noon with government officials, businessmen, and students who come for the comfortable if relatively unadorned environment, good beer, and honest food with no pretensions. This is a fine place for standards such as roast pork with mushroom sauce or, in season, venison. The standard menu card is available in English, but ask about the daily specials. In summer, the tables outside on the square are in great demand. ✉ *Judenpl. 10,* ☎ *01/533–4428. No credit cards. Closed weekends.*

$ ✕ Reinthaler. The atmosphere is thick enough to cut in this convenient neighborhood establishment, full of regulars. The fare is genuine Viennese: schnitzel, chicken, roast pork with *Knödel* (bread dumpling), and such. The ivy-fenced tables outside in summer are particularly popular. ✉ *Glückgasse 5,* ☎ *01/512–3366. No credit cards. Closed weekends. No dinner Fri.*

$ ✕ Rosenberger Marktrestaurant. Downstairs under a huge (artificial) tree you'll find a cluster of cafeteria islands offering soups, excellent grilled specialties, vegetables, pastas, salads, desserts, and fresh juices and other beverages, all prepared to order and attractively (if somewhat confusingly) presented. You can leave your valuables in one of the free lockers while you make and enjoy your selection. Look for seasonal specialties such as asparagus and fresh chilled melon. Take your choice to any of the side rooms, some decorated with musical instruments, some with antique kitchenware and dishes. ✉ *Maysedergasse 2/Führichgasse 3,* ☎ *01/512–3458. No credit cards.*

$ ✕ Schnitzelhaus. This local self-service chain specializes in pork schnitzel (pork cutlet breaded, deep fried), but you could have a turkey schnitzel, schnitzel cordon bleu or a schnitzelburger as an alternative. And there are smaller portions for children. The decor is relatively unadorned, but the schnitzels are certainly not bad (choose fries over the traditional but sometimes soggy potato salad accompaniment), and prices rock-bottom. Beer and wine in mini-bottles are available in addition to soft drinks. All items are available for take-out. ✉ *Krugerstr. 6,* ☎ *01/513–2560;* ✉ *Kettenbrückengasse 19,* ☎ *01/586–1774;* ✉ *Billrothstr. 18;* ✉ *Favoritenstr. 145;* ✉ *Brigittapl. 22. No credit cards.*

$ ✕ Trzesniewski. "Unpronounceably good" is the (correct) motto of this tiny sandwich shop, a Viennese tradition for decades. If a quick snack will suffice, three or four of the open sandwiches and a *Pfiff* (⅛ liter, or ⅒ quart) of beer, or a vodka, may be just the needed pickup. Share one of the few tables, or stand up at one of the counters. You'll be surprised at the elegance of many of the customers. ✉ *Dorotheergasse 1,* ☎ *01/512–3291. No credit cards. Closed Sun. No dinner Sat.*

Wine Taverns

In-town wine restaurants cannot properly be called *Heurigen,* since they are not run by the vintner, so the term is "wine restaurant," or "cellar" (*Keller*). Many of them extend a number of levels underground, particularly in the older part of the city. Mainly open in the evening, they are intended primarily for drinking, though you can always get something to eat from a buffet, and increasingly, full dinners are available. As at their country cousins, wine is served by the mug. Some of the better wine restaurants follow; no credit cards are accepted except where noted.

$$ ★ ✕ **Augustinerkeller.** This ground-floor-and-upstairs Keller is open at noontime as well. The grilled chicken is excellent, as is the filling *Stelze* (roast knuckle of pork). The open wines are first-class. ✉ *Augustinerstr. 1/Albertinerpl.,* ☎ *01/533–1026. MC, V.*

$$ ★ ✕ **Esterházykeller.** This maze of rooms offers some of the best Keller wines in town plus a typical Vienna menu noontime and evenings plus hot and cold buffet, but the atmosphere may be too smoky for some. ✉ *Haarhof 1,* ☎ *01/533–3482. Stüberl closed Sat., Keller closed weekends. No lunch Sun. at Stüberl.*

$$ ★ ✕ **Melker Stiftskeller.** Down and down you go, into one of the friendliest Kellers in town, where Stelze is a popular feature, along with outstanding wines by the glass or rather, mug. ✉ *Schottengasse 3,* ☎ *01/533–5530. MC. Closed Sun. No lunch.*

$ ✕ **Zwölf Apostel-Keller.** You pass a huge wood statue of St. Peter on the way downstairs to the two underground floors in this deep-down cellar in the oldest part of Vienna. The young crowd comes for the good wines and the atmosphere, and there's buffet food as well. ✉ *Sonnenfelsgasse 3,* ☎ *01/512–6777. No lunch.*

Heurigen

Few cities the size of Vienna boast wine produced within city limits, even fewer offer wines ranging from good to outstanding. But in various suburban villages—once well outside the center but now now parts of the urban complex—the fringes of the city have spawned characteristic wine taverns and restaurants, sometimes located in the vineyards themselves. Called *Heurigen* (the single appelation is a *Heuriger*) for the new wine that they serve, they are very much a part of and typical of the city (although not unique to Vienna). Heurigen sprang up in 1784 when Joseph II decreed that owners of vineyards could open their own private wine taverns.

These taverns in the wine-growing districts on the outskirts of the city vary from the simple front room of a vintner's house to ornate establishments. (The name means "new wine," and that's what is chiefly served.) The true Heuriger is open for only a few weeks a year to allow the vintner to sell a certain quantity of his production tax-free for consumption on his own premises. The commercial establishments keep to a somewhat more regular season, but still sell only wine from their own vines.

The choice is usually between a "new" and an "old" white wine and a red, but you can also ask for a milder or sharper wine according to your taste. Most Heurigen are happy to let you sample the wines before ordering. You can also order a *Gespritzter,* half wine and half soda water. The waitress will bring you the wine, usually in a ¼-liter mug or liter carafe, but you get your own food from the buffet. The wine tastes as mild as lemonade, but it packs a punch. If it isn't of good quality, you will know by a raging headache the next day.

Summer and fall are the seasons for visiting the Heurigen, though often the more elegant and expensive establishments, called *Noble-Heurige,* stay open year-round. No credit cards are accepted except where noted.

Heurige are concentrated in several outskirts of Vienna: Stammersdorf, Grinzing, Sievering, Nussdorf, Neustift, and a corner of Ottakring. Perchtoldsdorf, just outside Vienna, is also well known for its wine taverns.

Our favorite district is Stammersdorf, across the Danube. Try **Robert Helm** for good wines, a small but complete buffet including desserts from the house kitchen, and a wonderfully inviting tree-shaded garden. ✉ *Stammersdorfer Str. 121,* ☎ *01/292–1244. Closed Sun., Mon., and other periods during yr.*

Wine and food are both outstanding at **Wieninger,** with its spacious garden and series of typical vintner's rooms. Wieningers's bottled wines are ranked among the country's best. ✉ *Stammersdorfer Str. 78,* ☎ *01/292–4106. Closed Mon. and mid-Dec.–Jan. 2.*

The Grinzing district today suffers from mass tourism, with very few exceptions; one is **Zum Martin Sepp,** where the wine, food, service, and ambience are all good. ✉ *Cobenzlgasse 32,* ☎ *01/324–4875. DC, V.*

East of the Grinzing village center, **Zimmermann** has excellent wines and buffet foods, an enchanting tree-shaded garden, and an endless collection of small paneled rooms and vaulted cellars. ✉ *Armbrustergasse 5/Grinzinger Str.,* ☎ *01/318-8975. AE, DC, MC, V. Closed Sun. No lunch.*

In Sievering, vintner **Haslinger** offers both good wines and a small but tasty buffet. The atmosphere is plain but honest both indoors and in the small, typical vine-covered garden outside in summer. ✉ *Agnesgasse 3,* ☎ *01/440–1347. Closed Mon.*

In Neustift, **Wolff** has an enticing garden and outstanding food, as well as good wine. The small rooms inside are intimate and attractive. ✉ *Rathstr. 46,* ☎ *01/440–2335.*

In Nussdorf seek out **Schübel-Auer** for its series of atmospheric rooms and good wines. ✉ *Kahlenberger Str. 22,* ☎ *01/372222. Closed Sun., Jan., and July.*

Heiligenstadt is home to **Mayer am Pfarrplatz**—the legendary heuriger in Beethoven's former abode—where the atmosphere in the collection of rooms is genuine, the á la carte offerings and buffet more than abundant, and the house wines excellent. You'll even find some Viennese among the tourists. ✉ *Heiligenstädter Pfarrpl. 2,* ☎ *01/371287. AE, DC, MC, V. No lunch weekdays or Sat.*

Cafés

One of the quintessential Viennese institutions, the coffeehouse, or café, is club, pub, and bistro all rolled into one. For decades, a substantial part of Austrian social life has revolved around them (though now less than in the past) as Austrians by and large are rather reluctant to invite strangers to their homes and prefer to meet them in the friendly, but noncommittal, atmosphere of the café.

To savor the atmosphere of the coffeehouses you must take your time; set aside an afternoon, a morning, or at least a couple of hours, and settle down in one of your choice. Read or catch up on your letter writing: There is no need to worry about outstaying one's welcome, even over a single small cup of coffee, better identified as a *kleiner Schwarzer* (black) or *kleiner Brauner* (with milk). (Of course, in some of the more opulent coffeehouses, this cup of coffee can cost as much as a meal.)

Coffee is not just coffee in Austria. It comes in many forms and under many names. Morning coffee is generally *Melange* (half coffee, half milk), or with little milk, a *Brauner.* The usual after-dinner drink is *Mokka,* very black, and most Austrians like it heavily sweetened. Restaurants that serve Balkan food offer *Türkischer,* or Turkish coffee, a strong, thick brew. Most delightful are the coffee-and-whipped-cream concoctions, universally cherished as *Kaffee mit Schlag,* a taste that is easily acquired and a menace to all but the very thin. The coffee may be either hot or cold. A customer who wants more whipped cream than coffee asks for a *Doppelschlag.* Hot black coffee in a glass with one knob of whipped cream is an *Einspänner* (one-horse coach). Then you can go to town on a *Mazagran,* black coffee with ice and a tot of rum, or *Eiskaffee,* cold coffee with ice cream, whipped cream, and biscuits. Or you can simply order a *Portion Kaffee* and have an honest pot of coffee and jug of hot milk.

The typical Viennese café, with polished brass or marble-topped tables, bentwood chairs, supplies of newspapers, and tables outside in good weather, is a fixed institution of which there are literally hundreds. All cafés serve pastries and light snacks in addition to beverages. Many offer a menu or fixed lunch at noon, but be aware that some can get rather expensive. No credit cards are accepted except where noted.

Of course, when tourists think of Viennese cafés, Demel's and Café Sacher leap to mind, but they are hardly typical—for information on them, see the Kohlmarkt and the Albertina sections in the Exploring Vienna section, *above.* When you want a quick (but excellent) coffee and dessert, look for an **Aida** café; they are scattered throughout the city. Here's a sampling of the best of the traditional cafés. **Alte Backstübe** (✉ Lange Gasse 34, ☎ 01/406–1101), in a gorgeous Baroque house—with a café in front and restaurant in back—was once a bakery and is now a museum as well. **Bräunerhof** (✉ Stallburggasse 2, ☎ 01/512–3893) has music on some afternoons. **Café Central** (✉ Herrengasse 14, ☎ 01/535–4176–0) is where Stalin and Trotsky played chess. **Frauenhuber** (✉ Himmelpfortgasse 6, ☎ 01/512–4323) has its original turn-of-the-century interior and a good choice of desserts. **Haag** (✉ Schottengasse 2, ☎ 01/533–1810), with crystal chandeliers and a shaded courtyard garden in summer, serves snacks and desserts. **Landtmann** (✉ Dr. Karl Lueger-Ring 4, ☎ 01/532–0621) is where government officials gather. **Museum** (✉ Friedrichstr. 6, ☎ 01/586–5202), original interior by the architect Adolf Loos, draws a mixed crowd and has lots of newspapers. **Schwarzenberg** (✉ Kärntner Ring 17, ☎ 01/512–7393), with piano music in late afternoons, is highly popular, particularly its sidewalk tables in summer. **Tirolerhof** (✉ Tegetthoffstr. 8/Albertinapl., ☎ 01/512–7833), with ample papers and its excellent desserts, is popular with students.

Café Hawelka (✉ Dorotheergasse 12, ☎ 01/512–8230) deserves special mention; whole books have been written at and about this gathering place. Its international clientele ranges from artists to politicians; Hawelka is jammed any time of day, so you share a table (and the smoky atmosphere). In a city noted for fine coffee, Hawelka's is superb, even more so when accompanied by a freshly baked *Buchterln* (sweet roll, evenings only).

Pastry Shops

Viennese pastries are said to be the best in the world. In all shops you can buy them to enjoy on the premises, usually with coffee, as well as to take out. **Kurkonditorei Oberlaa** (✉ Neuer Markt 16, ☎ 01/513–2936; ✉ Landstrasser Hauptstr. 1, ☎ 01/714–6502) has irresistible confections, cakes, and bonbons, as well as light lunches and salad plates, served outdoors in summer. Traditionalists and tourists with fat pocketbooks still go to **Demel** (✉ Kohlmarkt 14, ☎ 01/533–5516–0), where the value is arguable but turn-of-the-century atmosphere prevails among velvet and polished brass in the older front rooms, stark modern in the new inner court, open in summer, covered in winter. The newer **Demel Vis-à-vis** opposite its mother shop (✉ Kohlmarkt 11, ☎ 01/533–6020) has an elegant buffet and stand-up tables, plus a mail-order service for Demel specialties. **Gerstner** (✉ Kärntner Str. 15, ☎ 01/

512–4963–0), while hardly inexpensive, is also recommended. **Heiner** (✉ Kärntner Str. 21-23, ☎ 01/512–6863–0; ✉ Wollzeile 9, ☎ 01/512–4838–0) is dazzling for its crystal chandeliers as well as for its pastries. **Sluka** (✉ Rathauspl. 8, ☎ 01/406–8896–0) has special dietetic desserts, snacks, and an appetizer buffet and serves outdoors in summer.

LODGING

In Vienna's best hotels the staff seems to anticipate your wishes almost before you express them. Such service of course has its price, and if you wish, you can stay in Vienna in profound luxury. For those with more modest requirements, ample rooms are available in less expensive but entirely adequate hotels. Pensions, mainly bed-and-breakfast establishments often managed by the owner, generally represent good value. A number of student dormitories are run as hotels in summer, offering about the most reasonable quarters of all. And several apartment-hotels accommodate those who want to stay longer.

When you have only a short time to spend in Vienna, you will probably want to stay in the inner city (the First District, or 1010 postal code) or fairly close to it, within walking distance of the most important sights, restaurants, and shops. Although most of the hotels there are in the upper categories, excellent and reasonable accommodations can be found in the Eighth District, which borders the First and puts you close to the major museums. You'll also find a group of moderate ($$) and inexpensive ($) hotels in the Mariahilfer Strasse–Westbahnhof area, within easy reach of the city center by subway.

For the high season, Easter through September, and around the Christmas–New Year holidays, make reservations a month or more in advance. Vienna is continually the site of some international convention or other, and the city fills up quickly.

Our hotel categories correspond more or less to the official Austrian rating system, with five stars the equivalent of our very expensive ($$$$) category. All rooms have bath or shower unless otherwise stated; color television is usual in the top two categories; breakfast is included with all *except* the highest category. Air-conditioning is rare except in the larger, newer chain hotels. These seem constantly to be hosting convention or seminar groups, making service somewhat less personal, but there are exceptions, as noted.

CATEGORY	COST*
$$$$	over AS2,700
$$$	AS1,200–AS2,700
$$	AS950–AS1,200
$	under AS950

**All prices are for two persons in a standard double room, including local taxes (usually 10%), service (15%), and breakfast (except in many $$$$ hotels).*

$$$$ **Ambassador.** This superbly located dowager (from 1866) wears well. An air of decadent elegance radiates from the red velvet and crystal chandeliers in the high-ceilinged guest rooms. The trade-off is room air conditioners and rather stuffy period furniture. But what was once good enough for Mark Twain—yes, he stayed here, but long before the 1990–91 renovations—is still very good, and you will know instantly that you are in Vienna. Unless you want the excitement of a direct view into the lively pedestrian Kärntner Strasse, ask for one of the quieter rooms on the Neuer Markt side. ✉ *Neuer Markt 5/Kärnt-*

ner Str. 22, A–1010, ☎ 01/514–66–0, FAX 01/513–2999. 107 rooms. Restaurant, bar. AE, DC, MC, V.

$$$$ ★ **Bristol.** This hotel has one of the finest locations in Europe, on the Ring next to the Opera House. The accent here is on tradition, from the brocaded walls to the Biedermeier period furnishings in the public rooms and many of the bedrooms. The house dates from 1896; renovations have left no trace of the fact that the Bristol was the U.S. military headquarters during the 1945–55 occupation. Like an old shoe, the hotel is seductively comfortable from the moment you arrive. The rooms on the Mahlerstrasse (back) side of the house are quieter, but the view isn't as gratifying as from rooms on the Kärntner Strasse or the Ring. ✉ *Kärntner Ring 1, A–1010, ☎ 01/515–16–0, FAX 01/515–16–550. 146 rooms. 2 restaurants, bar, sauna, exercise room. AE, DC, MC, V.*

$$$$ **Hilton.** The public areas have been restyled for a more contemporary look, and the air-conditioned bedrooms are a cut above the usual Hilton standard in size and individuality of decor. The suites are particularly spacious; who could resist breakfast on a suite balcony with a 180-degree view of the city? The upper rooms are quietest; the no-smoking floor is so popular that you need to book at least 2–3 weeks in advance. The airport bus terminal is part of the complex; the U3 and U4 subway lines, trains, and buses stop at the terminal across the street; yet you're within an easy walk of the city center. ✉ *Am Stadtpark, A–1030, ☎ 01/717–00–0, FAX 01/713–0691. 600 rooms. 2 restaurants, bar, café, sauna, health club, parking. AE, DC, MC, V.*

$$$$ ★ **Imperial.** The hotel is as much a palace today as when it was completed in 1869. The emphasis is on old Vienna elegance and privacy; heads of state stay here when they're in town. Service is deferential; the rooms have high ceilings and are furnished in classic antiques and Oriental carpets. The bath areas, in contrast, are modern and inviting; many are as large as guest rooms in lesser hotels. The staff will adjust the hardness (or softness) of the beds to your specific wants. Don't overlook the ornate reception rooms to the rear or the formal marble staircase to the right of the lobby area, newly restored to its original elegance. Rooms on the back overlooking the Musikverein are the quietest. ✉ *Kärntner Ring 16, A–1010, ☎ 01/501–10–0, FAX 01/501–10–410. 146 rooms. 2 restaurants, piano bar, no-smoking rooms. AE, DC, MC, V.*

$$$$ **InterContinental.** This "first" among Vienna's modern hostelries (1964) has taken on the Viennese patina, and its public rooms, with glittering crystal and red carpets, suggest luxurious comfort. The guest rooms lean more toward the chain's norm, adequate though unexciting, but you will get either a view over the city park across the street (preferred) or over the city itself. The higher you go, the more dramatic the perspective. One of the hotel restaurants is the famed Vier Jahreszeiten. ✉ *Johannesgasse 28, A–1030, ☎ 01/711–22–0, FAX 01/713–4489. 492 rooms. 2 restaurants, bar, no-smoking rooms, sauna, exercise room, parking. AE, DC, MC, V.*

$$$$ ★ **Palais Schwarzenberg.** You will know from your first glimpse of the elegant facade that this is no ordinary hotel. Set against a vast formal park, the palace, built in the early 1700s, seems like a country estate, and you can even jog in the garden. Your room will be furnished in genuine (but surprisingly comfortable) antiques, with some of the Schwarzenberg family's art on the walls. The baths are modern, although you might miss a shower curtain. Each room is individual; duplex suites 24 and 25 have upstairs bedrooms and views over the park; Room 26 has exquisite furniture, gorgeous draperies, and a winding stair leading up to the bedroom. If you have any reason to celebrate, do it here; this is the genuine old Vienna at its most elegant. ✉ *Schwarzenbergpl. 9, A–1030, ☎ 01/798–4515–0, FAX 01/798–4714. 38 rooms. Restaurant, bar, parking. AE, DC, MC, V.*

Altstadt, **5**
Ambassador, **20**
Austria, **16**
Biedermeier im Sünnhof, **15**
Bristol, **23**
Europa, **19**
Fürstenhof, **7**
Hilton, **28**
Hotel–Pension Zipser, **2**
Ibis Wien, **8**
Imperial, **29**
InterContinental, **30**
Kärntnerhof, **17**
König von Ungarn, **18**
Kugel, **6**
Mailberger Hof, **26**
Opernring, **21**
Palais Schwarzenberg, **31**
Pension Aclon, **11**
Pension Baroness, **1**
Pension Christina, **14**
Pension City, **13**
Pension Nossek, **9**
Pension Pertschy, **10**
Pension Suzanne, **24**
Pension Wild, **4**
Rathaus, **3**
Sacher, **22**
Vienna Marriott, **27**
Wandl, **12**
Zur Wiener Staatsoper, **25**

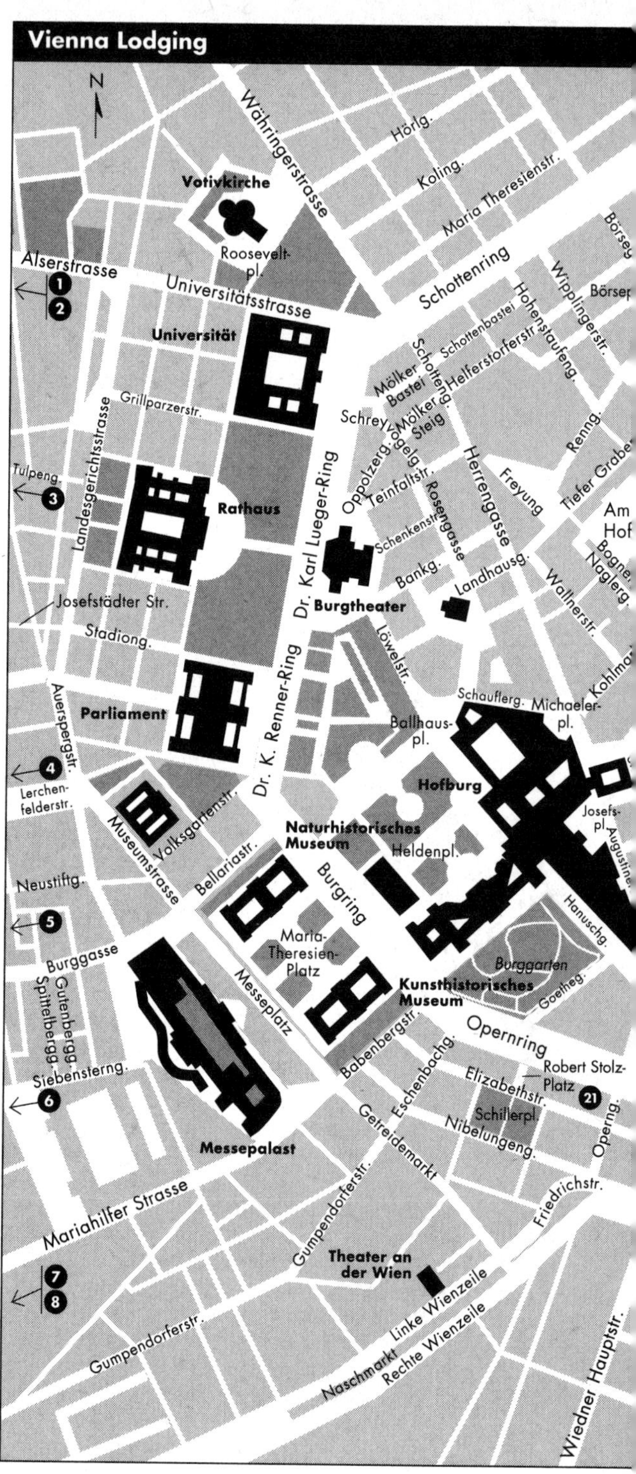

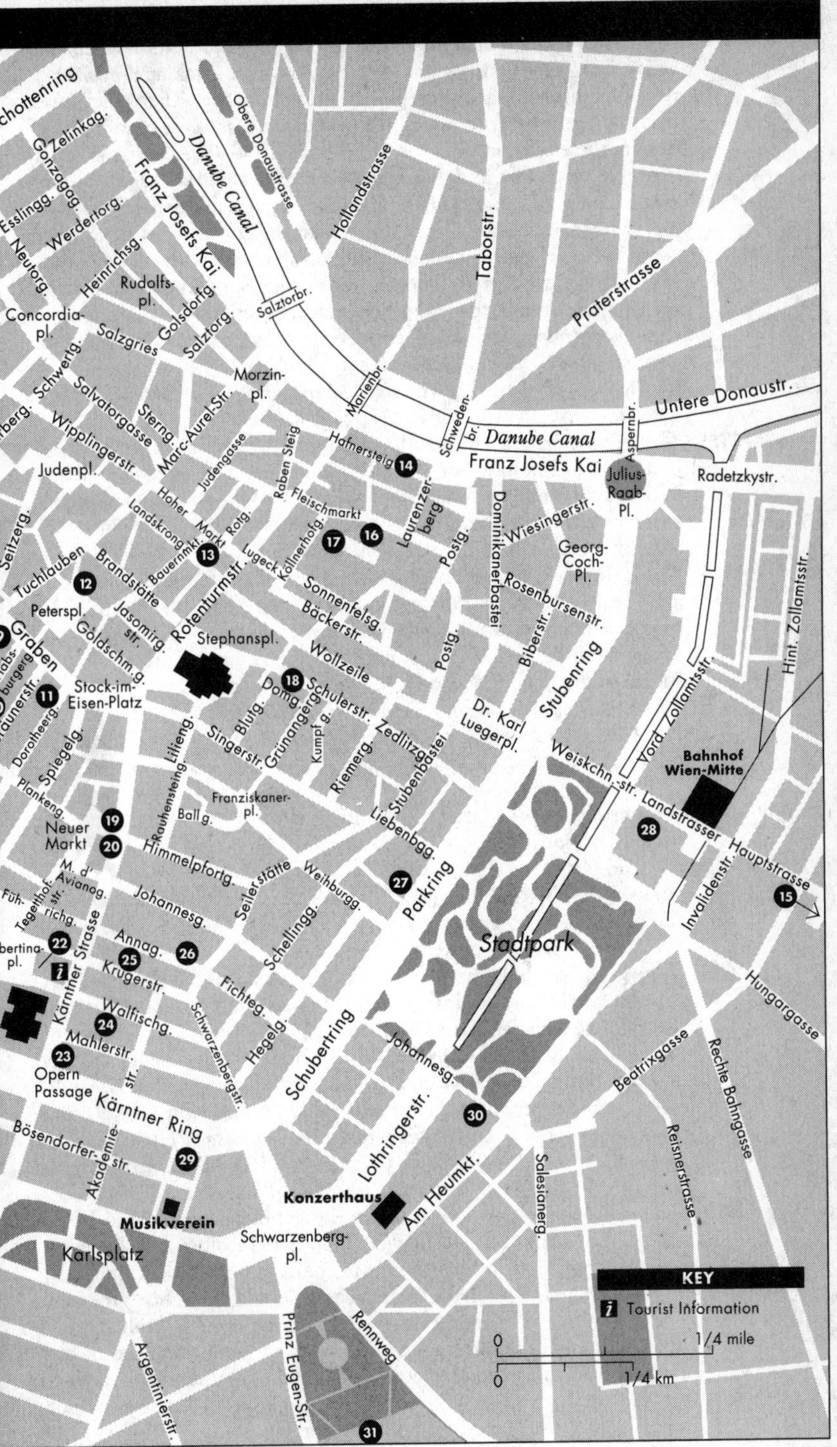

Danube Canal
Franz Josefs Kai
Obere Donaustrasse
Hollandstrasse
Taborstr.
Praterstrasse
Untere Donaustr.
Salztorbr.
Marienbr.
Schwedenbr.
Aspernbr.
Hafnersteig
Fleischmarkt
Laurenzerberg
Postg.
Dominikanerbastei
Wiesingerstr.
Julius-Raab-Pl.
Radetzkystr.
Georg-Coch-Pl.
Rosenbursenstr.
Biberstr.
Stubenring
Vord. Zollamtsstr.
Hint. Zollamtsstr.
Bahnhof Wien-Mitte
Weiskchn.-str.
Landstrasser Hauptstrasse
Invalidenstr.
Stadtpark
Hungargasse
Beatrixgasse
Rechte Bahngasse
Reisnerstrasse
Salesianerg.
Am Heumkt.
Konzerthaus
Lothringerstr.
Johannesg.
Parkring
Schubertring
Kärntner Ring
Schwarzenberg-pl.
Rennweg
Prinz Eugen-Str.
Argentinierstr.
Karlsplatz
Musikverein
Bösendorfer-str.
Akademie-str.
Opern Passage
Mahlerstr.
Walfischg.
Krugerstr.
Annag.
Johannesg.
Himmelpfortg.
Seilerstätte
Weihburgg.
Liebenbgg.
Schellingg.
Fichteg.
Hegelg.
Schwarzenbergstr.
Kärntner Strasse
Albertina-pl.
Führichg.
Tegetthof-str.
M. d'Avianog.
Neuer Markt
Plankeng.
Spiegelg.
Dorotheerg.
Bräunerstr.
Habsburgerg.
Graben
Stock-im-Eisen-Platz
Goldschm.g.
Jasomirg. str.
Stephanspl.
Rotenturmstr.
Liliens.
Rauhensteing.
Ball g.
Franziskaner-pl.
Singerstr.
Blutg.
Domg.
Grünangerg.
Kumpf g.
Riemerg.
Stubenbastei
Zedlitzg.
Schulerstr.
Wollzeile
Dr. Karl Luegerpl.
Bäckerstr.
Sonnenfelsg.
Lugeck
Köllnerhofg.
Rotg.
Bauernmkt.
Hoher Markt
Landskrong.
Brandstätte
Tuchlauben
Peterspl.
Seitzerg.
Judenpl.
Wipplingerstr.
Salvatorgasse
Sterng.
Marc-Aurel-Str.
Judengasse
Raben Steig
Morzin-pl.
Salztorg.
Golsdorfg.
Salzgries
Schwertg.
Concordia-pl.
Rudolfs-pl.
Heinrichsg.
Werdertorg.
Neutorg.
Esslingg.
Gonzagag.
Zelinkag.
Schottenring
KEY
Tourist Information
0
1/4 mile
0
1/4 km

$$$$ **Sacher.** Few hotels in the world have been featured so often in films or in history; you'll sense the musty atmosphere of tradition when you arrive. This is the house where the legendary cigar-smoking Frau Sacher reigned; Emperor Francis Joseph was a regular patron. The Sacher dates from 1876; the patina remains (Room 329 exudes a sense of well-being) despite the elegant new baths installed in 1990. The corridors are a veritable art gallery, and the location directly behind the Opera House could hardly be more central. The staff is particularly accommodating; it has long been an open secret that the concierge at the Sacher can miraculously produce concert and opera tickets when all other possibilities are exhausted. The restaurant is disappointing and overpriced, more average than innovative say many critics, but the Tafelspitz remains legendary. The Café Sacher, of course, is legendary (☞ Exploring Vienna, *above*). ✉ *Philharmonikerstr. 4, A–1010,* ☎ *01/514–56–0,* FAX *01/514–57–810. 116 rooms, 112 with bath. Restaurant, 2 bars, café, no-smoking rooms. AE, DC, MC, V.*

$$$–$$$$ **Vienna Marriott.** The metal-and-glass exterior gives the impression of a giant greenhouse, borne out by the minijungle of trees and plants in the vast atrium lobby. Some guests object to the perpetual waterfall in the bar-café area, but for Vienna the effect is certainly original. Despite the size, a friendly atmosphere pervades. For a hotel built in 1984, the air-conditioned rooms and suites are unusually spacious and furnished with extra attention to detail; the corner suites (No. 24 on each floor) give a superb view out over the city park opposite. The upper rooms in back offer a panorama of the inner city; these and the rooms on the inner court are the quietest. You're an easy stroll from the city center. ✉ *Parkring 12A, A–1010,* ☎ *01/515–18–0,* FAX *01/515–18–6722. 310 rooms. 2 restaurants, 2 bars, café, no-smoking rooms, pool, sauna, exercise room, parking. AE, DC, MC, V.*

$$$ ★ **Altstadt.** You're one streetcar stop or a short walk from the main museums in this old-Vienna residential building. Each of the spacious rooms has individual decor focusing mainly on period furniture, with fine wood set against light and blue-gray walls. Upper rooms have views out over the city roofline. The management is particularly personable and helpful. ✉ *Kirchengasse 41, A–1070,* ☎ *01/526–3399,* FAX *01/523–4901. 25 rooms with bath or shower. Bar. AE, DC, MC, V.*

$$$ ★ **Austria.** This older house, tucked away on a tiny cul-de-sac, offers the ultimate in quiet and is only five minutes' walk from the heart of the city. The high-ceilinged rooms are pleasing in their combination of dark wood and lighter walls; the decor is mixed, with Oriental carpets on many floors. Rooms without full bath are in the $$ category. You'll feel at home here, and the staff will help you find your way around town or get opera or concert tickets. ✉ *Wolfengasse 3 (Fleischmarkt), A–1010,* ☎ *01/515–23–0,* FAX *01/515–23–505. 46 rooms, 42 with bath or shower. AE, DC, MC, V.*

$$$ **Biedermeier im Sünnhof.** This jewel of a hotel is tucked into a renovated 1820s house that even with all modern facilities still conveys a feeling of old Vienna. The rooms are compact but efficient, the public areas tastefully done in the Biedermeier style, and the service is friendly. The courtyard passageway around which the hotel is built has attracted a number of interesting boutiques and handicrafts shops, but at times there is an excess of coming and going as tour groups are accommodated. It's about a 20-minute walk or a six-minute subway ride to the center of the city. ✉ *Landstrasser Hauptstr. 28, A–1030,* ☎ *01/716–71–0,* FAX *01/716–71–503. 204 rooms. Restaurant, bar, parking. AE, DC, MC, V.*

$$$ **Europa.** The hotel cannot quite hide its 1957 vintage, and the garish blue-and-pink entry canopies don't help. But the rooms are comfortable without being luxurious, and the baths are modern. You couldn't find a more central location. Rooms on the Neuer Markt side are quieter than those on Kärntner Strasse. ✉ *Neuer Markt 3/Kärntner Str. 18, A–1010,* ☎ *01/515–94–0,* FAX *01/513–8138. 102 rooms. Restaurant, bar, café. AE, DC, MC, V.*

$$$ **Fürstenhof.** This turn-of-the-century building, directly across from the Westbahnhof, describes its large rooms as "old-fashioned comfortable," and you reach them via a marvelous hydraulic elevator. Furnishings are a mixed bag. The side rooms are quieter than those in front. Rooms without bath are in the $$ category. ✉ *Neubaugürtel 4, A–1070,* ☎ *01/523–3267,* FAX *01/523–3267–26. 58 rooms, 39 with bath or shower. AE, DC, MC, V.*

$$$ **König von Ungarn.** In a 16th-century house in the shadow of St. Stephen's Cathedral, this hotel began catering to court nobility in 1815. (Mozart lived in the house next door when he wrote *The Marriage of Figaro*). A superb redesign turned it into a modern hotel, and you could hardly hope for a happier result. The hotel radiates charm, from the greenery in the wood-paneled atrium lobby to the antiques of various periods and the pine country furnishings in the bedrooms. The rooms are not overly large, but each is individually and appealingly decorated. Those in back are somewhat quieter. Insist on written confirmation of bookings. ✉ *Schulerstr. 10, A–1010,* ☎ *01/515–84–0,* FAX *01/515–84–8. 32 rooms. Restaurant, bar. DC, MC, V.*

$$$ ★ **Mailberger Hof.** This 14th-century house on a pedestrian street just off the Kärntner Strasse was once a Baroque town palace. In 1976 it was turned into an intimate family-run hotel with great success and is a favorite of stars from the nearby State Opera House. The rooms are so attractively decorated it's hard to imagine you're in a hotel; colors and furniture have been coordinated without fussiness to create a setting you won't want to leave. You'll have to book about a month ahead to get a room. ✉ *Annagasse 7, A–1010,* ☎ *01/512–0641,* FAX *01/512–0641–10. 40 rooms, 5 apartments with kitchenettes (available by month). Restaurant. AE, MC, V.*

$$$ ★ **Opernring.** This establishment's spacious, comfortable rooms, with homelike furnishings and bright, attractive tiled baths, are only one reason guests come back. The unusually friendly, personal attention of the owner, Susie Riedl, makes you feel as though you're the only guest. The hotel has Best Western affiliation. The rooms on the inner courtyard are sunny and quieter but have a dreary outlook; disregard the traffic noise (there's no air-conditioning, so you may want the windows open) and enjoy the extraordinary view of the Opera House, diagonally across the Ring. ✉ *Opernring 11, A–1010,* ☎ *01/587–5518,* FAX *01/587–5518–29. 35 rooms. AE, DC, MC, V.*

$$$ **Wandl.** The restored facade identifies a 300-year-old house that has been in family hands as a hotel since 1854. You couldn't find a better location, tucked behind St. Peter's Church, just off the Graben. The hallways are punctuated by cheerful, bright openings along the glassed-in inner court. The rooms are modern, but some are a bit plain and charmless, despite parquet flooring and red accents. Ask for one of the rooms done in period furniture, with decorated ceilings and gilt mirrors; they're palatial, if slightly overdone. ✉ *Peterspl. 9, A–1010,* ☎ *01/534–55–0,* FAX *01/534–55–77. 138 rooms. Bar. No credit cards.*

$$–$$$ ★ **Hotel-Pension Zipser.** This 1904 house, with an ornate facade and gilt-trimmed coat of arms, is one of the city's better hotel values. It's in a fascinating district of small cafés, shops, jazz clubs, and excellent restaurants, yet within steps of the J streetcar line direct to the city center. The rooms are newly redone in browns and beiges, with modern furniture to match; the baths are elegant and well lit. The balconies of some of the back rooms overlook tree-filled neighborhood courtyards. The friendly staff will help get theater and concert tickets. Book ahead

a month or two to be sure of a room. ✉ *Lange Gasse 49, A–1080, ☎ 222/404–54–0, FAX 01/408–5266–13. 47 rooms. Coffee shop, parking. AE, DC, MC, V.*

$$–$$$ ★ **Kärntnerhof.** Behind the "Schönbrunn yellow" facade of this elegant 100-year-old house on a quiet cul-de-sac lies one of the friendliest small hotels in the center of the city. Don't let the dated and uninteresting lobby put you off; take the gorgeously restored Art Deco elevator to the rooms upstairs. They have been done over in either brown or white reproduction furniture, and the baths are modern. The staff is adept at getting theater and concert tickets for "sold out" performances and happily puts together special outing programs for guests. For a small fee, parking can be arranged in the abbey courtyard next door. ✉ *Grashofgasse 4, A–1010, ☎ 01/512–1923–0, FAX 01/513–2228–33. 43 rooms. AE, DC, MC, V.*

$$–$$$ **Pension Aclon.** On the upper floors of a gray but gracious older building just off the Graben (with the famous Café Hawelka downstairs), this family-run hostelry (complete with sheepdog) is attractively done up in old-Vienna style, with lots of plants, 19th-century furniture, dark woods, and elegant marble baths. Rooms on the inner court are quieter, though the street in front carries no through traffic. New rooms were added in 1996, the smaller ones in modern decor, the larger in period Biedermeier style. ✉ *Dorotheergasse 6–8, A–1010, ☎ 01/512–7940–0, FAX 01/513–8751. 32 rooms, 21 with bath or shower. No credit cards.*

$$–$$$ **Pension Nossek.** This family-run establishment on the upper floors of a 19th-century office and apartment building lies at the heart of the pedestrian and shopping area. The rooms have high ceilings and are eclectically but comfortably furnished; those on the front have a magnificent view of the Graben. Do as the many regular guests do and book early. ✉ *Graben 17, A–1010, ☎ 01/533–7041–0, FAX 01/535–3646. 26 rooms, 22 with bath or shower. No credit cards.*

$$–$$$ ★ **Pension Pertschy.** Housed in a former town palace just off the Graben, this pension is as central as you can get. A massive arched portal leads to a yellow courtyard, around which the house is built. Anybody who has stayed in Room 220 with its stylish old blue ceramic stove (just for show) would be happy again with nothing less. Most rooms are spacious with antique furniture of mixed periods, but even the small single rooms are charming. Baths are satisfactory. Use the elevator, but don't overlook the palatial grand staircase. ✉ *Habsburgergasse 5, A-1010, ☎ 01/534–49–0, FAX 01/534–49–49. 43 rooms. DC, MC, V.*

$$ **Ibis Wien.** About an eight-minute walk from the Westbahnhof and easily identifiable by its bronze metal exterior, the Ibis offers its standard chain accommodations in contemporary air-conditioned rooms that are compact, complete, and very good value. The blue and blue-gray accents are refreshing against the white room walls. The rooms on the shady Wallgasse side are more comfortable; those on the upper floors have a superb panoramic view. ✉ *Mariahilfer Gürtel 22–24/Wallgasse 33, A–1060, ☎ 01/599–98–0, FAX 01/597–9090. 341 rooms. Restaurant, weinstube, parking. AE, DC, MC, V.*

$$ **Pension Baroness.** One flight up, behind the drab facade of this turn-of-the-century apartment house, are comfortable rooms with contemporary furnishings, many quite spacious and many completely renovated in 1990. The front rooms are noisy, but the nearby streetcar stop is a convenience. ✉ *Lange Gasse 61, A–1080, ☎ 01/405–1061, FAX 01/405–1061–61. 38 rooms. Bar. MC, V.*

$$ **Pension Christina.** This quiet pension, just steps from Schwedenplatz and the Danube Canal, offers mainly smallish modern rooms, warmly decorated with attractive dark-wood furniture set off against beige walls.

✉ *Hafnersteig 7, A–1010,* ☎ *01/533–2961–0,* FAX *01/533–2961–11. 33 rooms. MC, V.*

$$ ★ **Pension City.** You'll be on historic ground here: In 1791 the playwright Franz Grillparzer was born in the house that then stood here; a bust and plaques in the entryway commemorate him. On the second floor of the present 100-year-old house, located about three minutes away from St. Stephen's Cathedral, the rooms are newly outfitted in a successful mix of modern and 19th-century antique furniture against white walls. The baths are small but complete. ✉ *Bauernmarkt 10, A–1010,* ☎ *01/533–9521,* FAX *01/535–5216. 19 rooms. AE, DC, MC, V.*

$$ ★ **Pension Suzanne.** This 1950s building on a side street is just steps away from the Opera House. The rooms are smallish but comfortably furnished in 19th-century Viennese style; baths are modern, although short on shelf space. Suzanne has regular guests who book months in advance, so you'd be well advised to do the same. ✉ *Walfischgasse 4, A–1010,* ☎ *01/513–2507–0,* FAX *01/513–2500. 19 rooms, 7 apartments with kitchenette. AE, DC, MC, V.*

$$ ★ **Rathaus.** This friendly hotel, under the same management as the nearby Zipser, is in a 1908 building that has been attractively renovated: The spacious rooms have contemporary furnishings. You'll be within an easy walk of the main museums and close to public transportation. ✉ *Lange Gasse 13, A–1080,* ☎ *01/406–4302,* FAX *01/408–4272. 40 rooms. Garage. No credit cards.*

$$ **Zur Wiener Staatsoper.** The hotel's florid facade, with oversize torsos supporting its upper bays, is pure 19th-century Ringstrasse style. The rooms are less well defined in style, small yet comfortable. The baths are adequate. And you'll find yourself within steps of the Opera House and Kärntner Strasse. ✉ *Krugerstr. 11, A–1010,* ☎ *01/513–1274–0,* FAX *01/513–1274–15. 22 rooms. AE, MC, V.*

$ ★ **Kugel.** This older but recently redecorated hotel halfway between the Westbahnhof and the city center has rooms attractively furnished in lighter woods and contrasting textiles. The newer baths are elegantly tiled. Don't let the less appealing breakfast-TV room and reception areas put you off; the rooms themselves are in invitingly pleasant contrast. The staff is helpful and friendly. ✉ *Siebensterngasse 43, A–1070,* ☎ *01/523–3355,* FAX *01/523–1678. 38 rooms, 17 with bath or shower. No credit cards.*

$ ★ **Pension Wild.** This friendly, family-run pension on several floors of an older apartment house draws a liberal, relaxed, younger crowd to one of the best values in town. Rooms are simple but modern, with light-wood furniture and pine-paneled ceilings. Each wing has a kitchenette. The breakfast room/TV lounge is bright and attractive, and you're close to the major museums. ✉ *Lange Gasse 1, A–1080,* ☎ *01/406–5174,* FAX *01/402–2168. 14 rooms without bath. Sauna, exercise room. AE, DC, MC, V.*

Seasonal Hotels

Student residences, which operate as hotels July–September, can provide excellent bargains in the inexpensive ($) category. They have single or double rooms, all (unless noted) with bath or shower. You can book by calling any of the Rosenhotels (☎ 01/911–4910, FAX 01/910–0269) or central booking for the student residence hotels of the Albertina group (☎ 01/521–7493, FAX 01/521–1968). Unless otherwise noted, credit cards are accepted.

Academia. Among this group, a fairly luxurious choice. ✉ *Pfeilgasse 3a, A–1080,* ☎ *01/401–7655,* FAX *01/401–7620. 368 rooms. Restaurant, bar.*

Accordia. Belonging to the Albertina group, this is the newest of the seasonal hotels and is fairly close to the center. ✉ *Grosse Schiffgasse 12, A–1020,* ☎ *01/212–1668. 95 rooms with shower.*

Ambiente. This accommodation is an Albertina member near the U.S. embassy, a quiet location. ✉ *Boltzmanngasse 10, A–1090,* ☎ *01/310–3130–0. 50 rooms with shower.*

Auge Gottes. For bargain hunters, this choice is among the very cheapest. ✉ *Nussdorfer Str. 75, A–1090,* ☎ *01/319–4488. 79 rooms without bath.*

Avis. This option even features its own restaurant and bar. ✉ *Pfeilgasse 4, A–1080,* ☎ *01/408–3445,* FAX *01/405–6397. 72 rooms. Restaurant, bar. AE, MC, V.*

Haus Technik. An Albertina member, this place is fairly close to the center. ✉ *Schäffergasse 2, A–1040,* ☎ *01/587–6560–0. 104 rooms with shower. Restaurant, parking.*

Rosenhotel Burgenland 3. For weary travelers, the restaurant is a boon, but tips the house into the $$ category. ✉ *Bürgerspitalgasse 19, A–1060,* ☎ *01/597–9347,* FAX *01/597–9475–9. 140 rooms. Restaurant, bar, parking. AE, MC, V.*

Studentenheim der Musikhochschule. This choice offers the most central location of any of the seasonal hotels, in the heart of the city. ✉ *Johannesgasse 8, A-1010,* ☎ *01/514–84–0,* FAX *01/514–84–49. 85 rooms, some with bath or shower.*

NIGHTLIFE AND THE ARTS

The Arts

Dance

Other than ballet companies in the opera and Volksoper, Vienna offers nothing in the way of dance. Under new directors, the ballet evenings that are on the opera house schedules (☎ 01/514–44–0) are now much improved, and finally up to international standards.

Film

Film has enjoyed a recent renaissance, with viewers seeking original rather than German-dubbed versions. Look for films in English at **Burgkino** (✉ Opernring 19, ☎ 01/587–8406)—in summer, Carol Reed's classic *The Third Man* with Orson Welles is a regular feature; **de France** (✉ Schottenring 5/Hessgasse 7, ☎ 01/317–5236); **English Cinema Haydn** (✉ Mariahilfer Str. 57, ☎ 01/587–2262); **Top-Kino** (✉ Rahlgasse 1, ☎ 01/587–5557); and **Votiv-Kino** (✉ Währinger Str. 12, ☎ 01/317–3571). Art and experimental films are shown at the **Stadtkino** (✉ Schwarzenbergpl. 8, ☎ 01/712–6276). The film schedule in the daily newspaper *Der Standard* lists foreign-language films (*Fremdsprachige Filme*) separately. In film listings, *OmU* means original language with German subtitles.

The **Filmmuseum** in the Albertina shows original-version classics like *Birth of a Nation, A Night at the Opera,* and *Harvey* and organizes retrospectives of the works of artists, directors, and producers. The monthly program is posted outside, and guest memberships (AS40 per day) are available. It is closed July, August, and September. ✉ *Augustinerstr. 1,* ☎ *01/533–7054.* *AS45.* *Screenings Mon.–Sat. at 6 and 8.*

Galleries

A host of smaller galleries centers around the Singerstrasse and Grünangergasse, although there are many more scattered about the city.

Music

Vienna is one of the main music centers of the world. Contemporary music gets its hearing, but it's the hometown standards—the works of Beethoven, Brahms, Haydn, Mozart, and Schubert—that draw the Viennese public. A monthly program, put out by the city tourist board and available at any travel agency or hotel, gives a general overview of what's going on in opera, concerts, jazz, theater, and galleries, and similar information is posted on billboards and fat advertising columns around the city.

Vienna is home to four full symphony orchestras: the great Vienna Philharmonic, the outstanding Vienna Symphony, the broadcasting service's ORF Symphony Orchestra, and the Niederösterreichische Tonkünstler. There are also hundreds of smaller groups, from world-famous trios to chamber orchestras.

The most important concert halls are in the buildings of the Gesellschaft der Musikfreunde, called the **Musikverein** (⊠ Dumbastr. 3; ticket office at Karlspl. 6, ☎ 01/505–8190, FAX 01/505–9409) and the **Konzerthaus** (⊠ Lothringerstr. 20, ☎ 01/712–1211, FAX 01/712–2872). Both houses contain several halls; tickets bear their names: **Grosser Musikvereinssaal** or **Brahmssaal** in the Musikverein; **Grosser Konzerthaussaal, Mozartsaal,** or **Schubertsaal** in the Konzerthaus.

Concerts are also given in the small **Figarosaal** of Palais Palffy (⊠ Josefspl. 6, ☎ 01/512–5681–0), the concert studio of the broadcasting station (⊠ Argentinierstr. 30A, ☎ 01/501–01–8881), and the **Bösendorfersaal** (⊠ Graf Starhemberg-Gasse 14, ☎ 01/504–6651). Students of the music school regularly give class recitals in the school's concert halls during the academic year; look for announcements posted outside for dates and times (⊠ Seilerstätte 26 and Johannesgasse 8, ☎ 01/588–06–0).

Although the **Vienna Festival** (☎ 01/589–22–0), held early May to mid-June, wraps up the primary season, the summer musical scene is bright, with something scheduled every day. Outdoor symphony concerts are performed weekly in the vast arcaded courtyard of the Rathaus (entrance on Friedrich Schmidt-Pl.). You can catch musical events in the Volksgarten and in the St. Augustine, St. Michael's, Minorite, and University churches; at Schönbrunn Palace they're outside in the courtyard as well as part of an evening guided tour.

Mozart concerts are performed in 18th-century costume and powdered wigs in the large hall, or Mozartsaal, of the Konzerthaus (☞ *above*); operetta concerts are held in the Musikverein (☞ *above*), and the Hofburg and Palais Ferstel. There are no set dates, so inquire through hotels and travel and ticket agencies for availabilities. Note, however, that some of these concerts, including intermission lasting possibly an hour, are rather expensive affairs put on for tourists, and occasionally of disappointing quality.

Church music, the Mass sung in Latin, can be heard Sunday mornings during the main season at **St. Stephen's**; in the Franciscan church, **St. Michael's**; the **Universitätskirche**; and, above all, in the **Augustinerkirche.** The Friday and Saturday newspapers carry details. St. Stephen's also has organ concerts most Wednesday evenings from early May to late November.

The **Vienna Boys' Choir** (Wiener Sängerknaben) sing Mass at 9:15 AM in the **Hofburgkapelle** (⊠ Hofburg, Schweizer Hof, ☎ 01/533–9927) from mid-September to late June. Written requests for seats (standing room is free but limited) should be made at least eight weeks in advance to Hofmusikkapelle Hofburg, A–1010 Vienna. You will be sent a reservation card, which you exchange at the box office (in the Hofburg courtyard) for your tickets. Tickets are also sold at ticket agencies and at the box office every Friday at 5 PM, but you should be in line by 4:30. Each person is allowed a maximum of two tickets. If you've missed the Vienna Choirboys at the Sunday mass, you may be able to hear them in a more popular program in the Konzerthaus.

Most theaters now reserve tickets by telephone against a credit card; you pick up your ticket at the box office with no surcharge. The same applies to concert tickets. Ticket agencies charge a minimum 22% markup and generally deal in the more expensive seats. Expect to pay (or tip) a hotel porter or concierge at least as much as a ticket-agency markup for hard-to-get tickets. You might try **Vienna Ticket Service** (✉ Postfach 160, A–1043, ☎ 01/587–9843–0, FAX 01/587–9844), **Carta Austria** (✉ Goldschmiedgasse 10, ☎ 01/536–01), **American Express** (✉ Kärntner Str. 21–23, A-1015, ☎ 01/515–40–0, FAX 01/515–40–70), **Kartenbüro Flamm** (✉ Kärntner Ring 3, A–1010, ☎ 01/512–4225), or **Cosmos** (✉ Kärntner Ring 15, A–1010, ☎ 01/515–33–0, FAX 01/513–4147). Tickets to musicals and some events including the Vienna Festival are available at the "Salettl" gazebo kiosk alongside the Opera House on the Kärntner Strasse. Tickets to that night's musicals are reduced by half after 2 PM (☎ 01/588–85).

Opera and Operetta

The **Staatsoper** (State Opera House, ✉ Opernring 2, ☎ 01/51444–2656 or 01/514–44–0), one of the world's great opera houses, has been the scene of countless musical triumphs and a center of unending controversies over how it should be run and by whom. (When Lorin Maazel was unceremoniously dumped as head of the Opera not many years ago, he pointed out that the house had done the same thing to Gustav Mahler a few decades earlier.) A performance takes place virtually every night from September through June, drawing on the vast repertoire of the house, with emphasis on Mozart and Verdi. (Opera here is nearly always performed in the original language, even Russian.) Guided tours of the Opera House are held year-round. The opera in Vienna is a dressy event and even designer jeans are not socially acceptable. Evening dress and black tie, though not compulsory, are recommended for first-night performances and in the better seats.

Light opera and operetta are performed at the **Volksoper** (✉ Währingerstr. 78, ☎ 01/51444–3318) outside the city center at Währingerstrasse and Währinger Gürtel (third stop on Streetcar 41, 42, or 43, from "downstairs" at Schottentor, U2, on the Ring). Prices here are significantly lower than in the main opera, and performances can be every bit as rewarding. Mozart is sung here, too, but in German, the language of the house.

You'll find musicals and operetta also at the **Theater an der Wien** (✉ Linke Wienzeile 6, ☎ 01/588–30–0), the **Raimundtheater** (✉ Wallgasse 18, ☎ 01/599–77–0), and **Ronacher** (✉ Seilerstätte/Himmelpfortgasse, ☎ 01/514–02). Opera and operetta are performed on an irregular schedule at the **Kammeroper** (✉ Fleischmarkt 24, ☎ 01/513–6702).

In summer, look for outdoor opera performances on the grounds of Schönbrunn Palace (☞ Exploring Vienna, *above*); Mozart's *Don Giovanni* here is a memorable experience. The 1996 *Magic Flute* is likely to be held over to 1997. Book early, since the Schönbrunn performances are regular sellouts. There's standing room available. Also in summer, light opera or operetta performances by the Kammeroper ensemble are given in the exquisite **Schlosstheater** at Schönbrunn. Ticket agencies will have details.

Tickets to the state theaters (**Opera, Volksoper, Burgtheater,** or **Akademietheater**) can be charged against your credit card. You can order them by phoning up to a month before the performance (☎ 01/513–1513) or buy them in person up to a month in advance at the *Theaterkassen,* the central box office. ✉ *Theaterkassen, back of Opera, Hanuschgasse 3, in courtyard,* ☎ *01/514–44–2959 or 01/514–44–2960.* ⏲ *Weekdays 8–6, Sat. 9–2, Sun. and holidays 9–noon. Information and ticket office for Opera, Volksoper,* ✉ *Kärntner Str. 40, Staatsoper arcade,),* ☎ *01/514–44–2958.* ⏲ *Weekdays 10–1 hr before performance, Sat. 10–noon.*

You can also write ahead for tickets. The nearest Austrian National Tourist Office can give you a schedule of performances and a ticket order form. Send the form (no payment is required) to the ticket office (✉ Kartenvorverkauf Bundestheaterverband, Goethegasse 1, A–1010 Vienna), which will mail you a reservation card; when you get to Vienna, take the card to the main box office to pick up and pay for your tickets.

Theater

Vienna's **Burgtheater** (✉ Dr. Karl Lueger-Ring 2, A–1010 Vienna; *see* state theaters, *above,* for ticket details) is one of the leading German-language theaters of the world. Its current director has replaced the German classics with more modern and controversial pieces. The Burg's smaller house, the **Akademietheater** (✉ Lisztstr. 1), draws on much the same group of actors, for classical and modern plays. Both houses are closed during July and August.

The **Theater in der Josefstadt** (✉ Josefstädterstr. 26, ☎ 01/402–5127, FAX 01/402–7631–60) stages classical and modern works year-round in the house once run by the great producer and teacher Max Reinhardt. The **Volkstheater** (✉ Neustiftgasse 1, ☎ 01/523–3501–265) presents dramas, comedies, and folk plays. The **Kammerspiele** (✉ Rotenturmstr. 20, ☎ 01/533–2833) does modern plays.

For **theater in English** (mainly standard plays), head for **Vienna's English Theater** (✉ Josefsgasse 12, ☎ 01/402–1260). Another option is the equally good **International Theater** (✉ Porzellangasse 8, ☎ 01/319–6272).

Nightlife

Balls

The gala Vienna evening you've always dreamed about can become a reality: among the many balls given during the Carnival season, several welcome the public—at a wide range of prices (at press time; subject to change). You can book tickets with a Eurocheck or through hotel concierges; there are also ticket agencies, including ATT (✉ 6 Josefspl., A–1010, ☎ 0222/5124466, FAX 0222/5123355). Here is a run-down of some of the most popular Viennese balls. For a background on these festive events, *see* Stepping-Out in Three-Quarter Time *in* Pleasures and Pastimes, *above.*

Blumenball (✉ Stadtgartenamt, 2B Am Heurmarkt, A–1030, ☎ 0222/71116, Extension 97247), or Florists Ball, January 12 at the Rathaus. Tickets are AS374. **Philharmonic Ball** (✉ 12 Philharmoniker Bösendorferstr., A–1010, ☎ 0222/5056525), January 18 in the Goldmann Saal of the Vienna Musikverein; tickets are AS1305 (plus AS545 for a seat at a table). **Opera Ball** (✉ 1 Opernballbüro Goethegasse, A–1010, ☎ 0222/51440), February 15 at the Opera House; tickets are AS2942 (plus AS2182 for a seat at a table, AS171 for standing room on stage, AS160 to AS749 for balcony seats). **Kaffeesiederball** (✉ Club der Wiener Kaffeehausebesitzer Stubenring 8-10, A–1010, ☎ 0222/51450241), or Coffee Brewers' Ball, February 14 at the Hofburg Palace; tickets are AS706 (seats at tables from AS160). **Bonbon Ball** (✉ Zentralverband der Ssswarenhändler Österreichs Strasse, A–1020, ☎ 0222/3303121), February 16 at the Hofburg; tickets are AS492 (plus AS214 for a seat at a table).

Bars and Lounges

Vienna has blossomed in recent years with delightful and sophisticated bars. Head for the "Bermuda Triangle," an area in the First District roughly defined by Judengasse, Seitenstättengasse, Rabensteig, and Franz-Josefs-Kai. Here you will find dozens of bars, both intimate and large, like **Salzamt, Krah-Krah,** and **Ma Pitom.** Around Concordiaplatz and in Heinrichsgasse, **Puerto** and **Domicil** are highly popular. Back toward Stephansplatz, on Bäckerstrasse, check out **Weinorgel, Oswald & Kalb;** on Blutgasse, **Chamäleon;** on Singerstrasse, the **Galerie Bar. The American Bar** on Kärntner Durchgang has an original Adolf Loos turn-of-the-century interior.

Cabaret

Cabaret has a long tradition in Vienna. **Simpl** (✉ Wollzeile 36, ☎ 01/512–4742) continues earning its reputation for barbed political wit but has had to give way to some newcomers at **K&K** (✉ Linke Wienzeile 4, ☎ 01/587–2275) and **Kabarett Niedermair** (✉ Lenaugasse 1A, ☎ 01/408–4492). To get much from any of these, you'll need good German with some Viennese vernacular as well plus knowledge of local affairs.

Casinos

Try your luck at the casino **Cercle Wien** (✉ Kärntner Str. 41, ☎ 01/512–4836) in a former town palace redone in dark wood paneling and millions of twinkle lights. Games include roulette and blackjack. You'll need your passport for entry identification.

Discos

The disco scene is big in Vienna, and the crowd seems to follow the leader from one "in" spot to the next. A few continually draw full houses. Try **Atrium** (✉ Schwarzenbergpl. 10, ☎ 01/505–3594); **Queen Anne,** still very much "in" (✉ Johannesgasse 12, ☎ 01/512–0203); and **U–4,** popular with a mixed group, early thirties and younger (✉ Schönbrunner Str. 222, ☎ 01/858–3185).

Jazz Clubs

Vienna is increasingly good for jazz, though places where it can be heard tend to come and go. Nothing gets going before 9 PM. Try **Jazzland** (✉ Franz-Josefs-Kai 29, ☎ 01/533–2575); **Papa's Tapas** (✉ Schwarzenbergpl. 10, ☎ 01/505–0311); and **Roter Engel** (✉ Rabensteig 5, ☎ 01/535–4105), all of which offer live groups almost nightly. **Porgy & Bess** (✉ Spiegelgasse 2, ☎ 01/512–8438–0) has gained a reputation for good jazz, although the future of the club is uncertain.

Nightclubs

Vienna has no real nightclub tradition, although there are a number of clubs in town. Most of the ones with floor shows are horribly expensive and not very good; some are outright tourist traps. The two where you run the least risk are **Casanova,** where singles can sit reasonably peacefully at the upstairs bar (✉ Dorotheergasse 6, ☎ 01/512–9845), and upscale **Moulin Rouge** (✉ Walfischgasse 11, ☎ 01/512–2130). The leading spots for dancing are the **Eden Bar,** which always has a live band and is for the well-heeled mature crowd (✉ Liliengasse 2, ☎ 01/512–7450); **Chattanooga,** which often has a live band and draws a younger crowd (✉ Graben 29, ☎ 01/533–5000); and **Volksgarten** (✉ Volksgarten, Burgring 1, ☎ 01/533–0518–0), where a mixed younger set comes, particularly in summer for outdoor dancing.

OUTDOOR ACTIVITIES AND SPORTS

Participant Sports

Bicycling

Look for the special pathways either in red brick or marked with a stylized cyclist in yellow. Note and observe the special traffic signals at some intersections. You can take a bike on the subway (except during rush hours) for half fare, but only in cars with a blue shield on the door, and only on stairs or elevators with the "bike" shield, not the escalators. The city tourist office has a brochure in German with useful cycling maps, plus a leaflet "See Vienna by Bike" with tips in English. At most bookstores you can purchase a cycling map of Vienna put out by a local cycling organization known as ARGUS (✉ Frankenberggasse 11, ☎ 01/505–8435). You can rent a bike starting at about AS40 per hour, leaving your passport or other identification as a deposit.

Rent a bike year-round at the Westbahnhof, Wien Nord (Praterstern), or Floridsdorf rail stations, or pick up a bike at **Radverleih Hochschaubahn,** mid-March through October (✉ Prater amusement park, by Hochschaubahn, bear slightly right after you pass wheel, ☎ 12/729–5888); at **Radverleih Praterstern,** April–October (✉ street level under Praterstern North rail station); or at **Hammermayer/Radsport Nussdorf** (✉ Donaupromenade, next to Nussdorf DDSG dock, ☎ 01/374598). Other rental locations are available from tourist offices.

Boating

Both the **Alte Donau** (Old Danube), a series of lakes to the north of the main stream, and the **Neue Donau,** on the north side of the Donauinsel (the artificial island in the river), offer good waters for paddleboats, rowboats, kayaks, sailboats, and windsurfing. The Danube itself is somewhat fast-moving for anything but kayaks. Rent boats from **Auzinger Boote** (✉ Laberlweg 22, ☎ 01/235788), **Karl Hofbauer** (✉ Neue Donau at Reichsbrücke; ✉ Obere Alte Donau 185, ☎ 01/204–3435–0), **Eppel** (✉ Wagramer Str. 48, ☎ 01/235168), **Irzl** (✉ Florian Berndl-Gasse 33 and 34, ☎ 01/203–6743), and **Newrkla** (✉ Obere Alte Donau, ☎ 01/386105). For details about sailing and sailing events, check with **Haus des Sports** (✉ Prinz-Eugen-Str. 12, ☎ 01/505–3742–0).

Golf

The top in-town golf course is at **Freudenau** in the Prater (☎ 01/728–9564–0, FAX 01/728–5379). But this 18-hole par-70 course is so popular from April to November, even with the weekday AS800 fee, that you'll probably need to be invited or have an introduction from a member to play; on weekends, membership or an invitation is required. Alternatives are **Golfclub Am Wienerberg,** a 9-hole, par 35/70 course on the south side of Vienna, open March–Nov. (✉ Gutheil Schoder-Gasse 9, ☎ 01/66123–0); **Brunn am Gebirge,** an 18-hole par-72 course about 10 kilometers (6 miles) to the southwest (✉ Rennweg 50, ☎ 02236/33711, FAX 02236/33863); **Ebreichsdorf,** 27 kilometers (17 miles) south of Vienna, an 18-hole par-72 course (✉ Schlossallee 1, ☎ 02254/73888, FAX 02254/73888–13); **Colony Club Gutenhof,** 10 kilometers (6 miles) to the southeast, with two courses of 18 holes, par 73 each, at Himberg (✉ Gutenhof, ☎ 02235/87055–0, FAX 02235/87055–14); or **Hainburg,** 50 kilometers (31 miles) east of Vienna, with 18 holes, par 72 (✉ Auf der Heide, ☎ 02165/62628, FAX 02165/65331); but these, too, are generally overbooked. Weekdays, of course, will be best for any of the courses, particularly those farther from Vienna.

Health and Fitness Clubs

Try **Fitness Center Stadtpark** (✉ Kursalon, Johannesgasse 33, ☎ 01/714–7775), **Fitness Center Harris** (✉ Niebelungengasse 7, ☎ 01/587–3710), or **Zimmermann Fitness** (✉ Kaiserstr. 43, ☎ 01/526–2000; ✉ Kreuzgasse 18, ☎ 01/406–4625). (The latter club is for women only.)

Ice Skating

The **Wiener Eislaufverein** (✉ Lothringer Str. 22, behind InterContinental Hotel, ☎ 01/713–6353–0) has outdoor skating with skate rentals, October through March. Weekends are crowded. For indoor skating, check the **Wiener Stadthalle** (✉ Vogelweidpl. 14, U6 to Urban Loritz-Pl., ☎ 01/981–00–0).

Jogging

Jogging paths run alongside the Danube Canal, and runners also frequent the Stadtpark and the tree-lined route along the Ring, particularly the Parkring stretch. Farther afield, in the Second District, the Prater Hauptallee, 4 kilometers (2½ miles) from Praterstern to the Lusthaus, is a favorite.

Riding

Splendid bridle paths crisscross the Prater park. To hire a mount, contact the **Reitclub Donauhof** (✉ Hafenzufahrtstr. 63, ☎ 01/728–3646 or 01/728–9716), or **Reitclub Prater/Reitschule Sylvia Kühnert** (✉ Dammhaufen 62, ☎ 01/728–1335).

Skiing

Nearby slopes such as **Hohe Wand** (Bus 49B from the Hütteldorf stop of the U4 subway), west of the city in the 14th District, offer limited skiing, with a ski lift and man-made snow when the heavens refuse, but serious Viennese skiers (that includes nearly everybody) will take a train or bus out to nearby Niederösterreich (Lower Austria), with the area around the **Semmering** (about an hour from the city) one of the favorite locations for a quick outing.

Swimming

Vienna has at least one pool for each of its 23 districts; most are indoor pools, but some locations have an outdoor pool as well. An indoor favorite is **Rogner's,** complete with water slide (✉ Strohbachgasse 7–9, ☎ 01/587–0844–0). For a less formal environment, head for the swimming areas of the **Alte Donau** or the **Donauinsel.** The pools and the Alte Donau (paid admission) will be filled on hot summer weekends, so the Donauinsel can be a surer bet. Some beach areas are shallow and suitable for children, but the Donauinsel has no lifeguards, though there are rescue stations for emergencies. Changing areas are few, lockers nonexistent, so don't take valuables. And don't be tempted to jump into the Danube Canal; the water is definitely not for swimming, nor is the Danube itself, because of heavy undertows and a powerful current.

The city has information on all places to swim; contact City Hall (✉ Rathaus, Friedrich Schmidt-Pl., ☎ 01/4000–5). Ask for directions to reach the following:

Donauinsel Nord. This huge free recreation area has a children's section and nude bathing. **Donauinsel Süd** is free and offers good swimming and boating and a nude bathing area. It's harder to get to and less crowded than other areas, and food facilities are limited. **Gänsehäufel.** This bathing island in the Alte Donau (☎ 01/235392) has paid admission, lockers, changing rooms, children's wading pools, topless and nude areas, and restaurants; on sunny weekends, it's likely to be full by 11 AM or earlier. **Krapfenwaldbad** is an outdoor park/pool tucked among the trees on the edge of the Vienna Woods (☎ 01/321501), full of Vienna's beautiful people and singles. Get there early on a sunny Sunday or you won't get in. **Stadionbad.** This huge sports complex is popular with the younger crowd; go early. There is no direct transportation; take the Bus 80B from U3/Schlachthausgasse to the Hauptallee stop, or, for the fun of it, ride the miniature railway (*Liliputbahn*) from behind the Ferris wheel in the Prater amusement park to the Stadion station and walk the rest of the way (✉ Prater, Marathonweg, ☎ 01/720–2102).

Tennis

Though Vienna has plenty of courts, they'll be booked solid. Try anyway; your hotel may have good connections. **Sportservice Wien-Sport** (✉ Bacherpl. 14, ☎ 01/545–1201–0) operates a central court-booking service (100 courts in summer, three halls in winter), and **Vereinigte Tennisanlagen** (✉ Prater Hauptallee, ☎ 01/728–1811) has courts in other locations as well. Or you can try **Tennisplätze Arsenal** (✉ Arsenalstr. 1, by Südbahnhof, ☎ 01/798–2132; ✉ Faradaygasse 4, ☎ 01/798–7265; ✉ Gudrunstr. 31, ☎ 01/602–1521), which has 57 sand courts; **Tennisplätze Stadionbad** (✉ Prater Hauptallee, ☎ 01/720–2070); or **Wiener Eislaufverein** (✉ Lothringer Str. 22, behind Inter-Continental Hotel, ☎ 01/713–6353–0).

Top businessmen and political leaders head to **Tennis Point Vienna** (✉ Nottendorfergasse/Baumgasse, ☎ 01/799–9997) for the 10 indoor courts, squash, sauna, and an outstanding fitness studio; there is a bar and an excellent and remarkably reasonable restaurant as well.

Spectator Sports

Football (Soccer)

Matches are played mainly in the **Ernst-Happel-Stadion** (stadium) in the Prater (✉ Meiereistr., ☎ 01/728–0854) and the **Hanappi Stadium** (✉ Keisslergasse 6, ☎ 01/914–3490–0). Indoor soccer takes place in the **Stadthalle** (✉ Vogelweidpl. 14, ☎ 01/981–00–01). Tickets can usually be bought at the gate, but the better seats are available through ticket agencies. At the **Vienna Ticket Service** (✉ Postfach 160, A–1060, ☎ 01/587–9843–0, FAX 01/587–9844), tickets must be ordered a month in advance. Otherwise try **American Express** (✉ Kärntner Str. 21–23, ☎ 01/515–40–0, FAX 01/515–40–70), **Cosmos** (✉ Kärntner Ring 15, A-1010, ☎ 01/515–33–0, FAX 01/513–4147), **Kartenbüro Flamm** (✉ Kärntner Ring 3, A-1010, ☎ 01/512–4225, FAX 01/513–9962), or **Österreichisches Verkehrsbüro** (✉ Friedrichstr. 7, ☎ 01/588–00–0, FAX 01/587–7142).

Horse Racing

The race track (flat and sulky racing) is in the Prater (Galopprennpl. Freudenau, ☎ 01/728–9535–0), and the season runs April–November. The highlight is the Derby, which takes place the third Sunday in June.

Tennis

Professional matches are played in the Prater or in the Stadthalle (☞ Football, *above*). Ticket agencies will have details.

SHOPPING

Shopping Districts

The **Kärntner Strasse, Graben,** and **Kohlmarkt** pedestrian areas claim to have the best shops in Vienna, and for some items, such as jewelry, some of the best anywhere, although you must expect high prices. The

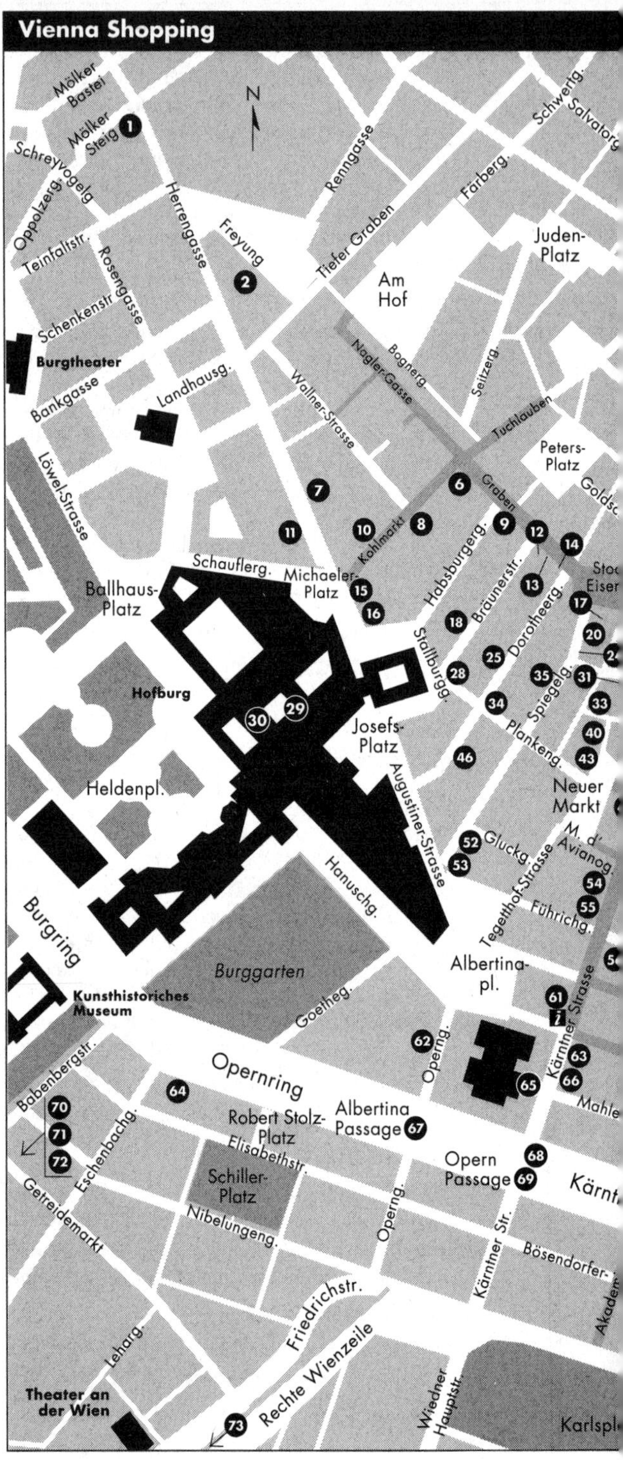
Vienna Shopping
N
Mölker Bastei
Mölker Steig
Schreyvogelg.
Oppolzerg.
Teinfaltstr.
Rosengasse
Schenkenstr.
Herrengasse
Freyung
Renngasse
Tiefer Graben
Färberg.
Schwertg.
Salvatorg.
Juden-Platz
Am Hof
Bognerg.
Nagler-Gasse
Seitzerg.
Tuchlauben
Peters-Platz
Graben
Burgtheater
Bankgasse
Landhausg.
Wallner-Strasse
Löwel-Strasse
Kohlmarkt
Habsburgerg.
Bräunerstr.
Dorotheerg.
Schauflerg.
Michaeler-Platz
Ballhaus-Platz
Stallburgg.
Spiegelg.
Plankeng.
Hofburg
Josefs-Platz
Augustiner-Strasse
Heldenpl.
Neuer Markt
Gluckg.
Tegetthof-Strasse
Führichg.
Hanuschg.
Burgring
Burggarten
Albertina-pl.
Kunsthistoriches Museum
Goetheg.
Operng.
Kärntner Strasse
Opernring
Babenbergstr.
Robert Stolz-Platz
Albertina Passage
Mahlerstr.
Eschenbachg.
Elisabethstr.
Schiller-Platz
Opern Passage
Nibelungeng.
Getreidemarkt
Operng.
Kärntner Str.
Bösendorfer-
Friedrichstr.
Lehárg.
Rechte Wienzeile
Theater an der Wien
Wiedner Hauptstr.
Karlspl.

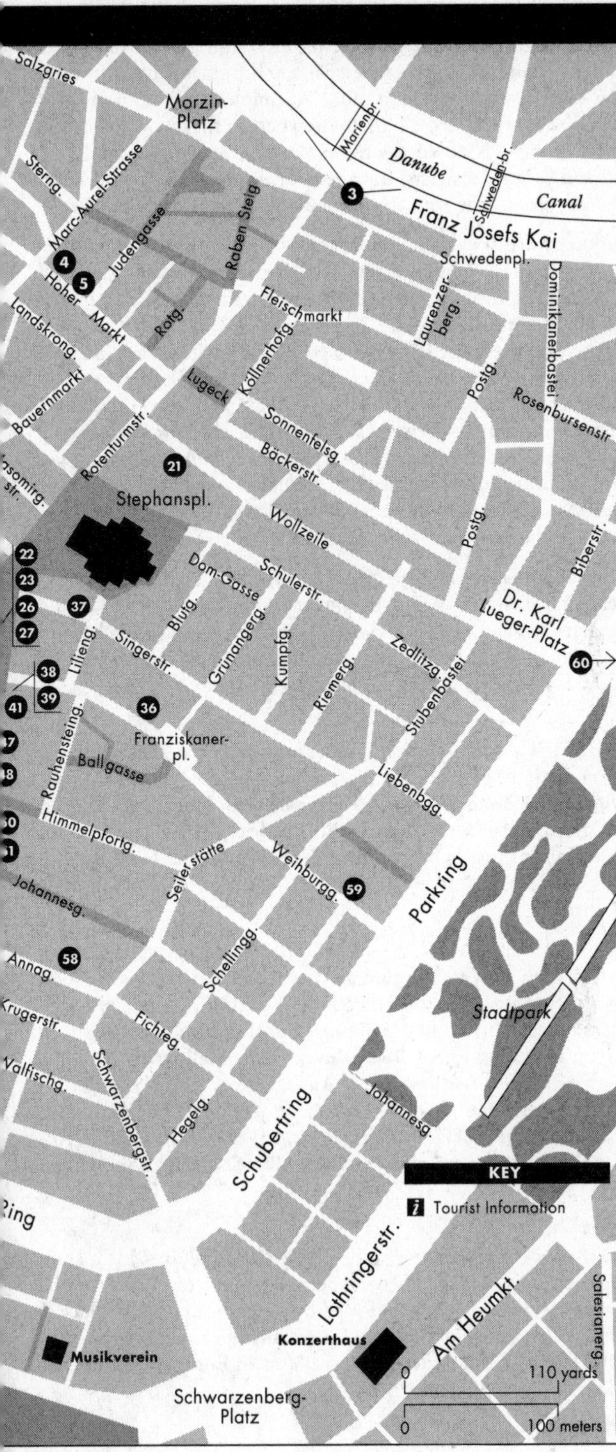

Souvenir in der Hofburg, **29**
Stafa, **72**
Steffl, **47**
Stransky, **30**
Tabletop, **2, 59**
Teller, **60**
Tostmann, **1**
Venturini, **24**
Wahliss, **39**
Wiener Geschenke, **16, 53**
Zach, **18**
Zak, **61**

side streets within this area have developed their own character, with shops offering antiques, art, clocks, jewelry, and period furniture. **RingstrassenGalerie,** the new shopping plaza at Kärntner Ring 5-7, brings a number of shops together in a modern complex, although most of these stores have other, larger outlets elsewhere in the city. Outside the center, concentrations of stores are on **Mariahilfer Strasse** straddling the Sixth and Seventh districts; **Landstrasser Hauptstrasse** in the Third District; and, still farther out, **Favoritenstrasse** in the 10th District.

A collection of attractive small boutiques can be found in the **Palais Ferstel** passage at Freyung 2 in the First District. A modest group of smaller shops has sprung up in the **Sonnhof** passage between Landstrasser Hauptstrasse 28 and Ungargasse 13 in the Third District. The **Spittelberg** market, on the Spittelberggasse between Burggasse and Siebensterngasse in the Seventh District, has drawn small galleries and handicrafts shops and is particularly popular in the weeks before Christmas and Easter. Christmas is the time also for the tinselly **Christkindlmarkt** on Rathausplatz in front of city hall; in protest over its commercialization, smaller markets specializing in handicrafts have sprung up on such traditional spots as Am Hof and the Freyung (First District), also the venue for other seasonal markets.

Vienna's **Naschmarkt** (between Linke and Rechte Wienzeile, starting at Getreidemarkt) is one of Europe's great and most colorful food and produce markets. Stalls open at 5 or 6 AM, and the pace is lively until 1 or 2 PM. Saturday is the big day, when farmers come into the city to sell at the back end of the market. It's closed Sunday.

ANTIQUES

You will find the best antiques shops located in the First District, many clustered close to the Dorotheum auction house, in the **Dorotheergasse, Stallburggasse, Plankengasse,** and **Spiegelgasse.** You'll also find interesting shops in the **Josefstadt** (Eighth) district, with prices considerably lower than those in the center of town. Wander up Florianigasse and back down Josefstädter Strasse, being sure not to overlook the narrow side streets.

D&S (✉ Dorotheergasse 12, ☎ 01/512–1011) specializes in old Viennese clocks. Look in at **Glasgalerie Kovacek** (✉ Spiegelgasse 12, ☎ 01/512–9954) to see a remarkable collection of glass paperweights and other glass objects. You'll find paintings and furniture in many shops in this area, including **Kunst Salon Kovacek** (✉ Stallburggasse 2, ☎ 01/512–8358). **Peter Feldbacher** (✉ Annagasse 6, ☎ 01/512–2408) has items ranging from glass to ceramics to furniture. For Art Deco, look to **Galerie Metropol** (✉ Dortheergasse 12, ☎ 01/513–2208). Another Art Deco option is **Galerie bei der Albertina** (✉ Lobkowitzpl. 1, ☎ 01/513–1416).

Auctions

The **Dorotheum** (✉ Dorotheergasse 17, ☎ 01/515–60–0) is a state institution dating to 1707, when Emperor Josef I determined that he didn't want his people being exploited by pawnbrokers. The place is intriguing, with goods ranging from furs to furniture auctioned almost daily. Information on how to bid is available in English. Some items are for immediate cash sale.

Flea Markets

Every Saturday (except holidays) rain or shine, from about 7:30 AM to 4 or 5, the **Flohmarkt** in back of the Naschmarkt, stretching along the Linke Wienzeile from the Kettenbrücken U4 subway station, offers a staggering collection of stuff ranging from serious antiques to plain junk. Haggle over prices.

On Thursdays and Fridays from late spring to midfall, an outdoor combination arts-and-crafts, collectibles, and flea market takes place on Am Hof.

On Saturday and Sunday in summer from about 10 to 6 an outdoor **art and antiques market** springs up along the Danube Canal, stretching from the Schwedenbrücke to beyond the Salztorbrücke. Lots of books are sold, some in English, plus generally better goods and collectibles than at the Saturday flea market. Bargain over prices all the same.

Department Stores

The **Steffl** department store (✉ Kärntner Str. 19, ☎ 01/512–0685) is moderately upscale without being overly expensive. The larger department stores are concentrated in Mariahilfer Strasse. By far the best is **Herzmansky** (✉ Mariahilfer Str. 26–30, ☎ 01/521–58–0), definitely upscale; outstanding gourmet shops and restaurants are in the basement. Farther up the street you will find slightly cheaper goods at **Gerngross** (✉ Mariahilfer Str. and Kirchengasse, ☎ 01/521–80–0) and cheaper still at **Stafa** (✉ Mariahilfer Str. 120, ☎ 01/523–3483–0).

Specialty Stores

BOOKS

Several good stores whose stock includes books in English are on the Graben and Kärntner Strasse in the First District. For bookstores specializing in English-language books, *see* Contacts and Resources *in* Vienna A to Z, *below*.

CERAMICS AND PORCELAIN

Ceramics are anything but dull at **Berger** (✉ Weihburggasse 17, ☎ 01/512–1434). Gmunden primitive country ceramics are at **Pawlata** (✉ Kärntner Str. 14, ☎ 01/512–1764). More country ceramics can be found at **Plessgott** (✉ Kärntner Durchgang, ☎ 01/512–5824). Check out Viennese porcelain patterns at **Augarten** (✉ Graben/Stock-im-Eisen-Pl. 3, ☎ 01/512–1494) and **Albin Denk** (✉ Graben 13, ☎ 01/512–4439), **Rosenthal** (✉ Kärntner Str. 16, ☎ 01/512–3994), and **Wahliss** (✉ Kärntner Str. 17, ☎ 01/512–1729–0).

CRYSTAL AND GLASS

Select famous Vienna glassware at **Bakalowits** (✉ Spiegelgasse 3, ☎ 01/512–6351–0) and **Lobmeyr** (✉ Kärntner Str. 26, ☎ 01/512–0508–0), which also has a small museum of its creations upstairs; the firm supplied the crystal chandeliers for the Metropolitan Opera in New York City, a gift from Austria. **Berndorf** (✉ Wollzeile 12, ☎ 01/512–2944) and **Rasper & Söhne** (✉ Graben 15, ☎ 01/534–33–0) have the exquisite Riedl glass; so do **Albin Denk** (✉ Graben 13, ☎ 01/512–4439) and **Tabletop** (✉ Passage, Freyung 2, ☎ 01/535–4256; ✉ Weihburggasse/Hotel Marriott, ☎ 01/513–3895), though readers have reported that goods purchased here for shipment were never received.

GIFT ITEMS

Österreichische Werkstätten (✉ Kärntner Str. 6, ☎ 01/512–2418) offers outstanding and unusual handmade handicrafts, gifts, and quality souvenirs ranging from jewelry to textiles.

Souvenir in der Hofburg (✉ Hofburgpassage 1 and 7, ☎ 01/533–5053) is another source of more traditional gift items.

Niederösterreichisches Heimatwerk (☞ Women's Clothing, *below*) has handmade folk objects and textiles.

Wiener Geschenke (✉ Reitschulgasse 4/Michaelerpl., ☎ 01/533–7078; ✉ Lobkowitzpl. 1, ☎ 01/513–3773) has a nice selection of quality gift and traditional souvenir items and is open Sunday during part of the year.

JADE

Discover interesting pieces of Austrian jade at **Burgenland** (✉ Opernpassage, ☎ 01/587–6266).

JEWELRY

Carius & Binder (✉ Kärntner Str. 17, ☎ 01/512–6750) is good for watches.

Haban (✉ Kärntner Str. 2, ☎ 01/512–6730–0; ✉ Graben 12, ☎ 0222/512–1220) has a fine selection of watches and jewelry.

A. Heldwein (✉ Graben 13, ☎ 01/512–5781) sells elegant jewelry, silverware, and watches.

A. E. Köchert (✉ Neuer Markt 15, ☎ 01/512–5828–0) has outstanding original creations.

Eleonora Kunz (✉ Neuer Markt 13, ☎ 01/512–7112) sells stunning modern pieces for men and women.

Schullin (✉ Kohlmarkt 7, ☎ 01/533–9007–0) has some of the most original work found anywhere.

MEN'S CLOTHING

Clothing in Vienna is far from cheap but is of good quality. The best shops are in the First district: **Sir Anthony** (✉ Kärntner Str. 21–23, ☎ 01/512–6835), **E. Braun** (✉ Graben 8, ☎ 01/512–5505–0), **House of Gentlemen** (✉ Kohlmarkt 12, ☎ 01/533–3258), **ITA** (✉ Graben 18, ☎ 01/533–6004–0), **Malowan** (✉ Opernring 23, ☎ 01/587–6296), **Silbernagel** (✉ Kärntner Str. 15, ☎ 01/512–5312), **Teller** in the Third district (✉ Landstrasser Hauptstr. 88–90, ☎ 01/712–6397) for particularly good value, **Venturini** (✉ Spiegelgasse 9, ☎ 01/512–8845) for custom-made shirts.

For men's *Trachten,* or typical Austrian clothing, including lederhosen, try **Loden-Plankl** (✉ Michaelerpl. 6, ☎ 01/533–8032), and go to **Collins Hüte** (✉ Opernpassage, ☎ 01/587–1305) to get the appropriate hat.

NEEDLEWORK

For Vienna's famous petit point, head for **Petit Point Kovacec** (✉ Kärntner Str. 16, ☎ 01/512–4886) or **Stransky** (✉ Hofburgpassage 2, ☎ 01/533–6098).

RECORDS

Look for records and tapes at **Arcadia** (✉ Kärntner Str. 40, Staatsoper arcade, ☎ 01/513–9568), which also features books and imaginative music-related souvenirs.

Carola is best for pop LPs and CDs (✉ Albertinapassage by Opera House, ☎ 01/564114). **EMI** (✉ Kärntner Str. 30, ☎ 01/512–3675) has a wide selection of pops plus classics upstairs.

Havlicek (✉ Herrengasse 5, ☎ 01/533–1964) features classics and is particularly knowledgeable and helpful. **da Caruso** (✉ Operngasse 4, ☎ 01/513–1326) specializes in classics, with an emphasis on opera.

SHOES AND LEATHER GOODS

Try **Humanic** (✉ Kärntner Str. 51, ☎ 01/512–5892; ✉ Singerstr. 2, ☎ 01/512–9101). For exclusive styles, go to **Zak** (✉ Kärntner Str. 36, ☎ 01/512–7257), **Popp & Kretschmer** (✉ Kärntner Str. 51, ☎ 01/512–6421–0), and **Nigst** (✉ Neuer Markt 4, ☎ 01/512–4303).

WOMEN'S CLOTHING

The couturier to Vienna is **Adlmüller** (⊠ Kärntner Str. 41, ☏ 01/512–6650–0). Check also **Flamm** (⊠ Neuer Markt 12, ☏ 01/512–2889), **E. Braun, ITA,** or **Malowan** (☞ Men's Clothing, *above*). You'll find modern young styling at **Maldone** (⊠ Kärntner Str. 4, ☏ 01/512–2761; ⊠ Kärntner Str. 12, ☏ 01/512–2234; ⊠ Graben 29, ☏ 01/533–6091; ⊠ Hoher Markt 8, ☏ 01/533–2555).

Check out the selection of dirndls and women's *Trachten,* the typical Austrian costume with white blouse, print skirt, and apron, at **Lanz** (⊠ Kärntner Str. 10, ☏ 01/512–2456), **Niederösterreichisches Heimatwerk** (⊠ Herrengasse 6–8, ☏ 01/533–3495), **Resi Hammerer** (⊠ Kärntner Str. 29–31, ☏ 01/512–6952), and **Tostmann** (⊠ Schottengasse 3a, ☏ 01/533–5331–0). (☞ Loden-Plankl *in* Men's Clothing, *above.*)

WROUGHT IRON

Weinhebers (wine dispensers with pear-shape glass containers) and other iron items can be found at **Franz Hamerle** (⊠ Annagasse 7, ☏ 01/512–4746) or **Zach** (⊠ Bräunerstr. 8, ☏ 01/533–9939).

VIENNA A TO Z

Arriving and Departing

By Boat

If you arrive in Vienna via the Danube, the DDSG/Blue Danube ship will leave you at **Praterlände** near Mexikoplatz (⊠ Handelskai 265, ☏ 01/727–50–0), although some upstream ships also make a stop at **Nussdorf** (⊠ Heiligenstädter Str. 180, ☏ 01/371257). The Praterlände stop is a two–block taxi ride or hike to or from the Vorgartenstrasse U1/subway station, or you can take a taxi directly into town.

By Bus

International long-distance bus service (Bratislava, Brno) and most postal and railroad buses arrive at the **Wien Mitte** central bus station (⊠ Landstrasser Hauptstr. 1b, ☏ 01/711–07–3850 or 01/711–01), across from the Hilton Hotel.

By Car

Vienna is 300 kilometers (187 miles) east of Salzburg, 200 kilometers (125 miles) north of Graz. Main routes leading into the city are the A1 Westautobahn from Germany, Salzburg and Linz, and the A2 Südautobahn from Graz and points south.

On highways from points south or west or from the airport, **Zentrum** signs clearly mark the route to the center of Vienna. From there, however, finding your way to your hotel can be no mean trick, for traffic planners have installed a devious scheme prohibiting through traffic in the city core (the First District) and scooting cars out again via a network of exasperating one-way streets. In the city itself a car is a burden, though very useful for trips outside town.

By Plane

Vienna's airport is at Schwechat, about 19 kilometers (12 miles) southeast of the city. For flight information, call 01/7007–2233. **Austrian Airlines** (☏ 01/717–99–0), **Air Canada** (☏ 01/515–55–31), **Delta** (☏ 01/512–6646–0), and **Lauda Air** (☏ 01/0660–6655) fly into Schwechat from North America. The North American services of Austrian, Delta, and Swissair are shared under joint flight numbers and may be flown in and out of Vienna by any of the three lines.

BETWEEN THE AIRPORT AND CITY CENTER

A **bus** leaves the airport every half hour from 5 AM to 6:30 AM, then every 20 minutes from 6:50 AM to 11:30 PM (the last bus is at midnight; after that, buses depart every hour to 5 AM), for the city air terminal (☎ 01/5800–35404 or 01/5800–33369) beside the Hilton Hotel. The trip takes about 25 minutes and costs AS70; you buy your ticket on the bus, so be sure to have Austrian money handy. A bus also runs every hour (every half-hour on weekends and holidays April–September) to the Westbahnhof (West Station) via the Südbahnhof (South Station); this bus might land you closer to your hotel, and taxis are available at the station. The introduction of improved rail service between the airport and the Wien-Mitte/Landstrasse rail station (opposite the Hilton) may bring changes to bus schedules this year.

Taxis will take about 30 minutes to most downtown locations, longer when traffic is heavy (weekdays 7–8:30 AM and 4:30–6:30 PM). Taxis from Vienna are not allowed to pick up passengers at the airport unless they've been ordered; only those from Lower Austria (where the airport is located, beyond the city limits) can take passengers into town. This means that taxis travel one way empty, so the meter fare is doubled; you'll end up with a bill of about AS350. You can cut the charge to about AS250 by phoning one of the Vienna cab companies from the airport (☎ 01/313–00, 01/601–60–0, or 01/401–00) and asking for a taxi to take you into town. They'll give you the last couple of digits of the taxi license, and you wait until it arrives. Be sure to arrange where the taxi will meet you. The same scheme applies when you leave: Not all Vienna cabs have permits for airport service, so call in advance to get one that can take you out for about AS300–AS320. The cheapest cab service is C+K Airport Service (☎ 01/60808), charging about AS270–AS300.

Mazur limos provide door-to-door transportation that's cheaper than a taxi. Look for the Mazur stand at the airport, or call 01/7007–6422, 01/604–9191, or 01/604–2233.

Fast **trains** run from the airport to the Wien Mitte station across the street from the Hilton Hotel and to the Wien Nord station, Praterstern, with service at half-hour intervals. The fare is AS30, or a Vienna streetcar ticket plus AS15. Check schedules, as the service is being expanded and changes are likely.

By Train

Trains from Germany, Switzerland, and western Austria arrive at the **Westbahnhof** (West Station), on Europaplatz, where the Mariahilfer Strasse crosses the Gürtel. If you're coming from Italy or Hungary, you'll generally arrive at the **Südbahnhof** (⊠ South Station, Wiedner Gürtel 1). The current stations for trains to and from Prague and Warsaw are **Wien Nord** (⊠ North Station, Praterstern) and **Franz-Josef Bahnhof** (⊠ Julius-Tandler-Pl.). Central train information will have details (☎ 01/1717; taped schedule information (in German) for trains to/from west, ☎ 01/1552; for trains to/from south, 01/1553).

Getting Around

Vienna is divided into 23 numbered districts. Taxi drivers may need to know which district you seek, as well as the street address. The district number is coded into the postal code with the second and third digits; thus A–1010 (the "-01-") is the First District, A–1030 is the Third, A–1110 is the 11th, and so on. Some sources and maps still give the district numbers, either in Roman or Arabic numerals, as Vienna X or Vienna 10.

Vienna is a city to tackle on foot. With the exception of the Schönbrunn and Belvedere palaces and the Prater amusement park, most sights are concentrated in the center, the First District (A–1010), much of which is a pedestrian zone anyway.

By Bus and Streetcar

Vienna's public transportation system is fast, clean, safe, and easy to use. Get public transport maps at a tourist office or at the transport-information offices (*Wiener Verkehrsbetriebe*), underground at Karlsplatz, Stephansplatz, and Praterstern. You can transfer on the same ticket between subway, streetcar, bus, and long stretches of the fast suburban railway, *Schnellbahn (S-Bahn)*. Buy single tickets for AS20 from dispensers on the streetcar or bus; you'll need exact change. The ticket machines at subway stations (*VOR-Fahrkarten*) give change and dispense 24-hour, 72-hour, and eight-day tickets, as well as single tickets separately and in blocks of two and five. At *Tabak-Trafik* (cigarette shops/newsstands) or the underground *Wiener Verkehrsbetriebe* offices you can get a block of five tickets for AS85, each ticket good for one uninterrupted trip in more or less the same general direction with unlimited transfers. Or you can get a three-day ticket for AS130, good on all lines for 72 hours from the time you validate the ticket; there's also a 24-hour ticket for AS50. If you're staying longer, get an eight-day ticket (AS265), which can be used on eight separate days or by any number of persons (up to eight) at any one time. These rates were valid at press time, but could be higher in 1997. A useful address is Tabak-Trafik Almassy (⊠ Stephanspl. 4, to the right behind cathedral, ☎ 01/512–5909); it is open every day from 8 AM to 7 PM and has tickets as well as film and other items. Ask at tourist offices or your hotel about a *Vienna-Card*; the card costing AS180 combines 72 hours' use of public transportation and discounts at certain museums and shops.

The first streetcars run about 5:15 AM, for those Viennese who start work at 8. From then on, service (barring gridlock on the streets) is regular and reliable, and most lines operate until about midnight. Where streetcars don't run, buses do; route maps and schedules are posted at each bus or subway stop.

Should you miss the last streetcar or bus, special night buses with an *N* designation operate at half-hour intervals over several key routes; the starting (and transfer) points are the Opera House and Schwedenplatz. The night-owl buses take a special fare of AS25, tickets available on the bus; normal tickets, your 72-hour or Vienna Card are not valid.

Within the heart of the city, bus lines 1A, 2A, and 3A are useful crosstown routes. These carry a reduced fare of AS8.50 per trip if you have bought the *Kurzstrecke* ticket (AS34), good for four trips or up to four people on one trip (with no transfer). The *Kurzstrecke* tickets are also valid for two stops on the subway or shorter distances on the streetcar lines.

By Car

Traffic congestion within Vienna has gotten out of hand and driving to in-town destinations generally takes longer than public transportation. City planners' solutions have been to make driving as difficult as possible, with one-way streets and other tricks, and a car in town is far more of a burden than a pleasure. Drivers not familiar with the city literally need a navigator. The entire First and Sixth through Ninth districts are limited parking zones and require that a "Parkschein," a paid-parking chit available at most newsstands and tobacconists, be displayed on the dash during the day. Overnight street parking in the First and Sixth through Ninth Districts is restricted to residents with special permits; all other cars are subject to expensive ticketing or even towing, so in these districts be sure you have off-street garage parking.

By Horse Cab

A *Fiaker,* or horse cab, will trot you around to whatever destination you specify, but this is an expensive way to see the city. A short tour of the inner city takes about 20 minutes and costs AS500; a longer one including the Ringstrasse takes about 40 minutes and costs AS800, for the whole Fiaker. The carriages accommodate four (five if someone sits next to the coachman). Starting points are Heldenplatz in front of the Hofburg, Stephansplatz beside the cathedral, and across from the Albertina, all in the First District. For longer trips, or any variation of the regular route, agree on the price first.

By Subway

Five subway lines (*U-bahn*), whose stations are prominently marked with blue *U* signs, crisscross the city. Karlsplatz and Stephansplatz are the main transfer points between lines. The last subway (U4) runs at about 12:30 AM.

By Taxi

Taxis in Vienna are relatively inexpensive. The initial charge is AS26 for as many as four people daytime, AS27 nighttime, weekends, and holidays. AS16 is added for radio cabs ordered by phone and for each piece of luggage that must go into the trunk, and a charge is added for waiting beyond a reasonable limit. It's customary to round up the fare to cover the tip. Taxis can be flagged on the street (when the roof light is on), taken from regular stands, or ordered by phone. To get a radio cab, call 01/313–00, 01/401–00, or 01/601–60–0. Service is usually prompt, but at rush hour, when weather is bad, or if you need to keep to an exact schedule, call ahead and order a taxi for a specific time. If your destination is the airport, ask for a reduced-rate taxi. For the cheapest taxi to the airport, *see* Between the Airport and City Center, *above.*

For a chauffeured limousine call **Tibor Adler** (☎ 01/216–0990), **Göth** (☎ 01/713–7196), **Mazur** (☎ 01/604–2233), or **Peter Urban** (☎ 01/713–5255 or 713–3781).

Contacts and Resources

Car Rentals

Rental cars can be arranged at the airport or in town. Major firms include **Avis** (✉ Airport, ☎ 01/7007–2700; ✉ Opernring 3–5, ☎ 01/587–6241), **Budget** (✉ Airport, ☎ 01/7007–2711; ✉ Hilton Hotel, Am Stadtpark, ☎ 01/714–6565–0), **EuroDollar** (✉ Airport, ☎ 01/7007–2699; ✉ Schubertring 9, ☎ 01/714–6717), **Hertz** (✉ Airport, ☎ 01/7007–2661; ✉ Kärntner Ring 17, ☎ 01/512–8677; international reservations, ☎ 01/713–1596), **National** (✉ Europcar/interRent at airport, ☎ 01/7007–3316; ✉ Denzel Autovermietung, Kärntner Ring 14, ☎ 01/505–4200; international reservations, 01/505–4166). **Buchbinder** (✉ Schlachthausgasse 38, ☎ 01/717–50–0) is a local firm with particularly favorable rates and clean cars.

Doctors and Dentists

If you need a doctor and speak no German, ask your hotel, or in an emergency, phone your consulate.

Embassies

U.S. embassy (✉ Boltzmanngasse 16). **U.S. consulate** (✉ Gartenbaupromenade, Parkring 12A, Marriott building). The telephone number for both is 01/313–39. **Canadian embassy** (✉ Fleischmarkt

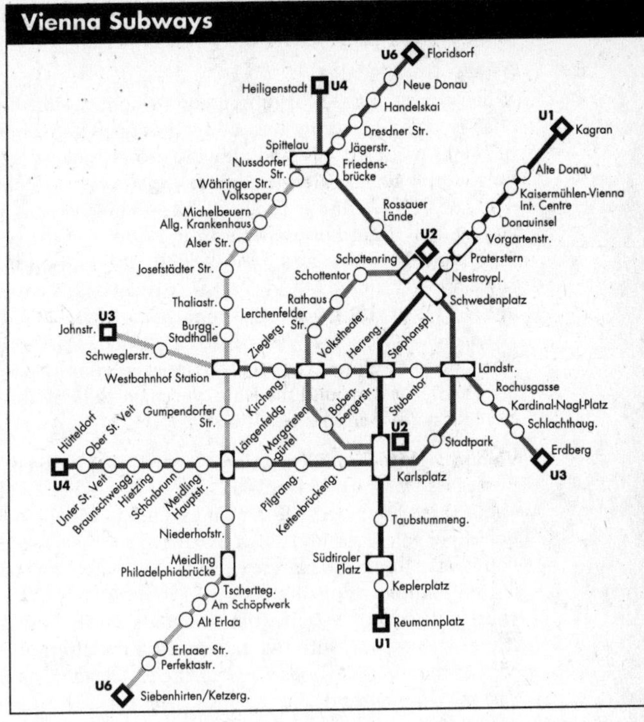

19/Laurenzerberg 2, ☎ 01/531–38–0). **U.K. embassy and consulate** (✉ Jauresgasse 12; embassy, ☎ 01/713–1575; consulate, ☎ 01/714–6117).

Emergencies

The emergency numbers are 133 for the **police,** 144 for an **ambulance,** 122 for the **fire department.**

English-Language Bookstores

The leading sources of books in English are **Big Ben Bookstore** (✉ Servitengasse 4a, ☎ 01/319–6412–0), **British Bookstore** (✉ Weihburggasse 24–26, ☎ 01/512–1945–0), and **Shakespeare & Co.** (✉ Sterngasse 2, ☎ 01/535–5053–0). **Pickwick's** (✉ Marc-Aurel-Str. 10–12, ☎ 01/533–0182) mainly rents videotapes.

English-Language Radio

"Blue Danube Radio" on FM at 103.8 and 91.0 MHz carries news, music, and information in English (and some in French) throughout the day and early evening, with major newscasts at 12 noon and 6 PM.

Guided Tours

BOAT TOURS

The **DDSG/Blue Danube Steamship Line** (☎ 01/727–50–0) runs a three-hour boat tour up the Danube Canal and down the Danube, from Schwedenbrücke, by Schwedenplatz, May through September, daily at 10:30 AM, 1, 2:30, and 4:30 PM. From early to late April and late September to the end of October, tours run daily at 1 PM. Check schedules and special cruise offerings, as the line has been under new management since last year, and trips as well as schedules are subject to change.

EXCURSIONS

All three bus tour operators (☞ Orientation Tours, *below*) offer short trips outside of the city. Check their offerings and compare packages and prices to be sure you get what you want. Your hotel will have brochures.

ORIENTATION TOURS

When you're pressed for time, a good way to see the highlights of Vienna is via a sightseeing-bus tour, which gives you a once-over-lightly of the heart of the city and allows a closer look at Schönbrunn and Belvedere palaces. **Vienna Sightseeing Tours** (✉ Stelzhammergasse 4/11, ☎ 01/712–4683–0, FAX 01/712–4683–77) runs a 1¼-hour "get acquainted" tour daily, leaving from in front of the Opera House at 10:30 and 11:45 AM and 3 PM (AS220). **CityTouring Vienna** (✉ Penzingerstr. 46, ☎ 01/894–1417–0, FAX 01/894–3239) runs a similar tour at 9:30 AM (AS180), leaving from the City Air Terminal by the Hilton Hotel, across from the Wien Mitte/Landstrasse U3/U4 subway station. You can cover almost the same territory on your own by taking either Streetcar 1 or 2 around the Ring, and then walking through the heart of the city (☞ Self-Guided Tours, *below*).

Vienna Sightseeing, CityTouring Vienna, and **Cityrama/Gray Line** (✉ Börsegasse 1, ☎ 01/534–13–12, FAX 01/534–13–22) all have tours of about three hours (AS320), including brief visits to Schönbrunn and Belvedere palace grounds. If you want to see the Schönbrunn interior, you'll have to pay a separate entrance fee, with some operators offering a 30-minute or one-hour stop, or in some cases leaving you to find your way back to the center of town yourself. The CityTouring Vienna trip breaks the day into two halves, with the afternoon taking in the edge of the Vienna Woods via Grinzing and heading along the Danube past the UN-Center, the Prater amusement park, and the Hundertwasser House. Cityrama and Vienna Sightseeing tours start daily at 9:30 and 10:30 AM, and 2:30 PM; the CityTouring Vienna tours are at 11, 3:15, and 4. All three firms offer a number of other tours as well (your hotel will have detailed programs), and provide hotel pickup for most tours. For other than the "get acquainted" tours, the Vienna Sightseeing buses leave the central loading point in front of the Opera House 10 minutes before scheduled tour departures to make the hotel pickups. Cityrama tours start from Johannesgasse at the Stadtpark station on the U4 subway line, diagonally across from the InterContinental hotel. CityTouring Vienna tours originate at the City Air Terminal by the Hilton Hotel, opposite the Wien Mitte/Landstrasse station on the U4 and U3 subway lines.

STREETCAR TOURS

From early May through September, a 1929 vintage streetcar leaves each Saturday at 11:30 AM and 1:30 PM and Sunday, Monday, and holidays at 9:30 and 11:30 AM and 1:30 PM from the Otto Wagner Pavilion at Karlsplatz for a guided tour. For AS200 (AS180 if you have the *Vienna-Card*), you'll go around the Ring, out past the big Ferris wheel in the Prater and past Schönbrunn and Belvedere palaces in the course of the two-hour trip. The oldtimer trips are popular, so get tickets in advance at the transport-information office underground at Karlsplatz, weekdays 7 AM–6 PM, weekends and holidays 8:30–4 (☎ 01/7909–44026).

PERSONAL GUIDES

Guided walking tours (in English) are a great way to see the city highlights. Tour topics range from "Unknown Underground Vienna" to "1,000 Years of Jewish Tradition" and "Vienna Around Sigmund Freud." Tours take about 1½ hours, are held in any weather provided at least three people turn up, and cost AS108 plus any entry fees. No reservations are needed. Get a list of the guided-tour possibilities at the city information office at Kärntner Strasse 38 (☎ 01/513–8892). Ask for the monthly brochure "Walks in Vienna," which details the tours, days, times, and starting points. You can also arrange to have your own privately guided tour for AS1,116 for a half day.

SELF-GUIDED

Get a copy of "Vienna Downtown Walking Tours" by Henriette Mandl from any bookshop. The six tours take you through the highlights of central Vienna with excellent commentary and some entertaining anecdotes, which most of your Viennese acquaintances won't know. The booklet "Vienna from A–Z" (in English, AS70; available at bookshops and city information offices) explains the numbered plaques attached to all major buildings.

Late-Night Pharmacies

In each area of the city one pharmacy stays open 24 hours; if a pharmacy is closed, a sign on the door will tell you the address of the nearest one that is open. Call 01/1550 for names and addresses (in German) of the pharmacies open that night.

Lost and Found

If you've lost something valuable, check with the police at the **Fundamt** (☒ Wasagasse 22, ☎ 01/313–44–0 or 01/313–44–9211). If your loss occurred on a train, check the **Bundesbahn Fundamt** (☒ railway lost property office, ☎ 01/5800). If you were coming in from Salzburg, call the office at the **Westbahnhof** (☎ 01/5800–32996) 8–noon; from Villach or the south, call the **Südbahnhof** (☎ 01/5800–35656). Losses on the subway system or streetcars can be checked by calling the **Zentrale Fundstelle** (☎ 01/7909–43500).

Travel Agencies

The leading agencies are **American Express** (☒ Kärntner Str. 21–23, ☎ 01/515–40–0, FAX 01/515–40–70), **Carlson/Wagon-Lits** (☒ Kärntner Ring 2, ☎ 01/501–60–0, FAX 01/501–60–65), **Cosmos** (☒ Kärntner Ring 15, ☎ 01/515–33–0, FAX 01/513–4147), **Ruefa Reisen** (☒ Fleischmarkt 1, ☎ 01/534–04–0, FAX 01/534–04–394), and **Österreichisches Verkehrsbüro** (☒ Friedrichstr. 7, opposite Sezession, ☎ 01/588–00–0, FAX 01/986–8533).

Visitor Information

The main point for information is the **Vienna City Tourist Office** (☒ Fremdenverkehrsstelle der Stadt Wien), in back of the Opera House and around the corner from the Hotel Sacher, at Kärntner Strasse 38 (☎ 01/513–8892–0), open daily from 9 to 7.

If you need a room, go to **Information-Zimmernachweis** operated by the Verkehrsbüro in the Westbahnhof (☎ 01/892–3392) and in the Südbahnhof (☎ 01/505–3132). At the airport, the information and room-reservation office in the arrivals hall (☎ 01/7007–2828) is open daily 8:30 AM–9 PM. The information office at the DDSG dock on the Danube (☎ 01/727–50–0 or 01/218–0114) is open when ships are docking and embarking. None of these offices can arrange room bookings by telephone; you must deal in person.

If you're driving into Vienna, get information or book rooms at **Information-Zimmernachweis** at the end of the Westautobahn at Wientalstr./Auhof (☎ 01/979–1271) or at the end of the Südautobahn at Triesterstrasse 149 (☎ 01/616–0071 or 01/616–0070).

3 Side Trips from Vienna

From the Vienna Woods to the Weinviertel

Is it the sun or the soil? The dreamy castle-capped peaks? Whatever the reason, the idyllic regions outside Vienna have always offered perfectly pastoral escapes for Viennese. Rich in scenic splendor, this countryside is also saturated with musical history. Here, Beethoven was inspired to write his Pastoral Symphony, *Johann Strauss set the Vienna Woods to music, and a glass of intoxicating* Retzer Wein *urged Richard Strauss to compose the Rosenkavalier Waltz. From the elegant spa of Baden to mysterious Mayerling, this region is a day-tripper's delight.*

THE VIENNESE ARE UNDENIABLY LUCKY. Few populaces enjoy such glorious—and easily accessible—options for day-tripping. City residents in the droves tie their bicycles to the roof racks of their Mercedes on Saturdays and Sundays; Vacationers to Vienna can share in the natives' obvious pleasure in the city's environs any day of the week. For many the first destination is, of course, the Wienerwald, the fabled Vienna Woods. This is not a natural park or forest, as you would think from listening to Strauss or the tourist blurbs. The Wienerwald is a large range of rolling, densely wooded hills, extending from Vienna's doorstep to the outposts of the Alps in the south. This region is crisscrossed by country roads and hiking paths, dotted with forest lodges and inns, and solidifies every now and then into quaint little villages and market towns. In addition to such natural pleasures, the regions outside of Vienna offer something for everyone. Turning south to Mayerling leads you to the site where the successor to the Austrian throne presumably took his own life after shooting his secret love—a mystery still unresolved. You can opt to head northeast, into wonderfully encompassing woods and gently rolling hills sprinkled with elegant summer palaces, and, to the north, to take one long liquid adventure by exploring the Weinstrasse (Wine Road), along which vast expanses of vineyard produce excellent, mainly white, wines. Another choice is to follow the trail of the defensive castles that protected the land from invaders from the north, or you can even trace the early days of Masonry in Austria—both Haydn and Mozart were members of what was then a secret and forbidden brotherhood.

Updated by Willibald Picard

These subregions of Lower Austria are simple, mainly agricultural, country areas. People live close to the earth, and on any sunny weekend from March through October, you'll find whole families out working the fields. This isn't to suggest that fun is forgotten; just as often, you'll stumble across a dressy parade with the local brass band done up in *Lederhosen* and feathered hats. Sundays here are still generally days of rest, although this generally means that on Sunday morning, wives and daughters go to mass while husbands and older sons retire to discuss weather and politics at the local *Gasthaus,* the families to be reunited after services over a simple but filling meal. Whichever destination you choose, however, the lakes are waiting, the biking paths are open, and the lovely countryside cafés beckon.

Pleasures and Pastimes

Bicycling

The Carnuntum region and the southeast corner of the Weinviertel, a region known as the Marchfeld, offer outstanding cycling, with a number of marked routes. Cycle paths follow the southern bank of the Danube past Carnuntum (Petronell) through Bad Deutsch–Altenburg to Hainburg, and other parts of the region are flat enough to offer fine cycling without exertion. In the Marchfeld, another marked route close to the March river includes the Baroque castles at Marchegg, Schlosshof, and Niederweiden.

Castles

To take advantage of the fact that the Danube forms a natural line of defense, barons and baliffs decided centuries ago to fortify bluffs along the river. Castles were the best answer and a wonderful string of these more or less follows the course of the Thaya river, starting in Weitra and Heidenreichstein close to the Czech border, then eastward to Raabs, Riegersburg and Hardegg. The 17th- and 18th-century structures vary from turreted hilltop fortresses to more elegant moated bastions, but all were part of a chain against invaders. Several are basically intact, the others restored, and all are impressive relics well worth visiting. Castle concerts have become popular during summer months, when the buildings are open for tours as well.

Dining

With very few exceptions, food in this region, while influenced by Vienna cuisine, is simple. The basics are available in abundance: roast meats, customary schnitzel variations, game in season, fresh vegetables, and standard desserts such as *Palatschinken,* crepes filled with jam or with nuts topped with chocolate sauce. Imaginative cooking is rare; this is not tourist country, and the local population demands little beyond reasonable quality and quantity.

Wines are equally taken for granted, although four of the areas included here are designated as separate wine regions—the Weinviertel, or wine quarter to the north of Vienna; the Kamptal, which divides the Weinviertel from the Waldviertel to the west; the Carnuntum–Petronell region just below the Danube to the southeast of Vienna, and the Thermen region south and southwest of the capital. The specialties are mainly white wines, with the standard types, Grüner Veltliner and Rieslings and increasingly Weissburgunder, predominating. Reds are coming more into favor, with lighter reds such as Zweigelt and even rosés to be found in the northern areas, the heavier reds such as Blaufränkisch and St. Laurent and the spicier Gewürztraminer and Müller–Thurgau whites in the south. Most of the vintners work small holdings, so output is limited. The wine market in Poysdorf, center of Austria's largest wine region, offers an opportunity to sample a wide choice of area wares.

Restaurant prices include taxes and a service charge, but it is customary to give the waiter an additional tip of 5%–7%, usually rounding up the bill to the nearest AS5 or 10.

CATEGORY	COST*
$$$$	over AS350
$$$	AS200–AS350
$$	AS100–AS200
$	under AS100

**per person for a typical two-course meal, including a small glass of wine or beer but excluding an additional tip*

Hiking and Walking

The celebrated Vienna Woods to the west and southwest of Vienna are crisscrossed by hundreds of easy hiking paths, numbered, color-coded, and marked for destinations. Excellent hiking maps available from most bookstores will give ideas and routes. Paths will take you through woods, past meadows and vineyards, alongside streams and rivers, with occasional *Waldschenke* hidden away deep in the woods where you can stop for refreshment or a cold snack. Deer, wild boar and a host of small animals inhabit these preserves. The area is protected, and development is highly restricted, making it ideal for pleasurable hiking.

Lodging

Accommodations in the countryside around Vienna are pretty basic. This is underdeveloped tourist territory, prime turf for the more adventuresome, with rooms frequently to be found as an adjunct to the local *Gasthaus*. Nearly all are family-run; the younger members will speak at least some school English. You'll probably have to carry your own bags, and elevators to upper floors are scarce. Booking ahead is a good idea, as most places have relatively few rooms, particularly rooms with full bath. Window screens are almost unknown in Austria as bugs are few, but in farming areas, both flies and occasionally mosquitoes can be a nuisance in the warmer seasons. Since you'll want windows open at night, take along a can of bug spray and you'll sleep more peacefully. The standard country bed covering is a down-filled feather bed, so if you're allergic to feathers or want more warmth, ask for blankets. Even the simpler hotels will be spotless, and almost without exception, you'll be offered a tasty breakfast which can range from fresh rolls with cold cuts and cheese and tea or coffee, to an ample buffet spread with cereals and fruit as well, included in the room price.

Hotel room rates include taxes and service, and usually breakfast—although check to be sure.

CATEGORY	COST*
$$$$	over AS1,000
$$$	AS800–AS1,000
$$	AS500–AS800
$	under AS500

**All prices are for a standard double room for two, including taxes and service charge.*

Exploring Vienna's Environs

The region surrounding Vienna divides itself logically into four areas. The Vienna Woods, that huge unspoiled belt of forest green stretching westward south of the Danube, was celebrated by composers Beethoven, Schubert, and Strauss, and remains a favorite of the Viennese today. The towns to the south, Mödling, Baden, and Bad Vöslau mark the east end of the rolling, wooded hills. There the fertile Vienna Basin begins, sweeping east to the low, wooded Leitha Mountains that shelter the Putzta Plain extending on into Hungary. The northern part of the basin widens into the Danube Valley, forming the Carnuntum agricultural and wine region, with Slovakia to the east.

North of the Danube, two great regions are divided by the Kamp River, with the wooded Waldviertel, or forest district, to the northwest adjoining the Czech Republic, and the rolling hills of the agricultural Weinviertel, or wine district, to the northeast, bordering in the north on the Czech Republic and in the east, where the March River flows into the Danube, on Slovakia.

Great Itineraries

The four districts surrounding Vienna are compact and each can be explored in a day or two. To pursue the lives of the famous composers Schubert and Beethoven, take the route to the south, to Mödling and Baden; for Haydn's birthplace, to the east to Rohrau, then possibly on to Eisenstadt (☞ Chapter 4). To tour a chain of defensive castles, head for the forested *Waldviertel*. For rolling hills, vast expanses of vineyards and to sample their output, seek out the *Weinviertel* to the north.

Baden and Environs

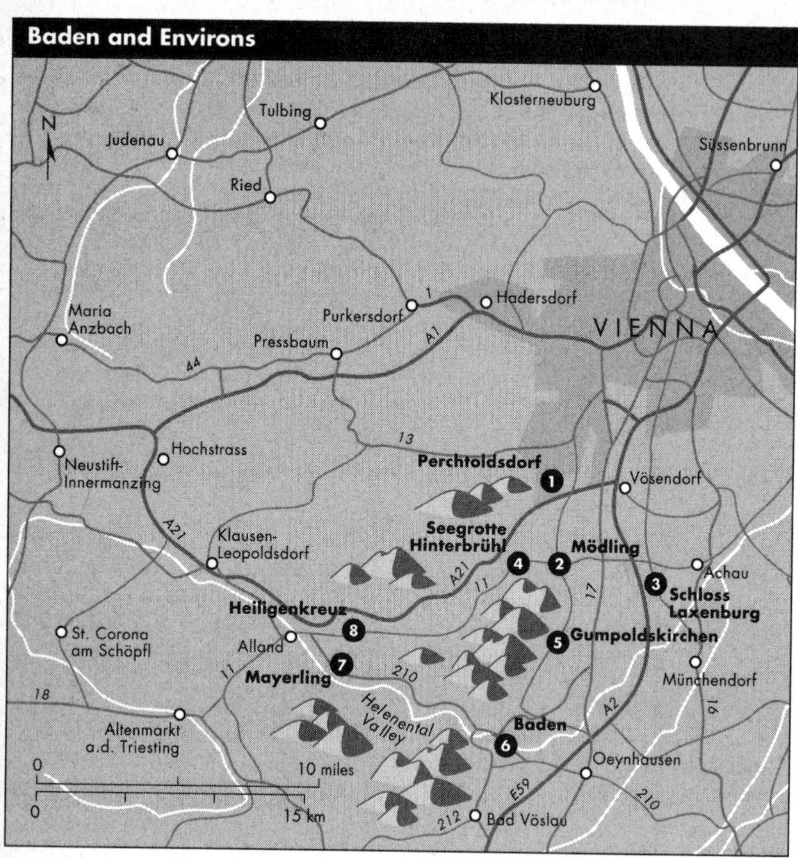

Numbers in the text correspond to numbers in the margin and on the Baden and Environs and Waldviertel/Weinvierte maps.

South of the Danube

IF YOU HAVE 1 DAY

To get a taste of the fringes of the Vienna Woods to the capital's south and west, head for **Mödling** ② and **Baden** ⑥. Both are smaller communities with unspoiled 17th-century town centers on a scale easy to assimilate. The route to Baden runs through the band of rolling wooded hills that mark the eastern edge of the Vienna Woods. The hills are skirted by vineyards forming a "wine belt," which also follows the valleys south of Vienna.

IF YOU HAVE 3 DAYS

With more time, you might spend two days in the Vienna Woods area, starting off with two particularly picturesque towns, **Perchtoldsdorf** ① and **Mödling** ②—with perhaps a look at the grand castle garden of **Laxenburg** ③—then following the scenic *Weinstrasse* ("wine road") through the lush vineyard country to the noted wine-producing village of

Gumpoldskirchen ⑤. Overnight in **Baden** ⑥, then spend your second day taking in the sights of the fashionable spa town, including its grand Kurpark and Casino. Set out in the afternoon for mysterious **Mayerling** ⑦. After an evocative dawn and morning here, set out for the great abbey at **Heiligenkreuz** ⑧, then head back to Vienna.

North of the Danube

IF YOU HAVE 1 DAY

The decision will have to be woods or wine, if you're tight on time. If woods, then head for **Waidhofen an der Thaya** ⑲, returning via picturesque **Raabs an der Thaya** ⑳ and **Geras** ㉓ and **Horn** ⑩. If wine, start at the bustling shipbuilding city of Korneuburg, then northward to the border town **Laa an der Thaya** ㉗, and return via **Poysdorf** ㉘, famous as a wine center.

IF YOU HAVE 3 DAYS

Spend a leisurely two days tracking the castles of the Waldviertel, starting at **Ottenstein** ⑫, moving on to **Zwettl** ⑬, with its magnificent abbey, overnighting at the noted castle-hotel/Masonic museum in **Rosenau** ⑭, and on to **Weitra** ⑮, with its painted facades, for the start of the defensive castles route. The next mighty castle is at **Heidenreichstein** ⑱; follow the castle route with an overnight in **Raabs an der Thaya** ⑳ and onward to **Riegersburg** ㉑ and **Hardegg** ㉒, overlooking the river forming the border with the Czech Republic. A stop in the ancient city of **Retz** ㉖ will give you a taste of the wine country; to end your excursion, head on to **Laa an der Thaya** ㉗ and **Poysdorf** ㉘.

When to Tour Vienna's Environs

Most of the regions around Vienna are best seen in the temperate seasons between mid-March and mid-November. The Waldviertel, however, with its vast stands of great forest offers picturebook scenery throughout the year. The combination of oaks and evergreens offers a color spectrum ranging from intense early spring green, through the deep green of summer into traces of autumn foliage, particularly in the Kamp River valley; in winter, occasional spectacular displays of hoar frost and snowswept vistas turn the region into a glittering three-dimensional Christmas card.

ON THE ROAD TO BADEN AND MAYERLING

This short, though history-rich, tour takes you to Baden through the legendary band of rolling wooded hills of the Vienna Woods (Wienerwald) that border Vienna on the west. The hills are skirted by vineyards forming a "wine belt," which also follows the valleys south of Vienna. You can visit this area easily in a day's outing, either by car or by public transportation, or you can spend the night in Baden, Mödling, or Alland for a more leisurely tour, visiting Mayerling, Heiligenkreuz, and a few other sights in the area.

By car from Vienna, head for Liesing (23rd District), then take Wiener Strasse to Perchtoldsdorf; from there, follow the signs south to Mödling and Baden. From Baden, take Route 210 (marked HELENENTAL) to Mayerling and on to Alland; return to Vienna via Route 11, stopping in Heiligenkreuz en route.

Perchtoldsdorf

1 *12 km (7½ mi) southwest of Vienna center.*

Just over the Vienna city line to the southwest lies Perchtoldsdorf, a charmingly picturesque market town with many wine taverns, a 13th-century Gothic parish church, and the symbol of the town—an imposing stone tower completed in 1511, once forming a piece of the town's defense wall. Familiarly known as Pedersdorf, the town is a favorite excursion spot for the Viennese, who come mainly for the good local wines. Wander around the compact town square to admire the Renaissance houses, some with arcaded courtyards. The "Pestsäule" (Plague Column) in the center of the square, which gives thanks for rescue from the dread 16th century plague, was created by the famous Baroque architect Fischer von Erlach, and is similar to the Plague Column that adorns the Graben in Vienna. Without a car, you can reach Perchtoldsdorf from Vienna by taking the S-Bahn, or train, from the Westbahnbof, to Liesing, and then a short cab ride to the town.

Dining

$$$$ ✕ **Jahreszeiten.** This elegant, formal yet relaxed restaurant is in the capable hands of Günter Winter, whose reputation as a top chef continues to grow. The menu reflects international cuisine with an Austrian flair. You might be offered game and spring lamb in season, or try any of the fish offerings, perhaps sweet-sour shrimp on saffron rice. Finish with *Topfensouffle*, a delicately light cheesecake concoction. Beyond the kitchen, the atmosphere, like the tables, is set to perfection, and the menu is supplemented by wines from an outstanding cellar, international as well as local. ✉ *Hochstr. 17,* ☎ *0222/865–3129. Reservations essential. AE, DC, MC, V. Closed Mon., Easter week, and late July–early Aug. No lunch Sat. or dinner Sun.*

Mödling

2 *20 km (12½ mi) southwest of Vienna.*

Founded in the 10th century, Mödling has a delightful town center, now a pedestrian zone. Here you can admire centuries-old buildings, most one- or two-story, which give the town an intimate feeling. Composers Beethoven and Schubert appreciated this in the early 1800s; Mödling was one of Beethoven's favored residences outside of Vienna. Note the domineering **St. Othmar Gothic parish church** on a hill overlooking the town proper, a Romanesque 12th-century charnel house (where the bones of the dead were kept), and the town hall, which has a Renaissance loggia. Later eras added Art Nouveau, which mixes happily with the several 16th- and 17th-century buildings.

3 A few kilometers east of Mödling is **Schloss Laxenburg,** a complex consisting of a large Baroque Neues Schloss (New Castle), a small 14th-century Altes Schloss (Old Castle), and an early 19th-century neo-Gothic castle set into the sizable lake. The large park is full of birds and small game, such as roe deer and hare, and is decorated with statues, cascades, imitation temples, and other follies. The park and grounds are a favorite with the Viennese for Sunday outings. The Altes Schloss was built in 1381 by Duke Albrecht III as his summer residence, and several Habsburg emperors spent summers in the Neues Schloss, which now houses the International Institute of Applied Systems Analysis. Opposite is the large Baroque Convent of the Charitable Sisters. The cas-

tle is currently occupied by a research institute and is generally not open to the public, but the gardens are open daily. ✉ *Schlosspl. 1,* ☎ *02236/712–26–0.*

4 West of Mödling on Route 11 is the **Seegrotte Hinterbrühl,** a fascinating but now somewhat commercialized underground sea, created years ago when a mine filled up with water. You can take a 45-minute motorboat trip and look at the reflections through the arched caverns of the mine. ✉ *Grutschgasse 2,* ☎ *02236/26364.* *AS50.* *Apr.–Oct. daily 9–12, 1–5; Nov.–Mar. daily 9–12, 1–3.*

NEED A BREAK? **Höldrichsmühle,** where a mill has turned since the 12th century, is now the spot for a famed 200-year-old country inn (✉ Gaadner Str. 34, ☎ 02236/26274–0). Legend holds that the linden tree and the well found here inspired composer Franz Schubert to one of his better-known songs. Stop at this traditional restaurant for fish, game or various Champignon dishes in season.

Dining and Lodging

$$$$ ✕ **Babenbergerhof.** Rooms in this renovated, older hotel are comfortably up-to-date. You're in the quiet pedestrian zone (parking available), and upper rooms on the street side have views of the ancient parish church. The garden is particularly pleasant for summer dining; try the fried chicken or boiled beef. ✉ *Babenbergergasse 6, A-2340,* ☎ *02236/22246,* FAX *02236/22246–6. 50 rooms. Restaurant, bar. AE, DC, MC, V.*

Gumpoldskirchen

From Mödling, follow the scenic "wine road" (an unnumbered road to the west of the rail line) through the lush vineyard country to the
5 famous wine-producing village of **Gumpoldskirchen,** home of one of Europe's pleasantest white wines. This tiny village on the eastern slopes of the last Alpine rocks has lived for wine for two thousand years, and its white wines enjoy a fame that is widespread. At one stage, there was more Gumpoldskirchner on the world markets than the village could ever have produced—a situation reminiscent of the medieval glut of pieces of the True Cross. **Vintners' houses** line the main street, many of them with the typical large wooden gates that lead to the vine-covered courtyards where the Heuriger (wine of the latest vintage) is served by the owner and his family at simple wooden tables with benches. Gumpoldskirchen also has an arcaded Renaissance town hall, a market fountain made from a Roman sarcophagus, and the (private) castle of the Teutonic knights, whose descendants still own some of the best vineyard sites in the area.

Dining

$$ ✕ **Mautwirtshaus.** For a snack or a full meal, any of the various rooms in this country-style *Gasthaus* with its antique decor accents will be a good choice. Offerings range from lighter sausage and sauerkraut to the traditional roast pork or chicken, with surprise specialties when asparagus, game and goose are in season. Occasional Sunday jazz brunches add a contemporary note. ✉ *Kaiserin-Elisabeth-Str. 22,* ☎ *02236/24481–0. DC, MC, V.*

Baden

6 *32 km (20 mi) southwest of Vienna, 24 km (15 mi) north of Wiener Neustadt.*

The wine road brings you to the famous spa of Baden. Since antiquity, Baden's sulfuric thermal baths have attracted the ailing and the fashionable from all over the world. When the Romans came across the springs, they dubbed the town Aquae; the Babenbergs revived it in the 10th century, and when the Russian Czar Peter the Great visited in 1698, Baden's golden age began. Austrian Emperor Franz II spent 31 successive summers here: Every year for 12 years before his death in 1835, the royal entourage moved from Vienna for the season. Later in the century, Emperor Franz Josef II was a regular visitor, becoming the inspiration for much of the regal trappings the city still sports. In Baden, Mozart composed his "Ave Verum"; Beethoven spent 15 summers here and wrote large sections of his Ninth Symphony and *Missa Solemnis* when he lived at Frauengasse 10; here Franz Grillparzer wrote his historical dramas; and Josef Lanner, both Johann Strausses (father and son), Carl Michael Ziehrer, and Karl Millöcker composed and directed many of their waltzes, marches, and operettas.

The loveliest spot in Baden, and for many the main reason for a visit, is the huge and beautiful **Kurpark,** where occasional outdoor public concerts still take place. Operetta is performed under the skies in the Summer Arena (the roof closes if it rains); in winter, it is performed in the Stadttheater. People sit quietly under the old trees or walk through the upper sections of the Kurpark for a view of the town from above. The old Kurhaus, now enlarged and renovated, incorporates a convention hall. The ornate **Casino**—with a bar, restaurant, and gambling rooms—still includes traces of its original 19th-century decor, but has been enlarged and overlaid with glitz that rivals Las Vegas. ✉ *Kurpark,* ☎ *02252/44496–0.* ⏲ *Daily from 1 PM, gambling daily from 3 PM.*

Music lovers will want to visit the **Beethoven House** (✉ Rathausgasse 10, ☎ 02252/86800–310). Admission is AS20, and hours are Tuesday–Friday 4–6, weekends and holidays 9–11 and 4–6. Children of all ages will enjoy the enchanting **Doll and Toy Museum** (✉ Erzherzog Rainer-Ring 23, ☎ 02252/41020). Admission is AS20, and the museum is open Tuesday–Friday 4–6, weekends and holidays 9–11 and 4–6.

One of the pleasures associated with Baden is getting there. You can reach the city directly from Vienna by bus or, far more fun, interurban streetcar, in about 50 minutes—the bus departs from the Ring directly opposite the Opera House; the streetcar departs from the Ring across from the Bristol Hotel. Both drop you in the center of Baden. By car from Vienna, travel south on Route A2, turning west at the junction of Route 305. It is possible, with advance planning, to go on to Mayerling and Heiligenstadt on post office buses (☎ 0222/711–01).

Dining and Lodging

$$$$ ✕🏨 **Grand Hotel Sauerhof.** "Schönbrunn yellow" marks this appealing country house that's been elegantly renovated, with rooms in old-Vienna style. The hotel caters heavily to seminars and group activities, but individual guests are not ignored, and accommodations are comfortable and modern. The hotel's Rauhenstein restaurant is excellent (try the beef fillet with mushrooms, or for dessert, the famous house crepes) if occasionally inconsistent. ✉ *Weilburgstr. 11–13, A–2500,* ☎ *02252/41251–0,* FAX *02252/48047. 88 rooms. Restaurant, bar, indoor pool, sauna, tennis court, exercise room. AE, DC, MC, V.*

$$$$ ✕🏨 **Schloss Weikersdorf.** You're in a restored renaissance castle, but just minutes away from the center of Baden. The setting on the edge of a vast public park offers bonuses of a rose garden and boating on the lake. Rooms and baths are luxuriously outfitted. ✉ *Schlossgasse 9–1, A-2500,* ☎ *02252/48301,* FAX *02252/48301–150. 78 rooms, plus 26 rooms in the annex. Restaurant, bar, indoor pool, sauna, tennis courts, bowling. AE, DC, MC, V.*

$$$–$$$$ ✕🏨 **Krainerhütte.** This friendly house, in typical Alpine style, with balconies and lots of natural wood, has been family-run since 1876. The location on the outskirts of town is ideal for relaxing or exploring the surrounding woods. Facilities are up-to-date, and the restaurant offers a choice of cozy rooms or an outdoor terrace along with international and Austrian cuisine, with fish and game from the hotel's own reserves. ✉ *Helenental, A–2500,* ☎ *02252/44511–0,* FAX *02252/44514. 60 rooms. Restaurant, indoor pool, sauna, tennis court. AE, MC, V. Closed mid-Jan.–early Feb.*

Mayerling

❼ *29 km (18 mi) west of Vienna, 11 km (7 mi) northwest of Baden.*

Scenic route 210 takes you through the quiet Helenental valley west of Baden to Mayerling, scene of a tragedy that is still impetuously discussed and disputed by the Austrian public, press, and historians at the slightest provocation as well as providing a torrid subject for movie-makers and novelists in many other parts of the world. On the snowy evening of January 28, 1889, the 30-year-old Habsburg heir, Crown Prince Rudolf, Emperor Franz Josef's only son, and his 17-year-old mistress, Baroness Marie Vetsera met a violent and untimely end at the emperor's hunting lodge at Mayerling. Most historians believe it was a suicide pact between two desperate lovers (the Pope had refused an annulment to Rudolf's own unhappy marriage). There are those, however, who feel Rudolf's pro-Hungarian political leanings might be a key to the tragedy. In an attempt to suppress the scandal—the full details are not known to this day—the baroness's body, propped up between two uncles, was smuggled back into the city by carriage (she was buried hastily in nearby Heiligenkreuz). The bereaved emperor had the hunting lodge where the suicide took place torn down and replaced with a rather nondescript Carmelite convent. Mayerling remains beautiful, haunted—and remote: the village is infrequently signposted.

Dining and Lodging

$$$$ ✕🏨 **Kronprinz Mayerling.** Close to both Mayerling and Heiligenkreuz, this stylish building set in a beautiful park has immaculate rooms, each with a whirlpool bath and balcony. The Kronprinz restaurant serves outstanding, adventuresome fare; each course is a concept unto itself, with inspiration coming from French and Chinese cuisine. Fish is particularly well handled, but you might find veal or lamb specialties offered. The associated Landgasthof Marienhof restaurant is simpler, cheaper, and generally far more crowded. ✉ *Mayerling 1, A–2534 Alland,* ☎ *02258/2378,* FAX *02258/2379–41. 28 rooms. Restaurant, sauna, tennis court, exercise room. AE.*

Heiligenkreuz

❽ *14 km (8¾ mi) northwest of Baden, 14 km (8¾ mi) west of Mödling.*

Slightly northeast of Mayerling, in the heart of the southern section of the Vienna Woods, is Heiligenkreuz, a magnificent Cistercian abbey with a famous Romanesque and Gothic church, founded in 1135 by Leopold III. The church itself is lofty and serene, with beautifully carved choir stalls (the Cistercians are a singing order) surmounted by busts of Cistercian saints. The great treasure here is the relic of the Cross which Leopold V is said to have brought back from his crusade in 1188. The cloisters are interesting for the Chapel of the Dead, where the brothers lie in state guarded by four gesticulating skeletons holding a candelabra. The chapter house contains the tombs of Babenberg rulers. ✉ *Heiligenkreuz 1,* ☎ *02258/2282.* 🎫 *AS35 (tours only).* ⏲ *Tours*

Mon.–Sat. 10, 11, 2, 3, 4 (summer only); Sun., hols., 11, 2, 3, 4 (summer only).

On a corner of the abbey grounds, follow the Baroque Stations of the Cross along chestnut and linden tree-lined paths. From Vienna, reach Heiligenkreuz by taking Route A21 southwest or via bus from Südtirolerplatz.

Dining and Lodging

$$$ ✕🏨 **Landgasthof Zur Linde.** In the heart of the Wienerwald, some 24 kilometers (15 miles) northwest of Mayerling, lies the small town of Laaben—equally distant (about 14 miles northwest of Mayerling) from Mayerling and Heiligenkreuz, in the shadow of the 2,900-foot Schöpfl Mountain. This charming, family-run country inn offers an excellent base from which to explore the countryside. Rooms are modest but complete and comfortable, with rustic decor. The popular restaurant, with its several wood-beamed rooms, sets the right atmosphere for international and regional cuisine, with seasonal specialties such as lamb, asparagus, and game featured. You might find roast pork marinated in apple cider or fresh local trout. ✉ *Hauptpl. 28, A-3053 Laaben,* ☎ *02774/8378–0,* FAX *02774/8378–20. 10 rooms. Restaurant. No credit cards. Closed Tues., Wed., mid-Feb.–Mar., and 2 wks in Nov.*

THE WALDVIERTEL

The "Forest District" north of the Danube and to the northwest of Vienna was long dormant, out of the mainstream and cut off from neighboring Czechoslovakia by a sealed border until 1990. Today, with the reopening of many crossing points, the Waldviertel has reawakened. Here, gentle hills bearing stands of tall pine and oak are interspersed with small farms and friendly country villages. The region can be seen in a couple of days, longer when you pause to explore the museums, castles, and other attractions. Zwettl and Raabs an der Thaya, where facilities are more modest and much less expensive than those of the major tourism routes, make good bases for discovering this area.

The main rail line from Vienna to Prague passes through the Waldviertel, making the region accessible by train. In addition, post office buses cover the area fairly well and with reasonable frequency. Bus hubs are Horn, Waidhofen, and Zwettl. An express bus service runs between Vienna and Heidenreichstein via Waidhofen an der Thaya.

If you're traveling by car, signs for Prague will head you in the right direction out of Vienna. At Stockerau take Route 4 to Horn, Route 38 west to Zwettl, an unnumbered road to Weitra, Route 41 to Gmünd and Schrems, Route 30 north to Heidenreichstein, Route 5 to Waidhofen an der Thaya, an unnumbered road via Gross Siegharts to Raabs an der Thaya, Route 30 to Riegersburg, and an unnumbered road to Hardegg. Return on Route 30 to Geras, Route 4 to Horn, Route 34 down the Kamp Valley past Langenlois, and Route 3 back to Vienna.

Kleinwetzdorf/Heldenberg

❾ *52 km (32½ mi) northwest of Vienna, 32 km (20 mi) southeast of Horn.*

The celebrated Austrian field marshal Joseph Wenzel Graf von Radetsky (1766–1858) is buried at Heldenberg near the tiny village of Kleinwetzdorf, in elegant but lugubrious surroundings. The great field marshal was instrumental in defeating Napoléon in 1814, thus saving the Habsburg crown for the young Francis Joseph II. His tomb, arranged for by a wealthy uniform supplier, is marked by an obelisk set in a park studded with dozens of larger-than-life busts of Austrian roy-

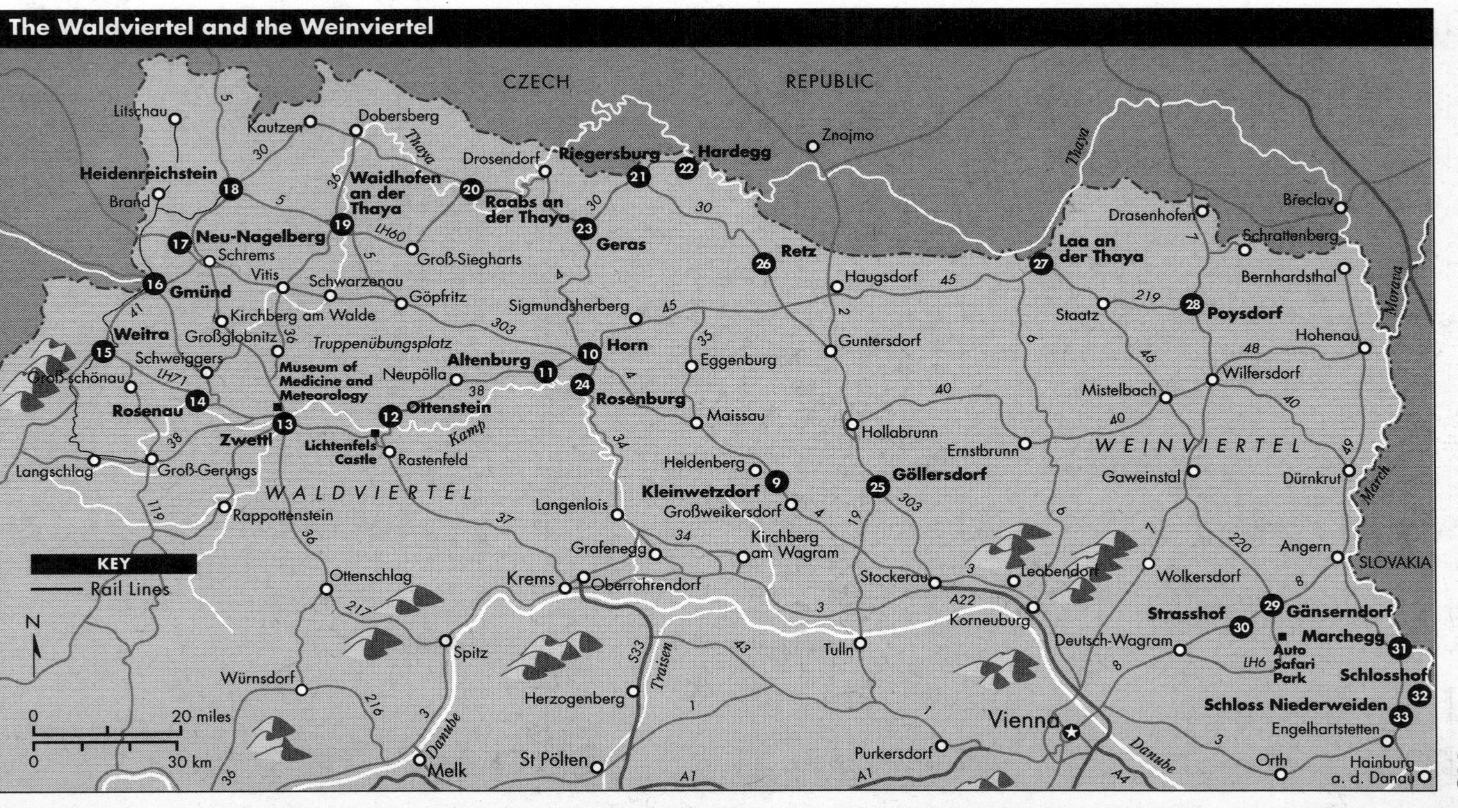
The Waldviertel and the Weinviertel
CZECH
REPUBLIC
Litschau
Kautzen
Dobersberg
Thaya
Drosendorf
Riegersburg
Hardegg
Znojmo
Heidenreichstein
Brand
Waidhofen an der Thaya
Raabs an der Thaya
Geras
Retz
Laa an der Thaya
Drasenhofen
Břeclav
Schrattenberg
Bernhardsthal
Neu-Nagelberg
Schrems
Groß-Siegharts
Vitis
Schwarzenau
Göpfritz
Gmünd
Kirchberg am Walde
Sigmundsherberg
Haugsdorf
Staatz
Poysdorf
Weitra
Großglobnitz
Truppenübungsplatz
Horn
Eggenburg
Guntersdorf
Hohenau
Morava
Schweiggers
Groß-schönau
Museum of Medicine and Meteorology
Altenburg
Neupölla
Rosenburg
Mistelbach
Wilfersdorf
Rosenau
Ottenstein
Maissau
Hollabrunn
Zwettl
Lichtenfels Castle
Rastenfeld
Kamp
Ernstbrunn
WEINVIERTEL
Langschlag
Groß-Gerungs
Heldenberg
Kleinwetzdorf
Göllersdorf
Gaweinstal
Dürnkrut
March
WALDVIERTEL
Großweikersdorf
Rappottenstein
Langenlois
Grafenegg
Kirchberg am Wagram
Angern
SLOVAKIA
KEY
Rail Lines
Ottenschlag
Krems
Oberrohrendorf
Stockerau
Leobendorf
Wolkersdorf
Strasshof
Gänserndorf
Korneuburg
Deutsch-Wagram
Marchegg
Auto Safari Park
Spitz
Tulln
Traisen
Schlosshof
N
Würnsdorf
Herzogenberg
Schloss Niederweiden
Engelhartstetten
Vienna
Danube
0
20 miles
0
30 km
Melk
St Pölten
Purkersdorf
Orth
Hainburg a. d. Danau

alty and nobility. Follow the marked path to the west back of the park past the memorial to young emperor Franz Josef II to reach the lion-guarded memorial to Radetzky's military campaigns in Italy and Hungary. The whole complex is a slighly eerie phantasmagoria—but historically fascinating. ✉ *Heldenberg 46,* ☎ *02956/2372.* 🎫 *Free.* ⏲ *Daily dawn–dusk.*

The small 17th-century Schloss Wetzdorf has a **Radetzky museum,** although of all the memorials to the field marshal, probably Johann Strauss father's "Radetzky March" is the best known. Half-hidden to the south of the castle is a free-standing arched gate surmounted with wonderful reclining lions. ✉ *Kleinwetzdorf 1,* ☎ *02956/2751.* 🎫 *Tour AS30, parking free.* ⏲ *Tour May–Oct., weekends and holidays at 2, 3, and 4.*

NEED A BREAK?

The **Schlosstaverne** in the Schloss Wetzdorf (☞ *above*) offers light snacks and basics such as Wiener schnitzel, coffee or a cooling drink (only open on weekends and holidays). The courtyard makes a delightful setting in good weather.

Dining and Lodging

$$–$$$ ✕🏨 **Restaurant Naderer.** A fine "food with a view" spot, the Naderer is located at the top of the hill above Maissau, 14 kilometers (9 miles) northwest of Kleinwetzdorf on Route 4. The cuisine is of a standard that draws guests from as far away as Vienna. You can expect the standards such as roast pork or chicken, but you'll also find excellent goose, duck, lamb and game in season. The cakes from the house kitchens are particularly good. Most of the excellent wines come from the surrounding vineyards. In summer, lunching on the terrace overlooking the valley can be a particularly pleasurable experience. Twelve hotel rooms are available for overnights. ✉ *Am Berg 44, A-3712 Maissau,* ☎ *02958/82334. 12 rooms with bath. AE, DC, MC, V.*

Horn

10 *81 km (50½ mi) northwest of Vienna.*

Horn lies at the eastern edge of the Waldviertel. Remnants of the impressive fortification walls with its watchtowers built in 1532 to defend against invading Turks are still obvious. Wander through the core of the old city, which dates from the 15th century. Note the painted Renaissance façade on the house (1583) at Kirchenplatz 3. The **St. Stephen's parish church** on the edge of the cemetery out of the center boasts a Gothic choir and late Gothic stone chancel. The Baroque **Piaristen church,** built in 1660, features a 1777 altar painting by the renowned regional artist Kremser Schmidt. The castle, started in the 1500s and completely rebuilt in the 18th century, sits at the edge of the large, attractive Schlosspark. Horn is host to an international chamber music festival in summer.

11 About 5 kilometers (3 miles) west of Horn, at **Altenburg** on Route 38, **Altenburg abbey** was built in 1144 and rebuilt in 1645–1740 after its destruction by the Swedes. The library and the frescoed translucent ceilings by the master artist Paul Troger are glorious. ✉ *Altenburg 1,* ☎ *02982/3451.* 🎫 *AS50 (tours only).* ⏲ *Daily; tours Easter–Nov. 1, daily at 10, 11, and 4, and Nov. 2–Easter by appointment.*

Almost 35 kilometers (21 miles) west of Altenburg on Route 38, the
12 castle at **Ottenstein,** now a hotel-restaurant, has a number of impressive reception rooms and parts dating to 1178. Ottenstein defied the invading Swedes in 1645 only to be devastated by the Russians in 1945. Sports enthusiasts will find boating and swimming in the reservoir-lake

and golf at Niedergrünbach. The ruined Lichtenfels castle nearby can be explored. ✉ *Ottenstein 1,* ☎ *02826/254.*

Zwettl

13 *125 km (78 mi) northwest of Vienna, 52 km (32½ mi) northwest of Krems, 49 km (30¾ mi) west of Horn.*

Zwettl lies in the heartland of the forest district. The town center, squeezed between a river bend, is attractive for its gabled houses and colorful pastel façades. The city wall, dating from the Middle Ages, still includes eight defensive towers. But Zwettl is best known for the vast **Cistercian abbey,** dating from 1138, about 2¼ kilometers (1½ miles) west of the town. The Zwettl abbey, perched above the Kamp River, was established as an outpost of the abbey at Heiligenkreuz in the Wienerwald (☞ Heiligenkreuz, *above*). The imposing south gate in the cloisters remains from the original edifice; the church with its massive Gothic choir was completed in 1348. Later renovations added the glorious Baroque touches, with the west wall crowned by a 292-foot tower. An international organ festival is held here annually from the end of June to the end of July. ☎ *02822/550–17.* *AS50.* *Tour May and June, Mon.–Sat. at 10, 11, 2, and 3, and Sun. at 11, 2, and 3; July–Sept. additional tour daily at 4.*

About 2 kilometers (1 mile) north of Zwettl on Route 36, at Dürnhof, a fascinating **Museum of Medicine and Meteorology** is housed in a cloister chapel built in 1294. Exhibits follow the development of medicine from earliest times to the present, and the courtyard garden of medicinal herbs adds another dimension to the history. ☎ *02822/53180.* *AS40.* *May–Oct., Tues.–Sun. 10–6.*

Dining and Lodging

$$ ✕ **Stiftsrestaurant.** Set within the Zwettl abbey, this spacious tavern complex serves good Austrian country fare such as grilled chicken and roast pork with bread dumplings and occasional regional specialties such as Waldviertel potato dumplings. The outstanding beer, fresh from the nearby brewery, alone is alone worth a stop, as are the wines, which come from the abbey's own cellars. ✉ *Stift Zwettl,* ☎ *02822/550–36. No credit cards. Closed Tues. and Nov.–Easter.*

$$ **Gasthof "Dichter Hamerling."** The cream-colored plain façade gives way to a relatively simple but modernized family-run hotel set somewhat to the east of the town center. Rooms are comfortable enough, and the buffet breakfast is ample. ✉ *Galgenbergstr. 3, A–3910,* ☎ *02822/54328,* FAX *02822/52344–85. 24 rooms with bath. Parking. No credit cards.*

Rosenau

14 *8 km (5 mi) west of Zwettl.*

Schloss Rosenau, with its prominent central tower, is an impressive Renaissance structure built in 1590 with later Baroque additions. The castle was ravaged by the Soviets in 1945, then rebuilt as a hotel and museum complex housing the unique **Freemasonry Museum** (Freimaurer-Museum). A secret room once used for lodge ceremonies was discovered during the renovations and is now part of the museum. Displays show the ties of Haydn and Mozart to freemasonry, and many exhibits are in English, reflecting the origins of the brotherhood. ☎ *02822/58221.* *AS45.* *Mid-Apr.–Oct., daily 9–5.*

Dining and Lodging

$$$–$$$$ ★ **Schloss Rosenau.** Set in an elegant castle, this small hotel offers country quiet and modern rooms furnished in period style. The wood-paneled restaurant is one of the best in the area, featuring garlic soup, bread soup, and lamb or game in season. In summer, food seems to taste even better on the sunny outdoor terrace, which overlooks great expanses of grain fields set about a jewel of a tiny castle. ✉ *A-3924,* ☎ *02822/58221,* FAX *02822/58222–8. 18 rooms. Restaurant, indoor pool, sauna, fishing. AE, DC, MC, V. Closed mid-Jan.–Feb.*

Weitra

15 *24 km (15 mi) northwest of Zwettl, 16 km (10 mi) southwest of Gmünd.*

The small town of Weitra, set along the main road of LH71, is renowned for its stunning ornate painted house façades (sgraffiti) dating from the 17th and 18th centuries. A charming small brewery has been in business here since 1321! And the tradition is well founded: In 1645, 33 Weitra citizens held the right to operate a brewery. At the local Brauhotel, you can even take a course in brewing. The domineering 15th-century defense **castle** with its Renaissance features is privately owned, but following extensive renovations in 1993 parts are now open to the public; the Rococo theater, ceremonial hall, the tower, and the extensive Schlosskeller with an exhibition on beer brewing are particularly worthwhile. This is the most westerly of the line of castles built to defend against possible invaders from the north. ☎ *02865/3311 or 02856/2998.* *AS60.* *Mid-May–late Oct., Wed.–Sun. 10–5.*

Dining and Lodging

$$$ **Brauhotel Weitra.** Riding on the town's tradition for beer brewing, this new hotel is tucked behind an ancient façade, blending well with the other buildings in the center. Rooms are comfortable and modern. The restaurant offers Austrian and regional standards plus some surprises, often based on the use of beer in cooking. The house mini-brewery keeps glasses filled, but wines are good, too. ✉ *Rathauspl. 6, A-3970,* ☎ *02856/2936–0,* FAX *02856/2936–222. 35 rooms. Restaurant, bar, sauna. No credit cards. Closed late Jan.–early Feb.*

Gmünd

16 *16 km (10 mi) north of Weitra, 55 km (34½ mi) northwest of Horn.*

The town of Gmünd was curiously divided in 1918 when the border with Czechoslovakia was established. The actual line passes through a few houses and backyards, but with the barbed-wire defenses removed, the border is now a harmless affair. The core of the old town remains in Austria, and is worth viewing for the painted façades (sgraffiti) around the main square. Adjacent to the square is the once-moated (private) castle which dates from the 16th century.

Railroad fans have a field day in Gmünd; the Czechs still use some steam locomotives for switching, and on the Austrian side Gmünd is one of the main points on the delightful narrow-gauge **Waldviertler Bahn** (☎ 02852/52588–365, 02852/51541, or 02812/228), which runs occasional steam excursions plus some regular services. The excursion runs generally include a club car with refreshments.

The **Naturpark Blockheide Gmünd-Eibenstein** nature park to the northeast of the town center, open free to the public all year, includes a geological open-air museum and a stone marking the 15th meridian east of Greenwich. No one knows the source of the huge granite boulders that adorn the park. ✉ *Grillensteiner Str.,* ☎ *02852/54964.*

17 Northwest of Schrems, a detour west from Route 30, on Route 303, leads to **Neu-Nagelberg,** pressed against the Czech border and a center of glass making since 1740. Among the operating glassworks you can visit to see how glass is made and blown is Glasstudio Zalto (✉ Neu-Nagelberg 58, ☎ 02859/7237-0). Another, Stölzle Kristall (✉ Hauptstr. 45, Alt-Nagelberg, ☎ 02859/7531-0), has a showroom and factory outlet.

Heidenreichstein

★ 18 *13 km (8¼ mi) north of Schrems, 51 ki (32 mi) northwest of Horn, 14 ki (9 mi) northwest of Waidhofen an der Thaya.*

The scenic route north from Schrems parallels the narrow-gauge railway to Heidenreichstein, noted for the massive moated **castle** with its corner towers, which has never been captured by enemy forces since it was built in the 15th century; some of the walls, 10 feet thick, went up in the 13th century. This is one of the most remarkable "water" castles in Austria. "Water"—or moated—castle were surrounded by a body of water (natural or artificial) for defense purposes whereas the "hill" castles used steep, often rocky and inaccessible, slopes for protection. The building is in remarkable condition, the best-preserved of all moated castles in Austria, and some of the rooms are furnished with pieces dating from the 15th and 16th centuries. ☎ *02862/52268.* *AS60 (tours only).* *Mid-Apr.–mid-Oct., Tues.–Sun. at 9, 10, 11, 2, 3, and 4.*

Waidhofen an der Thaya

19 *14 km (8¾ mi east of Heidenreichstein, 32 km (20 mi) north of Zwettl, 37 km (23¼ mi) northwest of Horn.*

Route 5 between Heidenreichstein and Waidhofen an der Thaya is particularly scenic. Waidhofen itself is a three-sided walled defense city typical of those of the 13th century. Fires destroyed much of the early character of the town, but the town square, rebuilt at the end of the 19th century, has a pleasing unity. The town is dominated by its Baroque parish church locally known as the "cathedral of the Thaya valley"; the Rococo chapel to Mary includes a Madonna of 1440 and distinguished portraits marking the Stations of the Cross. Outside the city walls, the **Bürgerspitalkapelle** has a side altar with a Gothic carved-wood relief of Madonna and child and 13 assistants, dating from about 1500.

Raabs an der Thaya

★ 20 *21 km (13 mi) northeast of Waidhofen an der Thaya, 42 km (26¼ mi) northwest of Horn.*

The Thaya River wanders leisurely thorough Raabs an der Thaya, an unusually attractive village watched over by an 11th-century castle perched dramatically on a rock outcropping and reflected in the river below. This was one of the chain of defensive castles through the Waldviertel region. The river is popular for fishing and swimming. ☎ *02846/365.* *AS50.* *June–Sept., weekends 10–5; call to confirm.*

The intriguing ruins of the Kollmitz castle to the southeast of Raabs can be explored, and a bit farther along are the ruins of Eibenstein castle, another link in the 16th- and 17th-century defense chain along the border with Bohemia.

Northeast of Raabs along Route 30 is the border town of Drosendorf, with a castle built in 1100 and an historic center typical of a small walled community. The encircling wall is virtually intact and complete with watchtowers.

Dining and Lodging

$$ ★ ✕ **Hotel Thaya.** A friendly, family-run hotel directly on the river, the Thaya offers comfortable, modern if slightly spartan rooms in the new annex. Rooms directly overlooking the river are the favorites. The restaurant prepares such solid local specialties as roast pork and veal. ✉ *Hauptstr. 14, A–3820,* ☎ *02846/202–0,* FAX *02846/202–20. 25 rooms. Restaurant, bar, beer garden, sauna, exercise room, dance club, parking. No credit cards.*

$$ **Pension Schlossblick.** This small modern pension has a homey atmosphere in its spacious lounge and cheery breakfast room. The rooms on the town side looking through the trees to the castle are the nicest. ✉ *Eduard Braith-Str. 7, A–3820,* ☎ *02846/437. 13 rooms. Restaurant, parking. No credit cards.*

Riegersburg

21 *28 km (17½ mi) east of Raabs, 33 km (20½ mi) north of Horn, 18½ km (11½ mi) northwest of Retz.*

The impressive **Schloss Riegersburg** was originally moated before the substantial edifice was given a Baroque makeover in 1731 and again virtually rebuilt after the Russians inflicted heavy damage in 1945. Note the window variations and the classic figures that ornament the roofline. The whole castle was renovated in 1992–93, highlighting the elegance of the public rooms and its period furnishings, now back in place. ☎ *02916/332.* *Tour AS85, combination ticket with Hardegg AS130.* *Apr.–June and Sept.–mid-Nov., daily 9–5; July and Aug., daily 9–7.*

22 **Hardegg,** about 6 kilometers (4 miles) east of Riegersburg on an unnumbered road, features a wonderfully eclectic **castle** that stands mightily on a rock promontory high above the Thaya River, watching over the Czech Republic. (The river midstream marks the boundary; as recently as 1990, the pedestrian bridge was unpassable, the border sealed, and Czech border defenses were concealed in the woods opposite.) The earliest parts of the castle date from 1140. The armory and armament collection, chapel, and the museum's exhibits on the emperor Maximilian in Mexico alone are worth a visit. In addition, the kitchen and other working rooms of the castle give a real feeling of the daily life of an earlier era. An English-speaking guide is available for small-group tours. ☎ *02949/8225.* *AS65, tour AS25.* *Apr.–June and Sept.–mid-Nov., daily 9–5; July and Aug., daily 9–6.*

Geras

23 *22 km (13¾ mi) north of Horn, 23 km (14½ mi) southeast of Raabs an der Thaya, 20 km (12½ mi) southwest of Hardegg.*

Another of the Waldviertel's great abbeys, the **Stift Geras,** is situated at Geras. Established in 1120, the impressive complex has had from its beginnings close ties to its agricultural surroundings. The abbey was given a glorious full-blown Baroque treatment in the course of rebuilding following a fire in 1730, including a translucent fresco by the noted Paul Troger in the 18th century Marble Hall, now often used for concerts. While the abbey still functions as a religious center, the complex is now also a noted school for arts and crafts. ✉ *Hauptstr. 1,* ☎

02912/345–289. AS50. Tour May–Oct., Tues.–Sat. at 10, 11, 2, 3, and 4; Sun. at 11, 2, 3, and 4.

Dining and Lodging

$$$ **Stiftsrestaurant und Hotel "Alter Schüttkasten."** A former granary outbuilding of the abbey has been turned into a modern hotel with all the amenities. Rooms are comfortable; those on the front look out over the fields toward the abbey. The restaurant offers seasonal specialties such as fish and game in addition to pork, beef and other regional standards. *Vorstadt 11, A–2093, 02912/332, FAX 02912/332-33. 26 rooms. Restaurant, bar, sauna, parking. DC.*

Kamptal

The gloriously scenic Kamp River valley (Kamptal), running from Rosenburg in the north some 30 kilometers (19 miles) south roughly to Hadersdorf am Kamp, technically belongs to the Waldviertel, though for the amount of wine produced here, it might as well be a part of the Weinviertel, the wine district to the east. The river, road, and railroad share the frequently narrow and twisting route which meanders some 25 kilometers (15½ miles) through the valley from Rosenburg south to Langenlois. The villages along the route—Gars am Kamp, Schönberg am Kamp, Zöbing, Strass, and Langenlois—are all known for excellent wines, mainly varietal whites. Strass in particular has become an active center of viticulture, and many vintners offer wine tastings. Castle ruins dot the hilltops above the woods and vineyards; the area has been populated since well before 900 BC. Scattered through the valley are some noted eateries and hotels; the best are reviewed below, listed under their particular village.

24 The massive defense castle at **Rosenburg** dates from 1200 and dominates the north entrance to the Kamptal Valley. Its features include the original jousting field as a forecourt and impressive reception rooms inside, where armor and other relics of the period are on display. Curious Renaissance balconies and small courtyards are incorporated into the design, although the variety in the 13 towers added in the 15th century is the touch that immediately catches the eye. *02982/2911. AS65, including tour; falconry demonstration AS65; combination ticket for tour and demonstration AS100. Apr.–mid-Nov., daily 9–5; falconry demonstration Apr.–Nov., daily at 11 and 3; tour begins 1 hr before demonstration.*

Dining and Lodging

GARS AM KAMP

$$–$$$ **Pfiffig.** The ruins of the ancient castle above Gars am Kamp provide the dramatic setting for this excellent family-run restaurant serving regional specialties and other choices such as *Tafelspitz* (delicate boiled beef). The rooms are elegant and offer a showcase for local artists. The excellent wines understandably come from the neighborhood. *A–3571 Gars am Kamp, 02985/30500. No credit cards. Closed Mon., Tues., and Jan.*

GRAFENEGG

$$–$$$ ★ **Schlosstaverne Mörwald.** Beyond the golden facade of this elegant tavern across from Schloss Grafenegg you'll find a friendly and welcoming atmosphere. Rooms are comfortably furnished in beiges and reds. The restaurant offers game in season and local cuisine with international touches. The strawberries in early summer taste even better outdoors on the sunny dining terrace. *A–3485 Haitzendorf, 02735/2616, FAX 02735/2298–6. 6 rooms. Restaurant. MC, V. Closed Jan. and Feb.*

KIRCHBERG AM WAGRAM

$$$$ ★ ✕ **Gut Oberstockstall.** A former cloister in Oberstockstall, just north of Kirchberg am Wagram, houses this country inn where the rustic setting indoors is charming and the courtyard garden idyllic in summer. Nearly all ingredients come from the farm itself, guaranteeing top freshness; preparation is individual and imaginative. The specialties of the house include beef, lamb, duck, game in season, and delicious desserts—all to the accompaniment of the house's own outstanding wines. ✉ *A–3740 Kirchberg am Wagram,* ☎ *02279/2335. No credit cards. Closed Sun.–Tues.; mid-Dec.–Feb.; and last 2 wks of Aug.*

LANGENLOIS

$–$$ ✕ **Brundlmayer.** This country Heuriger in the center of Langenlois offers outstanding wines from one of Austria's top vintners, as well as a tasty hot-and-cold buffet, all in an indoor rustic setting, or outdoors in the Renaissance courtyard. The simple but delicious fare might include variations on Schinkenfleckerl, the popular dish of baked ham and noodles, goat cheese, or dried, lightly-smoked ham. ✉ *Walterstr. 14, A–3550 Langenlois,* ☎ *02734/2883. No credit cards. Closed Mon.–Wed. and mid-Dec.–early Mar.*

Route 34 takes you through more vineyards to Kollersdorf, where Route 3 east will return you to Vienna.

THE WEINVIERTEL

Vines have a tendency to thrive in beautiful surroundings and, as attractive buildings and towns often develop close to vineyards, a journey through any wine region can be an alluring prospect. Luckily, Austria has been largely neglected by the "experts," and its deliciously fresh wines form an ideal treasure trove to reward those who enjoy drinking wine and dislike the all-too-frequent nonsense that goes with it. That's especially the case with the rustic and delightful "Wine District," the rolling countryside north of Vienna, which earns its name from the terrain and climate of the region, ideal for the cultivation of wine.

The Weinviertel is bounded by the Danube on the south, the Thaya River and the reopened Czech border on the north, the March River and Slovakia to the east. No well-defined line separates the Weinviertel from the Waldviertel to the west; the Kamp River valley, officially part of the Waldviertel, is an important wine region. Whether wine, crops, or dairying, this is farming country, its broad expanses of vineyards and farmlands broken by patches of forest and neat villages. A tour by car, just for the scenery, can be made in a day; you may want two or three days to savor the region and its wines—these are generally on the medium-dry side. Don't expect to find here the elegant facilities found elsewhere in Austria; prices are low by any standard, and village restaurants and accommodations are mainly *Gasthäuser* that meet local needs. This means that you'll rub shoulders over a glass of wine or a beer with country folk.

Göllersdorf

㉕ *10 km (6¼ miles) north of Stockerau West interchange on Rte. 303/E59.*

The rolling hills and agricultural lands of the southwest Weinviertel around Hollabrunn offer little excitement other than panoramas and scenic pleasures, but one exception is the **Schloss Schönborn** about 2 kilometers (1¼ mile:south of Göllersdorf. The castle was laid out in 1712 by that master of Baroque architecture, Johann Lukas von Hildebrandt. Today the castle is in private hands, but the harmony of design can be appreciated from the outside. The parish church in Göllersdorf is also a Baroque Hildebrandt design of 1740 overlaid on a Gothic structure dating to the mid-1400s.

Retz

★ 26 *70 km (43¾ mi) north of Vienna, 29 km (18¼ mi) northeast of Horn, 13 km (8¼ mi) southeast of Hardegg.*

Retz, at the northwest corner of the Weinviertel, is a charming town with an impressive rectangular central square formed by buildings mainly dating to the 15th century. Retz is best known for its red wines. Here you can tour **Austria's largest wine cellar,** tunneled 65 feet under the town, and at the same time taste wines of the area. Some of the tunnels go back to the 13th century, and at the end of the 15th century each citizen was permitted to deal in wines and was entitled to storage space in the town cellars. Efforts to use the cellars for armaments production during World War II failed because of the 88% humidity. The temperature remains constant at 8°C–10°C (47°F–50°F). Entrance to the cellars is at the Rathauskeller. ☎ *02942/2700.* *Tour AS70.* *Tour Mon.–Sat. at 10:30 and 2, Sun. at 10:30, 2, and 4; call to confirm tour times.*

Take time to explore Retz's tiny streets leading from the town square; the oldest buildings and the wall and gate tower defenses survived destruction by the Swedish armies in 1645 during the Thirty Years' War. The Dominican church (1295) at the southwest corner of the square survived, and it is interesting for its long, narrow design. The pastel Biedermeier façades along with the sgraffiti add appeal to the square, which is further marked by the impressive city hall with its massive Gothic tower in the center.

Dining and Lodging

$$$$ ✕ **Althof Retz/Hotel Burghof.** A new hotel has been tucked into an ancient estate building just off the town square. Take your choice of the upscale Hotel Burghof or the slightly less expensive Althof, which also serves as a training hotel. Both are done in whites and light wood. Rooms are modern, comfortable and with all facilities. The restaurant has been less successful, but the standards and regional specialties are fine. The excellent wines naturally come mainly from the area. ✉ *Althofgasse 14, A–2070,* ☎ *02942/3711–0,* FAX *02942/3711–55. 65 rooms. Restaurant, parking. No credit cards.*

Laa an der Thaya

27 *65 km (40¾ mi) north of Vienna, 39 km (24¼ mi) east of Retz, 26 km (16¼ mi) northwest of Mistelbach.*

From 1948 until about 1990, Laa an der Thaya, was a town isolated by the Cold War, directly bordering then–Czechoslovakia. Laa is considerably livelier now that the border is open. (As long as you have your passport with you, you can cross into the Czech Republic and return without complication.) The town's huge central square is adorned with a massive neo-Gothic city hall, in stark contrast to the low, colorful buildings that form the square. If you're traveling from Retz to Laa an der Thaya, retrace your way south on Route 30 to Route 45.

Laa boasts a **Beer Museum,** located in the town fortress, that traces the history of beer (the nearby Hubertus brewery has been in business since 1454) and maintains an imposing collection of beer bottles. ☎ *02522/2501–29.* *AS20.* *May–Sept., weekends and holidays 2–4.*

Dining

$$ ★ ✕ **Restaurant Weiler.** Light woods and country accessories set the tone in this family-run restaurant, and in summer dinner is served in the outdoor garden. Try the delicate cream of garlic soup or the house specialty, game in season. For dessert, the delicious cakes of the house are temptingly displayed in a showcase. ✉ *Staatsbahnstr. 60,* ☏ *02522/379–2379. No credit cards. Closed Mon., 2 wks in Feb., and July. No dinner Sun.*

Poysdorf

28 *61 km (38¼ mi) north of Vienna, 22 km (13¾ mi) southeast of Laa an der Thaya.*

Poysdorf is considered by many the capital of the Weinviertel. Winemaking here goes back to the 14th century. Poysdorf vintages, mainly whites, rank with the best Austria has to offer. Narrow paths known as *"Kellergassen"* ("cellar streets") on the northern outskirts are lined with wine cellars set into and under the hills. A festival in early September marks the annual harvest. At the wine market in the center of town, you can taste as well as buy (✉ Singerstr. 2); the market is open Monday–Thursday 8–5, Friday 8–6, and weekends and holidays 10–noon and 2–6. The town museum includes a section on viticulture and wine-making. ✉ *Brunner Str. 9,* ☏ *02552/2200–17.* *AS40.* ⏲ *Easter–Oct., Mon.–Wed. 9–noon and 1–5; call to confirm.*

Dining

MISTELBACH

$$–$$$ ★ ✕ **Zur Linde.** This friendly family-run restaurant with rustic decor 16 kilometers (10 miles) south of Poysdorf is setting higher standards for such traditional fare as roast pork, stuffed breast of veal, flank steak, and fresh game in season. Desserts are excellent; try the extraordinary *Apfelstrudel.* A major attraction here is the remarkable range of wines from the neighborhood at altogether reasonable prices. ✉ *Bahnhofstr. 49, A–2130 Mistelbach,* ☏ *02572/2409. AE, DC, MC, V. Closed Mon.; late Jan.–mid-Feb., and late July–mid-Aug. No dinner Sun.*

POYSDORF

$$ ✕ **Gasthaus Schreiber.** Choose the shaded garden under huge trees or the country rustic decor indoors. The typical Austrian fare—roast pork, stuffed breast of veal, boiled beef, filet steak with garlic—is commendable, as is the house-made ice cream. The wine card lists more than 60 area labels. ✉ *Bahnstr. 2, A–2170,* ☏ *02552/2348. No credit cards. Closed Tues. and late Jan.–mid-Feb. No dinner Mon.*

Gänserndorf

29 *30 km (18¾ mi) northeast of Vienna.*

Three kilometers (2 miles) south of Gänserndorf, the **Safari-Park und Abenteuerpark** (Safari Park and Adventure Park) allows visitors to drive through re-created natural habitats of live wild animals, many of which (lions and tigers) are hardly indigenous to Austria. The adventure takes five to six hours, allowing time for the petting zoo and the extra animal shows, which start every half hour. For those without a car, a safari bus leaves for the circuit every hour. ✉ *Siebenbrunner Str.,* ☏ *02282/70261–0,* FAX *02282/70261–27.* *AS162.* ⏲ *Palm Sun.–Oct., weekdays 9:30–4, weekends and holidays 9–4:30.*

Strasshof

30 *3 km (2 mi) southwest of Gänserndorf.*

The **Heizhaus** north of Strasshof is a fascinating private collection of dozens of steam locomotives and railroad cars stored in a vast engine house. Enthusiasts have painstakingly rebuilt and restored many of the engines; steam locomotives are up and running on the first Sunday of each month. The complex includes transfer table, water towers, and coaling station, and visitors can climb around among many of the locomotives awaiting restoration. The collection includes—at least for the time being—many of the operative locomotives from the Technical Museum in Vienna, now closed for extensive renovations. ✉ *Sillerstr. 123,* ☎ *02287/3027.* *AS60, steam days AS70, including parking and tour.* ⏲ *Mid-Apr.–Oct., Sun. and holidays 10–4.*

The area to the north of Gänserndorf includes one of Austria's few gas and oil fields, where operating pumps patiently pull up crude to be piped to the refinery about 20 kilometers (12½ miles) south. Underground, exhausted gas wells serve as natural storage tanks for gas coming to Western Europe from Russia.

Dining

$$$$ ✕ **Marchfelderhof.** Located in nearby Deutsch Wagram, this sprawling complex, with its eclectic series of rooms bountiously decorated with everything from antiques to hunting trophies, has a reputation for excess in the food department as well. The menu's standards—Wiener schnitzel, roast pork, lamb—are more successful than the more expensive efforts at innovation. Deutsch Wagram is 12 kilometers (7 miles) southwest of Gänserndorf on Route 8, 17 kilometers (11 miles) northeast of Vienna on Route 8. ✉ *Bockfliesser Str. 31, A–2232 Deutsch Wagram,* ☎ *02247/2243–0. AE, DC, MC, V. Closed Mon. and late Dec.–early Feb.*

Marchegg

31 *11 ki (7 mi) southeast of Gänserndorf.*

The tiny corner of the lower Weinviertel to the southeast of Gänserndorf is known as the Marchfeld, for the fields stretching east to the March River, forming the border with Slovakia. In this region—known as the granary of Austria—three elegant Baroque castles in the area are worth a visit; all have been totally renovated in recent years and given over to changing annual exhibits, concerts, and other public activities. These country estates have lost none of their gracious charm over the centuries. The northernmost of the group is the **castle** at Marchegg, the oldest parts dating to 1268. What you see today is the Baroque overlay added in 1733 to the basic building of the middle ages. The castle now houses a hunting museum. To reach Marchegg from Gänserndorf, take Route 8a 6 kilometers (4 miles) east to Route 49, then Route 49 10 kilometers (6 miles) south. ☎ *02285/224.* *AS30.* ⏲ *Mid-Mar.–Nov., Tues.–Sun. 9–noon and 1–5.*

32 The castle at **Schlosshof** is a true Baroque gem, a product of that master designer and architect Johann Lukas von Hildebrandt, who in 1732 reconstructed the four-sided castle into an elegant U-shaped building, opening up the eastern side to a marvelous Baroque formal garden that gives way toward the river. The famed Italian painter Canaletto captured the view before the reconstruction. The castle—once owned by Empress Maria Theresa—is now used for changing annual exhibits, but you can walk the grounds without paying admission. The castle is about 8 kilometers (5 miles) south of Marchegg. ☎ *02285/6580.* *AS50, tour AS20, combination ticket with Schloss Niederweiden AS80.* ⏲ *Apr.–Oct., daily 10–5.*

33 **Schloss Niederweiden,** about 4 kilometers (2½ miles) southwest of Schlosshof and north of Engelhartstetten, was designed as a hunting lodge and built in 1694 by that other master of the Baroque, Fischer von Erlach. This jewel was subsequently owned by Prince Eugene and Empress Maria Theresa, who added a second floor and the mansard roofs. Annual exhibits now take place here in summer, and in a vinothek you can sample the wines of the surrounding area. ☎ *02214/2803.* 🎫 *AS50, tour AS20, combination ticket with Schlosshof AS80.* ⏲ *Apr.–Oct., daily 10–5; Vinotek weekends and holidays 10–6.*

SIDE TRIPS FROM VIENNA A TO Z

Arriving and Departing

By Car

The autobahn A1 traverses the Wienerwald in the west; the A2 autobahn runs through the edge of the Wienerwald to the south. The A4 autobahn is a quick way to reach the Carnuntum region. The Waldviertel and Weinviertel are accessed by major highways but not autobahns.

By Plane

Vienna's Schwechat airport serves the surrounding region as well.

By Train

The main east–west train line cuts through the Wienerwald; the main north–south line out of Vienna traverses the eastern edge of the Wienerwald. The main line to Prague and onward runs through the Waldviertel. Train service in the Weinviertel is regular to Mistelbach, irregular after that. The rail line east out of Vienna to the border town Wolfstal cuts through the Carnuntum region. The line to the north of the Danube to Bratislava runs through the middle of the Marchfeld.

Getting Around

By Bus

Buses are a good possibility for getting around, although if you're not driving, a combination of bus and train is probably a better answer in many cases. Frequent scheduled bus service runs between Vienna and Baden, departing from across from the Opera House in Vienna to the center of Baden. Connections are available to other towns in the area. Bus service runs between Vienna and Carnuntum–Petronell, and on to Hainburg. Service to the Waldviertel is less frequent, but is available between Vienna and Horn, Zwettl, Waidhofen, and Raabs an der Thaya. From these points, you can get buses to other parts of the Waldviertel. An express bus service runs between Vienna and Heidenreichstein via Waidhofen an der Thaya. In the Weinviertel, bus service is fairly good between Vienna and Mistelbach, Laa an der Thaya, and Poysdorf.

By Car

Driving through these regions is by far the best way to see them, since you can wander the byways and stop whenever and wherever you like. Roads are good and generally well marked. To explore the Vienna Woods, from Vienna head for Liesing (23rd District), then take Wiener Strasse to Perchtoldsdorf; from there, follow the signs south to Mödling and Baden. From Baden, take Route 210 (marked HELENENTAL) to Mayerling and on to Alland; return to Vienna via Route 11, stopping in Heiligenkreuz en route.

Carnuntum–Petronell is easy to reach: from Vienna, simply follow signs to AIRPORT/BRATISLAVA (A4). Leave the divided highway for the more scenic

Route 9, which will be marked to Hainburg. At Petronell, you will have to take a sharp left off the bypass road, but signs are clear for the Roman ruins (Carnuntum), as they are for the other destinations in the region.

For the Waldviertel, signs for Prague will head you in the right direction out of Vienna. At Stockerau take Route 4 to Horn, Route 38 west to Zwettl, an unnumbered road to Weitra, Route 41 to Gmünd and Schrems, Route 30 north to Heidenreichstein, Route 5 to Waidhofen an der Thaya, an unnumbered road via Gross Siegharts to Raabs an der Thaya, Route 30 to Riegersburg, and an unnumbered road to Hardegg. Return on Route 30 to Geras, Route 4 to Horn, Route 34 down the Kamp valley past Langenlois, and Route 3 back to Vienna. If you're headed out of Vienna toward Langenlois and the lower Kamp Valley, follow signs to Krems; the turnoff onto Route 3 at Stockerau West is a bit tricky.

You've a choice of routes when heading out to the Weinviertel. One is to head out of Vienna to Stockerau on Route 3 or the autobahn A22/E49/E59, following the signs to Prague. After Stockerau, turn north on Route 303 to beyond Hollabrunn, then Routes 2 and 30 to Retz. From Retz, backtrack on Route 30 to Route 45 and head east to Laa an der Thaya. Then follow Route 46 to Staatz, Route 219 to Poysdorf, Route 7/E461 south beyond Gaweinstal, Route 220 to Gänserndorf, and Route 8 back to Vienna. The alternative is to take Route 7/E461 from Vienna/Floridsdorf north via Wolkersdorf; beyond Gaweinstal there's a choice of routes that will bring you to Mistelbach and on to Laa an der Thaya, or to Poysdorf.

By Train

Take the interurban train between Vienna and Baden for a delightful variation on the car or bus routine. Local trains on the Westbahn (main east–west line) will drop you off at stations in the Wienerwald, but connections can be tricky unless you plan on an "out-and-back" excursion.

The suburban trains (*Schnellbahn*) running from Wien-Mitte (Landstrasser Hauptstrasse) stop at Petronell, with service about once an hour. Carnuntum is about a 10-minute walk from the Petronell station. Trains go on to Hainburg, stopping at Bad Deutsch-Altenburg.

The main rail line from Vienna to Prague passes through the Waldviertel, making the region accessible by train, but you'll need a bus connection to reach the smaller towns.

Train service into the Weinviertel is fairly good but selective in the destinations you can reach on a direct trip. The suburban express line (*Schnellbahn*) runs between Vienna and Mistelbach, and to Gänserndorf and beyond to Bernhardsthal on the Czech border.

Contacts and Resources

Bicycle Rentals

The best bicycling territories in the regions surrounding Vienna are the Weinviertel, the Carnuntum–Petronell area and the Marchfeld. Larger towns have shops that rent bicycles, as do the key rail stations, but demand is great, so reserve in advance. The Lower Austrian information office (✉ Heidenschuss 2, A-1010 Vienna, ☎ 01/533–3114–0) can assist.

Car Rentals

Cars can be rented from all leading companies at the Vienna airport (☞ Vienna A to Z *in* Chapter 2) or in Baden, from Autoverleih Buchbinder (☎ 02252/48693) or Autoverleih Schmidt (☎ 02252/47047).

Emergencies

Police, ☏ 133, **fire,** ☏ 122. For **ambulance** or medical emergency, ☏ 144.

Guided Tours

The Wienerwald is one of the standard routes offered by the sightseeing-bus tour operators in Vienna, and it usually includes a boat ride through the "underground sea" grotto near Mödling. For details, check with your hotel or with **Cityrama** (☏ 01/534–13–12), **Vienna Sightseeing Tours** (☏ 01/712–4683–0), or **CityTouring Vienna** (☏ 01/894–1417–0). These short tours give only a quick taste of the region; if you have more time, you'll want to investigate further.

With the opening of the Czech and Slovak republics, more tours may be offered to the Waldviertel and Weinviertel regions of Lower Austria, but for now this is one area you'll probably have to explore on your own.

Visitor Information

Get information in Vienna before you start out, at the tourist office of Lower Austria (✉ Heidenschuss 2, ☏ 01/533–3114–0, FAX 01/535–0319). There are several helpful regional tourist offices. **Wienerwald** (✉ Hauptpl. 11, A–3002 Purkersdorf, ☏ 02231/2176, FAX 02231/5510). **March-Donauland** (✉ Hauptpl. 4, A-2405 Bad Deutsch–Altenburg, ☏ 02165/64820, FAX 02165/65322). **Waldviertel** (✉ Gartenstr. 32, A–3910 Zwettl, ☏ 02822/54109, FAX 02822/54144). **Weinviertel** (✉ Liechtensteinstr. 1, A-2170 Poysdorf, ☏ 02552/3515, FAX 02552/3715).

Local tourist offices are generally open weekdays. Here are the offices for the Wienerwald region. **Perchtoldsdorf** (☏ 01/869–7634–34). **Mödling** (✉ Elisabethstr. 2, ☏ 02236/26727, FAX 02236/41632). **Gumpoldskirchen** (✉ Schrannenpl. 1, ☏ 02252/62101–0). **Baden** (✉ Hauptpl. 2, ☏ 02252/44531–57, FAX 02252/80733).

The Waldviertel district has numerous tourist offices. **Gars am Kamp** (✉ Hauptpl. 82, ☏ 02985/2680). **Horn** (✉ Wiener Str. 4, ☏ 02982/2372). **Zwettl** (✉ Dreifaltigkeitspl. 1, ☏ 02822/52233). **Gmünd** (✉ Stadtpl. 19, ☏ 02852/53212, FAX 02852/54713). **Waidhofen an der Thaya** (✉ Hauptpl. 1, ☏ 02842/503–17). **Raabs an der Thaya** (✉ Hauptstr. 25, ☏ 02846/365–0, FAX 02846/365–21).

The Weinviertel region has several tourist centers. **Retz** (✉ Hauptpl. 30, ☏ 02942/2700). **Laa an der Thaya** (✉ Rathaus, ☏ 02522/2501–0). **Mistelbach** (✉ Hauptpl. 6, ☏ 02572/2515–248). **Poysdorf** (✉ Singergasse 2, ☏ 02552/2200–17). **Gänserndorf** (✉ Rathauspl. 1, ☏ 02282/2651–0).

4 Eastern Austria

Burgenland, Graz, and the Styrian Wine Country

Despite its proximity to vibrant Vienna, Eastern Austria offers rustic pleasures and simple treasures: the sight of a stork alighting on the chimney atop a Mother Goose house; an evening filled with the haunting sounds of Gypsy music; vistas of lush vineyards; and the city of Graz, whose preserved Old Town is a time-warped marvel. In Burgenland, discover vast Lake Neusiedl, so shallow you can wade across it, and Eisenstadt, alive with the sound of Joseph Haydn's celebrated music.

By Earl Steinbicker

Updated by Willibald Picard

NO PART OF THE NATION offers a greater range of scenery than the area loosely defined as Eastern Austria, yet, despite its proximity to Vienna, it is largely overlooked by foreign tourists. Not that the region lacks for visitors—long a favorite of Austrians, it is now becoming increasingly popular with Hungarians and other Eastern Europeans as border restrictions are relaxed. Accordingly, most of the visitors are cost-conscious and demand strict value for their money, ensuring that prices will remain lower here than in other parts of the country for some time.

There are no singularly great sights in the region—no Schönbrunn Palace, no Salzburg, no not-to-be-missed five-star attractions; still, the aggregate of worthwhile sights is most impressive. You'll find a largely unspoiled land of lakes, farms, castles, villages, and vineyards. It's also a sports-lover's paradise and is rich in history, with a distinguished musical past and—yes—one genuine city, Graz, whose sophistication and beauty may surprise you. In short, this is an ideal destination for experienced travelers who have already explored Vienna, Salzburg, the Tirol, and other better-known parts of Austria. It is a place to relax and mingle with Austrians who have not yet been overwhelmed by mass tourism.

Eastern Austria, as it is defined here, consists of Burgenland, most of Styria (Steiermark), and a small section of Lower Austria (Niederösterreich)—three distinct provinces with little in common. The geography varies from haunting steppes and the mysterious Lake Neusiedl in the east to the low, forested mountains of the south; the industrial valleys of the center and west; and the more rugged mountains of the north, where Austrian skiing began. Culturally, Eastern Austria is strongly influenced by neighboring Hungary and Slovenia, especially in its earthy and flavorful cuisines. Along with hearty food, the region is noted for its wines, many of which never travel beyond the borders.

We begin with Burgenland, intriguing both for its flatness and for the shallow Lake Neusiedl, with its reed-lined shore forming a natural nature preserve. Storks come in the thousands to feed in the lake and stork families, in turn, obligingly nest atop nearby chimneys—allegedly bringing luck to the household below (and assuring travelers of some great photos). Off to the east, the lake gives way to the vast Hungarian plain, interrupted by occasional thatch-roofed farmhouses and picturesque pole-and-pail wells. Music lovers will want to make the pilgrimage to Eisenstadt, where the great composer Joseph Haydn (1732–1809) was in the employ of Prince Esterházy. The impressive Esterházy castle stands as it did in Haydn's time, with its spacious theater/auditorium in which Haydn conducted his own operas and orchestral works almost nightly for the prince's entertainment.

The route from Burgenland southwest to Graz achieves an end-around run, circling the eastern tail of the Alps thorugh a territory marked by monumental defensive castles built to ward off invaders from the east. Graz, Austria's second largest city, boasts one of Europe's best preserved Renaissance town centers, dating to an era when Graz, not Vienna, was the capital. The compact pedestrian zone that forms the city core sets imaginations on fire, with eye-catching discoveries around every corner. History notwithstanding, the city today is a pulsating metropolis, a surprise even to many Austrians. North out of Styria offers the chance to visit one of Europe's oldest and still-revered religious pilgrimage sites at Mariazell. The dramatic onward route northward can be accomplished by rail or road; the latter climbs to above 3,000 feet at Annaberg in a series of over a dozen hairpin turns. The easier route to Vienna via the

Semmering pass achieves the same elevation and also offers some magnificent panoramas, including the snow-capped Schneeberg.

Pleasures and Pastimes

Dining

When choosing a restaurant, keep in mind that each province has its own cooking style. In Burgenland, the local Pannonian cooking, strongly influenced by neighboring Hungary, features such spicy dishes as *gulyas* (goulash) flavored with paprika. You'll also find fish from Lake Neusiedl, goose, game, and an abundance of fresh, local vegetables. Styria, bordering on Slovenia (formerly northern Yugoslavia), has a hearty cuisine with Serbian overtones; a typical dish is *Steirisches Brathuhn* (roast chicken turned on a spit), and *Kernöl,* a strange but tasty greenish-black pumpkinseed oil, is used as a dressing. Such Balkan specialties as *cevapcici* (spicy pan-fried sausages) are also often found on Styrian menus. You are most likely to encounter the more urbane Viennese cooking in Lower Austria, where you can get Wiener schnitzel nearly everywhere.

Eastern Austria is also **wine** country. Outstanding white wines predominate, although there are increasingly excellent reds and rosés as well. Burgenland's vineyards, mostly around Lake Neusiedl, produce wines that tend to be slightly less dry, with perhaps the best examples coming from the village of Rust and the areas around Donnerskirchen, Purbach, and Jois. Some of the dessert wines (Spätlese, Eiswein) are extraordinary, and all Burgenland wines are gaining a reputation for high quality. Many vintners happily share samples of their wares and will provide bread and cheese as accompaniment. In Styria, the wines from south of Graz along the Slovenian border and near Leibnitz are superb, especially the tangy Schlilcher rosé (☞ Wines, *below*).

Many of the restaurants listed in the chapter are actually country inns that provide overnight accommodations as well as meals, as noted in the reviews. Restaurant prices include taxes and a service charge, but it is customary to give the waiter an additional tip of 5%, a bit more in the nobler restaurants of Graz.

CATEGORY	COST*
$$$$	over AS500
$$$	AS300–AS500
$$	AS200–AS300
$	under AS200

**per person for a typical three-course meal, excluding drinks and additional tip*

The Great Outdoors

BOATING

All kinds of small craft—rowboats, pedal boats, electric boats, and sailboats—can be rented along the shores of **Lake Neusiedl,** by the hour or by the day. Though shallow, the lake can be treacherous, and less experienced sailors are warned against gusts and storms, which can come up suddenly.

HIKING

Eastern Austria is prime hiking country, and most tourist regions have marked trails. You'll need a local hiking map (*Wanderkarte*), usually for sale at the town's tourist office—whose staff can also suggest short rambles in the vicinity. Some particularly good places for walks are around **Lake Neusiedl** and **Güssing** in Burgenland; in the **Mur Valley** of Styria, especially the Bärenschützklamm at **Mixnitz**; around **Mariazell**; and atop the **Schneeberg, Rax** and **Semmering** in Lower Austria.

For the truly ambitious, several long-distance trails cut through this region, among them the **Nordalpen-Weitwanderweg** past the Raxalpe to Rust and the **Oststeiermärkischer Hauptwanderweg** from western Austria to Riegersburg. There's no need to carry either food or a tent, because you stay overnight in staffed huts. Camping is strongly discouraged for both safety and environmental reasons.

HORSEBACK RIDING

The *puszta* (steppe) known as the *Seewinkel* to the east of **Lake Neusiedl** is a perfect place for riding (*Reiten*), and horses (*Pferde*) can be hired in several villages. Ask at the local tourist office. Weekends are particularly popular, so book your steed well in advance.

SKIING

When you think of Austrian skiing, you naturally think of western and central Austria. The east has neither the tall mountains nor the highly developed facilities of other parts of the country, yet real Alpine skiing in Austria first began around **Mürzzuschlag,** in Styria. The town is still popular with Viennese skiers and has a fine museum of the sport's history. In the nearby regions of **Schneeberg, Rax,** and **Semmering,** all in Lower Austria, there's pleasant (if not too exciting) skiing within easy reach of Vienna. The gentler slopes near **Mariazell,** in Styria, are popular with families. All the eastern ski areas share a casual gemütlichkeit. The resorts mentioned have cross-country as well as downhill skiing and plenty of lifts, hotels, inns, restaurants, and even, occasionally, nightlife. Contact regional tourist offices for more details.

WATER SPORTS

The best swimming on Lake Neusiedl is at **Podersdorf,** whose 5-kilometer- (3-mile-) long beach (*Strand*) is virtually free of reeds. Neusiedl am See and Rust also have good beaches. Most towns in Eastern Austria have at least one public indoor swimming pool (*Hallenbad*), and many have outdoor pools (*Freibäder*). Ask at the local tourist office about conditions of use and fees. Lake Neusiedl is also excellent for windsurfing. You can take lessons and rent sailboards at most lakeside villages.

Lodging

Accommodations in Eastern Austria range from luxury city hotels to mountain and lakeside resorts to castles and romantic country inns, and all are substantially lower in price than those in Vienna or Salzburg. Every town and village also has simpler *Gasthäuser,* which give good value as long as you don't expect a private bath. Accommodations in private homes are cheaper still. These bargains are usually identified by signs reading ZIMMER FREI (room available) or FRÜHSTÜCKSPENSION (bed-and-breakfast).

The tourist information office (Fremdenverkehrsverein, Fremdenverkehrsamt, or Gästeinformation) in virtually every town can usually find you a decent place to sleep if you haven't made a reservation (☞ Visitor Information *in* Eastern Austria A to Z, *below*). Hotel room rates include taxes and service, and usually breakfast—although you should always ask about the latter.

CATEGORY	COST*
$$$$	over AS2,000
$$$	AS1,000–AS2,000
$$	AS600–AS1,000
$	under AS600

**All prices are for a standard double room for two, including taxes and service charge.*

Wines

Eastern Austria vies with Lower Austria as source of the country's best wines. In both Burgenland and Styria, you can travel among villages and sample local vintages on "wine routes." Burgenland offers reds—the Blauer Burgunder and slightly heavier Blaufränkisch can be outstanding; whites, ranging from the lighter Grüner Veltliner and Welschriesling to spicier Müller-Thurgau and Traminers; and full-fledged dessert wines. Styrian wines emphasize the whites, although the blush rosé Schilcher is indigenous to the province, as is an odd specialty called Uhudler, grown in a very limited area.

Exploring Eastern Austria

The Eastern Austrian countryside has been fought over many times, which in part explains the host of defensive hilltop castles overlooking the flatter outlands to the east. Both conqueror and conquered have left their marks. The topography here, which ranges from the flat puszta of the north to the rolling hills of the south, demonstrates that there's more to Austria than the Alps. Graz is the only real city here; other centers are little more than villages in comparison.

Great Itineraries

Travelers who tackle Eastern Austria usually design their trip around threee different destinations—Burgenland, the city of Graz, and the mountain route to Vienna—and the following suggested itineraries highlight these destinations.

Numbers in the text correspond to numbers in the margin and on the Burgenland, Eastern Styria and Lower Austria, and Graz maps.

IF YOU HAVE 1 DAY

Travelers with only a day at their disposal could head for **Eisenstadt** ⑧ and along the west shore of **Lake Neusiedl** to **Rust** ⑥, then return to Vienna via **Wiener Neustadt** ㊴. Another good (but full) one-day excursion is to **Mariazell** ㉟, or to **Puchberg am Schneeberg** ㊳, both reachable from Vienna by car or train.

IF YOU HAVE 3 DAYS

Pick **Eisenstadt** ⑧ as a first stop, spending a half day here, then onward to the west shore of **Lake Neusiedl** to **Rust** ⑥ for brief stops before continuing southward to **Graz** ⑬ for two overnights, with a day spent exploring the city. From Graz, head northward via **Bruck an der Mur** ㉗ over the **Semmering** ㊲ pass and **Wiener Neustadt** ㊴ to Vienna.

IF YOU HAVE 5–7 DAYS

A leisurely pursuit of Eastern Austria is highly rewarding. Get better acquainted with the curiously flat puszta on the eastern side of **Lake Neusiedl,** then head back over to the western side and spend your first overnight in **Rust** ⑥. The next day head to the historic town of **Eisenstadt** ⑧ and follow in the footsteps of famed Baroque-era composer Joseph Hayden and the Esterházy princes. Follow the Burgenland wine route south, and for contrast, spend two nights and a day discovering the delightful Altstadt and bustling metropolis that is **Graz** ⑬. Take in the magnificent **Seckau** ㉙ Abbey and the vast **Eisenerz** ㉜ open-pit iron ore mines, with an overnight in nearby **Leoben/Niklasdorf** ㉘ before continuing north for the attractions of Lower Austria. You might consider an overnight at **Semmering** ㊲ on the way back to Vienna.

When to Tour Eastern Austria

Spring, summer and fall are the seasons for Eastern Austria, unless you're a winter sports enthusiast, when downhill skiers head for Lower Aus-

Burgenland

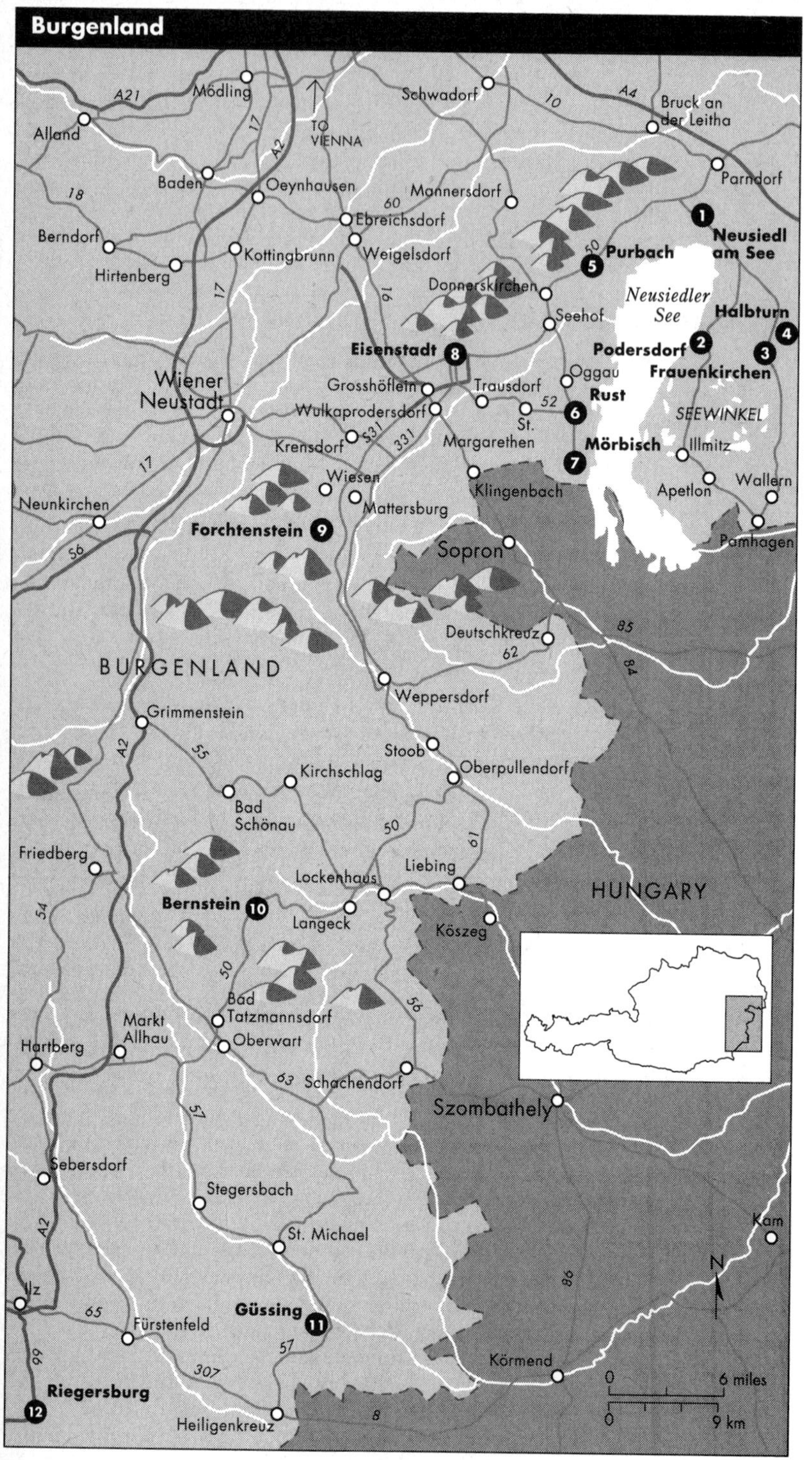

Mödling
Alland
A21
Baden
Oeynhausen
TO VIENNA
Schwadorf
Bruck an der Leitha
Parndorf
Mannersdorf
Ebreichsdorf
Berndorf
Hirtenberg
Kottingbrunn
Weigelsdorf
Neusiedl am See
Purbach
Donnerskirchen
Neusiedler See
Halbturn
Seehof
Eisenstadt
Podersdorf
Frauenkirchen
Wiener Neustadt
Grosshöflein
Oggau
Trausdorf
Rust
Wulkaprodersdorf
St. Margarethen
SEEWINKEL
Krensdorf
Mörbisch
Illmitz
Wiesen
Klingenbach
Apetlon
Wallern
Neunkirchen
Mattersburg
Pamhagen
Forchtenstein
Sopron
Deutschkreuz
BURGENLAND
Weppersdorf
Grimmenstein
Stoob
Oberpullendorf
Kirchschlag
Bad Schönau
Friedberg
Lockenhaus
Liebing
HUNGARY
Bernstein
Langeck
Köszeg
Bad Tatzmannsdorf
Markt Allhau
Hartberg
Oberwart
Schachendorf
Szombathely
Sebersdorf
Stegersbach
St. Michael
Kam
N
Ilz
Güssing
Fürstenfeld
Körmend
Riegersburg
Heiligenkreuz
0
6 miles
0
9 km

tria and the less crowded slopes of Styria. Other than festival-goers and, in summer, visitors to the shores of Lake Neusiedl, you'll find relatively few tourists in this region. Graz functions year-round but its treasures are less touted and crowds are unknown; Christmas in Graz is a visual spectacle, with whole sections of the city turned into a Christmas market. Winter in the area is an enigma: the Semmering mountains mark the eastern tail end of the Alps—north of the divide can be overcast and dreary while the area to the south basks in sunshine.

LAND OF CASTLES

Through Burgenland to Graz

This tour demonstrates that there's more to Austria than the Alps; it travels the length of Burgenland from the flat puszta of the north to the rolling castle-capped hills of the south before turning west to Styria, ending at Austria's second city, Graz. Although it is possible to cover the entire route of about 300 kilometers (185 miles) in a single day, a leisurely pace is preferable.

Burgenland, a region of castles, fields of grain, and vineyards, is a narrow, fertile belt of agricultural land stretching some 170 kilometers (106 miles) from the Slovak (former Czechoslovak) border, along the Hungarian frontier, and south to Slovenia (formerly northern Yugoslavia). Only 65 kilometers (40 miles) across at its widest point, its waist narrows to a mere 4 kilometers (2½ miles).

The name Burgenland, meaning land of castles, dates only from 1921; prior to World War I this area was a part of Hungary. Throughout its long history it has been a battleground between east and west. It was part of the ancient Roman province of Pannonia, occupied by Celts, Roman settlers, Ostrogoths, and Slavs. After them came the Bavarians, Hungarians, and Austrians, followed by invading Turks. This legacy of conflict has continued into the late 20th century, with the tensions of the Iron Curtain a stark fact of life until 1989. The opening of the Hungarian border has again brought change and increased Burgenland's appeal to tourists.

Lake Neusiedl (Neusiedler See)

Located in the north part of Burgenland and one of the region's chief attractions, Lake Neusiedl (Neusiedler See) occupies a strange world. One of the largest lakes in Europe, it is the Continent's only true steppe lake—a bizarre body of warm brackish water. Its sole tributary is far too small to replenish the water lost through evaporation, and there is no outflow at all. Underground springs feed it, but when they fail it dries up, which last happened in the 1860s. At present the water is nowhere more than about 7 feet deep; its many shallower sections make it possible (but dangerous) to wade across the lake. Its depth has varied dramatically, however, at times nearly engulfing the villages on its banks. Most of its 320-square-kilometer (124-square-mile) surface area is in Austria, but the southern reaches extend into Hungary.

What really sets Lake Neusiedl apart is the thick belt of tall reeds—in some places more than a mile wide—that almost completely encircles it. This is the habitat of a large variety of birds (more than 250 species) that nest near the water's edge. The lake is also a paradise for anglers, boaters, and windsurfers; other activities include swimming and, along its banks, bicycling.

Neusiedl am See

1 *51 km (32 mi) southeast of Vienna, 31 km (19½ mi) northeast of Eisenstadt.*

Neusiedl am See, at the north end of the lake for which it is named, is a pleasant resort town with good facilities. Direct hourly commuter trains from Vienna have made it very popular, so you won't be alone here. To reach the lake itself, follow the main street for three blocks east of the Hauptplatz and turn right on Seestrasse, a mile-long causeway that leads through the reeds to the lake, where you can rent small boats, swim, or just laze on the beach. Near the water's edge is the **Seemuseum,** which has a well-rounded exhibit of local flora and fauna. ✉ *Seebad,* ☏ *02167/2229.* 🎫 *AS20.* ⏲ *May–Oct., daily 9–noon and 1–5.*

In Neusiedel am See itself, visit the ruins of a 13th-century hill fortress *Ruine Tabor*), a 15th-century parish church near the town hall, and the **Pannonisches Heimatmuseum** (museum of local Pannonian life). ✉ *Kalvarienbergstr. 40,* ☏ *02167/8173.* 🎫 *Donation suggested.* ⏲ *May–Oct., Tues.–Sat. 2:30–6:30, Sun. and holidays 10–noon and 2:30–6:30.*

The flat plains around Lake Neusiedl, with their tiny hamlets and unspoiled scenery, are perfect for leisurely bicycling. Practically every village has a bike-rental shop (*Fahrradverleih* or *Radverleih*), but demand is so great that it's a good idea to reserve in advance. A bike route encircles the lake, passing through Hungary on the southern end (you can shorten the route by taking the ferry between Illmitz beach and Mörbisch). This and many other routes are described in a German-language map/brochure called "Radeln in Burgenland," available free at tourist offices.

Lodging

$$$ 🏨 **Hotel Wende.** This sprawling new three-story hotel complex is close to the lake and has many standard amenities, but don't expect the charm of a country inn. The comfortable rooms with balconies are of adequate size, and the restaurant is well regarded. ✉ *Seestr. 40, A–7100,* ☏ *02167/8111–0,* FAX *02167/8111–649. 105 rooms with bath. Restaurant, bar, indoor pool, sauna, exercise room, bicycles. No credit cards. Closed late Jan.–mid-Feb.*

Podersdorf

2 *14 km (8¾ mi) south of Neusiedl am See.*

The region east of Lake Neusiedl is the beginning of the unusual Hungarian puszta, the great flat steppe marked with occasional windmills and characteristic wells with long wooden poles for drawing up water—a circular tour of about 70 kilometers (44 miles) by car (or bicycle) would cover nearly everything of interest before returning you to Neusiedl am See. Some of the picturesque houses in Podersdorf have typical thatched roofs, and their chimneys are often adorned in summer with storks nesting after wintering in Egypt. Podersdorf has excellent swimming. The **Natur- und Tierlehrpfad**—a nature learning trail with cement casts of native bird and animal groupings—and a windmill (open for limited times only) educate tourists. ✉ *Mühlstr. 26,* ☏ *02177/2227.* 🎫 *AS25.* ⏲ *Mid-May–mid-Sept., daily 6–7* PM.

Dining and Lodging

$$ ★ ✕ **Gasthof zur Dankbarkeit.** The kitchen offers fine local fare as well as creative dishes with occasional Hungarian touches, served in comfortable *Stuben.* The menu changes daily, but you might find chicken-

liver paté, lamb sausages, rabbit, or rack of venison. The courtyard garden makes a delightful setting in summer. The excellent wines come from neighboring vineyards. ✉ *Hauptstr. 39,* ☎ *02177/2223. DC, V. Closed Mon.–Thurs.*

$$–$$$ **Haus Attila.** In this small, simple, family-run lakefront hotel, the balconied rooms overlooking the lake are especially appealing. The Karner family also runs the nearby smaller (and slightly cheaper) **Seewirt** (✉ Strandpl. 1, ☎ 02177/2415). ✉ *Strandpl. 8, A–7141,* ☎ *02177/2415,* FAX *02177/2465–30. 34 rooms with bath. Restaurant, sauna. No credit cards. Closed Jan. and Feb.*

En Route Podersdorf marks the beginning of the **Seewinkel,** a flat marshy area dotted with small lakes and ponds, much of which is a wildlife sanctuary. The national park in **Illmitz** has a noted biological station and a nature trail (☎ 02175/2328–0). Beyond Illmitz, the road goes through Apetlon to **Pamhagen,** a border hamlet with a small zoo exhibiting animals and birds native to the Hungarian steppes.

Frauenkirchen

❸ *16½ km (10¼ mi) southeast of Neusiedl am See, 7½ km (4½ mi) east of Podersdorf.*

Frauenkirchen is known mainly for its **Pilgrimage Church,** rebuilt in 1702 after its 14th-century predecessor was destroyed by invading Turks and again restored following World War II. The Baroque interior has a much-venerated wooden statue of the Virgin, from the 13th century. Note the miniature Mount Calvary depiction alongside the church.

Dining

$$ ✕ **Altes Brauhaus.** No signs of the old brewery, other than the hearty regional fare, remain at this attractive country inn directly opposite the Pilgrimage Church. The dining rooms have varying rustic decor (the large back one caters to groups), and in summer there's also garden dining under the huge chestnut tree. Try the smooth garlic soup and follow with lamb, goose, or venison during the specialty weeks. Keep an eye out for regional and Hungarian specialties, such as meat-filled pancakes. ✉ *Kirchenpl. 27,* ☎ *02172/2201. AE, DC, MC, V. Closed mid-Jan.–Feb. and Mon. and Tues. mid-Sept.–mid-July.*

Halbturn

❹ *14 km (8¾ mi) southeast of Neusiedl am See, 5 km (3¼ mi) northwest of Frauenkirchen.*

Halbturn contains the exquisite Baroque **Schloss Halbturn,** an imperial hunting lodge built in 1710 by Lukas von Hildebrandt, the great architect of the period. This restored jewel was once used by Empress Maria Theresa as a summer residence and is especially noted for its ceiling frescoes. Devastated by Russian troops in the occupation following World War II, then rebuilt in the 1970s, the castle in summer now houses special annual exhibitions. You can stroll through the large wooded surrounding park anytime, but in late spring when the red and pink chestnut trees are in bloom, the spectacle easily rivals a Monet landscape. In the courtyard, a shop sells excellent wines from the Halbturn vineyards, and a small art museum displays a copy of Gustav Klimt's impressive *Beethoven Frieze,* with the decided advantage over the Vienna original that here you can see the details up close. ✉ *Schloss Halbturn,* ☎ *02172/8577.* *AS60.* *May–Oct., daily 9–6.*

Purbach

5 *13 km (8¼ mi) southwest of Neusiedl am See, 15 km (9½ mi) northeast of Eisenstadt.*

Purbach, like the nearby wine villages of Breitenbrunn and Donnerskirchen, retains traces of its medieval fortifications. Look for the bust of a Turk atop a chimney in the town center; legend has it that when the invaders withdrew in 1532, one hungover, sleepy Turk missed the retreat and, fearing retribution, climbed down a chimney for safety. He was discovered, became an honored citizen, and lived in Purbach happily ever after. The wines of this area, the reds in particular, are outstanding and merit stopping for samples. In late fall and early winter you'll still see bunches of shriveled grapes on the leafless vines; these will be turned into rare *Spätlese* (late harvest) and still-rarer *Eiswein* (pressed from frozen grapes) dessert wines.

Dining and Lodging

$$$–$$$$ ★ ✕ **Nikolauszeche.** This is one of Burgenland's best restaurants, noted for its elegant country decor in a 15th-century Renaissance house (it is a member of the Romantik Hotels & Restaurants group) as well as for its excellent regional cuisine. Specialties vary with the season, but you might find local goat cheese with olive oil, roast leg of lamb with rosemary and scalloped potatoes, or a pink fillet of young goat with mushroom cream sauce. There is an excellent selection of local wines, including some from the house's own winery. ✉ *Bodenzeile 3,* ☎ *02683/5514,* FAX *02683/5077. AE, DC, MC, V. Closed Tues. and mid-Dec.–mid-Mar. No lunch Wed.*

$$–$$$ ✕🏨 **Am Spitz.** This country inn, at the end of an attractive row of wine cellars, is known for its local Burgenland and Pannonian cooking. The restaurant is in a former cloister, and the outside garden enjoys an exquisite floral setting, looking down over the lake. The menu changes daily but always features fresh fish, possibly including a spicy Hungarian fish soup, a cassoulet of lake fish in basil cream, and roast veal steak. The somewhat plain and modern associated *Gasthof* ($$) is pleasant but less gemütlich. ✉ *Waldsiedlgasse 2, A-7083,* ☎ *02683/5519,* FAX *02683/5519–20. 14 rooms with bath. No credit cards. Closed Mon., Tues., and late Dec.–Mar.*

Rust

6 *16 km (10 mi) east of Eisenstadt, 28 km (17½ mi) southwest of Neusiedl am See.*

Picturesque Rust is easily the most popular village on the lake for its colorful pastel facades and for lake sports. Tourists flock here in summer to see for themselves the famed sights of storks nesting atop the Renaissance and Baroque houses in the town's well-preserved historic center. There are wine-tasting opportunities at the **Weinakademie** (✉ Hauptstr. 31, ☎ 02685/6451, FAX 02685/6431). Visit the restored Gothic **Fischerkirche** (Fishermen's Church) off the west end of the Rathausplatz. Built between the 12th and 16th centuries, it is surrounded by a defensive wall and is noted for its 15th-century frescoes and an organ from 1705. If you're heading from Purbach, leave Route 50 at Seehof and follow the local road past Oggau to arrive in Rust. ✉ *Conradpl. 1,* ☎ *02685/502.* 🎫 *AS10.* ⏲ *May–Sept., Mon.–Sat. 10–noon and 2:30–6, Sun. and holidays 11–noon and 2–6.*

NEED A BREAK? You can sample the excellent local vintages, along with a light lunch, in a number of friendly cafés, cellars, and the typical *Heurige,* where young wines are served by their makers. A favorite spot is the **Rathauskeller** (✉ Rathauspl. 1) open daily except Wednesday from 11:30 AM. The Ruster Blaufränkisch red wine is particularly good, resembling a well-rounded Burgundy.

A causeway leads through nearly a mile of reeds to the **Seebad** beach and boat landing, where you can take a sightseeing round-trip or a boat to another point on the lake, rent boats, swim, or enjoy a waterside drink or snack at an outdoor table of the Seerestaurant Rust.

Dining and Lodging

$$$–$$$$ ✕ **Zur Backstube.** Try this tiny gem of a restaurant one flight up, over a bakery, for a change from the usual wine cellars. The menu lists only fresh items such as fish or lamb, which together with such specialties as chilled cream of cucumber soup, fish soup, salmon-trout in potato crust, and excellent desserts and wines add up to a fine meal. ✉ *Kirchengasse 3, ☎ 02685/6405. Reservations essential. V. Closed Thurs. and Nov.–mid-Apr.*

$$$ ✕ **Rusterhof.** A lovingly renovated *Burgher* house—the town's oldest—at the top of the main square, is home to an excellent and imaginative restaurant. Light natural woods and vaulted ceilings set the atmosphere in the series of smaller rooms; in summer there's an outside garden. The menu depends on what's fresh, and might include grilled fish or saddle of hare in *Eiswein* sauce. Finish with a rhubarb compote. The complex also includes four apartments for guests. ✉ *Rathauspl. 18, ☎ 02685/6414. V. Closed Mon. and Jan.–Apr.*

$$$ 🏨 **Seehotel.** Set on the very edge of Lake Neusiedl, this luxuriously modern complex contrasts strikingly with the bordering historic village. The comfortable guest rooms are contemporary Scandinavian in style; ask for one facing the lake. The kitchen is excellent. Golfers get reduced greens fees at the nearby Donnerskirchen course. ✉ *Am Seekanal 2–4, A–7071, ☎ 02685/381–0, FAX 02685/381–419. 110 rooms with bath. 3 restaurants, bar, indoor pool, sauna, tennis courts, exercise room, squash, beach, boating. AE, DC, MC, V.*

Mörbisch

7 *22 km (13¾ mi) southeast of Eisenstadt, 5½ km (3½ mi) south of Rust.*

Mörbisch is the last lakeside village before the Hungarian border. Considered by many to be the most attractive settlement on the lake, the town is famous for its low, whitewashed, Magyar-style houses, whose open galleries are colorfully decorated with flowers and bunches of grain. The local vineyards produce some superb white wines, especially the fresh-tasting Welschriesling and the full-bodied Muscat-Ottonel. Here, too, a causeway leads to a beach on the lake, where an international operetta festival is held each summer (☞ Nightlife and the Arts, *below*). A leisurely activity is to tour the countryside in a typical open **horse-drawn wagon.** Operators in several lakeside villages will arrange this, including Johann Mad (✉ Ruster Str. 14, ☎ 02685/8250), and Evi Wenzl (✉ Weinberggasse 12, ☎ 02685/8401).

Lodging

$$–$$$ 🏨 **Hotel Steiner.** Though in the center of the village, the family-run Steiner is also close to the vineyards and Lake Neusiedl. The somewhat plain modern exterior conceals rustic-style accommodations with all conveniences. ✉ *Hauerstr. 1, A–7072, ☎ 02685/8444–0, FAX 02685/8446–43. 52 rooms with bath. Restaurant, indoor pool, sauna, bicycles. No credit cards. Closed Dec.–Mar.*

Nightlife and the Arts

At the **Mörbisch Lake Festival,** held on Fridays, Saturdays, and Sundays from mid-July through August on Burgenland's Lake Neusiedl, operettas are performed outdoors on a floating stage. Special buses run from Vienna (✉ Blaguss, ☎ 0222/501–80–0). The 1997 choice is Jacques Offenbach's rollicking, high-kicking *Pariser Leben* (*Paris Life*). For information, contact the Mörbisch tourist office or the festival office (*Seefestspiele Mörbisch*) in Schloss Esterházy in Eisenstadt (☎ 02682/66210–0, FAX 02682/66210–14), or, during July and August, in Mörbisch itself (☎ 02685/8181–0, FAX 02685/8334).

Eisenstadt

8 *48 km (30 mi) south of Vienna, 26 km (16¼ mi) west of Wiener Neustadt.*

Burgenland's provincial capital, Eisenstadt, scarcely more than a village, nevertheless has an illustrious history and enough sights to keep you busy for a half if not a full day. It is connected to Neusiedl am See by train and to Vienna and places throughout Burgenland by bus. From Rust, take Route 52 west past St. Margarethen and Trausdorf to the capital.

Although the town has existed since at least the 12th century, it was not of any importance until the 17th, when it became the seat of the Esterházys, a princely Hungarian family that traces its roots to Attila the Hun. Esterházy support was largely responsible for the Habsburg reign in Hungary under the Dual Monarchy. At one time, the family controlled a far-flung agro-industrial empire, and it still owns vast forest resources. The composer Joseph Haydn lived in Eisenstadt for some 30 years while in the service of the Esterházys. When Burgenland was ceded to Austria after World War I, its major city, Sopron, elected to remain a part of Hungary, and so in 1925 tiny Eisenstadt was made the capital of the new Austrian province.

In addition to what's listed below, Eisenstadt has a few other attractions that its tourist office can tell you about, including the Museum of Austrian Culture, the Diocesan Museum, the Fire Fighters Museum, Haydn's little garden house, and an assortment of churches.

★ **Schloss Esterházy,** the yellow-facaded former palace of the ruling princes, reigns over the town. Built in the Baroque style between 1663 and 1672 on the foundations of a medieval castle, it was later modified and is still owned by the Esterházy family, who lease it to the provincial government for use mostly as offices. Part of the recently mounted exhibition on the Esterházy family is still open; the rooms alone are worth viewing. The lavishly decorated **Haydn Room,** an impressive concert hall where the composer conducted his own works from 1761 until 1790, is still used for presentations of Haydn's works, with musicians often dressed in period garb. It can be seen on guided tours (in English on request) lasting about 30 minutes. The **park** behind the Schloss is pleasant for a stroll or a picnic; in late August it is the site of the Burgenland wine week. ✉ *Esterházy Pl.,* ☎ *02682/63384–16.* 🎫 *AS60.* ⏲ *Easter–May and Oct., daily 8:30–5; June–Sept., daily 8:30–6; Nov.–Easter, weekdays 8:30–5; guided tour hourly.*

NEED A BREAK? The **Schloss-Café Zachs,** opposite the west end of the Schloss Esterházy at Glorietteallee 1, is open daily until 1 AM for snacks and refreshments.

At the crest of the Esterházystrasse perches the **Bergkirche,** an ornate Baroque church that includes the strange *Kalvarienberg*, an indoor Calvary Hill representing the Way of the Cross with life-size figures placed in cavelike rooms along an elaborate path. At its highest point, the trail reaches the platform of the belfry, offering a view over the town and this section of Burgenland. The magnificent wooden figures were carved and painted by Franciscan monks more than 250 years ago. The main part of the church contains the tomb of Joseph Haydn, who died in 1809 but whose body, sans head, was not moved here until 1932 (the head, stolen by admirers and kept in Vienna, was returned in 1954). ✉ *Kalvarienbergpl.,* ☎ *02682/62638.* 🎫 *AS25.* ⏲ *Apr.–Oct., daily 9–noon and 2–5.*

The short block around Wertheimergasse and Unterbergstrasse housed a barred Jewish ghetto from 1671 until 1938. During that time, Eisenstadt had a considerable Jewish population; today the **Austrian Jewish Museum** (Österreichisches Jüdisches Museum) recalls the experience of all Austrian Jews throughout history. A fascinating private synagogue in the complex survived the 1938 terror and is incorporated into the museum. ✉ *Unterbergstr. 6,* ☎ *02682/65145.* 🎫 *AS25.* ⏲ *Late May–late Oct., Tues.–Sun. 10–5.*

The **Landesmuseum** (Burgenland provincial museum) brings the history of the region to life with displays on such diverse subjects as Roman culture and the area's wildlife. There's a memorial room to the composer Franz Liszt, along with more relics of the town's former Jewish community. ✉ *Museumgasse 5,* ☎ *02682/62652–0.* 🎫 *AS30.* ⏲ *Tues.–Sun. 9–noon and 1–5.*

Joseph Haydn lived in the simple house at No. 21 Haydn Gasse from 1766 until 1778. Now the **Haydn Museum,** it contains several of the composer's original manuscripts and other memorabilia. The house itself, and especially its flower-filled courtyard with the small back rooms, is unpretentious but quite delightful. ☎ *02682/62652–0.* 🎫 *AS20.* ⏲ *Easter–late Oct., daily 9–noon and 1–5.*

Dining and Lodging

$$ ✕ **Schlosstaverne.** Gypsy music and candlelight accompany the food at the Schlosstaverne, housed in the former stables of Schloss Esterházy. This is a rather touristy place, but friendly and enjoyable nonetheless. Its cuisine is a satisfactory blend of Viennese and Hungarian styles, and its location just across from the princely palace couldn't be more convenient. You'll find old favorites like Wiener schnitzel and goulash on the menu, but the specialty is *Esterházy Rostbraten,* a rump steak lightly browned, then steamed in a vegetable broth and garnished with julienne vegetables. Finish with a rich, creamy *Esterházy Torte.* ✉ *Esterházypl. 5,* ☎ *02682/63102. No credit cards. Closed Mon. and mid-Dec.–mid-Mar.*

$ ✕ **Haydnbräu.** A red tiled floor against white stucco walls and lots of natural wood provide the right setting for the "First Burgenland Restaurant-Brewery." Indeed, the excellent beer comes directly from polished copper vats behind the bar. The food, too, is good, for either snacking or a main meal; try the delicate cream of garlic soup or any of the more substantial daily specials. ✉ *Pfarrgasse 22,* ☎ *02682/61561–17. No credit cards.*

$$$ ✕🏨 **Hotel Burgenland.** Considered the province's best, this strikingly contemporary hotel has everything you'd expect in a first-class establishment. It's near the town center and the large rooms are bright and airy. The restaurants, alas, have been inconsistent, although the glassed-in winter-garden café offers a pleasant pastel setting for a coffee or snack. ✉ *Schubertpl. 1, A–7000,* ☎ *02682/696,* FAX *02682/65531. 88 rooms with bath. Restaurant, bar, indoor pool, sauna. AE, DC, MC, V.*

$$ ✕🏨 **Gasthof Ohr.** This personal, family-run hotel and restaurant is about a 10-minute easy walk from the town center. The immaculate rooms are comfortably attractive, done in natural woods and white with color accents; those in the back are quieter. The rustic wood-paneled restaurant offers specialty weeks—goose, game, new asparagus—in addition to Austrian and regional standards such as schnitzel or Hungarian fish soup. In summer, the canopied outdoor dining terrace is a green oasis. Wine comes from the family vineyards. ✉ *Ruster Str. 51, A-7000,* ☎ *02682/62460,* FAX *02682/64481. 24 rooms with bath or shower. Restaurant. MC, V.*

Nightlife and the Arts

Eisenstadt devotes much cultural energy to one of its favorite sons. In the first half of September, it plays host to the annual **Haydn Festival** in the Esterházy Palace. Many of the concerts are by world-famous performers, and admission prices vary with the event. Other concerts featuring the works of Joseph Haydn run from mid-May to early October. Contact the Haydnfestspiele office (☎ 02682/61866–0, FAX 02682/61805) in Schloss Esterházy (☞ *above*) or the local tourist office. Eisenstadt's **Haydn Quartet**, in 18th-century costumes, plays short matinee concerts of the master's works at 11 AM Tuesday and Friday, from mid-May to late October, at the Esterházy palace (☎ 02682/63384–16, FAX 02682/63384–20); tickets are AS80.

Forchtenstein

❾ *23 km (14½ mi) southwest of Eisenstadt, 3 km (2 mi) southwest of Mattersburg.*

Heading southwest from Eisenstadt brings you to the narrow waist of Burgenland, squeezed between Lower Austria and Hungary. The leading attraction here is Forchtenstein; take Route S31 for 20 kilometers (12½ miles) to Mattersburg, then a local road 3 kilometers (2 miles) west. In the summer, people throng to the small village of Forchtenstein for its strawberries, but its enduring dominant feature is the medieval hilltop castle, **Burg Forchtenstein.** This formidable fortress was built in the early 14th century, enlarged by the Esterházys around 1635, and twice defended Austria against invading Turks. Captured enemy soldiers were put to work digging the castle's 466-foot-deep well, famous for its echo. As befits a military stronghold, there is a fine collection of weapons in the armory and booty taken from the Turks; there's also an exhibition of stately carriages. ✉ *Burgpl. 1,* ☎ *02626/81212.* 🎫 *AS50.* ⏲ *Apr.–Oct., daily 8–11:30 and 1–4.*

Dining and Lodging

$$$ ✕ **Reisner.** The delicately prepared traditional food served at this popular restaurant attracts people from all over the region. You can eat in the somewhat formal dining room or in a rustic tavern favored by the locals, with the offerings matching the setting. Some typical dishes are trout with a ragout of fresh vegetables; excellent steaks; and, for dessert, rhubarb tart and poppyseed parfait. ✉ *Hauptstr. 141,* ☎ *02626/63139. AE. Closed Wed., Thurs., and early Mar.*

$ 🏨 **Gasthof Sauerzapf.** This simple country inn on the main road just five minutes west of the castle has recently modernized its rooms. ✉ *Rosalienstr. 9, A–7212,* ☎ *02626/81217. 14 rooms, some with shower. Restaurant. No credit cards.*

Bernstein

❿ *12 km (7½ mi) west of Lockenhaus, 16 km (10 mi) north of Oberwart.*

The small village of Bernstein is one of few sources of *Edelserpentin*, a dark green serpentine stone also known as Bernstein jade. Jewelry and objets d'art made locally from the town's stone are on display in the **Felsenmuseum** (stone museum), located partly within a former mine. ✉ *Potsch, Hauptpl. 5,* ☎ *03354/6620–0.* *AS50.* ⏲ *Mar.–Oct., daily 9–noon and 1:30–6; Nov. and Dec., daily 9–noon and 1:30–5.*

Shops in town explain cutting and exhibit stones. A visit to the **Piringer** shop and museum includes a look into the caves from which the Edelserpentin is hewn. ✉ *Hauptpl. 3 and 7,* ☎ *03354/6504, 6506.* *AS15.* ⏲ *Mid-Mar.–mid-Dec., daily 9–noon and 1:30–5:30.*

Overlooking the village is **Burg Bernstein,** a 12th-century fortress that was rebuilt in the 17th century. Part of it is now a romantic castle-hotel, but the rest may be visited. ☎ *03354/6382.* *AS50.* ⏲ *By appointment May–Oct., daily 9–noon and 1–5.*

You can get to Bernstein from Forchtenstein by returning to the highway from Burg Forchtenstein and taking S31 and Route 50 south past Weppersdorf and Stoob, the latter famous for its pottery. The road then goes through Oberpullendorf and close to Lockenhaus, where a renowned music festival is held each summer in the 13th-century castle (☞ Nightlife and the Arts, *below*).

OFF THE BEATEN PATH

SOUTH BURGENLAND OPEN-AIR MUSEUM – South of Bernstein in Bad Tatzmannsdorf is the Freilichtmuseum (South Burgenland Open-Air Museum) which displays wonderfully restored old barns, farmhouses, and stables from the region, giving a feeling of life as experienced a century or more ago. ✉ *Josef-Hölzel-Allee 1,* ☎ *03353/8284 or 03353/8314.* *AS10.* ⏲ *Oct.–May, daily 8–4; June–Aug., daily 8–6.*

Dining and Lodging

$ ✕ **Gasthof Heanznhof-Frühwirth.** In this typical Gasthof in the center of town you'll find unusually good regional cooking with strong Hungarian overtones: thick spicy soups, goose, duck, and other game in season. ✉ *Hauptstr. 59,* ☎ *03354/6503. No credit cards. Closed Jan. and Thurs. Nov.–Mar.*

$$$ ★ **Burg Bernstein.** This medieval castle, built in the 12th century, became a hotel in 1953. Its hilltop location gives it a birds-eye view of the peaceful Tauchen valley, just west of the village of Bernstein. The rooms, which tend to be huge, are furnished with antiques and heated by traditional ceramic stoves. Meals are served with regional wines in a Baroque style baronial hall. ✉ *Schlossweg 1, A–7434,* ☎ *03354/6382,* FAX *03354/6520. 10 rooms with bath. Pool, sauna, fishing, hunting. AE, DC, MC, V. Closed Oct.–Easter.*

Nightlife and the Arts

The **International Chamber Music Festival** (*Kammermusikfest*) of Lockenhaus, 15 kilometers (9½ miles) east of Bernstein, takes place during the first half of July in a 13th-century castle. World-famous musicians are invited to this intimate festival, and the audience may attend morning rehearsals. Violinist Gidon Kremer is the musical sparkplug behind the festival. Call the local church office (*Pfarramt*) for information, reservations, and accommodations (☎ 02616/2023 or 02616/2224).

Güssing

⓫ *54 km (34 mi) south of Bernstein, 13 km (8 mi) north of Heiligenkreuz.*

Güssing is yet another of Burgenland's castle-dominated villages. From Bernstein many travelers arrive via Route 50 past Bad Tatzmannsdorf, then follow Route 57. The classic 12th-century fortress, **Burg Güssing,** perched high on a solitary volcanic outcrop, has wonderful views of the surrounding countryside. It also has a fine collection of Old Master paintings, weapons, and armor, and a Gothic chapel with a rare 17th-century cabinet organ. In recent years, an exhibition celebrating fairy tales has been on view, with rooms devoted to Hansel and Gretel and Snow White. ☎ *03322/43400 or 03322/42491.* *Castle museum and fairy-tale exhibition AS75.* *May–Oct., daily 10–6; last admission at 5.*

If you stop in Güssing to explore its castle, consider also visiting the **Naturpark Güssing** (Güssing Game Park) where a variety of wild animals indigenous to Eastern Austria reside in more than a square mile of open space. Observation posts are scattered throughout, and you should take your time at them—the animals have to come to you. ✉ *1 km (⅔ mi) northeast of Güssing,* ☎ *03322/42419–0.* *AS15.* *Daily dawn–dusk.*

Dining and Lodging

$$ ★ ✕ **Gasthof Gibiser.** Its proximity to Hungary (Heiligenkreuz is 13 kilometers, or 8¼ miles, southwest of Güssing) has inspired the creative dishes served at this classic, white, villa-style country inn. The Pannonian cuisine combines the best of Austrian and Hungarian culinary traditions to produce such specialties as cabbage soup and steak stuffed with goose liver. For overnight guests there are several quiet rooms plus a few rustic thatched-roof cottages in the garden. ✉ *Heiligenkreuz 81, A–7561,* ☎ *03325/4216–0,* FAX *03325/4246–44. 12 rooms with bath, 3 cottages. AE, DC, MC, V. Closed 1st 2 wks of Feb.; late Dec.; and Mon. in winter.*

Riegersburg

12 *13 km (8¼ mi) south of Ilz, 10 km (6¼ mi) north of Feldbach.*

Riegersburg is a quiet agricultural communiity overshadowed by the massive fortress which perches atop an extraordinary volcanic outcropping. The rock has had its attraction over the centuries; archeological finds have established that there were settlements here more than 6,000 years ago. Rising some 600 feet above the valley below is the mighty and well-restored **Riegersburg Castle,** one of Austria's great defensive bastions. Originally built in the 11th century on the site of Celtic and Roman strongholds, it has never been humbled in battle, not even in 1945 when its German occupants held out against the Russians. The present structure dates from the 17th century and is entered by way of a heavily defended, winding path, so be prepared to climb for 20 to 30 minutes. (Taxis will take travelers with disabilities up; check with the Zehethofer BP filling station in town, ☎ 03153/8281.) The castle has weapons displays, rooms with period furnishings, and a separate museum of witchcraft and magic. Needless to say, the views are magnificent. ☎ *03153/8213–0.* *Each museum AS60, both museums AS95.* *Apr.–Oct., daily 9–5.*

Adjacent to the Riegersburg Castle you can observe free flight of birds of prey at **Greifvogelwarte Riegersburg** (birds-of-prey keep). At various hours, falcons and eagles are set loose from a stand within the aviary preserve (returning to the keepers' care—and tempting meals, of course). ☎ *03153/7390.* *AS50.* *Mon.–Sat. at 11 and 3; Sun. and holidays at 11, 2, and 4, weather permitting.*

To arrive at Riegersburg from Güssing, stay on Route 57 to the frontier village of Heiligenkreuz-im-Laftnitztal, then take Route 65 west to Fürstenfeld, leaving Burgenland and crossing into Styria. Continue on to Ilz, then turn south on Route 66 to Riegersburg, a total distance of 57 kilometers (35 miles) southwest of Güssing. From Riegersburg to Graz—the province's main metropolis–it is 56 kilometers (35 miles) west via Route 65 or A2.

Dining and Lodging

$$ ★ **Gasthof Fink Zur Riegersburg.** This venerable family-run country inn near the foot of the castle is prettily adorned with flower boxes and shutters. Its large, paneled dining room—complete with ceiling beams—is bright and airy, and there's also garden dining in season. The Austrian cuisine is hearty, with such dishes as bratwurst with sauerkraut and dumplings, and roast beef with cornmeal. A fine selection of Styrian wines is offered. ✉ *Riegersburg 29, A–8333,* ☎ *03153/8216,* FAX *03153/7357. 33 rooms. AE, DC, MC, V. Closed Feb.*

GRAZ AND ITS ENVIRONS

Land of Gemütlichkeit

Every day at 11 AM and 6 PM two tall windows open above the Glockenspielplatz in the center of Graz. A wooden man adorned in lederhosen appears in one, a tankard of beer in his upraised fist; from the other emerges a dirndl-wearing Austrian maiden. An old folk tune strikes up and they dance on the window-ledges high above the square before returning to their mullioned windows. This mechanized glockenspiel show is one of the many delights that can tempt the tourist in Graz, the capital of Styria and the second-largest city in Austria. A preserved marvel, its *Altstadt* (Old Town) quarter is a threadwork of historic streets, so beautifully restored that the city has garnered international awards for historic preservation. Here, through medieval passageways and past Baroque churches, time seems to meander, whiling the hours away. The city embodies Austrian *gemütlichkeit*—easy-going good nature—but it also remains a city on the move: it's the seat of two universities and site of a lively cultural center.

Lying in a somewhat remote corner of the country and often overlooked by tourists, Graz is easily reached from Vienna or Salzburg and provides the urban highlight of an itinerary through southeastern Austria. The name Graz derives from the Slavic *gradec,* meaning small castle; there was probably a fortress atop the Schlossberg hill as early as the 9th century. This strategic spot guarded the southern end of the narrow Mur Valley—an important approach to Vienna—from invasion by the Turks. By the 12th century, a town developed at the foot of the hill, which in time became an imperial city of the ruling Habsburgs. Graz's glory faded in the 17th century when the court moved to Vienna, but the city continued to prosper as a provincial capital, especially under the enlightened 19th-century rule of Archduke Johann.

If you're staying in the city for more than a day, you might want to make a short excursion or two into the countryside. Ask at the information office for the detailed folder in English, "Excursions around Graz," with suggestions as well as travel directions. Three favorite trips—to Stübing bei Graz, Piber, and Bärnbach—can each be done in a few hours.

Graz

13 *200 km (125 mi) southwest of Vienna, 285 km (178 mi) southeast of Salzburg.*

Nearly all tourist attractions in Graz are conveniently located in the compact Altstadt, or **Old Town** quarter, which can easily be explored
★ 14 on foot in an hour or so, not including any stops. Begin at the **Haupt-**

Eastern Styria and Lower Austria

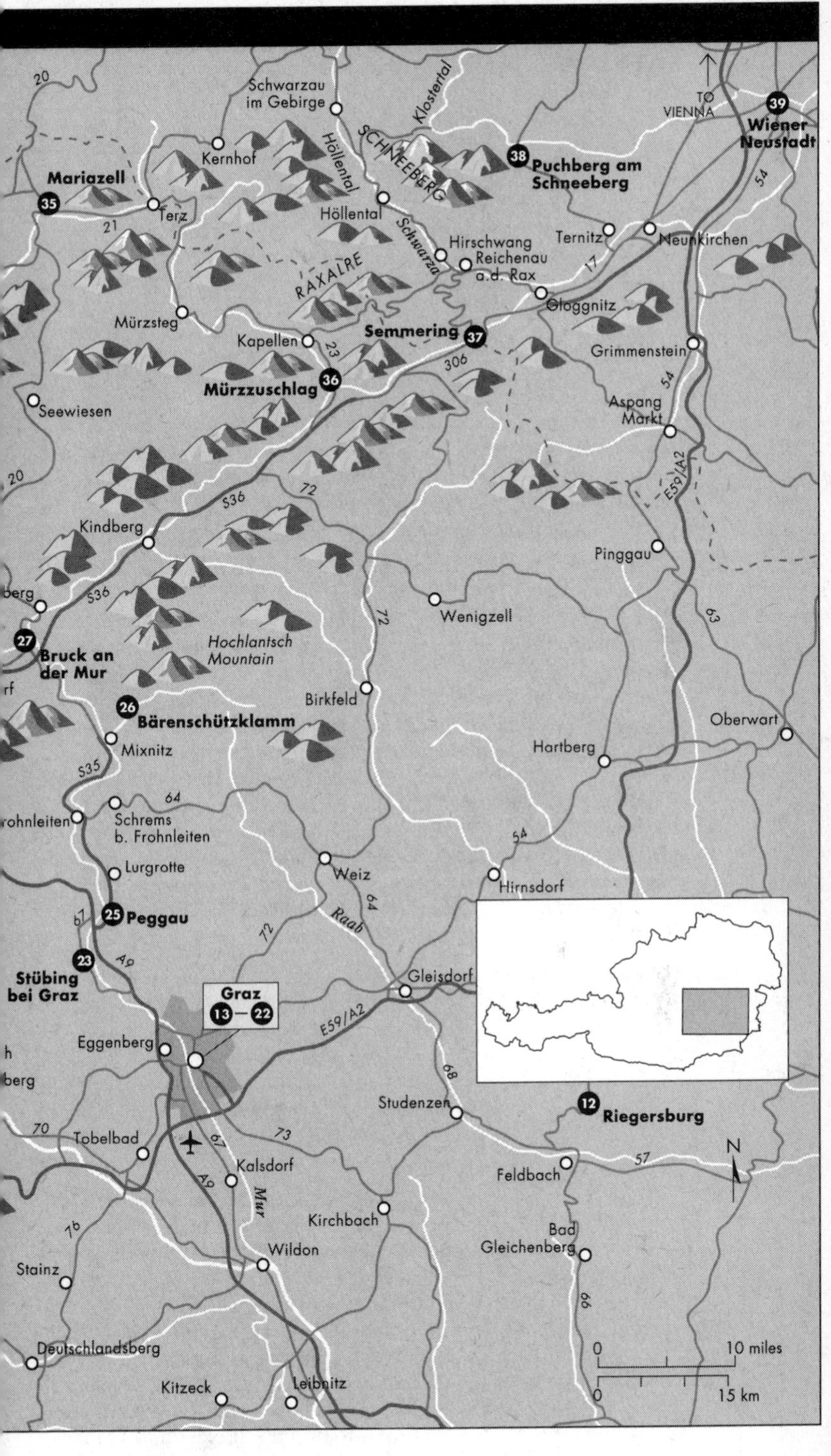
Schwarzau
im Gebirge
Klostertal
TO
VIENNA
Wiener
Neustadt
Kernhof
Höllental
SCHNEEBERG
Puchberg am
Schneeberg
Mariazell
Terz
Höllental
Schwarza
Ternitz
Neunkirchen
Hirschwang
Reichenau
a.d. Rax
RAXALPE
Gloggnitz
Mürzsteg
Semmering
Kapellen
Grimmenstein
Mürzzuschlag
Seewiesen
Aspang
Markt
Kindberg
Pinggau
Wenigzell
Bruck an
der Mur
Hochlantsch
Mountain
Birkfeld
Bärenschützklamm
Mixnitz
Oberwart
Hartberg
Schrems
b. Frohnleiten
Lurgrotte
Weiz
Hirnsdorf
Peggau
Raab
Stübing
bei Graz
Graz
Gleisdorf
Eggenberg
Studenzen
Riegersburg
Tobelbad
Kalsdorf
Feldbach
Mur
Kirchbach
Bad
Gleichenberg
Wildon
Stainz
Deutschlandsberg
Kitzeck
Leibnitz
10 miles
15 km

platz (main square), a triangular area first laid out in 1164 and used today as a lively open-air produce market. In its center stands the **Erzherzog Johann Brunnen** (Archduke Johann Fountain), dedicated to the popular 19th-century patron whose enlightened policies did much to develop Graz as a cultural and scientific center. The four female figures represent what were Styria's four main rivers; today only the Mur and the Enns are within the province. Behind the Brunnen statue, to the north, rises the **Schlossberg** (castle hill) with its 16th-century **Uhrturm** (clock tower), the very symbol of Graz. Take a careful look at the richly ornamented 17th-century **Luegg House** at the corner of Sporgasse, noted for its Baroque stucco facade, and at the Gothic and Renaissance houses on the west side of the square. The late-19th-century **Rathaus** (city hall) totally dominates the south side of the main square. From the Neue-Welt-Gasse and Schmiedgasse you get a superb view of the Hauptplatz.

Appropriately enough, the **Franziskanerkirche** (Franciscan church), which has a 14th-century choir, a 16th-century nave, and a 17th-century tower, is in the narrow Franziskanergasse. The tiny streets of this former butchers' quarter retain much of their medieval atmosphere and are worth exploring.

15 Near Hauptplatz is the **Landesmuseum Joanneum,** the oldest public museum in Austria, founded by Archduke Johann in 1811. Actually, this is part of a large complex of museums devoted to different subjects, several of which are in other parts of town. The entrance at Raubergasse 10 is for the natural history departments, while that at Neutorgasse 45 leads into the applied arts department and the **Alte Galerie** (old gallery), a world-famous collection of art from the Middle Ages through the Baroque period. Among its treasures are works by Pieter Brueghel the Younger and both Hans and Lucas Cranach, the noted *Admont Madonna* wood carving from 1400, and a medieval altarpiece depicting the murder of Thomas à Becket. *Natural history section, ☎ 0316/8017–0. ⏲ Weekdays 9–4, weekends and holidays 9–noon. Applied arts section, ☎ 0316/8017–4780. ⏲ Mon. and Wed.–Fri. 10–5, weekends and holidays 10–1. Alte Galerie, ☎ 0316/8017–4770. ⏲ Tues.–Fri. 10–5, weekends and holidays 10–1. 🎫 Each section AS25.*

The **Herrengasse** is the main business street. At No. 3 is the 15th-century **Gemaltes Haus** (painted house), a former ducal residence decorated with frescoes from 1742. Along the west side of the street stands the massive **Landhaus** (Styrian provincial parliament), built between 1557 and 1565 by Domenico dell' Allio in the Italian Renaissance style. Its arcaded courtyard is magnificently proportioned and features a 16th-century fountain that is an unusually fine example of old Styrian wrought-iron work.

16 Possibly the most noted attraction in Graz is the **Landeszeughaus** (provincial arsenal). Virtually unchanged since it was built in 1643, this four-story armory still contains the 16th- and 17th-century weapons intended for use by Styrian mercenaries in fighting off the Turks. Nearly 30,000 items are on display, including more than 3,000 suits of armor (some of which are beautifully engraved), thousands of halberds, swords, firearms, cannons, and mortars. (Pieces from this collection were shown in the United States and Canada in 1992.) Probably the most important collection of its type in the world, it is now being rearranged for better presentation—to turn the displays into a "living exhibition" highlighting unusual items in contrast to the sheer quantity on hand. Call for possible new winter and evening hours. *✉ Herrengasse 16, ☎ 0316/8017–4810. 🎫 AS25. ⏲ Apr.–Oct., weekdays*

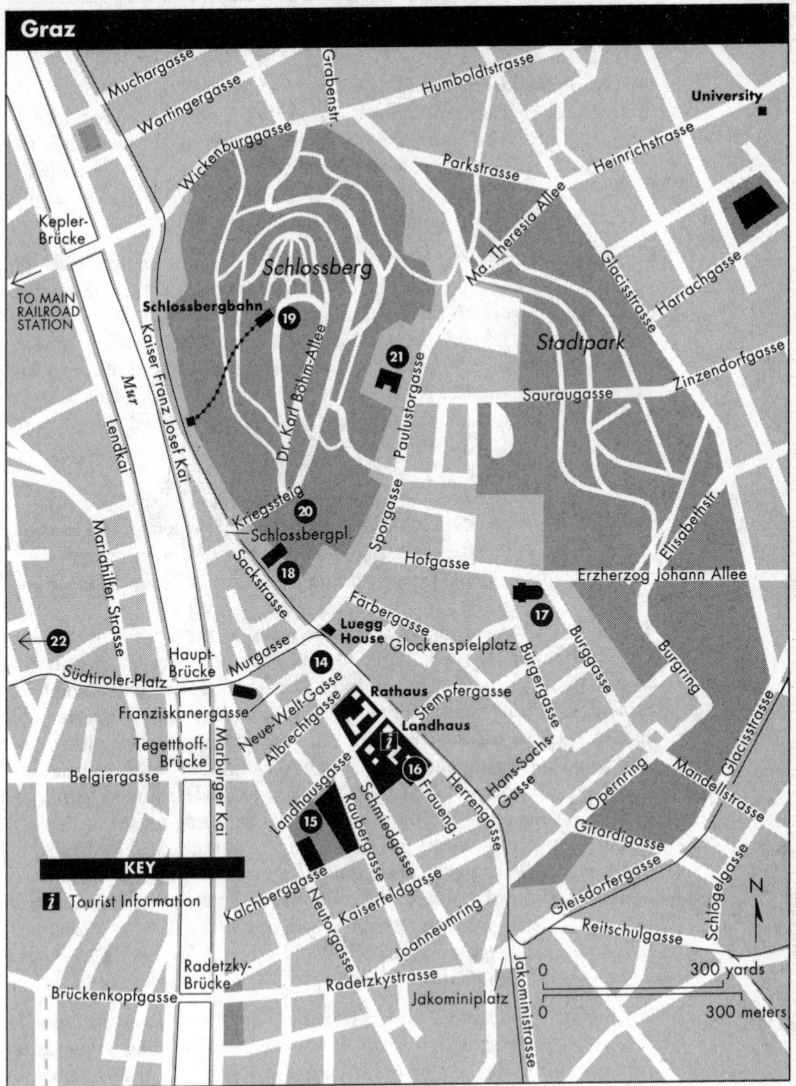

Domkirche, **17**
Hauptplatz, **14**
Herberstein Palace, **18**
Landesmuseum Joanneum, **15**
Landeszeughaus, **16**
Schlossberg, **19**
Schloss Eggenberg, **22**
Steirisches Volkskundemuseum, **21**
Uhrturm, **20**

9–5, weekends and holidays 9–1; tour hourly, last tour 1 hr before closing.

The **Stadtpfarrkirche** (city parish church) on Herrengasse was built early in the 16th century, and later received its Baroque facade and 18th-century spire. Tintoretto's *Assumption of the Virgin* decorates the altar. Across the street begins a narrow lane named after Johann Bernhard Fischer von Erlach, the great architect of the Austrian Baroque, who was born in one of the houses here in 1666.

From Herrengasse, walk up the narrow Stempfergasse, and turn left on Enge Gasse to the delightful **Glockenspielplatz,** the mechanical clock whose wooden figures emerge daily from a wall above a café, dancing to an old folk tune at 11 AM and 6 PM and at other times as well. Look into the courtyard at No. 5, which has an impressive 17th-century open staircase. The house at No. 7 has an arcaded Renaissance courtyard. Adjacent to the square is the **Mehlplatz,** lined with historic houses.

NEED A BREAK? You can wait for the musical show right under the glockenspiel at the trendy **Glockenspiel Café** (✉ Glockenspielpl. 4). The coffee, sandwiches, and pastries are all excellent, and there are plenty of outdoor tables from which to enjoy the passing parade. The café is closed Sunday.

An open staircase from Bürgergasse leads to the 15th-century late-
17 Gothic **Domkirche** (cathedral). On its south exterior wall, near the steps, is a rather faded 15th-century fresco called the *Landplagenbild,* which graphically depicts contemporary local torments—the plague, the locusts, and the Turks. Step inside to see the outstanding high altar made of colored marble, the choir stalls, Raphael Donner's 1741 tomb of Count Cobenzl, and Konrad Laib's *Crucifixion* of 1457. The 15th-century reliquaries on either side of the triumphal arch leading to the choir were originally the hope chests of Paola Gonzaga, daughter of Ludwig II of Mantua. The Baroque **Mausoleum** of Emperor Ferdinand II, who died in 1637, adjoins the cathedral. Its sumptuous interior is partly an early design by native son Fischer von Erlach and his only work to be seen in Graz. ✉ *Burggasse 3,* ☎ *0316/821683.* *Free.* *May–Sept., Mon.–Sat. 11–noon and 2–3; tour Oct.–Apr., Mon.–Sat. at 11.*

The scanty remains of a former imperial palace known as the **Burg** lie just north of the cathedral across Hofgasse. Now housing government offices, most of this uninspired structure is from the 19th and 20th centuries, but two noteworthy vestiges of the original 15th-century stronghold remain: the **Burgtor** (palace gate), which opens into the sprawling **Stadtpark** (municipal park); and the unusual 49-step, 26-foot carved stone double-spiral **Gothic staircase** of 1499, in the hexagonal tower at the far end of the grand courtyard.

Narrow, winding Sporgasse, one of the oldest streets in Graz, is lined with boutiques and cafés. It leads downhill to the Hauptplatz and Sack-
18 strasse, where the 17th-century **Herberstein Palace,** a former city residence of the ruling princes, now houses the **Neue Galerie** (new gallery). Its collection of paintings and sculpture from the 19th century to the present includes works by such Austrian artists as Egon Schiele, along with the newest in Styrian art. ✉ *Sackstr. 16,* ☎ *0316/829155.* *AS25.* *Tues.–Sat. 10–6, Sun. and holidays 10–1.*

Palais Khuenburg was the birthplace in 1863 of Archduke Franz Ferdinand, heir to the throne of the Austro-Hungarian empire. His assassination at Sarajevo in 1914 led directly to the outbreak of World War I. The palace is now home to the **Stadtmuseum** (city museum), whose exhibits trace the history of Graz and include an old-time pharmacy. ✉ *Sackstr. 18,* ☎ *0316/822580–0.* 🎫 *Free.* ⏲ *Tues. 10–9, Wed.–Sat. 10–6, Sun. and holidays 10–1.*

Schlossbergplatz marks the lower end of a stone staircase leading to the top of Graz's midtown mountain. The view from the summit takes in all of the city and much of central Styria, but since it is a 395-foot climb, you may prefer to use the **Schlossbergbahn** funicular railway (fare AS20). To reach it, follow Sackstrasse to Kaiser-Franz-Josef-Kai 38.

19 As its name implies, the **Schlossberg** (castle hill) was once a defensive fortification. The ramparts, which were built to prevent the invading Turks from marching up the Mur Valley toward Vienna, remained in place until 1809, when a victorious Napoléon had them dismantled after defeating the Austrians. The town paid a large ransom to preserve two of the castle's towers, but the rest was torn down and is today a well-manicured and very popular park. Atop the Schlossberg and a few steps east of the funicular station is the **Glockenturm** (bell tower), an octagonal structure from 1588 containing Styria's largest bell, the famous four-ton Liesl. This is also the departure point for guided walking tours of the Schlossberg, conducted daily, every hour from 9 to 5, except in winter. The **Open-Air Theater,** just yards to the north, is built into the old casemates of the castle and has a sliding roof in case of rain. Both opera and theater performances are held here in summer.

NEED A BREAK? The **Schlossberg Café,** at the top of the funicular railway, has garden tables with a sweeping view across Graz. Among its specialties are *Germknödel* (a sweet dumpling in poppyseed sauce) and *Most* (a light nonalcoholic wine).

20 A downhill walk from the Schlossberg toward the Old Town brings you to the 16th-century **Uhrturm** (clock tower), the most notable landmark of Graz. Its 18th-century clock mechanism has four giant faces that might at first confuse you—until you realize that the *big* hands tell the hour and the *small* hands, the minutes. At the time the clock was designed, this was thought to be easier to read at a distance.

21 The **Steirisches Volkskundemuseum** (Styrian Folklore Museum), which occupies parts of a former monastery in the Old Town, displays regional costumes, period room settings, and other items of local interest. ✉ *Paulustorgasse 13,* ☎ *0316/830416–0.* 🎫 *AS25.* ⏲ *Apr.–Oct., weekdays 9–4, weekends and holidays 9–noon.*

22 A major attraction of Graz, which requires at least a few hours to enjoy, is **Schloss Eggenberg,** a 17th-century palace on the very edge of the city surrounded by a large deer park. During the summer, candlelit chamber concerts are held in the palace. Take Streetcar 1 from the Hauptplatz or elsewhere to Schloss Strasse, then walk two blocks south to the entrance. Built around an arcaded courtyard lined with antlers, this fine example of the high-Baroque style contains gorgeous **Prunkräume** (state apartments), noted for their elaborate stucco decorations and frescoes, as well as three branch museums of the Joanneum. The largest is the **Jagdmuseum** (hunting museum) on the first floor, which displays antique weapons, paintings, and realistic dioramas. The **Abteilung für Vor- und Frühgeschichte** (Pre- and Early History Museum), has a remarkable collection of Styrian archaeological finds, including the small and rather strange **Strettweg Ritual Chariot** dating from the 7th century BC. The **Münzensammlung** (Numismatic Museum) is tucked away in a corner on the ground floor. The attractive outdoor café in the park surrounding the castle is the perfect place to fortify yourself before or after visiting the museums. ✉ *Eggenberger Allée 90,* ☎ *0316/53264–09.* 🎫

Park AS2; park, state apartments, and museums AS25. ⏲ *Park fall–spring, daily 8–6, and summer, daily 8–7; state-apartment tour Apr.–Oct., daily at 10, 11, noon, 2, 3, and 4; Numismatic Museum Feb.–Nov., daily 9–noon and 1–5; Hunting Museum Mar.–Nov., daily 9–noon and 1–5.*

Dining and Lodging

$$$–$$$$ ✕ **Casino-Restaurant.** It's no gamble when you dine in Graz's best restaurant, even if you have to pass the roulette wheels to reach the dining salons. The atmosphere is appropriately elegant and glitzy, if a bit dimly lit. Try the changing multicourse fixed menu or select from regional and international specialties such as rack of venison, roast lamb in cheese crust, or fillet of sturgeon with caviar. Desserts are excellent, berry compote with marzipan crust or elderberry sherbet being recommended examples. The wine list includes regional and international choices; wines by the glass are somewhat limited. ✉ *Landhausgasse 10,* ☎ *0316/832578–37. Jacket and tie. AE, DC, MC, V. Closed Good Fri., Nov. 1, Dec. 24. No lunch.*

$$$ ✕ **Gerlindes Gasthaus.** The *Gasthaus* reference notwithstanding, this is no rustic country inn magically relocated to a bustling city center. While a sportif crowd does settle in downstairs, the three eclectic and kitschy upstairs dining rooms attract more formal folk. Here, you'll find a mixed cuisine ranging from such regional specialties as lamb to more exotic offerings like medallions of venison or stuffed breast of chicken with watercress cream sauce and buckwheat dumplings. Only dinner is served. ✉ *Abraham-a-Santa-Clara-Gasse 2,* ☎ *0316/813830. Jacket and tie. AE, DC, MC. Closed Sun. and holidays. No lunch.*

$$$ ★ ✕ **Kaiser Josef.** The space is minuscule, the room modern, and the food among the best the city currently offers. The menu might offer cream of lobster soup, lobster in cognac sauce, or roast wild boar; ask about daily specials. ✉ *Schlögelgasse 1,* ☎ *0316/812512. No credit cards. Closed Sun., holidays, and Aug. No dinner Sat.*

$$$ ★ ✕ **Landhauskeller.** The Landhaus complex, which includes the provincial parliament and the armory, also includes a favorite traditional restaurant, with its comfortably rustic dining rooms and courtyard, set within the ancient arcaded Landhaus itself. Among the variety of hearty Styrian dishes that may be served are *Tafelspitz* (boiled beef) and ragout of veal. The menu is extensive and there are excellent Styrian wines, too. ✉ *Schmiedgasse 9,* ☎ *0316/830276. AE, DC, MC, V. Closed Sun., holidays, and late Dec.–mid-Jan.*

$$ ★ ✕ **Keplerkeller.** The astronomer Johannes Kepler is supposed to have lived here at the end of the 16th century, but, alas, there's no proof. It is, nevertheless, an atmospheric wine-cellar with heavy paneling and rustic decor, set between the Landeszeughaus and the Glockenspielplatz in the pedestrian zone of the Old Town. There is a lovely Renaissance courtyard for alfresco dining and live music after 9 PM. The menu features local specialties like Styrian beef salad, Styrian pan-roasted beef, or Tafelspitz, and locally made strudel, along with the usual schnitzels. The Keplerkeller is especially popular for its selection of local wines in open carafes. ✉ *Stempfergasse 6,* ☎ *0316/822449. AE, DC, MC, V. Closed Sun. and holidays. No lunch.*

$$ ★ ✕ **Stainzerbauer.** Local residents return again and again to this cheerful restaurant, one block south of the cathedral, to eat at their regular tables or, in summer, in the cool courtyard. The popular Styrian specialties may include such hearty dishes as pork chops on a wooden plank with garlic bread, *Fleischknödel* (bread-and-meat dumplings) in cream sauce, and a variety of crisp salads. ✉ *Bürgergasse 4,* ☎ *0316/821106. No credit cards. Closed Sun. and holidays.*

$ ✕ **Lustig Essen.** The concept in this stylishly modern restaurant is smaller portions, which means you can sample a wider range of such excellent Austrian and Styrian specialties as baked noodles with ham or grilled sausage with sauerkraut. Wine choices are somewhat limited but good. ✉ *Feuerbachgasse 8,* ☎ *0316/917885. No credit cards. Closed Sun. and holidays. No lunch.*

$$$$ ★ **Grand-Hotel Wiesler.** With five stars and a location just across the Mur river from the Old Town, the Wiesler is the doyen of Graz hotels. It dates from the turn of the century, as evidenced by high ceilings and large spaces, and was totally renovated in 1986. The decoration of both the public areas and the rooms is predominantly updated Art Nouveau, with much pale marble, cherry wood, and brass. ✉ *Grieskai 4, A–8020,* ☎ *0316/9066–0,* FAX *0316/9066–76. 98 rooms with bath. Restaurant, bar, sauna. AE, DC, MC, V.*

$$$$ ★ **Schlossberghotel.** This old inn, overlooking the Mur River at the foot of the Schlossberg, was rebuilt in 1982 and is a superb example of quiet good taste in a casually refined atmosphere. Each room is individually decorated and furnished with provincial antiques, although the creature comforts are thoroughly modern. An ultramodern annex offers convenient parking and also houses an excellent new restaurant, Donik, with international cuisine and panoramic view over the river. ✉ *Kaiser-Franz-Josef-Kai 30, A–8010,* ☎ *0316/8070–0,* FAX *0316/8070–160. 55 rooms with bath or shower. Restaurant, bar, pool, sauna, exercise room, parking. AE, DC, MC, V.*

$$$ ★ **Hotel Erzherzog Johann.** Travelers who prefer a traditionally elegant city hotel will be happy with this Old World establishment in a 16th-century building. Its location, just steps from the Hauptplatz in the Old Town, is perfect for tourists. Try to book one of the recently renovated rooms that open onto a charming atrium. ✉ *Sackstr. 3–5, A–8010,* ☎ *0316/811616,* FAX *0316/811515. 62 rooms with bath. Restaurant, bar, café, sauna. AE, DC, MC, V.*

$$$ **Hotel Europa.** Opened in 1986, this modern hotel is directly across from the main train station, 1½ kilometers (1 mile) west of the Old Town. Its thoroughly contemporary design and interiors and its ease of access make it popular with both businesspeople and tourists. An underground shopping mall connects it directly with the rail station and air terminal. ✉ *Bahnhofgürtel 89, A–8020,* ☎ *0316/9076–0,* FAX *0316/9076–606. 114 rooms with bath, 4 suites. Restaurant, bar, café, sauna. AE, DC, MC, V.*

$$$ **Hotel Gollner.** A friendly, atmospheric, older hotel near the Opera House on the edge of the Old Town, the Gollner has long been a favorite of the theatrical and operatic crowd. Its soundproof rooms are comfortably large and have been recently renovated; those still without a private bath are less expensive and rate in the $$ category. ✉ *Schlögelgasse 14, A–8010,* ☎ *0316/822521–0,* FAX *0316/822521–7. 50 rooms, 46 with bath or shower. Bar, sauna, exercise room. AE, DC, MC, V.*

$$$ **Hotel Mariahilf.** A comfortable old hotel in the center of things, the Mariahilf is just across the river from the Old Town. Although the location is fairly busy, the rooms are quiet thanks to soundproofing. Those without private bath rate in the $ category. ✉ *Mariahilferstr. 9, A–8020,* ☎ *0316/913163–0,* FAX *0361/917652. 44 rooms, 33 with bath or shower. Restaurant. AE, DC, MC, V.*

$$ **Rosenhotel Steiermark.** An exceptional value, this recent and very modern student accommodation, two blocks northeast of the university, functions as a hotel from early July until late September. Naturally, it attracts a young crowd and has an institutional feel, but if you want a clean room with a private bath at a low price, this is a good choice. ✉ *Liebiggasse 4, A–8010,* ☎ *0316/324041–0 or 0222/911–4910,* FAX *0316/381503–62 or 0222/910–0269. 121 rooms with shower. Restaurant, bar, parking. AE, DC, MC, V. Closed Oct.–June.*

Graz Dining and Lodging

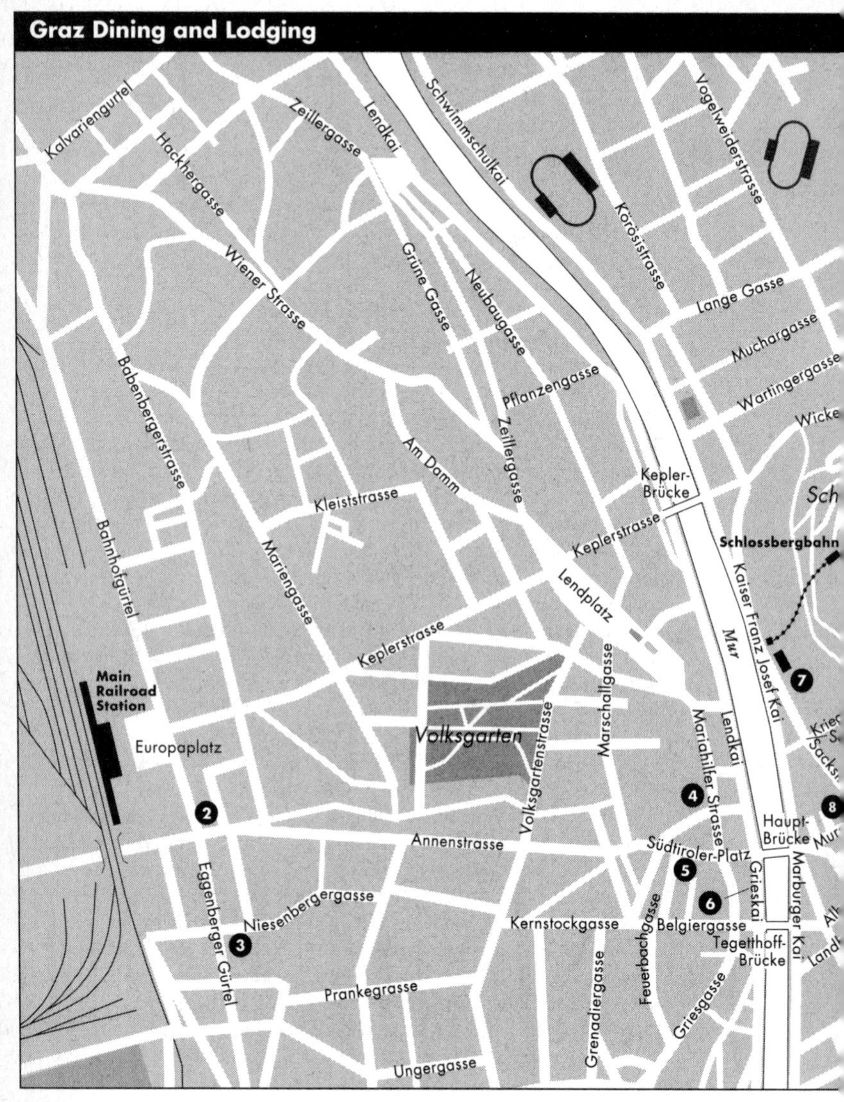

Dining
Casino-Restaurant, **9**
Gerlindes Gasthaus, **12**
Kaiser Josef, **15**
Keplerkeller, **10**
Landhauskeller, **13**
Lustig Essen, **5**
Stainzerbauer, **11**

Lodging
Grand-Hotel Wiesler, **6**
Hotel Erzherzog Johann, **8**
Hotel Europa, **2**
Hotel Gollner, **14**
Hotel Mariahilf, **4**
Hotel Strasser, **3**
Rosenhotel Steiermark, **1**
Schlossberg Hotel, **7**

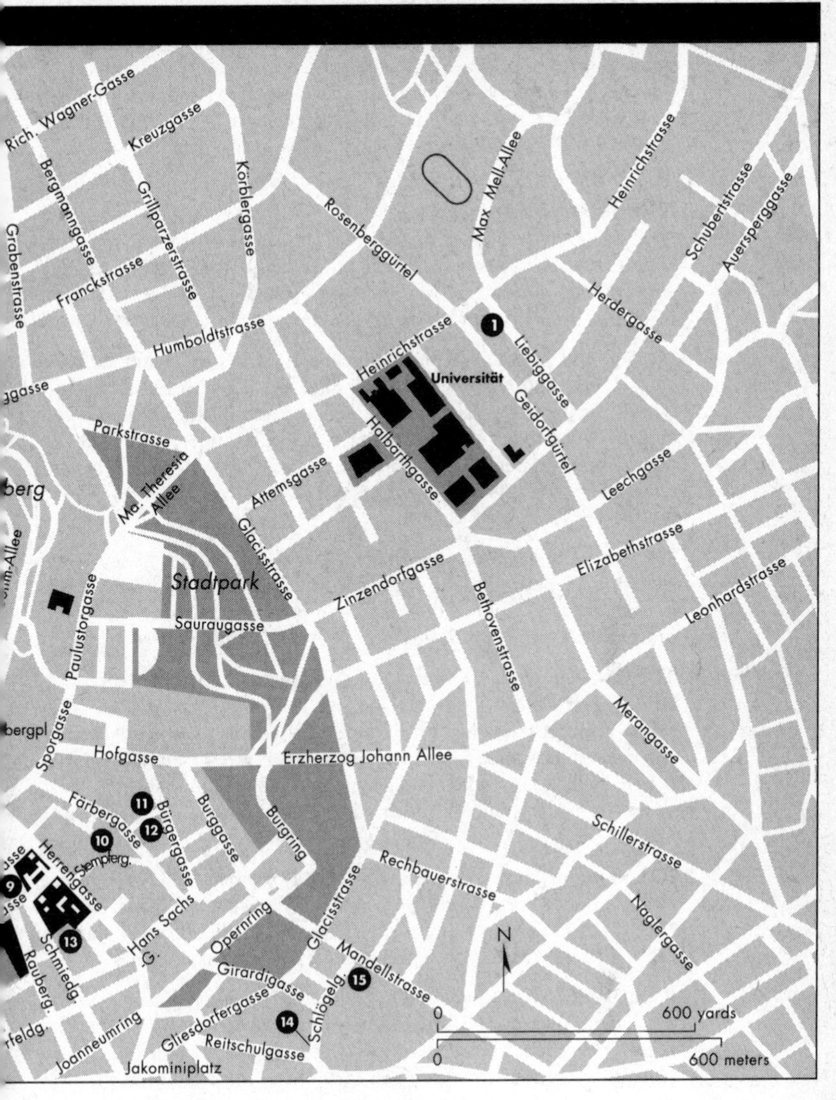

Rich. Wagner-Gasse
Kreuzgasse
Bergmanngasse
Grillparzerstrasse
Körblergasse
Grabenstrasse
Franckstrasse
Humboldtstrasse
Rosenberggürtel
Max Mell-Allee
Heinrichstrasse
Schubertstrasse
Auersperggasse
Herdergasse
Liebiggasse
Heinrichstrasse
Universität
Geidorfgürtel
Parkstrasse
Halbärthgasse
Attemsgasse
Ma. Theresia Allee
Leechgasse
Glacisstrasse
Stadtpark
Zinzendorfgasse
Elizabethstrasse
Leonhardstrasse
Paulustorgasse
Sauraugasse
Beethovenstrasse
Merangasse
Sporgasse
Hofgasse
Erzherzog Johann Allee
Färbergasse
Bürgergasse
Burggasse
Burgring
Schillerstrasse
Herrengasse
Stempferg.
Rechbauerstrasse
Glacisstrasse
Hans Sachs G.
Opernring
Naglergasse
Schmiedg.
Rauberg.
Girardigasse
Mandellstrasse
Schlögelg.
Gliesdorfergasse
Reitschulgasse
Joanneumring
Jakominiplatz
N
0
600 yards
0
600 meters

$ 🏨 **Hotel Strasser.** This friendly budget hotel, just two blocks south of the main train station, offers acceptable accommodations at rock-bottom prices. There is no elevator, the toilets are down the hall, and it is a bit noisy, but the rooms are large, comfortable, and clean, and the cozy restaurant is a good value. ✉ *Eggenberger Gürtel 11, A–8020,* ☎ *0316/913977,* FAX *0316/916856. 40 rooms, most with showers. Restaurant, parking. No credit cards.*

Nightlife and the Arts

Graz is noted for its avant-garde theater and its opera, concerts, and jazz. The Graz tourist office distributes the quarterly "Graz Guide," with information in English, and the "Graz Stadtanzeiger" (City Informer), a free monthly guide in German.

The **Styriarte** festival (late June to mid-July), under the direction of Nikolaus Harnoncourt, gathers outstanding musicians from around the world. Performances take place at Schloss Eggenburg and various halls in Graz. For program details contact the tourist office (☞ Visitor Information *in* Eastern Austria A to Z, *below*) or Styriarte (✉ Palais Attems, Sackstr. 17, A–8010 Graz, ☎ 0316/812941 or 0316/877–3835, FAX 0316/877–3836).

The annual **Styrian Autumn Festival** (*Steirische Herbst*), a sometimes shocking celebration of the avant-garde in experimental theater, music, opera, dance, jazz, film, video, and other performing arts, is held in Graz in October. Contact Styriarte (☞ *above*) or the tourist office for details.

The 19th-century **Graz Opera House,** with its resplendent Rococo interior, was completely renovated in 1984. Famed as a showcase for young talent and experimental productions as well as more conventional works, it stages three to five performances a week from late September through June. Tickets are generally available until shortly before the performances; call for information (✉ Kaiser-Josef-Pl. 10, ☎ 0316/8008–0 or 0316/8008–2000, FAX 0316/8008–91).

Graz, a major university town, has a lively **theater** scene known especially for its experimental productions. Its **Schauspielhaus,** built in 1825, is the leading playhouse, and there are smaller theaters scattered around town. Contact the tourist office for current offerings.

Popular **candlelight concerts** are held in the **Eggenberg Palace** on Monday evenings from mid-July to mid-September at 8 PM. Ask the Graz tourist office for details. During July and August, students and, occasionally, faculty of the **American Institute of Musical Studies** (AIMS) offer concerts. For information, check with the tourist office or the institute (☎ 0316/327066, FAX 0316/325574). Graz's **after-hours scene** is centered in the area around Prokopigasse, Bürgergasse, and Glockenspielplatz. Here you'll find activity until the early morning hours. The crowd moves around, so check with the tourist office for the current "in" spots. The **Casino Graz,** at the corner of Landhausgasse and Schmiedgasse in the Old Town, is open daily from 3 PM. It offers French and American roulette, blackjack, baccarat, and punto banco. The entrance fee of AS210 gets you AS250 worth of chips. A passport is required, you must be at least 21, and men are expected to wear a jacket and tie.

Shopping

Be on the lookout for traditional skirts, trousers, jackets, and coats of gray and dark green woolen loden cloth; dirndls; modern sportswear and ski equipment; handwoven garments; and objects of wrought iron. The **Heimatwerk** shop at Paulustorgasse 4 is associated with the local folklore museum and stocks a good variety of regional crafts and products. For a wide selection of conventional goods, try the leading department store, **Kastner & Öhler,** at Sackstrasse 7, just off the Hauptplatz. The many smart **boutiques** in the streets surrounding Sackstrasse carry typical cosmopolitan wares.

Stübing bei Graz

❸ 23 *15 km (9½ mi) northwest of Graz via Route 67 to Gratkorn, or 15 minutes by train to Stübing and a 2-km (1¼-mi) walk from there, or 40 minutes by municipal bus from Lendplatz.*

The attraction in Stübing bei Graz is the **Austrian Open-Air Museum** (Österreichisches Freilichtmuseum), which covers some 100 acres of hilly woodland. Here is a fascinating collection of about 80 authentic farmhouses, barns, Alpine huts, working water mills, forges, and other rural structures dating from the 16th century through the early 20th century, moved to this site from every province of Austria. Buildings that otherwise would have been lost in the rush to "progress" have been preserved complete with their original furnishings. Most of the buildings are open to visitors, and in several artisans can be seen at work, sometimes in period costume. There is a restaurant and outdoor café by the entrance. ✉ *Stübing bei Graz,* ☎ *03124/53700.* 💳 *AS60.* ⏲ *Apr.–Oct., Tues.–Sun. 9–5; last admission at 4.*

Piber

★ ❸ 24 *41 km (25 mi) west on Route 70 west to Köflach, and 3 km (2 mi) northeast of Köflach.*

The hamlet of Piber on the outskirts of Köflach is devoted to raising horses, and from the **Lippizaner Stud Farm** come the world-famous stallions that perform at the Spanish Riding School in Vienna. These snow-white horses trace their lineage back to 1580, when Archduke Karl of Styria established a stud farm at Lipiza near Trieste, using stallions from Arabia and mares from Spain. After World War I, when Austria lost Lipiza, the farm was transferred to Piber. Born black, the steeds gradually turn white between the ages of two and seven. To get to Piber, the train from Graz takes an hour (the bus 75 minutes), with departures every hour or two. Some trains split en route; be sure to board the correct car. Walk or take a taxi between Köflach and Piber. ✉ *Bundesgestüt Piber,* ☎ *03144/3323.* 💳 *Tour AS100.* ⏲ *Apr.–Oct.; 1-hr tour starts between 9 and 10:15 and 1:30 and 3:15.*

Bärnbach

3 km (2 mi) north of Voitsburg.

Bärnbach offers the amazing visual sight of the **Church of St. Barbara.** Completely redone in 1988 by the contemporary Austrian painter Friedensreich Hundertwasser, its exterior is a fantasy of abstract religious symbols in brilliant colors and shapes. At the interesting **Styrian glass center and museum,** you can watch glass blowing and purchase original glass articles. ✉ *Hochregisterstr. 1,* ☎ *03142/62950,* 💳 *AS55.* ⏲ *Weekdays 9–5, Sat. 9–1, Sun. and holidays May–Oct. 9–1.*

THROUGH STYRIA TO VIENNA

Realm of Iron

The mountainous green heartland of Styria embraces a region where ancient Romans once worked the surrounding mines of what are accurately called the Iron Alps. Here in West Styria, the atmosphere can change abruptly from industrial to tourist and can often combine the two—as at the Erzberg, literally a mountain of iron. The prime destination, however, remains Mariazell. In the past, royalty—not only the Habsburgs but princes of foreign countries as well—went there, not for social pleasures, but for religious reasons, for Mariazell has a double personality. It is a summer and winter pleasure resort and a renowned place of pilgrimage. The evening candlelit processions through the village to its famed basilica are beautiful and inspiring.

To tour this region, you can head southwest—after a scenic ride north through the Mur Valley to the historic crossroads of Bruck an der Mur—to Judenburg and possibly Murau and even continue into Salzburg province. Another option is to start toward Judenburg but turn northwest beyond Leoben to the abbey at Admont and then either return to Bruck via Eisenerz or continue north through Upper Austria to Amstetten or via Steyr to Linz on the Danube. Back at Bruck an der Mur, where several highways and rail lines converge, you can head north to Mariazell and then continue on one of the country's most scenic mountain drives (or rail trips) back to the Danube Valley.

Peggau

25 *20 km (12½ mi) north of Graz, 34½ km (21½ mi) south of Bruck an der Mur.*

Just north of the industrial town of Peggau (rail stop Peggau-Deutschfeistritz) is the famous **Lurgrotte,** the largest stalactite and stalagmite cave in Austria. Conducted tours lasting an hour follow a subterranean stream past illuminated sights, and there is a small restaurant at the entrance. To get to Peggau from Graz, head north on Route 67, driving through the heavily forested, narrow Mur Valley toward Bruck an der Mur. (A rail line parallels the road, with trains every hour or two making local stops near the points of interest.) ☎ *03127/2266, 03127/2580, or 03125/2218.* 🎫 *Tours AS50.* ⏲ *Nov.–mid-Apr., weekdays by appointment, tour weekends and holidays at 11 and 2; mid-Apr.–Oct., daily 10–4, tour at 11, 2, and 4.*

Mixnitz

14 km (8¾ mi) south of Bruck an der Mur.

Mixnitz is the starting point for a rugged 4½-hour hike through the
26 wild **Bärenschützklamm,** a savage gorge that can be negotiated only on steps and ladders but is nevertheless worth visiting for its spectacular foaming waterfalls. Beyond it are peaceful mountain meadows and finally the 5,650-foot **Hochlantsch** mountain.

Bruck an der Mur

27 *155 km (97 mi) southwest of Vienna, 55 km (34½ mi) north of Graz.*

Bruck an der Mur is known primarily as Styria's major traffic junction, a point where four valleys and two rivers converge and where several highways and main rail lines come together. Although most of the busy town is devoted to industry, its compact historic center, dating partially from the 13th century, is well worth a short visit.

The architecturally distinguished main square, **Koloman-Wallisch-Platz,** is four blocks west of the train station. On its northeast corner stands the late-15th-century **Kornmesserhaus,** a magnificent example of secular architecture in the late-Gothic style, noted especially for its elaborate loggia and arcades. The filigreed **Eiserner Brunnen** is across the square. This ornamental wrought-iron well housing dating from 1620 is considered to be the best piece of ironwork in Styria, a province noted for its metalwork. The **Rathaus** (town hall) facing it is also attractive and houses a small museum of local life (✉ Heimatmuseum, ☎ 03862/51521–0). On the hill behind is the **Pfarrkirche** (parish church), built between the 13th and 15th centuries, which has an interesting late-Gothic sacristy door of wrought iron.

Overlooking the town, just two blocks northeast of its center, are the remains of **Burg Landskron,** a 13th-century fortress that once defended the confluence of the Mur and Mürz rivers. Today only its clock tower remains intact, but the view is worth the short climb.

NEED A BREAK? The small park surrounding the Landskron ruins, on the Schlossberg hill, makes a wonderful spot for a **picnic.** Buy your supplies at one of the shops in the streets below.

Dining

$$$ ★ ✕ **Schnepf'n Wirt.** This comfortably elegant country inn is well regarded locally for its imaginative variations on Austrian cuisine. It is on the western edge of town, in the hamlet of Unteraich along the Mur river. Among the dishes you might find are a parfait of goose liver with leafy salad, fillet of sole with asparagus, beef tournedos broiled with horseradish crust, and chocolate mousse with fresh berries. Ask about the excellent regional wines, although others are also available. *✉ Unteraich 23, ☎ 03862/51474, FAX 03862/56024. AE, DC, MC, V. Closed Mon.; Tues.; and 2 wks in Aug. No dinner Sun. or holidays.*

Leoben

28 *16 km (10 mi) southwest of Bruck an der Mur.*

Interesting side trips fan out in several directions from the main junction of Bruck an der Mur. One takes you southwest by car (Route S6), train, or bus, to Leoben, the largest town in central Styria and the center of an important mining and heavy-industry region. Most of the attractions in the charming **Old Town** are near the Hauptplatz. Here, six blocks south of the train station, you will find some historic Altstadt sights, including the **Altes Rathaus** of 1568, the **Plague Column** (Pestsäule) of 1717, and the handsome 17th-century **Hacklhaus** with its densely decorated Baroque facade. Walking one block west brings you to the **Museum der Stadt Leoben,** a municipal museum of local history, industry, art, and nature (✉ Kirchgasse 6, ☎ 03842/4062–227). Next door is the **Stadtpfarrkirche** (city parish church) of 1660; a block to the south is the **Mautturm** (customs tower) of 1615, locally called the *Schwammerl,* because it resembles a mushroom.

Across the Mur river from the Mautturm is the **Maria-am-Wasser Kirche,** a Gothic church with outstanding 15th-century stained-glass windows. The suburb of **Göss,** 2 kilometers (1¼ miles) south, is home of the famous **Gösser beer,** made in a former monastery founded in 1020. The small beer museum is open weekdays; the brewery itself may be toured by prior arrangement (✉ Brauhausstr., ☎ 03842/2090–0).

Lodging

$$ ★ **Brücklwirt.** This low-slung, modern hotel-restaurant is on the main highway 116 in Niklasdorf, 5 kilometers (3¼ miles) northeast of Leoben. The smallish but comfortable hotel rooms are done in soothing browns and beiges and the tiled baths are immaculate and bright. With the advent of the autobahn, traffic noise on the street side has been greatly lessened, although trains still roll through across the street on the key north–south route; rooms in the back are quieter and have

a magnificent view across green fields to the hills beyond. The unintimate restaurant has enjoyed forays into creative elegance but has now settled back into a worthy selection of regional and Austrian specialties. In summer, dining on the outside candlelit terrace is a delight. ⊠ *Leobener Str. 90, A-8712 Leoben/Niklasdorf,* ☎ *03842/81727,* FAX *03842/81727–5. 21 rooms with bath. Restaurant, indoor pool, sauna, tennis, parking. AE, DC, MC, V.*

Seckau

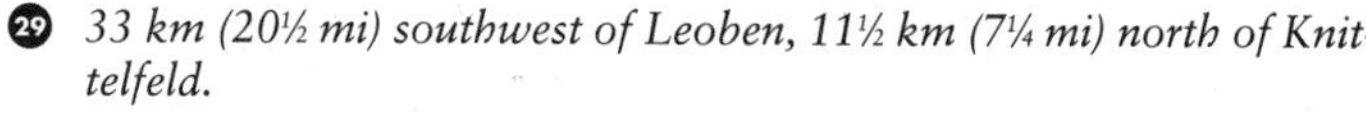

29 *33 km (20½ mi) southwest of Leoben, 11½ km (7¼ mi) north of Knittelfeld.*

For 550 years Seckau was the episcopal center of Styria, and its abbey is well worth a detour. The famed **Seckau Abbey** was founded in 1140 and over the years has been a significant religious center. The original Romanesque style of its church is visible despite later additions, and the complex contains several outstanding features of various periods, from the late-Renaissance mausoleum of Archduke Karl II to the strikingly modern apocalyptic frescoes in the Angels' Chapel by the 20th-century painter Herbert Boeckl. The whole complex of buildings bears rich testimony to the wealth that was lavished upon it—from stained-glass windows to wrought-iron fittings, paintings, and sculptures. To get to the abbey from Leoben, head southwest on Route S6/E7 along the Upper Mur Valley past St. Michael and on to Knittelfeld; About 16 kilometers (10 miles) north of this small industrial town is Seckau. ☎ *03514/234–300. Donation requested. Tour Sun. at 11:45 and 2:45, other days and times by appointment.*

Judenburg

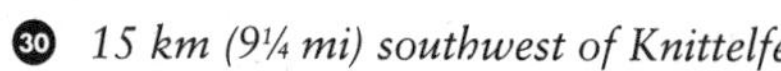

30 *15 km (9¼ mi) southwest of Knittelfeld.*

The ancient and attractive hill town of Judenburg overlooks the steelworks along the Upper Mur river valley. Its origins date to prehistoric times—the famous Strettweg Ritual Chariot (now on display at Schloss Eggenberg in Graz) was found here—but the town's name derives from a medieval colony of Jewish merchants. From its Hauptplatz rises the lofty **Stadtturm**, a 240-foot-high watchtower built between 1449 and 1520, which you can ascend. The tower is open May and June, Friday–Sunday 10–6; July–September, daily 10–6; and October, Friday–Sunday 10–5. The early 16th-century **Pfarrkirche** next to it has some excellent sculptures, especially of the Virgin. The small **Stadtmuseum** around the corner offers dioramas depicting local history and a display of minerals from nearby mines. ⊠ *Kaserngasse 27,* ☎ *03572/85053. Donation requested. Weekdays 9–noon.*

Just across the river from the Stadtmuseum, on Feldgasse, stands the 12th-century **Magdalenenkirche,** a Romanesque church with 14th-century frescoes and medieval stained-glass windows.

Murau

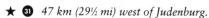

★ 31 *47 km (29½ mi) west of Judenburg.*

Murau is a stunningly picturesque, well-preserved medieval town where you can see stretches of the ancient **town wall**; the **Pfarrkirche** from 1296 with its ancient frescoes and late-Gothic "lantern of the dead" in the churchyard; the dominating **Schloss Obermurau,** a 13th-century castle that was rebuilt in the 17th century; and the **Altes Rathaus,** the old town hall that was once a part of the fortifications. Stroll along the river, looking up at the timbered houses atop the wall, to get the full effect of the town's medieval defensive character.

NEED A BREAK? The Murau brewery, with over 500 years brewing tradition, has a small museum and a souvenir shop, but stop in the ground-floor **Brauhaus** restaurant (✉ Raffaltpl. 17) to sample the brews and possibly have a filling meal of Styrian specialties as well.

If you ever dreamed of becoming a steam-locomotive engineer (*Lokführer*), Murau is your place. The narrow-gauge **Murtalbahn** (Mur Valley Railroad), which is more than 100 years old and is operated by the Steiermärkische Landesbahnen (Styrian Provincial Railways), gives engine-driving lessons on Thursday from early July until early September, ranging from 15 minutes on just a locomotive to longer periods with passenger cars attached; bring your friends, stock the bar car, and hire the local brass band to provide inspiration while you shovel the coal! The steam line also provides regular passenger service on the 37-kilometer (23-mile) stretch between Murau and Tamsweg several days a week from late June to mid-September. ☎ *03532/2233 or 0316/812581–26,* FAX *0316/812581–25.*

Eisenerz

★ 32 *30 km (18¾ mi) northwest of Leoben.*

The old mining town of Eisenerz is fascinating not only for its own attractions but also for the huge mountain of remarkably pure iron ore next to it. The community huddles around the Gothic parish **church of St. Oswald,** first built in 1282 and fortified as a bastion against the invading Turks in 1532. Its fantastically embellished interior is well worth seeing. West of the parish church stands the famous **Schichtturm,** an old tower whose bell once signaled the change of shifts at the mines. The 17th-century building now housing the **Stadtmuseum Eisenerz** was converted to an elegant hunting lodge by Emperor Francis Joseph; the museum today is devoted to mining and ironworking, as well as to local life and culture. ☎ *03848/3615.* 🎫 *AS36.* ⏲ *May–Oct., daily 9–5; Nov.–Apr., weekdays 9–noon.*

Just south of the town is its reason for being: the rust-colored, towering **Erzberg.** This mountain of iron ore has been worked since ancient times and still yields an ore that is 34% pure iron. Its present height is about 4,800 feet, although it was once much higher. Strip mining has given it a steplike appearance, similar to a ziggurat. Guided tours lasting about 1½ hours are conducted through the workings. It's cool inside no matter what the outside temperature, so take warm clothing. You can also tour the great stepped workings; transportation is via a crawler-truck fitted with seats. The trip takes about an hour. ✉ *Schau Bergwerke (inside), lower station of cableway near road from Präbichl,* ☎ *03848/4531–470 or 03848/3700.* 🎫 *Schau Bergwerke AS120, Tagebau (open mines) AS140, both tour AS230.* ⏲ *Schau Bergwerke tour May–Oct., daily at 10, 12:30, and 3; Tagebau tour May–Oct., daily by appointment with ticket office.*

Near Erzberg, southeast on Route 115, is the 6,250-foot **Polster** mountain that can be ascended by chairlift, offering great panoramic views to the west across the iron mountain.

En Route ★ Route 115 between Trofaiach and Hieflau to the northwest takes you through the scenic **Erzbach Valley,** with sensational vistas of snowcapped peaks to the southwest. The highway passes through the ancient mining town of **Vordernberg,** where Romans once worked with iron.

Northeast of Eisenerz is a hidden mountain lake of great beauty, the **Leopoldsteiner See**, worth the slight detour. Between Hieflau to Admont, Route 112 parallels the spectacular **Gesäuse Ravine,** where the Enns River with its plunging waterfalls surges through limestone formations. The magnificent 7,770-foot Hochtor peak can be seen to the south. This is among the wildest scenery in the Alps, and it's a favorite challenge for rock climbers.

Admont

★ 33 *40 km (25 mi) west of Eisenerz, 70 km (43¾ mi) northwest of Leoben, 20 km (12½ mi) east of Liezen.*

The small market town of Admont is dominated by its famous **Benedictine Abbey,** founded in the 11th century but almost entirely rebuilt after a disastrous fire in 1865. Of the earlier structures, only the glorious Baroque **library** survived intact. Fortunately, its treasures were also saved and are on view, including a Bible belonging to Martin Luther and a New Testament edited by Erasmus. The main building, 236 feet long, contains some 150,000 volumes and is noted for its 18th-century ceiling frescoes by Bartholomeo Altomonte as well as for its statues of *The Four Last Things* (Death, Judgment, Hell, and Heaven). There are also an extensive natural-history museum with lots of insects, an art museum, and a museum of local life. Many travelers visit this abbey from Bruck an der Mur, crossing mountainous country through western Styria. You can get there directly by taking Routes S6, 113, and A9 west and northwest almost to Liezen, then turning east on Route 117. The total distance is 100 kilometers (62 miles); both trains and a limited bus service operate over the entire route, with changes required. If you prefer picturesque back roads, follow the itinerary previously described to a point 6 kilometers (4 miles) west of Judenburg, take the steep but scenic Hohntaurern Pass Road (Route 114) north to Trieben, and then continue as above. ☎ *03613/2312–47.* *AS40.* *May–Sept., daily 10–1 and 2–5; Apr. and Oct., daily 10–noon and 2–4; Nov.–Mar. by appointment.*

Thörl

 *12 km (7½ mi) northwest of Kapfenberg, 42 ki (26¼ mi) south of Mariazell.*

A popular excursion from Bruck an der Mur takes you north 61 kilometers (38 miles) to Mariazell, a historic pilgrimage center. Along the way on Route 20, you'll discover the village of Thörl, dominated by the ruined 15th-century stronghold of **Schloss Schachenstein.** Nearby stands a curious roadside chapel with an unusually carved Calvary dating from 1530. Just north is the popular mountain health resort of **Aflenz Kurort,** from which a chairlift ascends the 5,110-foot **Bürgeralm.** It operates daily during the ski season, but only Friday through Monday and on holidays the rest of the year. The village church, dating partially from the 12th century, is noted for its rustic stonework.

The delightful narrow-gauge **Thörler Bahn** railroad, which marked its 100th anniversary in 1993, runs with its steam locomotives from Kapfenberg to Thörl-Aflenz on selected Tuesdays, Saturdays and Sundays from late June through mid-September. The rambling trip takes 1½ hours (☎ 03862/55288, 03862/21589, or 03862/56641).

En Route Headed north on Route 20, you'll climb to over 4,000 feet as the road crosses the **Seeberg Pass,** from which you can see the surrounding mountain ranges of Hochschwab and Veitschalpe. A descent to the valley is followed by another rise to Mariazell.

Mariazell

★ 35 *57 km (35¾ mi) north of Bruck an der Mur, 76 km (47½ mi) south of Ybbs an der Donau, 67 km (41¾ mi) southwest of St. Pölten.*

An excursion to Mariazell—famed for its pilgrimage church and gingerbread—is an adventure, thanks to the winding road that brings you there. The town has been a place of pilgrimage since 1157, when the Benedictines established a priory here. After Louis I, King of Hungary, attributed his victory over the Turks in 1377 to the intervention of its Virgin, Mariazell's reputation for miracles began to spread. As a year-round resort, Mariazell offers a wide range of sports and recreation; in winter there's a good ski school for beginners and young people.

The impressive **Mariazeller basilica** stands resolutely over the town square. The present structure replaced the original church during the 14th century and was itself enlarged in the late 17th century by the Italian architect Domenico Sciassia. Its exterior is unusual, with the original Gothic spire and porch flanked by squat, bulbous Baroque towers. Step inside to see the incredibly elaborate plasterwork and paintings. In the **Gnadenkapelle,** or Chapel of Miracles, the nave holds the main object of pilgrimage: the 12th-century statue of the Virgin of Mariazell. It stands under a silver baldachin designed in 1727 by the younger Fischer von Erlach and behind a silver grille donated by Empress Maria Theresa, who took her first communion here. Following her example, thousands of youngsters neatly turned out in white are brought annually from all over Austria to Mariazell for their first communion, usually on or around Whitsun. The bubbling **high altar** of 1704, by the elder Fischer von Erlach—the leading architect of the Austrian Baroque—is in the east end of the nave. Don't miss seeing the **Schatzkammer** (treasury) for its collection of votive offerings from medieval times to the present (open May–October 30, weekdays 10:30–noon and 2–3, weekends 10–3; admission is 20AS). Walls are covered with plaques, many of them illustrated, given in thanks for assorted blessings, including rescues ranging from runaway horses to shipwrecks.

Pay a visit to the **Heimatmuseum,** or Regional Museum of Local Life, at Wienerstrasse 35. Bruno Habertheuer's **mechanical Nativity figurines** are at the **Stations of the Cross** on Calvary Hill (✉ Kalvarienberg 1, ☎ 03882/2108). The nativity scene with its 130 moving figures took 18 years to build. Admission to the museum is AS10.

The skiing on 4,150-foot **Bürgeralpe** is quickly reached by the Bürgeralpebahn cable car from a lower station just two blocks north of the basilica. Paths from the upper station fan out in several directions for country walks in summer. ✉ *Wienerstr. 28,* ☎ *03882/2555.* 🎫 *Round-trip AS85.* ⏲ *Late Apr.–June, early–mid-Oct., and mid- to late Nov., daily 9–5; July and Aug., daily 8:30–5:30; Sept., daily 8:30–5; Dec. daily 8–4, Jan.–Mar., daily 8–5.*

The **Museumtramway,** the world's oldest steam tramway, dating to 1884, operates between Mariazell and the Erlaufsee, for a 20-minute ride of about 3½ kilometers (2 miles) to a lovely lake. For AS150 extra charge, you can accompany the engineer in the cab. ✉ *Bahnhof Mariazell,* ☎ *03882/3014,* FAX *03882/3393.* 🎫 *Round-trip AS50.* ⏲ *July–Sept., weekends and holidays, hourly 9:30–late afternoon.*

The famous narrow-gauge **Mariazellerbahn** rail line ambles over an 84 kilometer (52½ mile) route between Mariazell and St. Pölten, coursing magnificent valleys and surmounting mountain passes in the process. This remarkable engineering achievement—the line incorporates 21 tunnels and 75 bridges and viaducts—was built in 1907 and electrified in 1911. The cars are modern but the sensation is one of ages long past. About five trains a day traverse the route in each direction. In St. Pölten, the narrow-gauge line connects with the main east–west rail route. For schedules, contact the Austrian Federal Railways system (☎ 03882/2366).

Dining and Lodging

$$ ✕ **Jägerwirt.** In what is basically a tourist town, this restaurant, directly across from the basilica, offers traditional country atmosphere and solid Austrian cuisine at fair prices. Besides the usual steaks and Wiener schnitzels, the menu may include such items as boiled pork with grated horseradish and breast of veal with dumplings. ✉ *Hauptpl. 2, ☎ 03882/2362. No credit cards. Closed Mon., most of Dec., and 2 wks around Easter.*

$$$ **Hotel Feichtegger.** Although this is a five-story modern hotel near the basilica and the cable car, its ambience is one of quiet, understated luxury. The well-equipped guest rooms have balconies. ✉ *Wiener Str. 6, A–8630, ☎ 03882/2416–0, FAX 03882/2416–80. 48 rooms with bath. Restaurant, bar, indoor pool, sauna, exercise room. AE, DC, MC, V. Closed 2 wks in mid-Dec.*

$$$ **Mariazellerhof.** This small, cheerfully modern chalet-style hotel one block west of the basilica is known for its gingerbread snacks; the spicy aroma fills the house. Its comfortable rooms have balconies. ✉ *Grazer Str. 10, A–8630, ☎ 03882/2179–0, FAX 03882/2179–51. 10 rooms with bath, 4 with shower. Café. DC, MC. Closed last 3 wks of Jan.*

Shopping

Parts of town are permeated by the spicy aroma of baking **gingerbread** for which Mariazell is famous, and you'll see the decorated cookies everywhere.

THE MOUNTAIN ROUTE TO VIENNA

The most direct route from Bruck an der Mur northward to Vienna is also in some ways the most interesting. It takes you through the cradle of Austrian skiing, past several popular resorts, and over the scenic Semmering Pass and offers an opportunity to ride a 19th-century steam cogwheel train to the top of the highest mountain in this part of the country, a peak that often remains snowcapped into the summer. It also takes you to Wiener Neustadt, a small, historic city. This area's proximity to Vienna makes day trips or weekend excursions from the capital practical.

Mürzzuschlag

36 *37 km (23¼ mi) northeast of Bruck an der Mur, 14 km (8¾ mi) southwest of Semmering.*

The resort town of Mürzzuschlag is popular for both winter and summer sports. From Bruck an der Mur, head northeast on S6, past the industrial town of Kapfenberg, and take the exit marked for the resort. It is regarded as the birthplace of Austrian skiing and, in a sense, of the Winter Olympics, since the first Nordic Games were held here in 1904, but the main focus of ski activity has long since moved west to the Tirol. Mürzzuschlag is popular with the Viennese and preserves its past glories in the excellent **Winter-Sports-Museum,** which displays equipment past and present from around the world. ✉ *Wiener Str. 79, ☎ 03852/3504. AS30. Tues.–Sun. 9–noon and 2–5.*

Austria's only museum dedicated to composer Johannes Brahms, a German who adopted Austria as his home, is in Mürzzuschlag, where he spent many summers. The museum also hosts a number of chamber music concerts and recitals. ✉ *Wienerstr. 4,* ☎ *03852/3434 or 03852/3399.* *AS40.* ⏲ *May–Sept., daily 10–noon and 2–6; Oct.–Apr., daily 2–6.*

Semmering

37 *14 km (8¾ mi) northeast of Mürzzuschlag, 90 km (56¼ mi) southwest of Vienna.*

Climbing along Route 306, high atop the Semmering Pass, at a height of 3,230 feet, lies the boundary between the provinces of Styria and Lower Austria. A bridle path has existed on this mountainous route since at least the 12th century, but the first road was not built until 1728. Today's highway is an engineering wonder, particularly on the Lower Austrian side, where the new road high on concrete stilts leaps over deep valleys; the old road snakes up in a series of switchback curves. The Styrian side is less dramatic, but offers distant alpine vistas. Given the technologies of the era, the railway—completed in 1854—that crosses the divide is a technical marvel, with its great viaducts and tunnels, and is still the main north–south rail route. At the top is Semmering, the first town in Lower Austria, a resort on a south-facing slope overlooking the pass. Sheltered by pine forests and built on terraces reaching as high as 4,250 feet, Semmering is considered to have a healthy atmosphere and has several spa-type hotels and pensions. The Semmering area plus the nearby Rax and Schneeberg regions are immensely popular in winter with the Viennese skiers. This is the area in which most Viennese first learn to ski, meaning that there are slopes ranging from gentle to the more challenging, although they are no match for the rugged Alpine stretches of Tirol and Salzburg province.

OFF THE BEATEN PATH

HÖLLENTAL – A delightful side trip can be made from Semmering into the Höllental (valley of Hell), an extremely narrow and romantic gorge cut by the Schwarza stream between two high mountains, the Raxalpe and the Schneeberg (snow mountain). From Hirschwang, at the beginning of the valley you can ride the **Raxbahn cable car** to a plateau on the Raxalpe at 5,075 feet. ☎ *02666/2497.* *Round-trip AS165.* ⏲ *High season, daily 8–5:30 at ½-hr intervals; other months, daily 9–4:30 at ½-hr intervals.*

Dining and Lodging

$$$ **Panoramahotel Wagner.** The view over the surrounding mountains provides the setting for this renovated hotel, which delights in the personal touch. The kitchen has established itself as the best in the area; try the lamb or fish. The excellent beer comes from a tiny brewery in the valley below. ✉ *Hochstr. 267, A–2680,* ☎ *02664/2512–0,* FAX *02664/2512–61. 26 rooms with bath. Sauna. DC, MC. Closed Wed., Thurs., and Oct.–mid-Dec.*

$$–$$$ **Belvedere.** Recently renovated, this old Alpine-style mountain inn is well known for its hearty Austrian food. Though located in town, it has an outdoor garden for dining in fine weather. Expect to find such offerings as fresh cream of asparagus soup, pork chops, and roast chicken. ✉ *Hochstr. 60, A–2680,* ☎ *02664/2270,* FAX *02664/2267–42. 19 rooms. Indoor pool, sauna. AE, DC, MC, V. Closed mid- to late Apr.*

$$$–$$$$ **Hotel Panhans.** This classic and popular mountain lodge resort is set near the center of town; it is frequently booked for conventions. Built in 1888, the main lodge has retained its characteristic Art Nouveau ambience despite a 1982 modernization. In 1993 a luxurious annex connected by an enclosed walkway was added behind the main building; it offers imaginative minisuites for honeymooners, stargazers (telescopes provided), and those who want their own open hearth. The elegant *Kaiser Karl* restaurant is ambitious but inconsistent and occasionally disappointing; the more relaxed *Wintergarten* restaurant is a better choice. Wines are excellent, and the hotel has its own Vinotek for tastings. ✉ *Hochstr. 32, A–2680,* ☎ *02664/8181–0,* FAX *02664/8181–513. 112 rooms with bath. Restaurant, bar, café, indoor pool, sauna, exercise room, dance club. AE, DC, V.*

Puchberg am Schneeberg

38 *19 km (11¾ mi) northwest of Wiener Neustadt.*

People flock to the quiet mountain resort of Puchberg am Schneeberg largely to ride to the top of the Schneeberg mountain, Lower Austria's highest peak. You get to Puchberg via regular trains from Vienna, Wiener Neustadt, or points south. From Vienna, the railroads have a package ticket that includes the regular rail connection, the cog railway, and a chit for lunch at one of the mountaintop restaurants. From Höllental, continue north into the alley for 18 kilometers (11 miles), passing through the wildest section, to Schwarzau im Gebirge. Then circle the north slope of the Schneeberg via the Klostertal to the resort.

The marvelous, old narrow-gauge **Puchberg cog-wheel steam train** ascends to a plateau near Schneeberg's summit. Although many use the rail line as a starting point for mountain hiking, the journey itself is an exciting outing. Allow the better part of a day for this trip, since the ride takes 1⅓ hours each way and the trains are none too frequent, some running on a schedule and others according to demand. This excursion is very popular; make reservations well in advance—particularly for weekends and holidays—at any rail station in Europe. If you don't already have them, make reservations at Puchberg for the return down trip before you board for the trip up. Bring along a light sweater or jacket even in summer; it can be both windy and cool at the top. Ordinary walking shoes are sufficient unless you wander off the main trails, in which case you'll need hiking boots, along with some mountain experience.

The steam engines, dating from the 1890s, are built at a peculiar angle to the ground to keep their fireboxes level while climbing. The wooden cars they haul are of equal vintage, with hard seats; a rest stop is made at the **Baumgartner Haus,** where you can get refreshments before continuing up past the timberline and through two tunnels (close the windows or suffocate!). Near the upper station hut at altitude 5,892 feet is the small **Elizabeth Chapel** and the **Berghaus Hochschneeberg,** a simple lodge with a restaurant and overnight guest facilities. From here, you can walk to the **Kaiserstein** for a panoramic view and to the **Klosterwappen,** the highest peak, at 6,811 feet above sea level. Allow about 2–3 hours total for these walks. Maps are available at the lodge. The last train down usually leaves about 4:30 or 5:30 PM; later runs are made if traffic warrants. Eurailpass and Euro Domino card holders may use their passes but must make seat reservations. ✉ *Schneeberg Bahn, Bahnhof Puchberg,* ☎ *02636/2225–0.* *Round-trip AS250.* *Late Apr.–Oct.*

NEED A BREAK?

Real stick-to-your-ribs mountain food, draft beer, and plenty of gemütlichkeit are served up at the inexpensive **Damböck Haus,** a rustic hut operated by the Austrian Touring Club (ÖTK). It's only a 15-minute walk from the upper station of the Puchberg line.

Lodging

$ **Berghaus Hochschneeberg.** The only way to reach this simple mountaintop lodge, other than by climbing, is by the famous old steam cog railway from Puchberg. You arrive to find panoramic views and a sturdy stone hotel, as old as the railway (1898), set in peaceful surroundings. Although there are few modern conveniences (one bathroom per floor, running water in rooms, TV only in the reception room), staying here is an invigorating experience. There are wonderful paths to hike. ✉ *Hochschneeberg, A–2734,* ☎ *02636/2257. 25 rooms without bath. Restaurant, sauna. No credit cards. Closed Nov.–Apr.*

Wiener Neustadt

39 *45 km (28¼ mi) south of Vienna, 38 km (23¾ mi) northeast of Semmering, 27 km (16¾ mi) west of Eisenstadt.*

Although today's Wiener Neustadt is a busy industrial center built on the ashes of its prewar self, enough of its past glories survived World War II's bombings to make a visit worthwhile. The small city was established in 1194 as a fortress to protect Vienna from the Hungarians. During the mid-15th century it was an imperial residence, and in 1752 it became, and still is, the seat of the Austrian Military Academy. Begin your exploration of the Old Town at the **Hauptplatz,** the largely traffic-free main square, which contains several rebuilt medieval houses with Gothic arcades standing opposite the 16th-century **Rathaus** (city hall).

NEED A BREAK? The nicest place in town for pastries, ice cream, snacks, or even light meals is the **Café Witetschka** (✉ Allerheiligenpl. 1) located on a delightful and historic little square just half a block from the southwest corner of the Hauptplatz. You can sit at tables in the garden in good weather.

The mighty **Stadtpfarrkirche** (town parish church), also known as the Liebfrauenkirche, rises imposingly out of the center of Domplatz, or cathedral square. Begun in the 13th century, the church had cathedral status from 1468 until 1784, and a number of choirs and chapels were added during that period. Note the ornate entryway on the south side, dating to about 1230. Styles are mixed between Roman and Gothic, but the interior is impressive for its unity of columned walls and ribbed ceiling. Look for the painted wooden figures of the Apostles dating to about 1500, a mural of the Last Judgment from about 1300, and the splendid tomb of Cardinal Khlesl with a bust carved in 1630 attributed to the school of Giovanni Bernini, the master of the Italian Baroque.

A narrow lane called the Puchheimgasse leads to the 12th-century **Reckturm,** a defensive tower said to have been built with part of the ransom money paid to free Richard the Lionhearted. Down Baumkirchnerring at the corner of Wiener Strasse is the 14th-century **Church of St. Peter-an-der-Sperr,** once a defense cloister, now an exhibition gallery. The greatest treasure in the **Stadtmuseum,** which is in a onetime Jesuit residence on Wiener Strasse, is the *Corvinusbecher,* an elegant 32-inch-high goblet from 1487 that was a gift from the Hungarian king who conquered the town.

To the east of the Hauptplatz, on Neuklostergasse, is the **Neukloster Church,** part of a Cistercian convent founded in 1250. Behind the high altar in the richly Baroque interior is the tomb of Eleanor of Portugal (died 1467), wife of the emperor Frederick III.

The massive **Burg** on Grazer Strasse, a castle begun in the 13th century and rebuilt as an imperial residence in the 15th century, was designated the Austrian Military Academy by order of Empress Maria

Theresa in 1752. The Nazis took it over in 1938, and its first German commandant was General Erwin Rommel, the Desert Fox. The complex was battered by bombing in 1943 and 1945 but subsequently rebuilt. Enter its grounds to visit the famous 15th-century **Church of St. George,** whose gable is decorated with, among others, 14 Habsburg coats of arms. Beneath the gable is a statue of Friedrich III curiously inscribed "A.E.I.O.U." which some believe stand for the Latin words that mean "Austria will rule the world." Inside the church, under the steps of the high altar, the remains of Emperor Maximilian I are buried.

Dining and Lodging

$$$–$$$$ ✕ **Gelbes Haus.** The 1906 Art Deco "Yellow House" slightly north of the center offers limited but outstandingly prepared dishes served in tasteful surroundings. Look for consomée with meat-filled strudel, Tafelspitz and breast of duck with goose liver, and for dessert, figs with apple-cinnamon parfait. The homemade sherbets are also outstanding. The wine selection is broad, by the glass as well as the bottle. ✉ *Kaiserbrunngasse 11,* ☎ *02622/26400. DC, MC, V. Closed Sun. and holidays.*

$$$ ✕🏨 **Hotel Corvinus.** A low, modern, and exceptionally pleasant hotel next to the city park, the recently built Corvinus is two blocks east of the train station and only a few minutes' stroll from the main square. It caters primarily to business travelers. The restaurant is recommended. ✉ *Bahngasse 29–33, A–2700,* ☎ *02622/24134,* FAX *02622/24139. 68 rooms with bath. Restaurant, bar, sauna, meeting rooms. AE, DC, MC, V.*

Nightlife and the Arts

The **Wiesen Jazz Festival** attracts top-name performers from America and around the world for a couple of days in early July in Wiesen, Burgenland (12 kilometers, or 7½ miles, southeast of Wiener Neustadt). The Jazz Pub in Wieden has information (☎ 02626/81648–0 or 02626/81769–0, FAX 02626/81769–29).

EASTERN AUSTRIA A TO Z

Arriving and Departing

By Bus

The major bus services connecting Vienna to towns in Eastern Austria are **Bundesbus** (☎ 0222/71101); **Austrobus** (☎ 0222/534–11–0, FAX 0222/534–11–200); **Blaguss Reisen** (☎ 0222/501–80–0, FAX 0222/501–80–125); and **Dr. Richard** (☎ 0222/331–00–0, FAX 0222/330–9595). There is good service to Neusiedl am See, Eisenstadt, and Güssing in Burgenland; Mariazell in Styria; and Wiener Neustadt in Lower Austria. Direct express service to Graz is infrequent. Most buses leave Vienna from the Wien Mitte Bus Station on Landstrasser Hauptstrasse, opposite the air terminal and Hilton Hotel, but be sure to check first, since some services to the south may depart from the bus terminal area at Südtirolerplatz, to the west of the Südbahnhof rail station.

By Car

Two main autobahns traverse this region: the incomplete A3 between Vienna and Eisenstadt; and the heavily-traveled A2 between Vienna and past Wiener Neustadt to Graz and further south. Northern Burgenland can be reached via the A4 autobahn east out of Vienna.

By Plane

The northern part of Eastern Austria is served by Vienna's international airport at Schwechat, 19 kilometers (12 miles) southeast of the city center (☞ Chapter 2).

Graz has its own international airport at Thalerhof, just south of the city, with flights to and from Vienna, Innsbruck, Linz, Paris, Munich, Frankfurt, Düsseldorf, and Zürich. **Austrian Airlines** and its subsidiary **Tyrolean Airways,** and **Lufthansa** are the major carriers. Call for information (☏ 0316/291541–0).

By Train

Vienna or Graz are the logical rail arrival or departing points for this part of Austria. The main international north–south route connecting Vienna and northeastern Italy runs through this region and is traversed by **EuroCity** trains from Munich, Salzburg, Linz, Klagenfurt, and Venice, as well as other cities in neighboring countries. Nearly all long-distance trains going through this region meet at Bruck an der Mur, where connections can be made.

Getting Around

By Bus

Post office and railroad buses cover the area thoroughly, although services are less frequent in less populated areas further distant from city centers. Take trains for the main routes.

By Car

Driving is the best way to enter and explore Eastern Austria, especially if you're visiting the smaller towns and villages or if your time is limited. Route 10 from Vienna to Lake Neusiedl in Burgenland is the preferred scenic alternative to the new A4 autobahn. Graz is connected to Vienna by both A2 and a more scenic mountain road, Route S6 over the Semmering Pass to Bruck an der Mur, then south through the Mur Valley.

By Streetcar

In Graz, streetcars and buses are an excellent way of traveling within the city. Single tickets (AS20) can be bought from the driver, and one-day and multiple-ride tickets are also available. All six streetcar routes converge at Jakominiplatz near the south end of the Old Town. One fare may combine streetcars and buses as long as you take a direct route to your destination. For more detailed information, ☏ 0316/887411.

By Taxi

In Graz, taxis can be ordered by phone (☏ 0316/878, 0316/889, 0316/983–0, or 0316/2801). Driving in the city center is not advisable, since there are many narrow, one-way, and pedestrian streets and few places to park.

By Train

If you're not driving, take trains on the main routes; services are fast and frequent. Trains depart from Vienna's Südbahnhof (South Station) hourly for the one-hour ride to Neusiedl am See. Connections can be made there for Eisenstadt and Pamhagen. There is also express service every two hours from the same station in Vienna to Graz, 2½ hours away, with intermediate stops at Wiener Neustadt, Mürzzuschlag, and Bruck an der Mur, and connections to Puchberg am Schneeberg, Semmering, and points west. Trains for Mariazell depart from Vienna's Westbahnhof (West Station), with a change at St. Pölten. Call for information (departures from Vienna, ☏ 0222/1717; Graz's main station, ☏ 0316/1717).

Contacts and Resources

Bicycling

Bicycling is enormously popular in the flatlands around Lake Neusiedl. Try the following for rentals: in Neusiedl am See, **Bahnhof** (⊠ train station, ☎ 02167/2437) and **Hotel Wende** (✉ Seestr. 40, ☎ 02167/8111–0); in Podersdorf, **Fahrradverleih Tauber** (✉ Strandpl. 1, ☎ 02177/2204) and **Rad-Sport Waldherr** (✉ Hauptstr. 42, ☎ 02177/2297); in Illmitz, **Polay** (✉ Florianigasse 5, ☎ 02175/24192); in Rust, **Schneeberger** (✉ Rathauspl. 15, ☎ 02685/6442); in Mörbisch, **Posch** (✉ Blumentalgasse 9, ☎ 02685/8242).

Boating

You can hire boats (*Bootsvermietung* or *Bootsverleih*) around Lake Neusiedl from **Baumgartner** (✉ Neusiedl am See, ☎ 02167/2782), **Knoll** (✉ Podersdorf, ☎ 02177/2431), **Stefan Gangl** (✉ Illmitz, ☎ 02175/2158), **Ruster Freizeitcenter** (✉ Rust, ☎ 02685/595), and **Friedrich Lang** (✉ Mörbisch, ☎ 02685/8381). Expect to pay about AS50 per hour for a rowboat, AS80 for a pedal boat, and AS120 for an electric boat. Sailboat prices vary widely.

Car Rentals

Cars can be rented at all airports and in Graz from **Avis** (✉ Schlögelgasse 10 and airport, ☎ 0316/812920, FAX 0316/841178); **Buchbinder** (✉ Keplerstr. 93–95, ☎ 0316/917330, FAX 0316/918843); **Budget** (✉ Bahnhofgürtel 73, ☎ 0316/916966, FAX 0316/916683–4; airport, ☎ 0316/292506); **Europcar** (✉ Wiener Str. 15, ☎ 0316/914080–0, FAX 0316/911929); and **Hertz** (✉ Andreas-Hofer-Pl. 1, ☎ 0316/825007, FAX 0316/810288).

Emergencies

Police, ☎ 133. **Fire,** ☎ 122. **Ambulance,** ☎ 144; in Graz, **Medical Service,** ☎ 141. **Late-Night Pharmacies,** ☎ 18.

Guided Tours

Relatively few guided tours visit Eastern Austria, and those that do are in German, although English may be available on request. Inquire when booking. General orientation tours, departing from Vienna and lasting one to four days, are offered by the following reputable operators: **Vienna Sightseeing Tours** (✉ Stelzhammergasse 4/11, A–1031 Vienna, ☎ 0222/712–4683–0, FAX 0222/712–4683–77); **Cityrama Sightseeing** (✉ Börsegasse 1, A–1010 Vienna, ☎ 0222/534–13–0, FAX 0222/534–13–22); **CityTouring Vienna** (✉ Penzingerstr. 46, A–1140 Vienna, ☎ 0222/894–1417–0, FAX 0222/894–3239); **Blaguss Reisen** (✉ Wiedner Hauptstr. 15, A–1040 Vienna, ☎ 0222/501–80–0, FAX 0222/501–80–125); and **Austrobus** (✉ Dr. Karl Lueger-Ring 8, A–1010 Vienna, ☎ 0222/534–11–0, FAX 0222/534–11–200). The one-day tours are usually to Lake Neusiedl and include a boat ride, or to the Semmering mountain region with a cable-car ride.

Minibus sightseeing tours of Graz are conducted on weekdays from May through October. **Guided walking tours** of the Old Town, in English and German, are held April–October, daily at 2, and November–March, Saturday at 2. Guided tours of the Schlossberg are conducted daily April–mid-October, departing hourly 9–5 from the Glockenturm near the upper station of the Schlossberg funicular. For prices, bookings, and current schedules of all tours, contact the city tourist office (☞ Visitor Information, *below*).

Horseback Riding

The area around Lake Neusiedl is ideal for riding. Livery stables on the east side of the lake include two at Podersdorf, **Frankl** (☎ 02177/2251) and **Lang** (☎ 02177/2764). A different adventure is riding Icelandic ponies, possible at the **Schwarz** stables in Neckenmarkt in south Burgenland (☎ 02610/2020).

Travel Agencies

Check in Graz with **American Express** (✉ Hamerlinggasse 6, in pedestrian area off Opernring, ☎ 0316/817010–0, FAX 0316/817010–5) for travel and banking services; **Reisebüro Kuoni** (✉ Sackstr. 6, ☎ 0316/824571–0, FAX 0316/824571–6); or **Ruefa** (✉ Opernring 9, ☎ 0316/829775–0, FAX 0316/829775–23.

Visitor Information

The regional tourist information office for Burgenland province is the **Landesverband Burgenland Tourismus** (✉ Schloss Esterházy, A–7000 Eisenstadt, ☎ 02682/63384–16, FAX 02682/63384–20). For Styria, the provincial tourist office is **Steirische Tourismus** (✉ St. Peter Hauptstr. 243, A–8042 Graz, ☎ 0316/403033–0, FAX 0316/403033–10). Lower Austria has a tourist office in Vienna: the **Niederösterreichisches Landesreisebüro** (✉ Heidenschuss 2, A–1010 Vienna, ☎ 0222/533–3114–0, FAX 0222/535–0319).

For **Graz,** the quarterly *Graz-Guide* brochure, available from the tourist office (✉ Herrengasse 16, ☎ 0316/835241–11), includes a city map and provides information on current events.

There are several helpful local *Fremdenverkehrsamt* (tourist offices). **Bruck an der Mur:** Tourismusverband (✉ An der Postwiese 4, A–8600, ☎ 03862/54722, FAX 03862/54910). **Eisenstadt:** Eisenstadt Tourismus (✉ Franz-Schubert-Pl. 1, A–7000, ☎ 02682/67390, FAX 02682/67391). **Graz:** Grazer Tourismus (✉ Herrrengasse 16, A–8010, ☎ 0316/835241–11, FAX 0316/837987; ✉ Platform 1 of main train station, ☎ 0316/916837). **Mariazell:** Tourismusverband (✉ Hauptpl. 13, A–8630, ☎ 03882/2366, FAX 03882/3945). **Neusiedl am See:** Tourismusbüro (✉ Hauptpl. 1, A–7100, ☎ 02167/2229, FAX 02167/2637). **Rust:** Gästeinformation (✉ Rathaus, A-7071, ☎ 02685/202–18, FAX 02685/502). **Wiener Neustadt:** Fremdenverkehrsverein (✉ Hauptpl. 1–3, A–2700, ☎ 02622/23531–468, FAX 02622/23531–498).

5 The Danube Valley

A tonic in any season, a trip up the Austrian Danube unveils a parade of storybook-worthy sights: fairytale castles-in-air, medieval villages, and Baroque abbeys crowned with "candle-snuffer" cupolas. The Danube itself is a marvel—on a summer day it even takes on the proper shade of Johann Strauss blue. Along its banks, you'll discover the beautiful Wachau Valley, and cheery Linz, whose pastry shops produce the best Linzertortes around.

By George Hamilton

Updated by Willibald Picard

TO THE SIGHTSEER, a trip along the Austrian Danube unfolds rather like a treasured picture book of history. Roman ruins (some built by Emperor Claudius), remains of medieval castles-in-air, and Baroque monasteries crowned with "candle-snuffer" cupolas perch precariously above the river, compelling the imagination with their legends and myths. This is where Isa—cousin of the Lorelei—lured sailors to the shoals, where Richard the Lion-Hearted was locked in a dungeon for years, and where the Nibelungs—immortalized by Wagner—caroused operatically in battlemented forts. Once, Roman sailors used to throw coins into the perilous whirlpools around Grein to placate Danubius, the river's tutelary god. Today, thanks to the technology of modern dams, travelers have the luxury of seeing this part of Austria from the tame deck of a comfortable river steamer. In clement weather, the nine-hour trip upriver to Linz is highly rewarding. If you have more time to spare, the voyage onward to Passau may be less dramatic but gives more time to take in the picturesque vineyards and the castles perched like so many eagles' aeries on crags above bends in the river.

Even more of the region's attractions can be discovered traveling by car or bus. You can explore plunging Gothic streets, climb Romanesque towers, and linger over a glass at vaulted Weinkellers. River and countryside form an inspired unity here, with fortress-topped outcroppings giving way to broad pastures that swoop down to the very river banks. Many visitors classify this tour as one of Europe's great trips: here you feel you can almost reach out and touch the riverside towns and soak up the intimacy unique to this stretch of the valley. In this chapter, we follow the course of the Danube upstream from Vienna as it winds through Lower Austria (Niederösterreich) and a bit of Upper Austria (Oberösterreich) to Linz, past monasteries and industrial towns, the riverside vineyards of the lower Weinviertel, and the fragrant expanses of apricot and apple orchards.

Linz, Austria's third largest city (and its most underrated), is a key industrial center. It's also a fine town for shopping; the stores are numerous and carry quality merchandise, often at more reasonable prices than in Vienna or the larger resorts. Concerts and operas performed at Linz's modern *Brucknerhaus* make every bit as good listening as those in Vienna or Salzburg.

It is, however, the Danube, originating in Germany's Black Forest and emptying into the Black Sea, that is our focal point: The route that brought the Romans to the area and contributed to its development remains one of Europe's important waterways, with four national capitals on its banks—Vienna, Bratislava, Budapest, and Belgrade. It was not only the Romans who posited "Whoever controls the Danube, controls all Europe." The "Kuenringer"—the robber knights who built many of the hilltop castles—thrived by sacking the baggage caravans of the early Crusaders; later, castles were financed through slightly more legitimate means—Frederick Barbarossa, leading his army downstream, had to pay a crossing toll at Mauthausen. Subsequently, cities sprang up to serve as ports for the salt, wood, ores, and other cargo transported on the river. Today, modern railroads and highways parallel most of the Blue Danube's course.

This is a wonderful trip to take in early spring or in the fall after the grape harvest, when the vineyards turn reddish blue and a bracing chill settles over the Danube; the Empress Maria Theresa would arrive in Linz in May, just as the fruit trees were about to bloom. No matter when you come, be sure to try some of those fruits in a *Linzertorte*—a filling of brandy-flavored apricots, raspberries or plums under a latticed pastry crust—a treat as satisfyingly rich and copious as the Danube Valley itself.

Pleasures and Pastimes

Abbeys

While castles galore dot the area—ranging from crumbling mountaintop ruins to wonderfully restored edifices replete with gargoyles—the real gems in these environs are the abbeys, majestic relics of an era when bishops were as influential as kings. The greatest are Melk, Klosterneuburg, Kremsmünster, St. Florian and Göttweig, all of which have breathlessly imposing scope and elegance.

Bicycling

The trail along the Danube must be one of the great bicycle routes of the world. For much of the way (the exception being the Korneuburg–Krems stretch) you can bike on either side of the river. Some small hotels will even arrange to pick up you and your bike from the cycle path. You'll find bicycle rentals at most riverside towns and at rail stations. The terrain around Linz is relatively level, and within the city there are 89 kilometers (55 miles) of marked cycle routes. In the areas of Eferding, St. Florian, through the Enns River valley, and around Steyr, the territory is generally good for cycling, with gentle hills and special routes.

Dining

Wherever possible, restaurants capitalize on the river view, and alfresco dining overlooking the Danube is one of the region's unsurpassed delights. Simple *Gasthäuser* are everywhere, but better dining is more often found in the country inns. The cuisine is basically Austrian, although desserts are often brilliant local inventions, including the celebrated Linzertorte, basically a jam tart—almost a pie—topped with a lattice crust, and Linzer Augen, jam-filled cookies with three "eyes" in the top cookie.

Wine is very much the thing in the lower part of the Weinviertel, particularly in the Wachau region on the north bank of the Danube. Here you'll find many of Austria's best white wines, slightly dry and with a touch of fruity taste. In some of the smaller villages, you can sample the vintner's successes directly in his cellars. Restaurants, from sophisticated and stylish to plain and homey, are often rated by their wine offerings as much as by their chef's creations.

CATEGORY	COST*
$$$$	over AS500
$$$	AS300–AS500
$$	AS200–AS300
$	under AS200

**per person for a typical three-course meal with a glass of house wine*

Hiking

You could hardly ask for better hiking country: From the level ground of the Danube Valley, hills rise on both sides, giving great views when you reach the upper levels. There are *Wanderwege* (marked hiking paths) virtually everywhere; local tourist offices have maps and route details. Around Linz you might retrace the route of the Linz–Budweis horse-drawn tramway, Continental Europe's first railway, or trek from one castle to another. You can hike in the Mühlviertel from Freistadt to Grein and even get your pack transferred from hotel to hotel.

Lodging

Accommodation options range from castle hotels where you'll be treated like a king, to quieter but elegant, usually family-run country inns, to standard city hotels, in Linz. The region is compact, so you can easily stay in one place and drive to a nearby locale to try a different restaurant. Rates understandably reflect the quality of service and amenities and usually include breakfast, which may range from a fast to a feast.

CATEGORY	COST*
$$$$	over AS1,500
$$$	AS1,000–AS1,500
$$	AS700–AS1,000
$	under AS700

**All prices are for a standard double room, including tax and service.*

Exploring the Danube Valley

Although much of the river is tightly wedged between steep hills rising from a narrow valley, the north and south banks of the Danube present differing vistas. The hills to the north are terraced so that the vineyards can catch the sun; the orchards, occasional meadows, and shadowed hills on the south are as visually appealing if less dramatic. Upstream from the Wachau region the valley broadens, giving way to farmlands and the industrial city of Linz straddling the river.

Great Itineraries

The Wachau section of the Danube valley is a favorite outing for Viennese seeking a pleasant Sunday drive and a glass or two of good wine, but for foreign visitors to treat the region this casually would cause them to miss some of Austria's greatest treasures. Once there, castles and abbeys beckon, picturesque villages beg to be explored, and the vine-covered wine gardens prove nearly irresistible.

Numbers in the text correspond to numbers in the margin and on the Lower Danube Valley, Upper Danube Valley, and Linz maps.

IF YOU HAVE 3 DAYS

Start out early from Vienna, planning for a stop to explore the medieval center of **Krems** ③. The Vinotek Und's eponymous Kloster will give you a good idea of the regions's best wines. From Krems, you can scoot across the river to visit **Stift Göttweig** ㊹ or you can leave it until the return trip. Spend a night in a former cloister, now an elegant hotel, in **Dürnstein** ⑤ in the shadow of the ruined castle where Richard the Lion-Hearted was imprisoned. An early-morning climb up to the ruin, or a jog along the Danube shoreline will reward you with great views. Take time to explore the town before heading along the Danube, crossing to **Melk** ㊸, rated one of the greatest abbeys in Europe. This is high baroque at its most glorious. Follow the river road on to **Stift Göttweig** ㊹ and have lunch on the terrace. The Stift's Baroque chapel is breathtaking. Continuing eastward, follow the river as closely as possible (signs indicate Zwentendorf and Tulln) to **Klosterneuburg** ㊼, an imposing abbey once seat of the powerful Babenburger kings, and onward to Vienna.

IF YOU HAVE 5 DAYS

A more leisurely schedule would follow the same basic route but permit a visit at either **Burg Kreuzenstein** or **Schloss Grafenegg** before stopping in **Krems** ③ and Und, and an overnight in **Dürnstein** ⑤. Spend the morning exploring the town, including the colorfully restored baroque Stiftskirche. In the afternoon, discover the wine villages of **Weis-**

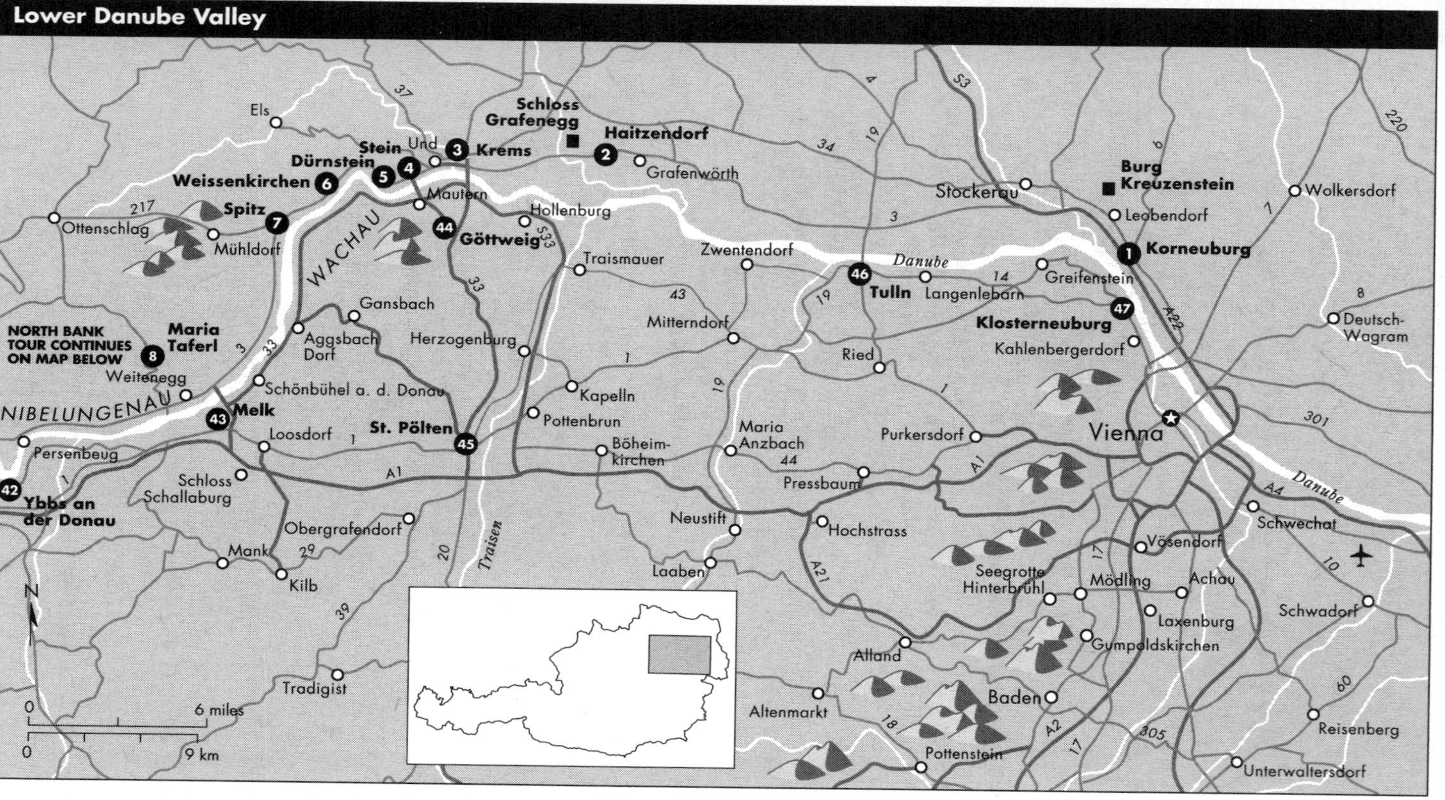
Lower Danube Valley
Els
Schloss Grafenegg
Haitzendorf
Grafenwörth
Stein
Und
Krems
Dürnstein
Weissenkirchen
Mautern
Spitz
Ottenschlag
Mühldorf
WACHAU
Göttweig
Hollenburg
Traismauer
Zwentendorf
Danube
Tulln
Langenlebarn
Greifenstein
Stockerau
Burg Kreuzenstein
Leobendorf
Korneuburg
Wolkersdorf
Deutsch-Wagram
Klosterneuburg
Kahlenbergerdorf
Gansbach
Aggsbach Dorf
Herzogenburg
Mitterndorf
Ried
NORTH BANK TOUR CONTINUES ON MAP BELOW
Maria Taferl
Weitenegg
Schönbühel a. d. Donau
Kapelln
Pottenbrun
NIBELUNGENAU
Melk
St. Pölten
Loosdorf
Maria Anzbach
Purkersdorf
Vienna
Persenbeug
Böheim-kirchen
Pressbaum
Schloss Schallaburg
Ybbs an der Donau
Neustift
Hochstrass
Schwechat
Obergrafendorf
Traisen
Vösendorf
Mank
Kilb
Laaben
Seegrotte Hinterbrühl
Mödling
Achau
Laxenburg
Schwadorf
Alland
Gumpoldskirchen
Tradigist
Altenmarkt
Baden
Reisenberg
Pottenstein
Unterwaltersdorf
N
0 6 miles
0 9 km

Upper Danube Valley

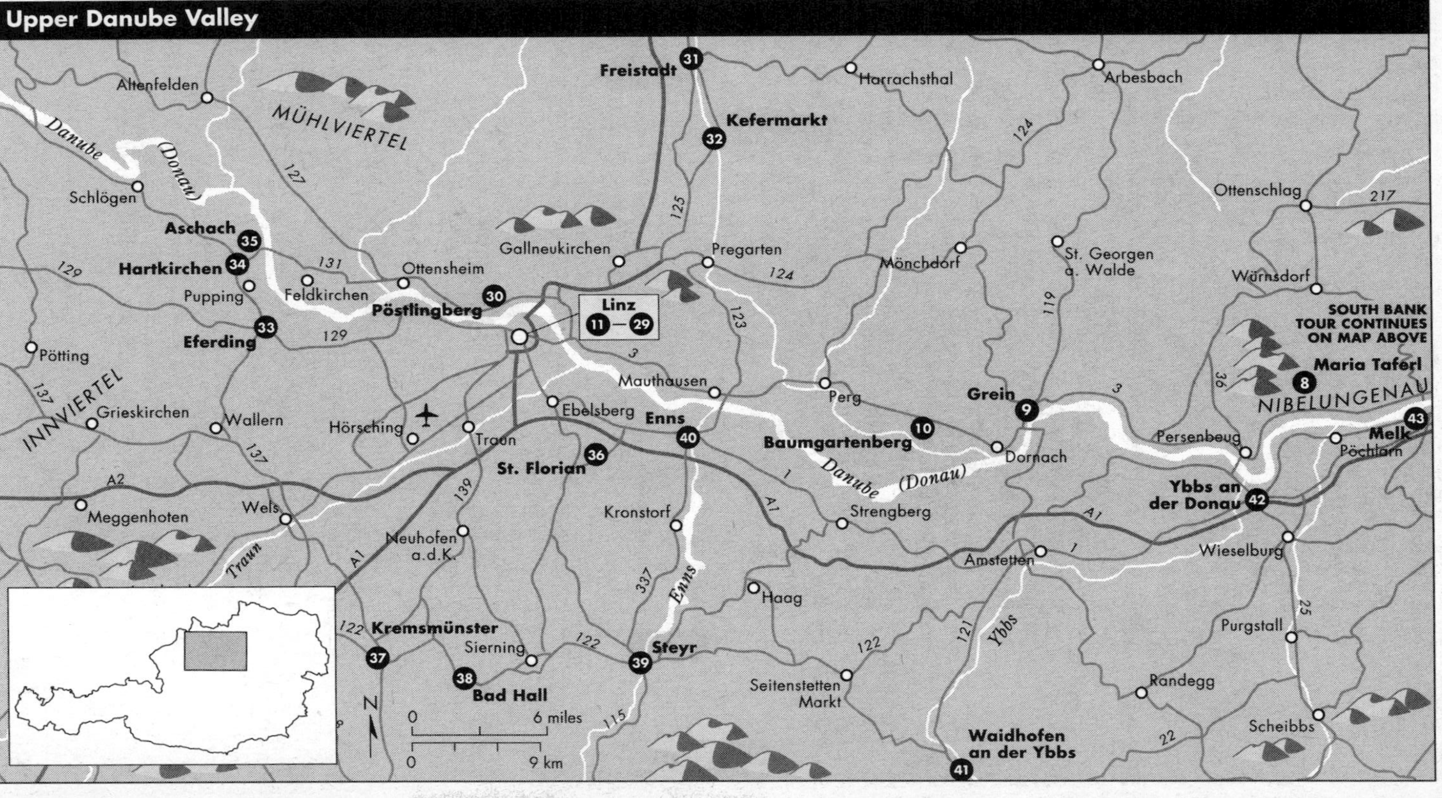

senkirchen ⑥ and **Spitz** ⑦. Plan on two overnights in **Linz** ⑪, to discover the city itself and to fit in a side trip across the river north to the walled city of **Freistadt** ㉛ and then on to **Kefermarkt** ㉜, to view the 42-foot high intricately carved wood winged altar dating to 1497. On day four, take in **Kremsmünster** ㊲ and **St. Florian** ㊱, then proceed to **Melk** ㊸. The fifth day will be full, but start with the Melk abbey, then **Stift Göttweig** ㊹, and onward to **Klosterneuburg** ㊼.

IF YOU HAVE 7 DAYS

Additional time would allow far better acquaintance with this region. Located to the northwest of the Wachau, the Mühlviertel—the mill region north of Linz—turned out thousands of yards of linen from flax grown in the neighboring fields in the last century. You might follow the "textile trail," which takes you to museums tracing this bit of history. On your way along the northern Danube bank, visit the fascinating theater in **Grein** ⑨ and view the curious chancel in the church at **Baumgartenberg** ⑩. From **Linz** ⑪, take trips upriver to **Eferding** ㉝, **Hartkirchen** ㉞, and **Aschach** ㉟, and south to **Steyr** ㊴; you might also consider an overnight in this charming medieval city with its vast center square framed in pastel facades. From Steyr, attractive back roads will bring you to the walled town of **Waidhofen an der Ybbs** ㊶, parts of which date to the Turkish invasion of the 1600s. Rather than try to pack three abbeys into one day, spread out the pleasures, dining in **Mautern** and overnighting in **Tulln** ㊻ before heading on to **Klosterneuburg** ㊼ and, finally, returning to Vienna.

When to Tour the Danube Valley

The Wachau—both north and south Danube banks—are packed wall-to-wall with visitors in late-April–early May, but of course there's a reason: the apricot and apple trees are in glorious blossom. Others prefer the chilly early to mid-autumn days, when a blue haze cradles the vineyards. Throughout the region, winter is drab. Seasons hardly withstanding, crowds jam the abbey at Melk; you're best off going first thing in the morning, before the tour buses arrive, or at midday when the throngs have receded.

THE WACHAU, NORTH BANK OF THE DANUBE

Storybook Castles and Wagnerian Legends

Unquestionably the most lovely stretches of the Danube's Austrian course run from the outskirts of Vienna, through the narrow defiles of the Wachau to the Nibelungengau—the region where the mystical race of dwarfs, the Nibelungs, are supposed to have settled, at least for a while. If you're taking the tour by train, take Streetcar D to Vienna's Franz Josefs Bahnhof, where you'll depart. If you're driving, the trickiest part may be getting out of Vienna. Follow signs to Prague to get across the Danube. Once across, avoid the right-hand exit marked Prague, which leads to the autobahn, and continue ahead, following signs for Prager Strasse and turning left at the traffic light. Prager Strasse (Route 3) heads you toward Langenzersdorf and Korneuburg.

Korneuburg

❶ *18 km (11¼ mi) northwest of Vienna.*

Until recently, Korneuburg was the center of Austrian shipbuilding, where river passenger ships, barges, and transfer cranes were built for Russia, among other customers. Stop for a look at the imposing neo-

Gothic city hall (1864), which dominates the central square and towers over the town.

Atop a hillside 3 kilometers (2 miles) beyond Korneuburg along Route ★ 3 sits **Burg Kreuzenstein,** a castle with fairy-tale turrets and towers. Using old elements and Gothic and Romanesque bits and pieces brought to this site of a previously destroyed castle, Count Wilczek built Kreuzenstein from 1879 to 1908, to house his late-Gothic collection of art objects. You would never suspect the building wasn't absolutely authentic if the tour guides weren't so forthcoming. You'll see rooms full of armaments, the festival and banquet halls, library, chapel, even the kitchens. You can also reach Kreuzenstein via the suburban train (*S-Bahn*) to Leobendorf and a ¾-hour hike up to the castle. ✉ *Leobendorf bei Korneuburg,* ☎ *02262/66102.* 🎫 *AS80.* ⏲ *Tour mid-Mar.–mid-Nov., Tues.–Sun. 9–5; last tour at 4.*

Haitzendorf

❷ *51 km (38½ mi) west of Korneuburg, 12 km (7½ mi) east of Krems.*

The tiny farming community of Haitzendorf—To reach it from Korneuburg, take Route 3, 33 kilometers (21 miles) past Stockerau, then turn right at Graftenwörth—features a church dating to the 14th century, but it best known for turreted Schloss Grafenegg nearby. In early summer, the vast strawberry fields surrounding the town yield a delicious harvest which you can pick yourself. A lush meadow and wood- ★ land area also surrounds **Schloss Grafenegg.** The moated Renaissance castle dating to 1533 was stormed by the Swedes in 1645 and rebuilt from 1840 to 1873 in the English Gothic Revival style. Greatly damaged during the 1945–1955 occupation, it was extensively restored in the 1980s. Look for such fascinating details as the gargoyle waterspouts, and don't miss the chapel. ☎ *02735/2205–14.* 🎫 *AS60.* ⏲ *Mid-Apr.–Oct., Tues.–Sun. daily 10–5.*

NEED A BREAK? The **Schlosstaverne Mörwald** (☎ 02735/2616–0) offers excellent food in a delightful setting, either in the Biedermeier-style dining room or under an umbrella in the garden.

Krems

★ ❸ *80 km (50 mi) northwest of Vienna, 26 km (16¼ mi) north of St. Pölten.*

Krems marks the beginning (when traveling upstream) of the Wachau section of the Danube. This delightful old town along Route 3 celebrated its 1000th birthday in 1995 and is closely tied to Austrian history; here the ruling Babenbergs set up a dukedom in 1120, and the earliest Austrian coin was struck in 1130. In the Middle Ages, Krems looked after the iron trade, while neighboring Stein traded in salt and wine, and over the years Krems became a center of culture and art. Today the area is the heart of a thriving wine production, and narrow streets, a Renaissance Rathaus, a parish church that is one of the oldest in Lower Austria, and a pedestrian zone make Krems an attractive city to wander through. Among the sights of Krems is the **Steiner Tor,** the massive square gate once set into the wall of the moated city, flanked by two stubby round towers and capped by candle-snuffer roofs. The oldest part of town is to the east. Along the **Obere and Untere Landstrasse,** you'll spot dozens of eye-catching buildings in styles ranging from Gothic to Baroque. It's easy to pick out the heavy Gothic **Piaristenkirche,** begun in 1470, with its distinctive square tower, central peak, and minitowers at each corner. The main altar and most of the side altars incorporate paintings by the local artist Martin Johann Schmidt (1718–1801), popularly known as Kremser Schmidt, whose translucent works you will repeatedly come across in the course of this trip. Close by is the parish church of **St. Veit,** completed in 1630. The interior is surprisingly spacious; Schmidt did the ceiling frescoes. On the entry portal of the **Bürgerspitalkirche** at Obere Landstrasse 15, you'll spot Friedrick III's legend *A.E.I.O.U.*, reputedly standing for *Austria Erit In Orbe Ultima,* Latin for "Austria will reach to the ends of the earth."

A 14th-century former Dominican cloister, farther along the street, now serves as the **Historisches Museum der Stadt Krems** (city historical museum), with a wine museum that holds occasional tastings. ✉ *Körnermarkt 13,* ☎ *02732/801–338.* 🎫 *AS30.* ⏲ *Easter–late Oct., Tues.–Sat. 9–noon and 2–5; Sun. and holidays 9–noon.*

Dining and Lodging

$$$ ✕ **Zum Kaiser von Österreich.** At this landmark located in the Old City district, you'll find excellent regional cuisine along with an outstanding wine selection (some of these vintages come—literally—from the backyard). The inside rooms are bright and pleasant but the outside tables in summer are even more inviting. Owner-chef Haidinger learned his skills at Bacher, across the Danube in Mautern, so look for fish dishes along with specialties such as potato soup and roast shoulder of lamb with scalloped potatoes. ✉ *Körnermarkt 9, A-3500,* ☎ *02732/86001. DC, MC, V. Closed Mon.*

$$$ ★ ✕🏨 **Am Förthof.** An inn has existed on the riverside site of this modern hotel for hundreds of years. The rooms are comfortable and balconied; those in front have a view of the Danube and Göttweig abbey across the river—and the sounds of the traffic. The dining room and in summer the inviting courtyard garden offer good regional cuisine; the chef's ambitions occasionally surpass his achievements, but the sumptuous breakfasts are an assured culinary experience. ✉ *Förthofer Donaulände 8, A–3500,* ☎ *02732/83345 or 02732/81348,* FAX *02732/83345–40. 20 rooms. Restaurant, pool, sauna. DC, MC, V.*

$–$$ ✕🏨 **Alte Post.** You're allowed to drive into the pedestrian zone to this romantic house in the heart of the old town, next to the Steinener Tor (Stone Gate). The rooms are in comfortable country style (full baths are scarce), but the real feature here is dining on regional specialties or sipping a glass of the local wine in the arcaded Renaissance courtyard. The staff is particularly friendly, and cyclists are welcome. ✉ *Obere Landstr. 32, A–3500,* ☎ *02732/82276–0,* FAX *02732/84396. 26 rooms, 7 with bath. Restaurant, bicycles. No credit cards. Closed Jan.–mid-Mar.*

En Route ★ Between Krems and Stein, in a beautifully restored Capuchin cloister in the tiny town of Und, is the **Weinkolleg Kloster Und.** The building also houses the tourist office and a small wine museum, where you can taste (and buy) more than 100 Austrian wines. ✉ *Undstr. 6, Krems–Stein,* ☎ *02732/73073,* FAX *02732/73074–85.* 🎫 *AS130, including tasting.* ⏲ *mid-Jan.–Dec. 24, daily 11–7.*

Stein

❹ *5 km (2 mi) east of Krems.*

A frozen-in-time hamlet that has become over time virtually a suburb of the adjacent city of Krems, Stein is dotted with lovely 16th-century houses, many on the hamlet's main street, Steinlanderstrasse. The former 14th-century **Minoritenkirche,** just off the main street in the pedestrian zone, now serves as a museum with changing exhibits. A few steps beyond the Minoritenkirche, an imposing square Gothic tower identifies the 15th-century **St. Nicholas parish church,** whose altar painting and ceiling frescoes were done by Kremser Schmidt. The upper part of the Gothic charnel house (1462), squeezed between the church and the hillside, has been converted to housing. Notice, too, the many architecturally interesting houses, among them the former tollhouse, with rich Renaissance frescoes. Stein was the birthplace of Ludwig Köchel, the cataloger of Mozart's works, which are referred to by their Köchel numbers.

Dürnstein

❺ *90 km (56 mi) northwest of Vienna, 9 km (5½ mi) west of Krems, 34 km (21¼ mi) northeast of Melk.*

If a beauty contest was held among the towns along the Wachau Danube, chances are Dürnstein would be the winner, hands down—as you'll see when you arrive along with droves of tourists. Set among terraced vineyards, the town is landmarked by its gloriously Baroque **Stiftskirche,** dating from the early 1700s, which sits on a cliff overlooking the river—this cloister church's combination of luminous blue facade and stylish Baroque tower is considered the most beautiful of its kind in Austria. More than 100 tiny angels decorate the heavens of its ceiling, and couples come from near and far to be married in the romantic setting. After taking in the Stiftskirche, most visitors head up the hill, climbing 500 feet over the town, to the famous **Richard the Lion-Hearted Castle** where Leopold V held Richard the Lion-Hearted of England, caught on his way back home from the Crusades. In the tower of this castle, Richard was imprisoned (1192–93) until he was rescued by Blondel, the faithful minnesinger. It's said that Blondel was able to locate his imprisoned king when he heard his master's voice completing the verse of a song he was singing. The rather steep 30-minute climb to the ruins will earn you a breathtaking view up and down the Danube Valley and over the hills to the south. The town is small; leave the car at one end and walk the narrow streets.

Dining and Lodging

$$$ ✕ **Loibnerhof.** Here, in an idyllic setting on the banks of the Danube, you'll dine on inventive variations on regional themes: Wachauer fish soup, crispy roast duck, and various grilled fish or lamb specialties. The house is famous for its *Butterschnitzel,* an exquisite variation on the theme of ground meat (this one's pan-fried veal with a touch of pork). The garden is enchanting in summer, but on weekends it's packed, and service tends to suffer. ✉ *Unterloiben 7,* ☎ *02732/82890–0,* FAX *02732/82890–3. No credit cards. Closed Mon., Tues., and mid-Jan.–mid-Feb.*

$$ ✕ **Zum Goldenen Strauss.** This onetime post station, long a simple *Gasthaus,* has ambitions to be something more. You'll be offered substantial portions of very good Austrian fare, prepared with a flair that helps compensate for the occasionally slow service. Try the garlic soup followed by *Tafelspitz,* tasty boiled beef. The dining rooms inside are cozy, the terrace a delight. ✉ *A–3601,* ☎ *02711/267. No credit cards. Closed Tues. and mid-Jan.–early Mar.*

$$$$ ★ 🏨 **Richard Löwenherz.** The impressive vaulted reception and dining rooms of this former convent are beautifully furnished with antiques, reflecting the personal warmth and care of the family management. The inviting open fire, stone floors, and friendly touches make this one of the most romantic of the Romantik Hotels group. Though all rooms are spacious and comfortable, the balconied guest rooms in the newer part of the house are more modern in decor and furnishings. Wander through the grounds and gardens, admiring the crumbling ruined walls from earlier centuries. A terrace overlooking the Danube offers stunning views. The outstanding restaurant is known for its regional specialties and local wines. ✉ *A–3601,* ☎ *02711/222,* FAX *02711/222–18. 40 rooms. Restaurant, bar, pool. AE, DC, MC, V. Closed Nov.–mid-Mar.*

$$$$ **Schlosshotel Dürnstein.** This 17th-century early Baroque castle, on a rocky terrace with exquisite views over the Danube, offers genuine elegance and comfort. The best rooms look onto the river, but all are unusually bright and attractive; of moderate size, they have comfortable seating and country antiques throughout. Half board is standard. The kitchen is not up to the quality of the excellent wines from the area, but the setting makes terrace dining a memorable experience. ✉ *A–3601,* ☎ *02711/212,* FAX *02711/351. 37 rooms. Restaurant, bar, indoor and outdoor pools, sauna, exercise room. AE, DC, MC, V. Closed Nov.–Mar.*

$$$ **Sänger Blondel.** Behind the yellow facade is a very friendly, traditional family hotel with elegant country rooms of medium size that have attractive paneling and antique decorations. The staff is particularly helpful and can suggest excursions in the area. The hotel is known for its restaurant, which features local specialties and a wide range of salads and lighter dishes. ✉ *A–3601,* ☎ *02711/253–0,* FAX *02711/253–7. 16 rooms. Restaurant. No credit cards. Closed mid-Nov.–mid-Mar. and 1 wk in early July.*

Weissenkirchen

❻ *14 km (8¾ mi) southwest of Krems, 22 km (13¾ mi) northeast of Melk.*

Tucked among vineyards, just around a bend in the Danube, is Weissenkirchen, a picturesque town that was fortified against the Turks in 1531. A fire in 1793 laid waste to much of the town, but the 15th-century parish church of **Maria Himmelfahrt,** built on earlier foundations, largely survived. The south nave dates to 1300, the middle nave to 1439, the chapel to 1460. The madonna on the triumphal arch goes back to the Danube school of about 1520; the Baroque touches date to 1736; and to complete the picture, the Rococo organ was installed in 1777. On the Marktplatz, check out the 15th-century **Teisenhoferhof,** which has a charming Renaissance arcaded courtyard. The building now houses the Wachau museum and contains many paintings by Kremser Schmidt. ☎ *02715/2268.* *AS20.* *Apr.–Oct., Tues.–Sun. 10–5.*

Dining and Lodging

$$$ ★ **Jamek.** Josef Jamek is known for his outstanding wines; his wife, Edeltraud, for what she and her chefs turn out in the kitchen of this fine restaurant, which is also their home. You dine in one of several rooms tastefully decorated with 18th-century touches. Creative variations on typical Austrian specialties are emphasized; lamb and game in season are highlights. Wines are from the nearby family vineyards. ✉ *Joching 45,* ☎ *02715/2235,* FAX *02715/2483. Reservations essential. No credit cards. Closed Sun., Mon., mid-Dec.–mid-Feb., and 1st 2 wks of July; but call, as closing times may vary. No dinner Thurs.*

$$$ ★ **Prandtauerhof.** The Baroque facade is the work of Jakob Prandtauer, the architect responsible for many of the greatest buildings in the area. Ornate details are carried over into the cozy guest rooms and the inner court; a sense of history pervades the house. The kitchen delivers excellent traditional cuisine such as stuffed breast of veal, and there's a separate fish menu. You'll also find game in season, tempting desserts such as rhubarb strudel, and wines from the house vineyards. ✉

Joching 36, ☎ 02715/2310, FAX 02715/2310–9. Reservations essential. No credit cards. Closed Tues.; Sun. and holiday evenings; and mid-Nov.–early Mar.

$$ ✕ **Heinzle.** The tree-shaded terrace overlooking the Danube is idyllic but the main dining room—with red tile floor and dark wood ceiling—is no less pleasant. This is a favorite on weekends and holidays, so come during the week or book ahead. The excellent fresh fish would be the logical (but not only) choice; start with a cream soup of smoked fish, and plan on one of the rich desserts. ✉ *Donaulände 280, ☎ 02715/2231. Reservations essential. No credit cards. Closed Jan.; Mon. in summer; and Mon. and Tues. in winter.*

$$$ ★ **Raffelsbergerhof.** This stunning Renaissance building (1574), once a shipmaster's house, has been tastefully converted into a hotel with every comfort. The rooms are attractively decorated without being overdone. The family management is particularly friendly, and there's a quiet garden to complement the gemütlich public lounge. ✉ *A-3610, ☎ 02715/2201, FAX 02715/2201–27. 12 rooms. MC. Closed Nov.–Apr.*

Spitz

7 *17 km (10½ mi) southwest of Krems, 17 km (10½ mi) northeast of Melk.*

Picturesque Spitz is set off the main road and back from the Danube, sitting like a jewel in the surrounding vineyards and hills. One vineyard, the "thousand bucket" hill, is said to produce that much wine in a good year. A number of interesting houses in Spitz go back to the 16th and 17th centuries. The late-Gothic 15th-century parish church contains Kremser Schmidt's altar painting of the martyrdom of St. Mauritius. Note the carved wood statues of Christ and the 12 apostles, dating to 1380, on the organ loft. Just beyond Spitz and above the road is the ruin of the castle Hinterhaus, to which you can climb. A side road here marked to Ottenschlag (Route 217) leads up the hill, and about 7 kilometers (4½ miles) beyond Mühldorf, to **Burg Oberranna,** a well-preserved castle surrounded by a double wall and dry moat. The original structure dates to 1114–1125, the St. George chapel possibly even earlier. Part of the castle has been renovated into a hotel (☞ *below*). ✉ *Ober-Ranna 1, Mühldorf, ☎ 02713/8221.* *AS20.* *May–Oct., Sat. 3–5, Sun. and holidays 2–6.*

Lodging

$$$ **Burg Oberranna.** This 12th-century castle—a noted historic sight in itself (☞ *above*)—has been successfully turned into a charming and comfortable hotel, great as a base for hiking and also perfect for those who just want to get away. Rooms include a kitchenette. ✉ *Ober-Ranna 1, A-3622, ☎ 02713/8221, FAX 02713/8366. 11 rooms with bath or shower and 4 apartments. Restaurant. AE, V. Closed Nov.–Apr.*

$$ **Wachauer Hof.** This appealing traditional house, set near the vineyards, has been under family management for generations. You can enjoy the wines in the *Gaststube,* the shaded garden, or the restaurant, which offers basic Austrian fare. The medium-size rooms have comfortable chairs, ample pillows, and rustic decor. ✉ *Hauptstr. 15, A-3620, ☎ 02713/2303–0, FAX 02713/2403. 30 rooms with bath or shower. Restaurant. MC. Closed mid-Dec.–mid-Feb.*

En Route The vistas are mainly of the other side of the Danube, looking across at Schönbühel and Melk, as you follow a back road via Jauerling and Maria Laach to Route 3 at Aggsbach. Shortly after Weitenegg the Wachau ends, and you come into the part of the Danube Valley known as the Nibelungenau, where the Nibelungs—who inspired the great saga, the *Nibelungenlied,* source of Wagner's Ring—are supposed to have settled for a spell. If you have always thought of the Nibelungs as a mythical race of dwarfs known only to old German legends and Wagner, dismiss that idea here. The Nibelungs existed, though not as Wagner describes them, and this area was one of their stamping grounds.

Maria Taferl

8 *13 km (8¼ mi) west of Melk, 7½ km (4½ mi) northeast of Persenbeug/Ybbs an der Donau.*

Crowning a hill on the north bank is the two-towered **Maria Taferl,** a pilgrimage church with a spectacular outlook. It's a bit touristy, but the church and the view are worth the side trip. About 5 kilometers (3 miles) up a back road is **Schloss Artstetten,** a massive square castle with four round defense towers at its corners. This is the burial place of Archduke Franz Ferdinand and his wife, Sophie, whose double assassination in 1914 in Sarajevo was one of the triggers that set off World War I. ☎ *07413/8302.* *AS58; combination ticket available with Melk abbey and Schloss Schallaburg (*☞ below*).* ⏲ *Apr.–Oct., daily 9–5:30.*

Lodging

$$$ **Krone-Kaiserhof.** Two hotels under the same family management share each other's luxurious facilities. The Krone looks out over the Danube Valley, while the Kaiserhof has views of the nearby Baroque pilgrimage church. Both have rooms done a bit slickly in country style, and the restaurants are popular. An associated guest house ($) is less elegant but also shares facilities. Cyclists staying overnight will be picked up free at Marbach or Klein Pöchlarn landing stations on the Danube. ✉ *A-3672,* ☎ *07413/6355–0 or 07413/6358,* FAX *07413/6355–83. 72 rooms. 2 restaurants, bar, café, indoor and outdoor pools, sauna, miniature golf, exercise room. V. Closed Jan. and Feb.*

Grein

9 *34 km (21¼ mi) east of Mauthausen, 20 km (12½ mi) west of Persenbeug/Ybbs an der Donau.*

Set above the Danube, Grein is a picture-book town complete with castle. The river bend below, known for years as "the place where death resides," was one of the most hazardous stretches of river until the reefs were blasted away in the late 1700s. Take time to see the intimate Rococo **Stadttheater** in the town hall, built in 1790 by the populace and still occasionally used for concerts or plays. ✉ *Rathaus,* ☎ *07268/6680.* *AS25.* ⏲ *Tour Apr.–late Oct., daily at 9, 10:30, and 2:30.*

NEED A BREAK? **Kaffeesiederei Blumensträussl** (✉ Stadtpl. 6) is a lovely spot for coffee and cake, amid the Viennese Biedermeier decor in winter or outdoors in the café garden in summer. The *Mozarttorte* is renowned.

Baumgartenberg

10 *11 km (6¾ mi) west of Grein, 17½ km (11 mi) east of Mauthausen.*

The small village of Baumgartenberg is worth a visit for its ornate Baroque parish church—note the lavish stucco-work and exquisitely carved 17th-century pews—and the unusual chancel supported by a tree trunk. The church is the only reminder of a once-famed Cistercian abbey, founded in 1141 by Otto von Machland, that used to thrive here. Outside the town is the picturesque castle of Klam, which used to belong to playwright August Strindberg; it now contains a small museum.

LINZ

The Rich Town of the River Markets

11 *130 km (81¼ mi) east of Salzburg, 185 km (115½ mi) west of Vienna.*

The capital of Upper Austria, set where the Traun River flows into the Danube, Linz has a fascinating old city core and an active cultural life. In 1832 it had a horse-drawn train to Czechoslovakia that was the first rail line on the Continent. Once known as "The Rich Town of the River Markets" because of its importance as a medieval trading post, it is today the center of Austrian steel and chemical production, both started by the Germans in 1938. A city of contrasts, Linz has Austria's largest medieval square and is home to one of the country's most modern multipurpose halls, the Brucknerhaus, which is used for concerts and conventions.

With the city's modern economic success, Linz's attractions for tourists have been generally overlooked. Nevertheless, Linz boasts beautiful old houses on the Hauptplatz, a Baroque cathedral with twin towers and a fine organ over which composer Anton Bruckner once presided, and its "city mountain," the Pöstlingberg, with a unique railway line to the top. Extensive redevelopment, restoration, and the creation of traffic-free zones continue to transform Linz. The heart of the city—the Altstadt (Old City)—has been turned into a pedestrian zone; either leave the car at your hotel or use the huge new parking garage under the main square in the center of town. Distances are not great, and you can take in the highlights in the course of a two-hour walking tour.

12 The lower end of the main square is marked by the **Altes Rathaus,** the old city hall. Although the original 1513 building was mainly destroyed by fire and replaced in 1658–59, its octagonal corner turret and lunar clock, as well as some vaulted rooms, remain, and you can detect traces of the original Renaissance structure on the Rathausgasse facade. The present exterior dates from 1824. The approach from Rathausgasse 5, opposite the Keplerhaus, leads through a fine arcaded courtyard. On the facade here you'll spot portraits of Emperor Friedrich III, the mayors Hoffmandl and Prunner, the astronomer Johannes Kepler, and the composer Anton Bruckner. ⊠ *Hauptpl.*

13 One of the symbols of Linz is the 65-foot Baroque **Pillar to the Holy Trinity** in the center of the Hauptplatz square. Completed in 1723 of white Salzburg marble, the column offers thanks by an earthly trinity—the provincial estates, city council, and local citizenry—for deliverance from the threats of war (1704), fire (1712), and plague (1713). From March through October, there's a flea market here each Saturday (except holidays), from 7 AM to 2 PM.

14 The **Minorite Church,** once part of a monastery, sits at the end of the Klosterstrasse. The present building dates from 1752–1758 and has a delightful Rococo interior with side altar paintings by Kremser Schmidt and the main altar by Bartolomeo Altomonte. The church is open October–June, Monday–Saturday 7:30–11 AM and Sunday 7:30–noon, and July–Sept., daily 7:30–4. The early-Renaissance monastery
15 adjoining the Minorite Church is now the **Landhaus,** with its distinctive tower, seat of the provincial government. Look inside to see the arcaded courtyard with the 1852 Planet Fountain and the Hall of Stone on the first floor, above the barrel-vaulted hall on the ground floor; for a more extensive look at the interior, inquire at the local tourist office for their scheduled guided tours. The beautiful Renaissance doorway (1570) is of red marble. ⊠ *Klosterstr. 7.*

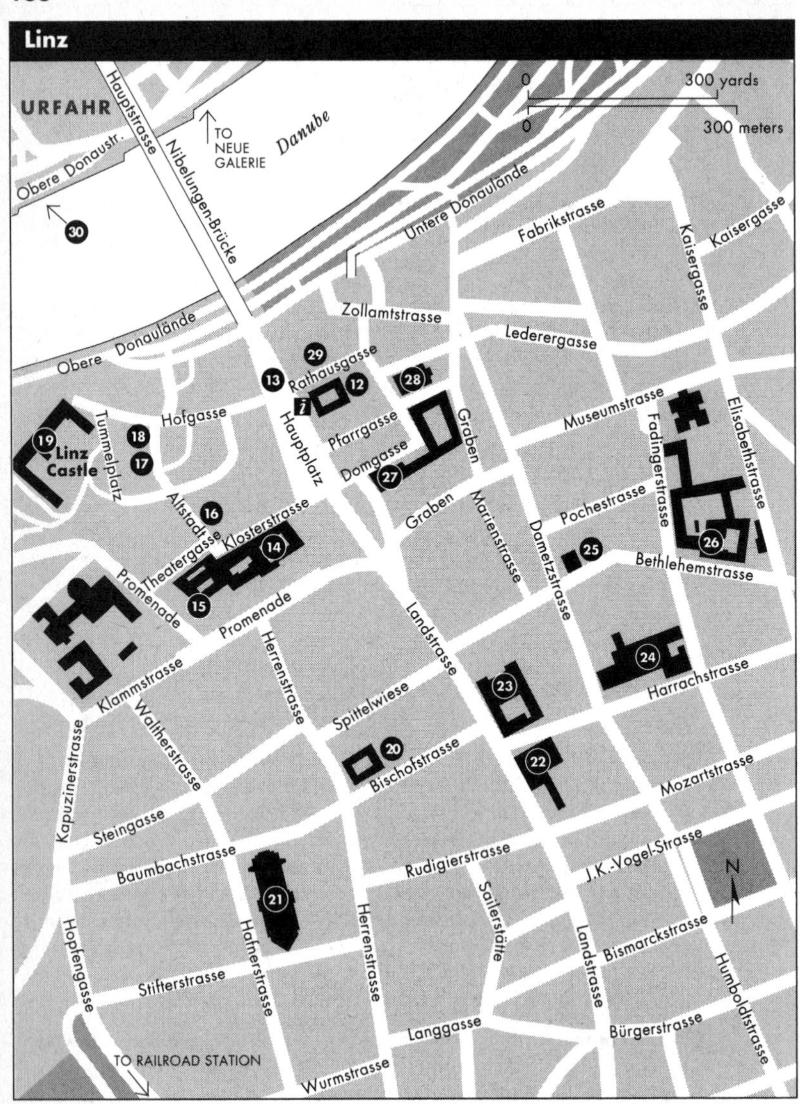

Alter Dom, **27**
Altes Rathaus, **12**
Bischofshof, **20**
Carmelite Church, **22**
Deutschordens-kirche, **24**
Elisabethinen-kirche, **26**
Kremsmünsterer-haus, **18**
Landhaus, **15**
Linz Castle, **19**
Minorite Church, **14**
Mozart Haus, **16**
Neuer Dom, **21**
Nordico (City Museum), **25**
No. 5 Rathausgasse, **29**
Pillar to the Holy Trinity, **13**
Pöstlingberg, **30**
Stadtpfarrkirche, **28**
Ursuline Church, **23**
Waaghaus, **17**

16 The three-story Renaissance **Mozart Haus** has a later Baroque facade and portal. Actually the Thun Palace, Mozart arrived here in 1783 with his wife to meet an especially impatient patron (Mozart was late by 14 days). As the composer forgot to bring any symphonies along with him, he set about writing one in the space of four days. The result: the sublime *Linz* symphony in 1783. The palace now houses the local tourist office and private apartments, but the courtyard can be viewed. ⊠ *Altstadt 17.*

17 The **Waaghaus,** bought by the city in 1524, is in the heart of the Altstadt on the tiny street of the same name. Once the public weighing
office, it's now an indoor market. Emperor Friedrich III is said to have
18 died in the **Kremsmünstererhaus** (⊠ Altstadt 10) in 1493. The building was done over in Renaissance style in 1578–1580, and a story was
added in 1616, with two turrets and onion domes. There's a memorial room to the emperor here; his heart is entombed in the Linz parish
church, but the rest of him is in St. Stephen's cathedral in Vienna. The
traditional rooms are now home to one of Linz' best restaurants, the
Kremsmünsterer Stuben (☞ Dining and Lodging, *below*).

19 The massive four-story building in Tummelplatz is the **Linz Castle,** rebuilt by Friedrich III about 1477, literally on top of a castle that dated from 799. Note the **Friedrichstor,** the Friedrich gate, with the same *A.E.I.O.U.* monogram also found in Krems, and the two interior courtyards. The castle houses the Upper Austrian provincial museum—weapons, musical instruments, nativity scenes, Upper Austrian art, and prehistoric and Roman relics. ⊠ *Tummelpl. 10,* ☎ *0732/774419.* 🎫 *AS40.* ⏲ *Tues.–Fri. 9–5, weekends and holidays 10–4.*

20 At the intersection of Herrenstrasse and Bischofstrasse is the **Bischofshof** (Bishop's Residence), which dates from 1721. Graced by a fine
wrought-iron gateway, this remains the city's most important Baroque
profane building. The design is by Jakob Prandtauer, the architectural
genius responsible for the glorious Melk and St. Florian abbeys. In 1862
the bishop of Linz engaged one of the architects of the Cologne cathedral to develop a design for a cathedral in neo-Gothic French-cathe-
dral style and modestly ordered that its tower not be higher than that
21 of St. Stephen's in Vienna. The result was the massive **Neuer Dom** (new
cathedral), its 400-foot tower shorter than St. Stephen's by a scant 6½
feet. ⊠ *Baumbachstr..* ⏲ *Daily 7:30–7.*

22 The **Carmelite Church,** on Landstrassem, was modeled on St. Joseph's
in Prague and is a magnificent Baroque church (open daily 7–11:30
and 3–6). Across the street from the Carmelite Church is another
23 Baroque wonder, the **Ursuline Church** (open daily 1–6). Its double-fig-
ured towers are one of the identifying symbols of Linz (open daily 8–
6). Inside is a blaze of gold and crystal ornament. Note the Madonna
figure wearing a hooded Carmelite cloak with huge pockets used to
24 collect alms for the poor. The former **Deutschordenskirche** (seminary
church, 1723) is a beautiful yellow-and-white Baroque treasure with
an elliptical dome, designed by Johann Lukas von Hildebrandt, who
also designed its high altar. ⊠ *Harrachstr..* ⏲ *Daily 8–6.*

At the corner of Dametzstrasse and Bethlehemstrasse, you'll find the
25 **Nordico** (city museum, 1610). Its collection follows local history from
pre-Roman times to the mid-1880s. ⊠ *Bethlehemstr. 7,* ☎ *0732/2393–
1912.* 🎫 *Free, except for special exhibits.* ⏲ *Weekdays 9–6, weekends 2–5.*

26 The **Elisabethinenkirche** (⊠ Bethlehemstr.) dates to the mid-18th century. Note the unusually dynamic colors in the dome fresco by Altomonte.
Hidden away off the Graben, a narrow side street off of the Tauben-
27 markt above the Hauptplatz, sits the Baroque **Alter Dom** (old cathe-

dral, 1669–78), whose striking feature is the single nave together with the side altars. Anton Bruckner was organist here from 1856 to 1868. ⏲ *Daily 7–noon and 3–7.*

28 The **Stadtpfarrkirche** (city parish church) dates to 1286 and was rebuilt in Baroque style in 1648. The tomb in the right wall of the chancel contains Friedrich III's heart. The ceiling frescoes are by Altomonte, and the figure of Johann Nepomuk (a local saint) in the chancel is by Georg Raphael Donner, in a setting by Hildebrandt. ✉ *Domgasse.* ⏲ *Mon.–Sat. 8–7, Sun. 9–7.*

29 At **No. 5 Rathausgasse,** the astronomer Johannes Kepler lived from 1622 to 1626; Linz's first printing shop was established in this house in 1745.

★ 30 For a splendid view over Linz and the Danube, ride up the **Pöstlingberg** on the electric **Pöstlingbergbahn.** To reach the base station for the railway, take Streetcar 3 across the river to Urfahr, Linz's left bank. Note the railway's unusual switches, necessary because the car wheel flanges ride the outside of the rails rather than the (usual) inside. When the line was built in 1898, it boasted the steepest incline of any noncog railway in Europe. In summer, the old open-bench cars are used. On a clear day the view at the top takes in a good deal of Upper Austria south of the Danube, with a long chain of the Austrian Alps on the horizon. At the Pöstlinberg summit is the **Church of Sieben Schmerzen Mariens,** an immense and splendidly opulent twin-towered Baroque pilgrimage church (1748), visible for leagues as a landmark of Linz. With a chilled glass of white wine, drink in the grand vista at one of the flower-hung restaurants located near the church. ☎ *0732/2801–7002.* 🎟 *Round-trip AS35, combined ticket with streetcar Line 3 AS48.* ⏲ *Daily every 20 min 5:30 AM–8:20 PM.*

A kid's treat at the top of the Pöstlinberg (that's entertaining for the rest of the family) is the **fairytale-grotto railroad,** which runs through a colorful imaginary world. 🎟 *AS40.* ⏲ *Sat. before Palm Sunday–Apr. and Oct., daily 9–4:45; May–Sept., daily 9–5:45.*

The exceptional **Neue Galerie,** across the river in the Urfahr district, is one of Austria's best modern art museums. The fine collection is well balanced, featuring mainly contemporary international and Austrian artists. ✉ *Blütenstr. 15, Urfahr,* ☎ *0732/2393–3600.* 🎟 *AS40.* ⏲ *May–Oct., Mon.–Wed. and Fri. 10–6, Thurs. 10–10, Sat. 10–1; Nov.–Apr., Fri.–Wed. 10–6, Thurs. 10–10.*

Dining and Lodging

$$$$ ✕ **Der neue Vogelkäfig.** In 1992 Georg Essig moved his restaurant, exotic bird cages and all, from an idyllic suburban location into this small house in an unfashionable part of town; the main trace of country remaining is the lovely garden under chestnut trees. But the interior setting, with its pastel colors, is both intimate and friendly. The kitchen is imaginative and up to Linz's highest standard, featuring such dishes as a selection of delicate fish filets or fillet of beef rolled with herbs. ✉ *Holzstr. 8,* ☎ *0732/770193. AE, DC, MC, V. Closed weekends and 3 wks weeks in Aug.*

$$$$ ★ ✕ **Kremsmünsterer Stuben.** In a beautifully restored historic house in the heart of the Old City you'll find an attractive wood-paneled restaurant offering everything from regional specialties to a six-course dinner. You might choose from saddle of hare or fillet of venison as a main course as you relax in the comfortable, traditional ambience of the city's best restaurant. ✉ *Altstadt 10,* ☎ *0732/782111,* FAX *0732/784130. Reservations essential. Jacket and tie. AE, DC, MC, V. Closed Sun., Mon., 2 wks in Jan., and 2 wks in Aug.*

$$$$ ✕ **Verdi.** Linz's favored dinner restaurant is in Lichtenberg, about 3 kilometers (2 miles) north of the center, off Leonfelder Strasse. The cuisine is regional Austrian, with Italian and French overtones; the name refers to the opulent green-hued decor. Some complain of overemphasis on presentation, but this hardly deters the many regulars. Choose game in season or tender lamb. ✉ *Pachmayrstr. 137,* ☎ *0732/733005. No credit cards. Closed Sun., Mon., and 3 wks in Jan.*

$$ ✕ **Stadtwirt.** First-class regional food is served along with colorful, genuinely local atmosphere (since 1622) unspoiled by frills, and at remarkably reasonable prices. If you long for a proper veal schnitzel, try it here—although the house specialty is variations on Tafelspitz. The strudels are outstanding, the service by the inexperienced staff less so. ✉ *Landstr./Bismarckstr. 1,* ☎ *0732/785122–0,* FAX *0732/785122–75. No credit cards. Closed Sun.*

$$ ★ ✕ **Traxlmayr.** Proud with the patina of age, this is one of Austria's great old-tradition coffeehouses. You can linger all day over one cup of coffee, reading the papers (*Herald Tribune* included) in their bentwood holders, and then have a light meal. All Linz gathers on the terrace in summer. Ask for the specialty, *Linzer Torte,* with your coffee. ✉ *Promenade 16,* ☎ *0732/773353. No credit cards. Closed Sun.*

$$ ✕ **Zum Klosterhof.** This complex in the former Kremsmünster abbey gives you a choice of upstairs and downstairs rooms that range from fairly formal to rustic-country to completely informal. The fare is traditional Austrian, and the beverage of choice is Salzburger Stiegl beer. ✉ *Landstr. 30,* ☎ *0732/773373–0,* FAX *0732/773373–21. AE, DC, MC, V.*

$$$$ 🏨 **Schillerpark.** You're close to the south end of the pedestrian zone but still reasonably near the center and the sights in this very modern complex (glass outside, marble and air-conditioned inside). The rooms have clean lines, with contemporary furnishings. The casino is in the same building. ✉ *Rainerstr. 2–4,* ☎ *0732/6950–0,* FAX *0732/6950–9. 111 rooms. 2 restaurants, 2 bars, café, sauna. AE, DC, MC, V.*

$$$ 🏨 **Trend.** In this multistory modern hotel, you'll be directly on the Danube, next to the Brucknerhaus concert hall, and within reasonable walking distance of the center. The rooms are compact, modern, and attractively decorated; ask for an upper room on the river side for the superb views. ✉ *Untere Donaulände 9,* ☎ *0732/7626–0,* FAX *0732/7626–2. 176 rooms. Restaurant, bar, café, indoor pool, sauna, exercise room, nightclub. AE, DC, MC, V.*

$$–$$$ ★ 🏨 **Wolfinger.** This charming, traditional hotel in an old building is a favorite of regular guests, in part because of the friendly staff, and its location couldn't be more central. The medium-size rooms have been recently modernized, with comfortable new furniture and bright fabrics. Those in the front are less quiet but give a view of city activities. ✉ *Hauptpl. 19,* ☎ *0732/773291–0,* FAX *0732/773291–55. 45 rooms. AE, DC, MC, V.*

$$ 🏨 **Zum Schwarzen Bären.** The "Black Bear" is a fine, traditional house near the center of the Old City, a block from the pedestrian zone, and incidentally was the birthplace of the renowned tenor Richard Tauber (1891–1948). The rooms are smallish and well worn, but the baths (most with shower) are modern, if compact. ✉ *Herrenstr. 9–11,* ☎ *0732/772477–0,* FAX *0732/772477–47. 35 rooms, 29 with bath. Restaurant, bar, weinstube. AE, DC, MC, V.*

Nightlife and the Arts

Linz is far livelier than even most Austrians realize. The local population is friendlier than that in either Vienna or Salzburg, and much less cliquish than in those top resort towns. Nor has Linz lagged behind other Austrian cities in developing its own hot section, known as the "Bermuda Triangle." Around the narrow streets of the Old City (Klosterstrasse, Altstadt, Hofgasse) are dozens of fascinating small bars and lounges, and as you explore, you'll probably meet some Linzers who can direct you to the current "in" location. A good starting point, where both the young and the older will feel comfortable, is **S'Linzerl** (✉ Hofberg 5), which is open Monday–Saturday 9 PM–3 AM.

The Linz casino, with roulette, blackjack, poker, and slot machines, is in the **Hotel Schillerpark;** the casino complex includes a bar and the Rouge et Noir restaurant. A passport is required for admission. ✉ *Rainerstr. 2–4,* ☎ *0732/654487–0,* FAX *0732/654487–24.* ⏲ *Dec. 25–Oct. and Nov. 2–Dec. 23, daily 3 PM–3 AM.* 🎫 *AS210, including 5 AS50 tokens.*

The tourist office's monthly booklet "Was ist los in Linz und Oberösterreich" ("What's on in Linz and Upper Austria") will give you details of theater and concerts. Two **ticket agencies** are Linzer Kartenbüro (✉ Herrenstr. 4, ☎ 0732/778800) and Ruefa (✉ Landstr. 67, ☎ 0732/662681–0, FAX 0732/662681–33).

The Linz **opera** company is talented and often willing to mount venturesome works and productions. Most performances are in the Landestheater, some in the Brucknerhaus. Concerts and recitals are held in the **Brucknerhaus,** the modern hall on the banks of the Danube. From mid-September to early October, it's the center of the International Bruckner Festival. In mid-June, the hall hosts the biggest multimedia event in the area, the Ars Electronica, a musical and laser-show spectacle ✉ *Untere Donaulände 7,* ☎ *0732/775230,* FAX *0732/783745.* ⏲ *Box office weekdays 10–6.*

Don't overlook the casual **wine gardens** set under huge trees on the north bank of the Danube (Urfahr district), west of the new city hall. This is anything but tourist territory, and you'll toast the friendly Linzers with mugs of wine on pleasant summer afternoons and evenings.

Shopping

Linz is a good place to shop; prices are generally lower than those in resorts and the larger cities, and selections are varied. The major shops are found in the main square and the adjoining side streets, in the old quarter to the west of the main square, in the pedestrian zone of the Landstrasse and its side streets, and in the Hauptstrasse of Urfahr, over the Nibelungen Bridge across the Danube. For local handmade items and good-quality souvenirs, try **O.Ö. Heimatwerk** (✉ Landstr. 31, Linz, ☎ 0732/773376–0), where you'll find silver, pewter, ceramics, fabrics, and some clothing. Items from clothing to china are sold at the **Flea Market** (open March–mid-November, Saturday 7–2) on the Hauptplatz (main square). From mid-November through February the market moves across the river next to the new city hall and runs from 8–2, also on Saturdays. The state-run **Dorotheum auction house** is at Fabrikstrasse 26 (☎ 0732/773132–0). Auctions take place every Wednesday at 1:30.

For **antiques** head for the old city, on the side streets around the main square. Try **Otto Buchinger** (✉ Bethlehemstr. 5, ☎ 0732/770117), **Richard Kirchmayr** (✉ Bischofstr. 3a, ☎ 0732/797711), **Kunsthandlung Kirchmayr** (✉ Herrenstr. 23, ☎ 0732/774667), and **Ute Pastl** (✉ Wischerstr. 26, Urfahr, ☎ 0732/737306). For **jewelry,** try **Pfaffenberger** (✉ Landstr. 42, ☎ 0732/772495) or **Wild** (✉ Landstr. 49, ☎ 0732/774105–0).

Sports and Outdoor Activities

Buy tickets for sports events at **Kartenbüro Ruefa** (✉ Landstr. 67, ☎ 0732/662681–0, FAX 0732/662681–33). The office is open weekdays 8:30–noon and 2–6 and Saturday 8:30–noon.

BICYCLING

Cyclists appreciate the relatively level terrain around Linz, and within the city there are 89 kilometers (55 miles) of marked cycle routes. Get the brochure *Cycling in Linz* from the tourist office. You can **rent a bike** through **Fahrradzentrum B7** (✉ Oberfelderstr. 12, ☎ 0732/330550); **LILO Bahnhof** (✉ Coulinstr. 30, ☎ 0732/600703); or at the **Hauptbahnhof** (✉ main rail station, Bahnhofstr. 3, ☎ 0732/6909–385).

GOLF

Fairly close to Linz is the 9-hole, par-72 **Golfclub St. Oswald-Freistadt** (✉ St. Oswald bei Freistadt, ☎ 07945/7938). The 18-hole, par-72 **Böhmerwald Golfpark** is near Linz (Ulrichsberg, ☎ 07288/8200). East of Linz is the relatively new 18-hole, par-71 **Linzer Golf Club Mühlviertel,** playable mid-March to November (✉ Luftenberg a.d. Donau, ☎ 07237/3893).

ICE SKATING

Linz is an ice-skating city; from late October to late February, there's outdoor skating at the **city rink** (daily 2–5 and Friday–Wednesday 6–9, weekends and holidays also 9–noon) and indoors at the adjoining indoor sports complex, the **Eishalle,** from late September to April, Wednesday 9–noon, Saturday 2–5, and Sunday 10–noon, 2–5, and 6–9. Hockey and skating competitions are also held in the Eishalle. ✉ *Untere Donaulände 11,* ☎ *0732/778513.*

SOCCER

Soccer matches are played in Linz in the **Stadion** (✉ Roseggerstr. 41, ☎ 0732/660670 or 0732/601115).

TENNIS

Tennis matches and other sports events are held at the **Stadthalle** (☎ 0732/657311–0).

WATER SPORTS

The Danube is not suitable for swimming, but alternatives exist. The closest swimming is at **Pleschinger Lake**; to get there, take Tram 1 to Urfahr/Reindlstrasse and Bus 32 to the lake. This is a pleasant spot for family swimming, although it tends to be crowded on sunny, warm weekends. The **Kral Waterskiing School** (✉ Talgasse 14, ☎ 0732/731494) offers waterskiing and other water sports.

EXCURSIONS FROM LINZ

Into the Hinterland

Many travelers find Linz the most practical point of departure for visits to the Mühlviertel and the Gothic and Baroque sights found in the towns of St. Florian, Kremsmünster, and Steyr, although Steyr certainly merits an overnight itself. The **Mühlviertel** (mill district now in the agricultural, not industrial, sense) north of Linz toward the Czech border is made up of meadows and gentle wooded hills interspersed with towns whose appearance has changed little since the Middle Ages. To the west of Linz, south of the Danube, lies the **Innviertel,** named for the Inn River (which forms the border with Germany before it joins the Danube), a region of broad fields and meadows, and enormous woodland tracts, ideal for cycling, hiking, and riding. To the south, the hilly landscape introduces the foothills of the Austrian Alps.

Freistadt

★ 31 *41 km (25¾ mi) northeast of Linz.*

To get to Freistadt, a preserved walled city in the eastern part of the Mühviertel, cross the Danube to Linz-Urfahr and turn right onto Freistädter Strasse (Route 125/E55). Freistadt developed as a border defense city on the salt route into Bohemia (now the Czech Republic), which accounts for the wall, towers, and gates, still wonderfully preserved today. Look at the late-Gothic **Linzertor,** the Linz Gate, with its steep wedge-shaped roof, and the **Böhmertor,** on the opposite side, leading to Bohemia. A walk around the wall gives an impression of how a city in the Middle Ages was conceived and defended; it takes about a half hour. The city's central square, aglow with pastel facades, is virtually the same as it was 400 years ago; only the parked cars intrude into the picture of antiquity. Pause for a local beer; the town's first brewery dated to 1573. While wandering through the alleys behind the **central square,** note the wealth of architectural details; plus, many of the arcades contain interesting small shops. The 15th-century parish **church of St. Catherine**'s was redone in Baroque style in the 17th century but retains its slender tower, whose unusual balconies have railings on all four sides. The late-Gothic castle to the northeast of the square now houses the **Mühlviertel Heimathaus** (district museum); the display of painted glass in the chapel and the hand tools in the 163-foot tower are especially interesting. ☎ *07942/2274.* 🎫 *AS10.* ⏲ *Tour May–Oct., Tues.–Sat. at 10 and 2, Sun. and holidays at 10; Nov.–Apr., Tues.–Fri. at 10, Tues. and Thurs. also at 2.*

Dining and Lodging

$$ ✕🏨 **Deim/Zum Goldenen Hirschen.** This romantic and atmospheric 600-year-old house full fits perfectly into the Old City. The rooms are up-to-date and attractive. The stone-arched ceiling adds to the elegance of the dining room, where you'll find international and local specialties and game in season. ✉ *Böhmergasse 8, A–4240,* ☎ *07942/2258–0, 07942/2111,* FAX *07942/2258–40. 32 rooms. Restaurant. DC. Closed 1st 2 wks of Jan.*

$$ ★ ✕🏨 **Zum Goldenen Adler.** Here you'll be in another 600-year-old house; it has been run by the same family since 1807, so tradition runs strong. The medium-size rooms are modern yet full of country charm; hotel service is exceptionally accommodating. The newly renovated garden, with a piece of the old city wall as background, is a delightful oasis. The restaurant can be variable but is known for regional specialties such as *Böhmisches Bierfleisch,* a cut of beef cooked in beer. The desserts are outstanding. ✉ *Salzgasse 1, A–4240,* ☎ *07942/2112–0,* FAX *07942/2112–44. 30 rooms. Restaurant, pool, sauna, exercise room. AE, DC, MC, V.*

Kefermarkt

32 *9 km (5¾ mi) south of Freistadt, either via marked back roads or by turning east off of Rte. 125/E14.*

The late-Gothic **church of St. Wolfgang** boasts one of Austria's great art treasures, a 42-foot-high winged altar intricately carved from linden wood, commissioned by Christoph von Zelking, and completed in 1497. So masterly is the carving that it has been ascribed to famous 15th-century sculptors Veit Stoss and Michael Pacher, but most historians now attribute it to Jürg Huber and Martin Kriechbaum. Some figures, such as the St. Christopher, are true masterpieces of Northern Renaissance sculpture. The church also has some impressive 16th-century frescoes.

Eferding

33 *25 km (15¾ mi) west of Linz, 22 km (13¾ mi) north of Wels.*

Eferding, a centuries-old community with an attractive town square, lies west of Linz. You can easily drive the 25 kilometers (16 miles) on Route 129, but the more adventurous route is via the *LILO* (Linzer Lokalbahn) interurban railway from Coulinstrasse 30 (☎ 0732/654376), near the main rail station. In the town itself, the double door in the south wall of the 15th-century **church of St. Hippolyte** is a gem of late-Gothic stonecutting, with the Madonna and Child above flanked by Saints Hippolyte and Agyd. Inside, note the Gothic altar with its five reliefs and the statues of Saints Wolfgang and Martin. Visit the **Spitalskirche** (built in 1325) and note the Gothic frescoes in the Magdalen chapel, which date to about 1430.

Dining and Lodging

$$$$ ★ ✕ **Dannerbauer.** Two kilometers (1½ miles) north of Eferding, on the road to Aschach and directly on the Danube, is one of the area's best restaurants. It serves many species of fish—some you probably never heard of—to your taste: poached, grilled, broiled, or fried. Many of the fish come from the river; some are raised in the house ponds, to ensure freshness. There are meat dishes, too, and game in season, and the soups (try the nettle soup) are excellent. The place has a pleasant outlook with lots of windows. ✉ *Brandstatt bei Eferding,* ☎ *07272/2471. AE, DC. Closed Mon., Tues., and mid-Jan.–mid-Feb.*

$ **Zum Goldenen Kreuz.** The golden facade indicates a typical country-style hotel, simple and with the appealing charm of a family-run establishment. You'll sleep under fluffy feather-bed coverlets. The restaurant is known for its good regional cuisine, and there are occasional specialty weeks. ✉ *Schmiedstr. 29, A–4070,* ☎ *07272/4247–0,* FAX *07272/4249. 21 rooms. Restaurant. AE, DC, MC. Closed Christmas wk.*

Hartkirchen

34 *12 km (7½ mi) north of Eferding, 26 km (16¼ mi) northwest of Linz.*

The **parish church** at Hartkirchen is worth a visit to see fine Baroque wall and ceiling frescoes, dated 1750, that create the illusion of space and depth. To reach Hartkirchen, take Rte. 130 north from Eferding to Pupping and continue 3 km (2 mi).

Aschach

35 *9 km (5½ mi) north of Eferding, 21 km (13¼ mi) northwest of Linz.*

Two kilometers (1 mile) farther (Route 131) along the Danube from Hartkirchen is Aschach, a small village that was once a river toll station and long famed as the birthplace of Leonard Paminger, one of the most noted 16th-century Austrian composers. It features several gabled-roof burghers' houses, a castle, and a late-Gothic church that are all well preserved. Less intact is the castle, now semi-ruined, that once belonged to the regal Counts of Harrach, located near the town.

Lodging

$$ ★ **Faust Schlössl.** Once a toll-collection station belonging to the Schaunberg family (ruins of the family castle are nearby), this castle is on the river directly across from Aschach. Rumor has it that the place is haunted by the Devil, who is said to have built it in a single night for Dr. Faustus. Ignore the tale and enjoy simple but modern comfort in the towers and turrets of the converted castle. ✉ *Oberlandshaag 2,*

A–4082 Feldkirchen, ☎ 07233/7402–0, FAX 07233/7402–40. 25 rooms. Restaurant, pool, fishing, bicycles. AE, MC, V.

$$ **Zur Sonne.** The welcome of the bright yellow facade carries over to the comfortable traditional decor inside. You're right on the Danube here, and the best rooms have a river view. This popular restaurant offers regional specialties and, of course, fish, including fresh trout. ⊠ *Kurzwernhartpl. 5, A–4082 Aschach/Donau, ☎ 07273/6308. 12 rooms with bath or shower. Restaurant. No credit cards.*

St. Florian

★ 36 *13 km (8¼ mi) southeast of Linz.*

St. Florian is best known for the great Augustinian abbey, considered among the finest Baroque buildings in Austria. Composer Anton Bruckner (1824–96) was organist for 10 years and is buried in the abbey. Take the road south to Kleinmünchen and Ebelsberg, or for a more romantic approach, try the **Florianer Bahn,** a resurrected electric interurban tram line, which runs museum streetcars on Sundays and holidays from May through the end of September, 6 kilometers (nearly 4 miles) from Pichling to St. Florian (☎ 07224/4333); streetcars depart at 10:40, 2:10, and 3:40.

Guided tours of the **Abbey of St. Florian** include a magnificent figural gate encompassing all three stories, a large and elegant staircase leading to the upper floors, the imperial suite, and one of the great masterworks of the Austrian Baroque, Jakob Prandtauer's **Eagle Fountain courtyard,** with its richly sculpted figures. In the splendid **abbey church,** where the ornate decor is somewhat in contrast to Bruckner's music, the Krismann organ (1770–74) is one of the largest and best of its period. Another highlight is the **Altdorfer Gallery,** which contains several masterworks by Albrecht Altdorfer, the leading master of the 16th-century Danube School and ranked with Durer and Grunewald as one of the greatest Northern painters. ⊠ *Stiftstr. 1, ☎ 07224/8902–10. AS58. 1½-hr tour Apr.–Oct., daily at 10, 11, 2, 3, and 4.*

Nightlife and the Arts

Summer concerts are held in June and July at the Kremsmünster (☞ *below*) and St. Florian abbeys; for tickets, contact Oberösterreichische Stiftskonzerte (⊠ Domgasse 12, ☎ 0732/776127). A chamber music festival takes place at Schloss Tillysburg in July (☎ 0732/775230). In July and August, a series of concerts on the Bruckner organ is given on Sunday afternoons at 4 in the church (☎ 07224/8903).

Kremsmünster

37 *36 km (22½ mi) south of Linz, 9 km (5½ mi) northwest of Bad Hall, 18 km (11¼ mi) southeast of Wels.*

The vast Benedictine **abbey** at Kremsmünster was established in 777 and remains one of the most important cloisters in Austria. Most travelers arrive there by taking Route 139 (or the train) heading southwest from Linz. Inside the church is the Gothic memorial tomb of Gunther, killed by a wild boar, whose father, Tassilo, duke of Bavaria (and nemesis of Charlemagne) vowed to build the abbey on the site. Centuries later, a Baroque extravaganza replaced the initial structures. There are magnificent rooms: the **Kaisersaal** and the frescoed library with more than 100,000 volumes, many of them manuscripts. On one side of the **Prälatenhof** courtyard are Jakob Prandtauer's elegant fish basins, complete with sculpted saints, holding squirming denizens of the deep, and opposite is the **Abteitrakt,** whose art collection includes the Tassilo Chalice, from about 765. The eight-story observatory houses an early museum of science. ☎ 07583/275–216. 🎫 *Rooms and art gallery AS45, observatory and tour AS50.* ⏲ *Rooms and art gallery tour (minimum 5 people) Easter–Oct., daily at 10, 11, 2, 3, and 4; Nov.–Easter at 11 and 2. Observatory tour (minimum 5 people) May, June, Sept., and Oct., daily at 10 and 2; July and Aug., daily at 10, 2, and 4).*

The castle at **Kremsegg,** on Route 139 near Kremsmünster, has a collection of old-fashioned cars and motorcycles. ☎ *07583/247–14.* 🎫 *AS70.* ⏲ *Sat. 1–5; Sun., holidays, and July–Aug., 10–noon, 1–5.*

Bad Hall

38 *36 km (22½ mi) south of Linz, 18 km (11¼ mi) west of Steyr.*

Bad Hall is a curious relic from earlier days when "taking the cure" was in vogue in Europe. It's still a spa and its saline-iodine waters are prescribed for internal and external application, but you can enjoy the town for its turn-of-the-century setting. Since those on the cure need amusement between treatments, the town lays on numerous sports offerings—-during warm weather, there are especially excellent opportunities for golf and tennis—and an operetta festival in summer.

Lodging

$$$$ ★ **Schlosshotel Feyregg.** You'll be in an exclusive setting in this Baroque castle just outside town, once the elegant summer residence of an abbot. The comfortable, spacious guest rooms on the ground floor are furnished in period style. The golf course is within an easy stroll. ✉ *A–4540 Bad Hall/Feyregg-Pfarrkirchen,* ☎ *07258/2591. 11 rooms. Bar. No credit cards.*

$$$–$$$$ **Herzog Tassilo Kurhotel.** The yellow exterior of this turn-of-the-century villa reflects the sunny attitude within. Rooms are comfortable if not luxurious, but the main attractions are the vast park in which the hotel is set and the opportunity to "take the cure" under medical supervision for eye, heart, or circulation complaints. Minimum half board is required. ✉ *Parkstr. 4, A–4540 Bad Hall,* ☎ *07258/2611–0,* FAX *07258/2611–5. 85 rooms. Restaurant, bar, café, indoor pool, sauna, exercise room. AE, DC, MC, V.*

Steyr

★ 39 *40 km (25 mi) south of Linz, 20 km (13½ mi) south of Enns.*

Steyr, a stunning Gothic market town, watches over the confluence of the Steyr and Enns rivers. If you travel from Kremsmünster, follow Route 139 until it joins Route 122 and take the road another 17 kilometers (10½ miles). Today the **main square** is lined with pastel facades, many with Baroque and Rococo trim, all complemented by the castle that sits above. The Bummerlhaus at No. 32, in its present form dating to 1497, has a late-Gothic three-story effect. On the Enns side, steps and narrow passageways lead down to the river. In Steyr you are close to the heart of Bruckner country. He composed his *Sixth Symphony* in the Parish House here, and there is a Bruckner room in the **Meserhaus** where he composed his "sonorous music to confound celestial spheres." So many of the houses are worthy of attention that you will need to take your time and explore. Given the quaintness of the town center, you'd hardly guess that Steyr in 1894 had Europe's first electric street lighting. The **Steyrertalbahn,** a narrow-gauge vintage railroad, wanders 17 kilometers (10½ miles) from Steyr through the countryside on weekends June–September (☎ 07252/46569 or 0732/250345). The **industrial museum** set in former riverside factories is a reminder of the era when Steyr was a major center of ironmaking and armaments production; hunting arms are still produced here, but the major output is powerful motors for BMW cars, including those assembled in the United States. ✉ *Wehrgrabengasse 7,* ☎ *07252/77351–0.* 🎫 *AS55.* ⏲ *Tues.–Sun. 10–5.*

Dining and Lodging

$$$ ✕ **Rahofer.** You'll have to search out this intimate restaurant, which is hidden away in one of the passageways off the main square down toward the river. The choice is limited but the Italian specialties are usually excellent; try the saltimbocca or lamb fillet broiled au gratin with herbs and olive oil. Soups and desserts are praiseworthy. ✉ *Stadtpl. 9,* ☎ *07252/54606. AE, DC, V. Closed Sun. and Mon.*

$$$ ✕🏨 **Minichmayr.** From this traditional hotel the view alone—out over the confluence of the Enns and Steyr rivers, up and across to Schloss Lamberg—will make your stay memorable. Ask for a room on the river side, but check before you register, since tradition has unfortunately, in some cases, become an excuse for shabbiness. No caveats apply to the excellent restaurant's creative, light cuisine and regional specialties. The hotel is one of the Romantik Hotel group. ✉ *Haratzmüllerstr. 1–3, A–4400,* ☎ *07252/53410–0,* FAX *07252/48202–55. 51 rooms. Restaurant, bar, weinstube, sauna, exercise room, bicycles. AE, DC, MC, V.*

$$ ★ 🏨 **Mader/Zu den Drei Rosen.** In this very old family-run hotel with small but pleasant modern rooms, you're right on the attractive town square. The restaurant offers solid local and traditional fare, with outdoor dining in a delightful garden area within the ancient courtyard. ✉ *Stadtpl. 36, A–4400,* ☎ *07252/53358–0,* FAX *07252/53358–6. 53 rooms. Restaurant, weinstube. AE, DC, MC, V.*

THE WACHAU ALONG THE SOUTH BANK OF THE DANUBE

South of the Danube and east of Linz, the gentle countryside is crossed by rivers that rise in the Alps and eventually feed the Danube. Little evidence remains today, in this prosperous country of small-industry and agriculture, that the area was heavily fought over in the final days of World War II. From 1945 to 1995, the river Enns marked the border between the western (U.S., British, and French) and the eastern (Russian) occupying zones.

Enns

40 *20 km (12½ mi) southeast of Linz.*

A settlement has continuously existed at Enns since at least AD 50; the Romans set up a major encampment shortly after that date. Contemporary Enns is dominated by the 184-foot square city tower (1565–68) that stands in the town square. A number of Gothic buildings in the center have Renaissance or Baroque facades. Guided tours of the town's highlights, starting at the tower, are available for a minimum of three persons daily at 9:15 and 10:30, May–mid-September (☎ 07223/3261). Visit the **St. Laurence basilica,** built on the foundations of a far earlier church, west of the town center, to view the glass-encased archaeological discoveries from earlier civilizations. And outside, look for the Baroque carved-wood Pontius Pilate disguised as a Turk, alongside a bound Christ, on the balcony of the old sanctuary.

Lodging

$$$ **Lauriacum.** You might overlook this plain contemporary building, set as it is among Baroque gems in the center of town, but it's the best place to stay. The bright rooms offer modern comfort, and the quiet garden is a welcoming spot. ✉ *Wiener Str. 5–7, A–4470,* ☎ *07223/2315,* FAX *07223/2332–29. 30 rooms. Restaurant, bar, café, sauna. MC, V.*

Waidhofen an der Ybbs

41 *30 km (18¾ mi) east of Steyr, 25 km (15¾ mi) south of Amstetten.*

Waidhofen an der Ybbs is well worth a slight detour from the more traveled routes. This picturesque river town developed early as an industrial center, turning Styrian iron ore into swords, knives, sickles, and scythes. These weapons proved successful in the defense against the invading Turks in 1532; marking the decisive moment of victory, the hands on the north side of the town tower clock remain at 12:45. In 1871, Baron Rothschild bought the collapsing castle and assigned Friedrich Schmidt, architect of the Vienna city hall, to rebuild it in neo-Gothic style. Stroll around the two squares in the Altstadt to see the Gothic and Baroque houses, and to the Graben on the edge of the old city for the delightful Biedermeier houses and the churches and chapels. From Enns, take the A1 autobahn or Route 1 east from Enns to just before Amstetten, where Route 121 cuts south paralleling the Ybbs River and the branch rail line for about 25 kilometers (16 miles).

Dining

$$$ ✕ **Türkenpfeiferl.** A relaxed atmosphere marks this restaurant. Set in a handsomely restored town house within the heart of the Old Town, it serves excellent regional standards. Try the breast of chicken, grilled trout with garlic butter, or lamb with creamed celery sauce. The wine cellar includes far more than is on the list, so ask for advice. The garden is particularly pleasant for summer dining, and children are welcome. ✉ *Hoher Markt 23,* ☎ *07442/53507. DC, MC. Closed Mon., Tues., and 1st wk of July.*

Ybbs an der Donau

42 *25 km (15¾ mi) northeast of Amstetten, 13 km (8¼ mi) west of Melk.*

Floods and fires have left their mark on Ybbs an der Donau, but many 16th-century houses remain, their courtyards vine-covered and shaded. The parish church of St. Laurence has interesting old tombstones, a gorgeous gilded organ, and a Mount of Olives scene with clay figures dating to 1450. To get to Ybbs an der Donau from Waidhofen an der Ybbs, make your way back to the Danube via Routes 31 and 22 east, then Route 25 north thorugh the beer-brewing town of Wieselburg.

Melk

★ 43 *22 km (13¾ mi) east of Ybbs an der Donau, 18 km (11¼ mi) west of St. Pölten, 33 km (20¾ mi) southwest of Krems.*

The ideal time to approach the magnificent abbey of Melk is mid- to late afternoon, when the sun sets the abbey's ornate Baroque yellow facade aglow. As one heads eastward paralleling the Danube, the classic view of the abbey, shining on its promontory above the river, comes into view—unquestionably one of the most impressive sights in all Austria. The glories of the abbey tend to overshadow the town—located along Route 1—but the riverside village of Melk itself is worth exploring. A self-guided tour (in English, from the tourist office) will head you toward the highlights and the best spots from which to photograph the abbey.

The **Abbey of Melk** by any standard is a Baroque masterpiece. Here the story of Umberto Eco's historical novel and film *The Name of the Rose* took place, and in fact, as in fiction, the monastery did burn in 1297, in 1683, and again in 1735. The Benedictine abbey was established in 1089; the building you see today dates to architect Jakob Prandtauer's reconstruction, completed in 1736, in which some earlier elements are incorporated. Part palace, part monastery, part opera set, Melk is a classic vision thanks greatly to the upward-reaching twin towers, capped with Baroque helmets and cradling a 208-foot-high dome, and a roof bristling with Baroque statuary. Symmetry here beyond the towers and dome would be misplaced, and much of the abbey's charm is due to the way the early architects were forced to fit the building to the rocky outcrop which forms its base. A tour of the building includes the main public rooms: a magnificent library, with more than 70,000 books, 2,000 manuscripts, and a superb ceiling fresco by the master Paul Troger; the marble hall, whose windows on three sides enhance the ceiling frescoes; the glorious spiral staircase; and the church of Saints Peter and Paul, an exquisite example of the Baroque style. ✉ *Abt Berthold Dietmayr-Str. 1,* ☎ *02752/2312.* 🎫 *AS50; with tour AS65; combination ticket available with Schloss Artstetten (☞ Maria Taferl,* above*) and Schloss Schallaburg (☞* below*).* ⏲ *Apr.–Sept., daily 9–5 (50-min tour hourly; last tour 1 hr before closing); Apr.–Oct., daily 9–5; tour Nov.–Mar., daily at 11 and 2.*

NEED A BREAK? The **Stiftsrestaurant** at the abbey of Melk (☞ *above*) offers standard fare, but the abbey's excellent wines elevate a simple meal to a lofty experience—particularly on a sunny day on the terrace. Closed November–April.

Dining and Lodging

$$–$$$ ✕🏨 **Stadt Melk.** This traditional hotel in the heart of town offers plain but adequate accommodations in smallish rooms (look before you register), but the main feature here is the excellent and attractive restaurant. The cuisine ranges from regional traditional to creative light; try one of the cream soups, stuffed chicken breast, or rack of lamb in an olive crust to enjoy the contrasts; dishes here are individually prepared. ✉ *Hauptpl. 1, A–3390,* ☎ *02752/2475,* FAX *02752/2475–19. 16 rooms. Restaurant. AE, DC, MC, V. Closed mid-Nov.–mid-Dec.*

$$ 🏨 **Goldener Ochs.** Here in the center of town you're in a typical village *Gasthof* with the traditional friendliness of family management. The rather small rooms were renovated in 1990, and the restaurant offers solid, standard fare. ✉ *Linzer Str. 18, A–3390,* ☎ *02752/2367–0,* FAX *02752/2367–6. 35 rooms, 25 with bath. Restaurant, sauna, exercise room, bicycles. AE, DC, MC, V.*

Schallaburg

6 km (3¾ mi) south of Melk.

From Melk, take a road south marked to Mank to arrive at the restored Protestant castle of **Schloss Schallaburg** (dating from 1573), which features an imposing two-story arcaded courtyard that is held to be the area's finest example of Renaissance architecture. Its ornate, warm brown terra-cotta decoration is unusual. The yard once served as a jousting court. Many centuries have left their mark on the castle: inside, the Romanesque living quarters give way to an ornate Gothic chapel. The castle now houses changing special exhibits. ☎ *02754/6317.* 🎫 *AS60; tour AS20 per person extra; combined ticket with Melk abbey AS75, with Schloss Artstetten AS95.* ⏲ *May–Oct., weekdays 9–5, weekends and holidays 9–6; last admission 1 hr before closing.*

En Route To return to the Wachau from Schallaburg, head back toward Melk and take Route 33 along the south bank. This route, attractive any time of the year, is spectacular (and thus heavily traveled) in early spring, when apricot and apple trees burst into glorious blossom. Among the palette of photogenic pleasures is **Schönbühel an der Donau,** whose unbelievably picturesque castle, perched on a cliff overlooking the Danube, is unfortunately not open to visitors. Past the village of Aggsbach Dorf you'll spot, on a hill to your right, the romantic ruin of 13th-century Aggstein castle, reportedly the lair of pirates who preyed on river traffic.

Mautern

1 km (½ mi) south of Stein.

Mautern, opposite Krems, was a Roman encampment mentioned in the tales of the Nibelungs. The old houses and the castle are attractive, but contemporary Mautern is known for one of Austria's top restaurants (☞ Dining and Lodging, *below*), in an inn run by Lisl Bacher; in nearby Klein-Wien there's another culinary landmark—also excellent—run by her sister (☞ Göttweig, *below*).

Dining and Lodging

$$$$ ★ ✕🏨 **Landhaus Bacher.** Lisl Bacher's creative, light cuisine has elevated this attractive restaurant to one of the top half-dozen in the country. Quality is consistently outstanding and the setting is delightful. The light-flooded rooms are elegant but not pretentious, and there's an attractive garden for al fresco dining. Offerings change regularly, reflecting the season and Bacher's remarkable inventiveness—simply perfection in the combination of ingredients and courses. Among main dishes, you might find local lamb with olives and artichoke hearts or guinea-fowl with truffles. Ask for advice on wines; the choice is wide. There are a few small and cozy rooms in an adjoining guest house. ✉ *Südtirolerpl. 208,* ☎ *02732/82937–0 or 02732/85429,* FAX *02732/74337. Reservations essential. DC, V. Closed Mon. and Tues. Nov.–Apr., and mid-Jan.–mid-Feb. No lunch Mon. and Tues. May–Oct.*

Göttweig

★ 44 *7 km (4½ mi) south of Krems, 18 km (11¼ mi) north of St. Pölten.*

You're certain to spot **Stift Göttweig** as you come along the riverside road: The vast Benedictine abbey high above the Danube Valley watches over the gateway to the Wachau. To reach it, go along Route 33, turn right into the highway south (marked to Stift Göttweig and St. Pölten), and turn right again (marked to Stift Göttweig) at the crest of the hill. Göttweig's exterior was redone in the mid-1700s in the classical style, which you'll note from the columns, balcony, and relatively plain side towers. Inside, it is a monument to Baroque art, with marvelous ornate decoration against the gold, brown, and blue. The stained-glass windows behind the high altar date to the mid-1400s. The church is open independent of guided tours. The public rooms of the abbey are splendid, particularly the Kaiserzimmer (emperor's rooms), in which Napoléon stayed in 1809, reached via the elegant emperor's staircase. ✉ *Furth bei Göttweig,* ☎ *02732/85581–0.* 🎫 *AS40.* ⏲ *Tour (minimum 8 people) Easter–Oct., daily at 10, 11, 2, 3, and 4.*

Dining

$$$ ★ ✕ **Schickh.** This restaurant, tucked away among lovely old trees below the north side of the Göttweig abbey, is worth looking for. Creative ideas out of the kitchen transform seasonal and regional specialties. You might be offered asparagus wrapped in smoked lamb or tender roast baby lamb. In summer you'll dine in the garden, probably rubbing elbows with the knowledgeable Viennese elite. There's a handful of guest rooms available for overnights. ✉ *Avastr. 2, A–3511 Klein-Wien/Furth bei Göttweig,* ☎ *02736/218–0,* FAX *02736/218–7. Reservations essential. No credit cards. Closed Wed., Thurs., and Mar.*

$–$$ ✕ **Stiftsrestaurant.** The terrace restaurant on the abbey grounds offers not only good standard Austrian cuisine but, on a fine day, a spectacular view. It's a great spot for lunch, coffee, or a drink. The grilled chicken can be recommended without reservation. You might try—and buy by the bottle—the excellent wines produced by the abbey. ✉ *Stift Göttweig, A–3511 Furth bei Göttweig,* ☎ *02732/84663. AE, DC, MC, V. Closed Nov.–Mar.*

St. Pölten

45 *65 km (40¾ mi:west of Vienna, 26 km (16¼ mi) south of Krems.*

St. Pölten, Lower Austria's capital to the south of the Danube, is a city of comfortable contrasts and, for some, will be worth a detour 20 kilometers (12½ miles) to the south of the main stretch of the Wachau. The old municipal center, now mainly a pedestrian zone, shows a distinctly Baroque face. The originally **Romanesque cathedral** on Domplatz has a rich Baroque interior; the Rococo **Franciscan church** at the north end of the Rathausplatz has four altar paintings by Kremser Schmidt. The Institute of English Maidens (a former convent, completed in 1769) on nearby Linzer Strasse is one of the finest Baroque buildings in the city. The east side of the river is abuzz with new glass and steel construction associated with the regional capital, which is moving here after centuries in Vienna. The capital is moving because of a political decision—supported by a one-sided referendum back in the mid-1980s—at enormous expense and rather against the current will of most Lower Austrian residents, who prefer the central convenience of Vienna. When completed in 1998, the St. Pölten government district will be a memorial to one of Lower Austria's powerful conservative politicians who initiated the project.

In a moated castle north of Pottenbrunn, 6½ kilometers (4 miles) east of St. Pölten, there's a fascinating museum, the ***Zinnfigurenmuseum*** devoted to authentically detailed tin soldiers. Imagine a bird's-eye view of entire armies in battle formation; you'll see thousands of soldiers at their posts in the battles of Leipzig (1813), Berg Isel (Innsbruck, 1809), Vienna (1683), and World War I. ✉ *Pottenbrunner Hauptstr. 77,* ☎ *02785/2337.* *AS50.* *Apr.–Oct., Tues.–Sun. 9–5.*

Dining and Lodging

$$$ ✕ **Galerie.** Mellow furnishings from long-gone dining rooms and hotels lend atmosphere to this stylish restaurant. In contrast to the antiques, the kitchen strives to do new things—generally successfully—with Austrian standards like pork fillet or turkey breast. ✉ *Fuhrmanngasse 1,* ☎ *02742/351305. AE, DC, MC, V. Closed Sun., Mon., and 2 wks around Easter.*

$$$ **Metropol.** Slick modern styling marks this new hotel on the edge of the pedestrian zone at the heart of the Old City. Rooms are comfortable, if lacking a broken-in quality. ✉ *Schillerpl. 1, A–3100,* ☎ *02742/70700–0,* FAX *02742/70700–133. 100 rooms. Restaurant, bar, sauna, parking. AE, DC, MC, V.*

OFF THE BEATEN PATH

HERZOGENBURG – The great Augustinian cloister of Herzogenburg is 11 kilometers (6¾ miles) north of St. Pölten (take Wiener Strasse/Route 1 out of St. Pölten heading east for 12 kilometers, or 8 miles, to Kapelln, then turn left to Herzogenburg). The present buildings date mainly to the mid-1700s. Fischer von Erlach was among the architects who designed the abbey. The church, dedicated to Saints George and Stephen, is wonderfully Baroque, with exquisitely decorated ceilings. ☎ *02782/3112–0.* 🎫 *AS40.* ⏲ *1-hr tour Apr.–Oct., daily 9–11 and 2–5 on the hr.*

En Route Small rural villages abound on the south bank plain, some quaint, some typical. Head north on Route S33 or the parallel road, marked to Traismauer, and pick up Route 43 east. If you're ready for back roads (too well marked for you to get lost), cut off to the left to Oberbierbaum (Upper Beer Tree!) and then on to Zwentendorf (there's a fascinating black madonna in the side chapel of the parish church here). If you follow Route 43, it will land you on Route 1 at Mitterndorf; drive east and after 4 kilometers (2½ miles), turn left off Route 1 onto Route 19, marked for Tulln.

Tulln

46 *41 km (25¾ mi) northeast of St. Pölten, 42 km (26¼ mi) west of Vienna.*

At Tulln, you'll spot a number of charming Baroque touches in the attractive main square. There's a new **Egon Schiele Museum** to honor the great modern artist, who was born here (1890–1918); the museum showing a selection of his works is in the one-time district prison, with a reconstruction of the cell in which Schiele—accused of producing "pornography"—was locked up in 1912. ✉ *Donaulände 28,* ☎ *02272/4570.* 🎫 *AS30.* ⏲ *Tues.–Sun. 9–noon and 2–6.*

A former **Minorite cloister** now houses a collection of museums. Among the more interesting are the **Limesmuseum,** which recalls the early Roman settlements in the area, and the **Landesfeuerwehrmuseum,** documenting rural firefighting. Also look inside the well-preserved, late-Baroque (1750) Minorite church next door. ✉ *Minoritenpl. 1,* ☎ *02272/61915.* 🎫 *AS30.* ⏲ *Weekdays 3–6, Sat. 2–6, Sun. 10–6.*

The Romanesque **St. Stephan Stadtpfarrkirche** (parish church) on Wiener Strasse is noteworthy for its west door and the six figures carved in relief circles on each side (presumably the 12 apostles). Alongside the church, the unusual combined chapel (upstairs) and charnel house (below) is in a structure that successfully combines late-Romanesque and early Gothic.

Dining and Lodging

$$$$ ★ ✕ **Zum Roten Wolf.** In an unpretentious but attractive rustic restaurant (one of Austria's top 20) in Langelebarn, 4 kilometers (2½ miles) east of Tulln, the stylishly elegant table settings complement the consistently outstanding food. Neither preparation nor presentation leaves anything to be desired. Try any of the lamb variations or the breast of duck. The service is especially friendly; ask for advice on the wines. You can get here by local train from Vienna; the station is virtually at the door. ✉ *Bahnstr. 58,* ☎ *02272/2567. Reservations essential. AE, DC, MC, V. Closed Mon. and Tues.*

$$ 🏨 **Zur Rossmühle.** From the abundant greenery of the reception area to the table settings in the dining room, you'll find pleasing little touches in this attractively renovated hotel on the town square. The rooms are done in grand-old yet brand-new Baroque. Take lunch in

the courtyard garden; here, as in the more formal dining room, you'll be offered Austrian standards. ✉ *Hauptpl. 12–13, A-3430,* ☎ *02272/2411,* FAX *02272/2411–33. 55 rooms. Restaurant, bar, sauna, horseback riding. AE, DC, V.*

Greifenstein

East of Tulln on Route 14; turn left at St. Andrä-Wördern and stay on the Danube shoreline.

Atop the hill at Greifenstein, yet another **castle** with spectacular views looks up the Danube and across to Stockerau. Its earliest parts date to 1135, but most of it stems from a thorough but romantic renovation in 1818. The view is worth the climb, even when the castle and inexpensive restaurant are closed. ✉ *Kostersitzgasse 5,* ☎ *02242/32353 or 02243/88105.* ⏲ *Mar.–Dec., Wed.–Sun.*

Klosterneuburg

47 *13 km (8¼ mi) northwest of Vienna.*

The great Augustinian **abbey** dominates the scene at Klosterneuburg. The structure has changed many times since the abbey was established in 1114, most recently in 1892, when Friedrich Schmidt, architect of Vienna's city hall, added neo-Gothic features to its two identifying towers. Klosterneuburg was unusual in that until 1568 it housed both men's and women's religious orders. In the abbey church, look for the carved wood choir loft and oratory and the large 17th-century organ. Among Klosterneuburg's treasures are the beautifully enameled 1181 Verdun Altar in the Leopold Chapel, stained-glass windows from the 14th and 15th centuries, Romanesque candelabra from the 12th century, and gorgeous ceiling frescoes in the great marble hall. In an adjacent outbuilding there's a huge wine cask over which people slide. The exercise, called *Fasslrutsch'n,* is indulged in during the *Leopoldiweinkost,* the wine-tasting around St. Leopold's day, November 15. ✉ *Stiftspl. 1,* ☎ *02243/36210–212.* 🎟 *AS50.* ⏲ *1-hr tour Mon.–Sat. hourly 9–11 and 1:30–4:30, Sun. and holidays at 11 and hourly 1:30–4:30.*

Dining

$$ ✕ **Stiftskeller.** The main dining rooms are on the ground floor, but instead seek out the atmospheric underground rooms in a historic part of the abbey. This is an authentic cellar in every sense of the word, with some of the fine wines even carrying the Klosterneuburg label. You can sample them along with standard Austrian fare, from Wiener schnitzel to rump steak with onions. ✉ *Albrechtsbergergasse 1,* ☎ *02243/32070. No credit cards.*

OFF THE BEATEN PATH

KAHLENBERGERDORF – Near Klosterneuburg and just off the road tucked under the Leopoldsberg promontory, is the charming small vintners' village of Kahlenbergerdorf, an excellent spot to stop and sample the local wines. You're just outside the Vienna city limits here, which accounts for the crowds on weekends.

DANUBE VALLEY FROM A TO Z

Arriving and Departing

By Boat

Large riverboats with sleeping accommodations ply the route between Vienna and Linz and between Passau on the German border and Linz, from late spring to early fall. Smaller day boats go between Vienna and the Wachau valley, and there you can change to local boats that crisscross the river between the colorful towns. For information on boat schedules, contact **DDSG/Blue Danube Schiffahrt** (✉ Handelskai 265, A–1020 Vienna, ☎ 0222/727–50–440, FAX 0222/218–9238; ✉ Untere Donaulände 10, A–4010 Linz, ☎ 0732/783607, FAX 0732/783607–9); for Linz–Passau service, **Wurm & Köck** (✉ Höllgasse 26, D–94032 Passau, ☎ 0049851/929292, FAX 0049851/35518); for Linz–Ottensheim and excursions, **Fitzcaraldo Donauschiffahrt** (✉ Ottensheimer Str. 37, A–4010 Linz, ☎ 0732/710008, FAX 0732/710009). Danube boat services from Melk to Krems with stops between within the Wachau region are operated by **Brandner Schiffahrt** (✉ Ufer 50, A–3313 Wallsee, ☎ 07433/2590–0, FAX 07433/2590–25.

By Car

A car is certainly the most comfortable way to see this region, as it conveniently enables you to pursue the byways. The main route along the north bank is Route 3; along the south bank, there's a choice of autobahn Route A1 or a collection of lesser but good roads.

By Plane

Linz is served mainly by **Austrian Airlines, Lufthansa, Swissair,** and **Tyrolean.** Regular flights connect with Vienna, Amsterdam, Berlin, Düsseldorf, Frankfurt, Paris, Stuttgart, and Zürich. The Linz airport (☎ 07221/72700–0) is in Hörsching, about 12 kilometers (7½ miles) southwest of the city. Buses run between the airport and the main railroad station according to flight schedules.

By Train

Rail lines parallel the north and south banks of the Danube. Fast services from Vienna run as far as Stockerau; beyond that, service is less frequent. The main east–west line from Vienna to Linz closely follows the south bank for much of its route. Fast trains connect German cities via Passau with Linz.

Getting Around

By Bicycle

A bicycle trail parallels the Danube for its entire length in Austria, in most stretches on both north and south banks. Tourist offices (☞ Visitor Information, *below*) have information, maps, and recommendations for sightseeing and overnight and mealtime stops.

By Boat

Bridges across the river are few along this stretch, so boats provide essential transportation; service is frequent enough that you can cross the river, visit a town, catch a bus or the next boat to the next town, and cross the river farther up- or downstream. You can take a day trip from Vienna and explore one of the stops, such as Krems, Dürnstein, or Melk. Boats run from May to late September.

By Bus

If you link them together, bus routes will get you to the main points in this region and even to the hilltop castles and monasteries, assuming you have the time. If you coordinate your schedule to arrive at a point by train or boat, you can usually make reasonable bus connections to outlying destinations. In Vienna you can book bus tours (☞ Guided Tours, *below*); in Linz, ask at the municipal bus station (✉ Bahnhofpl. 12, ☎ 0732/1671).

By Car

A car is certainly the most hassle-free way to get around. Roads are good and well marked, and you can switch over to the A1 autobahn, which parallels the general east–west course of the route (☞ Driving *in* the Gold Guide).

By Train

Every larger town and city in the region can be reached by train, but the train misses the Wachau Valley along the Danube's south bank. The rail line on the north side of the river literally clings to the bank in places, but service is infrequent. You can combine rail and boat transportation along this route, taking the train upstream and crisscrossing your way back on the river. From Linz, the delightful LILO interurban line (☎ 0732/654376) makes the run up to Eferding. A charming narrow-gauge line meanders south to Waidhofen an der Ybbs.

Contacts and Resources

Bicycle Rentals

For details on the scenic Danube river route, ask for the folder "Danube Cycle Track" (in English, from Niederösterreich-Information, ✉ Heidenschuss 2, A–1010 Vienna, ☎ 0222/533–3114–0 or 0222/53110–6200, FAX 0222/535–0319) for hints on what to see and where you'll find "cyclist-friendly" accommodations, repairs, and other services. You'll find bicycle rentals at Aggsbach–Markt, Dürnstein, Grein, Krems, Mautern, Melk, Persenbeug–Gottsdorf, Pöchlarn, Schönbühel/Aggsbach Dorf, Spitz, Weissenkirchen, and Ybbs. The terrain around Linz is relatively level, and within the city there are 89 kilometers (55 miles) of marked cycle routes. Ask for the brochure "Cycling in Linz" from the tourist office. You can rent a bike through **Fahrradzentrum B7** (✉ Oberfelderstr. 12, ☎ 0732/330550); **LILO Bahnhof** (✉ Coulinstr. 30, ☎ 0732/600703); or at the **Hauptbahnhof** (✉ main rail station, Bahnhofstr. 3, ☎ 0732/6909–385). Bicycles can be rented at the railroad stations in Freistadt (☎ 07942/2319) and Steyr (☎ 07252/595–385), or privately in Kremsmünster at **Tenniscenter Stadlhuber** (☎ 07583/7498–0). The brochure "Radfahren" is in German but lists contact numbers for cycle rentals throughout Upper Austria.

Canoeing

The Danube is fast and tricky, so you're best off sticking to the calmer waters back of the power dams (at Pöchlarn, above Melk, and near Grein). You can rent a canoe at Pöchlarn. You can also canoe on an arm of the Danube near Ottensheim, about 8 kilometers (5 miles) west of Linz. For information call Ruderverein Donau (☎ 0732/236250) or Ruderverein Ister-Sparkasse (☎ 0732/774888).

Car Rentals

Cars can be rented at the airports in Vienna or Linz. Linz contacts: **Avis** (✉ Schillerstr 1, ☎ 0732/662881); **Buchbinder** (✉ Untere Donaulände 15, ☎ 0732/773051); **EuroDollar** (✉ Coulinstr. 13, ☎ 0732/658360); **Hertz** (✉ Bürgerstr. 19, ☎ 0732/784841–0).

Emergencies

Police, ☎ 133. **Fire,** ☎ 122. **Ambulance,** ☎ 144. If you need a doctor and speak no German, ask your hotel how best to obtain assistance.

Fishing

This is splendid fishing country. Check with the town tourist offices about licenses and fishing rights for river trolling and fly-casting in Aggsbach-Markt, Dürnstein, Emmersdorf, Grein, Kleinpöchlarn, Krems, Mautern, Mauthausen, Persenbeug–Gottsdorf, Pöchlarn, Schönbühel/Aggsbach Dorf, Spitz, Waidhofen/Ybbs, and Ybbs. In Linz, check **Fischereiverband** (✉ Kärntnerstr. 12, ☎ 0732/650507), **Fischerhof AMBO** (✉ Landwiedstr. 69, ☎ 0732/670257), or **Weitgasser** (✉ Figulystr. 5, ☎ 0732/656566). In the streams and lakes of the area around Linz, you can fly-cast for rainbow and brook trout and troll for pike and carp. For details, contact the tourist offices or the numbers listed below: In Attersee, **Esso Station Nussdorf** (☎ 07666/80634); Bad Hall, **Gasthof Schröck "Hofwirt"** (hotel guests only, ☎ 07258/2274); Freistadt, **Sportgeschäft Gutenbrunner** (☎ 07942/2720) and **Sportgeschäft Juch** (☎ 07942/2532); Grein, **Die Erste Sparkasse Mauthausen** (☎ 07268/203); Kremsmünster, **Gerhard Fleck** (☎ 07583/6103); Steyr, **Angelsportverein Steyr** (☎ 07252/615443).

Golf

In addition to courses listed with towns, there are greens in Bad Ischl, Mondsee, and Wels.

Guided Tours

Tours out of Vienna take you to Melk and back by bus and boat in eight hours, with a stop at Dürnstein. Bus tours operate year-round except as noted, but the boat runs only April–October. Operators include: **Cityrama/Gray Line** (✉ Börsegasse 1, ☎ 0222/534–13–0, FAX 0222/534–13–22), for AS760; **Vienna Sightseeing Tours** (✉ Stelzhamergasse 4/11, ☎ 0222/712–4683–0, FAX 0222/712–4683–77), for AS890; and **Citytouring Vienna** (✉ Penzinger Str. 46, ☎ 0222/894–1417–0, FAX 0222/894–3239), for AS950, including a light snack.

Day boat trips with loudspeaker announcements in English run daily to and through the Wachau from Vienna from May through September. Contact the **DDSG/Blue Danube schiffahrt** (✉ Handelskai 265, ☎ 0222/727–50–440, FAX 0222/218–9238). The cruise trips leave from Schwedenbrücke, by Schwedenplatz, in Vienna, daily at 10:30, 1, 2:30, and 4:30. For information on daytime and evening excursions out of Linz, check with the tourist office or Fitzcaraldo Donauschiffahrt (☞ Getting Around by Boat, *above*).

Hiking

Local tourist offices have maps and route details of the fabulous trails in the area, and in Linz you can get the booklet "Urban Hiking Paths in Linz." For information on the Mühlviertel from Freistadt to Grein, call ☎ 0732/735020.

Tennis

You'll find tennis courts—indoors and out—in nearly every town. Ask at the tourist offices in Aggsbach-Markt, Dürnstein, Grein, Krems, Maria Taferl, Mautern, Persenbeug–Gottsdorf, Pöchlarn, Spitz, Waidhofen/Ybbs, and Weissenkirchen. In Linz, ask the tourist office about possible available courts.

Travel Agencies

In Linz, leading travel agencies include **American Express** (✉ Bürgerstr. 14, ☎ 0732/669013, FAX 0732/655334); **Carlson Wagonlit Travel** (✉ Bismarckstr. 8, ☎ 0732/771492–0, FAX 0732/771492–9); **Kuoni** (✉ Hauptpl. 14, ☎ 0732/771301, FAX 0732/775338); and **Oberösterreichisches Landesreisebüro** (✉ Hauptpl. 9, ☎ 0732/771061–0, FAX 0732/771061–49).

Visitor Information

For general information on the area, check with the following district tourist offices. **Lower Austria** (✉ Heidenschuss 2, A–1010 Vienna, ☎ 0222/533–3114–0, FAX 0222/535–0319). **Upper Austria** (✉ Schillerstr. 50, A–4010 Linz, ☎ 0732/771264, FAX 0732/600220). **Linz** (✉ Hauptpl. 5, ☎ 0732/7070–1777, FAX 0732/772873), where you can pick up the latest *Linz City News* in English as well as German.

Most towns have local *Fremdenverkehrsamt* (tourist offices). **Bad Hall** (✉ Kurhaus, A–4540, ☎ 07258/2031–0, FAX 07258/2031–25). **Dürn-**

stein (✉ Parkpl. Ost, A–3601, ☎ 02711/200, 02711/219, FAX 02711/422). **Eferding** (✉ Stadtpl. 1, A–4070, ☎ 07272/5555–20, FAX 07272/5555–33). **Freistadt** (✉ Hauptpl. 12, A–4240, ☎ 07942/2974, FAX 07942/3207). **Grein** (✉ Hauptstr. 3, A–4360, ☎ 07268/6680 or 07268/7290, FAX 07268/7290). **Klosterneuburg** (✉ Niedermarkt 4, A–3400, ☎ 02243/32038, FAX 02243/86773). **Krems/Stein** (✉ Undstr. 6, A–3500, ☎ 02732/82676, FAX 02732/70011). **Melk** (✉ Babenbergerstr. 1, A–3390, ☎ 02752/2307–32, FAX 02752/2307–37). **Pöchlarn** (✉ Regensburger Str. 11, A–3380, ☎ 02757/2310–30, FAX 02757/2310–66). **St. Pölten** (✉ Rathauspl. 1, A–3100, ☎ 02742/353354, FAX 02742/333–2819). **Steyr** (✉ Stadtpl. 27, A–4400, ☎ 07252/53229 or 48154, FAX 07252/48154–15). **Tulln** (✉ Albrechtsgasse 32, A–3430, ☎ 02272/5836, FAX 02272/5838). **Wachau** (✉ Undstr. 6, A–3500 Krems, ☎ 02732/85620, FAX 02732/87471). **Waidhofen an der Ybbs** (✉ Obere Stadtpl. 28, A–3340, ☎ 07442/511–165, FAX 07442/511–77). **Weissenkirchen** (✉ Gemeinde Weissenkirchen, A–3610, ☎ 02715/2232–11 or 02715/2600, FAX 02715/2232–22).

6 Salzkammergut

Remember the first five minutes of The Sound of Music? *Castles fronting on water, mountains hidden by whipped-cream clouds, and flower-strewn valleys crisped with cool blue lakes: Austria in all its Hollywoodian splendor. Those scenes were filmed here, not far from where the von Trapp children "Do-Re-Mi"-ed. Nearby, visit the towns of St. Wolfgang, Bad Ischl, and Hallstatt, and feel as though you were in an operetta—then discover Gosau, Austria's most beautiful lake.*

Updated by Charlotte van der Reyden

THE TRIPS IN THIS CHAPTER touch heights both material and spiritual. From the Schafberg, above St. Wolfgang, you can see forever, and in the pilgrimage church below, Michael Pacher's great winged altar, 10 years in the making, rises like a prayer. Whether mountain peak or nestled valley town, however, ready your camera, dust off your supply of *wunderschöns,* and prepare for enchantment as you head into this compact quarter of Austria. The Lake District of Upper Austria—centered in the region known as the Salzkammergut (literally, "salt estates")—presents the scenic-hungry traveler with soaring mountains and needlelike peaks; a glittering necklace of turquoise lakes; forested valleys that are home to the *Rehe* (roe deer) immortalized by Felix Salten in *Bambi*—Austria at its most lush and verdant. These lakes and valleys remain largely unspoiled, partly because the mountains act as a divider from busier, more accessible sections of the country. Another historic reason relates to the existence of the salt mines; with salt so common and cheap today, we forget it was once considered a luxury item mined under strict government monopoly. For that reason, the Salzkammergut region was banned to visitors for centuries, opening up only after Emperor Francis Joseph discovered its attractions and turned the town of Bad Ischl into the "drawing-room" of the Lake District. Lured by the idyllic landscape and the cosmopolitanism of Bad Ischl, the aristocracy, and soon the rest of the world, began to flock here.

To the west of Bad Ischl are the best known of all the Salzkammergut's 27 lakes—the Wolfgangsee, the Mondsee, and the Attersee (*See* is the German word for lake). Not far beyond these lakes the traveler will find one of Austria's loveliest spots, Gosau am Dachstein. Here, the three Gosau lakes are backdropped by a spectacular sight which acts as a landmark for many leagues: the Dachstein peak. Baron Friedrich von Humboldt, the 19th-century naturalist-traveler, called the Gosau am Dachstein one of the most beautiful spots in the world, and few persons at that time had seen more of the world than he. It is not surprising that Gosau inspired Wagner while he was writing *Parsifal.* Even today, Gosau remains a world's end, a place where people are content to simply drink in the view.

However, many activities beckon nearby. In summer, vacationers flock to the lakes, streams, meadows, and woods for boating, fishing, swimming (the taller the lakeside peak, the colder the water), and stimulating pine-needle baths. A favorite passion for Austrians is *Das Wändern,* or hiking. The Lake District has many miles of marked trails, with lovely stretches around Bad Ischl—with more than 100 kilometers (62½ miles) of trails alone; the Attersee area, which has one great 35-kilometer (22-mile) course that takes about 7½ hours to complete; the mountains in the Hallstatt and Alt-Aussee/Bad Aussee areas; and Bad Aussee, with more than 150 kilometers (93 miles) of trails. In winter, many come to the region to ski in the mountains of Salzburg Province and Styria. Amid this pastoral perfection, many enticing restaurants have sprung up; you can stay in age-old *Schloss* hotels or modern mansions. And shoppers come to buy the linens and ceramics, wood carvings, and painted glass of the region.

Pleasures and Pastimes

What's the Most Beautiful Place in the Lake District?

Whatever town or valley you pick, you'll have a battle on your hands insisting that your favorite spot in the Salzkammergut is *the* (only/best/unique) place in the region. The *whole* Salzkammergut is undeniably beautiful. As you explore the region, you'll note that if Austria were rated on a beauty-measuring gauge, the needle would fly off the scale in the Lake District. Hallstatt seems to rise out of Swan Lake itself, while the Dachstein massif—crowned in snowy ermine and reflected in the gorgeous Gosau lakes—puts Chamonix's Aiguilles to shame. Traveling through this region makes you feel like a judge in Mother Nature's own beauty contest. In this area, however, beauty is not only skin deep. Many of the most amazing sights lie *below* the surface of the earth, such as the Hallstatt salt mines or the Dachstein ice caves—it would be difficult to imagine a more impressive spectacle than these ice caverns, of which the largest is more than twenty miles long.

Dining

Whether it's cordon bleu or casual, expect wonderfully fresh, healthy cuisine in this region, often centered around fish—understandably, since many eateries are within eyeshot of the region's beautiful lakes. Carp, trout, and the smoked *seibling* are some specialties, often adorned with the omnipresent mayonnaise—ask for it on the side, or your trout may arrive drowned. Even when the food is on the bland side (carp can be insipid), you can always wake it up with the help of a *Salz Gurken,* the nearest thing to a New York-style dill pickle. In many of the towns of the Salzkammergut you'll find country inns that have dining rooms but few, if any, separate restaurants, other than the occasional, very simple *Gasthaus.* Then, again, you'll find culinary shrines around Mondsee. Prices for meals include taxes and a service charge, but not the customary small additional tip.

CATEGORY	COST*
$$$$	over AS500
$$$	AS300–AS500
$$	AS200–AS300
$	under AS200

**per person for a typical three-course meal, with a glass of house wine*

Lodging

In the grand old days, the aristocratic families of the region would take paying guests at their charming castles. Today, most of those castles have come down in the world: they're now schools or are in trade—actual hotels. You needn't stay in the Schloss Fuschl (once the hunting box of the prince-bishops of Salzburg and the former home of Joachim von Ribbentrop), to name but one example, to enjoy your Salzkammergut stay—there is a wide range of accommodations, ranging from luxurious lakeside resorts to small country inns or even guest houses without private baths, and in most places, the *Herr Wirt,* his smiling wife, and his grown-up children will do everything to make you feel comfortable. While we cover the best in every category, note that every village, however small, has a Gasthaüs or village inn. In peak summer season St. Wolfgang is packed, and you may find slightly less crowding and the same magnificent settings 3 kilometers (2 miles) up the lake at Ried or back at Strobl. Room rates include taxes and service and almost always breakfast, except in the most expensive hotels, but it is wise to ask. It is customary to leave a small additional tip (AS20) for the chambermaid. Happily, these hotels do not put their breathtakingly beautiful natural surroundings on the bill.

CATEGORY	COST*
$$$$	over AS1,500
$$$	AS1,000–AS1,500
$$	AS700–AS1,000
$	under AS700

**All prices are for a standard double room for two, including local taxes (usually 10%) and service (15%).*

Exploring the Salzkammergut

Whether you start out from Salzburg or set up a base in Bad Ischl—the heart of the Lake District—it's best to digest the riches of the region in two separate sections. For those heading to the region directly from the nearest major city, Salzburg, the first tour works eastward, starting with Mondsee, then heads south to St. Gilgen and St. Wolfgang, concluding with a side trip north to Gmunden. For those who prefer a base in Bad Ischl—the scenario for the itineraries below—note that you'll see these sights in reverse order, St. Wolfgang to Mondsee. The second tour takes you south to the Hallstätter See, Gosau am Dachstein, then to Bad Aussee and Altaussee, returning via the Pötschen mountain pass.

Numbers in the text correspond to numbers in the margin and on the Lake District/Salzkammergut map.

Great Itineraries

IF YOU HAVE 2 DAYS

Setting out early from Salzburg, head to the core of the Lake District, **Bad Ischl** ⑤. It will be an easy transition from the Imperial Austria of Salzburg to Franz Lehár—the composer of so many operettas which glorified the region—because Herr Lehár had a vacation villa here, joining the company of many other notables eager to holiday in Francis Joseph's favorite forgetaway. In the 19th century, the emperor set up his summer court in this town, building a lovely Kaiservilla, and welcoming such regal guests as Edward VII of England. After exploring the emperor's villa, the charming little house created for his Empress Elisabeth—the immortal "Sissi"—stop in at Zauner (just like Francis Joseph) for some of the best pastries in Europe. Delicious, but don't overestimate. *Two* to a person will be plenty! After quickly taking in this history-rich spa—today, it is one of the best equipped in Austria—head south on Route 145 toward Hallstatt, stopping at the cobbler's museum in **Bad Goisern** along the way if you want to buy some "Goiserer" (the finest hand-made mountain-climbing boots in the world). After Bad Goisern bear right past Au and then turn right over the bridge to cross the river Traun into Steeg. Traveling alongside the Hallstättersee, you will think you have made a magical detour into Norway: The lake, surrounded by towering peaks, seems to be a fiord. Eighteen miles distant from Bad Ischl you'll come to a junction with Route 166. Here you should turn right along the ravine of the Gosaubach river. After heading through seriously scenic territory for some twenty miles, you'll reach **Gosau** ⑧—home to the legendary Gosau lakes and one of Austria's most beautiful spots. There are three lakes here, several miles apart from each other, and all framed by the splendid Dachstein peak. After drinking in the views, spend the night in the village and awaken to a dazzling dawn over the Gosaukamm ridge.

Head back to Route 145 and south to **Hallstatt** ⑦, not just "the world's prettiest lakeside village" but the oldest settlement in Austria. After spending quality time with your Nikon, check out one of either two natural wonders: the Salzberg salt mines near Hallstatt or, continuing around the southern end of the lake for 3 miles, the **Dachstein Ice Caves** ⑨ at Obertraun. Leaving Upper Austria, head for **Bad Aussee** ⑩ along the road by the Traun river (beware that precipitous 23° gradient). Explore the town's picturesque 15th- and 16th-century architecture, feast on honey cakes at Lewandofsky's, and check out the sister town of **Alt-Aussee** ⑪, whose romantic setting inspired so many artists and poets. Return to Bad Aussee, taking Route 145 north through the Pötschen pass, enjoying spectacular vistas along the way back to Bad Ischl.

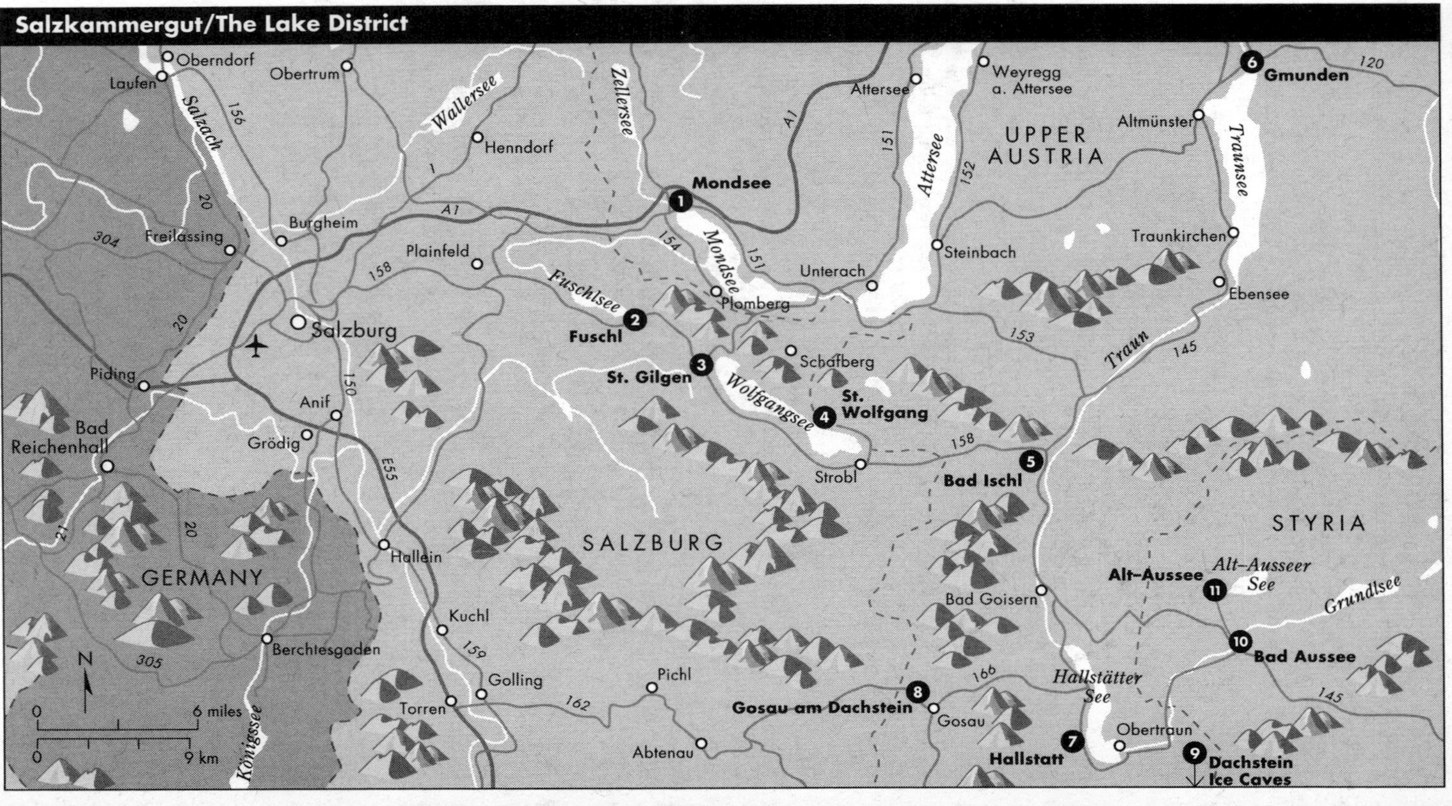
Salzkammergut/The Lake District
Oberndorf
Laufen
Salzach
Obertrum
Wallersee
Henndorf
Zellersee
Mondsee
Attersee
Weyregg a. Attersee
UPPER AUSTRIA
Gmunden
Altmünster
Traunsee
Traunkirchen
Ebensee
Freilassing
Burgheim
Plainfeld
Steinbach
Unterach
Plomberg
Fuschlsee
Fuschl
Salzburg
St. Gilgen
Schafberg
Wolfgangsee
St. Wolfgang
Traun
Piding
Anif
Grödig
Bad Reichenhall
Strobl
Bad Ischl
Hallein
SALZBURG
STYRIA
GERMANY
Alt-Aussee
Alt-Ausseer See
Grundlsee
Bad Goisern
Kuchl
Berchtesgaden
Bad Aussee
Golling
Pichl
Gosau am Dachstein
Gosau
Hallstätter See
Torren
Abtenau
Obertraun
Hallstatt
Dachstein Ice Caves
Königssee
N
0
6 miles
9 km
A1
E55
1
20
21
120
145
150
151
152
153
154
156
158
159
162
166
304
305

IF YOU HAVE 4 DAYS

After your first taste of Salzkammergut superlatives, as outlined above, head west to explore more of the Lake District. A magical mix of intimacy—simple gasthofs and rural hamlets—and publicity—celebrities and vacationing opera stars—will greet you at such destinations as St. Wolfgang and Mondsee. We once again start out from the unofficial "capital" of the region, **Bad Ischl** ⑤ (where, if you are doing this four-day tour of the region, you will have booked an overnight stay for your second night, after seeing the sights outlined above on your second day). Heading west on Route 158, then bearing right at Strobl, you'll reach **St. Wolfgang** ④—a town that all but clicks your camera shutter for you. Upon arriving—best by boat across the lake—take in one of the most beloved inns in Austria, the White Horse Inn, setting for an even more beloved operetta (bearing the same name), and the parish church, where Michael Pacher's triptych altarpiece—one of the greatest art treasures of the 15th century—holds pride of place. After an enchanting steamer trip on the lake (board outside the White Horse), enjoy the popular excursion to the top of the nearby Schafberg mountain, then return to St. Wolfgang for your dinner of trout *"blau"* and overnight. The next morning, backtrack to Strobl, then follow signs for Salzburg to join Route 158. Past Abersee, you'll reach **St. Gilgen** ③—a pleasant resort center. For lunch (be sure to make reservations), head for the famous Hotel Schloss Fuschl, former address to the prince-archbishops of Salzburg and Joachim von Ribbentrop; this is food with a view, as the dining room and terrace have grand vistas. Back on Route 158, **Mondsee** ① awaits, with its charming Marktplatz square and impressive Benedictine abbey church. From here, return west to Salzburg or east to Bad Ischl—vowing, undoubtedly, to return to the Lake District one day to buy a hillside chalet.

When to Tour the Salzkammergut

Year-round, vacationers flock to the Lake District, however late fall is the worst time to visit the lake country for it is the period of much rain. By far the best months are July and September. August, of course, sees the countryside overrun with visitors from the nearby Salzburg Music Festival (even so, who can resist a visit on August 18th to Bad Ischl, when Emperor Francis Joseph's birthday is still celebrated). Another seasonal highlight is the annual Narcissi Festival held at the beginning of June at Bad Aussee (the town is blanketed with flowers), also the site of an important Shrove Tuesday Carnival celebration. Others like to visit Hallstatt for its annual Corpus Christi procession across the lake.

ON THE ROAD TO ST. WOLFGANG AND BAD ISCHL

The Land of Operetta

As you enter the countryside that lies east of Salzburg, your eye begins to note mountains looming up. They may be less majestic than true Alps, but they are by the same token less stern; harbor lakes and villages nestle cosily in valleys instead of seeming in constant peril of being overwhelmed by towering peaks above. Little wonder that this nature-friendly setting has for centuries invited one and all to a lazy participation in the *dolce far niente* of Salzkammergut hinterland life. Here you'll find what travelers come to the Lake District for in spades: elegant restaurants, Baroque churches, meadows with getaway space and privacy, lakeside cabanas, and forests that could tell a story or two.

Mondsee

❶ *35½ km (22 mi) east of Salzburg, 100 km (62 mi) southwest of Linz.*

Mondsee is the gateway to the Salzkammergut for many tourists and Salzburgers alike, with most travelers heading eastward from Salzburg along the A1, the Salzburg-Linz main road. Without a car, you'll have to take a an hour-long bus ride from Salzburg's railway station to access the town (which has no rail service). *Mondsee* means **Moon Lake** and was named by the Romans, who were impressed by the beauty of this 8-kilometer-long, 1½-kilometer-wide (5-mile-long, 1-mile-wide) body of water, reflecting in its placid depths the mountain above it. The water is warmer than in any other of the high-placed lakes, which makes it a good place for swimming. Most travelers first head for the town square to visit the marvelously Baroque twin-tower **abbey church.** Mondsee takes pride in pointing out that that this church, built in 1470, is the largest in Upper Austria. The claim is a trifle spurious, since it was not originally constructed as a parish church, but for the more pretentious role of the abbey church of the Benedictine monastery established here in the eighth century. No matter. It holds a special place in the hearts of many travelers as they remember it as the church in which Maria finally wed her Captain von Trapp in *The Sound of Music.*

Once you've tasted some of your first delights of the region—swimming, sailing, and just relaxing—you're in for some of the best dining the Salzkammergut has to offer. Head out of the town along the west side of the lake to reach Plomberg, where Karl Eschelböck's restaurant draws gourmets from all over Austria. A bit farther along Route 154 is Schlössl, home of La Farandole. To the east of Mondsee on the east side of the lake, in the Loibichl/Au district, is the excellent Seehof restaurant. Whichever your choice, you won't be disappointed—unless you've failed to reserve in advance (☞ Dining and Lodging, *below*).

Dining

$$$$ ★ ✕ **La Farandole.** Just above Mondsee on Route 154, you'll find an intimate restaurant offering creative French-Swiss-Austrian cuisine, under the able hand of Wolfgang Buchschartner, who is manager, chef, and sommelier all in one. Specialties change with the season, but you may be offered a delicate cream of potato soup or crisp roast duck with pan-fried potatoes. The apple-cake dessert is superb. ✉ *Schlössl 150/Tiefgraben,* ☎ *06232/3475. Reservations essential. No credit cards. Closed Sun. and Mon. Sept.–June.*

$$$$ ✕ **Hotel/Restaurant Plomberg.** Karl Eschlböck, who apprenticed at Troisgros in France, is ranked among Austria's top chefs. His 300-year-old Alpine chalet overlooking the lake south of Mondsee is still a fine restaurant, although quality rollercoasters from superb to mundane while prices remain constant. Still, you're unlikely to be disappointed. What's offered in the individual dining rooms is what's fresh in the market that day; it could be anything from calf's tongue in mustard sauce to terrine of lake fish. The menu includes variations on classical Austrian dishes. ✉ *St. Lorenz 41, Plomberg-Mondsee,* ☎ *06232/2912–0,* FAX *06232/3166–20. Reservations essential. AE, DC, MC, V. Closed Tues.–Wed. Sept.–Mar.*

$$$$ ✕ **Seehof.** At this lakeside restaurant, the terrace setting is idyllic, the cuisine excellent, and the range of Italian, French, and Austrian wines comprehensive. Choices range more toward Austrian standards; specialities include venison on a bed of sauerkraut, spring lamb, and fresh fish from the lake. Located in the Park of the Seehof Hotel, this restaurant is a favorite of Mondseers-in-the-know. ✉ *Au 30, Loibichl-Mond-*

see, ☎ *06232/5031–0,* FAX *06232/5031–51. Reservations essential. AE, DC, MC, V. Closed mid-Sept.–mid-May.*

Outdoor Activities and Sports

GOLF

Golfclub am Mondsee. ☎ *06232/3835–0. 18 holes, par 72.* *Greens fee weekdays AS500, weekends AS600.* *Mar.–Nov.*

Fuschl

❷ *30½ km (19 mi) east of Salzburg, 20 km (12 mi) south of Mondsee.*

Fuschl is so close to Salzburg that many festival goers to the Salzburger Festspiele choose to stay in a hotel here, enjoying urban comforts while savoring rural pleasures at the same time. Located on Route 158, the town is on the Fuschlsee, a gem of a small lake surrounded by a nature preserve. There's not much to do in Fuschl—precisely why it gets so crowded with Salzburgers on the weekends. One good consequence is that the town now boasts many good places to eat and spend the night—including the finest hostelry in the Salzkammergut, the Schloss Fuschl.

Dining and Lodging

$$$$ ★ ✕ **Brunnwirt.** You'll have to knock to be admitted, but once inside, you'll find elegantly set tables in this atmospheric 15th-century house. Frau Brandstätter presides over a kitchen that turns out good-size portions of excellent Austrian and regional dishes. You might be offered game or roast lamb, but always with a light touch. Fish fresh from the lake is a regular specialty. ✉ *Brunn 8,* ☎ *06226/236. Reservations essential. Jacket and tie. AE, DC, MC, V. Closed Sun. and last 3 wks of Jan. No lunch except during Salzburg Festival wks.*

$$$$ ★ ✕ **Hotel Schloss Fuschl.** This noble hotel up the lake, built in 1450, was once the hunting castle of the prince-bishops of Salzburg. Now tastefully adapted and modernized, the blockhouse-style main building enjoys a setting about as perfect as you could imagine. Fireplaces and timbered ceilings abound amid the stonework. The hotel's elegant restaurant overlooking the lake is one of Austria's best. You can expect innovative variations on such regional specialties as rack of venison and lake fish. Schloss Fuschl is a member of Leading Hotels of the World. ✉ *A–5322 Hof bei Salzburg,* ☎ *06229/2253–0,* FAX *06229/2253–531. 62 rooms, 22 apartments. Restaurant, bar, indoor and outdoor pools, sauna, tennis court, golf, exercise room. AE, DC, MC, V.*

$$$$ ✕ **Parkhotel Waldhof.** This Alpine chalet, with bright red geraniums on the balconies, seems perfect in its setting against the lake and mountains. The hotel is a member of the Silence Hotel group. You'll feel comfortable in the paneled public room, warmed by the open fireplace. The restaurant emphasizes local duck and game dishes, and gourmands enjoy the variations on lake-caught fish. ✉ *Seepromenade, A–5330,* ☎ *06226/264,* FAX *06226/644. 64 rooms, 13 apartments. Restaurant, bar, indoor pool, lake, sauna, tennis court, archery, exercise room, windsurfing, boating. No credit cards. Closed Mar. and late Oct.–mid-Dec.*

St. Gilgen

❸ *34 km (21 mi) east of Salzburg, 10 ki (7 mi) south of Fuschl.*

South of Fuschl along Route 158 is St. Gilgen—the "Southampton" of the Salzkammergut. The many country castles here are the scene of glamorous parties, with persons innocent of any tincture of Austrian blood cavorting like characters in *The White Horse Inn* operetta; during festival time, Escadas are traded in for peasant dirndls. Today, the foreign invasion is nearly complete and all the local color left to St. Gilgen is its indirect musical ties: A Mozart fountain in the town square commemorates the fact that Mozart's mother was born here and his sister Nannerl later settled here. Rather overbuilt, the town is pleasant enough and features a nice beach at the northernmost location of the Wolfgansee.

Dining and Lodging

$$$ ✕ **Timbale.** Don't look for haute cuisine in St. Gilgen, but if you'd like something a bit different from the usual rustic atmosphere, this tiny restaurant may offer a pleasant surprise. The roast lamb and grilled shrimp are good but the specials not shown on the menu are usually better. ✉ *Salzburger Str. 2,* ☎ *06227/7587. No credit cards. Closed Thurs., mid- to late June, and various wks late Nov.–early Dec. No lunch Fri. Sept.–July.*

$$–$$$ ✕🏨 **Zur Post.** This house, one of the most attractive in town, dates to 1415. The rooms are comfortable and complete with modern baths. The restaurant emphasizes regional fare; try the cream of garlic soup or the boiled beef. ✉ *Mozartpl. 8, A–5340,* ☎ *06227/239–0,* FAX *06227/698. 15 rooms, some with bath. Restaurant, sauna. AE, MC. Closed early Nov.–early Dec.*

$$$–$$$$ 🏨 **Parkhotel Billroth.** This elegant villa, decorated in turn-of-the-century style, is set in a huge park 10 minutes from the town center but close to the lake. The house is pleasantly worn at the edges, yet spaciously arranged and luxuriously appointed, with a fine dining room. Sun terraces are particularly inviting. ✉ *Billrothstr. 2, A–5340,* ☎ *06227/217,* FAX *06227/218–25. 44 rooms. Restaurant, bar, sauna, tennis court, exercise room, beach. AE, V. Closed Oct.–May.*

St. Wolfgang

★ ❹ *50 km (31 mi) east of Salzburg, 13 km (8 mi) west of Bad Ischl.*

The best approach to the picture-book town of St. Wolfgang is to leave your car at Strobl at the southern end of the Wolfgangsee (a delightful setting, but not as fashionable as St. Wolfgang, a fact which, if you want a quiet vacation base, may increase its attraction for you) and take the lake steamer from the landing stage at Gschwendt; pulling into St. Wolfgang from the lake, you'll probably wind up shooting all your photographic film before you even draw up at the quay. The view of the town against the dramatic mountain backdrop is one you'll see again and again on posters and postcards. But there are other ways of traveling to the leading beauty-spot of the Wolfgangsee. Most cars take Route 158 east, while there are hourly buses from Bad Ischl, the hub of the Salzkammergut. Unless your hotel offers parking, you'll have to park on the fringes of town and walk a short distance, as the center is a pedestrian zone.

Here, you will find yourself—literally—in the Austria of operetta. For you can stay at a place called the **Weisses Rössl** (the White Horse Inn) with its landing stage on the lake, its pilgrimage church backdrop, and its gay dining terrace; this is *the* White Horse Inn, the one that was the setting for the famous 1890s operetta, *Im Weissen Rossl am Wolfgangsee,* and a later musical and film. The scenic town offers great hiking in the summer and fine skiing in the winter. Aside from immersing yourself in the sheer romance of St. Wolfgang, you shouldn't miss seeing **Michael Pacher's great carved altar** (1481) in the 16th-century pilgrimage church, one of the finest examples of Gothic wood carving to be found anywhere. The crowning of the Virgin is depicted in detail so exact that you can see the stitches in her garments. Surrounding her are various saints, including the local patron, the hermit St. Wolfgang. Since the 15th century, his namesake town has been a place of pilgrimage. ✉ *St. Wolfgang im Salzkammergut 5360,* ⏲ *May–Sept., daily 9–5; Oct.–Apr., daily 10–4; altar closed to view during Lent.*

OFF THE BEATEN PATH

SCHAFBERG – From May to mid-October the cog-railway trip from St. Wolfgang to the 5,800-foot peak of the Schafberg offers a great chance to survey the surrounding countryside from what is acclaimed as "the belvedere of the Salzkammergut lakes." On a clear day, you can see forever—or at least as far as the Lattengebirge Mountain Range west of Salzburg. Figure on crowds, so reserve in advance (☎ 06138/2232–0) or start out early. The train departs hourly: mid-May to mid-June, daily from 8:30 AM to 4:30 PM; mid-June to mid-September, daily from 7 AM to 6:26 PM; and mid-September to mid-October, daily from 8:30 AM to 6:00 PM. Allow at least a good half day for the outing, which costs AS250.

The Arts

MUSIC

Concerts are held in St. Wolfgang every Monday from June to September; there are also band concerts every Wednesday and Saturday evening at 8:30. Folk events are usually well publicized with posters. Not far from St. Wolfgang, the town of Strobl holds a Day of Popular Music and Tradition in early July—"popular" meaning brass band, and "tradition" being local costume. Check with the regional tourist office for details.

Dining and Lodging

$$$–$$$$ ★ ✕🏨 **Im Weissen Rössl.** Some say Im Weissen Rössl—the White Horse Inn—is really the *only* place to stay in St. Wolfgang. Others point out there are other excellent *Gasthäuser* in town—and most of those haven't been subjected to a brutal modernization. On the other hand, the golden yellow house, featured in films and theater over the years (thanks to the famous operetta set here), has kept its reputation for outstanding accommodations and service and is now part of the Romantik Hotel group. Despite the busloads that come "to have a look," the hotel holds a special charm for its regular guests. As you'd expect, the rooms are comfortable country-rustic. Nevertheless, the hotel's recent renovation sadly stripped much of its original old-world charm. The dining terraces, built on stilts over the water, remain enchanting; fresh lake fish is served to the sound of zither music. The kitchen is excellent. Keep in mind that this hotel is world famous; book well in advance, especially in the summer. ✉ *Markt 74, A–5360,* ☎ *06138/2306–0,* FAX *06138/2306–41. 72 rooms. Restaurant, bar, indoor pool, lake, sauna, tennis court, exercise room, windsurfing, boating, parking. AE, DC, MC, V. Closed Nov.–mid-Dec.*

$ ✕🏨 **Gasthof Zimmerbräu.** In this pricey town, it's a pleasant surprise to find a budget Gasthof. Once a beer brewery, this pension is in a house that is four centuries old; for the last hundred years, it's been run by the Scharf family. Centrally located, the Zimmerbräu is not near the lake but does feature its own bathing cabana by the water. The decor is traditional, most rooms have balconies, and the chef can even whip up some vegetarian specialties. ✉ *Im Stöck 85, A-5360.,* ☎ *06138/2204,* FAX *06138/242745. 24 rooms with bath. Restaurant. No credit cards.*

Outdoor Activities and Sports

BICYCLING

Much of the Salzkammergut is rather hilly for biking, but you'll find reasonably good cycling country around the lakes, including the Wolfgangsee. You can cycle the 14 kilometers (nearly 9 miles) from St. Wolf-

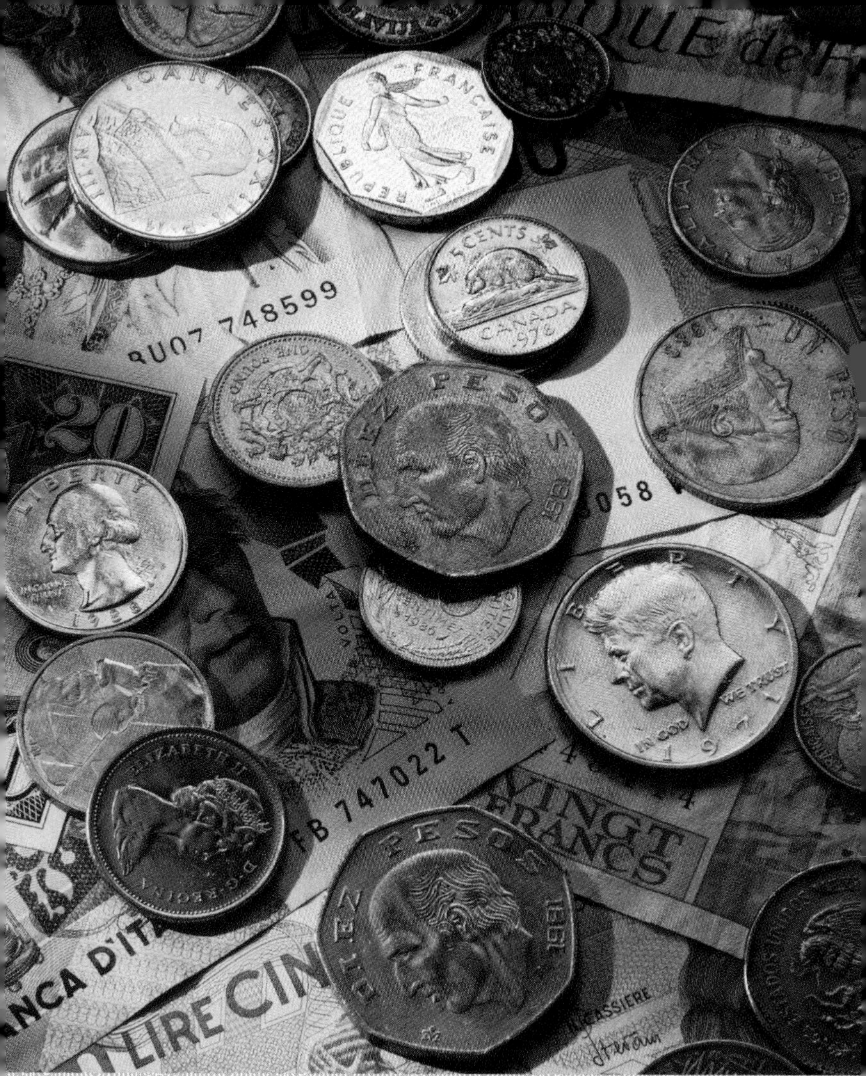
FRANCAISE
REPUBLIQUE
5 CENTS
CANADA
1978
748599
DIEZ PESOS
LIBERTY
FB 747022 T
VINGT
FRANCS
PESOS
LIRE CIN

gang to Bad Ischl on back roads. Bicycle rentals are available at the railroad station in St. Wolfgang (☎ 06138/2232–0) and at sports shops throughout the area; local tourist offices can point you to the right place.

Bad Ischl

❺ *56 km (35 mi) east of Salzburg, 16 km (10 mi) southeast of St. Wolfgang.*

Many travelers used to think of Bad Ischl primarily as the town where Zauner's pastry shop is located, to which connoisseurs drove miles for the sake of a cup of coffee and a *Torte.* Perhaps it is fitting that pastry continues to be the best-known drawing card of a community which symbolizes, more than any other place except Vienna itself, the old Austria of uniforms and balls and waltzes and operettas—in short, pastry. For Bad Ischl was the place where Emperor Francis Joseph chose to establish his summer court. Today, you can enjoy the same sort of pastries *mit Schlag* that the emperor loved. Afterward, you can hasten off to the town's modern spa, one of the best known in Austria. The town initially grew up around the curative mineral springs that are still the raison d'être for the classic 19th-century *Kurhaus* (spa) and the baths in the adjoining new buildings.

You'll want to stroll along the shaded **Esplanade,** where the pampered and privileged of the 19th century loved to take their constitutionals, usually after a quick stop at the spa pavilion of the **Trinkhalle,** still located in the middle of town on Ferdinand-Aübock-Platz. However, the quickest way to travel back in time to the 1880s in Bad Ischl is to head ★ for the **Kaiservilla,** the colorful imperial residence rather like a miniature Schönbrunn. Markus von Habsburg, great-grandson of Francis Joseph II, still lives here, but you can tour parts of the building to see the ornate reception rooms and the surprisingly modest residential quarters. ✉ *Kaiserpark,* ☎ *06132/23241.* 🎟 *Grounds AS45; combination ticket, including tour of villa, AS95.* ⏲ *Easter, Apr. weekends, and May–mid-Oct., daily 9–noon and 1–5.*

Don't overlook the small but elegant "marble palace" built nearby the Kaiservilla for Empress Elisabeth; it now houses the regional **photography museum.** (The marriage of Francis Joseph and Elisabeth was not a happy one. A number of houses in Bad Ischl bearing women's names are said to have been quietly given by the emperor to his various lady friends around town (☞ Villa Schratt, *in* Dining and Lodging, *below*). You'll first need to purchase a ticket to enter the park grounds. ✉ *Kaiserpark,* ☎ *06132/24422.* 🎟 *AS20.* ⏲ *Apr.–Oct., daily 9:30–5.*

Composers followed the aristocracy and the court to Bad Ischl. Bruckner, Brahms, Johann Strauss the Younger, and Oscar Straus all spent summers here, but it was Franz Lehar, composer of *The Merry Widow,* who left the most lasting musical impression. The operetta festival in summer (☞ Music *in* the Arts, *below*) always includes one Lehar work. **Lehar's villa** is now a museum, open for guided tours. ✉ *Pfarrgasse 11,* ☎ *06132/26992.* 🎟 *AS45.* ⏲ *Easter and May–Sept., daily 9–noon and 2–5; last tours at 11:30 and 4:30.*

Bad Ischl is accessed easily via various routes. From St. Wolfgang, backtrack south to Strobl and head eastward on Route 158. To get to the town directly from Salzburg, take the A1 to Mondsee, then Routes 151 and 158 along the Wolfgangsee and the Mondsee. There are many buses that depart hourly from Salzburg's main railway station; You can also travel by train via the junctions of Attnang-Puchheim or Stainach-Irdning (several transfers are required)—a longer journey than the bus ride, which is usually 90 minutes.

The Arts

MUSIC

The main musical events of the year in the Salzkammergut are the July and August operetta festival held here in Bad Ischl. In addition, performances of at least two operettas (*The Merry Widow* is a standard favorite) take place every season in the Kurhaus (☎ 06132/23766), where tickets are sold.

Dining and Lodging

$$$$ ✕ **Villa Schratt.** In this villa, where Emperor Franz Josef's most favored lady friend once lived, you'll be treated to some of the finest food in the area. Choose between modern decor or a rustic atmosphere replete with antlers; in either room, the setting is elegant and service attentive. Try any of the fish compositions, or beef tenderloins with mushrooms in a cream sauce. For dessert, order the traditional *Guglhupf* sponge cake. ✉ *Steinbruch 43,* ☎ *06132/27647,* FAX *06132/27647. Reservations essential. AE, MC. Closed Tues.; Wed.; early–mid-Nov.; and various wks during spring.*

$$–$$$ ★ ✕ **Weinhaus Attwenger.** This restaurant is set in a turn-of-the-century gingerbread villa under massive trees overlooking the river. In summer the garden alone is worth a visit; the question is whether new management will uphold a reputation for good food as well as service. Ask for seasonal recommendations, but the fish and game dishes are always particularly good. In the cozy wood-paneled rooms inside, the environment is rustic. ✉ *Leharkai 12,* ☎ *06132/23327. AE, DC. Closed Mon. and mid-Jan.–mid-Mar. No dinner Sun.*

$$ ★ ✕ **Café Zauner.** Unless you've been to Zauner, you haven't been to Bad Ischl. The desserts—particularly the house creation, *Zaunerstollen,* a chocolate-covered confection of sugar, hazelnuts, and nougat—have made this one of Austria's best-known pastry shops. Other possibilities include lunch or early dinner in the tree-shaded inner court or the garden restaurant alongside the river in summer. ✉ *Pfarrgasse 7,* ☎ *06132/23522,* FAX *06132/26716. No credit cards. Closed Tues. in winter.*

$$$ ✕🏨 **Kurhotel.** This fairly new and, for Bad Ischl, high-rise hotel, within a two-minute walk of the railroad station, serves as a training institute for the regional hotel school, so you're sure to get attentive, enthusiastic service. The rooms are modern in dark browns and beige; many have magnificent views of the mountains around the city. An underground passageway leads to the nearby mineral baths; use of the pool and sauna is free. The hotel restaurant specializes in regional dishes and game in season. ✉ *Voglhuberstr. 10, A–4820,* ☎ *06132/204,* FAX *06132/27682. 115 rooms. Restaurant, bar, pool, sauna, tennis court. AE, DC, MC, V.*

$$$ ★ ✕🏨 **Zum Goldenen Schiff.** This traditional family-run house, overlooking the river, offers typical country comfort. Rooms with a balcony on the river side are preferred, but all are appealing, with lots of natural wood in evidence. The restaurant specializes in fish. ✉ *Adalbert-Stifter-Kai 3, A–4820,* ☎ *06132/24241–0,* FAX *06132/24241–58. 56 rooms. Restaurant. AE, DC, MC, V.*

Outdoor Activities and Sports

GOLF

Salzkammergut Golfclub. ☎ *06132/26340,* FAX *06132/26708. 18 holes, par 71.* ⏲ *Apr.–Nov.*

TENNIS

The Salzkammergut is great tennis territory, with courts in almost every town. The best is probably the **Tennisclub Bad Ischl,** which has indoor and outdoor courts, ball-throwing machines, and equipment rentals (☎ 06132/23458 or 06132/23926).

Gmunden

❻ *76 km (47 mi) northeast of Salzburg, 40 km (25 mi) southwest of Linz, 32 km (20 mi) northeast of Bad Ischl.*

Gmunden, at the top of the Traunsee, is an attractive town to wander in. You can't overlook the gloriously ornate, arcaded yellow-and-white **town hall,** with its onion domes. Here in the town hall you'll find a famous carillon, with bells made from local clay.

The tree-lined esplanade along the lake is reminiscent of past days of the idle aristocracy and artistic greats—Schubert, Brahms, and the Duke of Württemberg were just some of the noted who strolled under the chestnut trees. You can easily walk to the **Strandbad,** the swimming area, from the center of town. The beaches are good, and you can sail, waterski, or windsurf. To get to Gmunden from Bad Ischl, take Route 145 along the Traunsee—note the Traunstein, Hochkogel, and Eriakogel peaks, which comprise the silhouette that Austrians have long nicknamed the *Schlafende Griechen* (Slumbering Greek Girl)—and then along the Traun River. You can also train to the town via the Attnang-Puchheim junction from Salzburg or Linz.

★ Take time to look at, or visit, the famous double castle, **Schloss Orth**—a *Landschloss* on the shore, a *Seeschloss* connected to the other by a causeway on an island in the lake. Its former owner, Archduke Johann, gave up his title and disappeared with the casket supposed to hold the secret of the Mayerling tragedy after Emperor Francis Joseph's son Rudolf died there. *Free. Daily 8 AM–dusk.*

★ From Gmunden, take a lake trip on the ***Gisela,*** built in 1872, the oldest, coal-fired steam side-wheeler running anywhere. It carried Emperor Francis Joseph 100 years ago and is now restored. For departure times, check with Traunseeschiffahrt Eder (☎ 07612/5215 or 07612/66700, FAX 07612/66741). Boat lines crisscross the whole 11-kilometer (7-mile) length of the lake.

From beyond the railroad station, take the 12-minute cable car ride to the top of the **Grünberg.** From here you will have a superb view out over the Traunsee, with the Dachstein glacier forming the backdrop. In the winter, there are good ski runs here. ✉ *Freygasse 4,* ☎ *07612/4977–0. Round-trip AS115, one-way AS81. May, June, and Sept., daily 9–5; July and Aug., daily 9–6; Oct., daily 9–4:30.*

OFF THE BEATEN PATH

TRAUNKIRCHEN – About 4½ kilometers (3 miles) north of Ebensee on Route 145 you'll come to Traunkirchen; stop for a look at the "fishermen's pulpit" in the parish church. This 17th-century Baroque marvel, carved from wood burnished with silver and gold, portrays the astonished fishermen of the Sea of Galilee pulling in their suddenly full nets at Jesus' direction.

Dining and Lodging

$$ ★ ✕ **Lambi Mambi.** Ignore the seemingly cute name—actually it's Finnish for warm and friendly—and try this chic but charming *Gasthaus* for some of the best food in the area. The choice is limited but imaginative; you might encounter an apple-celery soup with shrimp or fillet of lamb with a potato and leek crust. Finish with apple dumpling and

cinnamon cream. ✉ *Linzer Str. 37,* ☎ *07612/67488. No credit cards. Closed Sun. and Mon. No lunch.*

$$$ ★ 🏨 **Parkhotel am See.** This traditional-style house, separated from the lake by the promenade, is a five-minute walk from the town center. Although the building has recently been renovated, its antique furnishings continue to set the scene. There's a private pier for swimming. ✉ *Schiffslände 17, A–4810,* ☎ *07612/4230–0,* FAX *07612/4230–66. 50 rooms. Bar, brasserie, tennis court. MC, V. Closed Oct.–mid-May.*

$$–$$$ 🏨 **Schlosshotel Freisitz Roith.** On a hill overlooking the lake, this architectural amusement, a mixed-up Victorian wonder, now houses a modern hotel, but it has kept many of the old details, such as the vaulted ceilings. ✉ *Traunsteinstr. 87, A–4810,* ☎ *07612/4905,* FAX *07612/4905–17. 26 rooms. Restaurant, bar, sauna, exercise room, beach. AE, MC. Closed Jan. and Feb.*

Outdoor Activities and Sports

SWIMMING

Those who wish to get wet in the Salzkammergut know that swimming in Austrian lakes can be a *very* frigid affair. That's one reason why many hotels in Gmunden have lovely swimming pools—and why the town has become one of the most popular resorts of the region.

Shopping

Among the many souvenirs and handicrafts you'll find in Salzkammergut shops, the most famous are the handcrafted ceramics of Gmunden. You'll find them at the **Gmundner Keramik** shop (✉ Keramikstr. 24, ☎ 07612/5441–0). The green-trimmed, white country ceramics are decorated with blue, yellow, green and white patterns, including the celebrated 16th-century *Grüngeflammt* design.

HALLSTATT, GOSAU, AND BAD AUSSEE

Mountain Magic

It is hard to imagine anything prettier than this region of the Salzkammergut, which takes you into the very heart of the Lake District. The great highlight is Gosau am Dachstein—a beauty spot that even the least impressionable find easy to remember. But there are other notable sights, including Hallstatt, the Dachstein ice caves, and the spa of Alt-Aussee. Lording over the region is the Dachstein peak itself—the anchor post of Upper Austria, Styria, Land Salzburg, and monarch of all it surveys.

Hallstatt

7 *89 km (55 mi) southeast of Salzburg, 19 km (12 mi) south of Bad Ischl.*

As if rising from Swan Lake itself, the town of Hallstatt is the hero of thousands of travel posters. "The world's prettiest lakeside village" perches precariously on the lakeside, with what seems the smallest of toeholds to prevent it from tumbling into the dark waters of the Hallstättersee. Today, the town is a thriving tourist center and a bit too modernized, considering that Hallstatt is believed to be the oldest community in Austria. More than a thousand graves of prehistoric men have been found here, and it has been such an important source of relics of the pre-Christian Celtic period that this age is known as the Hallstatt epoch. Most of the early relics of the Hallstatt era are in Vienna (including the greatest Iron Age totem of them all, the *Venus of Willendorf,* now a treasure of Vienna's Naturhistorisches Museum) but some are here in the **Prähis-**

torisches Museum (Prehistoric Museum). ✉ *Seestr. 56,* ☎ *06134/8398.* *AS40.* ⏲ *Apr. and Oct., daily 10–4; May–Sept., daily 10–6.*

Salt has been mined in the area for at least 2,800 years, and the Hallstatt mines are the oldest in the world. Take the cable car up and tour the mines above town; after a 10-minute walk, you enter the mines, via either stairs or a wooden chute the miners used. There you'll see a subterranean lake and ride on the mile-long underground train. There is also an Iron Age cemetery and a restaurant here. ✉ *Salzberg (Salt Mountain),* ☎ *06134/8251–72.* *Cable car round-trip AS95, one-way AS55; mine and tour AS130.* ⏲ *Early Apr.–May and mid-Sept.–Oct., daily 9:30–3; June–mid-Sept., daily 9:30–4:30.*

The market square, now a pedestrian area, is bordered by colorful 16th-century houses. The charnel house beside the parish church by the lake is a rather morbid but regularly visited spot. Because there was little space to bury the dead over the centuries in Hallstatt, the custom developed of digging up the bodies after 12 or 15 years, piling the bones in the sun, and painting the skulls. Ivy and oak-leaf wreaths were used for the men, Alpine flowers for the women, plus names, dates, and often the cause of death. The myriad bones and skulls are now on view in ★ the charnel house. Be sure to visit the **parish church of St. Michael,** which is picturesquely sited near the lake. Within the 16th-century Gothic church, you'll find a beautiful winged altar, which opens to reveal nine 15th-century paintings. The lakeside vistas are spectacular, and people love to feed the fish by the shore.

In Gasthof Hallberg there is a curious **war museum** containing Nazi gold and propaganda materials that were to be air-dropped on Britain, discovered by the owner, Gerhard Zauner, on diving expeditions in nearby lakes. ✉ *Seestr. 113.,* ☎ *06134/8286.* *Free.* ⏲ *Daily.*

To get to Hallstatt from Bad Ischl, head south on Route 145 to Bad Goisern—which also has curative mineral springs but never achieved the cachet of Bad Ischl. Just south of town, watch the signs for the turnoff to the Hallstättersee. Since the lake is squeezed between two sharply rising mountain ranges, the road parallels the shore, with spectacular views. The Hallstatt railroad station is on the opposite side of the lake; if you arrive by train, a boat (*Hemetsberger,* Hallstättersee-Schiffahrt, ☎ 06134/8228) will take you across to the town, which clings precariously to the mountainside by the lake. Embark via train for Hallstatt from Bad Ischl or via the Stainach-Irdning junction. From Bad Ischl, you can also take a half-hour bus ride to Hallstatt.

Dining and Lodging

$$$$ ★ ✕ **Grüner Baum.** For such a major tourist destination, Hallstatt has alarmingly few decent guest accommodations. One of the best is this friendly house directly on the lake, in traditional yellow with white trim, dating from 1760. Most of the comfortable rooms overlook the lake, yet you're right in the center of town. The restaurant is known for its fish specialties. ✉ *Markpl. 104, A–4830,* ☎ *06134/8263–0,* FAX *06134/8420. 34 rooms. Restaurant, bar, lake. AE, DC, MC, V. Closed mid-Nov.–mid-Dec.*

Outdoor Activities and Sports

CANOEING

The lakes of the Salzkammergut are excellent for canoeing because most prohibit or limit powerboats. Try kayaking on the Hallstätter See (for information, call Alois Zopf (✉ Hauptstr. 327, Bad Goisern, ☎ 06135/8254, FAX 06135/7409) or white-water kayaking on the Traun River.

HIKING

There are many great hiking paths around Hallstatt; contact the local tourist office for information about the path along the Echerntal to **Waldbachstrub** past pleasant waterfalls, or the climb to the **Tiergartenhütte,** continuing on to the **Wiesberghaus** and, two hours beyond, the **Simony-Hütte,** spectacularly sited at the foot of the Dachstein glacier. From here mountain climbers begin the ascent of the **Hoher Dachstein,** the tallest peak of the Dachstein massif.

Gosau am Dachstein

★ 8 *10 km (6 mi) west of the Hallstättersee.*

Lovers of scenic beauty should not leave the Hallstatt region without taking in Gosau am Dachstein, considered the most beautiful spot in Austria by 19th-century travelers but unaccountably often overlooked today. This lovely spot is six miles west of the Hallstätter See, just before the Geschütt pass. You travel either by bus, rail, or motorboat as far as Gosaumühle—the village makes a good lunch stop (and, with its many *Gasthöfe* and pensions, could be a base for your excursion)—and from there you must walk, at the most an hour or two, depending on your speed, but you won't regret the hike. Of the three Gosauseen (Gosau lakes), the first—the Vorderer Gosausee—is the crown jewel, located some five miles to the south of the town itself. Beyond a sparkling, almost fjordlike basin of water rises the amazing Dachstein massif, majestically reflected in the mirrorlike surface of the lake. Other than a restaurant and a gamekeeper's hut, the lake is undefiled by man-made structures. At the right hour—well before 2:30 PM, when, due to the steepness of the mountain slopes, the sun is already withdrawing—the view is *königlich* (kingly) in its perfection. Following the path around the lake will clarify why some of the greatest passages in Richard Wagner's *Parsifal* were composed with these vistas in mind. Then you may choose to endure the stiff walk to the other two lakes (not as spectacularly sited), which will take another two hours, or take a cable car up to the Gablonzer Hütte on the Zwieselalm—you might consider skiing on the Gosau glacier—or tackle the three-hour hike up to the summit of the Grosser Donnerkogel. At day's end, head back for Gosau am Dachstein, settle in at one of the many *Gasthöfe* (reserve ahead) overhung with wild gooseberry and rosebushes (or stay at one of Gosau's charming *Privatzimmer* accommodations). Cap the day off with a dinner of fried *Schwarzrenterl,* a delicious regional lake fish. To get to Gosau, travel north or south on Route 145, turning off at the junction at Route 166, and travel 20 miles east through the ravine of the Gosaubach river.

Dining and Lodging

$$$ ★ **Hotel Koller.** One of the most charming hotels in Gosau, the Koller was originally the home of famed industrialist Moriz Faber, and it's one of the best preserved "Salzkammergut Landhous" villas in the valley. With enough peaked gables and weathervanes to make travelers dream of a White Christmas even in July, the Koller has a fairytale aura when seen from its pretty park. Inside, an open fireplace and warm woodwork create a beckoning atmosphere; guest rooms—many featuring breathtaking views—are newly renovated with blond-wood furniture. A special feature is the tavern's gala dinners, complete with folk music and regional barbecued specialties and health foods supplied fresh by the farmers of Gosau. Half board is required for the hotel's main dining room. Many guests say that a weekend at the Koller is as relaxing as a full week anywhere else. ✉ *A-4824 Gosau am Dachstein,* ☎ *06136/88410,* FAX *06136/884150. 18 rooms with bath, 5 suites. 2*

restaurants, bar, pool, playground. No credit cards. Closed late Oct.–mid-Dec.

Dachstein Ice Caves

★ 9 *5 km (3 mi) west of Hallstatt.*

Many travelers to Hallstatt make an excursion to one of the most impressive sights of the Eastern Alps, the Dachstein Ice Caves. From Hallstatt, take the scenic road around the bottom of the lake to Obertraun, then follow the signs to the cable car, the *Dachsteinseilbahn,* which will ferry you up the mountain (if you prefer, you can hike all the way up to the caves). From this landing, a 15-minute hike up takes you to the entrance (follow signs to "*Dachsteineishöhle*") of the vast ice caverns, many of which are hundreds of years old and aglitter with ice stalactites and stalagmites illuminated by an eerie light. The most famous sights are the *Rieseneishöhle* (Giant Ice Cave), the *Mammuthöhle* (Mammoth Cave), King Arthur's Cave, the Great Ice Chapel, and assorted frozen waterfalls. The cave entrance is at about 6,500 feet, still well below the 9,750-foot Dachstein peak farther south. Be sure to wear warm, weatherproof clothing; inside the caves it's cold, and outside, the slopes can be swept by chill winds. ☎ *06131/362 or 06131/273–0.* *Cable car round-trip AS155, Rieseneishöhle AS79, Mammuthöhle (mammoth caves) AS79, combined ticket for both caves AS110.* ⏲ *May–mid-Oct., daily 8:45–4:50 (5:50 for Mammuthöhle); last tours at 3:10 (Mammuthöhle) and 4:10 (Rieseneishöhle); cable cars for last tours depart at 2:10 (Mammuthöhle or combined) and 3:10 (Riesenhöhle), 1 hr later in July and Aug.*

Bad Aussee

10 *81 km (50 mi) southeast of Salzburg, 24 km (15 mi) west of Hallstatt.*

Following the road westward from Hallstatt, you'll find yourself in company with the railroad and the Traun River (watch out for the precipitous 23° gradient at one point). You now enter a region dotted with small lakes that seems, on contour maps, to push so illogically northward, but which is actually following the watershed with great geographic intelligence. The heart of this region is Bad Aussee, a great mecca in the summertime, for the town's towering mountains and glacier-fed lake keep the area cool. Even in midsummer, the waters of the lake are so cold that the presence of the municipal swimming pool is easy to account for. In the town, salt and mineral springs have been developed into a modern spa complex, yet the town retains much of its 15th- and 16th-century character in the narrow streets and older buildings, particularly in the upper reaches. The 1827 marriage of Archduke Johann to the daughter of the local postmaster brought attention and a burst of new construction, including some lovely 19th-century villas. Bad Aussee is a good base for hiking in the surrounding countryside in summer and for excellent skiing in winter. Many travelers come to Bad Aussee via the train from Salzburg, making a connection southward at the Attnang-Puchheim junction.

NEED A BREAK? Those "on the cure" can undo all the good in a single visit to **Kurhauskonditorei Lewandofsky,** a café where the pastries—particularly the honey cakes—are irresistibly tempting, especially when served in the summer garden with its overview of the central square, next to the Bad Aussee city park.

Dining and Lodging

$$$$ ★ ✕🏨 **Erzherzog Johann.** A golden yellow facade identifies this traditional house, which, though in the center of town, is quiet. A direct passageway connects the hotel to a spa next door, with a swimming pool and cure facilities. The hotel rooms are modern and immaculate in their country decor. The first-floor restaurant serves the best creative cooking in the area in an ambience that is elegant but nevertheless intimate. ✉ *Kurhauspl. 62, A–8990,* ☎ *03622/52507–0,* FAX *03622/52394–680. 62 rooms. Restaurant, bar, indoor pool, sauna, spa, exercise room. DC, MC. Closed late Nov.–mid-Dec.*

$$$ ★ 🏨 **Kristina.** Set in a lovely wooded park, this hotel is decorated with antlers and trophies in the style of a hunting lodge; its rooms are appropriately outfitted with older furniture. ✉ *Alt-Ausser Str. 54, A–8990,* ☎ *03622/52017,* FAX *03622/52017–1. 11 rooms. Restaurant. AE, DC, MC, V. Closed mid- to late Jan. and Nov.–mid-Dec.*

$$ 🏨 **Wasnerin.** This Styrian-style chalet above town offers magnificent views of the Dachstein peak. The rooms are simple but adequate, and the management is especially friendly. Half board is standard. ✉ *Sommersbergseestr. 19, A–8990,* ☎ *03622/52108. 33 rooms. Restaurant, bar, tennis court. No credit cards. Closed wk after Easter and Oct.–mid-Dec.*

Alt-Aussee

⓫ *4 km (2½ mi) north of Bad Aussee.*

Taking a fairly steep road from Bad Aussee, you'll find Alt-Aussee tucked away at the end of a lake cradled by the mountains that enclose it. This is one of the most magical beauty spots of the Salzkammergut, attracting so many noted artists and writers over the years that its lake has been called "the inkstand into which we all dip our quills." The town is completely unspoiled, perfect for those who simply want an Alpine idyll: to do nothing, hike in the meadows, climb the slopes, or row on the lake. Springtime is perhaps the best time to visit; the field flowers have burst forth and the town holds its annual narcissus festival at the beginning of June.

Salt is still dug in the nearby Sandling Mountains, and the mines are open to visitors. Check with the tourist office or phone for details of guided tours. ☎ *03622/71332–51.* 🎫 *AS120.* ⏲ *Apr.–Oct., daily 10–4; Nov.–Mar., tour daily at 2.*

The mines deep in the mountains have a more recent notoriety. During World War II, Nazi leaders stored stolen art in the underground caverns near Alt-Aussee. In their hurry to get the job done, they skipped a few details; one story has it that a famous painting from Vienna, possibly a Rubens or a Rembrandt, was overlooked and spent the remaining war years on the porch of a house near the entrance to the mines. At the end of the war, Allied forces were directed to the mines by the local populace, and, once unsealed, the caverns released a treasure unlikely to ever again be assembled in one place.

Dining and Lodging

$$$ ★ ✕🏨 **Seevilla.** This elegantly rustic hotel is one of the loveliest in the Salzkammergut, thanks to its site, which sits directly on the shores of Alt-Aussee's picture-book lake amid towering trees. The balconied rooms upstairs, reached by a stone staircase, are spacious and furnished in a modern country style; baths are elegant and efficient. The hotel was completely renovated in 1994 and now features a gracious café. ✉ *Fischerndorf 60, A–8992,* ☎ *03622/71302–0,* FAX *06322/71302–*

82. 46 rooms with bath, 7 apartments. Bar, café, indoor pool, sauna, beach, exercise room. AE, DC. Closed Nov.–mid-Dec.

$$ ✕🏨 **Zum Loser.** The rooms are simple but inviting in this attractive family-managed hostelry. The restaurant, specializing in fish, game, and pork, offers excellent local dishes. (You must order the delicious smoked trout a day in advance.) Local musicians entertain on Thursday evenings. ✉ *Fischerndorf 80, A–8992,* ☎ *03622/71373–0,* FAX *03622/71373–15. 8 rooms. Restaurant. AE, DC, MC, V. Closed Nov.–mid-Dec. and mid-Apr.–May.*

En Route To get back to Bad Ischl, your best bet is to return to Bad Aussee and then take Route 145 north. It's only 28 kilometers (18 miles), but a great deal of this consists of precipitous ups and downs, the highest point being at 3,200 feet before you head down through the Pötschen pass. Not surprisingly, the views are spectacular; don't miss the lookout point at a hairpin turn at Unter, far above the Hallstätter See.

SALZKAMMERGUT A TO Z

Arriving and Departing

By Car

Driving is by far the easiest and most convenient way to reach the Lake District. From **Salzburg,** you can take Route 158 east to Fuschl, St. Gilgen, and Bad Ischl or the A1 autobahn to Mondsee. Coming from **Vienna** or **Linz,** the A1 passes through the northern part of the Salzkammergut; get off at the Steyrermühl exit or the Regau exit and head south on Route 144/145 to Gmunden, Bad Ischl, Bad Goisern, and Bad Aussee. From the Seewalchen exit, take Route 152 down the east side of the Attersee, instead of the far less scenic Route 151 down the west side.

By Plane

The Lake District is closer to Salzburg than to Linz, but ground transportation is such that there is little preference for one departure point over the other. The **Salzburg** airport is about 53 kilometers (33 miles) from Bad Ischl, heart of the Salzkammergut; the **Linz** airport (Hörsching) is about 75 kilometers (47 miles). Both cities have good connections to European destinations, but no flights to or from North America. A number of charter lines fly into Salzburg, including some from the United Kingdom.

By Train

The geography of the area means that rail lines run mainly north–south. Trains run from Vöcklabruck to Seewalchen at the top end of the Attersee and from Attnang-Puchheim to Gmunden, Bad Ischl, Hallstatt, Bad Aussee, and beyond. Both starting points are on the main east–west line between Salzburg and Linz.

Getting Around

By Bus and Train

Railroad service is fairly good, but you won't get off the beaten path. Where the trains don't go, the post office or railroad buses do, so if you allow enough time, you can cover virtually all the area by public transport. Check at the railroad station in Salzburg or Bad Ischl on the availability of a "Salzkammergut Ticket" good for unlimited travel on all trains within the Salzkammergut region and for a 50% reduction on the lake steamers and Schafbergbahn mountain railway on any four days within a 10-day period from May to the end of October.

By Car

For sheer flexibility—plus being able to stop when you want to admire the view—travel by car is the most satisfactory way to see the Salzkammergut. Roads are good, and traffic is excessive only on weekends (although it can be slow on some narrow lakeside stretches).

Contacts and Resources

Canoeing

Helpful firms for the entire Salzkammergut region are **Intersport Steinkogler** (✉ Salzburger Str. 3, Bad Ischl, ☎ 06132/23655), and **Pro-Travel Salzkammergut aktiv** (✉ Markt 94, St. Wolfgang, ☎ 06138/2525–0, FAX 06138/3054).

Emergencies

The emergency numbers are 133 for the **police,** 144 for an **ambulance,** and 122 for the **fire department.** If you need a doctor and speak no German, ask your hotel how best to obtain assistance.

Fishing Licenses

The Salzkammergut is superb fishing country for casting or trolling—the main season runs from June through September—but you'll need a license. Check in **Alt-Aussee** and **Bad Aussee** with the local tourist offices. Many townships have their own licensing offices. **Attersee:** Matthäus Hollerweger (✉ Esso station, Nussdorf, ☎ 07666/8063–4). **Bad Ischl:** Ischler Waffen, Manfred Zeitler (✉ Schröpferpl. 4, ☎ 06132/23351). **Ebensee:** (✉ Baier/Landgasthof zur Kreh, Langbathsee 1, ☎ 06133/6235). **Gmunden:** Forstverwaltung Gmunden (✉ Klosterpl. 1, ☎ 07612/4529, FAX 07612/5664), Höller Kammerhof (✉ Kammerhofgasse 6, ☎ 07612/3308), Gasthof Steinmaurer (✉ Traunsteinstr. 23, ☎ 07612/4239–0). **Hallstatt:** Zentrasport Janu (✉ Seestr. 50, ☎ 06134/8298–0). **Mondsee:** Peter Schickl (✉ Pyrofex-Maximus-Str. 1, ☎ 06232/2881, FAX 06232/2040), Drogerie Maritsch (✉ Rainerstr. 1, ☎ 06232/3436). **St. Wolfgang:** Fischerhaus Höplinger (✉ Dr.-Rais-Promenade 79, ☎ 06138/2241). A number of hotels in the Alt-Aussee/Bad Aussee area have packages that combine a week's stay with the fishing license; for details and booking, contact **Steirischer Tourismus** (✉ St. Peter–Hauptstr. 243, A–8042 Graz, ☎ 0316/403033–0, FAX 0316/403033–10).

Guided Tours

You can take day-long tours of the Salzkammergut from Salzburg. Full-day tours to Salzburg from Vienna pass through the Salzkammergut via Gmunden and the Traunsee, Bad Ischl, the Wolfgangsee, St. Gilgen, and Fuschlsee, but these are such appealing areas it seems a shame to see them only briefly from a bus window. Of the tours from Vienna, those run by **Cityrama/Gray Line** (✉ Börsegasse 1, A–1010 Vienna, ☎ 0222/534–13–0, FAX 0222/534–13–22) and **Vienna Sightseeing Tours** (✉ Stelzhammergasse 4/11, A–1031 Vienna, ☎ 0222/712–4683–0, FAX 0222/712–4683–77) do not include lunch but cost substantially less than that of CityTouring Vienna. From Salzburg, half-day tours offered by **Albus/Salzburg Sightseeing Tours** (✉ Mirabellpl. 2, A–5020 Salzburg, ☎ 0662/881616, FAX 0662/882121) and **Salzburg Panorama Tours** (✉ Schrannengasse 2, A–5020 Salzburg, ☎ 0662/883211–0, FAX 0662/871618) whisk you all too quickly to St. Gilgen, St. Wolfgang, and Mondsee.

SPECIAL-INTEREST TOURS

At Bad Ischl you can arrange excursions to nearby glaciers or a tour of a salt mine, and the working mines in the Sandling mountains are also open to the public. Salzkammergut cycling tours take you past no fewer than 13 lakes; inquire at local tourist boards.

Swimming and Water Sports

There's every kind of water sport in the Salzkammergut, from windsurfing to yacht sailing. You can waterski at Strobl and St. Wolfgang on the Wolfgangsee, and at most towns on the Attersee and Traunsee. At Ebensee, check with **Diving School Gigl** (☒ Strandbadstr. 12, ☎ 06133/6381), which also offers skin diving. In Gmunden, contact **Wasserskischule** (☒ Traunsteinstr., ☎ 07612/3602). A "round" will cost you about AS120. You can explore the mysterious depths of the Hallstätter See by scuba diving via **Tauchschule und Bergefirma Zauner** (☒ Markt 113, ☎ 06134/8286–0).

Visitor Information

The main tourist offices for the provinces and regions covered in this chapter are:

Land Salzburg (☒ Wiener Bundesstr. 23, Pf. 1, A–5300 Hallwang bei Salzburg, ☎ 0662/6688–0, FAX 0662/6688–0; ☒ Mozartpl. 5, A–5020 Salzburg, ☎ 0662/843264). **Styria** (☒ St. Peter–Hauptstr. 243, A–8042 Graz, ☎ 0316/403033–0, FAX 0316/403033–10). **Upper Austria** (☒ Schillerstr. 50, A–4010 Linz, ☎ 0732/600–221–0, FAX 0732/600220). **Ausseer Land** (☒ Kurhauspl. 55, A–8890 Bad Aussee, ☎ 03622/54040–0, FAX 03622/54040–7). **Salzkammergut** (☒ Kaltenbachstr. 36, A–4820 Bad Ischl, ☎ 06132/26909–0, FAX 06132/26909–14).

Most towns in the Salzkammergut have their own *Fremdenverkehrsamt* (tourist offices). **Alt-Aussee** (☒ Fischerndorf 44, A–8992, ☎ 03622/71643–0, FAX 03622/71187). **Bad Aussee** (☒ Chlumeckypl. 44, A–8990, ☎ 03622/52324, FAX 03622/52324). **Bad Ischl** (Bahnhofstr. 6, A–4820, ☎ 06132/23520–0 or 06132/27757–0, FAX 06132/27757–77). **Gmunden** (☒ Am Graben 2, A–4810, ☎ 07612/4305 or 07612/794, FAX 07612/71410). **Gosau am Dachstein** (☒ Tourismusverband Gosau, A-4824, ☎ 06136/8295, FAX 06136/8255). **Hallstatt** (☒ Seestr. 169, A–4830, ☎ 06134/8208, FAX 06134/8352). **Mondsee** (☒ Dr.-Franz-Muller-Str. 3, A–5310, ☎ 06232/2270, FAX 06232/4470). **St. Gilgen** (☒ Mozartpl. 1, A–5340, ☎ 06227/348–0 or 06227/7267–0, FAX 06227/7267–9). **St. Wolfgang** (☒ Markt 28, A–5360, ☎ 06138/2239–0, FAX 06138/2239–81).

7 Salzburg

Mozart, Mozart, Mozart! Birthplace of the great 18th-century composer, Salzburg is a world-class music mecca that hosts the world's most elegant music festival every summer. But many come to tour this Golden City of High Baroque to the strains of music from the film that made Salzburg a household name. From Winkler Terrace to Nonnberg Convent, it's hard to go exploring without hearing someone hum "How Do You Solve a Problem Like Maria?"

A LL SALZBURG IS A STAGE," Count Ferdina ernin once wrote. "Its beauty, its tradition, its tory enshrined in the grey stone of which buildings are made, its round of music, its crowd of fancy-dressed people, all combine to lift you out of everyday life, to make you forget that somewhere far off, life hides another, drearier, harder, and more unpleasant reality." Shortly after the count's book, *This Salzburg,* was published in 1937, reality arrived, but having survived the Nazis, Salzburg once again became one of the Austria's top drawing cards. Art lovers call it the Golden City of High Baroque; historians classify it the Florence of the North, or the German Rome; and, of course, being the birthplace of Mozart, music lovers know it as the Festival City—home of the world-famous Salzburger Festspiele (Salzburg Festival).

Updated by Charlotte van der Reyden

The natural setting is perfect. Salzburg lies on both banks of the Salzach River, at the point where it is pinched between two mountains, the Kapuzinerberg on one side, the Mönchsberg on the other. In broader view are many beautiful Alpine peaks. Man's contribution is a trove of buildings worthy of such surroundings. Salzburg's rulers pursued construction on a grand scale ever since Wolf Dietrich von Raitenau—the "Medici prince-archbishop who preached in stone"—began his regime in the latter part of the 16th century. Astonishingly, they all seem to have shared the same artistic bent, with the result that Salzburg's many fine buildings blend into a harmonious whole. Perhaps nowhere else in the world is there so unanimous a flowering of Baroque architecture. Salzburg is a riot of the Baroque, which is quite proper, for Baroque is a riotous style.

While Salzburg is a visual pageant of Baroque motifs, music is the aural element that shapes the life of the city. It is heard everywhere: in the churches, castles, palaces, and, of course, the concert halls. Although the young Mozart was the wonder boy of Europe, Salzburg did him no particular honor in his lifetime. It is making up for it now. Since 1920, the Salzburg Festival has honored its native son, whose genius no superlatives can adequately describe, with performances by the world's greatest musicians. To see and hear them, crowds pack the city from mid-July until the end of August. Whether performed in the festival halls (Grosses und Kleines Festspielhaus) or outdoors with opulent Baroque volutes and scrolls of Salzburg's architecture as background, Mozart's music remains the heartbeat of the city.

Only the tourist who visits Salzburg outside of the festival season will have time to explore its other fascinating attractions. Many visitors love to make the town's acquaintance by visiting all the sights featured in *The Sound of Music,* filmed here in 1964. It's hard to take in the Mirabell Gardens, Winkler's Terrace, the Pferdeschwemme fountain, Nonnberg Convent, the Residenzplatz, and all the other filmed locations without imagining Maria and the von Trapp children trilling "Do-Re-Mi." (Like Mozart, the von Trapp family—who escaped the Third Reich by fleeing their beloved country—were little appreciated at home; Austria was the only place in the world where the film failed—it closed after a single week's showing in Vienna and Salzburg.) Whether it's the melodies of Rodgers and Hammerstein or Joannes Chrysostomus Wolfgangus Amadeus Theophilus Mozart filling your head, the city of Salzburg is a symphony of both sounds and sights.

Pastimes

of Night Music

n Salzburg is not just *Eine Kleine Nächtmusik* (*A Little Night* to mention one of Mozart's most famous compositions. The ity's nightlife is livelier than its reputation. Folklore performances are given twice a week during the summer season at the Augustinerbräu. In winter "in" areas include the "Bermuda Triangle" (Steingasse, Imbergstrasse) and Rudolfskai; young people tend to populate the bars and discos around Gstättengasse. Of course, Salzburg is most renowned for its **Salzburger Festspiele** summer festival of music and theatre (mid-July–August) and most visitors visit during this season. Much of Salzburg's very special charm can, however, best be enjoyed and discovered off season. For instance, real Mozart connoisseurs come to Salzburg in January for the **Mozart Week** (a 10-day festival held around Mozart's birthday on January 27). And in general music-lovers face an embarrassment of riches in this most musical of cities, ranging from concerts of chamber music held in the Marble Hall of the Mirabell Palace or the Golden Hall of the Fortress to the numerous concerts organized by the International Mozarteum Foundation from October to June in the Great Hall of the Mozarteum. Salzberg's concerts by the Camerata Academica under their director Sándor Végh are now just as much in demand as the subscription series by the Vienna Philharmonic in the Musikverein in Vienna. The **Landestheater** season runs from September to June and presents opera, operetta, plays, and ballet. No music lover should miss the chance to be enchanted and amazed by the skill and artistry of the world-famous **Salzburg Marionette Theater** performing operas by Mozart, Rossini, Johann Strauss, and Offenbach.

Bicycling

As most Salzburgers know, one of the best and most pleasurable ways of getting around the city and the surrounding countryside is by bicycle. Bikes can be rented and the tourist office has maps of the extensive network of cycle paths. The most delightful ride in Salzberg? The **Hellbrunner Allee** from Freisaal takes you past Frohnburg Palace and a number of elegant mansions on either side of the tree-lined avenue out to Hellbrunn Palace. The more adventurous can go farther afield taking the **Salzach cycle path** north to the village of Oberndorf or south to Golling and Hallein.

Dining

Salzburg has some of the best—and most expensive—restaurants in Austria; even better, the city is plentifully supplied with good eateries, offering not only solid good Austrian food (not for persons on a diet) but peppery Hungarian dishes, spiced Slav specialties, and newer-than-now *Neue Küche* (or nouvelle cuisine) delights. There are certain dining experiences that are quintessentially Salzburgian, including restaurants perched on the town's peaks that offer "food with a view"—in some cases, it's too bad the former isn't up to the latter!—or rustic inns that offer "Alpine evenings" with entertainment. A favorite dish is the *Forelle blau getsotten*—trout, served with its price tag attached, as you pay according to the weight of the fish—and don't forget to have a *Schmankerltorte* for dessert. Finally, everyone knows the top place at cocktail time is the gemütlich bar of the Goldener Hirsch, where countesses and opera divas use up every square inch of space from five to seven—and where you can get that rarity in Europe, a genuine martini.

CATEGORY	COST*
$$$$	over AS550
$$$	AS400–AS550
$$	AS200–AS400
$	under AS200

**per person, for a three-course meal including house wine, 10% service, and VAT, but excluding extra tip*

Lodging

The Old City has a wide variety of hotels and pensions, some with surprising locations and considerable atmosphere, but everything has its price and there are few bargains. In high season, and particularly during the festival (July and August), some prices soar and rooms are very difficult to find, so try to reserve at least two months in advance. Note that during the high season, rate differences may push a hotel into the next-higher price category. If you don't have a reservation, go to one of the tourist information offices or the accommodations service (*Zimmernachweis*) on the main platform of the railway station. If you're looking for something very cheap (less than AS400 for a double), clean, and comfortable, stay in a private home, though the good ones are all a little way from downtown. The tourist information offices don't list private rooms; try calling Eveline Truhlar of Bob's Special Tours (☎ 0662/849511–0), who runs a private-accommodations service.

CATEGORY	LOW SEASON*	HIGH SEASON*
$$$$	over AS2,200	over AS3,300
$$$	AS1,300–AS2,200	AS1,800–AS3,300
$$	AS900–AS1,300	AS1,200–AS1,800
$	under AS900	under AS1,200

**All prices are for a standard double room for two, with bath, including breakfast (except where noted) and VAT.*

Skiing

In the immediate vicinity of Salzburg, it is possible to ski down the **Gaisberg** or the **Untersberg.** These may not be ski resorts to please the expert; nevertheless, to take the cable car up the Untersberg and then ski down to the village of Fürstenbrunn can be a breathtaking experience—just right for a free morning or afternoon. Cross-country skiing is possible in **Hellbrunn Park** and around **the Gaisberg.** The tourist office on Mozartplatz will inform you about skiing facilities farther afield. In addition, Salzburg is a good base for excursions to the many ski resorts of Land Salzburg.

EXPLORING SALZBURG

The Altstadt, or Old City, where most of the major sights are concentrated, is a very compact area between the jutting outcrop of the Mönchsberg and the Salzach River. The cathedral and interconnecting squares surrounding it form what used to be the religious center, around which the major churches and the old archbishops' residence are arranged. The rest of the Old City belonged to the wealthy burghers: the Getreidegasse, the Alter Markt (old market), the town hall, and the tall, plain burghers' houses (like Mozart's Birthplace). The Mönchsberg cliffs emerge unexpectedly behind the Old City, crowned to the east by the Hohensalzburg Fortress. Across the river, in the small area between the cliffs of the Kapuzinerberg and the riverbank, is Steingasse, a narrow medieval street where the working people lived. Northwest of the Kapuzinerberg lie Mirabell Palace and its gardens, now an integral part of the city, but formerly a country estate on the outskirts of Salzburg.

We first explore the architectural and cultural riches of the Old City. In the second exploring section, we start at the fortress and then cross the river to explore the other bank. Ideally you should take one day for each tour. An alternative, if you enjoy exploring churches and castles, is to stop after visiting the Rupertinum and go directly up to the fortress, either on foot or by returning through the cemetery to the funicular railway. After exploring the city, the chapter concludes with a selection of short excursions from Salzburg.

Great Itineraries

IF YOU HAVE 1 DAY

It is the tourist who comes to Salzburg outside of the Festival who will have most time to explore its many fascinating attractions. But even for busy Festival visitors, making the acquaintance of the town is not too difficult, for most of its sights are compactly located in a comparatively small area. Of course, if you are doing this spectacular city in just one day, there is always a flip-book fast way to take a course in Salzberg 101—take one of those escorted bus tours through the city. However, since much of Salzburg's historic city center is for pedestrians only, the bus doesn't get you close to some of the best sights—so it's best just to join the army of bipeds and explore by foot.

Start at the **Mozartplatz**—not just to sweeten your tour with a few *Mozart Kugeln,* the omnipresent candy balls of pistachio-flavored marzipan rolled in nougat cream and dipped in dark chocolate—but to make a pit stop at the main tourist information office. Flower-bedecked cafés beckon but this is no time for a coffee—one of the glories of Europe is just a few steps away: the **Residenzplatz,** the veritable center of Baroque Salzburg. If a guided tour is about to leave, view the lavish state rooms of the **Residenz** here; if not, head for the **Dom,** Salzburg's grand cathedral and two of Salzburg's most opulent churches, **St. Peter's Abbey** and the **Franciscan Church.** Behind the cathedral, reflect in **St. Peter's Cemetery.** You're now ready to take the funicular (it's just behind the cathedral) up to the **Fortress Hohensalzburg**—the majestic castle atop the Mönchsberg peak that overlooks the city. All of Salzburg is below you as you walk along the Mönchsberg ridge. Head over to the famous **Winkler Terrace,** to enjoy a rest at the Grand Café Winkler or opt for enjoying some picnic provisions or lunch at the Burgerwehr-Einkehr restaurant. Descend back down to the city via the Mönchsberg express elevators which will deposit you back at No. 13 Gstättengasse. Head over to the **Pferdeschwemme**—the Baroque and royal horse trough that is a somewhat bewildering tribute to the chevaline race—then over to the **Getreidegasse,** the Old City's main shopping street, for some serious retail therapy. At No. 9 is **Mozart's Birthplace.** Welcome twilight with a Kaffee mit Schlag at the famous Café Tomaselli on the charming **Alter Markt** square. Choose one of the more than 40 pastries and congratulate yourself: You haven't seen everything in Salzburg, but you have missed few of its top sights.

IF YOU HAVE 3 DAYS

After completing "Salzburg for Beginners"—your first day—in the itinerary above, your second day will allow you to slow down and smell the *roses des Alpes.* Head for the New Town, although you'll wonder about that name when you enter the narrow little street of **Steingasse.** Soak in the history-rich atmosphere, note Number 9 (where Josef Mohr, the author of "Silent Night" was born), check out tiny **St. Johann am Imberg,** and head over to **Linzer Gasse** for shopping. Next stop is one of the marvels of Salzburg, the **Mirabell Gardens** (where Julie Andrews and her seven charges "do-re-mi"-ed). Explore the orangery, famed Dwarfs' Garden, and the **Mirabell Palace,** the "Taj Mahal of Salzburg."

If you're lucky, you'll catch one of the concerts given in the gardens most every week (usually between 8 and 10:30 PM). If you haven't been able to hear any Mozart divertimenti at the Mirabell, the **Mozarteum** nearby is a trove of Mozartiana. Not far away is the **Mozart Residence,** across from the Hotel Bristol; adjacent is the **Mozart Audio and Video Museum.** After spending part of the day visiting the sites of the most purely Austrian of all composers, in the evening catch a **concert**—hopefully of Wolfi's music—at one of the many music halls in the city (before you arrive in Salzburg, do some advance telephone calls to determine the music schedule of the city for the time you will be there and, if need be, book reservations; if you'll be attending the summer Salzburg Music Festival, this is a must). For your third day, try one of three options: Book a **Sound of Music tour**—who can resist seeing Maria von Trapp's Nonnberg Convent—then, in the afternoon, relax and take a ride up the **Untersberg,** or try to arrange an excursion to the beautiful **Salzkammergut,** to the picture-book towns of Mondsee or St. Wolfgang.

The Altstadt: In Mozart's Footsteps

To most people, Salzburg today means the city of Mozart. Ever since the film *Amadeus,* Wolfgang Amadeus Mozart has been the 18th-century equivalent of a rock star. Born in Salzburg on January 27, 1756, he crammed a prodigious number of compositions into the 35 short years of his life, many of which he spent in Salzburg. We explore the Altstadt (the Old City), and although we do not take you to all the landmarks of his Salzburg sojourn (he moved to Vienna in 1781), you'll explore the heart of the Baroque Salzburg he set to music. (Other Mozart-related sights are included in our second Salzburg tour.) Don't forget to take Mozart tapes along for your Walkman.

Numbers in the text correspond to numbers in the margin and on the Salzburg map.

A Good Walk

In Salzburg, as anywhere, if you have the right departure point, you will have a good journey and ultimately arrive at the right place. For this city, there is no more appropriate center-of-it-all than **Mozartplatz** ①, the square named to honor the genius who set lovely Salzburg to music. Get in the proper mood by taking in, near the statue of Mozart, the street violonists who are usually playing a Mozart sonata or two. Walk past the Glockenspiel café into the next square, the Residenzplatz, centered by the 40-foot-high Court Fountain, often illluminated at night. Take in the famous **Glockenspiel** ② atop the Neubau Palace (chances are the tunes it plays will be by you-know-who), then enter the **Residenz** ③, the opulent Baroque palace of Salzburg's prince-archbishops and Mozart's patrons. This is a Baroque jewel, thanks to its exquisite collection of Dutch and Flemish art, its *Kaisersaal* (Emperor Room), and the *Rittersaal* (Knight's Hall), one of the city's most regal concert halls. From the Residenzplatz, walk through the arches into Domplatz, the majestic Cathedral square of the city—in August, set out with seats for the annual presentation of Hofmannsthal's play *Jedermann.* The **Dom** ④ (Salzburg Cathedral) is among the finest Italian-style Baroque structures in Austria. Walk into the Kapitelplatz through the arches across the square and go through two wrought-iron gateways into **St. Peter's Cemetery** ⑤—one of the most historic and beautiful places in Salzburg. Enter the abbey church of **St. Peter's** ⑥: Above the main entrance the Latin inscription reads: "I am the door—by me if any man enters here, he shall be saved." If its nearing lunchtime, you may want to stop at the legendary Stiftskeller St. Peter—so legendary a restaurant that the story has it that Mephistopheles met Faust here.

As you leave the church of St. Peter's, look up to the right to see the thin Gothic spire of the **Franciscan Church** ⑦. Leave the courtyard in this direction, cross the road, and enter the church by the side entrance, which will bring you directly into the Gothic apse crowned by the ornate red marble altar designed by Fischer von Erlach. Go down the aisle and leave the church by the front entrance, which opens on Sigmund-Haffner Gasse. Opposite is the back entrance to Salzburg's museum of 20th-century art, the **Rupertinum** ⑧—its cafe is a handy spot for a lunch break. Turn left around the corner into **Toscaninihof** ⑨, the square cut into the dramatic Mönchsberg cliff. The wall bearing the harp-shaped organ pipes is part of the famed **Festspielhaus** ⑩. The carved steps going up the Mönchsberg are named for Clemens Holzmeister, architect of the festival halls. If you climb them, you get an intimate view of the Salzburg churches at the level of their spires, and if you climb a little farther to the right, you can look down into the open-air festival hall, cut into the cliffs. From Hofstallagasse, you can either walk directly up to Herbert-von-Karajan-Platz or, preferably, walk around by Universitätsplatz to take a look at one of Fischer von Erlach's Baroque masterpieces, the **Kollegienkirche** ⑪. In Herbert-von-Karajan-Platz is another point at which building and cliff meet: the **Pferdeschwemme** ⑫, a royal horse trough decorated with splendid paintings. To the left is the Neutor, the impressive road tunnel blasted through the Mönchsberg in 1764. Looking back toward Universitätsplatz, you'll see the famous hotel the Goldener Adler, its two buildings painted pink and blue. The arcaded Renaissance court on your left houses the **Spielzeugmuseum** ⑬, a delightful toy museum.

Pass by the tiny church of St. Blasius, built in 1350 and follow the road on through the Gstättentor to the **Mönchsberg elevator** ⑭ for a trip up the hill to the Winkler Terrace, Salzburg's most famous outlook. After you descend from the heights, turn left into the short street leading to Museumsplatz to explore the **Carolino Augusteum Museum** ⑮. Walk back toward the Blasius church, which stands at the beginning of the Old City's major shopping street, Getreidegasse, aglitter with numerous signs (featuring little wrought-iron cobblers and bakers—few people could actually read centuries ago). Amid all the boutiques and Salzburg's own McDonalds (featuring its own elegant sign) is **Mozart's Birthplace** ⑰ at No. 9. Continue down the street, pass the Rathaus (town hall), and enter the Alter Markt, the old marketplace adorned with historic buildings, including the Café Tomaselli (1703) and the Baroque Hofapotheke (court apothecary, 1591), still kept as it was back then. Finish up with some "I Was Here" photographs of the marble St. Florian's Fountain, then head back to Mozartplatz.

TIMING

Touring the Altstadt (Old Town)—the left bank of the Salzach River—contains many of the city's top attractions. Other than exploring by horse-drawn cabs (fiakers), which can be rented at Residenzplatz, most of your exploring will be done on foot since this historic section of town has banned cars. The center city is compact and cozy, so you can easily see it in one day. Note that many churches close at 6 PM, so unless you're catching a concert at one of them, be sure to explore them during daylight. In addition, several of the main attractions, such as the Residenz palace can only be seen by guided tour; refer to the hours we list and try to plan your day with such tours in mind.

Sights to See

⓳ **Alter Markt** (Old Marketplace). Right in the heart of the Old City is the Alter Markt, the old market-place and center of secular life in past centuries. The square is lined with 17th-century middle-class houses, col-

Alter Markt, **19**
Carolino Augusteum museum, **15**
Dom, **4**
Dreifaltigkeitskirche, **30**
Festspielhaus, **10**
Fortress Hohensalzburg, **21**
Franciscan Church, **7**
Funicular Railway, **20**
Getreidegasse, **16**
Glockenspiel, **2**
Kapuzinerberg Hill, **24**
Marionettentheater, **29**
Mirabell Gardens, **26**
Mirabell Palace, **27**
Mönchsberg elevator, **14**
Mozarteum, **28**
Mozartplatz, **1**
Mozart's Birthplace, **17**
Mozart Residence, **31**
Nonnberg Convent, **22**
Pferdeschwemme, **12**
Rathaus, **18**
Residenz, **3**
Rupertinum, **8**
St. Peter's Abbey, **6**
St. Peter's Cemetery, **5**
St. Sebastian's Cemetery, **25**
Spielzeugmuseum, **13**
Steingasse, **23**
Toscaninihof, **9**
Universitätskirche, **11**

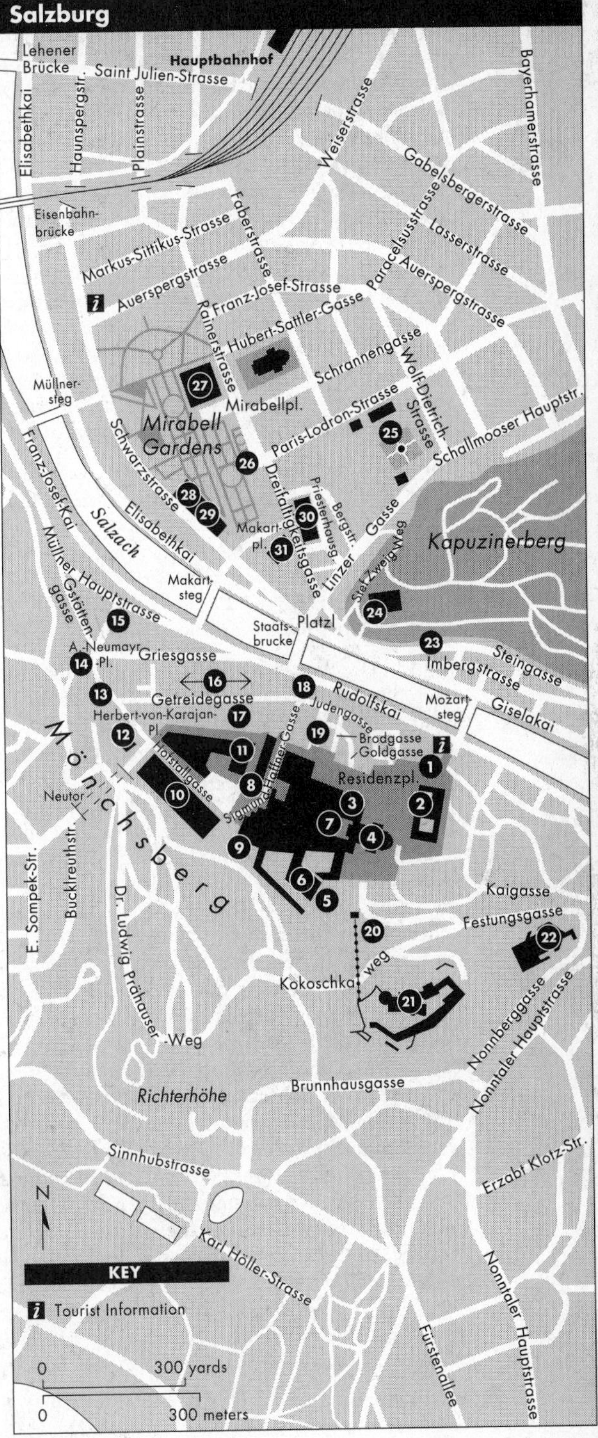

orfully hued in shades of pink, pale blue, and yellow ochre. Look in at the old royal pharmacy, the **Hofapotheke,** with its incredibly ornate black-and-gold Rococo interior built in 1760. Inside, you'll notice a curious apothecarial smell, thanks to the shelves lined with old pots and jars (labeled in Latin). These are not just for show: This pharmacy is still operating today. You can even have your blood pressure taken—but preferably not after drinking a *Doppelter Einspänner* (black coffee with whipped cream, served in a glass) in the famous **Café Tomaselli** just opposite. In warm weather, the café's terrace provides a wonderful spot for watching the world go by as you sip a mélange (another coffee specialty, served with frothy milk and cream), or, during the summer months, rest your feet under the shade of the chestnut trees in the Tomaselli garden at the top end of the square. Next to the coffee house, you'll find the **smallest house in Salzburg,** now an optician's. Note the slanting roof decorated with a dragon gargoyle. In the center of the square, surrounded by flower stalls, the marble **St. Florian's Fountain** was dedicated in 1734 to the patron saint of firefighters.

15 **Carolino Augusteum Museum.** Here you can see remains of Salzburg's old Roman ruins, the famous Celtic bronze flagon found earlier this century on the Dürrnberg near Hallein (10 kilometers, or 6 miles, south of Salzburg), and an outstanding collection of old musical instruments. Special exhibitions are mounted throughout the year. ✉ *Museumspl. 1,* ☎ *0662/843145, 0662/841134 or 0662/841137.* *AS40; combined ticket with toy museum AS60.* ⌚ *Tues. 9–8, Wed.–Sun. 9–5.*

★ 4 **The Dom** (Cathedral) and **Domplatz** (Cathedral Square). When you walk through the arches from the Residenzplatz into the Domplatz, it is not difficult to see why Max Reinhardt chose it in August of 1920 as the setting for the annual summer production of Hugo von Hofmannsthal's *Jedermann* (Everyman). The plaza is a complete, aesthetic concept and one of Salzburg's most beautiful urban set pieces. In the center rises the Virgin's Column, and at one side is what is considered to be the first early Baroque building north of the Alps and one of the ★ finest, the **Dom.** Its facade is of marble, its towers reach 250 feet into the air, and it holds 10,000 people. There has been a cathedral on this spot since the 8th century, but the present structure dates from the 17th century. Archbishop Wolf Dietrich took advantage of (some say he caused) the old Romanesque-Gothic cathedral's destruction by fire in 1598 to demolish the remains and make plans for a huge new building facing onto the Residenzplatz. His successor, Markus Sittikus, and the new court architect, Santino Solari, built the Renaissance-style cathedral, which was consecrated with great ceremony in 1628. The simple gray-and-white interior of the church, a peaceful counterpoint to the usual Baroque splendor, dates from a later renovation. Mozart was christened the day after he was born in the 13th-century font inside the cathedral, where he was organist from 1779 to 1781. Some of his compositions, such as the *Coronation Mass,* were written for the cathedral, and many were performed there for the first time. On Sunday, mass is sung here at 10 AM—the most glorious time to experience the cathedral in full splendor. Many of the church's treasures are in a special museum on the premises. ☎ *0662/844189 or 0662/842591–120.* *AS40.* ⌚ *Mid-May–mid-Oct., Mon.–Sat. 10–5; Sun. and holidays 11–5.*

10 **Festspielhaus** (Festival Hall Complex). To attend the world famous Salzburg Music Festivals, all music lovers head for the Hofstallgasse, the street where the three main festival theaters are located. The street owes its name to the fact that in the 17th century the court stables were located here. Now, instead of prancing horses, festival visitors promenade along the Hofstallgasse during the intervals of summer perfor-

mances, showing off their suntans and elegant attire. The festival complex consists of the **Kleines Festspielhaus** (the small festival hall, sometimes referred to as the Mozart Stage), built in 1937 and nowadays used mainly for productions of Mozart operas and chamber concerts; the **Grosses Festspielhaus,** built into the solid rock of the Mönchsberg and opened in 1960, with a maximum stage width of 104 feet and an auditorium seating over 2000. In recent seasons the Grosses Festspielhaus, nicknamed the Wagner Stage because of its width, has been the venue for spectacular productions such as *Boris Godunov* and *Der Rosenkavalier.* Stage-directors are faced with the greatest challenge in the **Felsenreitschule,** the former Summer Riding School, which—hewn out of the rock of the Mönchsberg during the 17th century—offers a setting more dramatic than anything on stage. Max Reinhardt made the first attempt at using the Summer Riding School for Salzburg Festival performances in 1926. With its retractable roof it gives the impression of an open-air theater; the three tiers of arcades cut into the rock of the Mönchsberg linger in the mind of lovers of *The Sound of Music* film, for here the von Trapps were portrayed as singing "Edelweis" in their last Austrian concert. The theaters are linked by tunnels (partially in marble and with carpeted floors) to a spacious underground car-park in the Mönchsberg. If you want to see the inside of the halls, it's best to go to a performance, but guided tours are given and group tours can be booked on request. ✉ *Hofstallgasse 1,* ☎ *0662/8045.* 🎫 *AS70.* ⏲ *Group tour July 22–Aug., daily at 9, 2, 4:30; individual tour July 22–Aug., daily at 10:30, 2, and 3:30.*

❼ **Franziskanerkirche** (Franciscan Church). The graceful, tall spire of the Franciscan Church stands out from all other towers in Salzburg and the church itself encompasses the greatest diversity of architectural styles. Even at the time of St. Virgil, in the 8th century, a church existed on this spot but it was destroyed by fire. The new one was consecrated with a Romanesque nave, still to be seen, as are other Romanesque features such as a stone lion set into the steps of the pulpit. In the 15th century the choir was rebuilt in Gothic style, crowned by an ornate red marble and gilt altar designed by Austria's most famous Baroque architect, Fischer von Erlach. Mass—frequently one of Mozart's—is celebrated here on Sunday at 9 AM. ✉ *Franziskanergasse 5,* ☎ *0662/843629 or 0662/840951.* ⏲ *Winter, daily 6:30–6; summer, daily 6:30 AM–8 PM.*

⓰ **Getreidegasse.** This is the main shopping street in the Old Town center. According to historians the historic name means "business street"—not "grain street" as many people believe. Today it is the address of famous and elegant fashion houses, international shoe chains, and MacDonalds (note its wrought-iron sign—one of many on the street—and classy bronze lettering: like all the other stores, it has conformed with Salzburg's strict Old City conservation laws). Other than shopping, visitors flock to this street because at No. 9, they'll find **Mozart's birthplace** (☞ *below*). Needless to say, in the summer the street is as closely packed with people as a corncob is with kernels. You can always escape for a while through one of the many arcades, mostly flower-bedecked and opening into delightful little courtyards, that link the Getreidegasse to the river and the Universitätsplatz.

❷ **Glockenspiel** (Carillon). The famous carillon tower is perched on top of the **Residenz Neubau** (New Residence), Prince-Archbishop Wolf-Dietrich's government palace and his first attempt at the Baroque style. The carillon is a later addition, brought from the Netherlands in 1688 and finally put in working order in 1702. The 35 bells play classical tunes (usually by Weber, Haydn, and you-know-who) at 7 AM, 11 AM, and 6 PM—with charm and ingenuity often making up for occasional musical inaccuracy. (You can get a deafening close-up of the action on a tour, at 10:45 AM and 5:45 PM in good weather; daily mid-Mar.–Oct.; weekdays Nov.–mid-Mar.) From Easter to October, the bells are immediately followed by a resounding retort from the 200-pipe "bull" organ housed in the Hohensalzburg Fortress. Details of the music are listed on a notice board across the square on the corner of the Residenz building. ✉ *Mozartpl. 1,* ☎ *0662/8042–2076,* 🎫 *AS20.*

14 **Mönchsberg Elevator.** Just around the corner from the Pferdeschwemme (☞ *below*), at Neumayr Platz, you'll find the Mönchsberg elevator which takes you up through solid rock to the **Winkler Terrace,** where you can walk along the paths through woods while enjoying spectacular vistas of Salzburg. In summer this can be a marvelous and fast way to escape the tiny crowded streets of the Old City. At the top of the Mönchsberg, follow the signs and path south to **Burgerwehr-Einkehr,** a popular café-restaurant open May–mid-October with a magnificent view of the churches and the fortress from its outdoor garden. ✉ *Gstättengasse 13.* 🎫 *Round-trip AS25, one-way AS15.* ⏲ *Tues.–Sun. 9 AM–11 PM, Mon. 9–7.*

31 **Mozarts Geburtshaus** (Mozart's Birthplace). Pilgrims to the city of Mozart's birth usually make this their first stop. Mozart was born on the third floor of this tall house on January 27, 1756, and the family lived here, when they were not on tour, until 1773 (the child prodigy composed many of his first compositions in these rooms). Mozart's piano and tiny violin are on display, as well as portraits of the family, autograph letters and manuscripts which are exhibited in cases illuminated by laser to make them easier to read. On the first floor, miniature stage models from various productions of Mozart operas are on display, and on the second floor a special annual exhibition is mounted which opens in the last week in January and runs until early October. ✉ *Getreidegasse 9,* ☎ *0662/844313.* 🎫 *AS65.* ⏲ *Sept.–June, daily 9–6; July and Aug., daily 9–7.*

NEED A BREAK? On the ground floor of Mozart's Birthplace stop in at **Trzesniewski's** (✉ Getreidegasse 9) for a light snack of open sandwiches (18 different spreads on fresh wholemeal bread) and an excellent cup of coffee.

1 **Mozartplatz** (Mozart Square). Right in the center of the square stands the statue of Wolfgang Amadeus Mozart, the work of sculptor Ludwig Schwanthaler and unveiled in 1842 in the presence of the composer's two surviving sons. It was the first sign of public recognition the great composer had received from his hometown since his death as a pauper in Vienna in 1791. As you will notice, the Mozart memorial industry has grown considerably since then. In fact, in 1991—the 200th anniversary of Mozart's death—a local sculptor caused an uproar, when, in protest against the overcommercialization of Mozart, he had the statue buried under a mountain of 200 supermarket shopping carts. The statue shows a 19th-century stylized view of Mozart, draped in a mantle, holding a page of music and a copybook. A more appropriate bust of the composer, modeled by Viennese sculptor Edmund Heller, is to be found on the Kapuzinerberg. It contains the inscription *Jung groß, spät erkannt, nie erreicht*—"Great while young, belatedly appreciated, never equaled."

12 **Pferdeschwemme** (Royal Horse Drinking Trough). At the western end of the Hofstallgasse is the Herbert-von-Karajan-Platz (named after Salzburg's second greatest son, maestro Herbert von Karajan, the legendary conductor and music director of the Salzberg Music Festival

for many decades). On the Mönchsberg side of the square is the Pferdeschwemme—a royal trough where prize horses used to be washed and watered, constructed in 1695; as they underwent this ordeal they could delight in the frescoes of their pin-up fillies on the rear wall. Looking back toward Universitätsplatz you'll see the famous hotel and restaurant the Goldener Hirsch, its two buildings painted pink and blue. ✉ *Herbert-von-Karajan-Platz.*

18 **Rathaus** (Town Hall). Where the Sigmund-Haffner-Gasse meets the Getreidegasse you will find the Rathaus, a remarkably insignificant building in the Salzburg skyline—apart from its clock which chimes every quarter hour—no doubt reflecting the historical weakness of the burghers vis-à-vis the church.

3 **The Residenz.** Situated at the very heart of Baroque Salzburg, the Residenz overlooks the spacious Residenzplatz and its famous horse fountain. The palace was built between 1600 and 1619 as the home of the prince-archbishops. The *Carabinierisaal* and the *Rittersaal* (Knight's Hall) can be seen with the rest of the state rooms on a guided tour. Today, the Residenz is often used for official functions, banquets and exhibitions. In recent seasons, its courtyard has been the lovely setting for opera productions of the Salzburg Festival. The **Residenzgalerie,** an art museum specializing in 17th-century Dutch and Flemish art and 19th-century paintings of Salzburg is situated on the second floor of the Residenz. ✉ *Residenzpl. 1,* ☎ *0662/8042–2270.* 🎫 *AS50. Art museum AS50, combined ticket AS80.* ⏲ *Apr.–Sept., daily 10–5, and Oct.–Mar., Thurs.–Tues. 10–5; tour July and Aug., daily 10–4:30 every ½ hr, and Sept.–June, weekdays at 10, 11, noon, 2, and 3.*

One of the most delightful ways to tour Salzburg is by horse-drawn carriage. Most of Salzburg's **Fiakers** are stationed in the Residenzplatz. In the Christmas season, large decorated horse-drawn carts take people around the Christmas markets. ✉ *Residenzpl.,* ☎ *0662/844772.* 🎫 *AS350 per Fiaker (up to 4 people) for 20–25 min.*

8 **Rupertinum.** If you are interested in 20th-century art don't miss the chance to see the outstanding permanent collection of paintings and graphic art on display here in this gallery. Take a rest in the museum's excellent café. ✉ *Wiener-Philharmoniker-Gasse 9,* ☎ *0662/8042–2336 or 0662/8042–2541.* 🎫 *AS40.* ⏲ *Tues. and Thurs.–Sun. 10–5, Wed. 10–9.*

13 **Spielzeugmuseum** (Toy Museum). On a rainy day this is a delightful diversion for both young and old with a collection of dolls, teddy bears, model railways, and wooden sailing ships. On certain days special Punch and Judy puppet shows are performed Wednesday and Friday at 3. ✉ *Bürgerspitalpl. 2,* ☎ *0662/847560.* 🎫 *AS30.* ⏲ *Tues.–Sun. 9–5.*

6 **St. Peter's Abbey.** The most sumptuous church in Salzburg, St. Peter's Abbey is where Mozart's Mass in C Minor premiered in 1783; the composer's *Requiem* is performed every year on the anniversary of his death. The porch has beautiful Romanesque vaulted arches from the original structure built in the 12th century, but the interior was decorated in the characteristically voluptuous late-Baroque style when additions were made in the 1770s. Note the side chapel by the entrance, with the unusual crèche portraying the flight into Egypt and murder of all first-born male infants. ✉ *St. Peter Bezirk,* ☎ *0662/844–578.* ⏲ *Fall–spring, daily 8–12:30 and 2–6; summer, daily 8–12:30 and 2–8.*

5 **St. Peter's Cemetery.** From the Kapitelplatz, walk through the arches across the square and go through two wrought-iron gateways (or access, instead, via the St. Peter's abbey courtyard) to discover this eerie

but intimate cemetery, the oldest Christian graveyard in Salzburg, dating back to 1627. Enclosed on three sides by wrought-iron grilles, Baroque vaults contain chapels belonging to old patrician families of Salzburg. The graveyard is far from mournful: The individual graves are tended with loving care, decorated with candles, fir branches or flowers—especially pansies (because their name means "thoughts"). In crypt XXXI is the grave of Santino Solari, architect of the cathedral; in XXXIX that of Sigmund Haffner, for whom Mozart composed a symphony and a serenade, naming them after his patron. The final communal crypt contains the body of Mozart's sister, Nannerl, and the torso of Joseph Haydn's brother, Michael (his head is inside an urn in St. Peter's church). ✉ *St. Peter Bezirk,* ☎ *0662/844578–0.* *AS12.* ⏲ *Tour May–Sept., daily 10–5 hourly; Oct.–Apr., daily at 11, noon, 1:30, 2:30, and 3:30; check times on notice board.*

9 **Toscaninihof** (Arturo Toscanini House). Crossing the two squares from St. Peter's you come into the much smaller Toscanini courtyard, named after the famous Italian maestro Arturo Toscanini, who conducted some of the most legendary performances at the Salzburg Festival during the 1930's. Throughout the summer months this courtyard is a hive of activity, with sets for the stage of the Kleines Festspielhaus being brought in through the massive iron folding gates.

11 **Universitätskirche** (Kollegienkirche), or Collegiate Church. Consecrated in 1707, this is architect Fischer von Erlach's masterpiece of the genre in Salzburg, as well as one of the finest examples of Austrian Baroque. The interior has a liberating feeling of space and light which stage-directors have used to great advantage in recent years for Salzburg Festival performances of contemporary music. ✉ *Universitätsplatz,* ☎ *0662/841–327–72.* ⏲ *Daily 9–6.*

Wiener Philharmonikergasse. Previously known as Marktgasse (Market Street), an open food market is held here every Saturday morning (note that a daily fruit and vegetable market is held on the Universitätsplatz every day). The street was renamed after the world famous Vienna Philharmonic Orchestra in recognition of the unique contribution they make annually to the Salzburg Festival by playing for most opera productions and for the majority of orchestral concerts.

The Fortress and the New Town

According to a popular saying in Salzburg, "If you can see the fortress, it's just about to rain; If you can't see it, then it's already raining." Fortunately there are plenty of days when spectacular views can be had of Salzburg and the surrounding countryside from the top of the fortress. Looking across the River Salzach you can pick out the Mirabell Palace and Gardens, the Landestheater, the Mozart Residence and the Mozarteum, the Church of the Holy Trinity and the Kapuzinerkloster perched on the Kapuzinerberg. Ranging from the "acropolis" of the city—the medieval Fortress Hohensalzburg—to the celebrated Salzburg Marionette Theater, this part of Salzburg captures the city in all its charm. If you want to see the most delightful Mozart landmark in this part of town, the *Zauberflötenhäuschen*—the mouthful used to describe the little summerhouse where he finished composing *The Magic Flute*—note you have to make a special appointment at the Mozarteum.

A Good Walk

Start with Salzburg's Number One sight—especially the case at night, when it is spectacularly spotlit—the famed **Fortress Hohensalzburg** (21), the 12th-century castle that dominates the town. Take the Mönchsberg elevator or the funicular railway on Festungasse, located behind the cathedral near St. Peter's Cemetery. If it's not running, you can walk up the zigzag path that begins a little farther up Festungsgasse; it's steep in parts but gives a better impression of the majesty of the fortress. Once you've explored the largest medieval fortress in central Europe, head back to the footpath but turn right toward the **Nonnberg Convent** ㉒ rather than taking the steps back into town. Explore the church—Maria von Trapp almost found her calling here—then return along the path to the first set of steps, walk down them into Kaigasse, and continue on to Mozartplatz. From here you can cross the Salzach River over the footbridge, Mozartsteg. Cross the road and walk west a minute or two along Imbergstrasse until you see a bookstore on the corner. Here a little street runs into **Steingasse** ㉓—a picturesque medieval street. After exploring this "Time Machine," walk through the Steintor gate, past the chapel of St. Johann am Imberg to the Hettwer Bastion on the **Kapuzinerberg Hill** ㉔ for a great vista of the city.

Continue up the path to the simple Kapuziner-Kloster. From here, follow the winding road down past the Stations of the Cross. Turn right at the bottom of the road into Linzer Gasse, the New Town's answer to the Getreidegasse. Continue up this street until St. Sebastian's church on the left. An archway will lead you into the tranquil **St. Sebastian's Cemetery** ㉕—if it looks somewhat familiar that's because this setting inspired the scene at the end of *The Sound of Music* where the von Trapps are nearly captured. When you leave the cemetery, walk north through a passageway until you reach Paris-Lodron-Strasse. To the left as you walk west down this street is the Loreto Church. At Mirabellplatz, cross the road to the **Mirabell Gardens** ㉖—the Pegasus Fountain (remember "Do-Re-Mi?") and the Dwarfs' Garden are highlights here.

Take in the adjacent **Mirabell Palace** ㉗ and its noted 18th-century Angel Staircase. Turn left out of the park on the busy Schwarzstrasse. Along this road you will find the **Mozarteum** ㉘. Next door is the **Marionettentheater** ㉙—home to those marionettes known round the world. Turn left at the corner, around the Landestheater, and continue into Makartplatz, which is dominated at the far end by Fischer von Erlach's **Dreifaltigkeitskirche** ㉚. Across from the Hotel Bristol is the **Mozart Residence** ㉛, where you can complete your homage to the city's hometown deity.

TIMING

Allow yourself half a day for the fortress, to explore it fully both inside and out. If you don't take an intermission at one of the restaurants on the Mönchsberg, you can stock up on provisions at Schwaighofer (Kranzlmarkt 3 in the Old Town) for a picnic in the beautiful Mirabell Gardens. Call the Mozarteum to see if there will be evening recitals in their two concert halls; hearing the "Linz" Symphony or the *Davidde Penitente* cantata could be a wonderfully fitting conclusion to your day.

Sights to See

30 **Dreifaltigkeitskirche** (Church of the Holy Trinity). The Makartplatz is dominated at the top (east) end by Fischer von Erlach's first architectural work in Salzburg, built 1694–1707. It was modeled on a church by Borromini in Rome and prefigures von Ehrlach's Karlskirche in Vienna. Dominated by a lofty, oval-shaped dome—which bears a painting by Michael Rottmayr—this church was the result of the archbishops' concern that Salzburg's new town was developing in a haphazard fashion. The Dreifaltigkeitskirche was intended to create order by introducing a spectacular monument of the Baroque—the signature style of the city—on the Makartplatz. The interior is small but perfectly proportioned, surmounted by its dome whose trompe l'oeil fresco seems

to open the church to the sky above. ✉ *Dreifaltigkeitasgasse 14,* ☎ *0662/877495–0.* ⏲ *Mon.–Sat. 6:30–6:30, Sun. 8–6:30.*

21 **Fortress Hohensalzburg.** Founded in 1077, the Fortress Hohensalzburg is Salzburg's "acropolis" and the largest preserved medieval fortress in Central Europe. Brooding over the city from atop the Festungsberg, it was originally built by Salzburg's Archbishop Gebhard, who had supported the pope in the political struggle against the Holy Roman Emperor. Over the centuries, the archbishops gradually enlarged the castle and used it first as a residence then as a siege-proof haven against invaders and the rebellions of their own subjects. Outside, the fortress may look grim, but inside there are lavish state rooms, such as the glittering **Golden Room,** the **Burgmuseum**—a collection of medieval art—and the **Rainersmuseum,** with its brutish arms and armour. Politics and church are in full force here: there's a torture chamber not far from the exquisite late-Gothic **St. George's Chapel,** which missed being 15th-century by only two years. One year later, in 1502, the fortress acquired the 200-pipe organ, played daily after the carillon in the Neugebäude. It is best to listen to it from a respectful distance, as it is not called The Bull without reason. Everyone will want to climb up the 100 tiny steps to the **Reckturm,** a lookout post for its sweeping view of Salzburg and the mountains. Remember that queues can be long to the fortress, so try to come early. ✉ *Mönchsberg 34,* ☎ *0662/8042–2123.* 🎫 *Fortress AS35, fortress and tour AS65.* ⏲ *Oct.–May., daily 8–6; June–Sept., daily 8–7; 50-min tour Nov.–Mar., daily 10–4:30 every ½ hr; Apr.–June, Sept., and Oct., daily 9:30–5 every ½ hr; July and Aug., daily 9–5:30 every ½ hr.*

20 You can either take the funicular railway, the **Festungsbahn,** up to the fortress (advisable with young children)—located behind St. Peter's Cemetery—or walk up the zigzag path that begins just beyond the Stieglkeller on the Festungsgasse. Note that descent on foot is possible only if you have a ticket for the fortress. ✉ *Festungsgasse 4,* ☎ *0662/842682.* 🎫 *Round-trip AS32, one-way AS22.* ⏲ *Oct.–mid-Nov., mid- to late Dec., and Feb.–Apr., daily 9–5 every 10 min; May–Sept., daily 8 AM–9 PM every 10 min.*

24 **Kapuzinerberg** and **Kapuzinerkloster** (Capuchin Monastery). The Kapuzinerberg hill—directly opposite the Mönchsberg on the other side of the river—is crowned by several interesting sights. By ascending a stone staircase near Steingasse No.9 you can start your climb up the peak. At the top of the first flight of steps is a tiny chapel, **St. Johann am Imberg,** built in 1681. Farther on is a signpost and gate to the **Hettwer Bastion,** part of the old city walls and offering one of the most spectacular viewpoints in Salzburg. At the summit is the gold-beige **Kapuzinerkloster,** the Capuchin Monastery, dating from the time of Prince-Archbishop Wolf-Dietrich. Pope John Paul II stayed here during his visit to Salzburg in 1988. The road downward is called Stefan Zweig Weg, after the great Austrian writer who had a house on the Kapuzinerberg until 1935 when he had to flee from Austria and the Anschluss. Along the road are the Stations of the Cross.

NEED A BREAK?

After scaling the Kapuzinerberg, you'll particularly appreciate a stop at the charming tavern **Zum fidelen Affen** (The Jolly Monkey), at Priesterhausgasse 8. It offers traditional Austrian food, light snacks, and tempting desserts in a cozy, informal atmosphere that has more than a passing likeness to an English pub.

29 **Marionettentheater** (Marionette Theater). This is both the world's greatest marionette theater and—surprise!—a sublime theatrical ex-

perience. Many critics have noted that viewers quickly forget the strings controlling the puppets, which assume lifelike dimensions and provide a very real dramatic experience. The Marionettentheater is identified above all with Mozart's operas, which seem particularly suited to the skilled puppetry; a delightful production of *Così fan Tutte* captures the humor of the work better than most stage versions. The company is famous for its world tours, but is usually in Salzburg around Christmas, during the late-January Mozart Week, Easter, and from May to September (schedule subject to change). ✉ *Schwarzstr. 24,* ☎ *0662/872406–0,* FAX *0662/882141.* 🎫 *AS250–AS400.* ⏲ *Box office Mon.–Sat. 9–1 and 2 hrs before performance; Salzburg season May–Sept., Christmas, Mozart Week, Easter.*

26 **Mirabell Gardens.** While there are at least four entrances to the Mirabell Gardens—from the Makartplatz, the Schwarzstrasse, and the Rainerstrasse—you'll want to enter from the Rainerstrasse and head for the Rosenhügel (Rosebush Hill): You'll arrive at the top of the steps where Julie Andrews and her 7 charges showed off their singing ability in *The Sound of Music.* This is also an ideal vantage point for admiring the formal gardens and offers one of the best views of Salzburg, as it shows how harmoniously architects of the Baroque period laid out the city. The center of the gardens—one of Europe's most beautiful parks, partly designed by Fischer von Erlach, and grand setting for the Mirabell Palace (☞ *below*)—is dominated by four large groups of statues representing the elements and designed by Ottavio Mosto who came to live in Salzburg from Padua. A bronze version of the horse Pegasus stands in front of the southern facade of the Mirabell Palace in the center of a circular water basin. The most famous part of the Mirabell Gardens is the **Zwerglgarten** (Dwarfs' Garden), which can be found opposite the Pegasus Fountain. Here you'll find 12 statues of dwarves sculpted in marble—the real-life models of which were presented to the bishop by the landgrave of Göttweig. Prince-Archbishop Franz Anton von Harrach had the stone figures made for a theater which was later closed. ✉ *Off Makartpl.* ⏲ *Daily 7 AM–8 PM.*

The Baroque Museum, beside the Orangery of the Mirabell Gardens, features a collection of late 17th and 18th century paintings, sketches and models, illustrating the development of the extravagant vision of life. Works by Giordano, Bernini and Rottmayr are some of the highlights of the collection. ✉ *Orangeriegarten,* ☎ *0662/877432.* 🎫 *AS40.* ⏲ *Tues.–Sat. 9–noon and 2–5, Sun. and holidays 9–noon.*

27 **Mirabell Palace.** The "Taj Mahal of Salzburg," the Mirabell Palace was built by Prince-Archbishop Wolf-Dietrich for his mistress, Salomé Alt, and their ten children: it was originally called *Altenau* in her honor. Over the centuries the Mirabell Palace, now the City Hall, has undergone many extensive alterations; Due to the fire which ravaged Salzburg in 1818, nothing remains of the original palace except the Marble Hall upstairs, nowadays regarded as the most beautiful registry office in the world because it is used for civil wedding ceremonies (candlelit chamber concerts are also held here in the evenings). Recently restored, the hall now looks more splendid than ever, with its marble floor in strongly contrasting colors and the walls of stucco marble ornamented with elegant gilt scroll-work.

The only other part of the palace to survive the fire was the magnificent marble staircase, sculpted by Georg Rafael Donner. Staircases of important buildings afforded many Baroque artists ideal opportunities for ingenious and exuberant ornamentation, and Donner produced a particularly charming example of this highly specialized art in Mirabell. Romantically draped with white marble putti, the staircase is adorned with a mulitude of these cherubs—their faces and gestures reflect a whole range of emotions, from questioning innocence to jeering mockery. Outdoor concerts are held at the palace and gardens, May though August, Sunday mornings and Wednesday evenings. ✉ *Off Makartpl.,* ☎ *0662/8485–86.* 🎫 *Free.* ⏲ *Weekdays and holidays 8–6.*

31 **Mozart Wohnhaus** (Mozart Residence). The Mozart family moved out of their cramped surroundings in the Getreidegasse to this house on the Hannibal Platz, as it was known then, in 1773. Wolfgang Amadeus Mozart lived here until 1780, his sister Nannerl stayed here until she married in 1784, and father Leopold lived here until his death in 1787. The house is, therefore, now referred to as "The Mozart Residence," signifying that it was not only Wolfgang who lived here. During the first allied bomb attack on Salzburg in October 1944, the house was bombed and partially destroyed. Despite international protest at the time a six-story office block was built in its place. Now, in an exemplary building and sponsorship project, the office block has been demolished and the house reconstructed according to how it used to look. Mozart composed the "Salzburg Symphonies" here, as well as violin concertos, church music and sonatas, and parts of his early operatic masterpieces. Besides an interesting collection of musical instruments, among the exhibits on display are the books Leopold Mozart had in his library. Autograph manuscripts and letters can be viewed, by prior arrangement only, in the cellar vaults. One room is devoted to more personal details about Mozart—his height, color of his hair, how he dressed, and his numerous travels across Europe. ✉ *Makartpl. 8,* ☎ *0662/88940–40,* FAX *0662/882419.* 🎫 *Mozart residence AS55, combined ticket for Mozart residence and birthplace AS100.* ⏲ *Daily 10–6.*

In the same building is the **Mozart Audio and Video Museum,** an archive of thousands of Mozart recordings as well as films and video productions, all of which can be listened to or watched on request. ✉ *Makartpl. 8,* ☎ *0662/883454.* 🎫 *Free.* ⏲ *Mon., Tues., and Fri. 9–1; Wed. and Thurs. 1–5.*

28 **Mozarteum.** Two institutions share the address here—the International Mozarteum Foundation, set up in 1870, and the Academy of Music and Performing Arts, founded in 1880. Both are important centers of academic research; the Mozarteum also organizes the annual Mozart Week festival in January and is sponsor of concerts from October to June in its two recital halls, the Grosser Saal (Great Hall) and the Wiener Saal (Vienna Hall). ✉ *Schwarzstr. 26,* ☎ *0662/88940,* FAX *0662/882419.*

The jewel of the Mozarteum is **Das Zauberflötehäuschen** (Magic Flute Summerhouse), set in the institute's garden. The modest wooden structure is a reconstruction of the summerhouse in Vienna in which theater-director Emanuel Schikaneder allegedly locked up Mozart to ensure that he finish composing the opera *Die Zauberflöte* (The Magic Flute) in time for the premiere on September 30, 1791. The house was brought to Salzburg in 1874 and first set up in the Mirabell Gardens, then on the Kapuzinerberg, and finally brought to the garden of the Mozarteum in 1950. The house contains facsimiles of the theater bill of the premiere of *Die Zauberflöte* as well as costume designs for a production in 1793. Unfortunately, the house can only be viewed by special appointment. ✉ *Schwarzstr. 26,* ☎ *0662/88940–0.*

22 **Nonnberg Convent.** Situated just below the south side of the Fortress Hohensalzburg—and best visited in tandem with it—this convent was founded around 700 A.D. by St. Rupert, and his niece St. Erentrudis was the first abbess (in the archway a late Gothic statue of Erentrudis welcomes the visitor). It's more famous these days as Maria's convent—

both the one in *The Sound of Music* and that of the real Maria. She returned to marry her Captain von Trapp here in the Gothic church. Each evening in May at 6:45, the nuns sing a 15-minute service called *Maiandacht*. Their beautiful voices can be heard also at midnight mass on December 24. Parts of the private quarters for the nuns, which feature some lovely, intricate woodcarving, can even be seen by prior arrangement. ✉ *Nonnberggasse 2,* ☎ *0662/841607.* ⏲ *Fall–spring, daily 7–noon and 1:30–5; summer, daily 7–noon and 1:30–7:30.*

23 **Steingasse.** This narrow medieval street, walled in on one side by the bare cliffs of the Kapuzinerberg, backed right onto the riverfront before the Salzach was regulated. Nowadays it's a fascinating mixture of artists' workshops, antiques shops, and trendy nightclubs, but with its high houses the street still manages to convey an idea of how life used to be in the Middle Ages. **Steingasse 9** is the house where Josef Mohr, who wrote the words to the Christmas carol "Silent Night, Holy Night," was born in 1792. The **Steintor** marks the entrance to the oldest section of the street; here on summer afternoons the light can be particularly striking. House No. 23 on the right still has deep, slanted peep-windows for guarding the gate.

25 **St. Sebastian's Cemetery.** Located in the shadows of St. Sebastian's Church, the Friedhof St. Sebastian is one of the most peaceful spots in Salzburg. Prince-Archbishop Wolf Dietrich commissioned the cemetery at the end of the 16th century to replace the old cathedral graveyard, which he planned to demolish. It was built in the style of an Italian *campo santo,* with arcades on four sides, and in the center of the square he had an unusual, brightly tiled, mannerist mausoleum built for himself, where he was buried in 1617. Several famous people are buried in this cemetery, including the physician and philosopher Paracelsus who settled in Salzburg during the early 16th century (the grave is by the church door); Mozart's wife, Constanze; and Mozart's father, Leopold (by the central path leading to the mausoleum). If the gate is closed, try going through church, or enter through the back entrance on Paris-Lodron-Strasse. ✉ *Linzergasse.* ⏲ *Daily 7 AM–7 PM.*

Short Side Trips from Salzburg

★ **Schloss Hellbrunn** (Hellbrunn Palace). Just 6½ kilometers (4 miles) south of Salzburg, the Lustschloss Hellbrun was the pleasure palace of the prince-archbishops. It was built in the early 17th century by Santino Solari for Markus Sittikus, after he'd imprisoned his uncle, Wolf Dietrich, in the fortress. The castle has some fascinating rooms, including an octagonal music room and a banquet hall with a trompe-l'oeil ceiling. From the magnificent gardens and tree-lined avenues to the silent ponds, Hellbrunn Park is often described as a jewel of landscape architecture. It became famous far and wide because of its **Wasserspiele,** or trick fountains: In the formal Baroque gardens, some of the exotic and humorous fountains spurt water from strange places at unexpected times—you will probably get wet. A visit to the gardens is highly recommended: nowhere else can you experience so completely the fantasy that the grand Salzburg archbishops delighted in. The **Monatsschlösschen,** the old hunting lodge, contains an excellent folklore museum; the palace deer park now sports a zoo featuring free-flying vultures and Alpine animals that largely roam unhindered. You can get to Hellbrunn by Bus 55, by car on Route 159, or by bike or on foot along the beautiful Hellbrunner Allee past several 17th-century mansions. The restaurant in the castle courtyard serves good food. ✉ *Fürstenweg 37, Hellbrunn,* ☎ *0662/820372.* 🎫 *Tour of castle, water* *gardens, and museum AS60; park free. ⏲ Apr. and Oct., daily 9–4:30; May–Sept., daily 9–5; evening tour July and Aug., daily 6–10 hourly.*

Oberndorf. This little village 21 kilometers (13 miles) north of Salzburg has just one claim to fame; it was where, on Christmas Eve, 1818, the organist and schoolteacher Franz Gruber composed the Christmas carol "Silent Night, Holy Night" to a lyric by the local priest, Josef Mohr. The church where the masterpiece was created was demolished and replaced in 1937 by a tiny commemorative chapel containing a copy of the original composition (the original is in the Carolino-Augusteum Museum in Salzburg); stained-glass windows representing Gruber and Mohr; and a nativity scene. The local **Heimatmuseum** opposite the chapel, about a 10-minute walk from the village center along the riverbank, documents the history of the carol. You can get to Oberndorf by the local train (opposite the main train station), by car along the Oberndorferstrasse, or by bicycle along the river Salzach. ✉ *Heimatmuseum, Stille-Nacht-Pl. 7, ☏ 06272/7569. 🎫 AS40. ⏲ Mar.–Jan., daily 9–noon and 1–5; memorial chapel Mar.–Jan., daily 8–5.*

Gaisberg and Untersberg. Adventurous people might like to ascend two of Salzburg's "house mountains" (not on the same day!). You can take the bus to the summit of the Gaisberg, where you'll be rewarded with a spectacular panoramic view of the Alps and the Alpine foreland. In summer the bus leaves from Mirabellplatz at 9 AM and 11 AM and the journey takes about half an hour. The Untersberg is the mountain Captain von Trapp and Maria climbed as they escaped the Nazis in *The Sound of Music.* In the film they were supposedly fleeing to Switzerland; in reality, the climb up the Untersberg would have brought them almost to the doorstep of Hitler's retreat at Eagle's Nest above Berchtesgaden! A cable car from St. Leonhard (about 13 kilometers, or 8 miles, south of Salzburg) takes you up 6,020 feet right to the top of the Untersberg, giving you a breathtaking view. In winter you can ski down (you arrive in the village of Fürstenbrunn and taxis or buses take you back to St. Leonhard); in summer there are a number of hiking routes from the summit. ✉ *Untersbergbahn, ☏ 06246/72477. 🎫 Round-trip AS200. ⏲ Mar.–June, daily 9–5; July–Sept., daily 8:30–5:30; Oct. 1–26, daily 9–5; Dec. 20–Feb. 28, daily 10–4.*

DINING

The prices in Salzburg's excellent restaurants are certainly higher than in much of the rest of Austria but, in general, justifiably so: You can experience some truly exquisite cuisine. Many restaurants favor the *Neue Küche*—a lighter version of the traditional, somewhat heavy specialties of Austrian cooking, but with more substance than *nouvelle cuisine.* The only truly indigenous Salzburg dish is *Salzburger Nockerln,* a snowy meringue of sweetened whisked egg whites with just a hint of lemon. But the Salzburgers have a wonderful way with fish—often a fresh catch from the nearby lakes of the Salzkammergut—than do chefs in most places in Austria. In the more expensive restaurants, the set menus give you an opportunity to sample the chef's best; in the less expensive ones, they help to keep costs down. Note, however, that some restaurants limit the hours during which the set menu is available. Many restaurants are open all day; otherwise, lunch is served from approximately 11 to 2 and dinner from 6 to 10. In higher category restaurants it's always best to make a table reservation. At festival time, most restaurants are open seven days a week and have generally more flexible late dining hours.

$$$$ ★ ✕ **Goldener Hirsch.** When you seek a very special night out in an atmosphere of demonstrative elegance, this hotel restaurant may be the place. The food is not especially innovative, but the chef, Herbert Pöcklhofer, is a master of traditional Austrian cooking: liver-dumpling soup, filet of lamb with thyme, smoked trout, and desserts, especially the *Eissoufflé Grand Marnier,* are outstanding. Everything is beautifully prepared and served and, of course, prices are high. At festival time the place is crowded, and service for noncelebrities suffers accordingly. If you want food from the same kitchen that's cheaper but less sophisticated, try the little s'Herzl, next door. ✉ *Getreidegasse 37,* ☎ *0662/8084,* FAX *0662/848511–845. Reservations essential. AE, DC, MC, V.*

$$$$ ✕ **Paris Lodron.** The restaurant in the Schloss Mönchstein is a retreat into Old World elegance. Antique furniture, exquisite porcelain, and heavy plated cutlery provide a wonderful contrast to the modern Austrian cuisine: cream of red-onion soup with cheese croutons, lamb wrapped in light pastry. The food is among the best Salzburg has to offer, and the sophisticated ambience makes dining here an especially memorable experience. Opt for the tiny terrace in summer. It's very popular, especially at festival time. ✉ *Mönchsberg 26,* ☎ *0662/848555–0,* FAX *0662/848559. Reservations essential. Jacket and tie. AE, DC, MC, V.*

$$$$ ★ ✕ **Purzelbaum.** Tucked away under the Nonnberg in the Nonntal district, this restaurant is a fine choice if you want to combine an outstanding gastronomic experience with enjoyable, relaxed surroundings and unobtrusive but attentive service. The light green and white decor has the flair of a Parisian bistro, with small square tables and subdued lighting in the rear room; in summer you can dine outside on the patio, discussing festival performances until well into the night. Specialties include fish caught in the lakes of the Salzkammergut served in delectable sauces. Ingenious combinations of vegetables are a delight for the eye as well as for the palate. But save enough room for a dessert—the variations on ice-cream truffles or even traditional Austrian curd-cheese dumplings are unequaled. ✉ *Zugallistr. 7,* ☎ *0662/848843,* FAX *0662/844352. Reservations essential. AE, DC, V.*

$$$ ✕ **Stadtkrug.** You'll receive a warm welcome from the owners of this family-run hotel and restaurant—the owners, Hugo and Eva, often wear traditional Austrian costume, and together with their team of charming waiters they ensure that any meal here is both a gastronomic and social occasion. The combination of Austrian rustic elegance and cosmopolitan flair makes this a favorite spot for theatergoers and music critics. Try the superb cream of lettuce soup, locally caught rainbow trout or char, or fillet of lamb from the Lech valley in Vorarlberg. This is also one of the best places in town for *Salzburger Nockerl*—but who can resist the *Heisse Liebe* (extra creamy ice cream with hot raspberries). Allow plenty of time to eat here: Service can be slow but the food is always well worth waiting for. ✉ *Linzergasse 20,* ☎ *0662/873545 or 0662/878244,* FAX *0662/879588. Reservations essential. AE, DC, MC, V. Closed Tues.*

$$$ ★ ✕ **Zum Eulenspiegel.** Ignore the Salzburgers who turn up their noses at the mention of this charming restaurant; go both for the food and the unique setting. The house is hundreds of years old and full of nooks and crannies. With numerous intimate corners, a winding staircase, and delicately elegant decor, it's one of the most romantic places in Austria. This isn't kitsch; it's genuine Old-World authentic. It's right in the middle of town, the friendly staff speak English, and the food is certainly nothing to complain about. Try the suckling pig with potato strudel or the pickled salmon trout with honey-mustard sauce—and note that these dishes seem to taste better at night when the candlelit atmosphere enhances everything. ✉ *Hagenauerpl. 2,* ☎ *0662/843180–0,* FAX *0662/843180–6. Reservations essential. AE, DC, MC, V. Closed Sun. except during Festival; Jan.–mid-Mar.*

Dining
Augustinerbräu, **1**
Fasties, **16, 22**
Goldener Hirsch, **6**
Humboldtstube, **4**
K+K StieglKeller, **15**
Paris Lodron, **2**
Purzelbaum, **21**
Stadtkrug, **26**
Sternbräu, **7**
Stiftskeller St. Peter, **20**
Wilder Mann, **8**
Zipfer Bierhaus, **11**
Zum Eulenspiegel, **9**
Zum fidelen Affen, **24**
Zum Mohren, **13**

Lodging
Altstadt Radisson, **14**
Amadeus, **28**
Blaue Gans, **5**
Elefant, **12**
Goldene Krone, **27**
Goldener Hirsch, **6**
Haus Wartenberg, **3**
Kasererbräu, **17**
Österreichischer Hof, **10**
Schloss Mönchstein, **2**
Schwarzes Rössl, **23**
Stadtkrug, **26**
Trumer Stube, **25**
Weisse Taube, **18**
Wolf, **19**

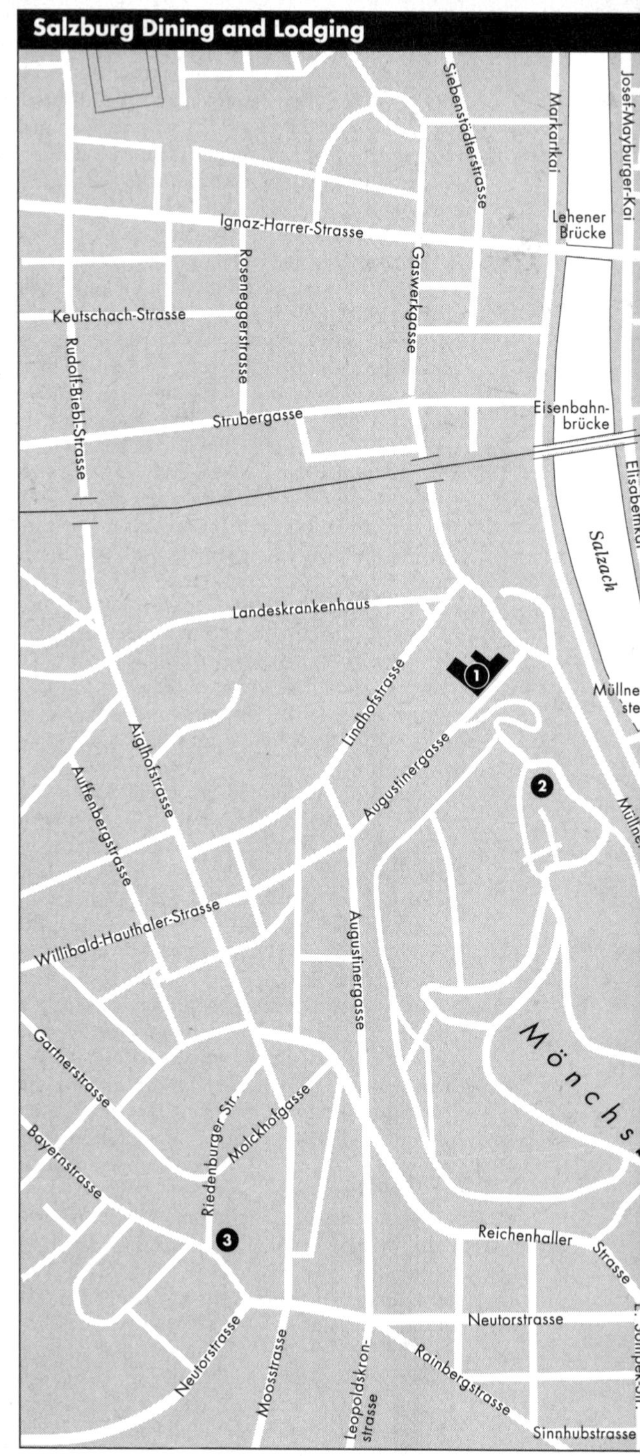

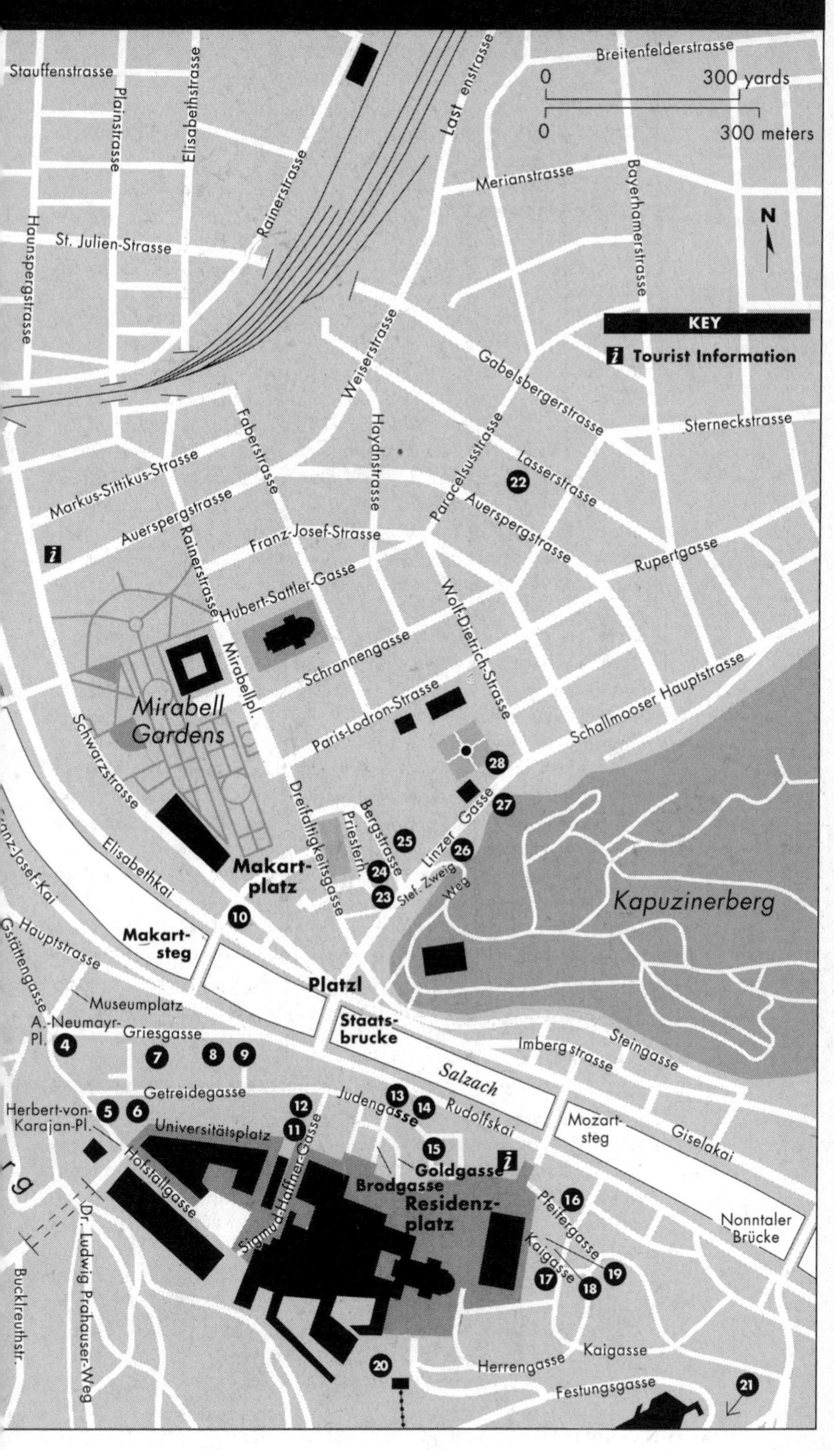

Stauffenstrasse
Plainstrasse
Elisabethstrasse
Rainerstrasse
Lastenstrasse
Breitenfelderstrasse
0
300 yards
0
300 meters
Merianstrasse
Bayerhamerstrasse
N
Haunspergstrasse
St. Julien-Strasse
KEY
Tourist Information
Weiserstrasse
Gabelsbergerstrasse
Haydnstrasse
Sterneckstrasse
Faberstrasse
Paracelsusstrasse
Lasserstrasse
Markus-Sittikus-Strasse
Auerspergstrasse
Franz-Josef-Strasse
Auerspergstrasse
Rainerstrasse
Rupertgasse
Hubert-Sattler-Gasse
Wolf-Dietrich-Strasse
Schrannengasse
Mirabellpl.
Mirabell Gardens
Paris-Lodron-Strasse
Schallmooser Hauptstrasse
Schwarzstrasse
Dreifaltigkeitsgasse
Bergstrasse
Priesterh.
Linzer Gasse
Stef. Zweig Weg
Makartplatz
Elisabethkai
Kapuzinerberg
Makartsteg
Hauptstrasse
Gstättengasse
Platzl
Museumplatz
Staatsbrucke
A.-Neumayr-Pl.
Griesgasse
Imbergstrasse
Steingasse
Salzach
Getreidegasse
Judengasse
Rudolfskai
Herbert-von-Karajan-Pl.
Universitätsplatz
Mozartsteg
Giselakai
Goldgasse
Brodgasse
Residenzplatz
Hofstallgasse
Sigmund-Haffner-Gasse
Pfeifergasse
Kaigasse
Nonntaler Brücke
Dr. Ludwig Prahauser-Weg
Bucklreuthstr.
Herrengasse
Kaigasse
Festungsgasse

$$ ✕ **K+K StieglKeller**. This restaurant is located near the cathedral and is divided into three different sections, each with a particular ambience. Upstairs the atmosphere is slightly more formal and local residents come here for business lunches or celebrations; downstairs, tourists form the main clientèle. Menu selections consist of traditional Austrian dishes, such as liver dumpling soup, locally caught fish, Tafelspitz with spinach and roast potatoes, Wiener Schnitzel, and game in season. ✉ *Waagpl. 2,* ☎ *0662/842156,* FAX *0662/84211770. AE, DC, MC, V.*

$$ ✕ **Stiftskeller St. Peter.** In what is said to be Europe's oldest *Gasthaus,* founded by Benedictine monks in the ninth century, choose between the fairly elegant, dark wood-paneled *Prälatenzimmer* or one of the several less formal rooms. Locals claim that Mephistopheles met Faust here. In summer the courtyard garden is a favorite. You'll find standards ranging from *Wiener schnitzel* to the delicate poached St. Peter's fish. Specialties include the *Klostertopf,* thick soup served in a loaf of bread, fish caught in local rivers and lakes, and, of course, Salzburger Nockerl. ✉ *St. Peter district 4,* ☎ *0662/848481,* FAX *0662/841268–75. AE, DC.*

$$ ✕ **Zipfer Bierhaus.** The arched ceilings, brick floors, and wooden tables provide the right setting for good, standard local fare such as roast pork with a dumpling, served with Zipfer beer, of course. This is one of Salzburg's oldest *Gasthäuser*; look down the ancient cistern in the passageway connecting the two main rooms. ✉ *Sigmund-Haffner-Gasse 12/Universitätspl. 19,* ☎ *0662/840745,* FAX *0662/853234. No credit cards. Closed Sun.*

$$ ✕ **Zum Mohren.** Good food, a central location by the river, a welcoming atmosphere, attentive service, and reasonable prices have made Zum Mohren very popular with both Salzburgers and tourists. The restaurant is in the basement of a 15th-century house; tables can be cramped. Offerings are not overly adventuresome but the menu always offers at least one vegetarian item and several fish dishes among a selection of Austrian specialties like sautéed veal liver and roast hare. ✉ *Judengasse 9/Rudolfskai 20,* ☎ *0662/842387. AE, MC, V. Closed Sun., bank holidays, and mid-June–mid-July.*

$ ✕ **Augustinerbräu.** Salzburg's homegrown version of a Munich beer house is located at the north end of the Mönchsberg. You can bring your own food; pick up a stone jug of strong, frothy (not fizzy) beer; and sit down in the gardens or at a dark-wood table in one of the large halls. Shops in the huge monastery complex sell salads which can look a little weary later on in the day, sausage, and fried chicken, and a little stall has tasty spirals of salted radish. If you don't feel up to cold beer, there's an old copper beer warmer in the main hall. ✉ *Augustinergasse 4,* ☎ *0662/431246,* FAX *0662/431246–20. No credit cards.* ⏲ *Daily 3–11 PM.*

$ ★ ✕ **Fasties.** An informal restaurant that serves excellent food is always useful. This neighborhood place not far from the Mirabell Gardens is decorated in a light, cheerful style. The second location, just off Mozartplatz, is equally informal, reminiscent of a bistro with its blackboard menu and more comfortable seating. The menu consists of excellent salads, soups, quiches, pâtés, sandwiches, and one or two larger dishes, prepared by a chef who has a superb way with sauces. The wine list is small but well chosen, and you can have the food packed to go. ✉ *Lasserstr. 19,* ☎ *06222/873876;* ✉ *Pfeifergasse 3,* ☎ *0662/844774. No credit cards. Lasserstr. closed weekends, Pfeifergasse closed Sun. No dinner Sat. at Pfeifergasse.*

$ ★ ✕ **Humboldtstube.** The main room, reminiscent of a hunting lodge, sets the atmosphere for good local food such as roast veal and pork with sauerkraut. Salad aficionados choose from 18 varieties. You can find hot food here until 2 AM year-round, and in summer dine outdoors at tables set on the street. ✉ *Gstättengasse 6,* ☎ *0662/843171. No credit cards.*

$ ✕ **Sternbräu.** This place seems big enough to have fed half the Austro-Hungarian army. The restaurant is divided into a series of rooms with varying degrees of formality. There are two beer gardens where you can sit on warm evenings in the shade of chestnut trees and enjoy local beer or a refreshing *weiss g'spritztzt* (white wine with water) and special Salzburg dishes with products supplied from local farms. One part of the restaurant (La Stella) also serves Italian food. ✉ *Griesgasse 23/Griesgasse 34,* ☎ *0662/842140–0,* FAX *0662/842140–81. No credit cards.*

$ ★ ✕ **Wilder Mann.** The atmosphere may be too smoky for some (choose the outside courtyard in summer), but the beamed ceiling and antlers are genuine, as are the food and value. There are no pretensions here. Try the boiled beef (*Tellerfleisch*) or game in season; the venison stew is outstanding. ✉ *Getreidegasse 20/Griesgasse 17 (passageway),* ☎ *0662/841787. No credit cards. Closed Sun.*

$ ★ ✕ **Zum fidelen Affen.** The name means "At the Jolly Monkey," which explains the monkey motifs in what is otherwise a traditional Austrian Gasthaus. The place is dominated by a large circular bar surrounded by tables, and the somewhat limited menu is not unusual for Austria: beef salad with pumpkinseed oil, dumplings with or without sauerkraut, and a wide variety of goulashes. What *is* unusual is the excellent quality of the food, particularly at these prices. Because half Salzburg knows this, the place is always packed. ✉ *Priesterhausgasse 8,* ☎ *0662/877361. No credit cards. Closed Sun. No lunch.*

LODGING

It is difficult for a Salzburg hotel not to have a good location—you can find a room with a stunning view over the Kapuzinergberg or Gaisberg or one that simply overlooks a lovely Altstadt street. Many hostelries are charmingly decorated in *Bauernstil*—the rustic, peasant-luxe look of Old Austria. Note that many hotels in the Old City have to be accessed via footpower, as cars are not permitted on many streets. If you have a car, of course, you may opt to do what many do—find a hotel or converted castle on the outskirts of the city. Needless to say, if you're planning to come at Festival time, you must book as early as possible. If you don't have a reservation, go to one of the tourist information offices or the accommodations service (*Zimmernachweis*) on the main platform of the railway station.

$$$$ 🏨 **Altstadt Radisson.** No two rooms or suites are alike in this luxurious and elegantly converted Old City hostelry dating to 1377. On one side, rooms overlook the river and the picturesque Capuchin cloister atop the hill opposite; on the other, upper rooms sneak a glance at the fortress. Despite smaller windows and original beamed ceilings, rooms are light and spacious. Added bonuses are the central yet quiet location, buffet breakfast, and the excellent restaurant. ✉ *Rudolfskai 28/Judengasse 15,* ☎ *0662/848571–0,* FAX *0662/848571–6. 41 rooms, 19 suites. Restaurant. AE, DC, MC, V.*

$$$$ ★ 🏨 **Goldener Hirsch.** The Golden Stag is a jewel among Salzburg's top hotels. The 800-year-old pink and blue houses, overlooking Getreidegasse on one side and Herbert-von-Karajan-Platz on the other, offer a variety of rooms furnished with antiques. The service is second to none—discreet, friendly, and incredibly polite. The hotel has recently acquired a new house across the road on Getreidegasse, where the rooms are larger and furnished in a slightly more contemporary style. If you want to be in the old building, specify it when reserving. Breakfast is not included in the room price. ✉ *Getreide-*

gasse 37, ☎ 0662/8084–0, FAX 0662/848511–845. 71 rooms. Restaurant, bar, parking. AE, DC, MC, V.

$$$$ **Österreichischer Hof.** The Gürtler Family, owners of the famous Hotel Sacher in Vienna, acquired the Österreichischer Hof in 1988, and extensive renovation work has made it one of Salzburg's top hotels with a commanding view of the Old City across the river Salzach. The rooms and suites facing the river are the most elegant and luxurious; if price is not a problem, ensure that you specify a river-view room when making a reservation. Room prices include a magnificent buffet breakfast catering to every taste. ✉ *Schwarzstr. 5-7,* ☎ *0662/88977,* FAX *0662/88977–14. 120 rooms. 5 restaurants, bar, conference facilities. AE, DC, MC, V.*

$$$$ **Schloss Mönchstein.** If you are a romantic with money to spend, look no further. This ancient, ivy-covered, fairy-tale castle, hidden in the woods at the top of the Mönchsberg, is a dream. The rooms are very uneven in size and decor, but the best are luxurious. Service is formal and discreet, and the restaurant is the epitome of Old World elegance. The castle has its own wedding chapel, which is particularly popular with American and Japanese couples. Getting in and out of town calls for a car or taxi, unless you are willing to negotiate steps or take the nearby Mönchsberg elevator which is about an 8-minute walk away. ✉ *Mönchsberg 26,* ☎ *0662/848555–0,* FAX *0662/848559. 17 rooms. Restaurant, bar, café, tennis court, chapel, parking. AE, DC, MC, V.*

$$$ **Kasererbräu.** A variety of tastes went into designing this hotel, resulting in a curious mixture of kitsch and elegance in the hallways and reception areas, with plain but adequate rooms. Apart from the friendly staff, the hotel has two big advantages: It's right next to Mozartplatz, and it has pleasant sauna and steam-bath facilities included in the price. ✉ *Kaigasse 33,* ☎ *0662/842445–0,* FAX *0662/842445–51. 43 rooms. Sauna, parking. AE, DC, MC, V.*

$$$ **Stadtkrug.** This historic family-run hotel is literally cut into the stone of the Kapuzinerberg, accounting for the various floor levels; the rock behind the reception desk is real, not decoration. In many of the rooms, dark wood contrasts with light walls and oriental carpets. The suites (Room 102, for example) are elegantly spacious, with original wood-beamed ceilings, canopied bed and period furniture. Marble baths are equally expansive. Side rooms have little or no view but are quieter, despite the pedestrian zone. The garden terrace adjacent to the fourth floor offers a hilltop view out over the city. ✉ *Linzer Gasse 20,* ☎ *0662/873545,* FAX *0662/879588. 34 rooms and suites. Restaurant, café. AE, DC, MC, V.*

$$ **Amadeus.** Rooms in this family-run house are tasteful and spacious, if simple, with natural wood and rustic accessories. Skillful renovations behind the period pink facade have turned a building that dates from the 1500s into a modern hotel that retains its intriguing winding stone stairs and original narrow hallways. It's centrally located and about a 10-minute walk from all the main sites . ✉ *Linzer Gasse 43–45,* ☎ *0662/871401,* FAX *0662/876163–7. 23 rooms with bath or shower. AE, DC.*

$$ **Blaue Gans.** Reasonable rates in a 500-year-old building in the heart of the Old City make the Blue Goose an extremely popular choice. Despite the building's undeniable atmosphere of a medieval inn, the rooms are unadorned, in white with gray furniture. Room 7 has a great view out over Herbert-von-Karajan-Platz; some inside rooms view the wall opposite. But stepping straight out onto Getreidegasse gives the hotel all the advantage it needs, so make reservations early. ✉ *Getreidegasse 43,* ☎ *0662/841317,* FAX *0662/841317–9. 45 rooms, 29 with bath. Restaurant. AE, DC, MC, V.*

$$ ★ **Elefant.** This 12th-century building, right in the middle of the Old City, has been a hotel for four hundred years, and has an atmosphere of traditional comfort rather than merely old age. The public areas, including a quiet writing room, and the high-ceilinged private rooms are well decorated with Persian carpets and Biedermeier furniture in dark woods. Double rooms are of three sizes. ✉ *Sigmund-Haffner-Gasse 4,* ☎ *0662/843397,* FAX *0662/840109–28. 36 rooms. 2 restaurants. AE, DC, MC, V.*

$$ ★ **Trumer Stube.** Readers repeatedly recommend this family-run pension, mentioning in particular its friendly atmosphere and helpful staff. It's in a well-kept old building on a narrow, winding street near Mirabellplatz and is scrupulously clean. It has a bright and cheerful breakfast room, although breakfast itself is on the light side for some. The attractively decorated, cheerful rooms would easily do justice to a far more expensive hotel. ✉ *Bergstr. 6,* ☎ *0662/874776–0,* FAX *0662/874326. 22 rooms. No credit cards. Closed Jan.*

$$ **Weisse Taube.** A traditional family-run hotel, close to the Mozartplatz, the White Dove is always heavily booked, though it does not take groups. The 14th-century house, with its uneven floors and strange nooks and crannies, is a historic property, which forced the owners to find original solutions to modern problems, such as bathrooms encapsulated in plastic, to protect the building from water. The rooms are a little dark and decorated with heavy patterned wallpaper and carpet. ✉ *Kaigasse 9,* ☎ *0662/842404,* FAX *0662/841783. 33 rooms, 29 with bath. Bar. AE, DC, MC, V. Closed 2 wks in Jan.*

$$ ★ **Wolf.** The embodiment of Austrian gemütlichkeit, just off the Mozartplatz, the Wolf offers spotlessly clean and cozy rooms at reasonable prices. The rooms in this small family-run hotel are idiosyncratically arranged on several upper floors, connected by narrow, winding stairs, and are decorated with a pleasing Salzburg mix of rag rugs and rural furniture. The staff is friendly and helpful; borrow a bright umbrella from the stand by the door for use against the inevitable Salzburg showers. ✉ *Kaigasse 7,* ☎ *0662/843453–0,* FAX *0662/842423–4. 12 rooms. AE. Closed mid-Feb.–mid-Mar.*

$ **Goldene Krone.** The feature here is the central location. Rooms come in all shapes and sizes (with a few large ones for families) but are a bit worn and unadorned, with furniture in plain natural wood. The least expensive rooms open onto ventilation shafts, so you may want to check before signing in. In contrast, those in front have splendid views of St. Sebastian's church across the street. Breakfast is definitely on the spartan side. ✉ *Linzer Gasse 48,* ☎ *0662/872300. 27 rooms. No credit cards.*

$ **Haus Wartenberg.** If you're looking for perfection, this is not the place to come. Nevertheless, it is one of the best values in Salzburg, with spacious double rooms at a reasonable price and tiny singles and doubles without bath at a steal. It's a rambling old house, a 10-minute walk from the town center, and all the rooms are furnished with antique peasant furniture; the family also runs an excellent restaurant on the premises. ✉ *Riedenburger Str. 2,* ☎ *0662/844284–0,* FAX *0662/848400–5. 18 rooms, 10 with bath. Restaurant. No credit cards.*

$ **Schwarzes Rössl.** Once a favorite with Salzburg regulars, this traditional *Gasthof* now serves as student quarters for most of the year but is well worth booking when available. Rooms are fresh and immaculate, if not elegant, and the location is excellent—close to the nighttime action. ✉ *Priesterhausgasse 6,* ☎ *0662/874426,* FAX *0222/401–76–20. 51 rooms with bath. AE, DC, MC, V. Closed Oct.–June.*

NIGHTLIFE AND THE ARTS

The Arts

Information and Tickets

Information and tickets for the main Salzburg Festival (late July–Aug.), the Easter Festival (early Apr.), and the Pentecost Concerts (late May) can be obtained from **Salzburger Festspiele** (✉ Hofstallgasse 1, A–5020 Salzburg, ☎ 0662/844501–0, FAX 0662/846682; Easter Festival, ☎ 0662/8045–361, FAX 0662/840124). You must reserve well in advance. Any office of the Salzburg Tourist Office (☞ Visitor Information *in* Salzburg A to Z, *below*) and most hotel concierge desks provide schedules for all arts performances, and you can find listings in the daily newspaper *Salzburger Nachrichten.* Tickets can be purchased directly at the box office, at your hotel, via the **Salzburg Ticket Service** (✉ Mozartpl. 5, ☎ 0662/842296 or 0662/840310, FAX 0662/842476), or at a ticket agency like **Polzer** (✉ Residenzpl. 3, ☎ 0662/846500, FAX 0662/840150) or **American Express** (✉ Mozartpl. 5, ☎ 0662/8080–0, FAX 0662/8080–9).

Film

Salzburg has very few movie theaters, and these few generally show English-language films dubbed into German—although these days more films are being shown in their original languages, particularly in *Das Kino* (✉ Giselakai 11, ☎ 0662/873100). Check the Kino listings in the *Salzburger Nachrichten* newspaper.

Music

There is no shortage of concerts in this most musical of cities. The **Salzburg Palace Concerts,** the **Fortress Concerts,** and the **Mozart Serenades** take place year-round. In addition, there are the **Easter Festival,** the **Pentecost Concerts, Mozart Week** (Jan. 24–Feb. 2), and the **Salzburg Cultural Days** (October). The Mozart Week is always special; in recent seasons, Nicholas Harnoncourt, Carlo Maria Giulini, and John Eliot Gardiner have conducted the Vienna Philharmonic. The 1997 programm includes an eagerly awaited stage version of Mozart's early opera *Mitridate, Re di Ponto,* directed by Jonathan Miller and conducted by Roger Norrington. For jazz, check **Jazzclub Live Salzburg** (✉ Urbankeller, Schallmooser Hauptstr. 50, ☎ 0662/878097) for its Friday events. The **Riff Bar und Musikcafé im Rockhaus** (✉ Schallmooser Hauptstr. 46, ☎ 0662/878097) has live music on Monday nights in a 400-year-old cellar.

Opera

The great opera event of the year is, of course, the **Salzburg Festival.** The **Easter Festival** in 1997 presents a new production of Alban Berg's *Wozzeck* directed by Peter Stein and conducted by Claudio Abbado, and the **Salzburg Cultural Days** will present operas as well as concerts. The **Marionettentheater** is also devoted to opera, with a particularly acclaimed production of *Così fan Tutte* to its credit, and gives performances the first week of January, during Mozart Week, May–September, and after December 25.

The season at the **Landestheater** (✉ Schwarzstr. 22, ☎ 0662/871512–0) runs from September to June. New productions in 1997 include Weber's *Der Freischütz* and Humperdinck's *Hänsel und Gretel,* and there will also be a revival of Mozart's *The Marriage of Figaro* from the previous season. You make place ticket orders by telephone Tuesday–Friday 10–1 and 5–5:30 and Saturday 10–1.

Theater

The Salzburg Festival performs Hugo von Hofmannsthal's morality play *Jedermann* (in German) annually in the forecourt of the cathedral. As is customary, the festival will feature the Vienna Philharmonic, but other orchestras can be expected to take leading roles as well.

Nightlife

Bars/Nightclubs

Chez Roland (✉ Giselakai 15, ☎ 0662/874335) is the haunt of "Loden-preppies," or the wealthy and stylish young, and is open Monday–Saturday 6 PM–1 AM. **Bazillus** (✉ Imbergstr. 2a, ☎ 0662/871631), on the other hand, is small, scruffy, and makeshift, but very cool; it's open daily 11 AM–1 AM. **Flip** (✉ Gstättengasse 7, ☎ 0662/843643), near the Mönchsberg elevator, is a 1950s neon bar, open daily 11 AM–3 AM. **Saitensprung** (✉ Steingasse 11, ☎ 0662/881377) is an elegant cocktail bar with food, open daily 8 PM–3 AM. Students gather at **Andreas Hofer** (✉ Steingasse 65, ☎ 0662/872769), open daily except Saturday 7 PM to midnight.

Casino

Salzburg's **Casino** (☎ 0662/845656–0) has found its new home in Schloss Klessheim, a bit out of the center. A free shuttle bus will bring you from the Mönchsberg lift or Mirabellplatz to Schloss Klessheim and back; your hotel can tell you the nearest departure point. Departures are hourly starting at 2:30 PM; check schedules if you also want to return by bus. Admission is free; you'll receive a free "welcome jeton" entitling you to purchase tokens worth AS250 for AS210. Open daily from 3 PM except Good Friday, Nov. 1, and Dec. 24. Remember to take your passport.

Discos

Disco Seven (✉ Gstättengasse 7, ☎ 0662/844181) is large, has a youngish crowd, and goes for the American market; it's open daily 9 PM–4 AM and takes credit cards. The **Half Moon** (✉ Anton-Neumayr-Pl. 5, ☎ 0662/841670) caters to yuppies and beautiful people and is open daily 10 PM–4 AM. The local disco scene has become more volatile, so check with the tourist office for the current best attractions.

OUTDOOR ACTIVITIES AND SPORTS

Bicycling

Getting Around *in* Salzburg A to Z, *below,* lists rental shops. The tourist office has maps of cycle paths. The Hellbrunner Allee out to Hellbrunn Palace and the Almkanal path out past Leopoldskron Palace are two of the nicest and least strenuous routes.

Fishing

There is plenty of fishing around Salzburg, largely for trout, carp, and pike. The season runs from May to December. Day licenses are available for around AS250, depending on season and waters, from **Sporthaus Markus Maier** (✉ Rainerstr. 2, ☎ 0662/871441), **Sport Rehm** (✉ Rudolf-Biebl-Str. 5a, ☎ 0662/435751), or **Starfish** (✉ Auerspergstr. 10, ☎ 0662/877000).

Golf

The **Golf and Country Club Salzburg** (✉ Schloss Klessheim, Salzburg-Wals, ☎ 0662/850851), just west of the city, is a 9-hole course at Klessheim castle. Take the A1 freeway to the Klessheim exit.

Skiing

Within Salzburg, the Gaisberg and the Untersberg have good ski slopes. Cross-country skiing is possible on the Hellbrunner Allee and around the Gaisberg (Rauchenbühelhütte). The tourist office at Mozartplatz will inform you about skiing facilities farther afield; Salzburg is often used as a base for excursions to the many ski resorts of the Land Salzburg district. Skis can be rented at **Sporthaus Markus Maier** (✉ Rainerstr. 2, ☎ 0662/871441). For snow reports in winter (in German) call 0662/1584.

Swimming

The **Paracelsus-Kurhaus** (✉ Auerspergstr. 2, ☎ 0662/883544–0) has a large swimming pool with a sauna and Turkish bath. There are several outdoor pools: Try **Freibad Alpenstrasse** (☎ 0662/620832), which you can reach on Bus 3; **Freibad Leopoldskron** (✉ Leopoldskronerstr. 50, ☎ 0662/829265–0); or **Freibad Volksgarten** (☎ 0662/623183–0), which you can reach via Bus 6 or 49.

Tennis

Salzburg has plenty of courts, although not in the center of town. The best tennis clubs are **Tennisklub Salzburg** (✉ Ignaz-Rieder-Kai 3, ☎ 0662/622403–0), which you can reach on Bus 6 or 49; **Salzburger Tenniscourts-Süd** (✉ Berchtesgardner Str. 35, ☎ 0662/820326), which you can reach via Bus 5; **Tennispoint Anif** (✉ Anif, ☎ 06246/72963); and **Tennishalle Liefering** (✉ Unter der Leiten/Lieferinger Spitz, ☎ 0662/432197), which you can reach on Bus 29.

SHOPPING

For a small city, Salzburg has a wide range of stores. The specialties are traditional clothing, like lederhosen and loden coats; jewelry; glassware; handicrafts; confectionery; dolls in native costume; Christmas decorations; sports equipment; silk flowers; and *Gewürzsträussl,* a bundle of whole spices bunched and arranged to look like a bouquet of flowers. Stores are open weekdays 8–6 and Saturday 8–noon. Many stores stay open until 5 on the first Saturday of the month and on Saturdays during the festival and before Christmas. Some supermarkets stay open until 8 on Thursday or Friday. Only shops in the railway station, the airport and near the general hospital are open on Sunday.

Shopping Streets

The most fashionable specialty stores and gift shops are to be found along Getreidegasse, Judengasse, and around Residenzplatz. Linzer Gasse, across the river, is less crowded and good for more practical items. There are also interesting antiques shops and jewelry workshops in the medieval buildings along Steingasse and in the Goldgasse.

Specialty Stores

Antiques

Along Gstättengasse you'll find, among others, **Kirchmayer** (✉ No. 3, ☎ 0662/842219), **Peter Paul Burges** (✉ No. 23, ☎ 0662/848115), **Schöppl** (✉ No. 5, ☎ 0662/842154), and **Marianne Reuter** (✉ No. 9, ☎ 0662/842136). For an amazing assortment of secondhand curiosities, try **Trödlerstube** (✉ Linzer Gasse 50, ☎ 0662/871453). An annual antiques fair takes place from Palm Sunday to Easter Monday in the state rooms of the Residenz.

Confectionery

If you're looking for the kind of *Mozartkugeln* (chocolate marzipan confections) you can't buy at home, try the two stores that claim to have discovered them: **Konditorei Schatz** (✉ Getreidegasse 3, Schatz passageway, ☏ 0662/842792) and **Konditorei Fürst** (✉ Brodgasse 13, ☏ 0662/843759–0).

Galleries

Salzburg is a good place to buy modern paintings, and there are several galleries on Sigmund-Haffner-Gasse. One of the best known, which also has an exhibition gallery plus a tiny coffee bar, is **Galerie Welz** (✉ Sigmund-Haffner-Gasse 16, ☏ 0662/841771–0).

Glass

Fritz Kreis (✉ Sigmund-Haffner-Gasse 14, ☏ 0662/841768) sells ceramics, wood carvings, handmade glass objects, and so on. The markets on the Universitätsplatz sell Gewürzsträussl, and at Christmas there is a special Advent market on the Domplatz.

Jewelry

For exquisite costume jewelry and antique pieces, go to **Anton Koppenwallner** (✉ Klampferergasse 2, ☏ 0662/841298), **Paul Koppenwallner** (✉ Alter Markt 7, ☏ 0662/842617; ✉ Universitätspl. 4, ☏ 0662/841449), or **Gerhard Lährm** (✉ Getreidegasse 27, ☏ 0662/843477–0), which is somewhat more expensive. Explore the **Schmuckpassage** (Jeweler's Passageway), which joins buildings between Universitätsplatz and Getreidegasse.

Men's Clothing

Men's outfitters are everywhere; the best are **Boss Herrenmoden** (✉ Schwarzstr. 12 ☏ 0662/874716), **Peter's Peter Bayer** (✉ Griesgasse 27, ☏ 0662/842213), and **Resmann M Exclusiv** (✉ Getreidegasse 25, ☏ 0662/843214–0).

Traditional Clothing

Salzburger Heimatwerk (✉ Residenzpl. 9, ☏ 0662/844119) has clothing, fabrics, ceramics, and local handicrafts at good prices. **Lanz** (✉ Schwarzstr. 4, ☏ 0662/874272) sells a wide selection of long dirndls, silk costumes, and loden coats. **Madl am Grünmarkt** (✉ Universitätspl. 12, ☏ 0662/845457) has more flair and elegance in their traditional designs. A more specialized place, selling wool and silk shawls and chamois-leather skirts and waistcoats, is **Wacht** (✉ Griesgasse 7, ☏ 0662/841622). For an enormous range of leather goods, some made to order, try **Jahn-Markl** (✉ Residenzpl. 3, ☏ 0662/842610).

Women's Clothing

If dirndls are not your style, try **Lady** (✉ Schwarzstr. 4, ☏ 0662/871247; ✉ Sigmund-Haffner-Gasse 6, ☏ 0662/840156), **La Femme** (✉ Hildmannpl. 1a, ☏ 0662/845203), **Opferkuch** (✉ Universitätspl. 9, ☏ 0662/842611) and **Resmann Couture** (✉ Rudolfskai 6/Getreidegasse 15, ☏ 0662/841213–0).

SALZBURG A TO Z

Arriving and Departing

By Bus

American Express (✉ Kärntnerstr. 21–23, 1010 Vienna, ☏ 0222/515–40–0, FAX 0222/515–40–70) and **Vienna Sightseeing Tours** (✉ Stelzhammergasse 4/11, 1030 Vienna, ☏ 0222/712–4683-0, FAX 0222/712–4683–77) run one-day bus trips Tuesday, Thursday, and Saturday to Salzburg from Vienna; the cost, AS1,190, includes a tour of the city. On Sunday, Wednesday, and Friday, **Cityrama/Gray Line** (✉ Börsegasse 1, 1010 Vienna, ☎ 0222/534–13–0, FAX 0222/534–13–22) offers a similar tour. The Monday and Friday tours of **Citytouring Vienna** (✉ Penzinger Str. 46, ☎ 0222/894–1417–0, FAX 0222/894–3239) include lunch and are slightly more expensive.

By Car

The fastest routes to Salzburg are the autobahns. From Vienna (320 kilometers, or 198 miles), take A1; from Munich (150 kilometers, or 93 miles), A8 (in Germany it's also E11); from Italy, A10. The only advantage to having a car in Salzburg is that you can get out of the city for short excursions or for cheaper accommodation. The Old City on both sides of the river is a pedestrian zone (except for taxis), and the rest of the city, with its narrow, one-way streets, is a driver's nightmare. A park/ride system covering the major freeway exits is being developed, and there are several underground garages throughout the city.

By Plane

Salzburg Airport (✉ Innsbrucker Bundesstr. 96, ☎ 0662/8580; flight information, ☎ 0662/8580–251), 4 kilometers (2½ miles) west of the city center, is Austria's second-largest international airport. There are direct flights from London and other European cities, but not from the United States. Americans can fly to Munich and take the 90-minute train ride to Salzburg. Alternatively, you can take a transfer bus from or to the Munich airport; in Salzburg the contact is **Salzburger Mietwagenservice** (✉ Ignaz-Harrer-Str. 79a, ☎ 0622/8161–0, FAX 0622/436324).

Taxis are the easiest way to get downtown; the ride costs around AS150 and takes about 20 minutes. City Bus 77, which goes by the airport every 15 minutes, takes you to the train station (about 20 minutes), where you change to Bus 1, 5, 6, 51, or 55 for the city center. Alternatively, you can take Bus 77 four stops to Aiglhof (look for a Mobil gas station on the corner), cross the road, and take Bus 29 (every 10–15 minutes) to the center of town.

By Train

You can get to Salzburg by rail from most European cities, arriving at **Salzburg Hauptbahnhof** (✉ Südtirolerpl., ☎ 0662/8887–0), a 20-minute walk from the center of town in the direction of Mirabellplatz. A taxi should take about 10 minutes and cost AS75. Train information is available by phone (☎ 0662/1717); don't be put off by the recorded message in German—eventually, you will be put through to a real person who should be able to speak English. You can buy tickets at any travel agency or at the station. The bus station and the suburban railroad station are across the street. Major building works are still in progress in front of the station and hamper access.

Getting Around

The Old City, composed of several interconnecting squares and narrow streets, is best seen on foot. An excellent bus service covers the rest of the city. A tourist map (available for AS10 from tourist offices in Mozartplatz and the train station) shows all bus routes and stops; there's also a color-coded graphic public transport network map that's free, so you should have no problem getting around. Virtually all buses and trolleybuses (O-Bus) run via Mirabellplatz and/or Hanuschplatz.

By Bicycle

Salzburg is fast developing a network of bike paths as part of its effort to get cars out of the city. A detailed bicycle map with suggested tours (about AS70–AS80) will help you get around. Bikes can be rented year-round at the **Salzburg Hauptbahnhof** railway station (✉ Südtirolerpl., Counter 3, ☎ 0662/8887–5427) for AS90 per day (AS50 if you have a train ticket for that day) or weekdays for AS360. You can rent a bike by the day or the week from **Zweirad Frey** (✉ Willibald-Hauthaler-Str. 4, ☎ 0662/431682) and, most cheaply, from **Albert Hager** (✉ Fürstenallee 39, ☎ 0662/823723, FAX 0662/829623). Also check **Top-Bike Handels-OEG** (✉ Aribonenstr. 18, ☎ 0662/862529, FAX 0662/434300–0) which is considerably more expensive but will deliver and pick up the bike. It's best to call and reserve in advance; you will need to leave your passport or a deposit.

By Horse-Drawn Carriage

Fiakers, carrying up to four people, will show you around the Old City for AS350 for 20–25 minutes and AS680 for 50 minutes. They are found on the Residenzplatz (☎ 0662/844772).

By Bus or Trolleybus

Single tickets bought from the driver cost AS19. Special multiple-use tickets, available at tobacconists (*Tabak-Trafik*), ticket offices (main office, ✉ Griesgasse 21, ☎ 0662/620551), and tourist offices, are much cheaper. You can buy five single tickets for AS15 each (not available at tourist offices), or transferable 24-hour tickets at AS32 each.

By Taxi

There are taxi stands all over the city; for a radio cab, call 0662/8111. Taxi fares start at AS30. Limousines can be hired for AS600 per hour (three-hour minimum) from Salzburg Panorama Tours (☎ 0662/883211–0 or 0662/874029, FAX 0662/871618).

Opening and Closing Times

Banks are open weekdays 8:00–12:30 and 2–4:30. You can change money at the railway station in summer daily 7 AM–10 PM, and in winter daily 7:30 AM–9 PM.

Contacts and Resources

Consulates

The U.S. consular agency (✉ Herbert-von-Karajan-Pl. 1, ☎ 0662/848776, FAX 0662/849777) is open Monday, Wednesday, and Friday 9–noon. The U.K. consular office (✉ Alter Markt 4, ☎ 0662/848133) is open weekdays 9–noon.

Emergencies

Emergency numbers are 133 for the **police,** 144 for an **ambulance,** 122 for the **fire department.** The main hospital is **the Landeskrankenhaus** (✉ Müllner Hauptstr. 48, ☎ 0662/44820), just past the Augustinian monastery heading out of town. If you need a doctor or dentist, call the **Ärtztekammer für Salzburg** (✉ Schrannengasse 2, ☎ 0662/871327–0); for emergency service on weekends and holidays, call the **Ärzte-Bereitschaftsdienst Salzburg-Stadt** (✉ Paris Lodron Str. 8A, ☎ 0662/141).

English-Language Bookstores

American Discount (✉ Alter Markt 1, ☎ 0662/845640), the only English-language bookstore in Salzburg, concentrates on popular paperbacks and magazines. You can, however, find some books in English in most good bookstores. **Hintermayer** (✉ Imbergstr. 23, ☎ 0662/875754–1), across the footbridge from Mozartpl., sells discount paperbacks in English.

Guided Tours

Because the Old City is largely a pedestrian zone, bus tours do little more than take you past the major sights. You would do better seeing the city on foot unless your time is really limited.

ORIENTATION

Salzburg Sightseeing Tours (✉ Am Mirabellpl. 2, ☎ 0662/881616, FAX 0662/882120), **Salzburg Panorama Tours/Gray Line** (✉ Mirabellpl./St. Andrä Church, ☎ 0662/883211–21 or 873646, FAX 0662/871618) and **Bob's Special Tours** (✉ Chiemseegasse 1/Kaigasse, ☎ 0662/849511–0, FAX 0662/849512) conduct 1½–2-hour city tours. The desk clerks at most hotels will book for you and arrange hotel pickup. Depending on the number of people, the tour will be in either a bus or a minibus; if it's the former, a short walking tour is included, since large buses can't enter the Old City. Tours briefly cover the major sights in Salzburg, including Mozart's Birthplace, the festival halls, the major squares, the churches, and the palaces at Hellbrunn and Leopoldskron. Depending on the operator, tours leave daily at 9, 9:30, 11, noon, 1, 2, 3 and 4 and cost AS220. Salzburg Sightseeing Tours also runs a shorter city tour daily at 10, 11, 1, 3, and 4, taking about 1 hour and costing AS170 excluding entrance fees to the various attractions.

SOUND OF MUSIC TOURS

The *Sound of Music* tour has been a staple of visits to Salzburg for the past 20 years and is still a special experience. All tour operators conduct one. The bus company actually featured in the film, Albus, offers a 3½-hour tour departing daily, which includes such sights as Anif Castle, Mondsee Church, and the little summerhouse in the gardens of Hellbrun—where Liesl and Rolf sang "I am 16 going on 17" (✉ Mirabellpl. 2, ☎ 0662/881616, FAX 0662/633790). Some travelers say the most personal approach is found with **Bob's Special Tours** (✉ Chiemseegasse 1/Kaigasse, ☎ 0662/849511–0, FAX 0662/849512). The four-hour minibus tour (AS300) begins with the major city sights, takes in outlying Leopoldskron—the lakeside terrace of this mansion was recreated for the film; this famous house is now owned by the Salzburg Seminar (whose headquarters are in Middlebury, Vermont)—and the Nonnberg convent, and explores the surrounding mountains, accompanied by music from the film. The twice-daily tour includes a stop at a lead-crystal workshop and toboggan-style slide rides in summer.

The Sound of Music dinner show (May–September, Thursday–Tuesday at 7) in the K+K StieglKeller restaurant (☞ Dining and Lodging, *above*) is immensely popular and performed with enthusiasm. Your hotel will have details, or call 0662/842681 for reservations. Bob's Special Tours also runs a 4-hour minibus tour (AS300) into the Bavarian mountains for a view of Hitler's Eagle's Nest, a one-hour stop in Berchtesgaden, and weekdays in summer, weather permitting, for AS50 a picnic in Untersberg Nature Park. Tours depart at 9 AM and at 2 PM.

WALKING

The tourist office's folder "Salzburg—The Art of Taking It All In at a Glance" describes a self-guided one-day walking tour that's marked on a map.

Pharmacies

In general, pharmacies are open weekdays 8–12:30 and 2:30–6, Saturday 8–noon. When they're closed, the name and location of a pharmacy that's open are posted on the door.

Travel Agencies

American Express (☎ 0662/8080–0, FAX 0662/8080–9) is next to the tourist office at Mozartplatz 5–7. **Thomas Cook** can be found under the name **Wagons-Lit Travel** (✉ Münzgasse 1, ☎ 0662/842755–0, FAX 0662/842755–5) in the Old City.

Visitor Information

The **Salzburg City Tourist Office** (✉ Auerspergstr. 7, A–5024 Salzburg, ☎ 0662/88987–0, FAX 0662/88987–32) handles written and telephone requests for information. You can get maps, brochures, and information in person from **Information Mozartplatz** in the center of the Old City (✉ Mozartpl. 5, ☎ 0662/847568) and from the **Railway Station** (✉ Platform 2A, ☎ 0662/871712).

All the major highways into town have their own well-marked information centers at the following addresses. **Salzburg-Mitte** (✉ Münchner Bundesstr. 1, ☎ 0662/432228), open April–October, daily 9–7, and November–March, Monday–Saturday 11–5. **Salzburg-Süd** (✉ Alpenstr. 67, ☎ 0662/620966), open November–March, Monday–Saturday 11–5, and April–October, daily 9–7. **Salzburg-West-Airport** (✉ Innsbrucker Bundesstr. 95, ☎ 0662/852451), open April, May, September, and October, Monday–Saturday 9–6, and June–August, daily 9–7. **Salzburg-Nord** (✉ Autobahn, Kasern service facility, ☎ 0662/663220), open March–June and October, Monday–Saturday 9–7, and July–September, daily 9–7.

8 Carinthia

Carinthia could be labeled "Extract of Austria" since it contains a greater variety of Austria's charms than any other province. Routine-numb Viennese dream of its Austrian Riviera, where waterside gaiety emanates from such resorts as Maria Wörth and Velden; the scenic cities of Klagenfurt and Villach beckon; and art treasures await—Spittal's Porcia palace, Gurk's great romanesque cathedral, and the model for the Gothic castle in Walt Disney's Snow White—*Fortress Hochosterwitz.*

By George Hamilton

Updated by Angela Walker

IN 1877 THE GERMAN COMPOSER Johannes Brahms wrote of an unexpected holiday he spent in Carinthia: ". . . the first day was so lovely that I determined to stay for a second, and the second was so lovely that I have decided to stay here for the time being." Little has changed since.

If you enter Carinthia along the main Vienna-Klagenfurt road between Bad Einöd and Friesach, you will be taking one of the main gateways into Austria's sunniest province. The broad, open countryside you will cross from there to the Wörther See—Austria's warmest lake and mecca of sun-worshippers—is only one aspect of Carinthia. If you approach the province from any other direction, you will get a very different impression—that of an area walled in by towering mountains, surmountable only through a few, mostly high-lying passes. This contrast is typical of the enticing variety of Carinthia. It has Austria's highest peak—the famous Grossglockner (which rises to more than 11,000 feet)—architectural treasures such as the Gothic Gurk Cathedral, Renaissance gems like Schloss Porcia in Spittal, and Baroque beauties everywhere. Then there is also the waterside gaiety of such resorts as Maria Wörth and Velden, set within the pleasure-land that is the Austrian Riveria. Carinthia has the best summer weather in all of Austria, which usually means reservations need to be booked well in advance for such towns.

Klagenfurt is the official seat of the government, but over the course of time, Villach, an equally attractive small city, has emerged as the "secret" capital, especially when the spirit of carnival captivates Austria; the Villach Carnival takes over during the week before Lent. Its costume parades, floats, parodies, and cabarets are now televised annually for international consumption. Also, a "Carinthian Summer" festival is held here in July and August.

Pleasures and Pastimes

Bicycling

Thanks to the many hills and mountains that crisscross the province, there are numerous ups and downs for Carinthia's backcountry pedalers. Roads often seem to never stop climbing, and the incline seems to grow with every inch. On the other hand, if some roads seem to scale the heights for 60% of their run, the second half is—*danke Gött!*—60% downhill. If you're not a serious biker, there are several lakeside paths ideal for a leisurely hour or two of cycling while gazing out across the water—and, even better, hopping in for a swim. You can rent bikes at lake resorts and local train stations.

Dining

Thanks to the region's many lakes and rivers, this is fish country. Carp, pike, crawfish (when in season, which is rather short), and, best of all, various trout are the best bets. Austrian brook trout and rainbow trout are delicious. The most popular way of serving them is "blue," the whole fish boiled in a court bouillon and accompanied by drawn butter. Or try it Müllerin—sautéed in butter to a crisp brown. Wonderful! In summer try cold smoked trout for a delicate entrée. Through much of Carinthia you'll discover that, other than simple *Gasthäuser*, pizzerias, and the ubiquitous Chinese, most restaurants are not independent establishments but belong to country inns. When a hotel dining operation is especially noteworthy, we flag it by including it under the heading of "Dining and Lodging." Prices for meals include taxes and a service charge but not the customary small additional tip of 5%–7%.

CATEGORY	COST*
$$$$	over AS500
$$$	AS300–AS500
$$	AS200–AS300
$	under AS200

**per person for a typical three-course meal, with a glass of house wine*

The Great Outdoors

FISHING

Having no seacoast, Austria must content its fishing aficionados with the freshwater varieties. In Carinthia, the Ossiacher See, Wörther See, and Faaker See all have excellent fishing. The crystal clear, warm waters provide an excellent breeding ground for fish, but you need to get a license from the local tourist office before you head out with your rod and reel—many of the fishing streams actually belong to the *Gemeinde,* the local rural authorities.

HIKING

Like the rest of the country, the hills and mountains scattered across Carinthia have a wealth of hiking opportunities (bookstores in your resort will have hiking maps of the area). Local tourist offices also publish maps and suggested itineraries, including treks to the many castle ruins which dot the landscape, and more leisurely strolls on well-marked lakeside paths. If you are planning high-altitude hiking, remember that cable cars tend to be closed for repairs out of season. Always take protection against the rain, an extra layer of clothing, and tell your hotel desk where you are going. A nice surprise: Rain in the valleys may give way to sunshine above 3,000 feet.

SKIING

Compared to the chic skiing destinations of St. Anton and Kitzbühel, Carinthia offers good terrain and facilities with much lower prices. The skiing season in the mountain area lasts from December to March, while high up in the Hohe Tauern it extends to late spring and even early June, for the Grossglockner glacier ski racing. Carinthia has slopes of all degrees of difficulty, from the gentler ones for novices to the seriously challenging for the experienced Alpine skier—since the mighty Grossglockner backs into the region, some ski runs even feature vertical drops of over 4,000 feet. When the altitude gets this high, the slopes are treeless. For more scenic runs, head for Villach and its environs, particularly the slopes of the Kanzelhöhe, which feature marvelous views of the Karawanken range. There are at least twenty ski towns in Carinthia. To determine which is best for you, contact the Austrian Tourist Board. Whether raw beginner or downhill racer, chances are you will ski down slopes of unforgettable loveliness.

WATER SPORTS

In winter, Austrians love to ski; in summer, they take to sail-skiing—just one of the many reasons they flock to the Carinthian lakes during warm weather. The Austrian Riviera resorts are a paradise for water sports—from windsurfing to sailing—with lakes that have public beaches and water pure enough to drink. Swimmers delight in the late summer water temperatures, which can reach 25°C (75°F)—due to the existence of subterranean thermal springs. Most beaches also have wading or supervised areas for small children. To avoid the crowds, book at a hotel that has its own private beach—most do.

Lodging

Accommodations range from luxurious lakeside resorts to small country inns or even guest houses without private baths. Room rates include taxes and service and almost always breakfast, except in the most expensive hotels, but it is wise to ask. When comparing prices, note that many hotels in the resort towns require half board (one meal in addition to breakfast). The larger hotels offer a choice of menu. When staying two or three days or longer, it is customary to leave a small additional tip (AS20) for the chambermaid.

CATEGORY	COST*
$$$$	over AS1,500
$$$	AS1,000–AS1,500
$$	AS700–AS1,000
$	under AS700

**per person for a standard double room with bath, including service and tax*

Exploring Carinthia

Carinthia's biggest draw is its chain of narrow, beautiful lakes, which run from east to west across the southern half of the province and comprise the heart of the Austrian Riviera—from the fashionable Wörther See to smaller spa towns where chic patrons pamper themselves with water cures. The province is ringed by mountains and castles perched precariously on mountain peaks. For history and architecture buffs, there's lots to discover from the medieval town of Friesach to the walled town of Gmünd to Celtic-Roman excavations.

Great Itineraries

You can get a taste of Carinthia in a weekend, or savor it all during a week-long stay. Our exploration of Carinthia begins with a visit to Villach, then a drive along the Ossiacher See and through the Gurktal up to the medieval town of Friesach, taking in a Disneyesque castle and a Roman excavation on our way to Klagenfurt. We then tackle the Austrian Riviera, begining in Klagenfurt, traveling a bit of both sides of the fashionable Wörther See, and making a loop by the Faakersee and the Feistritzer-Stausee back to Klagenfurt. Our last itinerary starts in Villach and goes northward to Spittal and the walled town of Gmünd, taking in the Millstätter See, and detouring to Bad Kleinkircheim—a ski area that is centered on a good spa town, giving the sports enthusiast the best of both worlds.

Numbers in the text correspond to numbers in the margin and on the Carinthia map.

IF YOU HAVE 3 DAYS

If your time is limited, head to the Austrian Riviera, balm to travelers who wish to simply sun and soak. Start off with a visit to the provincial capital **Klagenfurt** ①, before heading out to the most popular lake, the Wörther See. You can make stops along the way at resorts such as **Krumpendorf** ②, **Pörtschach** ③ before spending the night in chic **Velden** ⑤. For the next day and night, head to **Maria Wörth** ④, with its postcard-perfect spired chapel overlooking the lake. On your final day, take in the towns of Maria Gail, **Egg** ⑥, and **Viktring** ⑦, with its Cistercian Monastery dating back to 1142.

IF YOU HAVE 5 DAYS

The best place to start your trip is to take a day to explore **Spittal an der Drau** ⑧, the principal town in Upper Carinthia. After an overnight stay, head for the medieval-walled town of **Gmünd** ⑨ and continue on to the resorts on the Millstätter See, with your next night spent at **Millstatt** ⑩. The Roman baths at **Bad Kleinkirchheim** ⑪ are a treat for tired muscles on your third day; spend your third night at one of the spa's friendly chalet-style hotels. On your fourth day pass the quiet resort town of Feld am See on the Feldsee before pulling into

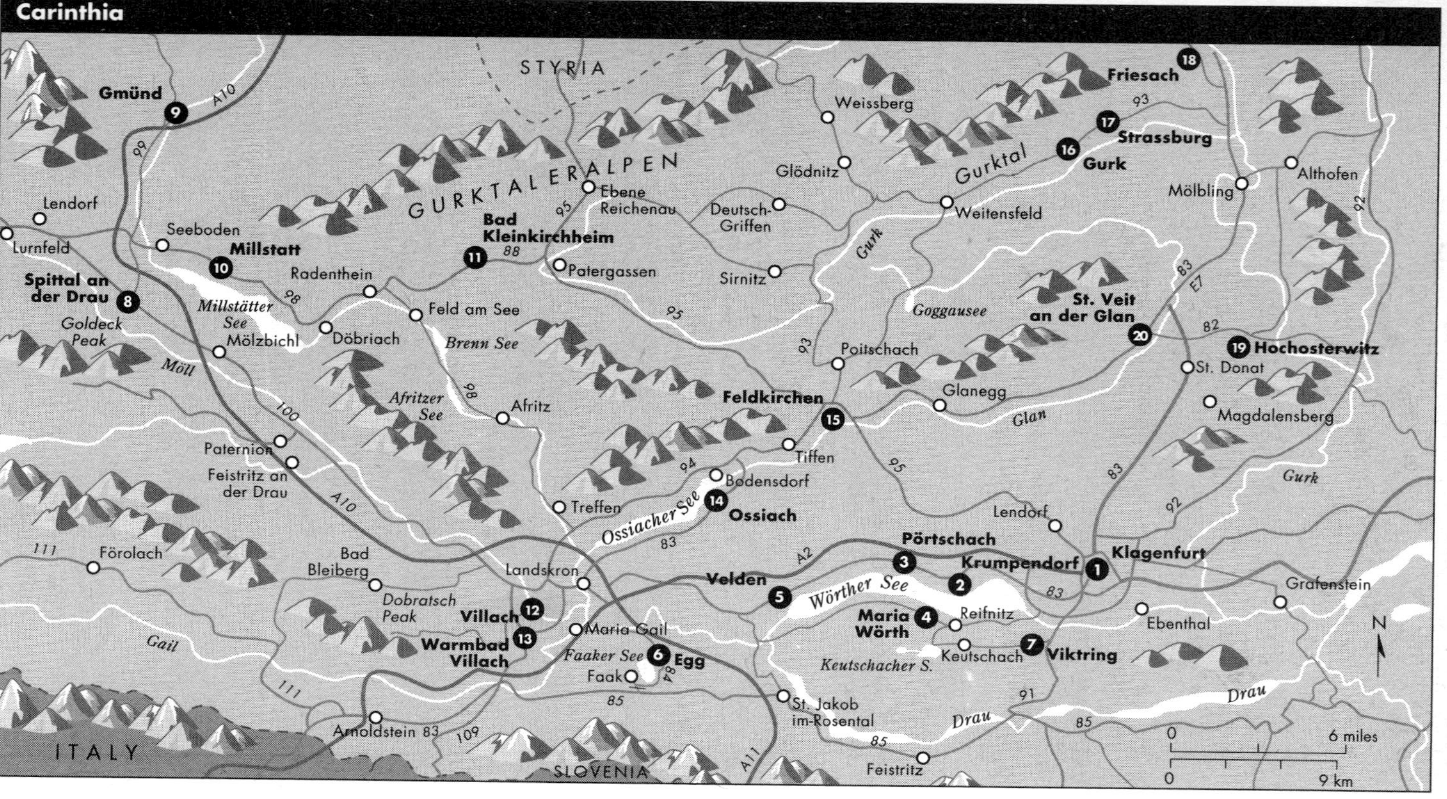
Carinthia
STYRIA
GURKTALER ALPEN
SLOVENIA
ITALY
Gmünd
9
Spittal an der Drau
8
Millstatt
10
Bad Kleinkirchheim
11
Villach
12
Warmbad Villach
13
Ossiach
14
Feldkirchen
15
Gurk
16
Strassburg
17
Friesach
18
Hochosterwitz
19
St. Veit an der Glan
20
Klagenfurt
1
Krumpendorf
2
Pörtschach
3
Maria Wörth
4
Velden
5
Egg
6
Viktring
7
Lendorf
Lurnfeld
Seeboden
Goldeck Peak
Millstätter See
Mölzbichl
Radenthein
Döbriach
Feld am See
Brenn See
Afritzer See
Afritz
Paternion
Feistritz an der Drau
Möll
Förolach
Gail
Bad Bleiberg
Dobratsch Peak
Arnoldstein
Landskron
Maria Gail
Faaker See
Faak
Treffen
Ossiacher See
Bodensdorf
Tiffen
Patergassen
Ebene Reichenau
Deutsch-Griffen
Sirnitz
Glödnitz
Weissberg
Weitensfeld
Gurktal
Gurk
Poitschach
Goggausee
Glanegg
Glan
Wörther See
Keutschacher S.
St. Jakob im-Rosental
Feistritz
Reifnitz
Keutschach
Drau
Lendorf
Ebenthal
Grafenstein
Magdalensberg
St. Donat
Mölbling
Althofen
N
0
6 miles
0
9 km
A10
A11
A2
E7
83
85
88
91
92
93
94
95
98
99
100
109
111

Villach ⑫—one of Carinthia's most historic cities—for your last night and day.

IF YOU HAVE 7 DAYS

Start your visit in **Villach** ⑫, nestled on the banks of the Drau River, wandering the meandering lanes of the Alte Stadt section. Spend the night in the city or head for the nearby spa of **Warmbad Villach** ⑬; the next day, relax with a massage or soak in the soothing hot springs, then check out the imposing ruins of Landskron Castle. Your third day is spent enjoying the resort town of **Ossiach** ⑭ and its 11th-century monastery where the soft sounds of music waft through summer nights during the annual music festival. Spend two nights there, for you'll want to get an early start on the day's full schedule of sightseeing attractions, including the medieval city of **Feldkirchen** ⑮, some possible detours along the way at the picturesque villages of Sirnitz, Deutsch-Griffen, Glodnitz and Weitensfeld, the massive Romanesque cathedral at **Gurk** ⑯, and a stop in **Strassburg** ⑰, formerly the seat of the bishopric. Pull into **Friesach** ⑱, where it's easy to imagine Lords and Ladies descended from the Middle Ages living in this village, for your fifth evening. A good base for touring, spend your fifth night back in Friesach. On the sixth day discover **St. Veit an der Glan** ⑳, Carinthia's capital until the 16th century, then move on to the amazing castle fortress of **Hochosterwitz** ⑲. For your last evening and day, return to **Klagenfurt** ①.

When to Tour Carinthia

If you wish to see the province in its best festive dress of blue and emerald lakes, framed by dark green wooded hills and rocky peaks, and also do some swimming, you should come between mid-May and early October. Early spring when the colors are purest and the crowds not yet in evidence, or fall, are perhaps the better times for quiet sightseeing.

ALONG THE AUSTRIAN RIVIERA

Klagenfurt and the Southern Lakes

Because of the resorts, the beautiful people, and the emphasis on dawn-to-dawn indulgences, the region surrounding Carinthia's pleasure lakes has been nicknamed Austria's Riviera. The most popular of the *"Funf Schwesterseen"* (Five Sister Lakes) is certainly the central lake, the Wörther See, sprinkled with such resorts as Krumpendorf, Velden, and Maria Wörth—once called the quietest village in all Austria, and subsequently overrun by hordes of tourists. The Wörther See is 17 kilometers (10½ miles) long and the warmest of Carinthia's large lakes; people swim here beginning in early May. A great way to see the lake is from one of the boats that run from end to end, making frequent stops along the way. Try to book passage on the SS *Thalia,* built in 1908, and now beautifully restored. You can follow the north shore to Velden by way of Pörtschach, bubbling with celebrities and excitement, or swing south and take the less traveled scenic route; in any case, you should visit picturesque Maria Wörth on the south shore.

Klagenfurt

❶ *329 km (192 mi) southwest of Vienna, 209 km (130 mi) southeast of Salzburg.*

Klagenfurt became the provincial capital in 1518, so most of what you see today dates from the 16th-century or later. And while Klagenfurt itself may not pulse with excitement, it's an excellent base for excursions to the rest of Carinthia. You can hardly overlook the *Lindwurm,* Klagenfurt's famous emblematic dragon with a twice-curled tail, which adorns the fountain on Neuer Platz (new square); the usual dragon tail was given a realistic undertone when the fossilized cranium of a prehistoric rhinoceros was found near Klagenfurt. Near the dragon square is the longish **Alter Platz,** the oldest square of the city and the center of a pleasant pedestrian area with tiny streets and alleys. South of the Neuer Platz is the **Domkirche,** or cathedral, completed as a Protestant church in 1591, given over to the Jesuits and reconsecrated in 1604. The 18th-century side-altar painting of St. Ignatius by Paul Troger is typical of his transparent style. One of the most notable sights of the city is the **Landhaus** (district government headquarters), with its towers and court with arcaded stairways. It was completed in 1591 and at the time formed a corner of the city wall. The only interior on view is a winner: the dramatic **Grosser Wappensaal** (hall of arms) contains 665 coats of arms of the communities of Carinthia and a stirring rendition of the Fürstenstein investiture ceremony portayed by Fromiller, the most important Carinthian painter of the Baroque period. ✉ *Alter Pl.,* ☎ *0463/57757. ß10AS.* ⏲ *Apr.–Sept., weekdays 9–12:30 and 1–5.*

From Klagenfurt, take the Villacher Strasse (Route 83) rather than the autobahn to the Wörther See, Austria's great summer-resort area. You'll pass by the extensive **Minimundus** park, a great place for children, with over 150 1:25-scale models of such structures as the White House, Independence Hall, the Statue of Liberty, the Eiffel Tower, and St. Peter's Basilica. ✉ *Villacher Str. 241,* ☎ *0463/21194–0.* *AS80.* ⏲ *Mid- to late Apr. and early–mid-Oct., daily 9–5; May, June, and Sept., daily 9–6; July and Aug., Sun.–Tues., Thurs., and Fri. 8–7, Wed. and Sat. 8* AM*–9* PM*; folklore performance July and Aug., Wed. at 8; live big band and jazz concerts Sat. at 8.*

OFF THE BEATEN PATH

PYRAMIDENKOGEL – On the banks of the Keutschacher lake, about 8 kilometers (5 miles) west of Klagenfurt, lies the town of Keutschach, with the Romanesque church of St. George, a Baroque castle and an 800-year-old linden tree. A winding 5-kilometer (3-mile) road ascends to the ★ observation tower atop the 2,790-foot Pyramidenkogel; on a clear day you can see out over half of Carinthia.

Dining and Lodging

$$$$ ★ ✕ **À la Carte.** This small and unpretentious restaurant in the center of the city has catapulted almost overnight into Austria's top ranks. Co-owner and chef Harald Fritzer trained under several of Europe's best cooks. Ask for help in translating the handwritten menu, and don't overlook the superb fish. The six-course evening feast can be trimmed to your appetite. Wines come from Austria, France, and Italy. ✉ *Khevenhüllerstr. 2,* ☎ *0463/516651. Jacket and tie. AE. Closed Sun., Mon., holidays, Easter wk, and mid-July–mid-Aug.*

$$$$ ✕ **Präsent–Lido am See.** The gorgeous setting, with a view out over the Wörther See, is the backdrop for some of the areas's best dining. Fish is the obvious choice, but don't overlook lamb chops, regional specialties, or such less predictable items as rabbit. Dishes are seasonal, depending on what's fresh in the market that day. The wine list features Austrian vintages but includes a good Bordelais selection as well. ✉ *Friedelstrand 1,* ☎ *0463/261723,* FAX *0463/262453. AE, DC, MC, V. Closed Tues. Sept.–June.*

$$ ★ ✕ **Peterwirt.** In Walddorf, about 6 kilometers (4 miles) north of Klagenfurt on Route 83, you'll find one of the better-kept restaurant secrets. This is country cooking at its best, with no pretensions. You won't need to ask for recommendations—there's no written menu; choose from such Austrian standards as roast chicken and beef roulade. ✉

Klagenfurt/Walddorf 1, ☏ 0463/42646. No credit cards. Closed 2 wks in May and Nov.

$$$ ★ **Musil.** Modern hotel amenities have been tastefully incorporated into a 15th-century nobleman's palace in the center of town, and the elegance is beautifully preserved. The style is personal and intimate, and each room is different. Decor ranges from overblown Baroque to elegant Biedermeier and simple Austrian rural. Rooms open onto a series of interior balconies. The popular café serves cakes from the hotel's own bakery. The candlelit restaurant is good; try the game in season. The hotel is a member of the Romantik Hotel group. You'll need to book a couple of months ahead. ✉ *10.-Oktober Str. 14, A–9010, ☏ 0463/511660–0, FAX 0463/511660–4. 15 rooms. Restaurant, bar, café. AE, DC, MC, V.*

$$ ★ **Moser-Verdino.** Renovations have kept pace with the times at this striking pink-and-white hostelry, the city's leading hotel for 100 years. The Art Deco design carries over into some of the rooms, no two of which are alike. The café is nearly always full and is a good spot for a snack. ✉ *Domgasse 2, A–9010, ☏ 0463/57878, FAX 0463/516765. 74 rooms. Bar, café, sauna. AE, DC, MC, V.*

$$ ★ **Sandwirt.** This centrally located hotel, incorporated into a 17th-century town house, has large rooms with high ceilings and traditional, comfortable furnishings. The family management is hospitable and friendly. The hotel is now part of the Best Western group. ✉ *Pernhartgasse 9, A–9010, ☏ 0463/56209, FAX 0463/514322. 40 rooms. Restaurant. AE, DC, MC, V.*

$ ★ **Wörthersee.** At the end of the lake, on its own beach, this glowing yellow mansion with fancy woodwork, towers, and balconies, will remind you of the era of the grand hotels. The rooms are modern and comfortable; the preferred ones overlook the lake. The restaurant has been restyled along the lines of an informal "Heuriger" weinstube. ✉ *Villacher Str. 338, A–9010, ☏ 0463/21158–0, FAX 0463/21158–8. 41 rooms. Restaurant, bar, café, sauna. AE, DC, MC, V.*

Nightlife and the Arts

Opera and operetta are performed at the Stadttheater in Klagenfurt year-round. For details and tickets, contact **Stadttheater Klagenfurt** (✉ Theaterpl. 4, A–9020, ☏ 0463/54064, FAX 0463/504663). The box office is open September–June, Tuesday–Saturday 9–noon and 4–6, and July and August, Tuesday–Saturday 9–noon and 5–7.

The chic Klagenfurt crowd gathers at **Scotch Club** (✉ Pfarrpl. 20, ☏ 0463/54097), currently the city's best disco. For a true after-hours scene in Klagenfurt, head for the Pfarrplatz/Herrengasse area, where you'll find a number of intimate bars and cafés.

Outdoor Activites and Sports

BICYCLING

You can rent bicycles at the Klagenfurt main station (☏ 0463/1700 or 0463/5811–0). Many visitors enjoy biking trips to the nearby Wörther See.

GOLF

Golfplatz Klagenfurt-Wörthersee at Schloss Seltenheim (☏ 0463/40223–0, FAX 0463/40223–20) recently expanded from 9 holes to a full 36-hole course. The greens fee is AS450, and the club is open March–October.

TENNIS

If you're in the mood to take to the courts check out Tenniscenter Allround (✉ Welzeneggerstr., ☏ 0463/31571) or Tennisplätze M. Schoklitsch (✉ Feschnigstr. 209, ☏ 0463/41140).

Krumpendorf

2 *10 km (6½ mi) west of Klagenfurt.*

The first town on the north side of the Wörther See is less chic and far less pretentious than the other resorts, but pleasant all the same, particularly for those families seeking to escape the higher prices and singles invasions of other areas. The resort's water sports and down-home atmosphere appeal to families.

Lodging

$ ★ **Schloss Hallegg.** Just east of Krumpendorf, a small road heading north leads to an early 13th-century castle, tucked away on the edge of a nature preserve above the lake. Now adapted as a hotel, its rooms are spacious and comfortable. You'll get breakfast only, but there is a choice of restaurants in town. There's a small lake for swimming and fishing, and ample grounds for hunting and riding. ✉ *Hallegger Str. 131, A–9201,* ☎ *0463/49311. 15 rooms. Lake, tennis court, horseback riding, fishing. No credit cards. Closed mid-Sept.–mid-May.*

Pörtschach

3 *6 km (4 mi) west of Krumpendorf.*

Midway along the Wörther See is Pörtschach, one of the two top vacation spots on the lake. Here, the water is often warm enough for swimming as early as May, which is very early indeed for an Alpine region. You'll find dozens of places to stay and even more things to do under the stars: the nightlife here is as varied as the daytime activities. Elegant villas line the peninsula, which is often abloom with flowers and verdant foliage during the summer months. Chicly dressed visitors head for the lakeshore promenade to enjoy the view.

Dining and Lodging

$$$ ✕ **Rainer's.** Make your way through the bar to this "in" restaurant. The most favored tables are on the balcony, although the two inside rooms have an intimacy of their own. Food choices are limited but good; try the grilled shrimp in herb sauce, the roast hare, or settle for a steak. ✉ *Monte-Carlo-Pl. 1,* ☎ *04272/3046. AE, MC, V. Closed mid-Sept.–mid-May. No lunch.*

$$–$$$ ★ ✕ **Schloss Leonstain.** This appealing 500-year-old castle, complete with tower and antique furnishings, is unfortunately situated between the railroad and the highway. Quiet is hard to find, but other attractions help compensate for this drawback. The restaurant is among the best in town and is well worth a visit on its own. In summer, tables are set up in the courtyard as well as in the historic rooms. ✉ *Hauptstr. 228, A–9210,* ☎ *04272/2816–0,* FAX *04272/2823. 35 rooms. Restaurant, lake, sauna, golf course, tennis court, boating. AE, DC, MC, V. Closed early Oct.–early May.*

$$$–$$$$ **Schloss Seefels.** At Töschling, about 3 kilometers (2 miles) west of Pörtschach, this hotel attracts a prominent international clientele. The sprawling, interconnected buildings are set in a huge park on the lake, the staff is friendly, and the elegantly furnished rooms are in the Grand-Hotel mode. You can go by boat directly to Klagenfurt and to the Kärntner golf course across the lake. Relax in the wicker-furnished café/restaurant or indulge in any of a dozen sports. The hotel can arrange rafting and fishing. You'll be expected to take half board. ✉ *A–9210, Pörtschach/Töschling 1,* ☎ *04272/2377–0,* FAX *04272/3704. 73 rooms. Restaurant, bar, indoor-outdoor pool, sauna, golf course, tennis court, exercise room, beach, boating. AE. Closed mid-Oct.–late Apr.*

$$$–$$$$ 🏨 **Werzer-Astoria.** Choose a room in one of the villas or in the hotel block, which has perhaps greater comfort but less charm. The setting, in a park running down to the shore, is splendid, and the family management has succeeded in blending the traditional with the new. The charming 19th-century boathouse contains a restaurant. ✉ *Werzerpromenade 8, A–9210,* ☎ *04272/2231–0,* FAX *04272/2251–113. 132 rooms. Restaurant, bar, indoor-outdoor pool, lake, sauna, golf course, tennis courts, exercise room, squash, boating, bicycles. AE, DC, MC, V. Closed early Oct.–Apr.*

$$–$$$ 🏨 **Europa.** This modern hotel, uninspired on the outside, stands directly on the water. Ask for a room on the lake side and enjoy the sunniest corner of the lake. Half board is standard. The view is wonderful from the restaurant. Fish is the best choice here—for example, the grilled lake perch, with just a touch of garlic, or smoked trout with caviar. ✉ *Augustenstr. 24, A–9210,* ☎ *04272/2244–0,* FAX *04272/2298. 47 rooms. Restaurant, lake, golf course, tennis court, boating, bicycles. No credit cards. Closed Oct.–Apr.*

Nightlife and the Arts

In Pörtschach, the crowd at **Rainer's** (✉ Monte-Carlo-Pl. 1, ☎ 04272/3046) is young, and the nights are lively, loud, and long; The restaurant, already earning a good reputation, is a recent addition to this popular watering-hole. Equally "in" are Montesol and the nearby Hausboot and Anna W.

Outdoor Activities and Sports

GOLF

You can improve your swing at the 18-hole, par-72 **Golfanlage Moosburg-Pörtschach** (☎ 04272/83486, FAX 04272/82055). The club is open April–early November.

WATER SPORTS

Pörtschach is a center of activity for windsurfing, parasurfing, and sailing. Check **Herbert Schweiger** (✉ 10.-Oktober-Str. 33, ☎ 04272/2655). Several hotels on the Wörther See offer sailing and surfing packages.

Maria Wörth

❹ *18 km (14 mi) southwest of Pörtschach.*

Maria Wörth's spired chapel reflected in the waters of the Wörther See is one of Austria's most photographed sights. This unpretentious little town is situated on a wooded peninsula jutting out toward the center of the lake, almost entirely surrounded by water. The present two churches date from the 12th century. The smaller **"Rosary" church** is basically Romanesque with later Gothic additions. The interior has a Romanesque choir with fragments of 12th-century frescoes of the apostles, a stained-glass Madonna window from 1420, and Gothic carved-wood figures. The larger **parish church,** despite its Romanesque portal, is mainly Gothic, with a Baroque interior. Skulls and bones can still be seen in the round Romanesque charnel house in the cemetery. These sights can be kept for a wet day; when the weather is good your time will be fully occupied with more important matters: bathing, tennis, sailing, aquaplaning, and golfing.

Lodging

$$$ 🏨 **Astoria.** This massive, comfortable villa on the lake is just 2 kilometers (1¼ miles) from the 18-hole, par-71 Kärntner Golf Club course at Dellach; the hotel offers golf-holiday packages. The rooms are attractively furnished; those overlooking the lake are preferred. You'll have to take half board. ✉ *A–9082,* ☎ *04273/2279,* FAX *04273/2279–*

80. 45 rooms. Restaurant, weinstube, indoor pool, sauna, tennis court. No credit cards. Closed mid-Oct.–mid-May.

Outdoor Activities and Sports

GOLF

Enjoy the scenic view while getting in your 18 holes at the **Kärntner Golf Club** at Oberdellach/Maria Wörth (☎ 04273/2515, FAX 04273/2606). The club is open April–October.

Velden

❺ *8 km (5 mi) west of Maria Wörth.*

Velden, the most noted resort on the lake, is perched at the west end of the Wörther See. The atmosphere here strives to retain its international chic—classy and lively—and the summer carnival in August adds to the action. The town's most famous beauty spot is the lakeside promenade, accented by turn-of-the-century lamps and mansions. Merrymaking includes a spin at the casino's tables and listening to orchestras at lakeside terraces. However, if you're looking for a tranquil holiday, Velden may be too exuberant. The town gets pricey in the July–August main season.

OFF THE BEATEN PATH

MARIA GAIL – The Romanesque parish church here has an unusually good 14th-century Gothic winged triptych altar. To get to Maria Gail, located 14 kilometers (10 miles) west of Velden, take the Villacher Strasse, Route 83 out of Velden. If you're heading on to Faaker See, you'll pass, several miles beyond Maria Gail, one of the most famous roadside shrines in Austria: framed by lake and mountain, this *Manternl* is a great photo op.

Dining and Lodging

$$$$ ✕ **Casino-Restaurant.** If you're looking for fine cuisine plus a view, this place offers a wondrous vista over the lake. A new chef has brought vast improvement to the kitchen in this dinner-only restaurant, specializing in international fare with a regional touch. The casino complex (☞ Nightlife and the Arts, *below*) is limited to those 18 and over, and you'll need your passport for identification. ✉ *Am Corso 17,* ☎ *04274/2948–57. AE, DC, MC, V.*

$$$–$$$$ ✕🏨 **Golf-Park-Hotel Velden.** This exclusive turn-of-the-century mansion, set in a park amid a stand of huge old trees, has been luxuriously renovated to offer every comfort. Not surprisingly, it has attracted the crème de la crème, from tennis stars to Saudi royals. From the spacious lobby to the modern guest rooms, you'll find elegance and attentive service. The gourmet restaurant is particularly noted and, for this region, is distinctively cordon-bleu in style and quality. ✉ *Seecorso 68, A–9220,* ☎ *04274/2298–0,* FAX *04274/2298–9. 89 rooms. 2 restaurants, bar, indoor pool, sauna, golf privileges, tennis. AE, DC, MC, V. Closed mid-Oct.–mid-Apr.*

$$–$$$ ✕🏨 **Hubertushof.** Two typical resort houses from the turn of the century comprise this family-run complex directly on the lake. A touch of the original Art Deco carries over into some of the rooms, most of which have balconies. The best rooms face the lake. The Hubertusstüberl is gaining a reputation for its way with regional specialties such as lamb. ✉ *Europapl. 1, A–9220,* ☎ *04274/2676–0,* FAX *04274/2657–60. 46 rooms. Restaurant, indoor pool, sauna, golf and tennis privileges, exercise room, boating. DC, MC, V. Closed mid-Oct.–mid-Apr.*

Nightlife

The casino in the center of **Velden** is a focal point of the evening, but you must be 18 or over. Along with the gambling tables and slot machines, the complex contains a disco, bars, and a restaurant (☞ Dining and Lodging, *above*), whose terrace overlooks the lake. You'll need your passport to enter the casino. ✉ *Am Corso 17,* ☎ *04274/2064,* FAX *04274/2982. Jacket and tie.* ⏲ *Daily 3 PM–3 or 4 AM.*

Egg am Faaker See

❻ *4 km (2½ mi) east of Maria Gail.*

With turquoise-green waters that seem almost Mediterranean, the Faaker See presents an idyllic setting for swimming and boating. Boating aficionados take to the lake in droves with a rainbow array of sails skimming across the horizon (motor boats are not allowed); even so, the round lake—with its tiny island in the middle—remains less crowded than other resort areas here. Watching over all is the mighty pyramid of the Mittagskogel of the Karawanken range. You can get to Egg am Faaker See from Velden by taking the E7 highway westward to the turnoff for Route 84, but you can also take a shorter route using secondary roads—ask for information in Velden.

Dining and Lodging

$$$$ ★ ✕🏨 **Karnerhof.** A chalet with a long, low extension, in a style that suits the dramatic landscape, is set in a park on the lake. The mountain range serves as a scenic backdrop. This affiliate of the Silencehotel group offers attractive rustic rooms and the excellent Götzelstube restaurant to complement the sensational setting. The food alone is worth a visit; all dishes are freshly prepared, and the fish is particularly fine. ✉ *Egger-Seepromenade 4/Karnerhofweg 10, A–9580,* ☎ *04254/2188,* FAX *04254/3650. 105 rooms. Restaurant, café, indoor-outdoor pool, sauna, tennis court, exercise room, beach. AE, DC, V. Closed mid-Oct.–Mar.*

$$$ ✕🏨 **Sonnblick.** The Hotel Sonnblick looks like it belongs in the pages of *Heidi* with its sun-drenched balconies and windows festooned with bright red geraniums. The family-run chalet has a cozy gemütlich atmosphere, with guests greeted with a "welcome" cocktail and evening barbecues on the terrace overlooking the mountains. You can also choose from set menus that change daily. The hotel justifiably prides itself on its extensive wine cellar featuring regional and European vintages. ✉ *Dreimuhlenweg 23, A-9580,* ☎ *04254/21670,* FAX *04254/21675. 32 rooms. Restaurant. AE, DC, V, MC.*

Outdoor Activities and Sports

GOLF

Take in a game of golf at the 18-hole, par-72 **Golfanlagen Velden-Köstenberg** (☎ 04274/7045, FAX 04274/708715). The club is open April–early November.

Viktring

❼ *17 km (10½ mi) east of Egg am Faaker See, 6½ km (4 mi) southwest of Klagenfurt.*

You can still see parts of the moat remaining from the Cistercian convent, established here in 1142. Don't miss the convent's arcaded cloisters, and look for the 14th- to 16th-century stained glass in the choir of the church, behind the Baroque high altar. From the west and the Faaker See, you can get to Viktring by following the valley on Route 85 until you come to the junction with Route 91 and then turn north toward Klagenfurt. From Viktring it's 6 ½ kilometers (4 miles) back to Klagenfurt.

THE DRAU VALLEY

A Carinthia for All Reasons

The Drau Valley is a Carinthia for all reasons—there's a little here of the best of everything you can find in the province. One of the most impressive Renaissance castles in the country can be found in Spittal an der Drau, which comes alive with a series of theatrical events and concerts during the summer months. Take a ride on the wild side with a visit to the Porsche Museum, which documents the history of the innovative carmaker. Or you can sooth tired muscles at a Roman bath before relaxing away from the crowds at the quiet lakeside resort on the Feldsee. We begin, however, at the main town in Upper Carinthia, Spittal an der Drau.

Spittal an der Drau

8 *26 km (16 mi) from northwest Villach.*

Even though Spittal an der Drau has an impressive Gothic church (on your left as you enter the town), it's most famous for its architecturally ★ superb **Schloss Porcia,** built in the 16th century by the imperial treasurer, Count Gabriel von Salamanca. This castle-palace, located in the center of town next to a lovely park, is one of the most beautiful Renaissance buildings in Austria, especially in its gracefully arcaded Italianate courtyard stairways and open corridors, which provide a dreamlike setting for summer performances of classical plays, often Shakespeare. The upper floors house a museum highlighting regional culture of the past. The town itself is unprepossessing. ☎ *04762/2890.* *AS45.* *Mid-May–Oct., daily 9–6, Nov.–mid-May, weekdays 1–4.*

The **Goldeckbahn,** the aerial tramway that leaves from behind the tennis hall on Ortenburgerstrasse (☎ 04762/2864–0), will take you up to the 6,960-foot peak of the Goldeck mountain, from which you get splendid panoramic views to the north and east.

To arrive at Spittal an der Drau from Villach, take Route 86 north to reach Route 100/E14 and head west through the Drau valley.

The Arts

In Spittal an der Drau, from mid-July through August, three or four plays are presented in the marvelous setting of **Schloss Porcia** (☞ *above*). The experience is exciting, even if the productions in German are not always as polished as you might expect. Call for program information and ticket details (☎ 04762/3161, 04762/3420, or 04762/5650–48, FAX 04762/3237).

Lodging

$ **Alte Post.** This traditional, friendly house in the center of town has comfortable modern rooms, a good restaurant, and the bonus of fishing rights on a reserved stretch of the Drau River. ✉ *Hauptpl. 13, A–9800,* ☎ *04762/2217–0,* FAX *04762/5125–57. 42 rooms. Restaurant, bar. AE, DC, MC, V. Closed Jan.*

$ **Ertl.** This salmon-fronted family-run hotel is just steps from the railroad station but away from heavy traffic. If you're touring by train, stay here; the rooms are large and attractively decorated. ✉ *Bahnhofstr. 26, A–9800,* ☎ *04762/2048–0,* FAX *04762/2048–5. 40 rooms. Restaurant, pool. AE, DC, MC, V. Closed Nov.*

Outdoor Activities and Sports

HIKING

There's unusually good hiking starting from Spittal, and even better from Gmünd, Seeboden, Millstatt, Bad Kleinkirchheim, Feld am See, and Afritz. Local visitor information offices will have suggestions for routes and for combining a hike with a return by local bus.

Gmünd

9 *19 km (12 mi) north of Spittal an der Drau via Rte. 99 (Gmündner Strasse).*

Not far from where the Malta mountain stream rushes into the Lieser is the colorful town of Gmünd. The warm pastels of the town's building facades on the oval-shaped central square stand in contrast to the dark green of the surrounding forested hills. This little 16th-century town with medieval walls has been carefully restored. The "new" **castle** (1651) is watched over by the old castle, in ruin above the town. See the **parish church** and the ancient fresco on the outside wall, which shows the town as it was in the 17th century, little different from the way it looks today, except that the old castle is complete. The town museum can be found in the lower gate tower.

The automobile designer Ferry Porsche was born and worked in Gmünd; an informative and fascinating **Porsche Museum** shows a series of the cars and experimental models he designed and built. The museum is located directly northwest of the old walled town. ☎ *04732/2471.* 🎫 *AS65.* ⏲ *Mid-May–mid-Oct., daily 9–6; mid-Oct.–mid-May, daily 10–4.*

Dining and Lodging

$$ ✕ **Alte Burg.** You might not expect to find a gemütlich setting within the ruins of a 13th-century castle, but you'll discover this attractive restaurant, set amid renovated dungeons and battlements, decorated with Carinthian wrought iron and antiques. On the menu, look for regional specialties such as roast lamb and Carinthian cheese noodles (a local form of ravioli with cream-cheese filling). This food comes with a view, as the castle picturesquely overlooks the town. ✉ *Alte Burg,* ☎ *04732/3639. AE, DC, MC, V. Closed Wed., Thurs. Sept.–June, and mid-Jan.–wk before Easter.*

$ 🏨 **Kohlmayr.** Behind the pinkish facade of this family-run hotel on the town square you'll find a particularly friendly staff and modern, attractive rooms in rustic decor. Up the stone steps is a large reception room furnished with country antiques (including a spinning wheel). The rooms in front have a stunning view over the square. The whole town gathers in the *Bierstube* in the late afternoon and on Sunday morning. The restaurant offers good standard Austrian country fare. ✉ *Hauptpl. 7, A–9853,* ☎ *04732/2149,* FAX *04732/2153. 22 rooms. Restaurant, weinstube. No credit cards. Closed Nov.*

Outdoor activities and sports

HIKING

In summer you can head up the scenic Malta Valley to see the massive hydroelectric dam and lake and hike at the top. During the winter, Gmünd makes an ideal base for skiing the nearby slopes—but après-ski entertainment is sparse.

Millstatt

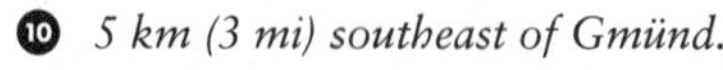

10 *5 km (3 mi) southeast of Gmünd.*

The largest resort on the Millstätter See is crowned by an impressive **Benedictine abbey** and adorned with imposing towers, antique courtyards, and centuries-old linden trees. The abbey was founded in the 11th century but secularized in the 18th. Parts can be seen only on conducted tours. The twin-towered Romanesque church of the abbey complex was partially rebuilt in Gothic style and later given some Baroque ornamentation, but its 12th-century Romanesque portal remains its outstanding feature. Note also the *Kreuzgang,* the arcaded cloister between the church and the monastery, with its complicated pillar ornaments. The abbey is the site of a series of music festivals that run continuously from mid-May through September. To get to Millstatt from Gmünd, turn east onto Route 98 heading for Seeboden at the north end of the Millstätter See; about 5 kilometers (3 miles) farther along is Millstatt.

Dining and Lodging

$$$ **Alpenrose.** This attractive house advertises itself as Austria's first "bio-hotel." It is constructed entirely of natural materials (primarily wood and brick) and uses no plastic or anything artificial in either the structure or the rooms, which are particularly inviting in their rustic design. The excellent restaurant continues the theme, featuring only natural ingredients (many of the vegetables are organically grown in the side garden). Try the cabbage soup or the Carinthian cheese noodles to start, and follow with the lake trout or pepper steak; hotel guests won't mind that half board is required. In winter there's free transport to nearby ski areas. ✉ *Obermillstatt 84, A–9872,* ☎ *04766/2500–0,* FAX *04766/3425. 34 rooms. Restaurant, pool, sauna. No credit cards. Closed late Nov.–mid-Dec.*

$$ **Die Forelle.** This four-story balconied house sprawls along the lake, its tree-shaded terrace directly over the water. The public rooms are elegant but comfortable, the guest rooms bright and welcoming. The hotel has its own stretch of fishing water. The restaurant is successfully ambitious; fish is featured here, but ask for recommendations. ✉ *Fischergasse 65, A–9872,* ☎ *04766/2050–00,* FAX *04766/2050–11. 68 rooms. Restaurant, pool, sauna, tennis court, boating, fishing. No credit cards. Closed Nov.–Apr.*

Nightlife and the Arts

In Millstatt there's something going on throughout much of the year: Musical Spring runs from mid-May through June; International Music Weeks take over during July and August, followed by Musical Autumn in September. Most events take place in the Benedictine abbey. For program details and ticket reservations, contact the secretariat (✉ Musikwochen Millstatt, Stiftgasse 1, A–9872, ☎ 04766/2165, FAX 04766/3479).

Outdoor Activities and Sports

BICYCLING

The area around the Millstätter See is good for cycling. You can rent bicycles at the **Spittal-Millstätter See railroad station** (☎ 04762/3976–0).

Bad Kleinkirchheim

11 *6 km (4 mi) north of Radenthein via Rte. 88.*

Barely known 30 years ago, the booming town of Bad Kleinkirchheim has become a stylish resort. Although it's popular in summer, the town is unquestionably Carinthia's top ski resort, and Austrians flock to the slopes here in winter for great cross-country skiing, snowboarding, and skating. Après-ski life centers on the hotels, Ronacher and Pulverer (☞ Dining and Lodging, *below*) being the current favorites. After a day on the slopes you can plunge into the (re-created) Roman baths, fed by thermal mineral springs. Nearby, the **Katharinenkapelle** (St. Catherine's chapel) marks the location of one of the springs. It has an organ loft with carved-wood reliefs and a late-Gothic winged altar. Stop at **St. Oswald**, north of town, to look at the unusual iron hinges on the doors of the late-Gothic church and to see its frescoes of 1514.

Lodging

$$$–$$$$ **Pulverer.** This friendly hotel, in a group of interconnected chalet-style buildings, is not only in the center of town but is one of the centers of activity. You can take a cure with the medicinal thermal waters, then undo the good work at the enticing buffets: breakfast, salad, strudel, and hors d'oeuvres. Half board is required. The reception area has a cathedral ceiling; the guest rooms are done in elegant country-rustic decor. ✉ *Bach 1, A–9546,* ☎ *04240/744–0 or 550,* FAX *04240/793. 40 rooms, 50 apartment-suites. Restaurant, indoor-outdoor pool, sauna, spa, exercise room. No credit cards. Closed mid- to late Apr. and Nov.–mid-Dec.*

$$$–$$$$ **Ronacher.** You can easily spoil yourself at this family-managed combination sports-and-cure facility, with its in-house thermal baths and luxurious balconied rooms in modern-rustic decor. The large hotel, in a typical country design—dark wood against white—is off the main road in the middle of town. It organizes many activities for those who dislike the chores of planning, but you'll have to take half board, although you can eat what and when you choose. ✉ *Bach 18, A–9546,* ☎ *04240/8615,* FAX *04240/282–606. 92 rooms. Restaurant, indoor-outdoor pool, sauna, spa, golf privileges, exercise room. AE, DC, V. Closed Apr. and late Oct.–mid-Dec.*

$$ **Putz-Römerbad.** This family-run chalet-style hotel, tucked away behind fir trees, is a bit east of the center, but a thermal mineral spring bath is just down the hall, and sports facilities are a short walk away. Public rooms are spacious, balconied guest rooms slightly less so; the warmth of the rustic decor creates a comfortable atmosphere. Rooms on the south side have a view of the mountains. Half board is required. ✉ *Zirkitzen 69, A–9546,* ☎ *04240/8234–0,* FAX *04240/8234–57. 32 rooms. Restaurant, sauna, exercise room, spa. AE, DC. Closed Nov.*

Outdoor Activities and Sports

GOLF

Golfclub Bad Kleinkirchheim (☎ 04275/594 or 04240/8282–16, FAX 04275/504 or 04240/8282–18) is challenging for beginners and advanced golfers alike, thanks to a fine 18-hole, par-72 course. The greens fee is AS400–AS600, depending on the season, and the club is open May–October.

SKIING

Made famous by local ski legend Franz Klammer, the ski resort at Kleinkirchheim has more than 100 kilometers of prepared trails. Less famous and glitzy that the resorts in neighboring Tirol, the region caters to parents and their children. Local hotels and tourist offices can provide information on lesson packages. More advanced skiers will be challenged by runs at altitudes of up to 2,440 meters.

OFF THE BEATEN PATH

TREFFEN – This town's Baroque castle dates from 1691, but the main attraction may be the 630 rosy-cheeked country dolls made by Elli Riehl at the **Puppenmuseum.** ✉ *Winklern 14,* ☎ *04248/2395.* *AS40.* ⏲ *Mid-Apr.–June and late Sept.–mid-Oct., daily 2–6; July–late Sept., daily 9–6.*

THE GURKTAL REGION

On the Road to Snow White's Castle

Storybook names, such as Tannhaüser, Snow White, and the "Holy Henna," are encountered throughout the Gurktal region of Carinthia. The region is populated with medieval strongholds, idyllic lakes, and towns that remain charming down to the last cobblestone. Here the fun is discovering which quaint town you like best—and which quaint town likes you.

Villach

⓬ *50 km (30 mi) west of Klagenfurt.*

Carinthia's "other" capital (Klagenfurt is the official one) sits astride the Drau River. The Romans may have been the first to bridge the river here for their settlement of Bilachium, from which the present name Villach is derived. The city is compact, with narrow, twisting lanes (restricted to pedestrians) winding through the Old City south of the river. Small, attractive shops are tucked into arcaded buildings, and each corner brings a fresh and surprising perspective. Renaissance houses surround the main square, which has a Baroque column in honor of the Trinity. At **Hauptplatz 14** lived the 16th-century alchemist and physician Theophrastus Bombastus von Hohenheim Paracelsus; his father was the town physician.

Curiously, the late-Gothic 14th-century **parish church of St. Jacob** was Protestant during the mid-1500s, making it Austria's first Protestant church. Its marble pulpit dates to 1555; the ornate Baroque high altar contrasts grandly with the Gothic crucifix. If the stair entry is open and you don't mind the rather steep climb, the view from the 310-foot tower is marvelous. Near the river, at the intersection of Ossiacher Zeile and Peraustrasse, the pinkish **Heiligenkreuz parish church,** with two towers and cupola, is a splendid example of fully integrated Baroque.

In the summer, a particularly lovely way to explore the Drau river from Villach is to take a cruise on the MS *Landskron*; watching the sun set over the mountains while you dine on board makes for a memorable evening. For schedule and details, check with the tourist office or Drau-Schiffahrt (✉ Neubaugasse 32, ☎ 04242/58071, FAX 04242/58072).

OFF THE BEATEN PATH

LANDSKRON – An interesting stopping point is this ruined castle, which has spectacular views over Villach, the Ossiach lake, and the Karawanken mountain range to the south. The original castle here dated from 1351 and was destroyed by fire in 1861; since then, sections have been rebuilt. To get there, take Route 83 northeast of Villach.

Dining and Lodging

$$$–$$$$ ★ ✕ **Bleibergerhof.** If you head north out of Villach on Route 86, you'll come to Untere Fellach, with a turnoff to the left marked to "Bleiberg" (there's also bus service out of Villach). About 13 kilometers (8 miles) up this scenic country road, Bad Bleiberg is the site of one of Austria's dozen top restaurants. You'll dine in elegant but unpretentious splendor on superb international and Carinthian specialties that vary with the season, with a choice of exquisite soups or light first courses. Further selections are based on a daily menu. The service is impeccable; ask for advice on wines. The family-run Bleibergerhof also has spa facilities, drawing on the hot mineral springs that flow from the mountain behind it. ✉ *A–9530,* ☎ *04244/2205–0,* FAX *04244/2205–70. Jacket*

and tie. No credit cards. Closed Nov.–mid-Dec. No dinner Sun.–Tues.; no lunch Mon.–Wed.

$$ ✕ 🏨 **Mosser.** You won't be able to miss the Hotel Mosser with its orange and green candy-striped columns and peach exterior. The welcome by the staff is equally cheery and exuberant. Located smack in the center of town, the Mosser is a short two-minute walk from the main station. The furnishings are a bit nondescript, but the rooms are large and comfortable; be sure to ask for one facing the courtyard to avoid the noise from the street below. The hotel's restaurant serves classic Austrian fare from Schnitzel to Wurst. ✉ *Bahnhofstr. 9, A-9500.* ☎ *04242/24115,* FAX *04242/24115–222. 30 rooms. Restaurant, massage. AE, DC, DC, V.*

$$ ★ ✕ 🏨 **Post.** This beautifully adapted Renaissance palace, which dates from 1500, is in the pedestrian zone in the heart of the old city. Architects have cleverly created an elegant, modern hotel while preserving Old-World features of the building such as the arcaded inner court. Service is personal and friendly. The ocher tones in the restaurant, with its arched ceiling, create a warm, inviting atmosphere; dishes range from light Austrian nouvelle cuisine to such traditional Carinthian specialties as cheese noodles. The Post is a member of the RomantikHotel group. ✉ *Hauptpl. 26, A–9500,* ☎ *04242/26101–0,* FAX *04242/26101–420. 77 rooms. Restaurant, bar, sauna, exercise room. AE, DC, MC, V.*

$ 🏨 **Europa.** You'll be across the river from the old city but just two minutes from the main rail station in this attractive yellow-and-white hostelry. The rooms are done with reproduction 19th-century furnishings; those on the inner side are quieter. The house is associated with the Best Western group. ✉ *Bahnhofstr. 10, A–9500,* ☎ *04242/26766,* FAX *04242/26766–50. 44 rooms. Café, bar, sauna, exercise room, parking. AE, DC, MC, V.*

Outdoor Activities and Sports

HIKING

Southwest of Villach, the extremely scenic 16-kilometer (10-mile) Villach Alpine highway climbs the mountain ridge to about 5,000 feet. From there, a lift gets you up to Hohenrain, then you can hike the marked trail—or take the train—up to the peak of the **Dobratsch mountain,** towering 7,040 feet into the clouds and providing a spectacular view. Close to parking lot 6, at 4,875 feet, is an Alpine botanical garden, which is open mid-June–August, daily 9–6. The 11 parking and outlook points along the highway offer great panoramas.

TENNIS

Most of the large towns have public courts, but you'll either have to book in advance or wait your turn. In the Villach area, try **Tennisplätze ASKÖ** (✉ Landskron, Süduferstr., ☎ 04242/41879) or **Tenniscamp Warmbad** (✉ Villach–Warmbad Villach, ☎ 04242/32564). Many hotels around the southern lakes have their own courts, some of them indoors.

Warmbad Villach

13 *3 km (1½ mi) southwest of Villach.*

On the southern outskirts of Villach lies Warmbad Villach, its name reflecting the hot springs of radioactive water, which is believed to combat aging. This remains one of the classic spas of Carinthia, and people also come to enjoy its thermal springs and swimming pools for various rheumatic ailments. Many hotels have been built around the *Kurpark,* the wooded grounds of the spa.

Dining and Lodging

$$$ ★ ✕🏨 **Warmbaderhof.** With a tranquil park setting seducing you into relaxation, the cure's the thing here. The feeling of quiet comfort in this meandering house carries over into the guest rooms. Ask for one of the modern, balconied rooms overlooking "Napoléon's meadow." The Bürgerstübe restaurant offers regional and national specialties, including game in season. The exclusive Das Kleines restaurant, with its wood and brass decor, changes its offerings with the seasons, so ask about current features. ✉ *Kadischenallee 22–24, A–9504,* ☎ *04242/3001–0,* FAX *04242/3001–309. 123 rooms. 2 restaurants, bar, indoor-outdoor pool, sauna, exercise room, horseback riding. AE, DC, MC, V.*

$$–$$$ 🏨 **Josephinenhof.** Modern without being impersonal, this newish hotel is set in the comfortable isolation of the Kurpark. Special programs are devoted to enhancing longevity and age-control. You need several days for a cure to be effective, and the hotel will book only full-week packages in the main season. The restaurant is unexciting, but ample other possibilities are close by. ✉ *Kadischenallee 8, A–9504,* ☎ *04242/3003–0,* FAX *04242/3003–89. 61 rooms. Restaurant, indoor-outdoor pool, sauna, spa, tennis court. AE, DC, MC, V. Closed late Nov.–mid-Dec.*

$$–$$$ 🏨 **Karawankenhof.** The larger rooms in this recently rebuilt hotel will appeal to those who want to take the cure or use this as a base for further excursions in Carinthia. Children are particularly welcome. An underground passageway leads to the spa, with its water slide and pools. The glassed-in terrace restaurant is a delight, but the kitchen, alas, does not quite live up to the decor. ✉ *Kadischenallee 25–27, A–9504,* ☎ *04242/3002–0,* FAX *04242/3002–61. 80 rooms, 9 apartments. Restaurant, bar, indoor-outdoor pool, sauna, exercise room. AE, DC, V.*

Ossiach

⑭ *10 km (6 mi) northeast of Warmbad Villach via Rte. 83.*

The resort town of Ossiach is now the center of the Carinthian Summer Festival (☞ Nightlife and the Arts, *below*) and is afflicted with wall-to-wall tourists during the high season. The festival specializes in the works of modern composers, though chestnuts by Mendelssohn and Vivaldi occasionally sneak in alongside Stravinsky. There are other attractions, including the 11th-century former monastery, a typical square building around an inner court, with a chapel at the side. The chapel, despite its stern, conservative exterior, is wonderfully Baroque. Legend has it that in the 11th century the Polish king Boleslav II lived incognito in the monastery for eight years, pretending to be mute, in penance for murdering the bishop of Cracow. A tombstone and a fresco on the church wall facing the cemetery commemorate the story.

Dining and Lodging

$ ✕ **Forellenstation Niederbichler.** This unpretentious, small dark-stained wood cabin serves some of the freshest fish you're likely to find in Austria. Caught right in the nearby pond, the trout—*bleu,* grilled, or breaded and fried—makes a memorable meal at a bargain price. Linger outdoors under the brightly colored umbrellas sipping a *G'spritzter* (wine with soda water). ✉ *Alt Ossiach 76,* ☎ *04243/8225. No credit cards.*

$ ✕🏨 **Seewirt Köllich.** This large rustic house in a quiet corner directly on the lake next to the monastery church offers simple but comfortable rooms with views over the lake (preferred) or of the lush green hills. The hotel has its own lakeside beach and paddle boats and is adjacent to the waterskiing school. The restaurant offers standard fare

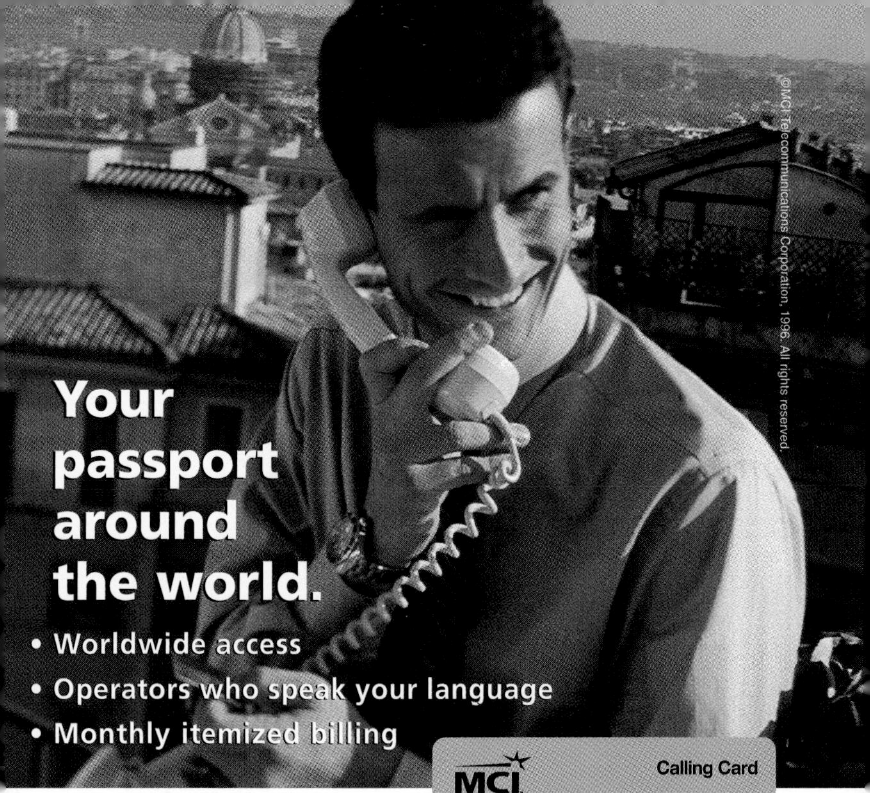

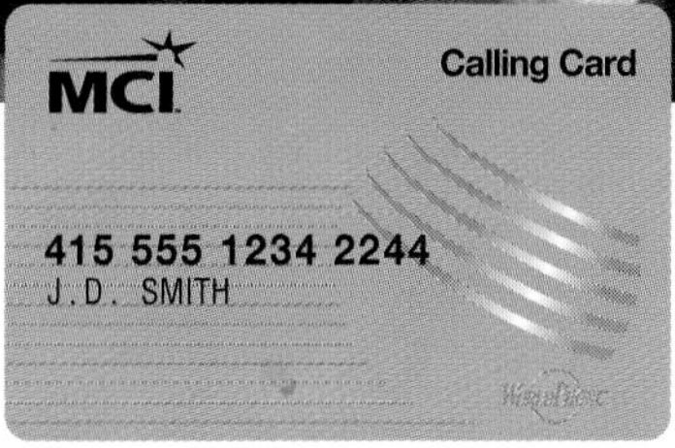

Use your MCI Card® and these access numbers for an easy way to call when traveling worldwide.

Austria (CC)♦†	022-903-012
Belarus	
From Gomel and Mogilev regions	8-10-800-103
From all other localities	8-800-103
Belgium (CC)♦†	0800-10012
Bulgaria	00800-0001
Croatia (CC)★	99-385-0112
Czech Republic (CC)♦	00-42-000112
Denmark (CC)♦†	8001-0022
Finland (CC)♦†	9800-102-80
France (CC)♦†	0800-99-0019
Germany (CC)†	0130-0012
Greece (CC)♦†	00-800-1211
Hungary (CC)♦	00▼800-01411
Iceland (CC)♦†	800-9002
Ireland (CC)†	1-800-55-1001
Italy (CC)♦†	172-1022
Kazakhstan (CC)	1-800-131-4321
Liechtenstein (CC)♦	155-0222
Luxembourg†	0800-0112
Monaco (CC)♦	800-90-19
Netherlands (CC)♦†	06-022-91-22
Norway (CC)♦†	800-19912
Poland (CC)✣†	00-800-111-21-22
Portugal (CC)✣†	05-017-1234
Romania (CC)✣	01-800-1800
Russia (CC)✣♦	747-3322
For a Russian-speaking operator	747-3320
San Marino (CC)♦	172-1022
Slovak Republic (CC)	00-42-000112
Slovenia	080-8808
Spain (CC)†	900-99-0014
Sweden (CC)♦†	020-795-922
Switzerland (CC)♦†	155-0222
Turkey (CC)♦†	00-8001-1177
Ukraine (CC)✣	8▼10-013
United Kingdom (CC)†	
To call to the U.S. using BT■	0800-89-0222
To call to the U.S. using Mercury■	0500-89-0222
Vatican City (CC)†	172-1022

To sign up for the MCI Card, dial the access number of the country you are in and ask to speak with a customer service representative.

MCI

http://www.mci.com

(CC) Country-to-country calling available. May not be available to/from all international locations. (Canada, Puerto Rico, and U.S. Virgin Islands are considered Domestic Access locations.) ♦ Public phones may require deposit of coin or phone card for dial tone. † Automation available from most locations. ★ Not available from public pay phones. ▼ Wait for second dial tone. ✣ Limited availability. ■ International communications carrier.

It helps to be pushy in airports.

Introducing the revolutionary new TransPorter™ from American Tourister®. It's the first suitcase you can push around without a fight. TransPorter's™ exclusive four-wheel design lets you push it in front of you with almost no effort–the wheels take the weight. Or pull it on two wheels if you choose. You can even stack on other bags and use it like a luggage cart.

Stable 4-wheel design.

TransPorter™ is designed like a dresser, with built-in shelves to organize your belongings. Or collapse the shelves and pack it like a traditional suitcase. Inside, there's a suiter feature to help keep suits and dresses from wrinkling. When push comes to shove, you can't beat a TransPorter.™ For more information on how you can be this pushy, call 1-800-542-1300.

Shelves collapse on command.

American Tourister

Making travel less primitive.®

©1996 American Tourister®

such as roast pork or goulash. ✉ *A-9570,* ☎ *04243/2268. 15 rooms. Restaurant, beach, boating. No credit cards. Closed Nov.–mid-May.*

$$$ **Stiftshotel Ossiach.** A monastery dating from the 1620s has been undergoing renovation to turn it into a first-class hotel while retaining much of its ancient charm. Try for one of the high-ceilinged rooms in front overlooking the lake. The rooms (particularly the front corner suites) are spacious, with reproduction period furnishings. The hotel has its own private pier and beach, and the lake boat docks in front. ✉ *A–9570,* ☎ *04243/8664–0,* FAX *0222/408–4976. 50 suites. Restaurant. AE, DC, MC, V. Sometimes closed Oct.–Apr.*

Nightlife and the Arts

Even though Ossiach is a small town (with a population of less than a thousand), it hosts an internationally renowned music event, the Carinthian Summer Festival, which has attracted many notable musicians, including Leonard Bernstein, the Collegium Musicum Pragense, and soloists from the London Symphony Orchestra. It is held in July and August and emphasizes 20th-century composition; along with Benjamin Britten's *Prodigal Son* opera, however, you might also hear some Mozart and Vivaldi, plus a little jazz and pop. Chamber concerts are all the more attractive for their setting in the Baroque chapel or the monastery in Ossiach. For a schedule or tickets, contact **Carinthischer Sommer** (✉ Stift Ossiach, A–9570 Ossiach, ☎ 04243/2510, FAX 04243/2353; ✉ Gumpendorfer Str. 76, A–1060 Vienna, ☎ 0222/596–8198, FAX 0222/597–1236).

In resort centers like Ossiach, you'll find regular evenings of folk music and dancing, some of them organized by the hotels. The local tourist offices will have details, and notices are often posted around the area.

Outdoor Activities and Sports

BICYCLING

The area around the Ossiacher See is excellent for cycling, and many of the main roads have parallel cycling paths. Rental bicycles are in great demand throughout this area, so reserve in advance. You can rent a bicycle at the **Ossiach-Bodensdorf railroad station** (☎ 04243/2218), where there's also a dock; you can put the bike on the boat, get off and cycle to the next boat landing, and return by boat when you run out of energy.

Feldkirchen

⓯ *6 km (4 mi) northeast of Ossiach.*

The colorful pastel facades dating back from the middle ages make one of Carinthia's oldest villages worth a stop. You can wander the pedestrian zone and the main square which remain surprisingly intact from the town's creation in 888. Some relics of the ancient wall around Feldkirchen remain, too. At the north end of town (Kirchgasse), look at the parish church in early Romanesque style, with a Gothic choir and Baroque decor. In addition, the town features some Biedermeier-style houses. Feldkirchen is an important crossroad. One road goes to Gurk while another climbs—at a gradient of 23%—23 miles through the mountainous Nockgebiet up to the Turracher Höhe, a high pass between Carinthia and Styria, a mountain summer resort and fine skiing center, on a pretty lake.

En Route Traveling north along Route 93 out of Feldkirchen are myriad small roads leading to colorful villages. The first, **Weitensfeld,** was the setting for one of Carinthia's most charming stories. In the 16th century, the plague decimated the population of this tiny town, southwest of Gurk.

Only three young men and a noblewoman who lived in nearby Thurnhof castle survived. A race was proposed to determine which of them should win her in marriage, and although history failed to record the outcome, the tradition of the race continues every Pentecost weekend. The winner now kisses the noblewoman's statue plus any other attractive female within reach, and the celebration goes on. Thurnhof Castle is up on the left after you leave Weitensfeld. Beyond Weitensfeld lie other storybook villages: **Goggau** on the right, with its small but charming lake; **Sirnitz** farther along to the left; also on the left, **Deutsch-Griffen** and its picturesque defense church; and then **Glödnitz.**

Gurk

16 *16 km (10 mi) northeast of Feldkirchen.*

Gurk's claim to fame is its massive Romanesque **Dom,** or cathedral, surmounted by two "candle-snuffer" cupolas and considered the most famous religious landmark in Carinthia. In the 11th century, the Countess Hemma, a wealthy woman devoted her life to building convents and churches, including the convent here. The local bishop decided to build a cathedral to honor her good works, and it was consecrated in 1200, although Hemma wasn't canonized until 1938. Her crypt is surrounded by 100 marble columns, and the small green-slate chair from which she personally supervised the construction is also there. The high altar is one of the most important examples of early Baroque in Austria; note the *Pietà* by George Rafael Donner, who is sometimes called the Austrian Michelangelo. The 900-square-foot Lenten altar cloth of 1458, showing 99 scenes from the Old and New Testaments, is displayed from Ash Wednesday to Good Friday—a beautiful example of a *Biblia Pauperum,* a "poor man's Bible," to teach the scriptures to those who could not read. The bishop's chapel includes rare late-Romanesque frescoes, among the oldest in Europe. The guidebook in English is helpful. ☎ *04266/8236–0.* *Donation requested; tour AS35.* *Daily 9–6; tour Ash Wednesday–Oct., daily at 11 and 2:30; May–mid-Oct., Mon.–Sat. at 9:30, 1:30, and 4:15, and Sun. at 9:30, 10:30, 1:30 and 4:15, church services permitting and given sufficient participation; tours at 1 and 3:45 are limited to 15 people and include bishop's chapel.*

A new attraction in Gurk is the **Zwergenpark,** a vast park area filled with amusing garden statuary in a natural setting; children can traverse the park via a miniature railway. The story of Snow White and her famous Seven Dwarfs comprise the main theme of the park. ☎ *04266/8077.* *AS55, with train ride AS35.* *May, June, and Sept.–mid-Oct., daily 10–6; July and Aug., daily 9–6.*

Strassburg

17 *3 km (1½ mi) northeast of Gurk.*

The seat of the Gurk bishopric until 1787, the episcopal palace, overlooking the Strassburg hamlet and now restored, houses small museums covering the history of the valley and of the diocese. The Gothic parish church, one of the most beautiful in Carinthia, has stained-glass windows dating from 1340. Also of note is the Heilig-Geist-Spital Church, constructed in the 13th century.

Outside Strassburg, at the intersection of Route 93 and Route 83/E7, you'll see the 18th-century **Pöckstein Castle,** belonging to the Carinthian bishops. In the distance off to the left, you'll notice a castle on a hilltop, which you can see close up by turning left at Mölbling on a road marked "Treibach/Althofen." The castle is actually in Ober Markt, an unusually picturesque town with 15th-century decorated houses.

Across the highway from the Pöckstein Castle is the northern terminal of a small narrow-gauge railway, the **Gurktaler Museumbahn.** The train meanders for 30 minutes under steam power down to Treibach on weekends and holidays, mid-June to mid-September. For an additional contribution, you can ride in the locomotive alongside the engineer. ☎ *04262/4783, 04242/317530, or 04229/3528. Round-trip AS60. Departures Sat. at 1, 2:30, and 4; Sun. and holidays at 10:30, 1, 2:30, and 4.*

NEED A BREAK? Heading north on Route 83/E7 toward Friesach, you'll come to **Brauerei Hirt,** a brewery since 1270. You might have a draft beer under the huge tree in the side garden or in one of the paneled rooms. The food is good, standard Austrian.

Friesach

18 *8 km (5 mi) north of Strassburg via Rte. 83/E7.*

One of the oldest settlements of Carinthia, romantic Friesach is great for wandering. You'll immediately find the **Hauptplatz** (main square), with its old town hall and picturesque, 19th-century facades, and as you stroll you'll discover parts of the medieval-era town: the double wall and the towers, gates, and water-filled moat. Among the medieval tournaments of gallantry that took place here, 600 knights participated in the famous one of May 1224; the Styrian minnesinger Ulrich von Liechtenstein, who appeared dressed and equipped all in green, alone broke 53 lances on his opposing adversaries. Look into the churches; the 12th-century **Romanesque parish church** on Wiener Strasse has some excellent stained glass in the choir. The 13th-century **Dominican church** north of the moat was the first of its order in Austria and contains a wonderful early Gothic choir. If you believe that Tannhaüser was a creation of Wagner's imagination, you will be surprised to learn that the descendants of his family were Salzburg administrators in Friesach; a **Tannhaüser Chapel** was erected in 1509 in this church, with a red marble tomb of Deputy Dean Balthasar Tannhaüser added after his death in 1516. From a footpath at the upper end of the main square, take a steep 20-minute climb up to the impressive remains of **Schloss Petersberg** to see 12th- and 13th-century frescoes and a museum with beautiful Late Gothic art.

The Arts

From late June to mid-August, there's open-air theater at the outdoor stage of the Dominican Monastery, performed in German, at Friesach. Check with the local tourist office (☎ 04268/4300) for details and tickets.

Lodging

$$ ★ **Metnitztalerhof.** This delightful hotel has overlooked Friesach's medieval town square for more than 400 years. Rooms are furnished with country charm from the rich, dark wood pieces to the floral fabrics covering chairs, curtains and beds. Make sure to ask for a room overlooking the imposing castle ruins. The hotel also hosts gatherings for guests from wine tastings to medieval feasts. ✉ *Hauptpl. 11, A–9360,* ☎ *04268/25100,* FAX *0468/2510–54. 30 rooms. Restaurant, garden. AE, DC, MC, V.*

$ ★ **Friesacherhof.** This comfortable hotel is incorporated into a centuries-old building on the main square. The rooms in front look out over the square and the Renaissance fountain, but can be somewhat noisy. ✉ *Hauptpl. 4, A–9360,* ☎ *04268/2123–0,* FAX *04268/2123–15. 20 rooms. Restaurant, café. AE, DC, MC, V. Closed mid- to late Jan.*

Outdoor Activities and Sports

HIKING

Trails crisscross the hills and mountains near Friesach. Local visitor information offices will have suggestions for routes and for combining a hike with a return by local bus.

SKIING

Friesach is developing as a ski area, particularly for cross-country enthusiasts. The local tourist office can offer you information on trails, maps, and ski rentals.

Hochosterwitz

19 *12 km (7½ mi) south of Friesach, 10 km (6 mi) east of St. Veit an der Glan.*

The dramatic 13th-century **Hochosterwitz Castle,** looking out of a fairy tale, literally crowns the steep, isolated mountain on which it is built. You can hardly ignore the Disneyland effect, and in fact, this was the inspiration for Walt Disney's *Snow White* castle. He and his staff stayed here for many weeks studying it, and you will find Walt's fantasy to be fact. Once the residence of the Counts of Khevenhüller, it is now the showplace of the castle-studded St. Veit region. It was in this castle that the besieged "Pocket-Mouthed Meg"—Margarethe Maultasch, the original of Feuchtwanger's *Ugly Duchess*—slaughtered the last ox of the starving garrison and dropped it onto the heads of the attacking Tyrolese. The stratagem succeeded and, dispirited by such apparent proof of abundant supplies, the Tyrolese raised the siege. The most recent fortifications were added in the late 1500s against the invading Turks; each of the 14 towered gates is a small fortress unto itself. Inside there's an impressive collection of armor and weaponry plus a café-restaurant in the inner courtyard. There's an elevator (which can accommodate wheelchairs; 🎫 AS40) from a point near the parking-lot ticket office. The hike up the rather steep path to the Hochosterwitz, of course, adds to the drama. It's easy to envision yourself as some sort of transplanted knight trying to vanquish the fortress. Your reward at the summit are spectacular vistas from every vantage point. Get to the castle on the back road from Treibach or via Route 83/E7. ✉ *Laundsdorf–Hochosterwitz,* ☎ *04213/2010.* 🎫 *AS40.* ⏲ *Easter–June, Sept., and Oct., daily 9–5; July and Aug., daily 8–6.*

St. Veit an der Glan

20 *9 km (5½ mi) west of Hochosterwitz via Rte. 82.*

Formerly the capital of Carinthia until 1518, this old ducal city remains largely unchanged, with the town hall's Baroque facade and ancient patrician houses forming the main square. Be sure to walk into the arcaded Renaissance courtyard of the **town hall,** overflowing with flowers in summer; the main state rooms can be seen on guided tours. The 12th-century Romanesque **parish church** was later given Gothic overtones; note the attractive entry. The **ducal palace** at the north end of town now houses a small medieval collection; the building itself has a marvelous arcaded stairway in the courtyard.

Dining and Lodging

$$$ ★ ✕ **Pukelsheim.** Despite its enlargement, this restaurant remains crowded—which testifies to its good reputation. You'll find regional specialties such as the ravioli-like *Nudeln* as well as variations on Austrian themes such as veal tongue with vegetables or stuffed roast chicken. The chef's recommendations are invariably good. But Pukelsheim is best known for its desserts: superb cakes and pies made

with fruit in season. ✉ *Erlgasse 11,* ☎ *04212/2473. AE, MC, V. Closed Mon., 1 wk in Feb., and 1st wk of Sept. No dinner Sun.*

$$$ **Weisses Lamm.** Originally built in 1412, the Hotel Weisses Lamm retains the romantic atmosphere of the bygone era when St. Veit an der Glan was the home of the Carinthian aristocracy. The hotel, painted a cheery yellow with flowers cascading from window boxes, was recently renovated. Full modern amenities have been provided, while the ancient charm of the sturdy rooms, furnished with rustic antiques, has been preserved. The delightful arcaded courtyard is just the spot to while away a lazy afternoon. The small dining room serves regional favorites with a strong selection of Austrian vintages on the wine list. ✉ *Unterer Pl. 4-5, A-9300,* ☎ *04212/2362,* FAX *04212/2362–62. 27 rooms. Restaurant, parking. AE, DC, MC, V.*

CARINTHIA A TO Z

Arriving and Departing

By Car

The most direct route from Vienna is via the Semmering mountain pass through Styria, entering Carinthia on Route 83 just above Friesach and going on to Klagenfurt. Route 95 leads into central Carinthia over the Turracher Höhe pass, a particularly scenic route. From Salzburg, the A10 autobahn tunnels beneath the Tauern range and the Katschberghöhe to make a dramatic entry into Carinthia, although the parallel Route 99, which runs "over the top," is the scenic route. Several mountain roads cross over from Italy, but the most traveled is Route 83 from Tarvisio.

By Plane

Carinthia is served—mainly by Austrian Airlines and its subsidiary Tyrolean Airways—through the Klagenfurt–Wörther See Airport just northeast of Klagenfurt. Several flights daily connect the provincial capital and Vienna. In summer, service is also available from Zürich, Rome, and Frankfurt. For flight information, call 0463/41500–0.

By Train

The main rail line south from Vienna parallels Route 83, entering Carinthia north of Friesach and continuing on to Klagenfurt and Villach. From Salzburg, a line runs south, tunneling under the Tauern mountains and then tracing the Möll and Drau river valleys to Villach. A line from Italy comes into the Drau valley from Lienz in East Tirol. The main line north from Udine in Italy runs through Tarvisio and up to Villach; other rail lines tie Slovenia with Klagenfurt.

Getting Around

By Bus

As in all of Austria, the post office or railroad (*Bundesbahn*) buses go virtually everywhere, but you'll have to allow plenty of time and coordinate schedules carefully so as not to get stranded in some remote location.

By Car

Highways in Carinthia are good, although you can hit some stretches as steep as the 23-degree gradient on the Turracher pass road (Route 95), for example. Hauling trailers is not recommended (or is forbidden). The north–south passes are kept open in winter as far as possible, but the tunnels under the Tauern and Katschberg mountains ensure that Route A10 is now passable all year.

By Train

Much of Carinthia's attractive central basin is bypassed by the rail routes. Though you can get into and through Carinthia fairly easily by train, to see the inner province you'll need to rely on a car or the network of buses.

Contacts and Resources

Adventure

Carinthia offers just about any activity you might want, ranging from extreme sheer-face climbing to ballooning and white-water rafting. Details are in a set of brochures from the regional Kärntner Tourismus tourist board office (✉ Casinopl. 1, A–9220 Velden, ☎ 04274/52100–0); ask for the specific sports that interest you.

Bicycling

Rental bicycles are in great demand throughout this area, so reserve in advance. The area around the Ossiacher See is excellent for cycling as are the larger resort towns around the Wörther See along the Austrian Riviera: rent bikes at **Faak am See** ☎ 04254/2149), **Klagenfurt main station** (☎ 0463/1700 or 0463/5811–0), and **Velden** (☎ 04274/2115–0). The area around the Millstätter See is about the only area good for cycling north of Villach. You can rent bicycles at the **Spittal-Millstätter See railroad station** (☎ 04762/3976–0).

Fishing

The Ossiacher See, Wörther See, and Faaker See all have excellent fishing. You'll need a license, issued by the tourist office. Some lakeside hotels offer fishing packages and allow you to fish in reserved waters. The booklet *Kärnten Fischen* from Kärntner Tourismus gives details (in German) about fishing waters, season, possible catch, bait, and local license-issuing authorities. Check also with your hotel or boat-rental shops (*Bootsverleih*); some can issue licenses.

Golf

Many hotels have special arrangements with the courses around the southern lakes. Ask for the booklet *Golf* (in German) from the Kärntner Tourismus office. Here is a selection of the leading golf courses of Carinthia.

Golfanlage Moosburg-Pörtschach is 18 holes, par 72. ☎ *04272/83486,* FAX *04272/82055.* ⏲ *Apr.–early Nov.* **Golfanlagen Velden-Köstenberg** is 18 holes, par 72. ☎ *04274/7045,* FAX *04274/708715.* ⏲ *Apr.–early Nov.* **Golfclub Bad Kleinkirchheim** (18 holes, par 72) is challenging for beginners and advanced golfers alike. ☎ *04275/594 or 04240/8282–16,* FAX *04275/504 or 04240/8282–18.* ⏲ *May–Oct.* **Golfclub Klopeiner See,** at St. Kanzian/Grabelsdorf, is 18 holes, par 72. ☎ *04239/3800–0,* FAX *04239/3800–18.* ⏲ *Late-Mar.–early Nov.* **Golfplatz Klagenfurt-Wörthersee,** at Schloss Seltenheim, should be fully playable by 1997 if construction on the full 36-hole course is completed. ☎ *0463/40223–0,* FAX *0463/40223–20.* ⏲ *Mar.–Oct.* **Kärntner Golf Club,** at Oberdellach/Maria Wörth, is 18 holes, par 71. ☎ *04273/2515,* FAX *04273/2606.* ⏲ *Apr.–Oct.*

Hiking

Trails crisscross the hills and mountains of the Ossiacher See area, and hiking is also good around Friesach and Hochosterwitz. From every community around the southern lakes, marked paths radiate out over mountains and through valleys. There's unusually good hiking starting from Spittal, and even better from Gmünd, Seeboden, Millstatt, Bad Kleinkirchheim, Feld am See, and Afritz. Local visitor information offices will have suggestions for routes and for combining a hike with a return by local bus.

Horseback Riding

Carinthia offers superb riding terrain, from mountains to woodlands. In nearly 50 towns you'll find stables and a number of hotels that offer riding package holidays. Otherwise an hour's outing will cost you about AS150; day rates are negotiable. The brochure *Reiten* (in German), from Kärntner Tourismus, has details.

Swimming and Water Sports

To avoid the crowds, book at a hotel that has its own private beach (most do), or try one of the smaller lakes. Pörtschach and Velden on the Wörther See are the centers of activity for windsurfing, parasurfing, and sailing. For rentals, **Herbert Schweiger** (☒ 10.-Oktober-Str. 33, Pörtschach, ☎ 04272/2655); **Segel-und-Surfschule Wörthersee/Berger** (☒ Seecorso 40, Velden, ☎ 04274/2691–0 or 04274/2956–0). Several hotels on the Wörther See offer sailing and surfing packages. You can also rent boats at Seeboden, Millstatt, Dobriach, and Feld am See.

Tennis

Most of the large towns have public courts, but you'll either have to book in advance or wait your turn. In the Villach area, try **Tennisplätze ASKÖ** (☒ Landskron, Süduferstr., ☎ 04242/41879); **Tenniscamp Warmbad** (☒ Villach–Warmbad Villach, ☎ 04242/32564). Many hotels around the southern lakes have their own courts, some of them indoors. In Klagenfurt, check **Tenniscenter Allround** (☒ Welzeneggerstr., ☎ 0463/31571); **Tennisplätze M. Schoklitsch** (☒ Feschnigstr. 209, ☎ 0463/41140). In Feld am See, the **Hotel Alte Post** specializes in tennis packages.

Visitor Information

The official tourist office for the province is Kärntner Tourismus in **Velden** (☒ Casinopl. 1, A–9220, ☎ 04274/52100–0, FAX 04274/52100–50). For other offices, look for the sign *Fremdenverkehrsamt.*

The following are the leading regional *Fremdenverkehrsamt* (tourist offices). **Bad Kleinkirchheim** (☒ A–9546, ☎ 04240/8212, FAX 04240/8537). **Gmünd** (☒ Hauptpl. 20, A–9853, ☎ 04732/2197–14 or 040732/2222, FAX 04732/2197–21 or 04732/3978). **Klagenfurt** (☒ Rathaus, A–9010, ☎ 0463/537223, FAX 0463/537295). **Maria Wörth** (☒ Verkehrsamt, A–9081, ☎ 04273/2240, FAX 04273/3703). **Millstatt** (☒ Kurverwaltung, Marktpl. 8, A–9872, ☎ 04766/2022–31, FAX 04766/3479). **Ossiach Lake area** (☒ A–9520 Sattendorf, ☎ 04248/2005, FAX 04248/3148; ☒ A–9570 Ossiach, ☎ 04243/497 or 04243/2246, FAX 04243/363). **Pörtschach** (☒ Hauptstr. 153, A–9210, ☎ 04272/2354, FAX 04272/3770). **Spittal an der Drau** (☒ Burgpl. 1, A–9800, ☎ 04762/3420, FAX 04762/3237). **Velden** (☒ Kurverwaltung, Seekorso 2, Box 91, A–9220, ☎ 04274/2103, FAX 04274/51078; ☒ Villacher Str. 14, ☎ 04274/3919). **Villach** (☒ Europapl. 2, A–9500, ☎ 04242/24444–0, FAX 04242/24444–17).

9 Eastern Alps

If you want a region that packages the panoramic, the most gemütlich little towns in Austria, and an all-out array of sports, head for the Eastern Alps, beautifully situated within East Tirol, Carinthia, Salzburg province, and western Styria. It's easy to feel on top of the world if you take the Grossglockner High Alpine Highway—the most thrilling pass over the Alps. Nestled in a nearby valley is Heiligenblut, a town commemorated in a thousand postcards. Everywhere, breathtaking Alpine vistas and centuries-old castles polka-dot the landscape.

By George W. Hamilton

Updated by Angela Walker

YOU CAN GET INTO SERIOUS MISCHIEF by judging where to go in Austria on the alluring photographs found in books and travel brochures. Pictures can be misleading—and using the sheer joy of nature's (and some of mankind's) creative magnificence as a measure, they can end up embracing the whole country. One place that truly lives up to its pictures is Heiligenblut, which, as the most photographed village in the country, is the icon of the Eastern Alpine region. With the majestic Grossglockner—Austria's highest mountain—for a backdrop, it cradles the pilgrimage church of St. Vincent. Though every Austrian hamlet seems to have a church, nowhere else does a steeple seem to find such affirmation amid a setting of soaring peaks.

While this little town is a visual treat, the whole Eastern Alps region is dramatic countryside, with breathtaking scenery and great winter sports equal to those in Switzerland. Here, majestic peaks, many well over 9,750 feet, are home to slow-drifting glaciers that give way to sweeping Alpine meadows, ablaze with wildflowers in spring and summer. Long, broad valleys (many with the suffix "au," meaning meadow are basins of rivers that cross the region between mountain ranges, sometimes meandering, sometimes plunging. The land is full of ice caves and salt mines, deep gorges, and hot springs. Today, most tourism is concentrated in relatively few towns, but wherever you go you'll find good lodging, solid local food, and friendly folk; it is countryside to drive and hike and ski through, where people live simply, close to the land.

Western Carinthia and East Tirol are dotted with quaint villages that boast charming churches, lovely mountain scenery, and access to plenty of outdoor action—from hiking and fishing in summer to skiing in winter. Across the southern tier, a series of scenic routes pass from Carinthia to that political anomaly, Osttirol (East Tirol). In 1918, after World War I, South Tirol was ceded to Italy, completely cutting East Tirol off from the rest of Tirol and the administrative capital in Innsbruck. The mountains along the Italian border and those of the Hohe Tauern, to the north, also isolate East Tirol, which has consequently been neglected by tourists.

We start out from Villach, in Carinthia, and travel to Lienz, in East Tirol, then into the Defereggental, north to Matrei and back to Lienz. The next itinerary takes you from Heiligenblut—perhaps Austria's most beautiful Alpine village—over the Grossglockner mountain pass (only in summer), through Salzburg province to the charming Zell am See and beyond. We then head east along the Salzach river valley from Zell am See, with a side trip to Badgastein, then on to Radstadt and Schladming, just over into Styria. Finally, we take in the magnificent Dachstein mountain complex and retrace our steps to go up through the Salzburg Dolomite range, ending about 40 kilometers (25 miles) from Salzburg. You can do it all in a rather full three days, or you could take a leisurely week, exploring the smaller towns and byways.

Pleasures and Pastimes

Dining

While this region contains fine restaurants—in fact, two of the country's top dozen dining establishments are here—most of the dining you'll do in the small towns of the Eastern Alps will take place in a *Gasthof/Gasthaus* (inn), where the dining rooms are not necessarily separate restaurants. Note that, in many cases, such inns are open only in the peak season. In resort areas, you may be required to take half board (that is, breakfast and one other meal). Prices for meals include taxes and a service charge but not the customary small additional tip.

CATEGORY	COST*
$$$$	over AS500
$$$	AS300–AS500
$$	AS200–AS300
$	under AS200

**per person for a three-course meal, with a glass of house wine*

The Great Outdoors

FISHING

The streams and lakes of the Eastern Alps provide some of the best trout fishing in Austria, so slip on your waders and head out to Matrei and St. Jakob in Defereggen in East Tirol. Several hotels around Filzmoos and Altenmarkt offer fishing packages.

HIKING

Whether you're an avid walker or less inclined to exercise, the area's spectacular mountain trails beg to be hiked. Local tourist offices can provide information on hiking clubs, equipment rentals, guides, maps, and any other information you need for your mountain trek. And for those interested in more leisurely walks amid the wildflowers that blanket the hills during the spring and summer, there are cable cars that will whisk you to the tops of peaks, enabling you to descend only.

SKIING AND SNOWBOARDING

There's superb downhill skiing in Badgastein, St. Jakob in Defereggen, Matrei in Osttirol, Grosskirchheim/Döllach, Heiligenblut, Saalfelden, Saalbach/Hinterglemm, St. Johann in Pongau, Radstadt, Schladming, Ramsau am Dachstein, Filzmoos, and Abtenau. Schladming is the most fashionable, and Heiligenblut and the Dachstein (Schladming and Ramsau am Dachstein) are for more advanced skiers. For cross-country, go to Abtenau, Zell am See, Saalfelden, and Radstadt. You can ski or snowboard year-round on the Dachstein glacier above Ramsau. Winter resorts such as Badgastein, Saalbach/Hinterglemm, St. Johann im Pongau, Schladming, and Ramsau am Dachstein have dedicated snowboard runs.

TENNIS

Many of the larger hotels in the resort centers have their own courts, and virtually every town has municipal courts that you can arrange to use. Call the local tourist office for information. You'll find concentrations of courts around Saalbach (17 courts), Badgastein (24), Zell am See (22), Saalfelden (21), and St. Johann im Pongau (20).

Lodging

When you think of Alpine hotels, you probably think of chalet-style inns with flower-decked balconies and overhanging eaves. Not surprisingly, that's mainly what you find in the Eastern Alps, though the range runs from family-run country inns to professionally managed resorts. Interiors are generally done in a rustic, country decor that's very homey. This part of Austria is relatively inexpensive, except for the top resort towns of Saalbach, Badgastein, and Zell am See. Even there, however, cheaper accommodations are available outside the center of town or in pensions. Prices out of season may be as low as half those of the high season. Room rates include taxes and service and almost always breakfast, except in the most expensive hotels, but it is wise to ask. Half board is required in some lodgings. It is customary to leave a small additional tip (AS20) for the chambermaid.

CATEGORY	TOP RESORTS*	OTHER TOWNS*
$$$$	over AS2,200	over AS1,500
$$$	AS1,500–AS2,200	AS1,000–AS1,500
$$	AS900–AS1,500	AS700–AS1,000
$	under AS900	under AS700

**for a standard double room with bath in high season*

Exploring the Eastern Alps

Austria's Eastern Alps straddle four different provinces: Carinthia (abbreviated C.), East Tirol (E.T.), Salzburg (S.P.), and Styria (S.)—you'll find these abbreviations next to the heads for each destination below. Imposing mountain ranges ripple through the region, isolating quaint Alpine villages whose picture-postcard perfection has remained unspoiled through the centuries. The mountainous terrain makes some backtracking necessary if you're interested in visiting the entire area, but driving through the spectacular scenery is part of the appeal of touring the region.

Great Itineraries

Numbers in the text correspond to numbers in the margin and on the Eastern Alps map.

IF YOU HAVE 3 DAYS

Start in the charming villages of **Hermagor** ① and **Kötschach** ②, stopping off at the Geo-Trail, which traces 50 million years of geological history. Then spend the afternoon exploring the East Tirolean capital of **Lienz** ③. Castle ruins, picturesque churches, and more spectacular landscapes are in store on your second day, as you visit **St. Jakob in Defereggen** ④ and **Matrei in Osttirol** ⑤ before returning to Lienz. On your final day, crown your trip with a visit to that Alpine jewel **Heiligenblut** ⑦, making stops at **Döllach** ⑥ and elsewhere along the imposing Grossglockner highway.

IF YOU HAVE 5 DAYS

Begin your trip in East Tirol's capital, **Lienz** ③, before heading to picture-perfect **Heiligenblut** ⑦. As long as it's not wintertime, your second day can be spent taking the scenic Grossglockner High Alpine Highway through the Hohe Tauern National Park to the lake resort of **Zell am See** ⑨. On day three, make a day trip to the mountain resorts of **Saalbach** ⑩ and **Saalfelden** ⑪, and descend into the depths with a tour of the **Lamprechtsofenlochöhle caves**. On your fourth day, travel to **Badgastein** ⑫, and take the cure. Then use your last day to visit the cathedral in **St. Johann im Pongau** ⑭ and the **Liechtensteinklamm** ⑬, the deepest, most dramatic gorge in the Eastern Alps.

IF YOU HAVE 7 DAYS

With a week at your disposal, you can see even more of the charming Alpine towns that dot the awesome landscape. Explore **Lienz** ③ and the lovely town of **Heiligenblut** ⑦ on your first day. Then take on the twists and turns of the Grossglockner highway before lingering by the lake at the resort town of **Zell am See** ⑨. On your third day, see the spectacular **Liechtensteinklamm** ⑬ gorge, and then overnight in **St. Johann im Pongau** ⑭. Villages seemingly unchanged by the years are on the agenda for the fourth day, with visits to the charming town of **Altenmarkt** ⑮, the medieval haven of **Radstadt** ⑯, and the former silver-mining town of **Schladming** ⑰. A cable car will whisk you to the top of the Hunerkogel the next day during a stop at **Ramsau am Dachstein** ⑱, and then it's on to the resort town of **Filzmoos** ⑲. On your sixth day, make an excursion to the dramatic underworld of the **Eisriesenwelt** ice caves. Wind up your journey with a trip to the mag-

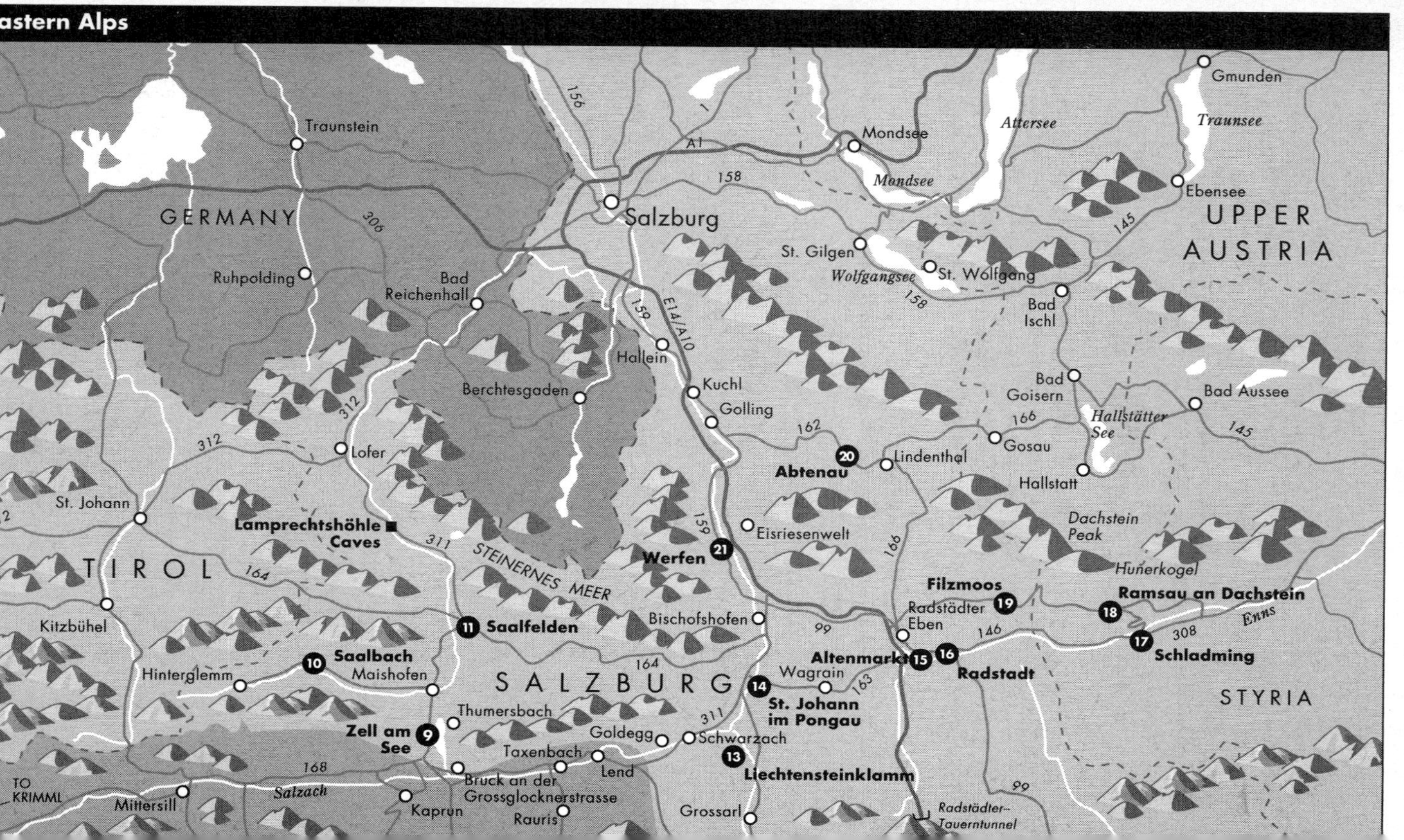
Traunstein
GERMANY
Ruhpolding
Bad Reichenhall
Salzburg
A1
156
158
306
Mondsee
Mondsee
Attersee
Gmunden
Traunsee
Ebensee
UPPER AUSTRIA
145
St. Gilgen
Wolfgangsee
St. Wolfgang
158
Bad Ischl
Bad Goisern
Bad Aussee
Hallstätter See
145
Hallein
159
E14/A10
Berchtesgaden
Kuchl
Golling
162
166
Gosau
Hallstatt
Lofer
312
312
20 Abtenau
Lindenthal
St. Johann
312
Lamprechtshöhle Caves
Eisriesenwelt
159
21 Werfen
Dachstein Peak
Hunerkogel
166
TIROL
164
311
STEINERNES MEER
Filzmoos 19
Radstädter Eben
18 Ramsau an Dachstein
Enns
Kitzbühel
11 Saalfelden
Bischofshofen
99
146
308
17 Schladming
10 Saalbach
Hinterglemm
Maishofen
164
SALZBURG
14 St. Johann im Pongau
Wagrain
163
Altenmarkt 15
16 Radstadt
STYRIA
Zell am See 9
Thumersbach
311
Goldegg
Schwarzach
Taxenbach
Lend
13 Liechtensteinklamm
168
Salzach
TO KRIMML
Mittersill
Kaprun
Bruck an der Grossglocknerstrasse
Rauris
Grossarl
99
Radstädter-Tauerntunnel

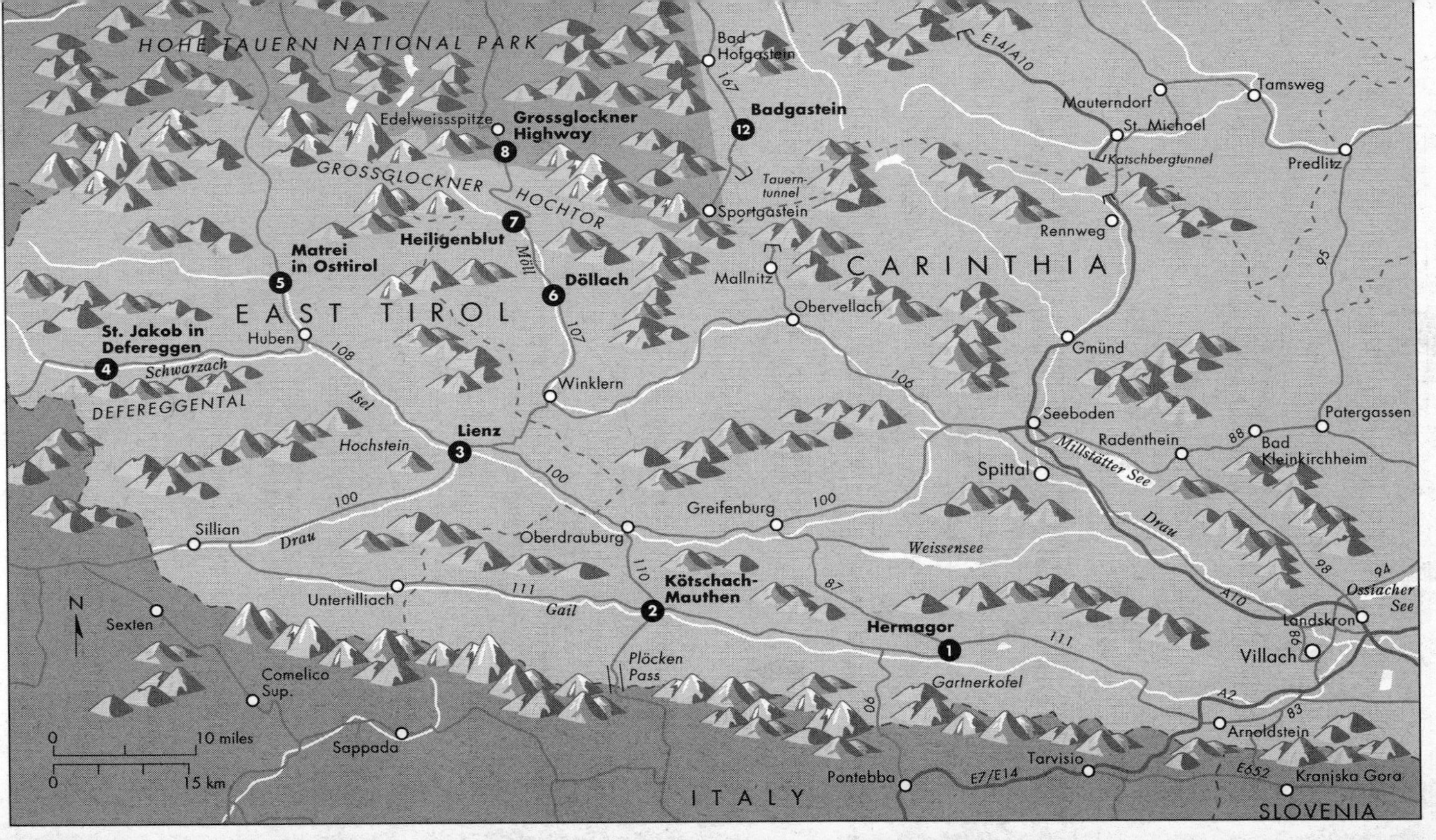
HOHE TAUERN NATIONAL PARK
EAST TIROL
CARINTHIA
ITALY
SLOVENIA
GROSSGLOCKNER
HOCHTOR
DEFEREGGENTAL
Tamsweg
Predlitz
Mauterndorf
St. Michael
Katschbergtunnel
Rennweg
Gmünd
Seeboden
Millstätter See
Radenthein
Bad Kleinkirchheim
Patergassen
Ossiacher See
Landskron
Villach
Arnoldstein
Kranjska Gora
Tarvisio
Spittal
Weissensee
Drau
Hermagor
Gartnerkofel
Pontebba
Obervellach
Mallnitz
Tauern-tunnel
Sportgastein
Badgastein
Bad Hofgastein
Greifenburg
Kötschach-Mauthen
Plöcken Pass
Oberdrauburg
Winklern
Döllach
Grossglockner Highway
Heiligenblut
Möll
Edelweissspitze
Lienz
Gail
Untertilliach
Sappada
Hochstein
Isel
Matrei in Osttirol
Huben
Schwarzach
St. Jakob in Defereggen
Sillian
Comelico Sup.
Sexten
E14/A10
A10
A2
E652
E7/E14
167
106
100
107
108
110
111
87
90
88
98
94
95
86
83
1
2
3
4
5
6
7
8
12
N
0
10 miles
15 km

nificently medieval castle at **Werfen** ㉑, where birds of prey still swoop over the imposing fortress and a final evening culinary blow-out at Obauer, one of the finest restaurants in Austria.

When to Tour the Eastern Alps

Depending on your interests, the Eastern Alps make a good destination at various times of year. Snowy conditions can make driving a white-knuckle experience, but winter also brings extensive, superb skiing throughout the region—often at a fraction of the cost of the more famous resorts in Tirol. In summer, the craggy mountain peaks provide a challenge to hikers, while cavers head into the bowels of the behemoths. Placid lakes and meandering mountain streams attract anglers for some of the best fishing to be found in the country.

TO LIENZ, INTO THE DEFEREGGENTAL, AND BACK

Summer Snow and Winter Sun

Take Route 86 south out of Villach, through Warmbad Villach, and then Route 83 to Arnoldstein, about 10 kilometers (6 miles) away. You're in the Gail River valley here, with the magnificent Karawanken mountains rising in Yugoslavia on your left. Just beyond Arnoldstein, turn right onto Route 111, marked for Hermagor. On the way up, the views now will be on the right, the dramatic Gailtal Alps in the background as you head west.

Hermagor (C.)

❶ *46 km (29 mi) west of Villach.*

Did the creation of the world take place in this area? Geologists from all over the world are fascinated by the possible answers that are believed to lie within the nearby Gartnerkoftel mountain south of Hermagor off Route 90. Amateur sleuths can join in the experience by ★ following the **"Geo-Trail,"** along which you can gather fossils and trace 50 million years of geological history. Maps are available from the local tourist office. Botanists are equally intrigued by the blue *Wulfenia,* which blankets the Nassfeld mountain area farther along Route 90 on the Italian border each June. The flower, which is protected under Austrian law, can be found only here and in the Himalayas.

This town is best known as a summer resort, accessible to hiking, climbing, and swimming in the nearby Pressegger Lake, but it also has skiing in winter. During the Middle Ages, villagers believed that the decorated keystones in Hermagor's late-Gothic **parish church** symbolized Jesus Christ's efforts to hold the framework of the church together. Dating from 1484, the church is also notable for its intricately carved and painted winged altar in the south Wolkenstein chapel.

En Route From Hermagor, both Route 87, running northwest to Greifenburg, and Route 111 up to Kötschach–Mauthen offer gorgeous views, and the distances to Lienz on both are about 55 kilometers (35 miles). If you choose Route 87, you can turn right shortly before Greifenburg for a detour to the blue-green **Weissensee,** a virtually undeveloped narrow lake 11 kilometers (almost 7 miles) long, tucked in between high mountain ridges, where there's excellent fishing and boating. Then, at Greifenburg, turn west onto Route 100 up the Drau river valley toward Lienz.

Kötschach–Mauthen (C.)

❷ *25 km (16 mi) west of Hermagor.*

Most visitors travel to this town, just off Route 111, for the natural beauty the area has to offer and to pay a call on the Kellerwand, one of Austria's top restaurants. The year-round resort is a good base for excursions via the Plöcken pass over the border into Italy or up the picturesque Lesach valley through the Austrian (Lienzer) Dolomites. The early frescoes and unusual decorated arched ceiling that adorn Kötschach's **parish church,** which dates from 1527, make it worth a stop, too.

Dining and Lodging

$$$–$$$$ ★ ✕🏨 **Kellerwand.** The restaurant, one of the top dozen in Austria, is the focal point here. Elegant tables in a quiet, luxurious atmosphere highlight the superb quality of the food. Frau Sonnleitner, who handles the kitchen, was named cook of the year in 1990, and her reputation remains justified. The cuisine that draws gourmets from all over the country is an uncommonly imaginative treatment of area specialties; recommendations include any of the outstanding delicate pasta dishes, roast lamb or venison, and, among desserts, the rhubarb strudel and warm chocolate cake served with frozen yogurt and berries. The unpretentious residence includes a small hotel, where rooms and eight luxury apartments are attractively decorated in a country style with tile floors. ✉ *Mauthen 24, A–9640,* ☎ *04715/269–0 or 04715/378–0,* FAX *04715/378–16. 12 rooms. Restaurant, bar, sauna. AE, DC, MC, V. Closed 1 wk in mid-Apr., and mid-Nov.–mid-Dec.*

$$$ ✕🏨 **Post.** This interesting house of eccentric design, with odd balconies and a triangular garden, is in the center of town. Excursions, climbing, rafting, and fishing are offered, and rooms are attractively decorated. ✉ *Hauptpl. 66, A–9640,* ☎ *04715/221,* FAX *04715/222–53. 24 rooms. Restaurant, bar, café, pool, sauna, exercise room, fishing. No credit cards. Closed late Apr. and mid-Nov.–mid-Dec.*

En Route The scenic Route 110 north over the Gailberg will bring you, after about 8 kilometers (5 miles) and some dramatic twists and turns, to Route 100 at Oberdrauburg. From here to Lienz (20 kilometers, or 12 miles) the highway follows the Drau river valley, with splendid views up into the Kreuzeck mountain range on your right. The Romans recognized the strategic importance of the region and about AD 50 established **Aguntum** here to protect the important trade route against possible usurpers. About 5 kilometers (3 miles) before you reach Lienz, you'll come to the excavations. You can explore the site, where archaeologists have been unearthing remains of this ancient civilization.

Lienz (E.T.)

❸ *55 km (34 mi) northwest of Kötschach–Mauthen.*

Tucked in at the confluence of the Drau and Isel rivers, with the Dolomites a dramatic backdrop to the south, Lienz, a summer and winter resort, is now the capital of the region. The awe-inspiring peaks rising around the town might make your first impression one of human insignificance in the face of overwhelming power and glory. Such feelings of reverence may account for the number of notable churches in Lienz; at least five are worth a visit, particularly the parish church of **St. Andreas,** on Patriadorfer Strasse, which you can reach by walking up Muchar Gasse and Schweizergasse or by following the Rechter Iselweg along the river. A Romanesque lion decorates the doorway, giving witness to the church's early roots. The present-day Gothic edifice was completed in 1457, while the interior is Baroque, from the winged high altar to the vividly colored ceiling fresco (1761). Note the ornate marble tombstones of the noble Görz family.

Three blocks away from St. Andreas—cross the Pfarrbrücke into Beda Weber-Gasse and turn left into Patriadorferstrasse—you'll find the **war memorial chapel,** designed by Clemens Holzmeister, the architect responsible for Salzburg's Festspielhaus and Felsenreitschule (the festival theaters). The wall paintings are by Albin Egger-Lienz (1868–1926), who is renowned for his ability to portray human strength and weakness and who is also buried here. Close to the center of town, the **Franciscan church** on the Muchargasse was originally a Carmelite cloister, founded in 1349 by the Countess Euphemia of Görz. The church was taken over by the Franciscans in 1785 and restored in 1947–48. A Gothic *pietà* from about 1400 adorns the left side altar at the back; its wall frescoes are from the 15th century. A wooden statue dedicated to St. Wolfgang can be found in the 1243 **Dominican church,** on the Schweizergasse, which was subsequently rebuilt in late-Gothic style. **St. Michael's** on Michaeler Platz on the north side of the Isel was completed in 1530, but the north tower, with its onion dome, dates only to 1713. Note the fancy ceiling ornamentation, the 1683 high altar, and the gravestones. The Rococo **St. Joseph's,** by the Spitalsbrücke, was badly damaged in 1945 and rebuilt in 1957. **St. Antonius** on the Hauptplatz dates to the 16th century. The recently restored 16th-century **Lieburg palace** on the Hauptplatz, with two towers, now houses provincial government offices.

A massive tower looms over the **Schloss Bruck,** a battlemented residential castle that dates to 1280 and now serves as the city museum. The remarkably well-preserved castle also has a Romanesque chapel with a late-15th-century ceiling and wall frescoes. Works by Egger-Lienz and Franz Defregger (1835–1921), another Tirolean painter, are displayed here, along with Celtic and Roman relics from nearby excavations. ⊠ *Iseltaler Str.,* ☎ *04852/62580.* *AS45.* ⏲ *Palm Sunday–mid-June and mid-Sept.–Oct., Tues.–Sun. 10–5; mid-June–mid-Sept., daily 10–6.*

Dining and Lodging

$$$$ ★ ✕🏨 **Traube.** In summer, the striped awnings of this central hotel (part of the Romantik Hotel group) shade the cafés on the street and balcony. The atmosphere is elegant, thanks to a mix of older furniture and antiques, and rooms are spacious and comfortable. The hotel has its own fishing waters and a rooftop swimming pool with wonderful views of the surrounding mountains. The restaurant's food is not quite up to the setting, but take the recommendations and you won't be unhappy; the cellar disco offers evening entertainment. ⊠ *Hauptpl. 14, A–9900,* ☎ *04852/64444,* FAX *04852/64184. 51 rooms. 2 restaurants, bar, café, indoor pool, sauna, fishing, dance club. AE, DC, MC, V. Closed weekends in Nov.*

$$$ ★ ✕🏨 **Tristachersee.** A little more than 4 kilometers (about 2½ miles) southeast of Lienz (take the road via Amlach marked to Tristacher See) is a small lake hidden away up a hill. It's a magical setting for this diminutive, totally renovated country hotel, whose rooms, which include 28 studios and 8 apartments, sport dark paneled walls and lots of fabrics. A lakeside terrace provides opportunity for relaxation, and an excellent restaurant features regional cuisine, including fresh fish from the hotel's own ponds. ⊠ *A–9900,* ☎ *04852/67666–0,* FAX *04852/67699. 48 rooms. Restaurant, bar, indoor pool, lake, sauna. No credit cards. Closed Nov.–mid-Dec. and last 2 wks of Apr.*

$$ ✕🏨 **Gasthof Haisenhof.** Nestled on a mountain slope overlooking the city, this traditional chalet is adorned with lush flowers hanging from the carved-wood balconies. Rooms are spacious if simply furnished in white linens and blond wood furniture. You can relax on a covered guest terrace with a spectacular view of the surrounding peaks. The restaurant serves up classic Austrian fare in ample portions as well as fresh fish dishes. ✉ *Grafendorfer Str. 12, A–9900,* ☎ *04852/62440,* FAX *04852/62440–6. 25 rooms. Restaurant, bar, sauna, exercise room. AE, DC, MC, V.*

Outdoor Activities and Sports

HIKING

Lienz has miles of marked trails, and detailed maps are available that show mountain lodges and other facilities. Trails in Tirol are designated as easy, moderate, or difficult. Just before Schloss Bruck (☞ *above*), you'll find a chairlift which rises nearly to the crest of the 6,685-foot **Hochstein** mountain, from which you get a splendid panoramic view over Lienz and to the east. You'll have to hike the last kilometer (½ mile) to reach the very top.

If you want to learn to climb, contact Leo Baumgartner at the **Alpinschule Lienz** (✉ Gaimberg, A–9900, ☎ 04852/68770).

WHITE-WATER RAFTING

Stretches of the **Isel** river from Matrei down to Lienz are raftable from May to mid-October. For outfitters, check with a tourist office, or contact **Dieter Messner** (✉ A–9951 Ainet, ☎ 04853/5231). The cost is AS450 and upwards per person, and a minimum of five people is required for a run.

St. Jakob in Defereggen (E.T.)

❹ *20 km (12 mi) northwest of Lienz.*

Few tourists venture into the Defereggental mountain range, although its craggy slopes are sprinkled with unspoiled villages. The small resort of St. Jakob in Defereggen is one of the most charming and picturesque in East Tirol. Sports enthusiasts flock to the area for hiking, climbing, and fishing in summer and skiing in winter. There are also sulfur baths at nearby St. Leonhard and a waterfall at Mariahilf. To reach St. Jakob from Lienz, head northwest on Route 108, following the Isel Valley, and turn left at the village of Huben, about 20 kilometers (12 miles) out of Lienz, onto a scenic side roadway that takes you up the Defereggental.

Dining and Lodging

$$$$ ✕🏨 **Alpenhof.** A large chalet set against a velvet green hillside is an ideal starting point for summer hiking and for skiing. The comfortable rooms all have flower-decked balconies, and the hotel pays particular attention to families with children. The restaurant features regional dishes; ask for recommendations. ✉ *Innerrotte 35, A–9963,* ☎ *04873/5351–0,* FAX *04873/5351–500. 85 rooms. Restaurant, bar, indoor pool, sauna, nightclub, children's programs. AE, DC, MC, V. Closed May and mid-Oct.–mid-Dec.*

Matrei in Osttirol (E.T.)

❺ *10 km (6 mi) northeast of St. Jakob in Defereggen.*

Because of its strategic location on the most secure north–south route over the Alps to Italy, Matrei in Osttirol was settled first by the Romans and then by the Celts. Every year on the eve of St. Nicholas's day (December 6), fantastically dressed characters with furs and bells storm through town in an old tradition called *Klaubaufgehen.* You can see a 15th-century carved-wood statue of St. Nicholas in the church dedicated to his honor in town. Late-13th-century frescoes depicting Adam and Eve also adorn the church, while remarkably well-preserved 14th-century frescoes decorate the outside walls. Just north of Matrei is Schloss Weissenstein, a 12th-century castle that underwent substantial rebuilding in the 1800s and is now privately owned.

Dining and Lodging

$$$–$$$$ ★ ✕🏨 **Rauter.** With an ultramodern facade, clean lines, and slick surfaces, this fashionable house offers elegant comfort in stark contemporary contrast to the usual rustic Alpine style. Here, too, are many diversions and the best restaurant in East Tirol. The fish comes from the hotel's own waters, the lamb from the nearby mountains, and the house bakery supplies the café. A hotel bus brings you to and from hiking areas in summer, ski slopes in winter. Fishing is available for guests staying three days or longer, and there is riding nearby. ✉ *Rauterpl. 3, A–9971,* ☎ *04875/6611,* FAX *04875/6613. 50 rooms. Restaurant, bar, café, indoor and outdoor pools, sauna, exercise room, fishing. No credit cards. Closed Nov.–mid-Dec.*

$ ★ ✕🏨 **Alpengasthof Tauernhaus.** There's quiet comfort in this simple rustic Gasthof, about 14 kilometers (9 miles) up the Tauern valley at the base of the Felbertauern pass. The hotel began as a rest house, founded in 1207 by the archbishops of Salzburg. It is a good starting point for hiking and skiing. ✉ *A–9971,* ☎ *04875/8811,* FAX *04875/8812. 41 rooms, 21 with full bath, 12 with shower. Restaurant, sauna. No credit cards. Closed Nov.*

ACROSS THE GROSSGLOCKNER PASS

From Heiligenblut to Zell am See

This is the excursion over the longest and most spectacular highway through the Alps, the Grossglockner High Alpine Highway, an engineering achievement of the first magnitude. There is one thrill every hundred yards along this scenic route, but your first will be sighting Heiligenblut, one of Austria's prettiest towns, at the foot of the Grossglockner. To explore this region, winter travelers have no choice but to drive north out of Lienz on Route 108, arriving in Mittersill in Salzburg province via the 5-kilometer (3-mile) Felbertauern toll tunnel (winter AS110, summer AS190) under the Tauern mountains, and taking Route 168 east to Zell am See. But if the road is open, go north over the Grossglockner mountain highway. (The trip can be done by car or bus.) Leave Lienz via Route 107, but stop on the way up the hill outside Iselsberg–Stronach for a great panoramic view over the city. As you go over the ridge, you'll be entering Carinthia again. At Winklern the road follows the Möll river valley, and after about 11 kilometers (7 miles) you'll come to Döllach.

Döllach (C.)

❻ *11 km (7 mi) northeast of Lienz.*

Prospectors once searched for gold in Döllach (Grosskirchheim), in the Möll river valley. Today, the history of local gold mining is chronicled in a museum in the **Schloss Grosskirchheim.** ☎ *04825/226.* 🎟 *AS30.* ⏲ *May–Oct., Mon.–Sat. 10–noon and 1:30–5; tour Mon.–Sat. at 10, 11, 1:30, 3, and 4:30.*

Don't overlook the Gothic **St. Maria Cornach church,** with its ornate Baroque interior.

Dining and Lodging

$$$–$$$$ ✕🏨 **Schlosswirt.** Rooms range from somewhat spartan to elegant in this appealing chalet hotel at the base of the mountains on the fringe of the

Grossglockner national park. In season you can climb, hike, ski, and ride horseback in the gorgeous "hidden valley" of the Graden brook. The hotel has its own fishing streams and lake, and it organizes dinners and wine tastings in the local 500-year-old castle. The restaurant has slipped since it started serving tour groups but is still worth a try; ask for recommendations. ✉ *A–9843,* ☎ *04825/211–0 or 04825/411–0,* FAX *04825/211–165. 25 rooms. Restaurant, bar, pool, lake, sauna, tennis court, horseback riding, fishing. No credit cards. Closed 3 wks in Apr.*

Heiligenblut (C.)

★ ❼ *17 km (10½ mi) north of Döllach.*

Some say the best time to experience this little slice of paradise is after a leisurely dinner at one of the many Gasthöfe, gazing out at the starry firmament over the Hohe Tauern range. Others relish standing around an early morning thaw-out fire, used by hikers setting out to conquer the mighty foothills of the Grossglockner peaks, the highest in Austria. This small town nestled in a valley is known for its picturesque church set against an equally picturesque mountain backdrop, but it's the famed mountain-climbing school and climbing and skiing facilities that draw flocks of all-out active types.

According to local legend, St. Briccius, after obtaining a vial of the blood of Jesus, was buried by an avalanche, but when his body was recovered, the tiny vial was miraculously found hidden within one of the saint's open wounds. The town gets its name, Heiligenblut (Holy Blood), from this miraculous event. Today the relic is housed in the *Sakramenthäuschen,* the chapel of the small but beautiful Gothic parish **church of St. Vincent.** Completed in 1490 after more than a century of construction under the toughest conditions, the church is marked by its soaring belfry tower. Sublimely, the sharply pointed spire finds an impressive echo in the conic peak of the Grossglockner. St. Vincent contains a beautifully carved late-Gothic double altar nearly 36 feet high, and the Coronation of Mary is depicted in the altar wings, richly carved by Wolfgang Hasslinger in 1520. The region's most important altarpiece, it imparts a feeling of quiet power in this spare, high church. The church also has a noble crypt and graveyard, the latter sheltering graves of those lost in climbing the surrounding mountains.

To get to Heiligenblut without a car, you need to travel via bus from Lienz or Zell am See (note that some buses stop in the tiny hamlet of Winkl directly below the town). During the winter, buses run from Heiligenblut to nearby ski runs. Heiligenblut loves tourists and special deals are usually offered, ranging from bargain cards issued to visitors staying more than three days to cut-rate one-day ski passes.

Dining and Lodging

$$$$ ✕🏨 **Glocknerhof.** This dark-wood chalet in the center of the village fits perfectly into the surroundings. You'll feel comfortable in its cozy, attractive rooms. Close to climbing in summer and skiing in winter, the hotel has its own fishing streams for guests. Tour groups stop here on the way over the Grossglockner road, but the restaurant is good. ✉ *Hof 3, A–9844,* ☎ *04824/2244,* FAX *04824/2244–66. 52 rooms. Restaurant, bar, indoor pool, sauna, fishing, children's programs. No credit cards. Closed mid-Apr.–mid-June and Oct.–early Dec.*

$$$–$$$$ ✕🏨 **Kärntnerhof.** Several chalet-style houses set close together have been combined to make up this intimate, family-run complex on the edge of thick woods about 2 kilometers (1¼ miles) from the center of town. There's entertainment twice weekly. ✉ *Winkl 3, A–9844,* ☎ *04824/2004–0,*

FAX 04824/2004–89. 43 rooms. Restaurant, bar, indoor and outdoor pools, sauna, exercise room. DC. Closed Easter–May and mid-Oct.–mid-Dec.*

$$$–$$$$ ✕🏨 **Panoramagasthof Lächenhof.** This charming Gasthaus lives up to its name, thanks to spectacular views of the surrounding Alpine scenery from balconied rooms festooned with flowers. The chalet-style building is perched on a mountain slope and surrounded by lush forest, so it's easy to feel you've left civilization behind. Rooms are comfortably appointed with pastel fabrics and sturdy wood furniture. ✉ *Hof 70, A–9844,* ☎ *04824/2262,* FAX *04824/2262–45. 23 rooms. Restaurant, bar, sauna. AE, DC, MC, V.*

$$$–$$$$ ✕🏨 **Senger.** Weathered wood and flowered balconies highlight this old farmhouse chalet, which has been cleverly enlarged while keeping its original rustic atmosphere. The rooms and romantic apartments, with lots of pillows and country prints, continue the attractive rural theme. It's a bit outside the center of town. ✉ *Heiligenblut 23, A–9844,* ☎ *04824/2215–0,* FAX *04824/2215–9. 9 rooms, 8 apartments. Restaurant, bar, sauna, exercise room. No credit cards. Closed 1 wk after Easter–June and mid-Oct.–mid-Dec.*

Outdoor Activities and Sports

DIGGING FOR GOLD

From mid-June to mid-September, you can pan for gold in the streams around Heiligenblut. Buy a ticket for an excursion at the "gold-digging" office in the town (✉ Tourismusverband, Hof 4, ☎ 04824/2001–21). The price includes a picnic lunch, necessary equipment, and a permit to take home your finds.

HIKING AND MOUNTAIN CLIMBING

This is a hiker's El Dorado, with (in summer) more than 240 kilometers (150 miles) of marked pathways and trails in all directions. There are relatively easy hikes to the Kalvarienberg (½ hour), Wirtsbauer-Alm (two hours), and the Leiterfall, a 400-foot-high waterfall (two hours). For serious Alpine climbers who wish to tackle the Grossglockner peak, one of the most famous mountain-climbing schools, the Institut Franz-Josefs-Höhe, has its cold-weather base here—during warm weather, the school shifts to a mansion on a Grossglocker mountain spur.

Grossglockner Highway

★ ❽ *14 km (10 mi) north of Heiligenblut.*

From Heiligenblut the climb begins up the Carinthian side of the Grossglockner. You'll be tapped here for a AS350 toll (AS340 from season opening to June 16 and from Sept. 16 to season closing) allowing you to use the Grossglockner High Alpine Highway as much as you like on the same day. There's also a ticket for AS480 good on any two days within a calendar year or for AS450 on any eight consecutive days. The peak itself—at 12,470 feet, the highest point in Austria—is off to the west. You can get somewhat closer than the main road takes you by following the highly scenic but steep Gletscherstrasse westward up to the Gletscherbahn on the Franz-Josef-Plateau, where you'll be rewarded with absolutely breathtaking views of the Grossglockner peak and surrounding Alps, the vast glacier in the valley below, and, on a clear day, even into Italy.

The Grossglockner road twists and turns as it struggles to the 8,370-foot Hochtor. At this point you've crossed into Salzburg province. Completed in 1935, the highway provides the only passage over the high mountain ranges anywhere between the Brenner pass and the Radstadt Tauern pass, which are 160 kilometers (100 miles) apart. You're now on Edelweiss-Strasse, where the rare white-starred edelweiss grows. A stop at the **Edelweissspitze** yields a view out over East Tirol, Carinthia, and Salzburg. The rare white-starred edelweiss—the von Trapps sang its praises in *The Sound of Music*—grows here. Though the species is protected, don't worry about the plants you get as souvenirs; they are cultivated for this purpose. Be sure to visit the **Visitor's Center and Alpine Museum.** An excellent short film (in English) tells the story of the area, and computer-driven dioramas show how animals survive the extreme climatic changes atop the mountain range. *Free. Early May–late Oct., daily 9–5.*

Zell am See (S.P.)

★ 9 *8 km (5 mi) northwest of the Grossglockner.*

After the toll station on the north side of the Grossglockner peak, the highway finally exhausts its hairpin turns (more than 30) and continues to Bruck an der Grossglocknerstrasse. From here it's only about 8 kilometers (5 miles) west on Route S11 and then north on Route 311 to Zell am Zee. This lovely lakeside town got its name from the monks' cells of a monastery founded here in about AD 790. In the quaint town center, visit the 17th-century Renaissance **Schloss Rosenberg,** now the town hall. The **city tower,** built around 1100, was originally a granary. Unusually fine statues of St. George and St. Florian can be found on the west wall of the splendid Romanesque **parish church of St. Hippolyte.** Built in 1217, the church was beautifully renovated in 1975. Several locations offer up stunning vistas of the town and its environs. On ground level, take a boat ride to the village of Thumersbach, on the opposite shore, for a wonderful reflected view of Zell am See. For a bird's-eye view, a cable car leads virtually from the center of Zell am See up to the **Schmittenhöhe** for a 180° panorama that takes in the peaks of the Glockner and Tauern granite ranges to the south and west and the very different limestone ranges to the north. This sweep will impress upon you the geology of Austria as no written description ever could. In addition, there are four other cable-car trips up this mountain, offering some of the most spectacular vistas of the Kitzbühel Alps.

The romantic narrow-gauge **Pinzgauer railroad** winds its way under steam power on a two-hour trip through the Pinzgau, following the Salzach River valley westward 54 kilometers (34 miles) to Krimml. Nearby are the famous Krimmler waterfalls, with a 1,300-foot drop, which you can see from an observation platform or explore close at hand (if you can manage a hike of about 3½–4 hours). Be sure to take a raincoat and sneakers. *06542/2600–0. Round-trip AS220. Trains depart July and Aug., Tues., Thurs., and weekends at 9:15; Sept., Sat. at 9:15.*

Dining and Lodging

$$$$ **Grand.** In the style of the great turn-of-the-century resort hotels, this totally renovated house right on the lake is, as its name implies, probably the grandest place to stay in Zell. It stands on its own peninsula, is decorated with mansard roofs and whipped-cream stuccowork, and serves up some fine dining. It may not offer all the amenities and health facilities of other Zell hotels provide, but no other choice offers such charm. Most of the accommodations are small apartments, complete with kitchenette and fireplace; some are duplexes; and the best are those farthest out on the small peninsula. Of the restaurants, the Seerestaurant serves fish fresh from the lake, the Wünderbar is set in a semicircular glass-enclosed room offering great views of the lake, while the Rendezvous is a nice spot for cocktails at dusk. *Esplanade 4, A-5700, 06542/2388–0, FAX 06542/2388–305. 111 rooms. 2*

restaurants, bar, indoor pool, lake, sauna, squash, boating, dance club. AE, DC, MC, V.

$$$$ ★ ✕🏨 **Salzburgerhof.** Sophisticated travelers often pick this impressive family-managed chalet, not far from the lake and the ski lift, as the town's foremost hotel; comfort and personal service are the rule. Each of the attractive rooms and suites has a flower-bedecked balcony. The restaurant is truly excellent; try the Tafelspitz or rack of lamb in an herbed pastry crust. The pleasant garden is used for barbecues and evenings of folkloric entertainment. Golfer guests get a 30% discount at the local club. ✉ *Auerspergstr. 11, A–5700,* ☎ *06542/2828–0,* FAX *06542/2828–66. 36 rooms, 8 suites, 16 junior suites. Restaurant, bar, indoor pool, lake, sauna, exercise room. AE, DC, MC, V. Closed Apr.–early May and Nov.–mid-Dec.*

$$$$ ★ ✕🏨 **Schloss Prielau.** Sporting turreted towers and striped shutters, this castle looks as if it stepped out of a fairy tale. Elegantly furnished rooms with sumptuous fabrics and traditional carved wooden furniture can be a bit dim, however, because of the narrow, old-fashioned windows. But the service will make you feel as if you are the newest member of royalty to take up residence here. The restaurant serves classic Austrian dishes like schnitzel but with a lighter, more refined touch than you find in most establishments. ✉ *Hofmannsthalstr., A–5700,* ☎ *06542/2609,* FAX *06542/2609–55. 12 rooms. Restaurant, bar, lake, sauna. AE, DC, MC, V.*

$$ ✕🏨 **St. Hubertushof.** On the opposite side of the lake from town, this sprawling hotel complex offers a great view across the water. Paneling and antlers over the fireplace in the lounge add to its rural style. Golfers get a 30% reduction at the local course. The dance bar draws a regular crowd, and the restaurant offers a wide range of international and local dishes. ✉ *Seeuferstr. 7, A–5705 Zell am See/Thumersbach,* ☎ *06542/3116–0,* FAX *06542/3116–71. 112 rooms. Restaurant, bar, café, sauna. AE, DC, MC, V. Closed Nov.*

Nightlife and the Arts

The emphasis in Zell is more on drinking than on dancing, but the scene does change periodically. At the moment, one of the "in" places is the **Crazy Daisy** (✉ ☎ 06542/2516), a dance pub near the Kurhaus. Also near the Kurhaus and popular is the pub **Zuckersake** (☎ 06542/4151). A mature crowd gathers at the **Wunderbar** (☎ 06542/23870), in the Grand Hotel (☞ Dining and Lodging, *above*). Check out the action in the cellar of the **Sporthotel Lebzelter** (☎ 06542/24110).

Outdoor Activities and Sports

BICYCLING

The area around Zell am See is a gorgeous spot for bicycling. If you left your wheels at home, you can rent some at the train station (☎ 06542/3214–380) for AS90 (AS50 if you have a valid rail ticket). From April to October, bike tours run from south of Zell am See via St. Johann up to Salzburg via the Tauern cycle route. Check with **Austria Radreisen** (✉ Holzingerstr. 546, A–4780 Schrading, ☎ 07712/5511, FAX 07712/4811).

FISHING

The lake's tranquil waters offer fine fishing. Many hotels in the area have packages for avid anglers.

GOLF

Zell am See/Kaprun has two 18-hole courses (each par 72). ✉ *Golfstr. 25,* ☎ *06542/56161,* FAX *06542/56035.* ⏲ *Apr.–Oct.*

WATER SPORTS

Boating—from paddleboats to sailboats—and swimming are excellent on the uncrowded Zeller See. Since powerboats are restricted on many Austrian lakes, you won't find much waterskiing, but there is a waterskiing school, **Wasserskischule Thumersbach** (✉ Strandbad, Thumersbach, ☎ 06542/4362), on the lake.

Saalbach/Hinterglemm (S.P.)

⑩ *14 km (9 mi) northwest of Zell am See.*

These noted skiing meccas are part of an area, comprising Saalbach, Kaprun, Zell am See, and Hinterglemm, that becomes a ski circus in winter. A clever layout of lifts and trails enables you to ski slopes without duplication and still get back to your starting point. When the snow melts, the region offers sensational hiking and both towns offer a wide variety of sports. Both Saalbach and Hinterglemm have banned cars from the village center. You can drive to your hotel to unload baggage; watch carefully for signs or ask for specific directions—the routes are convoluted and confusing. Take the **Kohlmais cable car** north out of Saalbach to the top of the ridge for a superb 360° view of the surrounding mountain ranges. To get to Saalbach from Zell am Zee, continue north on Route 311 to Maishofen, where the Glemm valley opens to the west, then continue about 9 kilometers (5 miles) to the west. For those traveling by train or bus, head first to Zell am See for transfers up the valley.

Dining and Lodging

$ ★ ✕ **Iglsbergerhof.** This utterly unpretentious family-run Gasthof serves up some of the best authentic regional specialties in the area. Start with beef bouillon with *Pinzgauer Käspressknödel* (cheese dumplings), then *Speckknödel* (bread dumpling with bacon chunks) with sauerkraut, and finish with a *Pinzgauer Bauernkrapfen,* a delicious filled doughnut. ✉ *Vorderglemm 340, Saalbach,* ☎ *06541/6491. No credit cards. Closed Wed. and Nov.–mid-Dec.*

$$$–$$$$ ✕🏨 **Glemmtalerhof.** This massive chalet is surprisingly intimate inside, with pleasant paneled rooms and 20 apartments in Alpine style, most with balconies. It is mainly a winter resort, but there's still plenty to do in summer. Golfers get a 30% reduction on greens fees at Zell am See courses. ✉ *Glemmtaler Landstr. 150, A–5754,* ☎ *06541/7135,* FAX *06541/7135–63. 62 rooms. 2 restaurants, 2 bars, café, indoor pool, sauna, golf privileges, exercise room, horseback riding, nightclub, children's programs, parking. AE, DC, MC, V. Closed mid-Apr.–mid-May and mid-Oct.–mid-Dec.*

$$$–$$$$ ✕🏨 **Saalbacher Hof.** This family-run chalet complex in the center of town is identified by a rustic bell tower and overflowing pots of red geraniums against weathered dark wood. Warm paneling and a large fireplace welcome you; the rooms are spacious and comfortable. The hotel can make arrangements for golf and tennis. ✉ *Dorfstr. 27, A–5753,* ☎ *06541/7111,* FAX *06541/7111–42. 90 rooms. 2 restaurants, bar, pool, sauna, golf privileges, tennis court, nightclub. AE, DC, MC, V. Closed mid-Apr.–May and Oct.–Nov.*

$$$–$$$$ ✕🏨 **Theresia.** The term "garden hotel" applies here. Intimate wood-paneled reception rooms spill over into a garden area topped with pools tucked into the hillside behind. On the quieter edge of Hinterglemm, the hotel is close to ski lifts and hiking trails. Spacious rooms feature light wood, and the restaurant is excellent. Zell am See courses offer a 30% greens fee reduction. ✉ *Glemmtaler Landestr. 208, A–5754,* ☎ *06541/7414–0,* FAX *06541/7414–121. 37 rooms. Restaurant, bar,*

3 heated outdoor pools, 1 indoor pool, sauna, golf privileges, exercise room. DC. Closed mid-Apr.–mid-May and Nov.–mid-Dec.

Outdoor Activities and Sports

SKIING

In addition to tobogganing, sleigh rides, and curling, Saalbach and Hinterglemm have some of the finest skiing in Land Salzberg. There are more than 40 ski lifts, numerous cross-country ski trails, and for ski potatoes, races and competitions are often run on the Saalbach-Hinterglemm Slalom. The most popular run is on the Schattberg mountain—a cable car takes you there from the center of Saalbach—where, on high, a restaurant offers fine dining and even better *Sonnengrill.* Ski schools are also here for beginners.

Saalbach has a number of places that crowd up quickly as the slopes are vacated. The tourist office has a list of bars and discos, but try the **Hinterhagalm** disco/bar (☎ 06541/7212) or the **Visage** disco in the Hotel Kristall (☎ 06541/6376–45). The **Alpenhotel** (☎ 06541/6666–0) and **Neuhaus** (☎ 06541/7151–0) feature small local bands. There's action at the **Almbar** in the Hotel Glemmtalerhof (☎ 06541/7135–0) and at the **Pinzgauer Stüberl** in Hotel Wolf in Hinterglemm (☎ 06541/6346–37). The **Londoner** and **Knappenkeller** in the Hotel Knappenhof (☎ 06541/6497) in Hinterglemm offer disco or live music in winter and are currently among the "in" spots. Among bars, **Stamperl, Flockerl, Pfiff,** and, in Hinterglemm, **Lumpie's, Bla-Bla,** and **Rudi's Kneipe** are current favorites.

Saalfelden (S.P.)

11 *10 km (6 mi) northeast of Saalbach.*

Saalfelden nestles at the foot of the **Steinernes Meer** (Sea of Stone), the formidable ridge that divides Austria from Germany. The town, farther up Route 311 from Saalbach, is a climber's mecca, but only for those who are experienced and who can tackle such challenges as the 9,560-foot Hochkönig. At the edge of the Steinernes Meer, signs lead you to a late-Gothic **cave chapel,** containing a winged altarpiece near a stone pulpit and hermit's cell. Saalfelden is a main stop on the Innsbruck–Salzberg train route. Sights in town include a 19th-century Romanesque parish church with a late-Gothic winged altar, the nearby 14th-century Farmach Castle which is now a retirement home, and the 13th-century Lichtenberg Castle which is now privately owned. For many, the most interesting attraction is the **Ritzen Castle** museum, where the Christmas manger collection of artisan Xandl Schläffer, and exhibits on minerals, native handicrafts, and local history, are on view. ☎ *06582/2759.* *AS30.* *Jan.–Easter and mid-Sept.–Oct., Wed., weekends, and holidays 2–4; mid-June–mid-Sept., daily 10–noon and 2–5; Dec., daily 2–4.*

Teenagers will enjoy the 1½-kilometer (1-mile) **summer toboggan run.** With 63 curves, it is the longest such run in Europe. Other well-marked attractions in the area include the **Vorderkaserklamm gorge.** The **Hirschbichl pass** was a strategic route where several battles were fought during the Napoleonic wars.

OFF THE BEATEN PATH

LAMPRECHTSOFENLOCHOHÜLE CAVES – About 14 kilometers (8 miles) north of Saalfelden, you come to Weissbach bei Lofer. Here you find these interesting caves, which have great domes and waterfalls. ☎ *06582/8343.* *AS30.* *Late Apr.–early Nov., Fri.–Wed. 8–7; early Nov.–late Apr., Tues., Thurs., and weekends 10–4, and Mon., Wed., and Fri. 10–10.*

Dining and Lodging

$$–$$$ ★ ✕ **Schatzbichl.** The reputation of this simple Gasthaus slightly east of Saalfelden draws guests from near and far. The pine-paneled interior is bright and cheerful, as is the usually overworked staff. Regional dishes are simply prepared and presented; try the garlic soup, lamb chops, or any of the fish offered. ✉ *Ramseiden 82,* ☎ *06582/3281,* FAX *06582/3281–4. Reservations essential. No credit cards. Closed Tues. Mar.–May, Sept., and Oct.; 2 wks in Apr.; and Nov.*

$$$$ ✕🏨 **Sporthotel Gut Brandlhof.** This sprawling ranch, about 5 kilometers (3 miles) outside town, is perfect for an active vacation. The vast complex provides all manner of sports facilities, including the 18-hole, par-72 Saalfelden golf course, which belongs to the hotel. The comfortable rooms are done in Alpine-country style. ✉ *Hohlwegen 4, A–5760,* ☎ *06582/2176–0,* FAX *06582/2176–598. 150 rooms. Restaurant, 2 bars, indoor and outdoor pools, sauna, 18-hole golf course, tennis courts, bowling, exercise room, horseback riding, squash, fishing, children's programs. AE, DC.*

$$$ ✕🏨 **Gasthof Hindenburg.** This 500-year-old inn in the center of town has been newly renovated from top to bottom to provide modern comfort while retaining historic touches. Room colors are warm and inviting, complementing the wood flooring and the combination of antique and modern furnishings. Some apartments have a duplex layout. In summer, the garden restaurant is particularly inviting. ✉ *Bahnhofstr. 6, A–5760,* ☎ *06582/2303,* FAX *06582/4114–78. 38 rooms, 6 apartments. 4 restaurants, bar, sauna. AE, DC, MC, V.*

Outdoor Activities and Sports

BICYCLING

The valley leading to Saalfelden is a great place for seeing sights on two wheels. You can rent a bike at the **railroad station** (☎ 06582/2344–0) for AS90 (AS50 if you have a valid rail ticket).

GOLF

The tricky 18-hole, par-72 course crisscrosses the wild Saalach stream. ✉ *Hohlwegen 4,* ☎ *06582/2176–555,* FAX *06582/2176–598.* ⊙ *Apr.–Oct.*

HIKING

From Saalfelden, you can head off through the magnificent Saalach Valley on any of three 5- or 6-day self-guided expeditions called **"Hiking without Luggage."** Your bags are transported, your choice of accommodation is pre-booked, and guidebooks are available in English. The exhilaration can't be described in words. Information is available from Saalfelden's Pinzgau regional tourist office (✉ Lofererstr. 5, Postfach 116, A–5760, ☎ 06582/4017, FAX 06582/4017–4).

MOUNTAIN SPAS AND ALPINE RAMBLES

From Badgastein to the Salzburger Dolomitenstrasse

Icy Alps and hot springs, luxurious hotels and tranquil lakes are the enticing combinations this Austrian region superlatively serves up. Gold mined from the mountains here gave rise to numerous burger fortunes; today, glittering gold jewelry finds many buyers in the shops of Badgastein's Empress Elisabeth Promendade. To set off on this trip, head south from Salzberg on the A10 and turn west at the Route 311 junction, or from Zell am See, turn east on Route 311 to pass Bruck again, continue through Taxenbach, and turn south at the intersection of Route 167.

Badgastein (S.P.)

12 *42 km (26 mi) southeast of Saalfelden.*

Though it traces its roots all the way back to the 15th century, this resort, one of Europe's leading spas, really gained renown in the last century, when aristocrats and other notables flocked to the area to "take the cure." Today, Badgastein retains much of its 19th-century ambience. The stunning setting—a mountain torrent, the Gasteiner Ache, rushes through the unusual town—adds to the attraction. Although some say the town has fallen into a bit of a trance, with most attempts to rejuvenate this turn-of-the-century jewel unsuccessful, many travelers still come to its noted Felsenbad baths and **Kur-und-Kongresszentrum** (Treatment Complex) to rejuvenate themselves with radioactive mineral-water cures. The most unusual spa is the natural sauna at **Böckstein,** near the Empress Elisabeth Promenade, where an abandoned gold mine contains thermal passageways. For complete information on the town's main spas, contact the Badgastein tourist office. In the winter, the skiing at the nearby **Graukogel, Stubnerkogel,** and **Kreuzkogel** (☞ Skiing, *below*) peaks are the equal of any in Land Salzburg. Badgastein is serviced by many rail lines, with many expresses running from Salzberg and Klagenfurt. You can also reach the town by bus from Salzberg.

Dining and Lodging

$$$$ ✕🏨 **Elisabethpark.** The public rooms go on and on in this elegant hotel—modern, but of the old school—in the center of town. The grand-hotel atmosphere is underscored by Oriental carpets, marble, and crystal chandeliers. Rooms, with period furnishings, are particularly comfortable, and service has a pleasantly personal touch. ✉ *A–5640,* ☎ *06434/2551–0,* FAX *06434/2551–10. 109 rooms. Restaurant, bar, café, indoor pool, sauna, spa, exercise room. AE, DC, MC, V. Closed mid-Apr.–early June and Sept.–mid-Dec.*

$$$$ ✕🏨 **Villa Solitude.** In this central turn-of-the-century villa overlooking the gorge below, six elegant suites offer every comfort. Rooms are wood-paneled, with furnishings appropriate to the period. The management is the same as at the Grüner Baum. In the excellent restaurant, the Brasserie, try fish or fillet of beef; if you're here in summer, you can enjoy them on the terrace. ✉ *Kaiser-Franz-Josef-Str. 16, A–5640,* ☎ *06434/5101–0,* FAX *06434/5101–3. Restaurant. AE, DC, MC, V. Closed May and Nov.*

$$$–$$$$ ✕🏨 **Grüner Baum.** You're out of the center of town here, in a relaxing, friendly hotel village set amid meadows and woodlands. The guest list in this Relais et Châteaux group hotel has included Austrian Empress Elisabeth and Saudi King Saud. Five separate houses have comfortable rustic, wood-paneled rooms, giving the complex a feeling of intimacy and personality. Children are well looked after. The elegant restaurant has an excellent reputation. ✉ *Kötschachtal, A–5640,* ☎ *06434/2516–0,* FAX *06434/2516–25. 80 rooms. Restaurant, bar, indoor and outdoor pools, sauna, tennis court, exercise room, children's programs. AE, DC, MC, V. Closed mid-Oct.–mid-Dec.*

$$ 🏨 **Krone.** Most of the pleasant, bright rooms in this in-town hotel have balconies, and you're about three minutes from the cable car up the mountain. In addition, the thermal spa is next door. ✉ *Bahnhofspl. 8, A–5640,* ☎ *06434/2330–0,* FAX *06434/2330–86. 60 rooms. Restaurant, bar, spa. MC, V. Closed mid-Apr.–mid-May and Oct.–mid-Dec.*

Nightlife and the Arts

The **Grand Hotel de l'Europe casino** has baccarat, blackjack, roulette, and slot machines. A passport is required. ✉ *Kaiser-Franz-Josef-Str. 14,* ☎ *06434/2465–0.* ⏲ *July–mid-Sept. and Dec. 26–Mar., daily 7 PM–2 AM.*

Outdoor Activities and Sports

GOLF

The **Golfclub Gastein** has an attractive 9-hole, par-36 course. ☎ *06434/2775,* FAX *06434/2775–4.* 🎟 *Greens fee weekdays AS390, weekends AS500.* ⏲ *Late Apr.–Oct.*

SKIING

Though other Austrian winter sports areas are more popular, don't let this discourage you from trying the excellent facilities and good slopes in Sportgastein, some 9 kilometers (5½ miles) south of Badgastein. The main ski run near Badgastein is the Graukogel peak, which also offers a restaurant and great alpine hiking. To reach the winter-sports region, turn right at Böckstein onto the Gasteiner Alpenstrasse toll road. The toll is included in a winter ski pass. *Road conditions,* ☎ *06434/2398.* 🎟 *Toll AS45.*

Liechtensteinklamm

13 *20 km (15 mi) north of Badgastein.*

Traveling from Badgastein along Route 311, turn east toward Schwarzach in Pongau, where the road heads north, to find, between Schwarzach and St. Johann, the Liechtensteinklamm, the deepest (1,000 feet), narrowest (12½ feet), and most spectacular gorge in the Eastern Alps. At its far end is a 200-foot waterfall. A tour on a walkway crisscrossing the gorge takes about 45 minutes. ☎ *06412/8572.* 🎟 *AS30.* ⏲ *Early May–Oct., daily 8–5.*

St. Johann im Pongau (S.P.)

★ 14 *18 km (11 mi) north of Badgastein.*

St. Johann has developed into a full-fledged year-round resort. The area is favored by cross-country and intermediate downhill skiers, as the gentle slopes provide an almost endless variety of runs. The huge twin-spired parish church, built in 1861 in neo-Gothic style, is known locally as the **Pongau Cathedral**—a mammoth structure that some feel appears unnecessarily overbearing compared to the tiny town. Every four years during the first week of January, the populace of St. Johann celebrates *Pongauer Perchtenlauf,* which can be poetically translated to mean "away with Winter's ghost." Taking to the streets, they ring huge cowbells and wear weird masks and costumes to drive away evil spirits. The next celebration will be in the year 2000; check with the tourist office for the exact date. St. Johann is on the rail lines connecting Munich, Klagenfurt, and Salzburg.

Dining and Lodging

$$$–$$$$ ✕🏨 **Sporthotel Alpenland.** The newest hotel in town has a somewhat more commercial approach to innkeeping than do the family-run chalets, but you get an attractive room, efficient service, and plenty of facilities. Three restaurants offer pizza, steaks, and such local specialties as lamb. ✉ *Hans-Kappacher-Str. 7–9, A–5600,* ☎ *06412/7021–0,* FAX *06412/7021–51. 137 rooms. 3 restaurants, bar, indoor and outdoor pools, sauna, tennis court, exercise room. AE, DC, MC, V.*

Outdoor Activities and Sports

GOLF

An 18-hole, par-70 course is open May–October. ✉ *Off Rte. 311, Box 6, Goldegg, near Schwarzach in Pongau,* ☎ *06415/8585,* FAX *06415/8585–4.* ⏲ *May–Oct.*

SKIING

Linked by buses and 50 miles of ski runs with other towns in the Pongau Valley, St. Johann remains the ski capital of the area, with more than 40 ski lifts plus several cable-car ascents. Along with other Pongau Valley runs, the town offers a *Drei-Taler-Skischaukel* (three-valley) pass.

Altenmarkt (S.P.)

⓯ *14 km (9 mi) east of St. Johann im Pongau.*

Traveling north on Route 311 from St. Johann in Pongau (about 3 kilometers, or 2 miles, beyond Bischofshofen, take Route 99/E14 where it cuts off east to Radstadt) will take travelers to Altenmarkt. Nearby streams make the town a prime fishing site in summer, while skiing takes the spotlight during the winter months. The **parish church of St. Mary's** contains the *Schöne Madonna,* an outstanding statue of the Virgin Mary that dates to before 1384. Outside of town, look for the **Schloss Tantalier,** built in 1450 for a noble family, reconstructed in 1569, and now serving as a youth hostel. The castle is unusual for its virtually square shape, with round towers on the south side and square ones on the north.

Dining and Lodging

$$$$ ★ ✕🏨 **Lebzelter.** Even though it's in the center of town, this comfortable, family-run hotel has its own fishing stream. The excellent, window-filled, country restaurant has a broad reputation. Dishes range from steaks to fish to vegetarian meals, but the emphasis is on traditional fare. ✉ *Marktpl. 79, A-5541,* ☎ *06452/6911,* FAX *06452/7823. 29 rooms. Restaurant, bar, sauna, exercise room, fishing. AE, DC, MC, V.*

$$–$$$ ✕🏨 **Markterwirt.** This traditional house in the center of town dates back 900 years. The personal style of the family who runs it is reflected in the charming country decor of the comfortable rooms. The main dining room and the informal *Stube* are good, and half board is required. The hotel has its own lake for fishing. ✉ *Marktpl. 4, A–5541,* ☎ *06452/5420,* FAX *06452/5420–31. 28 rooms. Restaurant, café, sauna, fishing. MC, V. Closed Nov.*

Radstadt (S.P.)

⓰ *4 km (2½ mi) east of Altenmarkt.*

Despite wars and fires, the picturesque walled town of Radstadt still retains its 12th-century character. Standing guard over a key north–south route, Radstadt was once granted the right to warehouse goods and to trade in iron, wine, and salt, but the town's present prosperity is due to tourism: The area is growing in popularity as a skiing destination and has been a long-time mecca for hiking in the summer. Radstadt's north and west walls, dating to 1534, are well preserved, as are three of the towers that mark the corners of the old town. Most of the buildings around the square are also from the 16th century. The late-Romanesque **parish church,** north of the square, dominates the town, but reconstructions over the ages have destroyed much of its original character. The interior contains several Baroque altars. To get to Radstadt, motorists usually take the A10 from Salzberg, from which trains also frequently depart for Radstadt; a transfer has to be made at Bischofshofen.

Dining and Lodging

$$$ ✕🏨 **Sporthotel Gründler.** The emphasis here is on water, and the sport is fishing; the hotel has rights on 16 kilometers (10 miles) of the Enns river. It also has ties to the Radstadt golf club. In summer, huge outdoor pools and a water slide offer great fun for children. The restaurant specializes in trout. ✉ *Schlossstr. 45, A–5550,* ☎ *06452/5590–0,* FAX *06452/5590–28. 10 rooms, 18 apartments. Restaurant, 3 indoor and outdoor pools, sauna, fishing. MC, V. Closed mid-Apr.–mid-May and mid-Oct.–mid-Dec.*

Golf

During the April–November season, hills and a 16th-hole island pose challenges on the town's 18-hole, par-72 course. ✉ *Römerstr. 18,* ☎ *06452/5111,* FAX *06452/7336.* ⏲ *Apr.–Nov.*

Schladming (S.)

17 *18 km (11 mi) east of Radstadt.*

In the 14th and 15th centuries, Schladming was a thriving silver-mining town; then in 1525 the town was burned in an uprising by miners and farmers. Most of what you see today dates to 1526, when reconstruction began, but traces of the earlier town wall and the old miners' houses stand as testament to the town's former glory. Dominating the skyline is the Romanesque tower of the **St. Achaz parish church.** Schladming is popular as a year-round resort. This is an area where sport is taken seriously; not only does it attract the world's best skiers, but it also gives beginners ample scope. And in happy contrast to fashionable resorts in Tirol and Vorarlberg, Schladming and its surroundings are reasonably priced. To get to Schladming from Radstadt, take scenic Route 146 east along the Enns River valley for about 18 kilometers (11 miles) over the provincial border at Mandling. The town is also accessible by rail via the Salzberg–Graz line.

Dining and Lodging

$$$–$$$$ ★ ✕🏨 **Alte Post.** This traditional house in the center of town dates to 1618 and is notable for its particularly attractive *Stuben* and the older rooms with vaulted ceilings. Guest rooms are cozy and comfortable. The restaurants offer good regional and Austrian cuisine in an appropriately genuine atmosphere. Golf arrangements can be made for the nearby Dachstein-Tauern club. ✉ *Hauptpl. 10, A–8970,* ☎ *03687/22571,* FAX *03687/22571–8. 40 rooms. 2 restaurants, bar, tennis court. AE, DC, MC, V. Closed mid- to late Apr., mid- to late Nov.*

Outdoor Activities and Sports

FISHING

From May to mid-September you can cast a fly for trout in the nearby Enns river. Contact **Walter Dichtl** (✉ Hauptpl. 28, ☎ 03687/23539).

GOLF

Schladming-Haus has an Alpine setting that's reason enough to play the 18-hole, par-71 course at the **Golf & Country Club Dachstein-Tauern.** ☎ *03686/2630–0,* FAX *03686/2630–15.* ⏲ *May–Oct.*

SKIING

The main ski runs here are on the Hochwurzen and Planai peaks, both offering cable cars, chair lifts, and expert downhill runs. The Dachstein-Südward cable car ascends to a height of almost 9,000 feet, allowing skiing well into June. Another lure here is the bustling après-ski scene.

Ramsau am Dachstein (S.)

18 *6 km (4 mi) north of Schladming.*

Heading north out of Schladming on a breaktakingly gorgeous local road to Ramsau am Dachstein, and about 4½ kilometers (about 3 miles) west of Ramsau, a small road (AS30 per adult) turns north toward the Dachstein itself, a majestic craggy outcrop of 9,826 feet. Take the impressive 20-minute **Hunerkogel cable car ride** to the top of the Alps (round-trip without skis AS245, open May–Mar.); a phone call to ☎ 03687/81315 will tell you in German what the weather's like up there. To the north lie the lakes of the Salzkammergut, to the west, the Tennen mountain range. South and east lie the lower Tauern mountains. A snowmobile ride will take you very close to the Dachstein peak, or you can hike over if you're wearing hiking or ski boots. In summer the south cliff at Hunerkogel is a favorite "jumping-off spot" for paragliders. To get to Ramsau without a car, you need to take a bus from Schladming.

Dining and Lodging

$$$ ★ 🏨 **Peter Rosegger.** This rustic chalet in a quiet area on the forest's edge is decorated with homey mementos—framed letters and embroidered mottoes—of the Styrian writer for whom it is named. This is the place to stay when you've come for climbing, as Fritz Walcher heads the Alpine school. Rooms are country comfortable, and though the kitchen is the best in the area, the restaurant is only for hotel guests, who are treated to such local specialties as house-smoked trout, Styrian corned pork, and stuffed breast of veal. ✉ *A–8972,* ☎ *03687/81223–0,* FAX *03687/81223–8. 13 rooms. Restaurant, sauna, exercise room. No credit cards. Closed mid-Apr.–May and Nov.–mid-Dec.*

$$–$$$ ✕🏨 **Pehab-Kirchenwirt.** *Kirchenwirt* implies "next to the church," and that's exactly where this rustic family-run hotel is. Many of the comfortable rooms have balconies; those in the back have the best mountain view. You're close to hiking trails in summer and the hotel-operated ski lift and ski runs in winter. Hotel guests can use the nearby indoor pool, which has a sauna and solarium. The restaurant serves good local food. ✉ *A–8972,* ☎ *03687/81732,* FAX *03687/81655. 40 rooms, 4 apartments. Restaurant, café, weinstube. AE. Closed Nov. and 1 month after Easter.*

Outdoor Activities and Sports

HIKING

If you're interested in learning to climb in the difficult Dachstein area, contact the **Alpinschule Dachstein** (✉ Ramsau am Dachstein 233, A–8972, ☎ 03687/81223–0) or **Bergsteigerschule Dachstein** (✉ Ramsau am Dachstein 101, A–8972, ☎ 03687/81424).

SKIING

The famous **Dachstein glacier** can be skied year-round, although summer snow conditions require considerable expertise. Marked trails lead down the north side and along the ridge to the northwest.

Shopping

In the nearby village of Rössing, you'll find Richard Steiner's **Lodenwalker** (☎ 03687/81930), which, since 1434, has been turning out that highly practical felt-like fabric called loden. Here you can find various colors and textures at reasonable prices. It's open weekdays.

Filzmoos (S.P.)

19 *14 km (9 mi) west of Ramsau am Dachstein.*

Filzmoos is a well-kept secret. Though skiing in the nearby Dachstein mountains is excellent, the not terribly expensive winter resort has yet to be discovered by foreign tourists. During the summer months, meandering mountain streams and myriad lakes attract anglers eager for trout, while hikers come to challenge the craggy peaks.

Dining and Lodging

$$$ ★ **Hubertus.** In this highly personal hotel in the center of town, every last detail—from romantic furnishings to modern conveniences—is done to perfection. Fishing enthusiasts have 20 kilometers (12 miles) of mountain streams and two small lakes at their disposal. The restaurant is the best in the area: Frau Maier's way with trout (which you might have caught yourself) is exquisite, but don't overlook the game, roast poultry, or veal sweetbreads. Finish with *Topfenknödel* (cream cheese dumpling), a house specialty. ✉ *Am Dorfpl. 1, A–5532,* ☎ *06453/204,* FAX *06453/2066. 17 rooms. Restaurant, bar, café, sauna, exercise room, fishing. No credit cards. Closed mid-Apr.–mid-May and mid-Oct.–mid-Dec.*

$$–$$$ **Alpenkrone.** From the balconies of this chalet complex, you'll have a great view of the surrounding mountains. Rooms are simple and in no particular style, but the friendly management has succeeded in providing four-star comfort at three-star prices even when the customary half board is considered. ✉ *Filzmoos 133, A–5532,* ☎ *06453/280–0,* FAX *06453/280–48. 51 rooms. Restaurant, bar, indoor pool, sauna, exercise room. DC, MC, V. Closed Easter–mid-May and mid-Oct.–mid-Dec.*

En Route From Filzmoos, rejoin Route 99/E14 again at Eben im Pongau. Here you can take the A10 autobahn north to Salzburg, if you're in a hurry. But if you have time for more majestic scenery and an interesting detour, continue about 4 kilometers (2½ miles) on Route 99/E14, and turn north on Route 166, the **Salzburger Dolomitenstrasse** (Salzburg Dolomites Highway), for a 43-kilometer (27-mile) swing around the Tennen mountains. Be careful, though, to catch the left turn onto Route 162 at Lindenthal; it will be marked to Golling. Head for Abtenau.

Abtenau (S.P.)

20 *37 km (23 mi) northwest of Filzmoos.*

Highlighting this town are the saltwater springs that feed the local spa, which is surrounded by waterfalls and the Tricklfall caves. A charming old village square is flanked by colorful burgher's houses and the 14th-century **St. Blasius parish church,** which has late Gothic frescoes and a Baroque high altar.

Dining and Lodging

$$$$ **Moisl.** This group of typical Alpine chalet–style houses in the center of town, with flower-laden balconies and overhanging eaves, dates back to 1764, but its services and facilities are absolutely up-to-date. Rooms are done in country decor. Evening entertainment includes folk dancing and wine and grill parties. ✉ *Markt 26, A–5441,* ☎ *06243/21630,* FAX *06243/2232–612. 75 rooms. Restaurant, bar, café, indoor pool, sauna, tennis court, bowling. No credit cards. Closed Apr. and mid-Oct.–mid-Dec.*

$$$ **Post.** This older, centrally located hotel, decorated in rustic style with natural wood, has comfortable rooms with up-to-date facilities. And transportation is at the door; the Windhofer family also runs the

town's taxi and bus service. The restaurant is good; try the rump steak Tirol or any of the other beef dishes. ✉ *Markt 39, A–5541,* ☎ *06243/2209–0,* FAX *06243/3353. 40 rooms. Restaurant, café, indoor pool, sauna. DC. Closed Apr. and Nov.–mid-Dec.*

Outdoor Activities and Sports

BICYCLING

The hilly town of Abtenau has a program of mountain biking and plenty of rental bikes. To find out more about individual biking tours, contact **Austria Radreisen** (✉ Holzingerstr. 546, A–4780 Schrading, ☎ 07712/5511, FAX 07712/4811).

WHITE-WATER RAFTING

From May to the middle of October, you can raft the Salzach and Lammer rivers. The Lammer, with its "Hell's Run," is particularly wild. Call either of Abtenau's two active clubs, **Alpin Sport** (☎ 06243/3088, FAX 06243/3244) or **Club Zwilling** (☎ 06243/3069), for details. Runs cost AS450–AS790 per person.

Werfen (S.P.)

21 *28 km (17 mi) southwest of Abtenau.*

The small town of Werfen, adorned with 16th-century buildings and a lovely Baroque church, belies its importance for it actually is the base for exploring three extraordinary attractions: the largest and most fabulous ice caverns in the world, one of Austria's most spectacular castles, and a four-star culinary shrine, Obauer. The riches of Werfen, in other words, place it on a par with many larger, much touted Austrian cities.

★ From miles away, you can see **Burg Hohenwerfen,** one of the most formidable fortresses of Europe (it was never taken in battle), which dates to 1077, that looms over Werfen. Though fires, reconstructions, and renovations, most recently in 1948, have altered the appearance of the formidable fortress, it still maintains its medieval grandeur. Hewn out of the rock on which it stands, the castle was once called by Maximilian I "a plume of heraldry radiant against the sky." Inside, it has black-timber beamed state rooms and an enormous frescoed Knights' Hall. It even has a torture chamber. Eagles, falcons, and other birds of prey swoop dramatically above the castle grounds, adding considerably to the Middle Ages feel. ☎ *06468/7603–0.* *Admission, tour, and birds-of-prey performance AS100.* ⏲ *Easter–Oct., daily (may be closed Mon. in Apr. and Oct.); tour Apr. and Oct., Tues.–Sun. 10–4; May and Sept., daily 10–3; July and Aug., daily 11–5; Birds of prey performance Apr.–early July and late Aug.–Oct., daily at 11 and 3; early July–late Aug., daily at 11, 2, and 4.*

OFF THE BEATEN PATH

EISRIESENWELT – The World of the Ice Giants, just southwest of Abtenau, houses the largest known complex of ice caves, domes, galleries, and halls in Europe. It extends for some 42 kilometers (26 miles) and contains a fantastic collection of frozen waterfalls and natural statuesque formations. If you're not setting off by bus from Werfen, drive to the rest house, about halfway up the hill and be prepared for some seriously scenic vistas. Then walk 15 minutes to the cable car, which takes you to a point about 15 minutes by foot from the cave, where you can take a 1¼-hour guided tour. You can also take a bus to the cable car from the Werfen railroad station (☎ 06468/293), but be sure to leave at least an hour before the start of the next scheduled cave trip. The entire adventure takes about half a day. And remember, no matter how warm it is outside, it's below freezing inside, so bundle up, and wear appropriate shoes. ☎ *06468/291 or 06468/248–0.* *AS170, including cable* *car. ⏲ Tours May, June, and Sept.–early Oct., daily 9:30–3:30 hourly; July and Aug., daily 9:30–4:30 hourly.*

Dining and Lodging

$$$$ ★ ✕ **Obauer.** Worth a detour on your way back to Salzburg, this *Landgasthaus* (country inn) is one of Austria's top half dozen restaurants—some would argue the best. The gourmet temple draws people from around the nation, so reserve well in advance and allow plenty of time: This is superlative cuisine. The menu constantly changes to match the imagination of the Obauer brothers, who share responsibilities as chef. Diners choose a fixed menu or order à la carte, but either way, you'll find perfection in every offering. Ask for advice on the appropriate wines. You can also stay overnight here; the house has seven rooms (reserve in advance). ✉ *Hauptstr. 46, A–5450,* ☎ *06468/212–0,* FAX *06468/212–12. Reservations essential. AE. Closed 2 (varying) days per wk; annual holiday closing also varies.*

$ **Gästhaus Erzherzog Eugen.** You can't miss this hot pink Gasthaus with window boxes trailing garlands of geraniums. It's smack in the middle of town. Though the decor is basic and a bit bland—traditional white lace curtains and nondescript furniture—the staff extends a warm and hospitable welcome to its guests. The lodging is under the same management as the nearby Obauer. ✉ *Weng 17, A–5453,* ☎ *06468/210–0,* FAX *06468/210–3. 12 rooms. Bar. No credit cards.*

EASTERN ALPS A TO Z

Arriving and Departing

By Car

If you're coming from northern Italy, you can get to Villach on the E56 autobahn; from Klagenfurt, farther east in Carinthia, taking the A2 autobahn is quickest. The fastest route from Salzburg is the A10 autobahn.

By Plane

The closest airport is at Klagenfurt, 50 kilometers (31 miles) from Villach. It is served by Austrian Airlines, Tyrolean Airways, and Swissair. Salzburg, too, has its own airport (☞ Salzburg A to Z *in* Chapter 7). Both have frequent connections to other Austrian cities and other points in Europe, but neither has scheduled overseas connections.

By Train

Villach and Salzburg are both served by frequent rail service from Vienna. Villach is also connected to Italy, whereas Salzburg has links to Germany and beyond.

Getting Around

By Bus

As is typical throughout Austria, where trains don't go, the post office and railroad buses do, though some side routes are less frequently covered. You'll need to coordinate your schedule with that of the buses, which is not as difficult as it sounds. The Austrian travel offices are helpful in this regard. Handy numbers for bus information are ☎ 0660/5188; in Villach, ☎ 04242/44410 or 04242/2020–4041; and in Salzburg, ☎ 0662/167 or 0622/872150. You can take a post office bus from the Zell am See rail station (☎ 06542/2295) up and over the mountains to the glacier at Kaiser-Franz-Josefs-Höhe, a 2½-hour trip, or from the Lienz rail station (☎ 04852/67067) via Heiligenblut to the glacier, about 2 hours on this route. Buses run from early June to mid-October.

By Car

A car is by far the preferred means of seeing this area; the roads are good, and you can stop for picnics or just to marvel at the scenery. Be aware that the Grossglockner High Alpine Highway is closed from mid-November or possibly earlier (the first heavy snow) to mid-May or early June. Though many of the other high mountain roads are kept open in winter, driving them is nevertheless tricky, and you'll probably need chains.

By Train

You can reach most of the towns in the Eastern Alps by train, but the Grossglockner and Dachstein mountains are reachable in a practical sense only by road. If you do travel by rail, you can go from Villach to Hermagor, to Lienz, and northward (north of Spittal an der Drau) via Mallnitz and Badgastein to the main line at Schwarzach. There you can cut back westward to Zell am See or continue onward to Bischofshofen, connecting there via Radstadt to Schladming or staying on the main line north to Salzburg.

Contacts and Resources

Guided Tours

Bus tours from Salzburg include the Grossglockner mountain highway (☞ Salzburg A to Z *in* Chapter 7).

Visitor Information

For information about **Carinthia,** contact Kärntner Tourismus (✉ Casinopl. 1, A–9220 Velden, ☎ 04274/52100, FAX 04274/52100–50). The central tourist board for **East Tirol** is Tirol-Information (✉ Wilhelm-Greil-Str. 17, A–6010 Innsbruck, ☎ 0512/5320–170, FAX 0512/5320–174). For information about **Salzburg Province,** contact Salzburger Land Tourismus (✉ Wiener Bundesstr. 23, Postfach 1, A-5300 Hallwang bei Salzburg, ☎ 0662/6688, FAX 0662/6688–0). The main tourist bureau for **Styria** is Steiermark Information (✉ St. Peter–Hauptstr. 243, A–8042 Graz, ☎ 0316/403033–0, FAX 0316/403033–10).

Many individual towns have their own *Fremdenverkehrsamt* (tourist offices. **Badgastein:** Kurverwaltung (✉ Kaiser-Franz-Josef-Str. 1, A–5640, ☎ 06434/2531–0, FAX 06434/2531–37). **Grosskirchheim/Döllach:** Verkehrsamt (✉ A–9843, ☎ 04825/521–0, FAX 04825/522–30). **Heiligenblut:** Tourismusverband (✉ Hof 4, A–9844, ☎ 04824/2001–21, FAX 04824/2001–43). **Hermagor:** Verkehrsamt (✉ Wulfeniapl. 1, A–9620, ☎ 04282/2043–0, FAX 04282/2043–50). **Kötschach-Mauthen** (✉ Kötschach 390, A–9640, ☎ 04715/8516, FAX 04715/8513–30). **Lienz** (✉ Europapl. 1, A–9900, ☎ 04852/65265, FAX 04852/65265–2). **Matrei in Osttirol** (✉ Rauterpl. 1, A–9971, ☎ 04875/6527, FAX 04875/6527–40). **Radstadt** (✉ Stadtpl. 17, A–5550, ☎ 06452/4305 or 06452/7472, FAX 06452/6702). **Ramsau am Dachstein** (✉ Kulm 40, A–8972, ☎ 03687/81925 or 03687/81833, FAX 03687/81085). **Saalbach-Hinterglemm** (✉ A–5753, ☎ 06541/7272–0, FAX 06541/7900). **Saalfelden** (✉ Bahnhofstr. 10, A–5760, ☎ 06582/2513, FAX 06582/5398). **St. Jakob in Defereggen** (✉ Unterrotte 75AH, A–9963, ☎ 04873/5483 or 04873/5484, FAX 04873/5265). **St. Johann im Pongau** (✉ Hauptstr. 16, A–5600, ☎ 06412/6036–0, FAX 06412/6036–74). **Schladming** (✉ Hauptpl. 18, A–8970, ☎ 03687/22268–0, FAX 03687/24138). **Werfen** (Verkehrsverein, ✉ Hauptstr., A–5450, ☎ 06468/388). **Zell am See:** Kurverwaltung (✉ Brucker Bundesstr. 1, A–5700, ☎ 06542/2600 or 06542/2601, FAX 06542/2032).

10 Tirol and Innsbruck

Tirol has a great deal, if not everything: the Holy Roman Empire splendors of Innsbruck, Hansel-and-Gretel villages, majestic mountain peaks, masked carnival revelers, and more—much more. Shine up your best lederhosen and set out to shop for cuckoo clocks, then try out your vibrato on some Jodeln, *Tirolian singing. Then head for the great ski resorts—St. Anton, Kitzbühel and St. Johann—where sport* und Spiel *are always in high gear.*

TIROL IS SO DIFFERENT FROM THE REST OF AUSTRIA that you might think you've crossed a border. In a way, you have. The frontier between the provinces of Salzburg and Tirol is defined by mountains; four passes make traffic possible. The faster trains cut across Germany rather than agonizing through the Austrian Alps. To the west, Tirol is separated from neighboring Vorarlberg by the Arlberg Range.

Updated by Angela Walker

Relatively small as the province of Tirol is, the idea of Tirol remains all encompassing—it is virtually the shop window of Austria. Its very name conjures up visions of great chains of never-ending snow-capped mountains, remote winding Alpine valleys, rushing mountain torrents, and spectacular glaciers that rise out of the depths like brilliant, icy diamonds; in the winter you'll find masses of deep, sparkling powder snow, unrivaled skiing and tobogganing, bizarre winter carnivals with grotesque masked mummers; in the summer, breathtaking picture-postcard Alpine scenery, cool mountain lakes, and rambles through forests; and throughout the year, yodeling and zither music, villagers in lederhosen and broad-brimmed, feathered hats, and, of course, the sounds of those distinctive cowbells.

As if the sheer physical splendor of Tirol weren't enough, the region can look back on a history filled with romance. Up to the beginning of the 16th century, Tirol was a powerful state in its own right, under a long line of counts and dukes, including personages of such varying fortunes as Friedl the Penniless and his son Sigmund the Wealthy. (On the whole, Tirolean rulers were considerably more wealthy than penniless.) The province reached the zenith of its power under Emperor Maximilian I (1459–1519), when Innsbruck was the seat of the Holy Roman Empire. Maximilian's tomb in Innsbruck gives ample evidence of this onetime far-reaching glory. Over the centuries, the Tiroleans became fiercely nationalistic. In 1809–10 Andreas Hofer led bands of local patriots against Napoléon in an effort to break free from Bavaria and rejoin Austria. After three successful battles, including the battle of Bergisel just outside Innsbruck, Hofer lost the fourth attempt against combined French and Bavarian forces, was executed in Mantua, and became a national hero. The spirit of Tirolean identity remains strong. Today, Tirol looks to Vienna for political support in its perpetual dispute with Italy over the South Tirol, a large and prosperous wine-growing region that was ceded to Italy after World War I. Many Austrian Tiroleans still own property in South Tirol and consider it very much a part of their homeland. Yet even Austria's Tirol is physically divided: East Tirol, a small enclave of remarkable natural magnificence wedged between the provinces of Salzburg and Carinthia, belongs to Tirol, except that it can be reached only by trespassing through Italy or the province of Salzburg.

And what about the Tiroleans themselves? Like most mountain peoples, the Tiroleans are very proud and independent—so much so that for many centuries, the natives of one narrow valley fastness had little communication with their "foreign" neighbors in the next valley (it's still possible to find short, dark, and slender residents in one valley, and strapping blond, blue-eyed giants in the next). But Tirol can also be very cosmopolitan, as any visitor to Innsbruck can attest. The city is Tirol's treasure-house—historically, culturally, and commercially. It's also sited smack dab in the center of the Tirolian region and makes a convenient base from which to explore. Even if you are staying at an area resort, spend a day or two in Innsbruck first: It will give you a far better perspective on the rest of the region.

Pleasures and Pastimes

Dining

Tirolean restaurants range from grand-hotel dining salons—favored spots for chic Innsbruckers—to little Tirolean *Bauernstube,* where you can enjoy hearty carrot, *Knödel* (dumpling), and zucchini soups while sitting on highly polished wooden seats—rather hard ones! When you hit pay dirt and find a really good kitchen, you're in luck: the helpings in Tirol are always more than ample. Don't forget to enjoy some of the fine Innsbruck coffee houses, justly famous for their scrumptuous cakes—mainly of the whipped cream variety—and remember that some daytime eating places turn into wine taverns late in the evening. Outside of Innsbruck, you'll find country inns that have dining rooms, but there are few if any separate restaurants. Prices for meals include taxes and a service charge but not the customary small additional tip.

CATEGORY	COST*
$$$$	over AS400
$$$	AS300–AS400
$$	AS200–AS300
$	under AS150–AS200

**per person for a typical three-course meal, with a glass of house wine*

Hiking

Tirol has a good share of the more than 50,000 kilometers (about 35,000 miles) of well-maintained mountain paths that ribbon the country. Hiking is one of the best ways to truly experience the awesome grandeur of the Alpine scenery, whether you just want to take a leisurely stroll around one of the crystal blue lakes reflecting the mountains towering above them or trek to the top of one of the mighty peaks. **Mountain-climbing** is a highly organized sport in Tirol, a province that features some of the greatest challenges to lovers of this sport: the Kaisergebirge (base: Kufstein), the Zillertaler and Tuxer Alps (base: Mayrhofen), the Wettersteingebirge and Karwendel ranges (base: Seefeld), the Nordkette range (base: Innsbruck), and the Oetz (base: Obergurgl). The instructors at the **Alpine School Innsbruck** are the best people to contact when making arrangement for a mountain climbing holiday or if you wish to attend a mountain climbing school; if you already know how, contact the **Österreichischer Alpenverein** (☞ Outdoor Activities and Sports *in* Innsbruck, *below*).

Lodging

For one reason or another, travelers do not stay very long in Innsbruck itself. The rival attractions of the magnificent countryside, the lure of the mountains and the countless Alpine valleys prove perhaps too strong—in any case, Innsbruck hotels report the average stay is usually two to three days, so there is a fast turnover and always a room to be had. Even so, if you travel during the high season, July–August and in the winter, it's best to book in advance. If you're driving, you may want to seek out a hotel in Innsbruck that has parking, since otherwise cars must be left some distance from the city center. Hotel rates vary widely by season, with the off-peak periods being March–May and September–November. Some travelers opt to set up their base not in Innsbruck, but *overlooking* it, on the Hungerburg Plateau, on the top of a hill 3,000 feet above sea level, or in one of the hotels and inns perched still higher up on the Nordkette chain, both reached by funicular. If you choose these lofty eyries, you will have invigorating mountain air and a wonderful view of the Alps with Innsbruck spread at your feet (commutation to the city, of course, will add to your expenses).

In the popular resort towns, many hotels operate on a half-board basis (breakfast and one other meal a day must be taken) during the ski season, and some take no credit cards. Summer prices are often as much as 50% lower than during the ski season. If you're out for savings, it's a good idea to find lodgings in small towns nearby, rather than in the resorts themselves; local tourist offices may be able to help you, possibly even with accommodations in private homes if you book well ahead. In our listings, Kitzbühel, St. Anton, and Seefeld are the higher-priced resorts. Prices include tax and service.

CATEGORY	RESORTS*	SMALL TOWNS*
$$$$	over AS2,200	over AS1,000
$$$	AS1,500–AS2,200	AS800–AS1,000
$$	AS900–AS1,500	AS550–AS800
$	under AS900	under AS550

**per person for a standard double room with bath, including breakfast (except in $$$$ hotels), generally half board in resorts in winter*

Powder-Perfect Skiing

Downhill was practically invented in Tirol, which came to the forefront as a prime tourist destination because of the excellence of its skiing. Modern ski techniques were developed here, thanks to the legendary skiing master Hannes Schneider, who took the Norwegian art of cross-country skiing and adapted it to downhill running. No matter where your trip takes you, worldclass—and often gut-numbing—skiing is available, from the glamour of Kitzbühel in the east to the imposing peaks of St. Anton am Arlberg in the west. And even on the sultriest summer day, it's still possible to slip on your skis and glide down the nearest glacier.

Close to the Arlberg Pass is **St. Anton,** which, at 4,300 feet, is home to one of the finest ski schools in the world. The specialty at St. Anton is piste skiing—enormously long runs studded with mogels (and few trees), some so steep and challenging that the sport is almost more like mountain climbing. In fact, this is the only place you can heli-ski in Austria. It was here that Hannes Schneider started the school that was to become the model for all others. A short bus ride to the top of the Pass brings you to **St. Christoph,** at 5,800 feet. Many excellent tours, served by the Galzip cable railway, start here, but the *Skihaserl,* or ski bunny, would do well to stay down at St. Anton where there are better—and gentler—nursery slopes.

Farther along the Inn is the Ötz Valley. From the Otztal station, you can go by bus to **Soelden,** a resort at 4,500 feet that is not as expensive as others, nor as highly organized. The village of **Obergurgl,** at 6,321 feet, lies at the head of the Ötz Valley, where you can ski until early summer. Not far from Innsbruck is **Seefeld,** at 3,870 feet, long the town of one of Austria's best known aces, Toni Seelos. At the farther end of Tirol lies **Kitzbühel,** chic and *charmant,* perhaps most famous for its "ski circus," a system of ski lifts and trails, floodlit at night, whereby skiers can ski for weeks without retracing their steps. The best time for skiing around **Innsbruck** is January through March.

Exploring Tirol and Innsbruck

Great Itineraries

Numbers in the text correspond to numbers in the margin and on the Innsbruck, Eastern Tirol, and Western Tirol maps.

IF YOU HAVE 3 DAYS

Head straight to the heart of Tirol to the provincial capital of **Innsbruck** ①–⑩; the city is conveniently situated for the traveler to Tirol, for it lies almost exactly in the center of the province on the Inn river. Even if you have already settled on a resort for your holiday, you should spend at least a day in the capital first to check out the beautiful buildings built by the Emperor Maximilian—from the **Goldenes Dachl** ① to the **Hofburg** ⑤—and by Austria's Empress Maria Theresa, who gave her name to the principal street of the town, the Maria-Theresien-Strasse (any sightseeing in Innsbruck begins on this street, which runs through the heart of the city from north to south and is the main shopping center). Far from being exhausting to explore, Innsbruck is only a half-hour walk from one end of the old town to the other. The next day, let the funicular whisk you up the **Hungerburg** for the breathtaking views of Innsbruck below. You can take a leisurely hike along the mountain trail and see the flora and fauna at the Alpine zoo. After returning to the capital city, set out on your final day to visit **Schloss Ambras** with its impressive collections of medieval curiosities—pack a picnic and stay for a concert if you're traveling during the summer season. More ambitious travelers should consider a quick day trip to the seriously scenic **Stubatial Valley,** one of the showpieces of the Tirol—via the narrow-gauge electric Stubaitalbahn.

IF YOU HAVE 5 DAYS

Begin your Tirolian soujourn with two days in attraction-studded **Innsbruck** ①–⑩—but don't forget to experience your first taste of the region's grand Alpine setting by fitting some quick excursions to the outlying **Hungerburg** peak, the **Schloss Ambras,** or the **Stubatial Valley.** On day three, charming alpine villages are on the agenda with a visit to the Ötz Valley: head for **Telfs** ㉖, **Ötz** ㉘, and **Sölden** ㉙, ending your journey at Austria's highest mountain town, **Obergurgl** ㉚. On the fourth day, spend time exploring castle ruins, Baroque churches, and yet more spectacular scenery in **Imst** ㉗, **Landeck** ㉛, and **Ried** ㉜, with an overnight in **Serfaus** ㉝. For the peak experience of your trip—literally—head to the slopes on your final day at **St. Anton am Arlberg** ㉞. Keep in mind that modern highways can get you to your destination quickly, but often the most beautiful scenic views lie on off-the-beaten-track roads: ask your hotel concierge for advice on finding the best beauty spots.

IF YOU HAVE 7 DAYS

Innsbruck ①–⑩ makes a good base for discovering the entire region but is well worth spending two days exploring on its own. After seeing the riches of the old town of the imperial city and its neighboring attractions, the **Hungerburg** peak and **Schloss Ambras,** set out on the morning of the third day to see how the Habsburgs amassed their vast wealth: visit the mint at **Hall in Tirol** ⑪ and the silver mines at **Schwaz** ⑫. Then spend the night overlooking the pristine **Achensee** ⑬ or at **Pertisau** ⑭. On your fourth day, head south following the Ziller river with stops along the way in **Zell am Ziller** ⑮ and **Mayrhofen** ⑯. From there you can head west to explore the beautiful Tuxer Valley and the classic alpine villages of **Lanersbach** and **Hintertux** or save your breath and head east to climb the impressive Kreuzjoch mountain in nearby **Gerlos** ⑲. On the fifth day, challenge the slopes at either of the world-famous resorts of **St. Johann** ㉔ or **Kitzbühel** ㉕—two towns that have become almost more fashionable as warm-weather destinations than skiing meccas. On day six, visit the smaller resorts of **Going, Ellmau,** and **Söll** before visiting Emperor Maximilian's pleasure palace in **Kufstein** ㉓. On your final day, visit the medieval town of **Rattenberg** ㉒ and the castles of **Brixlegg** ⑳ on your way back to Innsbruck.

When to Tour Tirol and Innsbruck

Tirol is a province for all seasons, and the physical geography of the province makes it an especially ideal place in which to enjoy the outdoor life year-round. Ski-crazy travelers descend on the resorts during the winter months; in the summer, when the mountains are awash with

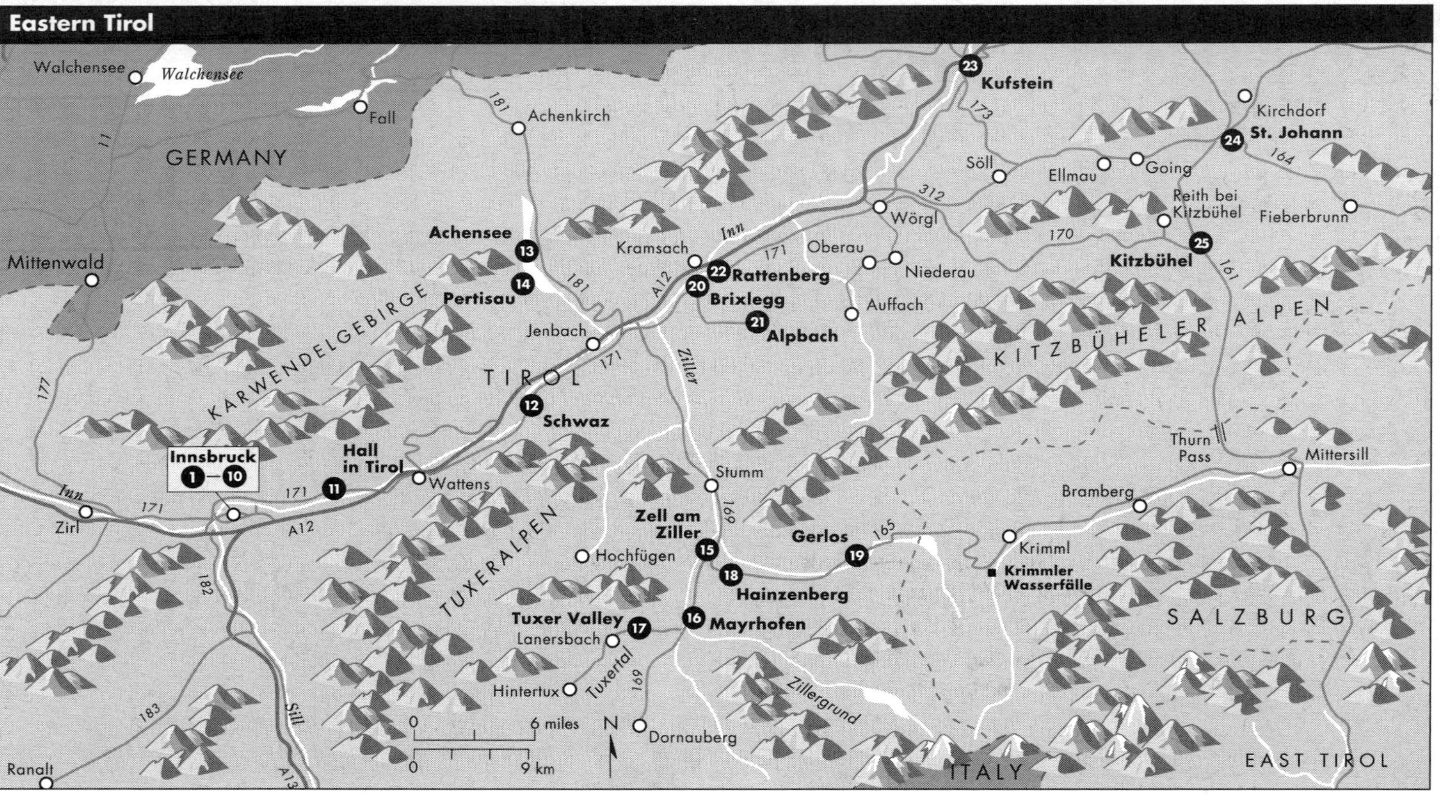
Eastern Tirol
Walchensee
Walchensee
Fall
11
GERMANY
Mittenwald
181
Achenkirch
Achensee
13
14
Pertisau
181
KARWENDELGEBIRGE
177
Jenbach
TIROL
171
12
Schwaz
Innsbruck
1—10
Hall in Tirol
11
Wattens
Inn
171
171
Zirl
A12
182
183
Ranalt
Sill
A13
Kramsach
A12
Inn
171
22
Rattenberg
20
Brixlegg
21
Alpbach
Oberau
Niederau
Auffach
Ziller
TUXERALPEN
Stumm
169
Zell am Ziller
15
Hochfügen
18
Hainzenberg
Gerlos
19
165
Tuxer Valley
17
16
Mayrhofen
Lanersbach
Hintertux
Tuxertal
169
Dornauberg
Zillergrund
0
6 miles
0
9 km
N
23
Kufstein
173
Söll
Wörgl
312
Ellmau
Going
170
Reith bei Kitzbühel
25
Kitzbühel
161
24
St. Johann
Kirchdorf
164
Fieberbrunn
KITZBÜHELER
ALPEN
Thurn Pass
Mittersill
Bramberg
Krimml
Krimmler Wasserfälle
SALZBURG
ITALY
EAST TIROL

Western Tirol

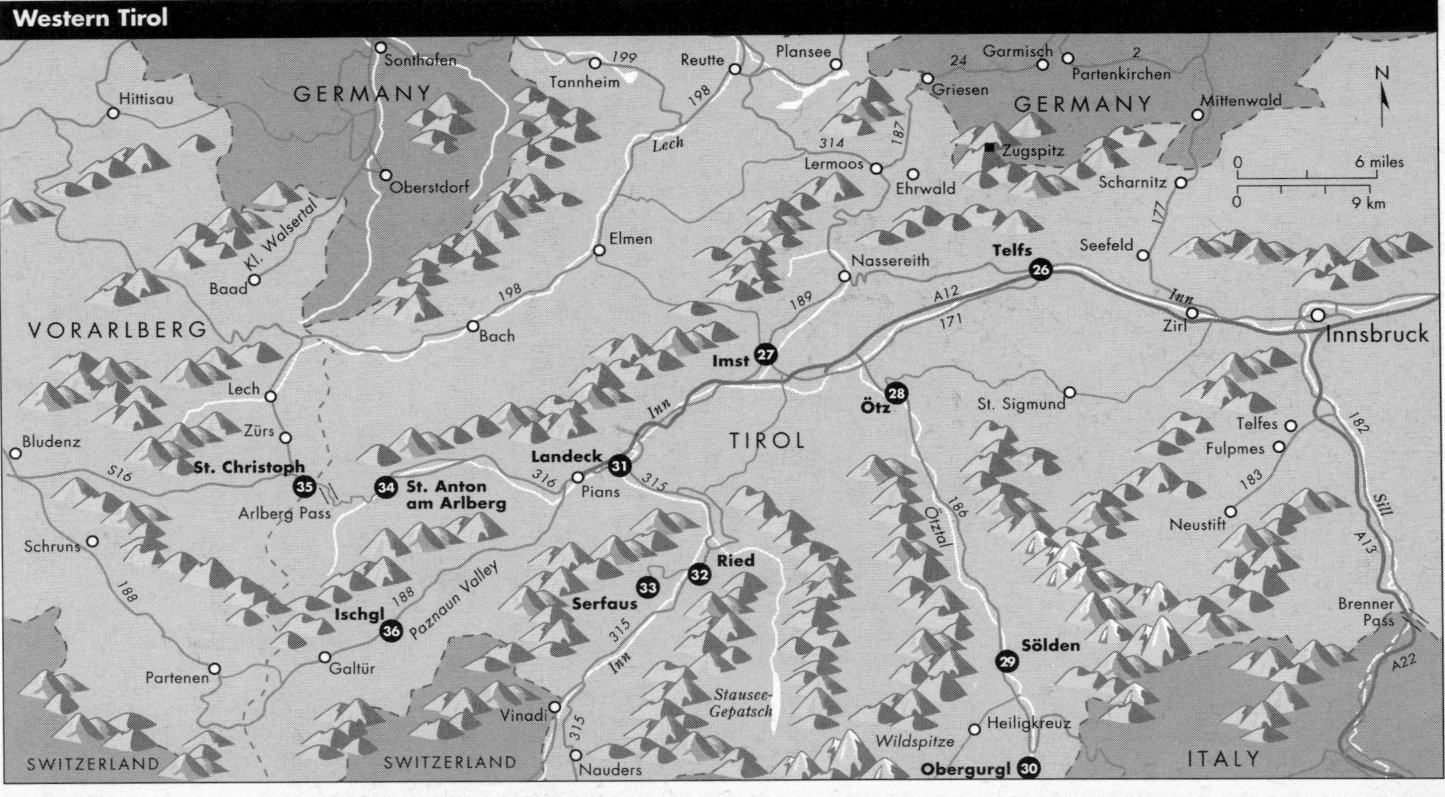

wildflowers, camping tents spring up like mushrooms in the valleys as hikers, cavers, and mountain climbers take advantage of the palatial peaks. The annual Tirolean calendar is packed with special events: the famous *Schemenlaufen*, a procession of picturesque woodcarved masks, held in February in Imst; the Fasching balls, which reach their peak at the end of February in Seefeld; the Hahnenkamm ski race and curling competition held in winter in Kitzbühel; the glacier ski races in April at Obergurgl; the world-famous *Gauderfest* at Zell am Ziller during the first weekend in May; and the castle concerts at Kufstein and the folk festival in Mayrhofen during July and August.

INNSBRUCK

190 km (118 mi) southwest of Salzburg, 471 km (304 mi) southwest of Vienna.

The capital of Tirol is one of the most beautiful towns of its size anywhere in the world, owing much of its charm and fame to its unique setting. To the north, the steep, sheer sides of the Alps rise, literally from the edge of the city, like a shimmering blue-and-white wall—an impressive backdrop for the mellowed green domes and red roofs of the Baroque town tucked below. To the south, the peaks of the Tuxer and Stubai ranges undulate in the hazy purple distance.

Innsbruck has been an important crossroads for hundreds of years. When it was chartered in 1239, it was already a key point on the north–south highways between Germany and Italy and the east–west axis tying eastern Austria and the lands beyond to Switzerland. Today Innsbruck is the transit point for road and rail traffic between the bordering countries.

The charming Old World aspect of Innsbruck has remained virtually intact and includes ample evidence of its Baroque lineage. The skyline encircling the center suffers somewhat from high-rises, but the heart, the **Altstadt,** or Old City, remains much as it was 400 years ago. The protective vaulted arcades along main thoroughfares, the tiny passageways giving way to noble squares, and the ornate restored houses all contribute to an unforgettable picture.

Squeezed by the mountains and sharing the valley with the Inn River (Innsbruck means "bridge over the Inn"), the city is compact and very easy to explore on foot. Reminders of three historic figures abound: the local hero Andreas Hofer, whose band of patriots challenged Napoléon in 1809; Emperor Maximilian I (1459–1519); and Empress Maria Theresa (1717–80), the last two of whom were responsible for much of the city's architecture. Maximilian ruled the Holy Roman Empire from Innsbruck, and Maria Theresa, who was particularly fond of the city, spent much time here.

A Club Innsbruck pass (☞ Getting Around *in* Tirol A to Z, *below*) entitles you to reduced-price admissions to the Olympic Museum, Hofkirche, Volkskunstmuseum, Ferdinandeum, Alpenverein Museum, Bergisel Museum, and the Alpenzoo. A special visitor's card (*Besucherkarte Innsbruck-Igls*; AS360) available at the tourist information office offers entry to most of the city's museums, plus the Alpenzoo, and free use of all city transportation for one day, including the Hungerburg, Patscherkofel, and Nordketten cable cars. If museums alone are your target, get a Museum Card at the tourist information office or at the first museum you visit; it provides entry to virtually all of the city's museums between May and September, and at AS150, it's a good value.

❶ Any walking tour of Innsbruck should start at the **Goldenes Dachl** (the Golden Roof), which made famous the late-Gothic mansion whose balcony it covers. In fact, the roof is made of gilded copper tiles, and its recent refurbishment is said to have taken 14 kilograms (nearly 31 pounds) of gold. The house was built in 1420 for Duke Friedrich (otherwise known as Friedl the Penniless), and it is said that the indignant duke had the original roof covered with gold to counter the rumor that he was poor; the balcony was added in 1501 by Maximilian I as a sort of "royal box" for watching street performances in the square below. The structure was altered and expanded at the beginning of the 18th century, and now only the loggia and the alcove are identifiable as original. The magnificent coats of arms representing Austria, Hungary, Burgundy, Milan, the Holy Roman Empire, Styria, Tirol, and royal Germany are copies. You can see the originals (and up close, too) in the Ferdinandeum. The Goldenes Dachl building now houses an **Olympic Museum,** which features videotapes of past Innsbruck winter Olympics. A combined-admission ticket with the Goldenes Dachl also covers entry to the Stadtturm (☞ *below*). ✉ *Herzog Friedrich-Str. 15,* ☎ *0512/5360–575.* 🎫 *AS22; combination ticket with Stadtturm AS32.* ⏲ *Mar.–Oct., daily 9:30–5:30; Nov.–Feb., Tues.–Sun. 9:30–5:30.*

2 Across the street from the Goldenes Dachl is the **Stadtturm,** the 15th-century city tower, with a steep climb of 148 steps to the top. ✉ *Herzog-Friedrich-Str. 21,* ☎ *0512/5759–62.* 🎫 *AS20.* ⏲ *Mar.–June, Sept., and Oct., daily 10–5; July and Aug., daily 10–6.* 🎫 *Combination ticket Olympic Museum AS32.*

3 Nearby is the dramatic blue-and-white **Helbling House,** originally a Gothic building (1560) to which the obvious, ornate Rococo decoration was added in 1730.

4 The main attraction of the Baroque **Domkirche zu St. Jakob** (Cathedral of St. James Pfarrgasse) is the high-altar painting of the Madonna by Lucas Cranach the Elder, dating from about 1520. The cathedral, built in 1722, was dedicated to St. Jacob. The ornate Baroque interior also has dramatic painted ceilings. ✉ *Dompl. 6,* ☎ *0512/5839–02.* ⏲ *Sat.–Thurs. 6–noon and 2–5, Fri. 2–5.*

5 One of the most historic attractions of Innsbruck is the **Hofburg** imperial palace, which Maximilian I commissioned in the 14th century. (The booklet in English at the ticket office will tell you more interesting tidbits about the palace than the tour guide will.) Center stage is the **Giant's Hall**—designated a marvel of the 18th-century as soon as it was topped off with its magnificent trompe l'oeil ceiling, painted by Franz Anton Maulpertsch in 1775. The Rococo decor and the portraits of Habsburg ancestors in the ornate white-and-gold great reception hall were added in the 18th century by Maria Theresa; look for the portrait of "Primal" (primrose)—to use the childhood nickname of the empress's daughter, Marie-Antoinette. ✉ *Rennweg 1,* ☎ *0512/587186–13.* 🎫 *AS50.* ⏲ *Tour mid-May–mid-Oct., daily 9–5 hourly; mid-Oct.–mid-May, Mon.–Sat. daily 9–5 hourly.*

6 Close by the Hofburg is the **Hofkirche** (Court Church), built as a mausoleum for Maximilian I (although he is actually buried in Wiener Neustadt, south of Vienna). The emperor's ornate black marble tomb is surrounded by 24 marble reliefs portraying his accomplishments, as well as 28 larger-than-life statues of his ancestors, including the legendary King Arthur of England. Andreas Hofer is also buried here. Don't miss the 16th-century **"Silver" Chapel,** up the stairs opposite the entrance, with its elaborate altar and silver Madonna. The chapel was built in 1578 to be the tomb of Archduke Ferdinand II and his wife, Philippine Welser, a commoner, the daughter of a rich and powerful merchant family. Visit the chapel in the morning to take pictures; the blinding after-

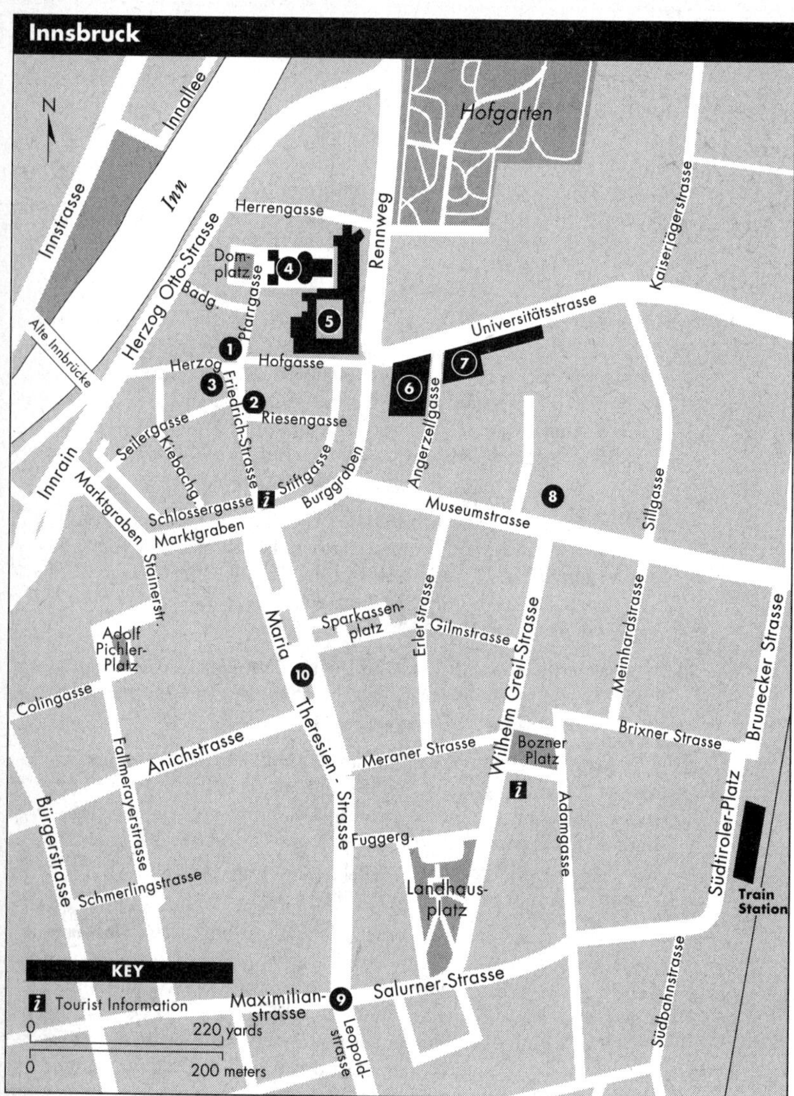

Annasäule, **10**
Domkirche zu St. Jakob, **4**
Ferdinandeum, **8**
Goldenes Dachl, **1**
Helbling House, **3**
Hofburg, **5**
Hofkirche, **6**
Stadtturm, **2**
Tiroler Volkskunstmuseum, **7**
Triumphpforte, **9**

noon sun comes in directly behind the altar. ✉ *Universitätsstr. 2,* ☎ *0512/584302.* 🎫 *AS20; combined ticket with Volkskunstmuseum AS50.* ⏲ *July and Aug., daily 9–5:30; Sept.–June, daily 9–5.*

7 The **Tiroler Volkskunstmuseum** (Tirolean Folk-Art Museum), in the same complex as the Hofkirche, exhibits Christmas mangers, costumes, rustic furniture, and entire rooms from old farmhouses and inns, decorated in styles ranging from Gothic to Rococo. Displays are somewhat static, and the information cards are in German. The small Christmas Manger Museum, on the other hand, is fascinating. ✉ *Universitätsstr. 2,* ☎ *0512/584302.* 🎫 *AS40; manger museum AS20.* ⏲ *July and Aug., Mon.–Sat. 9–5:30, Sun. 9–noon; Sept.–June, Mon.–Sat. 9–5, Sun. 9–noon.*

The **Schmetterlinghaus** (Butterfly House) in a corner of the Hofgarten is home to a fascinating collection of exotic live butterflies flitting about the sunny, flower-filled greenhouse. ✉ *Rennweg 2,* ☎ *0512/584803–27.* 🎫 *AS40.* ⏲ *Mid-June–mid-Sept, daily 10–5.*

8 The **Ferdinandeum** (Ferdinandeum Tyrol Museum) houses Austria's largest collection of Gothic art, 19th- and 20th-century paintings, and medieval arms. Here you'll find the original coats of arms from the Goldenes Dachl balcony. ✉ *Museumstr. 15,* ☎ *0512/59489.* 🎫 *AS50.* ⏲ *Oct.–Apr., Tues.–Sat. 10–noon and 2–5, Sun. 10–1; May–Sept., daily 10–5, Thurs. 7–9.*

9 The **Triumphpforte,** or Triumphal Arch, (✉ Salurner-Str.) was built in 1765 to commemorate both the marriage of emperor-to-be Leopold II and the death of Emperor Franz I, husband of Empress Maria Theresa.

10 The **Annasäule,** or St. Anna's Column (✉ Maria Theresien-Str.), commemorates the withdrawal of Bavarian forces in the war of the Spanish Succession in 1703 on St. Anna's Day. From here you'll have a classic view of Innsbruck, with the glorious mountains in the background.

A visit to the 400-year-old **Grassmayr Bell Foundry** will give you an idea of how bells are cast and tuned. Take Bus J, K, or S south to Grassmayrstrasse. ✉ *Leopoldstr. 53.,* ☎ *0512/59416–34.* 🎫 *AS20.* ⏲ *Weekdays 9–6, Sat. 9–noon.*

Three Excursions

Hungerburg

Just barely outside the city here at the Hungerburg, a combination of funicular and cable car will take you soaring above Innsbruck's skyline. Take Streetcar 1 or Bus "C" to the base station (✉ Rennweg 41, ☎ 0512/586158). From here you take the funicular up to the Hungerburg (2,800 feet), then a two-stage cable car to Seegrube at 6,250 feet and Hafelekar at the dizzying height of 7,500 feet. The round-trip to Hungerburg costs AS46; the round-trip to Hafelekar is AS268. At all three stops you'll find hotels and restaurants commanding breathtaking views over the Tirolean Alps and Innsbruck.

If you're staying in Innsbruck for a few days, you may want to break up this excursion into stages. Starting with Hungerburg, visit a different altitude and perspective each day, enjoying a leisurely lunch at each level. For hikers, there's a three-day mountain hiking pass (AS400) good for three consecutive days on the Hungerburg railway and Nordkette and Patscherkofel cable cars.

The **Alpenzoo,** a short walk from the Hungerburg station, has an unusual collection of Alpine birds and animals, including endangered species. The zoo alone is worth the trip up the Hungerburg; if you buy your ticket for the zoo at the base station, the trip up and back is free. ✉ *Weiherburggasse 37A,* ☎ *0512/292323.* 🎫 *AS60.* ⏲ *Spring–fall, daily 9–6; winter, daily 9–dusk.*

Schloss Ambras

One of the country's finest and best-preserved castles dates originally from the 11th century but was rebuilt by Archduke Ferdinand in the late 16th century. His commoner wife, Philippine Welser, lived here. The large Renaissance Spanish hall was added around 1573. Most of the original art is now in the Kunsthistorisches Museum in Vienna, but there is still a large collection of pictures, weapons, armor, furniture, ingenious household gadgets, and other curiosities dating from medieval times. Look around the grounds as well to see the fencing field and a small cemetery with samples of earth from 18 battlefields around the world. Schloss Ambras is 3 kilometers (2 miles) southeast of the city and easily reached by bus or streetcar. ✉ *Schloss Str. 20,* ☎ *0512/348446.* 🎫 *AS60; tour additional AS20.* ⏲ *Tour Apr.–Oct., Wed.–Mon. 10–5; Dec.–Mar., weekdays 2–3.*

The Stubaital Valley

The delightful little Stubaital Valley, less than 40 kilometers (25 miles) long, is one of the showpieces of the Tirol, with no fewer than 80 glistering glaciers and more than 40 towering peaks. If you just want to look, you can see the whole Stubaital in a full day's excursion from Innsbruck. The narrow-gauge electric **Stubaitalbahn** (departure from the center of Innsbruck and in front of the main rail station as well as from the station just below the Bergisel ski jump) goes as far as Fulpmes, partway up the valley. You can take the bus as far as Ranalt and back to Fulpmes, to see more of the valley, then return on the quaint rail line. Buses leave from Gate 1 of the Autobusbahnhof, just behind the rail station at Südtiroler Platz, about every hour (✉ Stubaitalbahn, ☎ 0512/5307–184).

Dining

$$$$ ✕ **Europa-Stüberl.** Warm wood paneling sets the tone for this fairly formal, elegant restaurant, once considered by many to be the city's best. The kitchen has happily settled down after a rapid succession of chefs, offering interesting variations on regional themes, such as the different treatments of lamb. The wine cellar stocks a good choice of Austrian vintages, as well as international specialties. ✕ *Brixner Str. 6, in Europa Tyrol hotel,* ☎ *0512/5931,* FAX *0512/587800. Reservations essential. AE, DC, MC, V.*

$$$$ ★ ✕ **Goldener Adler.** The address for celebrities and duchesses, this famous hotel (☞ Lodging, *below*) also features an even more famous restaurant. A true rarity, the place is as popular with Austrians as it is with travelers. Two of the rooms are exceptionally beautiful; the others are by no means the poor man's hussar, offering luxe peasant decor. If you wish to top the night off with zither music, be sure to book a table in the Goethe Stube (only open in the evening). The liveliest crowds favor the Batzenhäsl on the arcade ground-floor level. The menu offers superb Tirolean-style food, including a hearty cabbage soup with bacon. ✉ *Herzog Friedrich-Str. 6, A–6020,* ☎ *0512/586334. Reservations essential. AE, DC, MC, V.*

$$$$ ★ ✕ **Schwarzer Adler.** Of the comfortable restaurants in the Schwarzer Adler hotel, the preferred one is this intimate restaurant on the ground floor, with wood-paneled rooms and lead-paned windows. The other *Stube* rooms are in Tirolean country style. You'll be offered local and national specialties, including roast duck and a good schnitzel. The wine

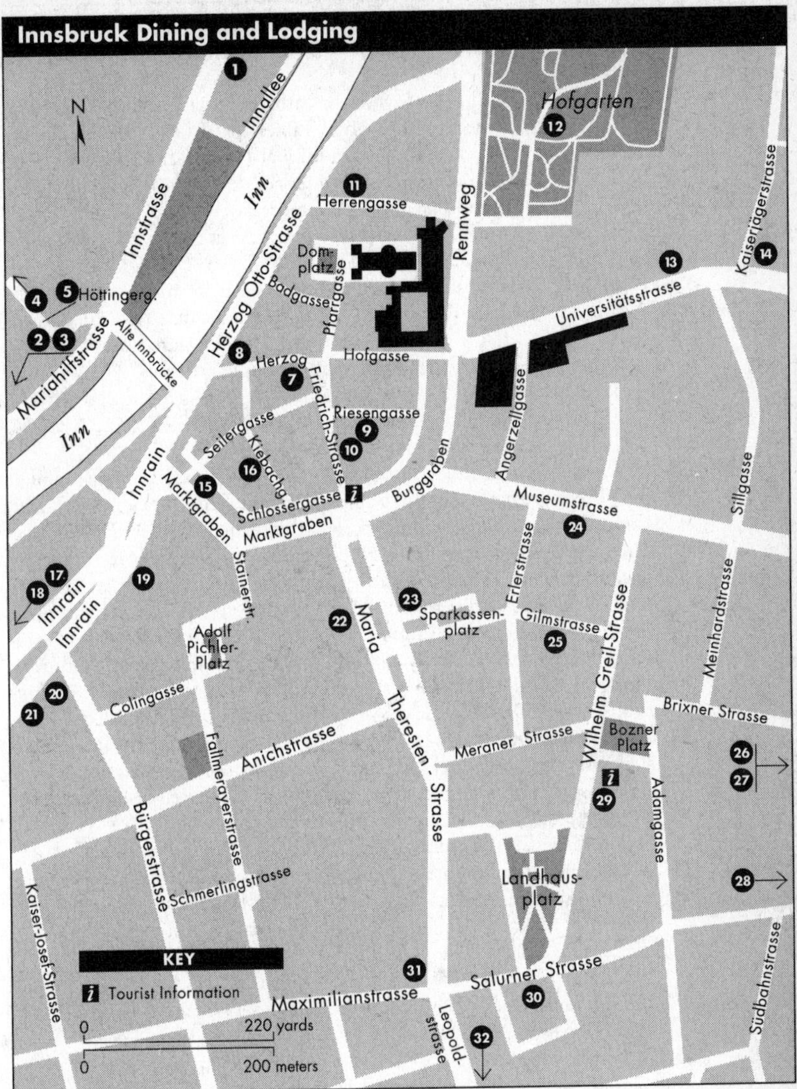

Dining

Central, **25**
Europa-Stüberl, **26**
Fischerhäsl, **11**
Gasthaus Engl, **1**
Goldener Adler, **7**
Herzog–Friedrich/Alte Teestube, **9**
Hofgarten Café, **12**
Jörgele, **8**
Ottoburg, **6**
Schnitzelparadies, **20**
Schwarzer Adler, **14**
Stieglbräu, **29**
Tiroler Stuben, **19**
Weisses Rössl, **16**
Wienerwald, **22, 24**

Lodging

Alpotel, **19**
Binder, **28**
Europa Tyrol, **27**
Goldene Krone, **31**
Goldener Adler, **7**
Grauer Bär, **13**
Innsbruck, **21**
Innsbrücke, **5**
Internationales Studentenhaus, **18**
Kapeller, **32**
Maria Theresia, **23**
Maximilian, **15**
Rosen–Hotel Höttinger Au, **2**
Rössl in der Au, **3**
Royal, **17**
Scandic Crown, **30**
Schwarzer Adler, **14**
Tautermann, **4**
Weisses Kreuz, **10**

list includes mainly Austrian and South Tirolean vintages. ✉ *Kaiserjägerstr. 2, A–6020,* ☎ *0512/587109,* FAX *0512/561697. AE, DC, MC, V.* ⏲ *Closed Sun.*

$$$ ✕ **Fischerhäsl.** In the shadow of the cathedral, the Fischerhäsl is a welcome relief from the tourist throngs. Tables are tucked into cozy alcoves decorated in warm earth tones. Traditional Tirolean favorites are served here, but the restaurant also has a wide selection of pasta and fish dishes for lighter appetites. If you prefer a more lively atmosphere, you can rub elbows with the locals at picnic benches set in the tree-lined guest garden. ✉ *Herrengasse 8,* ☎ *0512/583535. AE, DC, MC, V.*

$$$ ★ ✕ **Jörgele.** This flower-bedecked restaurant is located in the heart of the old quarter near the Goldenes Dachl. Traditional Tirolean classics such as game stew with mushroom and spinach dumplings and liver with bacon and tomatoes are served in ample portions. The wine list is extensive with vintages from around the globe including Argentina, California, and France. ✉ *Herzog-Friedrich Str. 13,* ☎ *0512/571006. AE, DC, MC, V.*

$$$ ★ ✕ **Tiroler Stuben.** Almost anything on the fairly wide-ranging menu at the *Tiroler Stuben* restaurant is likely to be excellent. Fresh fish and lamb come in twice weekly from France, and the kitchen under Friedrich Wolf's direction has a brilliant touch. For proof, try the delicate cream of potato and leek soup or the exceptional *Bauernschopsenes,* a country lamb stew. End with *Profiteroles,* vanilla ice-cream–filled cream puffs covered with chocolate sauce. Despite the fact that the restaurant is always packed, service is attentive. Ask for help with the wine list, although the open wines, particularly the red St. Laurent, are excellent. ✉ *Innrain 13,* ☎ *0512/577931. Reservations essential. AE, MC, DC, V.*

$$ ✕ **Gasthaus Engl.** Here is a *Gasthaus* in the best sense of the word: a simple setting, moderately attentive but overworked personnel, and large servings of delicious food. Look for pork and chicken dishes here, but check the daily specials as well. ✉ *Innstr. 22,* ☎ *0512/283112. AE, DC, MC, V. Closed Sun.*

$$ ★ ✕ **Ottoburg.** It's fun just to explore the rabbit warren of paneled rustic rooms upstairs in this red-and-white shuttered house built in 1494. Several of the bay-window alcoves have great views toward the Goldenes Dachl square. The *Gaststube* downstairs is less intimate but offers a lower-cost selection. Try the trout, if it's on the menu, but the chicken and duck dishes are also excellent. ✉ *Herzog Friedrich-Str. 1,* ☎ *0512/574652. AE, DC, MC, V. Closed 2 wks in mid-Nov.*

$$ ✕ **Stieglbräu.** At this popular spot you'll find an extensive menu of standard Austrian fare, including liver-dumpling soup, roast meats, and chicken, egg, and pasta dishes. The usual accompaniment is beer (Stiegl is brewed in Salzburg). The *Braustube* to the right is slightly less formal, and in the summer the garden is a pleasant oasis. ✉ *Wilhelm Greil-Str. 25,* ☎ *0512/584338. No credit cards.*

$$ ★ ✕ **Weisses Rössl.** In the authentically rustic rooms upstairs, an array of antlers and a private art gallery add to the decor. This is the right place for solid local standards, like *Tiroler G'röstl,* a tasty hash treatment, as well as veal cutlet, both of which taste even better on the outside terrace in summer. Child and senior portions are available. ✉ *Kiebachgasse 8,* ☎ *0512/583057. AE, MC, V. Closed Sun., early Nov., mid-Apr., and holidays.*

$ ✕ **Schnitzelparadies.** The specialty is schnitzel and variations, but there's a daily special and the mixed grill and salads are good, too. The atmosphere is casual Old London, with Tiffany lamps, oak floors, and even an English telephone booth. ✉ *Innrain 25,* ☎ *0512/572972. No credit cards. Closed Sun. and holidays.*

$ ✕ **Wienerwald.** This chain started out with grilled chicken (and very good indeed) but now serves pastas as well as roast and grilled meats in a modern rustic environment. In summer, the gardens of both locations are particularly pleasant and are open till 11 PM. ✉ *Maria Theresien-Str. 12,* ☎ *0512/584165;* ✉ *Museumstr. 24,* ☎ *0512/588994. AE, DC, MC, V.*

Cafés

★ ✕ **Central.** Since 1878 this large traditional café in the Viennese style has been *the* place to relax over a coffee. Recent renovations have also stripped away some atmosphere, but newspapers and magazines are still available, as is a variety of food and pastries. ✉ *Gilmstr. 5, in the Central Hotel,* ☎ *0512/5920–0. AE, DC, MC, V. Closed Nov.*

✕ **Herzog-Friedrich/Alte Teestube.** In an intimate set of rooms, choose from some four dozen kinds of tea, and an array of pastry accompaniments. ✉ *Riesengasse 6,* ☎ *0512/582309. No credit cards. Closed Sun., 2 wks in Apr., and Nov.*

✕ **Hofgarten Café.** Coffee or even lunch under the trees takes on a romantic feel in the center of the court gardens. This place is active from morning until night, with jazzfests and evening dancing outdoors in summer, inside in winter. ✉ *Rennweg 6a,* ☎ *0512/588871. No credit cards.*

Lodging

$$$$ **Europa Tyrol.** Crystal chandeliers and red velvet convey the traditional elegance of this hotel opposite the railroad station yet only a short walk from the Old City. For more than 100 years the Europa has been *the* place to stay in Innsbruck. Rooms are furnished mainly in period style, but some are contemporary; those on the inner court are considerably quieter. Warm wood paneling sets the tone at the fairly formal, elegant Europa-Stüberl restaurant (☞ Dining, *above*). ✉ *Südtiroler Pl. 2, A–6020,* ☎ *0512/5931,* FAX *0512/587800. 125 rooms. Restaurant, sauna, parking. AE, DC, MC, V.*

$$$$ ★ **Goldener Adler.** Dukes, princes, presidents, and ambassadors have stayed here over the years; look for their names and the dates of their visits on plaques over the second-floor rooms. This traditional hotel, a 600-year-old house with stone walls, winding staircases, and a variety of nooks and crannies, has spacious rooms with baths. It's in the heart of the Old City, directly across from the Goldenes Dachl. The rooms are luxuriously furnished in period or elegant Tirolean style. The ancient rooms with their timbered ceilings create just the right setting for a luxurious stay in Innsbruck. The hotel features one of Innsbruck's most renowned restaurants (☞ Dining, *above*). ✉ *Herzog Friedrich-Str. 6, A–6020,* ☎ *0512/586334,* FAX *0512/584409. 35 rooms. 2 restaurants, weinstube. AE, DC, MC, V.*

$$$$ **Maria Theresia.** Behind the elegant 1920s facade you'll find a freshly renovated hotel, now part of the Best Western chain. You couldn't be more central; choose between a room on the street overlooking the Anna Column and the active main thoroughfare or one on the inside, where it's considerably quieter. The rooms are stylishly furnished in neo-Baroque. ✉ *Maria Theresien-Str. 31, A–6020,* ☎ *0512/5933,* FAX *0512/575619. 105 rooms. Restaurant, parking. AE, DC, MC, V.*

$$$$ **Scandic Crown.** This modern high-rise close to the railroad station looks out of place but offers contemporary, air-conditioned comfort in friendly Scandinavian style. The rooms are luxurious yet efficiently modern. Look for Scandinavian specialties in the restaurants; the Sunday noon smorgasbord is justifiably popular. ✉ *Salurner Str. 15, A–6020,* ☎ *0512/5935–0,* FAX *0512/5935–220. 172 rooms. 2 restaurants, bar, indoor pool, sauna, parking. AE, DC, MC, V.*

$$$$ **Schwarzer Adler.** This member of the RomantikHotel group radiates tradition, and recent renovations have updated the rooms. The wood paneling, antique furniture, and other Old World touches in the lobby are repeated in the rooms, making them unusually inviting. You're only a few steps from the heart of the Old City. ✉ *Malser Str. 8, A–6500,* ☎ *05442/62316,* FAX *05442/62316–50. 32 rooms. Restaurant. No credit cards. Closed Nov.–mid-Dec.*

$$$ ★ **Alpotel.** All rooms are quiet in this modern hotel tucked into a small square on the edge of the Old City. The building was designed for apartments, so many rooms are almost miniature suites; furnishings throughout are in warm colors and natural wood. The rooms are particularly light and welcoming; those on the upper floors on the city side have a truncated view of the distant mountains. The *Tiroler Stuben* restaurant is one of the best in town (☞ Dining, *above*). ✉ *Innrain 13, A–6020,* ☎ *0512/577931,* FAX *0512/577931–15. 73 rooms. Restaurant, sauna, parking. AE, DC, MC, V.*

$$$ **Grauer Bär.** Despite renovations that have added baths as well as color, the Gray Bear remains a family-run hotel in the old style, with vast public areas, generous, comfortable rooms, and spacious baths. The bar in rustic decor completes the picture, and it's just steps from the Old City center. ✉ *Universitätsstr. 5, A–6020,* ☎ *0512/5924–0,* FAX *0512/574535. 81 rooms. Restaurant, bar, parking. AE, DC, MC, V.*

$$$ **Innsbruck.** Here, in one of the city's newest hotels, the mood is modern, from the lobby to the efficiently air-conditioned rooms with their accents of finished wood. From some of the rooms you'll get gorgeous views of the Old City, and from those on the river side, of the Nordkette mountains directly behind. ✉ *Innrain 3, A–6020,* ☎ *0512/59868–0,* FAX *0512/572280. 91 rooms. Restaurant, indoor pool, sauna, parking. AE, DC, MC, V.*

$$$ **Kapeller.** Outside the center in Amras (take Streetcar 3), this friendly *Gasthof* offers cozy rooms as well as the advantage of an excellent in-house restaurant. ✉ *Philippine-Welser-Str. 96, A–6020,* ☎ *0512/343101,* FAX *0512/343106–68. 36 rooms. Restaurant, parking. AE, DC, MC, V.*

$$$ **Maximilian.** From the pine-paneled lobby to the dark-wood furnishings in the compact rooms, you'll feel at home in this attractive hotel built in 1982. Tucked away in a peaceful corner of the Old City, it's convenient to most of the sights and shops. Best views are from the back, over the Old City roofs. Meals are for hotel guests only. ✉ *Marktgraben 7–9, A–6020,* ☎ *0512/59967–0,* FAX *0512/577450. 40 rooms. Dining room. AE, DC, MC, V.*

$$ **Goldene Krone.** The colorful facade of this older house conceals a set of smallish rooms that are modern and clean, and you couldn't ask for a better location: within two longish blocks of the railroad station and overlooking the main square. Rooms 1–11 on each floor are on the noisier Maximilianstrasse side but have great views of the *Jugendstil* building across the street. The plastic bath cubicles are adequate but unheated in winter. ✉ *Maria Theresien-Str. 46, A–6020,* ☎ *0512/586160,* FAX *0512/580189–6. 35 rooms. Café. AE, DC, MC, V.*

$$ **Royal.** This modern hotel overlooks the river and is only steps from the Old City. Rooms are simple but spacious and comfortable. ✉ *Innrain 16, A–6020,* ☎ *0512/586385,* FAX *0512/586385–10. 20 rooms. Breakfast room, parking. AE, DC, MC, V.*

$$ ★ **Tautermann.** This red-shuttered house within walking distance of the city's center has been successfully turned into a friendly, family-run hotel with rooms in natural woods and white. Some upper rooms on the west side have bay windows with gorgeous views of the imposing Hungerburg mountain. Bus A from the main station to Höttinger Kirchenplatz gets you close to the door. ✉ *Stamser Feld 5/Höttinger-*

gasse, A–6020, ☎ 0512/281572, FAX 0512/281572–10. 28 rooms. Breakfast room, parking. AE, DC, MC, V.

$$ ★ **Weisses Kreuz.** At first encounter, you'll fall in love with this hotel, set over the stone arcades in the heart of the old city. It has seen massive renovations since the first Gasthof stood on this site in 1465, and the rooms are simple but comfortable, with mainly rustic furniture and lots of light wood. The service is friendly and accommodating; there are special rooms on the ground floor in which you can keep your skis; hotel reception and a restaurant are upstairs. ✉ *Herzog Friedrich-Str. 31, A–6020, ☎ 0512/59479, FAX 0512/59479–90. 39 rooms. 2 restaurants. AE, MC, V.*

$ ★ **Binder.** A short streetcar trip (No. 3) from the center of town brings you to the less-costly comforts of this small, friendly, family-run hotel. Rooms are modest but modern and attractive. Book well ahead, as Binder has many regular guests. ✉ *Dr.-Glatz-Str. 20, A–6020, ☎ 0512/33436–0, FAX 0512/33436–99. 32 rooms. Bar, café, parking. AE,MC, V.*

$ **Innsbrücke.** Rooms at the front of this modest but comfortable hotel look across the river toward the Old City. You're five minutes from the center on foot, or to the railroad station by Bus A or K. Rooms are in beige and light wood and a few have baths. ✉ *Innstr. 1, A–6020, ☎ 0512/281934. 30 rooms, 8 with bath. Café. AE, DC, MC, V.*

Summer Hotels

Student accommodations in Innsbruck are turned into hotels from July to October and are extremely good value if you don't require the amenities of a full hotel; you may discover that Austrian university students don't live too badly. Check prices, as these can vary considerably from one hotel to another.

Internationales Studentenhaus. Not only the best located but also the cheapest option. ✉ *Rechengasse 7, A–6020, ☎ 0512/59477–0, FAX 0512/59477–15. 275 rooms. Parking. AE, DC, MC, V.*

Rosen-Hotel Höttinger Au. Across the Inn river, this choice overlooks the city. ✉ *Höttinger Au 84, A–6020, ☎ 0512/2206–0 or 0222/597–0689–0, FAX 0222/597–0689–89. 74 rooms. Restaurant, parking. AE, DC, MC, V.*

Rössl in der Au. Located across the Inn river, it affords a pleasant cityscape view. The associated **Atrium** (✉ Technikerstr. 7, ☎ 0512/286846) is slightly farther from the center but cheaper. ✉ *Höttinger Au 34, A–6020, ☎ 0512/2215 or 0512/286846, FAX 0512/293850. 125 rooms. Parking. AE, DC, MC, V.*

Nightlife and the Arts

The Arts

MUSIC

Concerts take place in the modern Saal Tirol of the **Kongresshaus** (✉ Rennweg 3, ☎ 0512/5936–0). Each year at Pentecost the churches resound with organ music during the annual International Organ Week. In summer, concerts are held in various historic places around Innsbruck, including Schloss Ambras, and there are brass-band folk-music concerts in the public squares almost every day. It's said that Tirol has more bandleaders than mayors. Folk shows at the Hotel Europa Tyrol and other spots around the city feature authentic Tirolean folk dancing, yodeling, and zither music. The tourist office and hotels have details.

THEATER AND OPERA

Innsbruck's principal theater is the **Tiroler Landestheater** (✉ Rennweg 2, ☎ 0512/52074–4). Both opera and operetta are presented in the "large house," usually starting at 7:30; plays in the Kammerspiele start at 8. Get tickets at the box office or at the main tourist office.

Nightlife

The jazzy **casino** adjacent to the Scandic Crown hotel offers blackjack, baccarat, roulette, and plenty of slot machines, as well as a bar and good restaurant. You must present your passport to enter the casino. ✉ *Salurner Str. 15,* ☎ *0512/587040–0.* 💴 *AS210, exchangeable for AS250 worth of chips; admission free for those not playing.* ⏲ *Daily 3 PM–3 AM.*

One of the more intriguing bars is the relaxed—or jammed, depending on the hour—**Café Brasil** (✉ Leopoldstr. 7, ☎ 0512/583466), with its fireplace and comfortable, if stylishly shabby, furnishings. The atmosphere is cool modern at **Das Büro** (✉ Badgasse 3, ☎ 0512/575633), by the cathedral. The beautiful people gather at **Café Adi** (✉ Burggraben 17, ☎ 0512/574411); another popular spot is **Arcos** (✉ Salurner Str., ☎ 0512/582423), next to the arch.

Currently the basement **Blue Chip** disco (✉ Wilhelm-Greil-Str. 17, ☎ 0512/565000) and the upstairs **Jimmy's** bar (✉ Wilhelm-Greil-Str. 19, ☎ 0512/570473) are hot spots and packed nightly. Of the classic discos, the best and most enduring is **Kandinsky** (✉ Anichstr. 7, ☎ 0512/582420).

Along the nightclub circuit, start first at **Filou** (✉ Stiftgasse 12, ☎ 0512/580256), where in summer you can sit in an attractive garden until 10 PM, when things move indoors for the sake of neighborhood peace and quiet. **Lady O** (✉ Brunecker Str. 2, ☎ 0512/586432) is the traditional striptease nightclub; you can see a teaser program on the ground floor at 9 PM for an AS20 admission charge, but the first drink costs AS140.

Outdoor Activities and Sports

Gliding

The mountains create updrafts, which makes Innsbruck a good place for sail gliding. Call **Flugsportzentrum Innsbruck** (☎ 0512/283157) for details.

Golf

Golfclub Innsbruck/Igls in Lans, about 9 kilometers (6 miles) outside the city, has two 9-hole courses, par 66 (☎ 0512/377165). It is open April–November. **Golfclub Innsbruck/Igls** in Rinn, about 12 kilometers (7½ miles) away, has 18 holes, with a par 71 (☎ 05223/8177). The course is open April–October. Both courses charge a AS460 greens fee on weekdays, AS580 on weekends, but you must be a member of a recognized club to use the courses. Several hotels—Europa-Tyrol in Innsbruck, Sporthotel Igls and Gesundheitszentrum Lanserhof at Lans, and the Geisler at Rinn—have special golfing arrangements.

Health and Fitness Clubs

In Innsbruck, try **City Fitness** (✉ Hunoldstr. 5, ☎ 0512/385696).

Hiking

Both easy paths and extreme slopes await hikers and climbers. From June to September, members of Club Innsbruck (☞ Getting Around *in* Tirol A to Z, *below*) can take free daily guided mountain hikes. The tourist office has a special hiking brochure. If you want to learn to climb, look to the **Alpine School Innsbruck** (✉ Natters, In der Stille 1, ☎ 0512/546000–0). If you're already a pro, check in with the the **Österreichischer Alpenverein** (✉ Wilhelm Greil-Str. 15, ☎ 0512/59547–0). If you'll be taking the cable-car lifts with any frequency, get a *Super-Bergbahnkarte* for three days' unlimited use on the Hungerburg, Nordketten, and Patscherkofel runs (💴 AS400). The card is available at the city office of the Innsbrucker Verkehrsbetrieb (✉ Museumstr. 23, ☎ 0512/5307).

Riding

Horseback riding can be arranged through **Reitclub Innsbruck** (⊠ Langer Weg, ☎ 0512/347174).

Skiing

In winter, check with the tourist office for information on snow conditions and how to get to the six ski areas. Your Club Innsbruck membership card will get you free transportation to the areas and reductions on a number of ski lifts. If you're a summer skier (and can take the altitudes), there's year-round skiing on the Stubai glacier, about 40 kilometers (25 miles) from Innsbruck, via the "ST" bus from the train station. You can book with the **Schischule Innsbruck** (☎ 0512/582310) or at the hotel information stand (☎ 0512/583766) in the station. A ski kindergarten in winter will teach smaller children to ski, while parents run the more advanced slopes. Ski schools and hotels have details.

Swimming

Around Innsbruck there are plenty of lakes, but in town you have little choice other than pools, indoor and out. Outdoors, try the **Freischwimmbad Tivoli** (⊠ Purtschellerstr. 1, ☎ 0512/342344); indoors, try **Hallenbad Amraser Strasse** (⊠ Amraser Str. 3, ☎ 0512/342585), **Hallenbad Höttinger Au** (⊠ Fürstenweg 12, ☎ 0512/282339), or **Hallenbad Olympisches Dorf** (Kugelfangweg 46, ☎ 0512/261342).

Tennis

Innsbruck has an abundance of courts, although they tend to be scattered and booked well ahead. Your hotel or the tourist office can help. Try the **Olympia-Eissportzentrum** (⊠ Olympiastr. 10, ☎ 0512/33838) or the **Tennisclub IEV** (⊠ Reichenauer Str. 144, ☎ 0512/346229); your Club Innsbruck card will get you a reduction at both.

Shopping

The best shops are along the arcaded Herzog Friedrich-Strasse in the heart of the old city; along its extension, Maria Theresien-Strasse; and the cross-street Maximilianstrasse in the newer part of town. Innsbruck is *the* place to buy native Tirolean clothing, particularly lederhosen. Look also for cut crystal and wood carvings; locally handmade delicate silver-filigree pins make nice gifts. A lively flea market takes place each Saturday from 8 to 1 on Innrain, near St. John's church (Johanneskirche). **Tiroler Heimatwerk** (⊠ Meraner Str. 2–4, ☎ 0512/582320) is the first place to look for local mementos and souvenirs of good quality. The extremely attractive shop carries textiles and finished clothing, ceramics, carved wooden chests, and some furniture. You can also have clothing made to order. **Trachten Wenger** (⊠ Herzog Friedrich-Str. 12, ☎ 0512/588336) is an outstanding source of dirndls, those attractive country costumes for women, with white blouse, dark skirt, and colorful apron. It also has children's clothing. **Rudolf Boschi** (⊠ Kiebachgasse 8, ☎ 0512/589224) turns out reproductions of old pewterware, using the original molds when possible. Among other items, he has locally produced hand-decorated beer mugs with pewter lids. **Galerie Thomas Flora** (⊠ Herzog Friedrich-Str. 5, ☎ 0512/577402) sells graphics by the droll Tirolean artist Paul Flora; you'll find much to smile at here, and maybe even to take home.

TIROL: A MOUNTAIN WONDERLAND

During each season of the year Tirol's awesome mountain scenery is defined by a different color: the fresh green of the high pastures in spring, the deep blue of the lakes in summer, the golden red of the rocky mountain slopes during the fall sunsets, and the brilliant white of snowy inclines reflecting the winter sun. Every season has its particular allure here, but Tirol remains the best winter sports area in Austria and one of the best skiing regions in the world. This is the home country of such legendary skiing masters as Hannes Schneider and Toni Seelos, of such record holders of today as Toni Sailer, Josl Rieder, and Andreas Molterer. It all started with the British Kandahar Ski Club, which hired Hannes Schneider in the 1920s to teach his revolutionary ski technique, thus popularizing the sport and making Austrian skiing world-famous. Travelers had already made inroads. In 1906 the railroad millionaire J. Pierpont Morgan spent a holiday in Innsbruck, and from that point on, Tirol was promoted in the United States as a vacation playground.

The awe-inspiring scenery of western Tirol looks as if it could have been fashioned by giants with its towering peaks and dramatic valleys speckled with sparkling glaciers. In fact, the mythic giants, goblins, and gnomes come magically alive during Lenten carnival season when masked revelers take to village streets.

Tirol's gorgeous geography precludes the convenient loop tour; you must go up into the valleys to discover the hundreds of charming villages and hotels, and a certain amount of backtracking is necessary. We've outlined six tours over familiar routes, touching on the best of the towns and suggesting side trips and pleasures off the beaten track.

Tour 1 will take you east of Innsbruck through the lower Inn Valley, then south into the Ziller and Tuxer valleys, with detours to the Achensee and to Gerlos. Tour 2, also east of Innsbruck, continues up the Inn Valley to Kufstein on the German border and to the ski resorts of St. Johann and Kitzbühel. Tour 3 explores the Inn Valley west of Innsbruck to Imst, then goes south up the Ötz Valley. Tour 4 heads west from Imst, takes in Landeck and the upper Inn Valley, ending with St. Anton and the Arlberg.

Whether you mix or match these tours or do them all, they'll allow you to discover a cross section of Tirol's highlights: the old and the new, glossy resorts, medieval castles, and always that superlative scenery.

Around the Lower Inn Valley

Northeast of Innsbruck the Inn River valley broadens out and courses right through Tirol toward Kufstein and the German border. Route 171 along the valley is a much pleasanter route than the autobahn running parallel.

Hall in Tirol

11 *9 km (5 mi) east of Innsbruck.*

Hall in Tirol (Solbad Hall), a bare 9 kilometers (5 miles) from Innsbruck, is an old city founded by salt miners. The picturesque old part of the town is made up of narrow lanes running east–west, interrupted by a few short cross alleys. Stop and look around; from the main road, you cannot get a proper perspective of the fine old buildings. The **Rathaus**, built in the mid-15th century, has ornately carved councillors' rooms and beautifully worked mosaics covering the walls. The **mint tower**, symbol of the town, and the 17th-century **monastery church**, the oldest Renaissance ecclesiastical building in Tirol, are both interesting examples of local craftsmanship. The mint was moved to Hall from Meran, and the first coins were struck here in 1477. Legend has it that Duke Sigmund the Wealthy, son of Friedl the Penniless, got his nickname by tossing handfuls of Hall-minted coins to the populace wherever he went. The Inntal (Inn Valley) gave its name to the coin, known as the *Taler,* from which came the word "dollar."

Dining and Lodging

$$$ ✕🏨 **Hotel Restaurant Heiligreuz.** Perched on a hillside shrouded with trees, the Hotel Restaurant Heiligreuz is an intimate home away from home. Dark wood paneling and comfortable, overstuffed furniture decorate the hotel. Rooms are equally elegant and welcoming, as is the friendly staff. The restaurant offers traditional rib-sticking classics such as *G'röstl,* a concoction of eggs, bacon, and potatoes guaranteed to satisfy the heartiest of appetites. ✉ *Reimmichlstr. 18, A–6060,* ☎ *05223/57114,* FAX *05223/571145. 38 rooms. Restaurant, bar. V.*

Shopping

Traveling east between Hall in Tirol and Schwaz, you'll pass the home of the of the Swarovski glass empire in Wattens. Stop at the **Crystal Shop** (✉ Innstr. 1, ☎ 05224/5886–0) not only to buy the famous crystal and glassware but to watch the glass cutting and blowing and the cutting of precious stones upstairs.

Schwaz

⓬ *16 km (10 mi) northeast of Hall in Tirol.*

The Hapsburg emperors in the 15th and 16th century owed much of their wealth to the silver and copper extracted from the mines here by the Fugger family, who emigrated from Augsburg. Founded in the 12th century, Schwaz, on the south bank of the Inn, evolved into a rich and important mining center—the **Silbergbergwerk Schwaz**—dug deep under the towering Tuxer Alps. Those mines indeed may have been the reason for setting up the mint in nearby Hall. ✉ *Alte Landstr. 3a,* ☎ *05242/72372–0.* ⏲ *Jan.–mid Nov., daily 8:30–5 in summer, 9:30–4 in winter.*

The 15th-and 16th-century houses built during those prosperous times still stand, and the marketplace has kept its atmosphere. Look at the vast **parish church,** the largest Gothic hall-church in Tirol. The church was expanded in 1490 and divided into two parts (once they were separated by a wooden wall): the southern chancel for the miners, and the northern, or the "Prince's chancel," for the upper classes.

En Route **Jenbach,** 8 kilometers (5 miles) north of Schwaz, across the river, is notable mainly as a rail and highway junction; from here Route 169 follows the Ziller River valley (Zillertal) south, past the Gerlos Valley (Route 165) and the Tuxer mountain range to Mayrhofen. The Achensee lies on the plateau to the north, fed by the Achen river rising high in the mountains beyond, on the German border. Both regions have become immensely popular.

Achensee

⓭ *17 km (12 mi) north of Jenbach.*

From Jenbach, many travelers head to the **Achensee.** If you're driving, take Route 181; the initial stretch involves hairpin turns and a steep climb, but the views over the Inn Valley are exquisite. You could take a bus, too, but the most adventuresome and romantic way to reach the Achensee is on the steam-powered, and more than a century old, train, the **Achenseebahn,** built in 1889 as Tirol's first mountain cog railway (☎ 05244/2243). The line does its 1,300-foot climb in a nearly straight line over 7 kilometers (4 miles) to the lower end of the Achensee (Seespitz), where you can get a lake steamer on to Buchau and Pertisau and to the north end.

The Achen Valley has fine skiing in winter, but the Achensee in summer, with water sports and excellent fishing, is the main attraction. It is the largest and most beautiful lake in Tirol—10 kilometers (6 miles) long—with the great mountains of the Karwendel and Sonnwend ranges rising from its blue-green waters. The lake steamer connects the villages strung along its length.

Lodging

$$$$ **Posthotel.** This comfortable Alpine chalet is also a health center; you'll find every convenience for taking care of fitness, weight loss, and exercise. Horseback riders will find mounts ranging from Haflingers to Shetland ponies. Rooms are in typical Tirolean country style. ⊠ *Achenkirch, A–6215,* ☎ *05246/6205–0,* FAX *05246/6205–468. 97 rooms. Restaurant, indoor and heated outdoor pools, sauna, tennis court, exercise room, horseback riding, squash. No credit cards. Closed mid-Nov.–mid-Dec.*

Pertisau

14 *25 km (16 mi) north of Schwaz.*

This small, picturesque village set into the thick pine forest of a nature preserve, is the only community on the western shore of the Achensee. It offers excellent swimming, sailing, tennis, fishing, and a golf course, all at budget prices. Although less popular, the eastern side of the lake enjoys at least two hours of sunshine more every day, and the water is consequently warmer. Because this area is so close to Innsbruck, the lake is crowded on summer weekends; try to visit on a weekday.

Dining and Lodging

$$$–$$$$ ★ ✕ **Fürstenhaus.** Duke Sigmund the Wealthy knew what he was doing when he built this massive house in 1469. A later Sigmund—Freud—stayed here in 1900. The elegant hotel, directly on the lake, has its own boats, and rooms are spacious and luxurious. The inviting restaurant features fresh lake fish. Use the hotel's spa facilities to help work off the results. ⊠ *A–6213,* ☎ *05243/5442–0,* FAX *05243/6168. 61 rooms. Restaurant, bar, café, indoor pool, beauty salon, sauna, spa, exercise room. AE, DC, MC, V. Closed Apr. and Nov.–mid-Dec.*

$$–$$$ ✕ **Kristall.** This chalet lodge set against a wooded mountain offers friendly comfort in ample, elegant public rooms and cheerfully decorated bedrooms. You can take half board or not, and the restaurant is open to the public. ⊠ *A–6213,* ☎ *05243/5490,* FAX *05243/5374–19. 52 rooms. Restaurant, bar, indoor and outdoor pools, sauna, exercise room. No credit cards. Closed Nov.–mid-Dec.*

Outdoor Activities and Sports

GOLF

Golf-Club Achensee in Pertisau is an attractive 9-hole, par-70 Alpine course with 18 tees and many long straight runs. ☎ *05243/5377.* ⊙ *May–Oct.*

En Route Scenic Route 181 leads along the eastern shore of the lake through Buchau to the northern end, passing through Achenseehof and Scholastika, among various small settlements belonging to the community of Achenkirch. Because this area is so close to Innsbruck, the lake is crowded on summer weekends; try to visit on a weekday.

The drive south from Jenbach on Route 169 follows the Ziller River, which rises high in the Alps to the south, in an area of perpetual glacier, then flows north. Route 169 parallels the narrow-gauge Ziller ★ railway, the **Zillertalbahn,** which makes daily runs between Jenbach and Mayrhofen, some under steam power. If your childhood dream was to drive a train, check in Jenbach (☎ 05244/5353–0, FAX 05244/3983–39) about renting this one; you can take a crash course in railroad operations and play engineer of the steam locomotive, all for a modest fee.

The first part of the Zillertal is broad and shallow, and the scenery is not very inspiring. But from Stumm onward, where you pass through some pretty Alpine villages, and particularly the stretch south of Zell am Ziller, the valley starts to live up to its reputation.

Zell am Ziller

15 *25 km (16 mi) southeast of Jenbach.*

The main town of the Zillertal—the biggest and most famous of the many beautiful Alpine valleys of the Tirol—is noted for its traditional 400-year-old Gauderfest (contact the local tourist board, ☎ 05282/2281), held on the first weekend in May, when thousands of tourists from far and wide pack the little market town of Zell am Ziller for the colorful skits, music, and singing—and great quantities of *Gauderbier,* a strong brew run up for the occasion. You can hear some of the country's best singing, by the valley residents, and listen to expert harp and zither playing, for which the valley is famous throughout Austria. Tradition runs strong here: witness the *Perchtenlaufen,* processions of colorfully masked well-wishers going the neighborhood rounds on January 5, or the annual *Almabtrieb* during the last September and first October days, when the cows are hung with wreaths and bells and, amid celebrations, are herded back from the high Alpine pastures into the lower fields and barns. This is a typical Tirolean country town, with Alpine lodges and a round-domed pink village church (note the Baroque painting of the Holy Trinity); in winter it's a center for skiing and sports.

Dining and Lodging

$$–$$$ ★ ✕🏨 **Bräu.** The core of this thick-walled, five-story, frescoed building in the center of town dates to the 16th century; subsequent renovations and a new wing have brought it quite up to date. The rooms are decorated in warm Alpine style, in beiges, greens, and browns. The hotel can arrange fishing trips. The three-room restaurant complex serves fine food, with emphasis on fish and game. Reserve for the *Bräustübl,* and enjoy the house beer; the house brewery is also the source of the *Gauderbier.* ✉ *Dorfpl. 1, A–6280,* ☎ *05282/2313,* FAX *05282/2313–17. 36 rooms. Restaurant, café, sauna. No credit cards. Closed Apr. and mid-Oct.–mid-Dec.*

$$–$$$ ✕🏨 **Zellerhof.** This variation on the traditional Alpine chalet is now a hotel school for most of the year, so you'll be looked after by a young and enthusiastic staff. The house is tastefully decorated in the local style, with ample natural wood, and the Tirolean ambience carries over to the comfortable rooms. The hotel can arrange fishing. The intimate restaurant upstairs is excellent. ✉ *Bahnhofstr. 3, A–6280,* ☎ *05282/2612–0,* FAX *05282/2612–65. 40 rooms. Restaurant, bar, café, sauna. AE, DC, MC, V. Closed mid-Oct.–mid-June, except Christmas and Easter holidays.*

Mayrhofen

16 *10 km (6 mi) south of Zell am Ziller.*

Down the road you'll come to Mayrhofen, end of the line for the narrow-gauge railway. This is the valley's main tourist base and the favorite summer resort of the British for many years. Mayrhofen is the starting point for summer hiking into the highly scenic valleys that branch off to the southeast, south, and southwest and for excursions into the Ziller glacier areas at heights of 9,750 feet and more.

At Mayrhofen the valley splits into three *Gründe* (grounds): the Zillergrund, Stillupgrund, and Zemmgrund—prime examples of picture-postcard Alpine areas, swept at the top with glittering, pale-blue glaciers.

Dining and Lodging

$$$ ★ ✕ **Wirtshaus zum Griena.** The restaurant tucked into this 400-year-old farmhouse is about a 10-minute drive north of Mayrhofen. The route is not simple, but everybody knows Griena's—ask at your hotel for directions. Once you get there, you'll find yourself in rustic surroundings of natural wood paneling. Such local favorites as beer soup, pasta dishes, and schnitzel are tempting. The beer is local and excellent, the wines somewhat disappointing. ✉ *Dorfhaus 768,* ☎ *05285/2778. No credit cards. Closed June–early July and Nov.–early Dec.*

$$$$ ★ ✕🏨 **Elisabeth.** This newish house, in Tirolean style, radiates elegance without being too formal. The same is true of the well-decorated bedrooms, which have every imaginable amenity, including room safes. Some have lovely old-fashioned canopied beds and ceramic heating stoves. The excellent Gute Stube restaurant, done in natural woods and reds, offers international and local specialties such as roast veal or trout. ✉ *Einfahrt Mitte 432, A–6290,* ☎ *05285/2929,* FAX *05285/4535. 40 rooms. 2 restaurants, bar, café, indoor pool, sauna, exercise room, dance club. AE, DC, MC, V.*

$$–$$$ ★ ✕🏨 **Kramerwirt.** Here's the center of the action in Mayrhofen, where the crowd gathers. The welcoming warmth of natural wood in the lobby and *Stuben* is accented by the Asian carpets and Tirolean antiques. Still family-run, this hostelry has been around for centuries. You'll feel at home in the comfortable rooms. ✉ *Am Marienbrunnen 346, A–6290,* ☎ *05285/2615,* FAX *05285/2615–502. 72 rooms. Restaurant, bar, sauna, exercise room, dance club, parking. No credit cards. Closed 2 wks in Dec.*

Outdoor Activities and Sports

CLIMBING

For the adventuresome, Peter Habeler at the **Alpinschule u. Schischule Mount Everest** (✉ Hauptstr. 458, ☎ 05285/2563 or 05285/2829, FAX 05285/2563–4) gives instruction in ice climbing.

Tuxer Valley

⓱ *15 km (9 mi) west of Mayrhofen.*

The fourth arm and highest in altitude of the Inn Valley is the Tuxer Valley, a summer ski region, which ends at the foot of the massive Olperer and Rifflerspitz glaciers, nearly 11,000 feet high. Frequent buses leave Mayrhofen for **Lanersbach**, a small mountain village, and **Hintertux**, right at the doorway of the great glaciers. Hintertux is also a popular spa, with a small thermal swimming pool, and the center of an ancient wood-carving industry. Rubies (called Tirolean garnets) were once mined in this area, and you might run across local amethyst in the shops as well.

Dining and Lodging

$$$ ✕🏨 **Neu Hintertux.** In the shadow of the nearby mountains, this turreted hotel decorated with frescoes and carved wood exudes traditional Alpine charm. Rooms are delightfully decorated with canopied beds, brocaded fabrics and tiled stoves. You can enjoy a drink after a day on the slopes around an open hearth in the bar that is covered in dark, carved wood. Tirolean classics are served in the restaurant. ✉ *A–6294*

Hintertux, ☎ 0587/325, FAX 05287/318409. 54 rooms. Restaurant, bar, sauna, bowling, billiards. No credit cards. Closed Sept.

$$$ ✕🏨 **Rindererhof.** This comfortable Alpine lodge at the end of the line is a good starting point for either climbing or skiing, since you're right at the base station for the cable cars up to the glacier. The outdoor Schirmbar (Umbrella Bar) is the "in" spot for après-ski in Hintertux. ✉ *A–6294 Hintertux, ☎ 05287/501, FAX 05287/502. 30 rooms, 30 suites. Restaurant, bar, sauna. No credit cards. Closed mid- to late July and early–mid-Dec.*

$$$ ✕🏨 **Tuxerhof.** The welcoming open fireplace in the lounge sets the relaxed style for this attractive Alpine inn, whose rooms and restaurant are comfortably appointed. In winter, skiing starts literally at the door; in summer, hiking paths will lead you into the surrounding forests and mountains. ✉ *Vorderlanersbach 185, A–6293 Lanersbach, ☎ 05287/211, FAX 05287/222–50. 42 rooms, 4 apartments. Restaurant, bar, pub, indoor pool, sauna, children's programs, parking. No credit cards. Closed May–June.*

$ ★ ✕🏨 **Forelle.** This friendly mountain inn offers comfortable rooms in typical Alpine decor and a good restaurant specializing in trout. The hotel has its own fishing stream. ✉ *Vorderlanersbach 216, A–6293 Lanersbach, ☎ 05287/214, FAX 05287/543. 34 rooms. Restaurant, bar, indoor pool, sauna, exercise room. No credit cards. Closed mid-Apr.–May and Nov.–mid-Dec.*

Outdoor Activities and Sports

CLIMBING

Those particularly interested in ice climbing should contact Anton Tomann at the **Hochgebirgs-und Wanderschule Tuxertal** (✉ Juns 424, A–6293 Lanersbach, ☎ 05287/372).

Hainzenberg

⓲ *6 km (4 mi) south of Zell am Ziller.*

Hainzenberg was once a gold-mining town. Stop at the **Maria Rast pilgrimage church,** built in 1739 by the prospectors, to see its stuccos and fine ceiling paintings. Don't look for the western transept wing of the church; it slid down the precipice in 1910.

Gerlos

⓳ *18 km (10 mi) east of Zell am Ziller.*

The sensationally scenic Route 165 climbs east out of Zell am Ziller up to Gerlos, a less glitzy but still splendid choice for a summer or winter holiday, with the 8,300-foot Kreuzjoch mountain looming in the background. Scheduled buses make the run up from Zell am Ziller. The Gerlos ski slopes are varied, and in summer the same slopes offer excellent hiking. Check in advance about hotel arrangements; many of the better houses in Gerlos require a minimum of half board.

Lodging

$$$$ 🏨 **Gaspingerhof.** The three Alpine chalets that make up this family-run, rustically furnished complex in the center of town are connected by underground passages. Rooms are done in the bright local custom, with natural woods and colorful fabrics. The nightlife is active. ✉ *A–6281, ☎ 05284/5216, FAX 05284/5355–49. 73 rooms. Restaurant, indoor pool, sauna, tennis court. DC. Closed mid-Apr.–mid-May and mid-Oct.–early Dec.*

$$ 🏨 **Almhof.** In typical Tirolean style, this Alpine inn about 2 kilometers (1¼ miles) out of the center offers a friendly reception area and comfortable rooms. ✉ *Gerlos–Gmünd, A–6281, ☎ 05284/5323–0,*

℻ *05284/5386–53. 45 rooms. Restaurant, indoor pool, sauna, tennis court, exercise room, parking. No credit cards. Closed May–early June and mid-Oct.–mid-Dec.*

En Route Beyond Gerlos, the highway climbs the 5,300-foot **Gerlos pass** and plunges into the province of Salzburg in a series of double-back hairpins close to the dramatic 1,300-foot Krimmler Wasserfälle (waterfalls). You can complete the circuit back into Tirol by continuing east to Mittersill and cutting north to Kitzbühel via the Thurn pass.

From Jenbach to Kitzbühel

Brixlegg

20 *16 km (10 mi) northeast of Jenbach.*

Starting again from Jenbach in the main Inn Valley, continue northeast on Route 171 until you hit Brixlegg, a former copper-mining town. It is the home of the Schloss Kropfsberg, built to defend the Ziller Valley from marauding invaders. Another castle from the 12th-century, the Schloss Matzen, is perched on a mountainside. For years, sufferers of rheumatism also have flocked to Brixlegg to soak in the radioactive sulfur waters of the Mehrn spa.

Dining and Lodging

$$$–$$$$ ✕ **Sigwart's Tiroler Weinstuben.** The wood-paneled rooms set a country atmosphere in this relaxed *Gasthaus.* The difference here lies in the food; try the sole with mushroom sauce or any of the roast meats. Even the breads are from the house kitchen. The open wines are excellent. ✉ *Marktstr. 40, A–6230,* ☎ *05337/62358,* ℻ *05337/63390–15. AE. Closed Mon., Tues., and early June–mid-July.*

$ ✕🏨 **Brixleggerhof.** This friendly, family-run house is small, but all the amenities are there. In the rustic restaurant, the standard dishes—roast pork and schnitzel—are the favorites. ✉ *Herrnhauspl. 12, A–6230,* ☎ *05337/62630. 10 rooms. Restaurant, bar. No credit cards. Closed May and Oct.*

Alpbach

21 *8 km (5 mi) southeast of Brixlegg.*

From Brixlegg a small side road runs down a valley to the unspoiled picture-book village of Alpbach. The town is nominally a winter-sports center, but it takes the international spotlight once a year in the spring when world leaders of government and industry gather to discuss global issues at the European Forum.

Dining and Lodging

$$$–$$$$ ★ ✕🏨 **Böglerhof.** Much of the original character has been preserved in this beautifully restored old double chalet, with its heavily beamed ceilings and stonework. The rooms are attractively decorated in Tirolean style. The excellent restaurant, with its small *Stuben* (side rooms), is known for such Austrian specialties as cabbage soup or fillet points in light garlic sauce. The hotel is a member of the RomantikHotel group. ✉ *A–6236,* ☎ *05336/5227 or 05336/5228,* ℻ *05336/5227–402. 50 rooms. Restaurant, bar, indoor and outdoor pools, sauna, tennis court, exercise room. MC, V. Closed mid-Apr.–May and mid-Oct.–mid-Dec.*

$$$ ✕🏨 **Alpbacher Hof.** The massive fireplace sets the keynote in the public rooms of this typical chalet hotel, and the welcoming feeling carries over to the bedrooms. You may be asked to take minimum half board, but the policy is flexible. ✉ *A–6236,* ☎ *05336/5237,* ℻ *05336/*

5016. 55 rooms. Restaurant, café, indoor pool, sauna. No credit cards. Closed Apr.–mid-May and Oct.–mid-Dec.

Rattenberg

22 *24 km (15 mi) southwest of Kufstein, 5 ki (3 mi) northeast of Brixlegg.*

Just up the road from Brixlegg is this quaint medieval town once famous for its silver mines. When the mines were exhausted, Rattenberg lapsed into a deep sleep lasting, like Rip van Winkle's, for centuries. Were it not for the constant procession of cars and trucks (which the residents are trying to ban), you might think you were back in the Middle Ages. Narrow old streets full of relics of its past glory twine around the town, which has remained remarkably unchanged for centuries. Local legend purports that the ruins of Emperor Maximilian's massive castle, which looms above the town, are haunted by ghosts from a bygone era.

Shopping

Across the river from Rattenberg, lies Kramsach, a glass-production center since the 17th century. At the **glassworks school** (call 05337/62623 to arrange a visit) you can see etching, engraving, and painting on glassware.

Back on Route 171, the road leads to **Wörgl,** a rail junction where the main Austrian east–west line and the shortcut via the "German corner" come together. From Wörgl an extremely scenic road leads south to the small resort villages of Niederau, Oberau, and Auffach.

Kufstein

23 *13 km (8 mi) north of Söll, 32 ki (24 mi) northeast of Brixlegg.*

Kufstein marks the border with Germany. The town was captured from Bavaria in 1504 by Emperor Maximilian I, who added it to the Habsburg domains. You'll immediately notice that Kufstein is dominated by a magnificent fortress right out of a Dürer etching, the **Schloss Geroldseck,** originally built as a "castle for contemplation" in 1200. But Maximilian decided it was better suited for merrymaking and expanded and strengthened it in 1504, rechristening it as *Lustschloss,* or "pleasure palace." The fortress, considerably renovated, contains a small museum and boasts the famed "Heroes' Organ" (said to burst into sound when a national hero dies). With sumptuous rooms and terraced gardens, Geroldseck ranks among the finest of the 1,001 Tirolian castles. The town of Kufstein itself has some beautiful medieval-period streets. *Castle, ☎ 05372/62207; museum, ☎ 05372/67038. Castle free, museum AS34. Castle May–Oct., daily 9–7; museum late Apr.–Oct., Tues.–Sun., tour Tues.–Sun. at 9:30, 11, 1:30, and 4:30.*

The center of town boasts a remarkable concentration of Art Nouveau buildings, both public and private. The **Burgher's Tower** houses the *Heldenorgel,* the world's largest outdoor organ, with 26 registers and 1,800 pipes. The instrument is played year-round daily at noon and in summer at noon and 6 PM.

Dining and Lodging

$$–$$$ ★ **Alpenrose.** This recently renovated house, on the edge of town in green surroundings, welcomes you immediately with its friendly lobby that seems to continue the outdoors; the feeling of relaxed comfort carries over into the attractive bedrooms as well. The elegant restaurant is the best in the area; the *Tafelspitz* (boiled beef) and fish, game, and goose in season are particularly recommended, as is the orange souf-

flé. ✉ *Weissachstr. 47, A–6330,* ☎ *05372/62122,* FAX *05372/62122–7. 19 rooms. Restaurant, bar. AE, MC. Closed wk before Easter.*

Shopping

Kufstein is home to the world-famous **Riedel glass works;** a visit to the factory (☎ 05372/64896–0) may be possible. Otherwise you can buy pieces at the factory outlet (✉ Weissach Str. 28–34, ☎ 05372/64896–0), which is open weekdays 9–noon and 1–5:30, and Saturday 9–noon.

En Route At Wörgl most travelers begin to head east toward the great resorts of St. Johann and Kitzbühel, destinations described below. Route 312 takes you to St. Johann, the noted vacation center, about 30 kilometers (19 miles) away. You can do the circuit of St. Johann and its more famous neighbor, Kitzbühel, by taking Route 161 for 10 kilometers (6 miles) between the two resorts and returning to Wörgl via Route 170. Heading eastward, you first encounter the charming towns of Going, Ellmau, and Söll.

Going, Ellmau, and Söll

10 km (7 mi) to 40 km (25 mi) south of Kufstein.

The towns of Going, Ellmau, and Söll have developed into attractive, small winter and summer resorts. Their altitudes (and their snow) are about the same as those in Kitzbühel and St. Johann, and their prices are half as high, but rising, as popularity grows. Some of the region's finest restaurants and hotels are located around these towns.

Dining and Lodging

$$$$ ★ ✕ **Rautnerwirt.** In its two small rooms with seven tables, this attractive restaurant in a country house offers imaginative local cuisine; depending on the season, you might find roast young goat or braised venison in a delicate mushroom sauce. You can watch the preparation through the picture window that divides kitchen and dining areas. ✉ *A–6353 Going,* ☎ *05358/2784. AE, DC, MC, V. Closed June–early July. No lunch Mon. or Tues.*

$$ ✕ **Schindlhaus.** Original variations on Austrian dishes are served up in a modern setting at this restaurant. Try the lightly braised fillet of venison with red cabbage or one of the fish specialties, served with a delicate sauce. The gemütlich atmosphere and friendly staff provide the perfect finishing touches. ✉ *Dorf 134, A–6303 Söll,* ☎ *05333/5161. AE, DC, MC, V. Closed Mon.*

$$$$ ★ ✕🏨 **Der Bär.** Within walking distance of the village center, the Bear, a member of the Relais & Châteaux group, is known throughout Austria as one of the foremost country inns. An elegant but friendly atmosphere pervades, with relaxed comfort in every respect, attractive bedrooms in Tirolean style included. The kitchen does best with local dishes; try roast lamb, game, or seafood. The wine list also has an extensive choice of Austrian, French and Italian vintages. ✉ *Kirchbichl 9, A–6352 Ellmau,* ☎ *05358/2395,* FAX *05358/2395–56. 45 rooms. Restaurant, indoor and outdoor pools, sauna, exercise room. No credit cards. Closed mid-Apr.–May and early Nov.–mid-Dec.*

$$$$ 🏨 **Stanglwirt.** A 300-year-old coaching inn forms the core of this centrally located health-and-fitness complex that's also a popular mealtime stop for tour buses. Rooms in the new section are spacious; some are studios with old-fashioned ceramic stoves, in keeping with the Tirolean decor. Guests can ride, swim, hunt, or ski in season, or play tennis and squash. This hotel is a great favorite with Germans, who

have ranked it among the top 12 resort hotels in Europe. ✉ *Sonnseite 50, A–6353 Going,* ☏ *05358/2000,* FAX *05358/2000–31. 62 rooms, 6 apartments. Restaurant, indoor and outdoor pools, tennis courts, sauna, exercise room, horseback riding, squash. AE, DC, MC, V.*

St. Johann

24 *32 ki (24 mi) southeast of Kufstein, 14 km (9 mi) northeast of Kitzbühel.*

For years, St. Johann lived in the shadow of Kitzbühel, but today the town, with its colorfully painted houses, has developed a personality of its own and for better or worse is equally mobbed, winter and summer. The facilities are similar, but prices are still lower, although climbing. (The dark horse here could be Kirchdorf, 4 kilometers or 2 miles north of St. Johann, where costs appear to be holding, or Fieberbrunn, 12 kilometers or 7 miles east on Route 164.) While in St. Johann, don't miss the magnificently decorated Baroque **parish church** or the Gothic **Spitalskirche,** with its fine late-medieval stained glass, just west of town in Weitau.

Dining and Lodging

$$$ **Alpenapartment Europa.** This apartment hotel next to the recreation center (swimming, sauna, tennis) is attractively furnished in Baroque and regional decor. Many rooms have Tirolean four-posters and furnished kitchenettes. Exhausted skiers delight in knowing that breakfast is served until 11 AM. ✉ *Achenallee 18, A–6380,* ☏ *05352/2285–0,* FAX *05532/5167. 16 apartments. No credit cards.*

$$$ ✕ **Goldener Löwe.** This traditional chalet-style hotel is festooned with bright red geraniums in summer and white fairy lights in winter. The staff extends the gemütlich atmosphere through their friendly and outgoing service. Rooms are decorated in cool pastels and blond-wood furniture. Never mind that the decor seems a bit dated: The views from the room balconies of the surrounding mountain scenery are spectacular. The restaurant serves up hearty Tirolean specialties. ✉ *A-6380,* ☏ *05352/2251,* FAX *05352/2981. 64 rooms. Restaurant, café, bowling. AE, DC, MC, V.*

$$$ ✕ **Post.** The painted stucco facade identifies this traditional hotel in the center of town. Natural woods and reds carry over from the public spaces and restaurant into the guest rooms. ✉ *Speckbacherstr. 1, A–6380,* ☏ *05352/2230,* FAX *05352/2230–3. 46 rooms. Restaurant, café. AE, DC, MC, V. Closed Apr. and Nov.*

Kitzbühel

25 *20 km (12 mi) south of St. Johann, 71 km (44 mi) northeast of Gerlos.*

Long before Kitzbühel became one of the fashionable winter resorts, the town had gained a reputation for its summer season. Now, however, the main accent is almost completely on skiing, with facilities among the finest in the world. The famous Ski Circus, a carefully planned, clever combination of lifts, cable railways, and runs, that let you ski for over 80 kilometers (50 miles) without having to exert yourself climbing a single foot, originally put this town on the map. Today, Kitzbühel is in perpetual motion, packed with celebrities in December and again in February. But at any time during the season there's plenty to do, from sleigh rides to fancy-dress balls.

Built in the 16th century with proceeds from copper and silver mining, the town itself is picturesque enough, but take time to also check out the churches: **St. Andrew's parish church** (1435–1506) has a lavishly Rococo chapel, the Rosakapelle, and the marvelously ornate tomb (1520) of the Kupferschmid family; the **Church of St. Catherine,** built about 1350, houses a Gothic winged altar dating to 1515.

In summer, get a guest card stamped by your hotel for substantial reductions on various activities (some of which are then free) like tennis, riding, and golf. The best swimming is in the nearby Schwarzsee (Black Lake). To see Alpine flowers in their natural glory, take the cable car up the Kitzbühler Horn to the **Alpine Flower Garden Kitzbühel** at 6,500 feet; it leaves every half hour.

Dining and Lodging

$$$$ ✕ **Wirtshaus Unterberger Stuben.** In this former residence done up in typical Tirolean fashion, with beige and red decor, you may have to reserve weeks ahead to get a table in winter; the celebrities book the place solid. The international cuisine is good if not always a match for the prices, offering such temptations as creamed pumpkin soup and stuffed oxtail. ✉ *Wehrgasse 2,* ☎ *05356/2101,* FAX *05356/71996. Reservations essential. No credit cards. Closed mid-May–June and Nov. No lunch Tues. or Wed. except during high season.*

$$ ★ ✕ **Praxmair.** Après-ski can't begin early enough for the casually chic crowds who pile into this famous pastry shop–café, known for its Florentines. ✉ *Vorderstadt 17,* ☎ *05356/2646. AE, DC, MC, V. Closed Apr. and Nov.*

$$$ ★ ✕🏨 **Tennerhof.** Hidden away slightly out of the center, this RomantikHotel is an elegant old country estate house set in a huge garden near the golf course. Emphasis here is on family, including a special supervised children's room. The bedrooms are done in Tirolean country furnishings, all different, some with ceramic stoves, some with hunting trophies. The restaurant enjoys a top reputation on its own; the Rosa Stube (pink room) is the more intimate and a favorite of celebrities. Try any of the local specialties, such as the roast lamb with herbs, sometimes picked fresh from the garden outside the door. ✉ *Griesenauweg 26, A–6370,* ☎ *05356/3181,* FAX *05356/3181–70. 44 rooms. Restaurant, indoor and outdoor pools, sauna, beauty salon. AE, DC, MC, V. Closed Apr.–mid-May and mid-Oct.–mid-Dec.*

$$$ 🏨 **Schloss Lebenberg.** A onetime 16th-century castle on a hilltop outside town has been transformed into a wholly modern owner-managed family hotel. The bedrooms are contemporary in flavor. You can literally start skiing at the front door, and if the youngsters are too small to go along, there's a nursery. ✉ *Lebenbergstr. 17, A–6370,* ☎ *05356/4301–0,* FAX *05356/4405. 109 rooms. Restaurant, indoor pool, sauna, tennis court, exercise room, nursery. AE, DC, MC, V.*

$$$ 🏨 **Schloss Münichau.** Four kilometers (2½ miles) outside town, just beyond the romantic Schwarzsee on the road to Reith, you'll find this quaint 15th-century hunting lodge from which you can still go hunting and fishing. The rooms are individual, with much Tirolean woodcarving in evidence. ✉ *A–6370 Reith bei Kitzbühel,* ☎ *05356/2962,* FAX *05356/2332–50. 58 rooms. Restaurant, sauna. AE, DC, MC, V. Closed mid–late Apr.–May and Nov.*

$$ ★ 🏨 **Goldener Greif.** The original building dates from 1271; renovations in the 1950s gave the house a more contemporary but still traditional Tirolean charm, emphasized by the magnificent vaulted lobby with open fireplaces and antiques. The rooms, too, are charming, some with four-posters, and a few apartments have fireplaces. The hotel is the locale of the Kitzbühel casino. ✉ *Hinterstadt 24, A–6370,* ☎ *05356/4311,* FAX *05356/5001. 47 rooms. Restaurant, bar, sauna, casino. AE, DC, MC, V. Closed Apr.–mid-June, Oct., and Nov.*

$$ **Weisses Rössl.** This elegant but friendly hotel in the middle of town has open fireplaces ablaze in winter. The spacious rooms display much light pine and are particularly comfortable. ✉ *Bichlstr. 3–5, A–6370,* ☎ *05356/2541–0,* FAX *05356/3472. 38 rooms. Restaurant, 2 bars, tennis court, dance club. AE, DC, MC, V. Closed mid-Apr.–mid-May and mid-Oct.–early Dec.*

Nightlife and the Arts

Much activity centers on the **casino** in the Goldener Greif hotel, where you'll find baccarat, blackjack, roulette, and one-armed bandits galore. There's a restaurant and a bar. You'll need your passport to enter the casino. There is no set closing time. ☎ *05356/2300.* *Free.* *Dec. 25–Mar. and July–mid-Sept., daily 7 PM.*

The **Tenne** has for generations been *the* evening spot in Kitz. It's partly because of the friendly atmosphere, the capacity, and the music (live), but most of all it's because you can meet people here. There's food, but emphasis is on drink and dance. ✉ *Hotel zur Tenne, A–6370,* ☎ *05356/4444–0,* FAX *05356/4803–56. AE, DC, MC, V.* *Bar Dec. 25–mid-Mar. and Aug., daily 9 PM–3 AM.*

The disco crowd moves from place to place, but check out **Take Five,** the town's newest hot spot (✉ Hinterstadt 22, ☎ 05356/74131). Take Five's competition, which also attracts celebrities, is **T-5** disco (✉ Bichlstr. 8, ☎ 05356/3425). Current among "in" spots are the **Stamperl** bar (✉ Franz-Reisch-Str. 7, ☎ 05356/2555); **The Londoner** (✉ Franz-Reisch-Str. 4, ☎ 05356/71428); and the **Fünferl** bar in the **Kitzbüheler Hof** (✉ Franz-Reisch-Str. 1, ☎ 05356/71300).

Outdoor Activities and Sports

GOLF

Golfclub Kitzbühel has 9 holes, par 72. ☎ *05356/3007.* *Apr.–Oct.* **Golf-Club Kitzbühel-Schwarzsee** has 18 holes, par 72. ☎ *05356/71645.* *Apr.–Oct.* Golf privileges can be arranged between the Kitzbühel courses and the Bichlhof, Erika, Rasmushof, Reisch, and Tennerhof hotels.

West from Innsbruck to Imst and the Ötz Valley

The upper Inn Valley from Innsbruck to the Swiss border is beautiful countryside, particularly the narrow valleys that branch off to the south. Take Route 171 west from Innsbruck along the banks of the Inn, rather than the autobahn, which hugs the cliffs along the way. From Telfs you have a choice of taking the very scenic Route 189/E6 to Nassereith and down to Imst, or following the rail line along the river on Route 171. All three towns are attractive for their richly decorated 15th- and 16th-century buildings and churches.

Telfs

26 *32 km (20 mi) southeast of Reutte.*

Mythical masked figures invade the streets of Telfs every five years when the town hosts its traditional Carnival celebration of **Schleicherlaufen.** Just before Lent in the year 2000 the whole population will celebrate in a festive masked procession. Some of the grotesque masks can be seen in the local museum.

Dining and Lodging

$$$$ **Interalpen Tyrol.** This new resort, outside town at 3,900 feet up the slopes, is simply huge, from the lobby with its vast expanse of carpet to the modern rooms. But the lobby's crackling fire is welcoming, and you'll find this a far quieter, more relaxing spot than you might guess from its original impression. ✉ *A–6410,* ☎ *05262/606,* FAX *05262/606–190. 300 rooms. Restaurant, indoor pool, sauna, spa, tennis courts, exercise room. AE, DC, MC, V. Closed Apr.–early May and Nov.–mid-Dec.*

$ ✕🏨 **Tirolerhof.** You're within a couple of blocks of the center of town in this comfortable balconied family-run hotel, convenient also to the indoor and outdoor pools, and tennis and squash courts. The restaurant offers standard regional fare. ✉ *Bahnhofstr. 28, A–6410,* ☎ *052652/62237,* FAX *05262/62237–9. 37 rooms. Restaurant. AE, DC, MC, V. Closed 3 wks before Easter.*

Imst

27 *35 km (22 mi) west of Telfs.*

Imst, a popular summer resort, lying a kilometer or so back from the Inn River and the railway line, makes an excellent base from which to explore the Paznaun Valley and the upper Inn Valley, leading into Switzerland and Italy. Here the **Schemenlaufen,** a masked procession depicting the struggle between good and evil, takes place on Shrove Tuesday. Many of the magnificently carved masks worn by the mummers—especially those of the fearsome witches—are very old and works of art. The event is scheduled every four years, and will next occur in the year 2,000. The tradition is ancient, and as in Telfs, you can see some of the 100-year-old carved masks in the local museum (✉ Ballgasse 1); check with the tourist office for opening times. A great feature of these rustic carnivals is the ringing of cow bells of all shapes, sizes, and tones, and the resulting noise is quite deafening when the procession hits its stride. Don't overlook the 15th-century frescoed **parish church** in the upper part of Imst.

Dining and Lodging

$$ ★ ✕🏨 **Post.** A 15th-century former castle, complete with onion-dome towers and set in the center of town next to a large park, is the heart of this member of the RomantikHotel group. The friendly interior is furnished with antiques, and the modern bedrooms are cheerful. The restaurant is recommended, particularly for game. ✉ *E.-Wallnöfer-Pl. 3, A–6460,* ☎ *05412/2554,* FAX *05412/2519–55. 35 rooms. Restaurant, indoor pool. AE, DC, MC, V. Closed Nov.–Jan.*

$$ 🏨 **Linserhof.** This double-chalet hotel is outside town, set in a lush Alpine meadow at the base of a wooded hillside. The attractive rooms are in rustic Tirolean decor, with much natural wood; those on the south side with balconies are preferred. ✉ *A–6460 Imst/Teilwiesen,* ☎ *05412/2415,* FAX *05412/2415–133. 42 rooms, 20 apartments. Restaurant, bar, indoor pool, lake, sauna, tennis court, exercise room, bicycles. AE, DC, MC, V.*

$ 🏨 **Zum Hirschen.** This comfortable *Gasthof-Pension,* attractively renovated and close to the center of town, pays particular attention to families with children. ✉ *Th.-Walsch-Str. 3, A–6460,* ☎ *05412/2209,* FAX *05412/2209–7. 53 rooms. Restaurant, bar, sauna. AE, DC, MC, V. Closed early–mid-Dec.*

En Route The Ötz Valley climbs in a series of six great natural steps for nearly 42 kilometers (26 miles) from the Inn River to the glaciers around Obergurgl, at 6,200 feet above sea level. The entire distance offers stunning scenery, with the most dramatic part beginning around Sölden, where the final rise begins to the 8,100-foot pass over the Timmel Alps and across the Italian border into South Tirol. To reach the valley, turn south off Route 171 onto Route 186.

Ötz

28 *21 ki (12 mi) southeat of Imst, 23 km (14 mi) southwest of Telfs.*

Gothic houses with colorful fresco decorations grace this typically Tirolean mountain village. The parish church of **St. George and St. Nicholas,** its tower once a charnel house, sits on a rock promontory above the village. The small St. Michael's chapel also has a splendid altar dating to 1683.

Lodging

$ **Alpenhotel.** This solid house fits the center of town well; here you'll find traditional country warmth, friendliness, and comfortable rooms. Minimum half board is required in winter. ✉ *Bielefeldstr. 4, A–6433,* ☎ *05252/6232,* FAX *05252/6232–16. 45 rooms. Restaurant. No credit cards. Closed mid-Apr.–May and Oct.–mid-Dec.*

$ **Drei Mohren.** You can't miss the roof of this inn, with its wonderful collection of odd towers and onion domes. Fortunately, the interior is less exotic; the comfortable rooms are elegantly paneled, and most have balconies. The restaurant, offering standard local fare, is intended primarily for hotel guests, and is tastefully decorated with old etchings. ✉ *Hauptstr. 54, A–6433,* ☎ *05252/6301,* FAX *05252/2464. 22 rooms. Restaurant, tennis court. AE, DC, MC, V. Closed Nov.–mid-Dec.*

Sölden

29 *28 km (18 mi) south of Ötz.*

The highest cable car in Austria squires skiers swiftly from Sölden over the glaciers to a permanent-snow area at almost 9,910 feet on Gaislacher Kogel, where you can ski all year. Sölden is the most famous village in the Ötz Valley, earning an international reputation for its natural skiing conditions. The towering **Hochsölden** (6,800 feet) ensures excellent snow for the whole season.

Dining and Lodging

$$$$ ✕ **Central.** Huge arches and heavy wooden timbers accent the antique furniture and set the atmosphere in this massive riverside hotel where the prominent are said to gather. The bedrooms are spacious and luxuriously furnished. Half board is standard. The intimate Ötztaler Stube restaurant is the best in town; sample the fillet of venison, and don't overlook the excellent desserts. ✉ *Hochsölden Hof 418, A–6450,* ☎ *05254/2260–0,* FAX *05254/2260–511. 92 rooms. Restaurant, indoor pool, sauna. No credit cards. Closed June–mid-July.*

$$$–$$$$ **Liebe Sonne.** You'll be right next to the chairlift to Hochsölden if you stay in this sprawling complex, recently rebuilt to include a new array of amenities. Its atmosphere is rustic, and the paneled rooms are cozy. Half board is required. ✉ *Rainstadl 85, A–6450,* ☎ *05254/2203,* FAX *05254/2423. 59 rooms. Restaurant, bar, indoor pool, sauna, spa, exercise room. No credit cards. Closed May and June.*

Outdoor Activities and Sports

CLIMBING

The nearby Venteral Valley burrows still farther into the Ötztal Alps, ending in the tiny village of **Vent,** a popular resort center. In summer, the village is transformed into a base for serious mountain climbers, experienced in ice and rock climbing, who want to attempt the formidable **Wildspitze** (12,450 feet) or other even more difficult neighboring peaks. Hiring a professional local guide is strongly advised. To reach Vent from Sölden, turn off at the road marked to Heiligenkreutz.

Obergurgl

30 *11 km (7 mi) south of Sölden.*

Austria's highest village, tiny Obergurgl gained its reputation not only for superb winter sports but also as the place where the Swiss physicist Auguste Piccard landed his famous stratospheric balloon in the 1930s. In winter, a vast expanse of snow and ice shimmers all around you, and all year, the great peaks and glaciers of the Ötztal Alps appear deceptively close at hand. A high Alpine road takes you from Obergurgl to the hotel settlement at **Hochgurgl,** another excellent skiing spot, and farther up to the Timmelsjoch pass through magnificent mountain scenery. From Hochgurgl, a three-stage chairlift brings you into an area of year-round skiing. In summer, ask at the tourist office about river-rafting possibilities.

Lodging

$$–$$$$ ★ **Bellevue.** This friendly Alpine chalet lives up to its name in every respect: Is there another Bellevue among the probable millions in the world with a vista to equal the one here? You can ski right out the front door. Rooms are cozily comfortable, but you'll have to take half board. ✉ *A–6456,* ☎ *05256/228,* FAX *05256/413. 26 rooms. Restaurant, indoor pool, sauna, exercise room. No credit cards. Closed May, June, and Sept.–early Dec.*

$$–$$$$ ★ **Edelweiss und Gurgl.** Traditionally, this is *the* place to stay. Renovations have turned the massive house into an excellent family-run hotel with a comfortable, relaxed ambience. The cheery rooms have attractive natural-wood touches. Minimum half board is required. ✉ *A–6456,* ☎ *05256/223,* FAX *05256/449. 100 rooms. Restaurant, bar, indoor pool, sauna. AE, DC, MC, V. Closed May–mid-June, Oct., and Nov.*

Landeck, Upper Inn Valley, and St. Anton

Back on Route 171, heading westward, you'll come to Landeck, 24 kilometers (15 miles) from Imst, a popular place in summer and a good base from which to explore the Paznaun Valley and the upper Inn Valley, leading into Switzerland and Italy.

Landeck

31 *24 km (15 mi) southwest of Imst.*

Landeck is known for an ancient and awe-inspiring rite that takes place on **"Cheese Sunday,"** the first Sunday following Ash Wednesday. At dawn the young men set out to climb to the top of the great rocky crags that overshadow and hem in the old city on three sides. As dusk falls, they light huge bonfires that can be seen for miles around and then set fire to great disks of pinewood dipped in tar, which they roll ablaze down to the valley below. The sight of scores of these fiery wheels bounding down the steep slopes toward town is a fearsome spectacle worthy of Ezekiel.

The 13th-century **Burg Landeck castle** dominates from its position above the town. Climb up and catch the superb views from this vantage point. Also note the 16th-century winged altar in the 15th-century Gothic parish **church of the Assumption.** Downhill and, increasingly, cross-country skiing can be found in Landeck and throughout the Upper Inn Valley. Equipment is available for rent, though the selection and quality will vary from place to place.

Lodging

$ **Schrofenstein.** Directly in the middle of town, this older house still shows its original beamed ceilings and marble floors in the public areas. The rooms are comfortably modern, those overlooking the river preferred. ✉ *Malser Str. 31, A–6500,* ☎ *05442/62395,* FAX *05442/64954–55. 54 rooms. Restaurant. AE, DC, MC, V. Closed mid–late Apr. and Nov.–mid-Dec.*

$ **Schwarzer Adler.** Virtually in the shadow of the town castle, this traditional, family-run hotel offers solid comfort in typical Tirolean style, with red checks and light wood. ✉ *Malser Str. 8, A–6500,* ☎ *05442/62316,* FAX *05442/62316–50. 32 rooms. Restaurant. No credit cards. Closed Nov.–mid-Dec.*

Outdoor Activities and Sports

HIKING

Would-be climbers can take lessons by contacting Hugo Walter at the **Bergsteigerschule Piz Buin-Silvretta** (✉ A–6563 Galtür, ☎ 05443/260).

Ried

32 *19 km (12 mi) south of Landeck.*

At Landeck the Inn River turns southward along the edge of the Silvretta mountains. The valley, tucked between two dramatic ranges, climbs toward the Italian border. As you follow Route 315/S15 beside the river, you'll come across **Schloss Sigmundsried,** a small castle built by Duke Sigmund the Wealthy about 1470 around an earlier tower; the castle holds intriguing 16th-century coat-of-arm paintings. Today, you can canoe or raft the river along the edge of the Silvretta mountains.

Serfaus

33 *8 km (5 mi) southwest of Ried.*

At Ried, turn west off route 315 for the scenic but steep climb up to Serfaus. This old village, perched on a plateau above the valley, has taken on new class in recent years as an important winter-sports center. There are several ski lifts, and the Komperdell cable car takes you in summer, too, up to points from which you can either hike or just enjoy the views.

Dining and Lodging

$$$–$$$$ ✕ **Maximilian.** The transformation of a former Serfaus Gasthof into a modern hotel seems to have worked, successfully blending the old and the new, and the house is now a member of the Silence Hotel group. Rooms in the new section, some with open fireplaces, are more spacious, but all are comfortable. A separate, excellent restaurant in a cozy side room is open to the public in the evening, with two fixed menus available. ✉ *Herrenanger 4, A–6534,* ☎ *05476/6520,* FAX *05476/6520–52. 36 rooms. Restaurant, indoor pool, sauna, exercise room, children's programs. No credit cards. Closed May, June, and Oct.–mid-Dec.*

$$$–$$$$ **Cervosa.** This typical twin chalet is not only close to the center of town, it's the center of action in Serfaus. The family owners have preserved the hotel's informal ambience despite its rather elegant reconstruction. Rooms are welcoming and modern; there are apartments of various sizes as well. Half board is standard in winter. ✉ *Herrenanger 11, A–6534,* ☎ *05476/6211,* FAX *05476/6211–141. 70 rooms. Restaurant, indoor and outdoor pools, beauty salon, sauna, bowling, exercise room, squash. AE, DC, V. Closed mid-Apr.–mid-June and mid-Oct.–mid-Dec.*

St. Anton am Arlberg

34 *22 ki (15 mi) west of Landeck, 49 km (30 mi) northwest ofSerfaus.*

Tucked between the entrance to the Arlberg tunnel and the railway (if you're coming from Serfaus, backtrack to Landeck and take Route 316/S16 west toward Vorarlberg), St. Anton seethes with visitors at the height of the season. The wealthy, the prominent, and, occasionally, the royal appear regularly to see and be seen—some even to enjoy the winter sports. Their presence boosts prices into the very-expensive-to-outrageous category, but if you shop around, you can find accommodations outside the center of the action at a bearable price. St. Anton is a particularly lovely town in summer—which seems on the verge of becoming the more fashionable season.

Modern skiing techniques were created and nurtured in St. Anton. In 1921, Hannes Schneider (1890–1955), an unknown young ski instructor with innovative ideas, set up a ski school to teach his new technique, at the invitation of the just-founded Kandahar Ski Club. This "Arlberg School" method, developed by Schneider in the '20s and '30s, laid down the basic principles followed by all skiing courses the world over. St. Anton's remains one of the world's leading ski schools. Thanks to an amazing system of funicular trains, double chair lift, and interconnected T-bars, St. Anton can access skiers to the Arlberg's region's enormous 200-odd miles of marked runs. If you decide to take to the slopes, remember that skiing remains serious business in St. Anton: many slopes are so steep you'll be sharing them with mountain climbers!

Dining and Lodging

$$$$ ★ ✕🏨 **Brunnenhof.** Set in the intimate, homey atmosphere of an old farmhouse in nearby St. Jakob is one of the best restaurants in the area. From the excellent Tirolean and international menu you might choose a mushroom, garlic, or cheese soup and follow it with roast rack of lamb in an herb crust. The wine list is good. The 10-room hotel offers cozy comfort from December to April and from June to September at moderate prices. ✉ *St. Anton/St. Jakob,* ☎ *05446/2293,* FAX *05446/2293–5. No credit cards. Closed May, June, Oct., and Nov.*

$–$$$ ★ ✕🏨 **Schwarzer Adler.** The beautifully frescoed facade of this 420-year-old inn in the center of town creates the right setting for the open fireplaces, Tirolean antiques, and colorful Oriental carpets inside. Rooms are tastefully furnished in Alpine style and fully equipped. An annex across the street has somewhat less elegant (and cheaper) rooms. The lively Disco Klause is in the basement of the main house. ✉ *A–6580,* ☎ *05446/2244–0,* FAX *05446/2244–62. 63 rooms. Restaurant, café, sauna, exercise room, dance club, baby-sitting. AE, DC, MC, V. Closed mid-Apr.–May, Oct., and Nov.*

$–$$ ✕🏨 **Karl Schranz.** Your first impression of this new and spacious Alpine lodge is made by the lobby's welcoming fireplace—a showcase for trophies won by the champion skier and owner-manager, Karl Schranz, from 1957–1972. A shuttle bus takes guests to and from the center of town. The rooms are large and modern, with elegant wood paneling. The Jägerstube restaurant features Austrian and Tirolean fare. ✉ *A–6580,* ☎ *05446/2555–0,* FAX *05446/2555–5. 23 rooms. Restaurant, bar, sauna, exercise room, baby-sitting. No credit cards. Closed May, June, Oct., and Nov.*

Nightlife and the Arts

For some visitors to St. Anton, the show, not the snow, is the thing. Nobody complains about lack of action! Check out the popular après-ski **Drop In** (✉ Sporthotel St. Anton, ☎ 05446/3131), the **Underground Piano Bar** (☎ 05446/2000), the **Postkeller** cellar disco (✉

Hotel Neue Post, ☎ 05446/2213–274), the **terrace of the Hotel Alte Post** (☎ 05446/2553) in early springtime, and in St. Christoph, the **Siglu** at the Arlberghöhe (☎ 05446/2635–0). In Moos, Gunnar Munthe's **Krazy Kanguruh** bar with its cellar disco is a favorite gathering spot; it opens at 3:30 PM (☎ 05446/2633). Some of the best, original, local Alpine atmosphere for drinking and dining can be found at **Rodelalm** (☎ 0663/858855) and **Sennhütte** (☎ 05446/20048).

Outdoor Activities and Sports

SKIING

The *Skihaserl,* or ski bunny, as the beginner is called, usually joins a class on St. Anton's good "nursery" slopes, where he or she will have plenty of often very distinguished company. The school here is excellent and is considered by some to be the "Harvard" of ski schools. Once past the Skihaserl stage, skiers go higher in the Arlberg mountains to the superlative runs from the top of the Galzig and the 9,100-foot Valluga above it. Check with your hotel or at ski-lift ticket offices about an **Arlberg Skipass**, which is good on cable cars and lifts in St. Anton and St. Christoph on the Tirol side and on those in Zürs, Lech, Oberlech, and Stuben in Vorarlberg—77 in all.

St. Christoph

35 *2 km (1 mi) west of St. Anton am Arlberg.*

A hospice was founded, in what is now St. Christoph, as early as the 15th century to care for imperiled travelers stranded by the snows on the pass. Today, the snow is what attracts visitors to the area. Even the Austrian government has gotten in on the act, holding its exacting courses for aspiring ski instructors here.

While St. Christoph hasn't the same social cachet as St. Anton, the skiing facilities are precisely the same (and even closer at hand). If you take your skiing seriously and are willing to forgo the high life as too distracting or too expensive, you may find winter sports per se more fun at St. Christoph.

Dining and Lodging

$$–$$$$ ★ ✕🏨 **Arlberg Hospiz.** This huge pink building re-creates much of the legendary ancient hospice that stood here until a fire in the 1950s. Carved wood paneling and rich Oriental carpets abound. The rooms are luxurious in the extreme; service is attentive but not obtrusive. The associated Hospizalm restaurant has earned a reputation for creative cooking: You might be offered cream of lobster or oyster soup, veal or venison, or fish dishes. The wine list is outstanding. ✉ *A–6580 St. Anton/St. Christoph,* ☎ *05446/2611,* FAX *05446/3545. 102 rooms. Restaurant, bar, indoor pool, sauna, exercise room, baby-sitting, dance club. No credit cards. Closed May, Oct., and Nov.*

Ischgl

36 *67 km (42 mi) southeast of St. Christoph.*

Ischgl, the largest town in the Paznaun Valley, offers excellent skiing, particularly in the small Fimber Valley to the south, and in summer is a popular high-altitude health resort. You can get to the 7,500-foot Idalpe via the 4-kilometer-long Silvretta cable-car run.

The enchanting Paznaun Valley follows the course of the Trisanna river for over 40 kilometers (25 miles). The valley runs into the heart of the Blue Silvretta mountains, named for the shimmering ice-blue effect created by the great peaks and glaciers. They are dominated by the Fluchthorn (10,462 feet) at the head of the valley near Galtür.

Slightly higher up the valley is Galtür, the best-known resort in the Paznaun, equally popular for winter sports, as a summer resort, and as a base for mountain climbing. Although Galtür is a starting point for practiced mountaineers, many of the climbs up the Blue Silvretta are very easy and lead to the half-dozen mountain huts belonging to the Alpenverein. Galtür and the Silvretta region inspired Ernest Hemingway's novella *Alpine Idyll*; the author spent the winter of 1925 here, and the town still remembers him.

Dining and Lodging

$$–$$$$ ✕ **Madlein.** This modern chalet-style hotel not far from the center is the place to stay for sheer Alpine elegance and to see the town's action. The rooms are attractive, but you'll be tempted to spend your time in such places as the beamed Almbar with its large dance floor and friendly atmosphere. The main restaurant has a fine kitchen. ✉ *A–6561,* ☎ *05444/5266,* FAX *05444/5636. 65 rooms. 2 restaurants, bar, indoor pool, sauna, nightclub. No credit cards. Closed May, June, Oct., and Nov.*

TIROL AND INNSBRUCK A TO Z

Arriving and Departing

By Bus

Innsbruck is connected by bus to other parts of Tirol, and the terminal (✉ Südtiroler Platz, ☎ 0512/1717 or 0512/585155) is beside the main train station.

By Car

To get to Innsbruck, exit from the east–west autobahn (Route A12/E60), or from the Brenner autobahn (Route A13/E45) running south to Italy. Since the Old City is a pedestrian zone and much of the rest of the downtown area is paid parking only, you'll be best off leaving the car in a central garage, unless your hotel has parking.

By Plane

The airport, 3 kilometers (2 miles) west of the city, is served principally by **Austrian Airlines** and **Tyrolean.** Call for 0512/22220 for flight information. Buses (Line F) to the city center (Maria-Theresien-Strasse) take about 20 minutes. Get your ticket from the bus driver; it costs AS18. Taxis should take no more than 10 minutes into town, and the fare is about AS100–AS150. Transfer services operated by Four Seasons Travel (✉ Müllerstr. 14, ☎ 0512/584157, FAX 0512/585767) run from and to the "Zentralbereich" at Munich airport, departing Munich at 7, 9, 11 AM and 4 PM. Service from Innsbruck to Munich is on demand; make arrangments in advance, allowing 2½ hours for travel. One-way fare is AS420, round-trip AS720; reservations are recommended.

By Train

Direct trains serve Innsbruck from Munich, Vienna, Rome, and Zürich, and all arrive at the railroad station at Südtiroler Platz. Call 0512/1717 for information and reservations.

Getting Around

By Bus and Streetcar

In Innsbruck, most bus and streetcar routes begin or end at Maria-Theresien-Strasse, nearby Bozner Platz, or the main train station (Hauptbahnhof). You can get single tickets costing AS18 on the bus or streetcar. Multiple-ride tickets bought in advance at most tobacconists (*Tabak-Trafik*), the Verkehrsbetriebe office at Museumstr. 23, or the tourist office at Burggraben 3 are cheaper; a block of four tickets is AS44. A 24-hour ticket good for the city costs AS25; other 24-hour network tickets cover areas outside the immediate city. A weekly ticket costs AS105. For information, check with the tourist office. You can transfer to another line with the same ticket as long as you continue in more or less the same direction in a single journey. The bus is also the most convenient way to reach the six major ski areas outside the city. A Club Innsbruck pass (free from the tourist office or your hotel if you spend one night or more) gives you free transportation to the ski areas; many hotels provide shuttle service to the special ski bus stop. The public ski buses leave from the Landestheater on Rennweg, across from the Hofburg. Check with your hotel or the tourist offices for schedules.

In Tirol, as throughout Austria, where the train doesn't go, the post office or railroad bus does, and except in the most remote areas, buses are frequent enough so that you can get around. But bus travel requires time and planning. In summer, tour-bus operators run many sightseeing trips through Tirol that often include East and South Tirol. Check with your travel agent or the nearest tourist office.

By Car

Private cars are not allowed in Innsbruck's Old City, and parking anywhere near the center in Innsbruck requires vouchers, which you buy from tobacconists, the tourist office (✉ Burggraben 3), post offices, or blue coin-operated dispensers found around parking areas. Each half hour costs AS5. Maximum parking time is 1½ hours. Large blue *P* signs direct you to parking garages. The bus is about as convenient as a car for reaching the ski areas if you have to cope with chains and other complications of winter driving.

Driving is the best way to see the rest of Tirol, since it allows you to wander off the main routes at your pleasure or to stop and admire the view. Roads are good, but a detailed highway map is recommended. In winter, check with one of the automobile clubs for road information (☎ 0222/71199–7) before starting out. Watch your gas gauge, particularly on Sunday and holidays, when some stations may be closed.

The autobahns are fastest, but for scenery you'll be best off on the byways. One important exception is the 1¾-kilometer (1-mile) Europa Bridge on the Brenner autobahn running south into Italy, although if you follow the parallel route from Patsch to Pfons, you'll have the views without the traffic. Roads with particularly attractive scenery are marked on highway maps with a parallel green line.

By Horse-Drawn Carriage

Horse-drawn cabs, still a feature of Innsbruck life, can be hired at the stand in front of the Landestheater. Set the price before you head off; a half-hour ride will cost around AS320.

By Taxi

In Innsbruck, taxis are not much faster than walking, particularly along the one-way streets and in the Old City. Basic fare is AS52 for the first 1½ kilometers (1 mile). Call to order a radio cab (☎ 0512/5311, 0512/45500, or 0512/1718).

By Train

The railroad follows nearly all the main routes in Tirol, with highways and tracks sharing the same narrow valleys. Some of the most fascinating and memorable side trips can be made by rail: Two narrow-gauge lines steam out of Jenbach, for example, one up to the Achensee, the other down to Mayrhofen in the Zillertal. From Innsbruck, the narrow-gauge Stubaitalbahn runs south to Telfes and Fulpmes.

The main railway line of Tirol runs east–west, entering Tirol via the Griessen pass, then heading on to St. Johann and Kitzbühel before wandering over to Wörgl and onward to Jenbach, Hall in Tirol, and Innsbruck. From Innsbruck on, the line follows the Inn Valley to Landeck, then to St. Anton, where it plunges into an 11-kilometer (7-mile) tunnel under the Arlberg range, emerging at Langen in Vorarlberg. From Innsbruck, a line runs north into Germany to Garmish-Partenkirchen and onward back into Austria, to Ehrwald and Reutte in Tirol and beyond, into Germany again. A line from Innsbruck to the south goes over the dramatic Brenner pass (4,465 feet) into Italy.

Contacts and Resources

Car Rentals

Avis (✉ Tourist Center, Salurner Str. 15, ☎ 0512/571754, FAX 0512/577149). **Budget** (✉ Michael-Gaismayr Str. 7, ☎ 0512/588468, FAX 0512/584580). **Europcar** (✉ Salurner Str. 8, ☎ 0512/582060, FAX 0512/582060–9).

Emergencies

For emergency medical help, call 0512/144, or call the university clinic in Innsbruck (✉ Anichstr. 35, ☎ 0512/504–0). If you need a doctor during a weekend or holiday, check with your hotel or call the weekend hot line (☎ 0512/360006).

Exchange

In addition to banks (open weekdays 7:45–12:30 and 2:15–4) and the American Express office (✉ Brixnerstr. 3, ☎ 0512/5829–91), you can change money at any post office and at Innsbruck's main train station (the office is open daily 7:30–12:30, 12:45–6, and 6:30–8:15) and city tourist information office (☞ *below*). But compare rates; you'll probably do best at a post office or bank. Cash machines in Innsbruck can be found at Hofgasse 2 and Herzog-Friedrich-Strasse 7.

Guided Tours

In Innsbruck, bus tours with English-speaking guides cover the city highlights (two hours), leaving daily at noon, year-round, from the hotel information office at the Südtiroler Platz station. In summer, additional buses are scheduled at 10 AM and 2 PM; and a shorter, hour-long tour leaves the Volkskunstmuseum Monday–Saturday at 10:15, noon, 2, and 3:15. Guided 1½-hour walking tours on Saturday and Sunday highlight historic personalities and some offbeat features associated with the city. Your hotel or one of the tourist offices will have tickets and details, or phone 0512/273700.

Late-Night Pharmacies

Several pharmacies stay open late in Innsbruck on a rotational basis. The newspaper will give their names, addresses, and phone numbers. Ask your hotel for help. Otherwise, try phoning the university clinic (☎ 0512/504–0).

Lodging

If you arrive in Innsbruck without a hotel room, check with the *Zimmernachweis* next to the railroad station (✉ Südtiroler Pl., ☎ 0512/583766–0). The office is open summer, daily 8 AM–10 PM. and winter, daily 9–9. The same organization also has offices on the incoming west autobahn (☎ 0512/573543), the east autobahn (☎ 0512/346474), the Kranebitter Allee (north) autobahn exit (☎ 0512/284991), and the Brenner (south) autobahn (☎ 0512/577933). Call for information on youth hostels (☎ 0512/346179 or 0512/346180). The booklet "Children's Hotels" (in English, available from the Tirolean tourist office) lists Tirolean hotels that cater particularly to families with children.

Travel Agencies

American Express. ✉ *Brixner Str. 3,* ☎ *0512/582491–0,* FAX *0512/573385.* ⏲ *Weekdays 9–5:30, Sat. 9–noon.*

Visitor Information

Most small-town tourist offices have no specific street address and are accommodated in the village hall. Address letters to Tourist Information and include the postal code of the town. Innsbruck's main tourist office (✉ Burggraben 3, ☎ 0512/5356, FAX 0512/5356–43) is open daily 8 AM–7 PM. The main office for Tirol is also in **Innsbruck** (Wilhelm-Greil-Str. 17, ☎ 0512/5320–170, FAX 0512/5320–174) and is open weekdays 8:30–6, Saturday 9–noon.

The following are the regional Fremdenverkehrsamt (tourist offices) of Tirol.

Achenkirch (✉ A–6215, ☎ 05246/6270, FAX 05246/6780). **Brixlegg** (✉ Marktstr. 6b, A–6230, ☎ 05337/62581, FAX 05337/63882). **Gerlos** (✉ A–6281, ☎ 05284/5244–0, FAX 05284/5244–24). **Imst** (✉ Johannespl. 4, A–6460, ☎ 05412/2419, FAX 05412/4783). **Ischgl** (✉ A–6561, ☎ 05444/5266–0, FAX 05444/5636). **Jenbach** (✉ Achenseestr. 37, A–6200, ☎ 05244/3901, FAX 05244/3552). **Kitzbühel** (✉ Hinterstadt 18, A–6370, ☎ 05356/2272, FAX 05356/2307). **Kufstein** (✉ Münchner Str. 2, A–6330, ☎ 05372/62207, FAX 05372/61455). **Landeck** (✉ Malserstr. 10, A–6500, ☎ 05442/62344, FAX 05442/67830). **Mayrhofen** (✉ Dursterstr. 225, A–6290, ☎ 05285/2305, FAX 05285/4116–33 or 05285/2305–33). **Obergurgl/Hochgurgl** (✉ A–6456, ☎ 05256/258 or 05256/353, FAX 05256/353–77). **Rattenberg** (✉ Klostergasse 94, A–6240, ☎ 05337/63321, FAX 05337/65130 or 05337/65417). **St. Anton am Arlberg** (✉ A–6580, ☎ 05446/2269–0, FAX 05446/2532). **St. Johann in Tirol** (✉ Poststr. 2, A–6380, ☎ 05352/2218, FAX 05352/5200). **Schwaz** (✉ Franz-Josef-Str. 26, A–6130, ☎ 05242/63240–0, FAX 05242/65630). **Serfaus** (✉ Unteres Dorf 13, A–6534, ☎ 05476/6239–0, FAX 05476/6813 or 05476/6239–77). **Sölden/Hochsölden** (✉ Rettenbach 288, A–6450, ☎ 05254/2212–0, FAX 05254/3131). **Tux/Lanersbach/Hintertux** (✉ A–6293 Lanersbach, ☎ 05287/606, FAX 05287/624). **Zell am Ziller** (✉ Dorfpl. 3a, A–6280, ☎ 05282/2281, FAX 05282/2281–80).

11 Vorarlberg

"What God has put asunder by a mountain, let no man join by a tunnel"—so said the Vorarlbergers of old. Once the Arlberg Tunnel linked Austria's westernmost province to the rest of the country, the secret was out. Vorarlberg—nicknamed the Ländle, *the "Little Province"—was really Austria's Switzerland: cheaper in some ways, perhaps less efficient in others. The world at large discovered skiing slopes that rival those of Austria's neutral neighbor, gorgeous Lake Constance, and the lush forests of the Bregenzerwald. In the winter, a winter* wunderland *is the main lure—especially at Lech, now more in fashion than ever since Princess Diana vacationed there.*

By George W. Hamilton

Updated by Angela Walker

THEY SAY YOU CAN LEARN ALL ABOUT AUSTRIA just by going to the Vorarlberg. Like studying the ocean in a drop of water, this postage stamp–sized province seems to be Austria in miniature—it features a sampling of the best of everything the country has to offer. Music devotees descend every summer on Hohenems for its elegant Schubertiade—held in a regal Renaissance castle—and on Bregenz for its famed lakeside music festival. Nature lovers head to the Bregenzerwald—a wide area of hunter-green forests, charming valleys, and lush meadows dotted with thick clusters of red, white, and yellow Alpine flowers—a region that remains decidedly private, unostentatiously beautiful. Literature buffs arrive to see the sun set in the village of Schruns, where Hemingway spent several winters writing *The Sun Also Rises*. And merrymakers like to throng Lech and Zürs, two top ski resorts where the perfumes of hot chocolate and Pfefferminz Tee always seem to mingle with Joy and Shalimar.

Tiny Vorarlberg covers an area of less than 1,000 square miles, and is the smallest (with the exception of Vienna) of Austria's federal states. As its name implies, the state lies "before the Arlberg," that massive range of Alps, the watershed of Europe, mecca of winter sports, and forms the western tip of Austria. Until the tunnel was cut through, the Arlberg was passable only in summer; in winter, Vorarlberg was effectively cut off from the rest of the country. And while Austrians from the east may go skiing or take vacations in neighboring Tirol, and although they may be well traveled, many never make it to Vorarlberg in the course of their lives. The Viennese semi-affectionately refer to Vorarlberg as the *Ländle,* meaning "the little province."

Nowhere in Austria will you find such determined adherence to old customs as in the villages and towns of the Vorarlberg. You'll see folk costumes on people on the street, not in museums, and your chances are good of running into a local celebration at any time of year. The province has much in common with neighboring Switzerland. Not only are the dialects similar, but the landscape flows across the border with continuity. Both peoples descended from the same ancient Germanic tribes that flourished in the 3rd century BC. Both have the same characteristics of thrift, hard work, and a deep-rooted instinct for democracy and independence. In fact, after the collapse of the Habsburg monarchy following World War I, Vorarlberg came very close to becoming a part of Switzerland. In 1919, 80% of the populace voted in favor of negotiating with the Swiss to join the confederation, but the St. Germain peace conference put an end to such ideas, and Vorarlberg remained Austrian.

Travelers approaching from the Western Alps take the tunnel under the Arlberg mountain range into Vorarlberg. Today, most visitors begin in Bregenz, the capital and usually end up in Lech, more than ever in fashion as a ski resort since Princess Diana and her two children visited.

Pleasures and Pastimes

Dining

Vorarlberg's cuisine is lighter than in neighboring Tirol and the rest of Austria. Fresh ingredients from the region's farms, lakes, and forests are the norm with an emphasis on dairy products from the cows that graze the mountains and meadows of the region. Be sure to try a slab of *Schweizer* cheese from one of the huge rounds produced at local farms. Cheese is also added to soups and noodle dishes and fried in fritters. Fresh river trout is caught in the waters of Lake Constance and in the surrounding lakes and streams. You'll see fish fried, broiled, and steamed on restaurant menus throughout Vorarlberg.

In small towns throughout the region, restaurants are often the dining rooms of country inns. The bill will include service and taxes, but it is customary to leave a small additional tip, rounded to the nearest 10 schillings.

CATEGORY	COST*
$$$$	over AS500
$$$	AS300–AS500
$$	AS150–AS300
$	under AS150

**for a typical three-course meal with a glass of house wine, service, and tax, but excluding additional tip*

Lodging

Vorarlberg has loads of accommodation options from sharing the chores at a local farmhouse to converted castle hotels to ski chalets perched on the slopes of the Western Alps. In ski resorts in Vorarlberg, hotel rates in season are often well above the range of our chart. At most of those hotels, the price includes a mandatory two meals a day, and often no credit cards are accepted. The tourist offices can usually help lead you to more moderate lodgings in private houses. In summer you can often find bargain rates at 50% of the winter tariff. In some towns, such as Bregenz, summer is the high season and may put the establishment into the next-higher price category.

CATEGORY	LECH/ZÜRS*	OTHER TOWNS*
$$$$	over AS2,200	over AS1,200
$$$	AS1,500–AS2,200	AS900–AS1,200
$$	AS900–AS1,500	AS600–AS900
$	under AS900	under AS600

**per person per night for a standard double room in high season, including breakfast (in resorts, including one additional meal in winter), service charge of 10%, and tax*

Skiing

One of the main attractions of a stay in Vorarlberg is the world-class skiing available in Austria's Western Alps. Afterall, modern ski techniques were developed in Vorarlberg by local Hannes Schneider. From intimate rustic resorts to the glamour of Lech and Zürs, the province has slopes to suit all tastes and levels, and fewer crowds than in the rest of the country.

The Sound—and Sights—of Music

Festival fever seizes the Vorarlberg every summer and summons the faithful to some of the finest concerts in Austria. Grand opera is offered lakeside at the **Bregenzer Festspiele** (Bregenz Summer Music Festival) while elegant recitals of the **Schubertiade** take place in the gilded ballrooms of Hohenems's palatial castle of Marcus Sitticus as well as in the auditoriums of the neighboring town of Feldkirch. The Bregenz festival is famed for its floating stage—in truth, a group of man-made islands mounted on pilings; now, when raindrops fall, there is a new indoor theater to accommodate the festivities. In Feldkirch and Hohenems—a spot some historians believe inspired the *Nibelungenlied*—Schubert *Lieder*-lovers come to hear fine musicians pay their homage to the great Biedermeier-era composer during a 10-day period in late June.

Exploring Vorarlberg

This chapter divides Vorarlberg into three sections. Our first exploring tour takes you through Bregenz, the region's historic capital. Then, we head out to the glorious countryside, taking in the legendary Bregenzerwald to Bludenz, following the Inn Valley to Feldkirch, and heading north again to Bregenz. Here, you can relax in a true backwoods atmosphere, while enjoying the beautiful, if somewhat hair-raising country roads as you pass through mountain hamlets, some with Au—sit on a pincushion and you will be pronouncing this name correctly—in their name, all with an Old World charm of their own, and few discovered by the guidebooks. The last excursion takes in the Arlberg ski resorts.

Great Itineraries

Numbers in the text correspond to numbers in the margin and on the Vorarlberg map.

IF YOU HAVE 2 DAYS

If you only have a weekend to visit Vorarlberg, head to the capital of **Bregenz** ① on the banks of the Bondsee (Lake Constance). Spend a day wandering around the lakeshore and the lovely, romantic remains of the once fortified medieval town. The next day take a boat ride into neighboring Switzerland or Germany. Around the lake are extensive hiking and biking trails for those who'd rather see the sites on their own steam.

IF YOU HAVE 5 DAYS

Visit the resorts in the Arlberg and the Montafon Valley, which have attracted such notaries as Ernest Hemingway and Britain's Princess Diana. Start off your trip in **Schruns** ⑫, visiting Hemingway's haunts. Now, you're ready for the Arlberg resorts. On your second day, head up north for **Stuben** ⑬, the hometown of skiing pioneer Hannes Schneider, moving on for your next overnight in **Zürs** ⑭. After a little hobnobbing with film stars and royalty, spend your final two overnights in Vorarlberg's most famous ski resort, **Lech** ⑮.

IF YOU HAVE 7 DAYS

If you have more time in Vorarlberg, begin by exploring the natural marvels of the **Bregenzerwald** and the history-rich sights of **Bregenz** ①. After two overnights in Bregenz, you can venture off the beaten track on your third day by stopping for discount shopping in Egg on your way to the picturesque town of **Schwarzenberg** ②. Then head to **Bezau** ③ to savor the beauty of the surrounding forests and mountains with a hike into the hills on your fourth day. That afternoon, visit breathtaking **Damüls** ④, where flowers blanket the hillsides during the summer and great skiing welcomes visitors in winter. Head for **Bludenz** ⑤ to explore one of the five magical valleys surrounding the town. The fifth day, follow the Inn valley to the medieval town of **Feldkirch** ⑦, and spend two days meandering through the narrow, winding streets admiring the burgher homes and castle from an earlier age when lords and ladies peopled the province. Make a stop in **Hohenems** ⑧ on your last day for a visit to the local Jewish Museum and **Dornbirn** ⑨, famous for its textiles, on your way back to the capital.

When to Tour Vorarlberg

Vorarlberg has something to offer visitors during every season. If you're in the province during warm weather, make sure to stop in Bregenz when the city comes to life with the Bregenzer Festspiele (Bregenz Summer Music Festival). Boat excursions to Switzerland and Germany are also a must. History buffs will enjoy the sights in Bregenz,

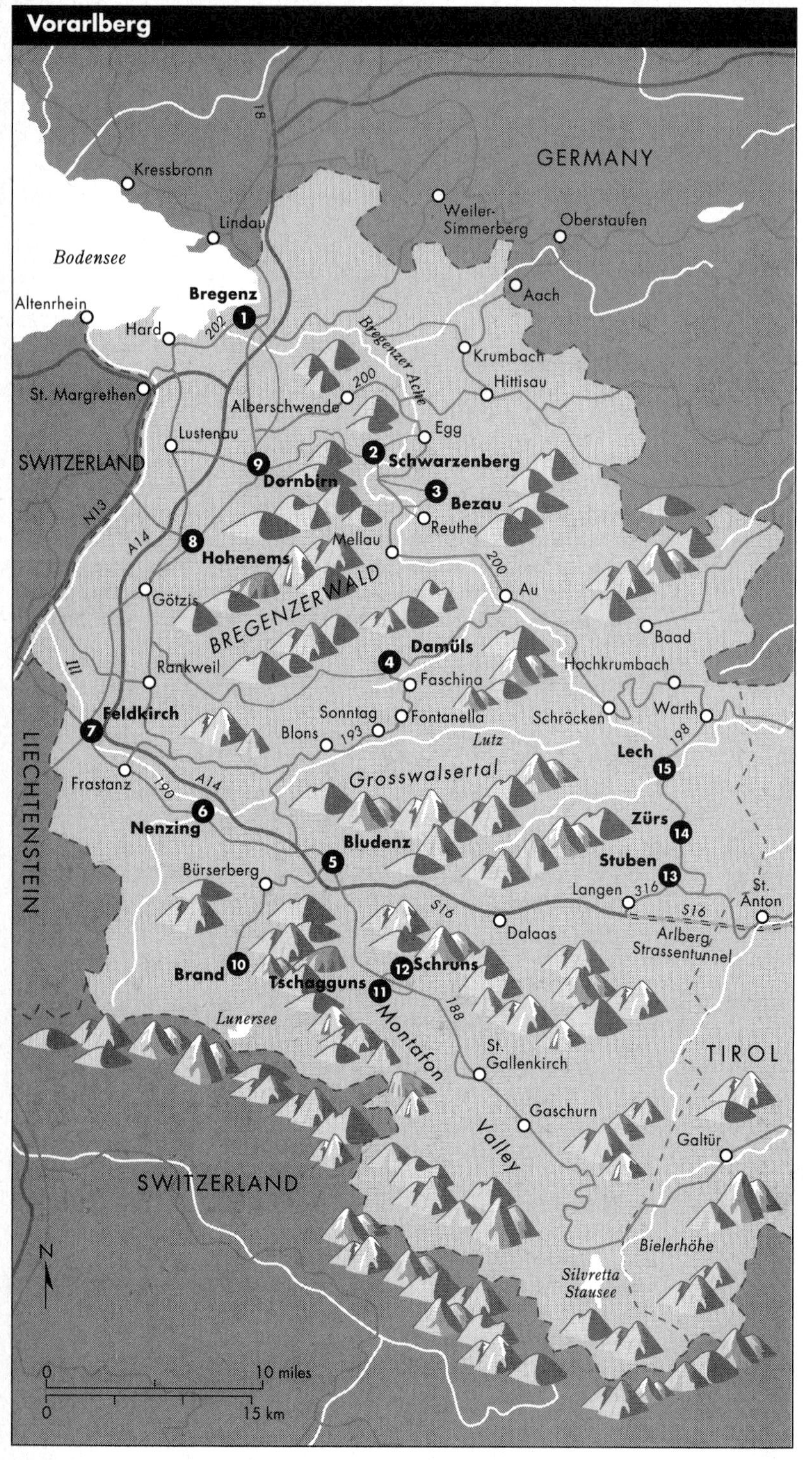
Vorarlberg
GERMANY
Kressbronn
Lindau
Weiler-Simmerberg
Oberstaufen
Bodensee
Bregenz
Altenrhein
Hard
Aach
Bregenzer Ache
Krumbach
Hittisau
St. Margrethen
Alberschwende
Egg
Lustenau
SWITZERLAND
Schwarzenberg
Dornbirn
Bezau
Reuthe
Mellau
Hohenems
BREGENZERWALD
Au
Götzis
Baad
Damüls
Hochkrumbach
Rankweil
Faschina
Feldkirch
Sonntag
Fontanella
Schröcken
Warth
Blons
Lutz
Lech
LIECHTENSTEIN
Frastanz
Grosswalsertal
Nenzing
Zürs
Bludenz
Stuben
Bürserberg
Langen
St. Anton
Dalaas
Arlberg Strassentunnel
Brand
Schruns
Tschagguns
Lunersee
Montafon Valley
St. Gallenkirch
TIROL
Gaschurn
Galtür
SWITZERLAND
Bielerhöhe
Silvretta Stausee
N
0
10 miles
0
15 km

Bludenz and especially Feldkirch. And sports enthusiasts will love the wealth of hiking, biking, sailing and fishing that is available around the region. Of course, if you travel to Vorarlberg during the winter months, then fasten on your bindings and head to the slopes.

BREGENZ

On the Shores of Lake Constance

❶ *150 ki (90 mi) west of Innsbruck, 660 km (409 mi) west of Vienna, 120 km (75 mi) east of Zurich, 193 km (120 mi) southwest of Munich.*

Part-medieval time machine, part-Coney Island, Bregenz is where Vorarlbergers come to make merry. Along the lakeside **Strand- und Friebad,** cabanas and candy floss lure starched collars to let loose, while nearby, the world-famous floating stage is the site for magnificent performances of Wagner and Strauss under the stars. Bregenz is also the capital of Vorarlberg and has been seat of the provincial government since 1819. The face of the town has changed dramatically in recent years, owing to much building in the lower or "new" section of the city. The rail yards were relocated outside town, and the main highway and railroad were put into tunnels, thereby allowing the development of acres of lakeside land as a recreation area and connecting the town to the waterfront. Bregenz is pleasant at any time of year, but the best time ★ to visit is during the **Bregenzer Festspiele** (Bregenz Summer Music Festival; ☞ Nightlife and the Arts, *below*). Acclaimed artists from around the world perform operas, operettas and musical comedies on the festival's floating stage, part of the Festspiel-und Kongresshaus (Festival Hall and Congress Center) complex. In front of the stage, the orchestra pit is built on a jetty, while the landlubberly audience of 6,000 is safely accommodated on the thirty-tier amphitheater, built on dry land—a unique and memorable setting you are sure to enjoy. Reserve your tickets in advance as performances sell out early.

The lake itself is a prime attraction with boat trips available to nearby Switzerland and Germany. Don't forget to bring along your passport. The Bodensee White Fleet ferries offer several trip options. You can travel to the "flower isle" of Manau or make a crossing to Konstanz, Germany, with stops at Linau, Friedrichshaften, and Meersburg. The longest round-trip excursion is the Drei-Länder Rundfahrt, which includes stops in Germany and Switzerland. ✉ *Ticket office, Seestr. 4,* ☎ *05574/42868.* ⏲ *Manau May, Tues., Thurs., Fri., and Sun. at 11; Konstanz trip June–mid-Aug., 5 trips daily; Drei-Länder July–Sept., daily at 2:30.*

Most of the important sights of Bregenz can be seen in the course of a walk of about two hours. The town's neo-classical main **Post Office** (✉ 5 Seestr.) was built in 1893 by Viennese architect Friedrich Setz. Because of the marshy conditions of the land, the post office is built on wood pilings to prevent it from sinking. Behind the post office, the **Nepomuk-Kapelle** (✉ Kaspar Moosbrugger Pl.) was built in 1757 to serve the city's fishermen and sailors. Today, the town's Hungarian community celebrates mass here. To the right of the Nepomukkapelle along Kornmarktstrasse is the **Gasthof Kornmesser,** built in 1720 and a gorgeous example of a Baroque town house. Just after the alley simply marked "Theater" along Kornmarktstrasse you'll reach the **Theater am Kornmarkt,** originally constructed in 1838 as a grain storehouse when Bregenz was still an important commercial port; in 1954, the granary was converted into a 700-seat theater. Next door to the Theater am Kornmarkt is the **Landesmuseum** (Provincial Museum), where relics from Brigantium, the Roman administrative city that once stood where Bregenz is today, are housed. Gothic and Romanesque ecclesiastical works are also on display in this turn-of-the-century building. ✉ *Kornmarktpl. 1,* ☎ *05574/46050.* 🎫 *AS20.* ⏲ *Sept.–June, Tues.–Sun. 9–noon and 2–5; July and Aug., daily 9–noon and 2–5.*

Originally used as a grain warehouse when it was built in 1685, the **Rathaus,** on the Rathausgasse, was turned over to the city in 1720. The ornate facade and tower were only added to the city hall in 1898. Next door to the Rathaus is the **Seekapelle** (Lake Chapel) topped with an onion dome. The chapel was put up over the graves of a defeated band of Swiss, who in 1408 attempted to incorporate Bregenz into Switzerland.

NEED A BREAK? Behind the Seekapelle is the traditional **Gösser Braugaststätte** (✉ Anton-Schneider-Gasse 1). This might be just the moment for a cool beer, a cup of coffee, or the daily vegetarian special.

Take the pedestrian subway, surface in Maurachgasse, take a left on Belrupstrasse, and you'll find the **Pfänderbahn** cable car which takes you up to the 3,460-foot peak overlooking the city. You can see four countries—and almost 240 Alpine peaks—from here, and the restaurant is open from June to mid-September. Children will enjoy a 30-minute circular hike to a small outdoor zoo, with deer, Alpine goats, mouflon, and wild boar. Admission is free. An added attraction is the **Adlerwarte,** where eagles and other birds of prey demonstrate their prowess in free flight. ☎ *05574/42160.* 🎫 *Round-trip AS110.* ⏲ *Dec.–Mar., daily 9–6; Apr.–Nov. 15., daily 9–7; service on hr and ½ hr. Closed last 2 wks of Nov. Adlerwarte,* ☎ *0663/053040.* 🎫 *AS40.* ⏲ *Flight exhibition May–Sept., daily at 11 and 2:30.*

On Belruptstrasse, the **Sacred Heart Church** was built in 1908 in brick Gothic style. The stained-glass windows by Martin Hausle are especially notable. Walking up Maurachgasse, you'll reach the **Stadtsteig** (stone gate) guarding the entrance to the old city, which bears the emblem of a Celtic-Roman equine goddess (the original is now housed in the Landesmuseum; ☞ *above*). Inside the gate are the coats of arms of the dukes of Bregenz and of the dukes of Montfort, the latter crest now the Vorarlberg provincial emblem. On Martinsplatz, explore the the interior of the tiny chapel called **Martinskirche** next to the Stadtsteig for its fine fourteenth-century frescoes. Next door to the Martinskirche, the **Martinsturm** (✉ Martinsg. 3B) boasts the largest onion dome in central Europe. The tower (1599–1602) has become a symbol of Bregenz and was the first Baroque construction on Lake Constance. The remains of the ancient **city wall** are to the right of the tower on Graf Wilhelm Strasse. The coats of arms of several noble Bregenz families still remain on the house next to the wall's remains. On Graf Wilhelm Strasse is the brightly shuttered **Altes Rathaus** (Old City Hall). The ornate half-timber construction was completed in 1622. At the head of Eponastrasse stands the former **Gesellenspital** (Journeymen's Hospital); remnants of a fresco still visible on its wall depict St. Christopher, St. Peter, and a kneeling abbot. Close by the Journeymen's Hospital is the **Ehreguta Inn** (✉ Eponastr. 4), named for the legendary woman who saved Bregenz during the Appenzell War. Every Ash Wednesday, the **Montfortbrunnen fountain** on Ehreguta Square is the scene of a ritual washing of wallets and change purses, when the carnival jesters clean out their empty pockets and spin tales about the events of the previous year. The fountain honors the minnesinger Hugo von Montfort, who was born in the city in 1357. The small parallel streets running uphill from the square where the fountain is located roughly outline the boundaries of the town in the Middle Ages. The **parish church of St. Gallus,** on Schlossbergstrasse, combines Romanesque, Gothic and Rococo elements. Empress Maria Theresia donated the money for the high-altarpiece. You'll notice the monarch's features on one of the shepardesses depicted there. The **Meissnerstiege** (Meissner steps) that lead from the old town down to the church are named after a local poet. The **Kunstlerhaus Thürn und Taxis** at No. 8 Belruptstrasse was owned by the regal Thürn und Taxis family until 1915. The building, erected in 1848, now contains a modern gallery. The **Thürn-und Taxispark** contains rare trees and plants from around the world.

Children and parents alike will enjoy a ride on the ***Hohentwiel,*** a restored old-time paddle-wheel lake steamship that cruises Lake Constance out of Hard, 8 kilometers (5 miles) southwest of Bregenz. Sailings are scheduled irregularly; call for information (☎ 05574/42467–80).

Dining and Lodging

$$ ✕ **Ilge-Weinstube.** This cozy, intimate *Keller* is old Bregenz at its best. Rustic decor in the basement of a 300-year-old house close to the oldest section of town draws the youngish "in" crowd. The atmosphere alone makes the Ilge-Weinstube worth a visit. ✉ *Maurachstr. 6,* ☎ *05574/43609. MC, V. Closed Mon., and 2 wks during Oct. or Nov.*

$$ ✕ **Maurachbund.** The elegant furnishings and soft lighting make dining at this restaurant an enjoyable, intimate experience. A glassed-in porch enables diners to "eat out" no matter what it's like outside. The menu features a wide variety of fish to choose from as well as traditional Austrian dishes. ✉ *Maurachgasse 11,* ☎ *05574/44020. MC, V.*

$$ ✕ **Wirtshaus am See.** This pyramid-shaped restaurant is right on the banks of Lake Constance, next to the floating stage used for the Bregenz Festival. The menu has the usual Austrian favorites from schnitzel to zweibelbraten. The main attraction here is the spectacular lake view. You can watch the world go by from the restaurant's extensive outdoor terrace. ✉ *Seeanlagen,* ☎ *05574/42210,* FAX *05574/42210–4. No credit cards.*

$ ★ ✕ **Goldener Hirschen.** Allegedly the oldest tavern in Bregenz and close to the oldest part of town, this restaurant offers traditional fare and drink in a lively atmosphere. Try any of the roast meats. ✉ *Kirchstr. 8,* ☎ *05574/42815. No credit cards. Closed Tues. and Sept.*

$$$$ ★ ✕ **Deuring-Schlössle.** The Huber family offers accommodations in this more than 400-year-old castle set in a park. Rooms are luxuriously furnished in rather formal antiques, which fit perfectly with the inlaid floors and the plaster ceiling ornamentation. The family also has established an exceptional restaurant—one of the very best in Austria. The period furniture contributes to the atmosphere and complements the cuisine. Everything is absolutely fresh, and the cuisine is imaginative; Austrian standards (like the freshwater fish soup) become outstanding. The wine list includes an international selection. ✉ *Ehre-Guta-Pl. 4, A–6900,* ☎ *05574/47800,* FAX *05574/47800–80. Restaurant. AE, DC, MC, V. Closed Mon.*

$$$ ★ ✕ **Kaiser Hotel.** The Kaiser Hotel has recently changed hands and has been extensively refurbished. The hotel successfully combines antiques with funky, modern decor. Guests will feel pampered in rooms complete with whirlpool, VCRs, and compact disc players. The hotel's Restaurant Heitinger specializes in dishes from Austria's southern neighbor, Italy. Two cafés on site serve lighter fare and drinks. ✉ *Kaiserstr. 2, A–6900,* ☎ *05574/52980,* FAX *05574/52982. 8 rooms. Restaurant, 2 cafés. AE, DC, MC, V.*

$$–$$$ **Mercure.** Adjacent to the festival hall and housing the casino, this is a good choice if you're in Bregenz mainly for the music or the money. The house is typical of the chain: functionally modern, all rooms with balconies. Rooms looking out over the lake are best. ✉ *Pl. der Wiener Symphoniker, A–6900,* ☎ *05574/46100–0,* FAX *05574/47412. 94 rooms. 2 restaurants, bar, parking. AE, DC, MC, V.*

$–$$ **Weisses Kreuz.** This traditional, family-run, turn-of-the-century house has been renovated with care and charm and is now a Best Western hotel. The location on the edge of the pedestrian zone is central, and the staff is particularly friendly. The rooms are comfortable and modern; those overlooking the private park out back are quieter. ✉ *Römerstr. 5, A–6900,* ☎ *05574/4988–0,* FAX *05574/4988–67. 44 rooms. Restaurant, bar, parking. AE, DC, MC, V. Closed Dec. 25–mid-Jan.*

Nightlife and the Arts

The cultural year starts with the **Bregenzer Frühling,** the spring music and dance festival that runs from mid-April to mid-May. Information and tickets are available through the tourist office (✉ Anton-Schneider-Str. 4a, A–6900, ☎ 05574/43391–0, FAX 05574/43391–10). The big cultural event in Bregenz is the **Bregenzer Festspiele** (Bregenz Summer Music Festival) held mid-July to mid-August (☞ *above*). For information and tickets, contact the festival office (✉ Box 311, A–6901, ☎ 05574/4920–223, FAX 05574/4920–228). Tickets are also available at the Bregenz tourist office. In case of rain, the massive **Festival Hall and Congress Center** next door to the floating stage can accommodate at least half of the 4,200 seats for performances on the floating lake stage.

The **casino** is the site of much activity (✉ Pl. der Wiener Symphoniker, A–6900, ☎ 05574/45127). The house opens at 3 PM. Bring your passport. Outdoor concerts are held during the summer months in the horseshoe-shaped **Music Pavilion** at the end of the promenade on the lake.

Outdoor Activities and Sports

Bicycling

The area around the lake offers superb cycling, and trails have been laid out to offer varying distances and degrees of difficulty. Maps and rental bikes are available; ask the tourist office for details.

Skiing

Skiers head for **Pfänder** mountain, literally in the backyard of Bregenz, which has a cable tramway and two drag lifts. The views are stunning from atop the peak, stretching as far as the Black Forest and the Swiss Alps.

Water Sports

With the vast lake at its doorstep, Bregenz offers a variety of water sports. You can even learn to sail, although a minimum of two weeks is required for a full course at **Segelschule Lochau.** ✉ *Box 7, Alte Fähre,* ☎ *05574/252793.*

THROUGH THE BREGENZERWALD TO BLUDENZ AND FELDKIRCH

Directly behind Bregenz lies the **Bregenzerwald** (Bregenz forest), a beautiful area studded with densely wooded highlands, sweeping valleys and lush meadows radiant in summer with wildflowers, all set against a fabulous backdrop of majestic, towering Alps. As you go along, you come across one town after another with *au*—meaning meadow—in its name: As the area developed, names were given to the meadows in which settlements were established. Here you will see the Vorarlbergers as they really are. In the little villages, you can spot women still wearing the handsome, stiffly starched folk dress of their ancestors. On festive occasions the girls wear a golden headdress shaped like a small crown, and the married women a black or white pointed cap. Men's costume is worn by musicians in the local bands (which seems to include nearly everyone), with the shape of the cap and the color of various parts of the clothing differing from town to town. Secure in their mountains, and, until quite recently, feeling no call to mix with the outside world, Vorarlbergers have remained true to the traits of their forebears.

To reach the Bregenzerwald, travelers can take one of the daily bus services which leave Bregenz or Dornbirn, on the main line from Feldkirch to Lindau in Germany—there are few train routes servicing the area. By car, leave Bregenz headed south on Route 190, then make a sharp left after crossing the river on a road marked to Wolfurt and Schwarzach. About 21 kilometers (13 miles) farther, at Alberschwende, you'll come to Route 200; follow the signs for **Egg**—a name easy to remember—where you should note the old country houses and if you've not yet bought your Alpine hat, go to the Capo hat and cap factory outlet here (✉ Mühle 534, ☎ 05512/2381–0). It's open weekdays 1–4:30 and sells fashionable headgear as well as Alpine styles. Head on from Egg to Schwarzenberg.

Schwarzenberg

❷ *31 km (19 mi) southeast of Bregenz.*

One of the region's most colorful villages is Schwarzenberg. The artist Angelika Kauffmann (1741–1807), who spent much of her time in England, considered this her home. Even though she became the most prominent female artist of the 18th century, few people in Austria east of the Arlberg mountains knew of her until her picture appeared on a new issue of Austrian currency a few years ago. You can see several of her larger works in the Baroque village church, including an altar painting from about 1800. The Landesmuseum in Bregenz has her portrait of the Duke of Wellington. The town hall has a room dedicated to her. ✉ *Hof 765,* ☎ *05512/3166.* *AS35.* *Tues., Thurs., and weekends 2–4, or by appointment.*

Bezau

❸ *4 km (2 mi) south of Schwarzenberg, 35 km (23 mi) east of Bregenz.*

According to local legend, Bezau's district hall was built on tall columns and was accessible only by ladder. Once the councillors were gathered inside, the ladder was removed until they came to a decision. The **Heimatmuseum,** slightly south of the center, contains more on the town's interesting past, including local folk costumes. ✉ *Ellenbogen 181,* ☎ *05514/2295.* *AS30.* *June, Tues. and Thurs. 2–4; July–Sept., Tues., Thurs., and Sat. 2–4, Wed. 10–noon; Oct.–May, Tues. 2–3.*

At the **Bregenzerwald Museumsbahn,** visitors can see all that is left of the onetime narrow-gauge railroad that ran from Bregenz to Bezau and was abandoned in 1980. The museum has managed to preserve more than 6 kilometers (almost 4 miles) of track to Bersbuch, beyond Schwarzenau, and runs diesel and steam excursions from June to mid-October. ✉ *Bahnhof 147,* ☎ *05514/3174 or 05514/2295.* *Round-trip by steam AS75, by diesel AS55.* *Weekends and holidays at 11, 2, and 3:30; also Thurs. 11 and 2 during July and Aug.*

Dining and Lodging

$$ ★ ✕ **Gasthof Engel.** The Gathof Engel has some of the best Italian food you'll find in Austria. Fresh regional ingredients are served with elegant simplicity here. A whole page of fresh pasta dishes are featured on the menu as well as traditional meat and fish dishes. The wine list has a fine selection of Austrian and Italian vintages. The service is also exceptional; you'll feel like a long lost member of the family. ✉ *Pl. 29,* ☎ *05514/2203. No credit cards. Closed Wed. and Nov.*

$$ ★ ✕🏨 **Gasthof Gams.** Dating from the 17th century, this friendly house in the center of town offers every comfort and is a great spot as a base. The rooms are in attractive country-rustic decor, and the hotel welcomes families. ✉ *Pl. 44, A–6870,* ☎ *05514/2220,* FAX *05514/2220–24. 22 rooms, 5 apartments. Restaurant, bar, pool, sauna, tennis court, exercise room. No credit cards. Closed Nov.–mid-Dec.*

Outdoor Activities and Sports

SKIING

Bezau has four regular trails for cross-country skiers and one lift that takes downhill skiers up to the 5,300-feet Baumgartenhöhe.

Damüls

4 *14 km (9 mi) south of Bezau, 59 km (37 mi) southeast of Bregenz.*

If you turn right onto Route 193 at Au, you'll be on the way leading to Damüls—the road is narrow, with a 14-degree gradient at one point, but when you reach the town, you'll agree the climb was worth it. You're at 4,640 feet, the top of the Bregenzerwald. This is great skiing country in winter. There are enough slopes and lifts, and the crowds are generally elsewhere. In summer the area is knee-deep in wildflowers, but don't pick them; it's against the law. Check the frescoes in the parish church, which date to 1490, just after the church was built, but were rediscovered under later plaster only about 40 years ago.

Lodging

$–$$$ 🏨 **Damülser-Hof.** This group of chalets, spread over a meadow, forms an elegant but friendly hotel complex. It's warmly decorated and cozy, with brick, exposed wood, carpets, and open fireplaces. The rooms—also in country rustic decor—in the older section have been renovated, the ones in the new section are well designed and executed. ✉ *NR 147, A–6884,* ☎ *05510/210–0,* FAX *05510/543. 37 rooms. Restaurant, bar, café, indoor pool, sauna, tennis court, bowling. MC, V. Closed Nov.*

En Route The **Grosswalsertal** (Great Walliser Valley) is extremely scenic. As you start the descent from Damüls heading toward Bludenz along Route 193, look across at the St. Gerold monastery to your right, but after reaching Blons, keep your eyes on the road: It's full of hairpin turns.

Bludenz

5 *22 km (13 mi) southwest of Damüls, 60 km (37 mi) south of Bregenz.*

Bludenz is full of architectural surprises: late 17th-century houses and relics of the ancient town defenses, arcaded shopping streets, and old buildings, all sheltered by mountains rising on the edge of the city—including the Muttersberg peak, nicknamed the "Sun Balcony. Bludenz sits at the junction of five valleys, all of which are well endowed with lifts, good slopes, and hiking trails. People here are pleased when you ask for a hot chocolate instead of coffee. Bludenz is a major chocolate-producing center, as you may detect if the wind is coming from the direction of the factories. The town, adorned with houses and pergolas that seem more Italian than Austrian, is a major transportation crossroads, serviced by frequent bus and train routes.

Dining and Lodging

$–$$ ★ ✕🏨 **Schlosshotel.** Perched on a hill above the castle and overlooking the town, this modern hotel with balconies offers splendid views of the Rätikon mountain range to the south, on the Swiss border; ask for a room in front above the café terrace. The pseudo-rustic decor of the house (lots of plastic) continues into the guest rooms, whose clean lines and modern furnishings are, in fact, attractive. ✉ *Schlosspl. 5, A–6700,* ☎ *05552/63016–0,* FAX *05552/63016–8. 42 rooms. Restaurant, café, miniature golf. AE, DC, MC, V.*

Nenzing

6 *12 km (8 mi) northwest of Bludenz.*

Nenzing is the jumping-off spot for the wildly romantic Gamperdonatal, the valley of the Meng river which rises towards peaks that are 6,500 feet or higher. The valley is hikable, but it's barely passable for cars. The top of the valley is called *Nenzinger Himmel,* literally Nenzing Heaven.

Feldkirch

7 *15 km (9 mi) northwest of Nenzing, 33 km (22 mi) southwest of Bregenz.*

Feldkirch is Vorarlberg's oldest town, with parts dating from the Middle Ages that contribute greatly to the town's romantic character. Picturesque arcades line the narrow main street, and wrought-iron oriels festoon some of the quainter town houses. Marvelous towers and onion domes top some of the buildings, watched over by an assembly of imposing stone blockhouses, which comprise the Schattenburg castle complex just above the town. Although the composer Schubert had no ties to the town, Feldkirch is now home to the annual **Schubertiade** (☞ Nightlife and the Arts, *below*), a small but elegant music festival that has won world renown for the quality of performers—including Jessye Norman and Cecelia Bartoli—with events offered in May, June, and Sept.

An easy walk around the center of Feldkirch will take you to most of the town's highlights. Start at the **St. Nicholas cathedral** on Domplatz. The mystical light in this church built in 1478 comes through the unusual glass windows. From the cathedral, walk toward the river past the district government offices (once a Jesuit monastery) and past the bishop's palace, a block back of Herrengasse, to the **Katzenturm** (literally, "cats' tower," figuratively, "the clergy"), reconstructed by Emperor Maximilian I (1491–1507). This is the most prominent remnant of the town's fortifications and now holds the 7½-ton town bell. Down the Hirschgraben, you'll come to the Chur gate and beside it the **Frauenkirche** (women's church), dedicated to St. Sebastian in 1473. Head down Montfortgasse to where the **Wasserturm** (water tower) and the **Diebsturm** (thieves' tower) stand guard over the Schillerstrasse bridge. Wander down Vorstadt to the **Pulverturm** (powder tower) and across to the **Mühlenturm** (mill tower), whose contrast to the modern Leonhardsplatz is considerable. Turning left, you'll find the St. Johann Church (1218); behind it, the **market square** (market days Tuesday and Saturday), with its arcades; and at the far end, a five-story, half-timbered house. The square is the site of the annual wine festival during the second week of July. Across the pedestrian zone you'll come to Liechtenstein Palace, once the administrative center. On your right is the **Rathaus** of 1493 with its frescoes and paneled rooms.

Overlooking Feldkirch, in the Neustadt, is the 12th-century **Schattenburg,** a massive castle that now houses a museum devoted to the decorative arts and armor. Arcades climb up the hill to frame the castle in an intriguing vista. ✉ *Burggasse 1,* ☏ *05522/71982 or 05522/73467.* *AS25.* *Mar.–Oct., Tues.–Sun. 9–noon and 1–5; Nov.–Feb. by appointment.*

The Arts

The **Schubertiade** presents an impressive series of concerts devoted to Franz Shubert and his circle, offered in churches, castles, and auditoriums in and around Feldkirch and Hohenems during May, June, and September. Everyone from Vladimir Ashkenazy to Dietrich Fischer-Dieskau has performed here, starring along with the Vienna Philharmonic and Vienna Symphony. For tickets and full information, contact the Schubertiade GmbH. ✉ *Schubertiade GmbH, Schubertpl. 1, A–6803,* ☏ *05522/38001–0,* FAX *05522/38005.*

Dining and Lodging

$$$ ✕ **Schäfle.** Tucked away in the heart of the old town, this *Gasthaus* offers atmosphere and food more typical of the countryside. The tables are elegantly set, and you can expect such regional fare as tongue, beef fillet, or perch from Lake Constance, all with delicate sauces and a fine touch. ✉ *Naflastr. 3,* ☏ *05522/72203–0,* FAX *05522/72203–17. AE, DC, MC, V. Closed Sun. and mid-Dec.–mid-Jan. No lunch Mon.*

$$$ ✕ **Central Lowen.** The rooms are large and comfortable but lacking a bit in the charm department. However, the hotel staff is friendly and outgoing. A steam room and sauna are on the premises to help you relax. The hotel's restaurant has a huge selection of Austrian and international favorites. The schnitzel is especially good. ✉ *Schlossgraben 13, A–6800,* ☏ *05522/72070–0,* FAX *05522/72070–5. 68 rooms. Restaurant, sauna, steam room. D, MC, V.*

$$ ★ **Alpenrose.** This charming old burgher house in the center of the old town has been renovated outside and in and offers unusually personal service. Rooms are tastefully done in period furnishings. The house is part of the Best Western group. ✉ *Rosengasse 6, A–6800,* ☏ *05522/72175–0,* FAX *05522/72175–5. 24 rooms. AE, DC, MC, V.*

Hohenems

8 *9 km (6 mi) northeast of Feldkirch, 24 km (15 mi) southwest of Bregenz.*

"The antiquity of Hohenems is so apparent, so forceful, it looms like a presence, a mysterious knight, armored cap-a-pie, visor lowered," observed James Reynolds in his 1956 book *Panorama of Austria,* probably the most beautifully written book about the country (according to some critics). Hohenems is a town dominated by castles, both ruined—the 12th-century Alt-Ems citadel atop the Schlossberg—and ravishing, especially the Schloss Glopper and the **Schloss of Prince-archbishop Marcus Sittcus von Hohenems,** whose elegantly ornate Rittersaal today hosts Schubertiads to rival any in the world. Empress Elizabeth of Austria used to stay in this castle toward the end of her tragically shortened life and, in fact, used the title of Countess Hohenems when she traveled "anonymously" around the world. In conjuction with the **Schubertiade festival** based in Feldkirch every summer, the Schloss Hohenems also becomes the elegant setting for concerts during the latter half of June; for information, *see* The Arts *in* Feldkirch, *above*. The **parish church,** dedicated to St. Carlo Borromeo (half-brother of the wife of Marcus Sittcus) and rebuilt in 1797, has a noted painted altarpiece of the Coronation of the Virgin.

Dornbirn

9 *4 km (2 mi) northeast of Hohenems, 13 km (8 mi) southwest of Bregenz.*

Dornbirn, the industrial center of Vorarlberg, is known as the "city of textiles." The annual Dornbirn Fair, held in mid-summer to tie in with the Bregenz Music Festival, shows a range of goods and technologies, but textiles are especially featured.

Dining

$$$ ★ ✕ **Rotes Haus.** The "red" in the name of this 1639 gabled wood house in the center of town refers to bull's blood, originally used as pigment for the facade, which is still basically red, with decorative panels. Traditional cuisine is served here in a series of charming small rooms. You'll find lamb, game, and fish on the unusual menu. ✉ *Marktpl. 13,* ☎ *05572/31555,* FAX *05572/31625. AE, DC, MC, V. Closed Sun.*

THE ARLBERG AND MONTAFON RESORTS

The Western Alps are a haven for those who love the great outdoors. It's also a region that provides great getaway space and privacy—Ernest Hemingway came to Schruns to write *The Sun Also Rises* and, more recently, Princess Di came to Lech with William and Harry to escape from the media. In the spring, summer, and fall, travelers delight in riding, tennis, swimming and, of course, hiking the Montafon valley, which is dominated by the "Matternhorn of Austria," the Zimba peak, and probably the most attractive of Vorarlberg's many tourist-frequented valleys. When the first snowflakes begin to fall, skiers head to the hills to take advantage of the Arlberg mountain range, the highest in the Lechtal Alps. If you'll be avoiding the crowds that can clog Austria's other resorts, keep in mind that Lech and Zürs are resorts where the seeing is almost as important as the skiing. If you're traveling by train, **Langen** is the stop closest to the ski resorts; Route S16/316 takes you by car from Bludenz to Langen and beyond to Route 198 heading north.

Brand

10 *70 km (43 mi) south of Bregenz.*

Since it was first settled by Swiss exiles centuries ago, the lush and beautiful Brand Valley has attracted many travelers interested in visiting the enormous glaciers and one of the largest lakes in the Alps located near the town. Today, the town is known as a winter sports center and as a health resort. Brand's hotels lie at the foot of the Scesaplana mountain group (which marks the Swiss border and is the highest range in the Rätikon), and if you are fond of hiking, you can climb by easy stages along the forest paths without much exertion to the famous glacier lake, the **Lünersee.** In winter, the skiing is excellent, and there is a short, modern gondola-type cable railway up the Niggenkopf (5,500 feet) to take you up to the finest ski slopes in just a few minutes. Anyone interested in geology should pay a visit to the tiny village **"trowel stone" chapel.** It's built of local rock which can be cut into shape quite easily with an ordinary saw; when exposed to the air, the masonry then shrinks slightly and hardens and becomes rather brittle. There are no rail lines to Brand, so the best way to reach the resort is to train to Bludenz and take the bus from there to Brand.

Dining and Lodging

$$ ✕🏨 **Sporthotel Beck.** The Beck family runs this sports hotel in the shadow of the nearby mountains. Rooms are comfortably furnished and light-filled and have flower-bedecked balconies that look out over the spectacular view. The hotel's restaurant features classic Austrian fare like schnitzel but also lighter dishes for those watching their waistlines. Sports enthusiasts will like the wide range of activities available in the hotel, as well as the great mountain-climbing nearby. ✉ *A-6708,* ☎ *05559/306,* FAX *05559/306–70. Restaurant, pool, massage, driving range, exercise room, horseback riding. AE, DC, MC, V.*

Outdoor Activities and Sports

GOLF

Golf Club Brand, set in a stunning Alpine valley and Vorarlberg's first course, has 9 holes, par 68. ☎ *05559/450,* FAX *05559/450–20.* ⏲ *May–Oct.*

HIKING

From a leisurely stroll to serious mountain trekking, Brand has hiking galore. The most noted trail runs from Brand via Innertal (with a chair-lift up to Melkboden) and the Schattenlagant-Alpe to the lower end of the Lünersee. Inquire at the local tourist office for maps.

SKIING

The Brandnertal has ski passes good for three, six, or 13 days, with rates for adults, children, and senior citizens varying according to season. The regional tourist office has details. Rental equipment is available.

Schruns-Tschagguns

⓫–⓬ *10 km (6 mi) northeast of Brand, 60 km (39 mi) south of Bregenz.*

Author Ernest Hemingway spent many winters at the Schruns–Tschagguns skiing area in the Montafon valley. Today, neither of the towns—sited across the Ill river from each other—is as fashionable as the resorts on the Arlberg, but the views over the Ferwall Alps to the east and the mighty Rätikon on the western side of the valley are unsurpassed anywhere in Austria. In winter, the powdery snow provides wonderful skiing. Thanks to an integrated system of ski passes and lifts, the Montafon Valley is considered a "ski-stadium" by skiers-in-the-know. They love to head for the Hochjoch-Zamang—the main peak at Schruns—to have lunch on the spectacularly-sited sun terrace of the Kapell restaurant, then on to Grabs-Golm over the river in Tschagguns. Others prefer the Silvretta-Nova run at Gaschurn. In summer, the heights are given over to climbers and hikers, the mountain streams to trout fishermen, and the lowlands to tennis players.

Dining and Lodging

$$$–$$$$ ✕🏨 **Löwen.** The modified chalet design of this hotel in the center of town makes it look huge, but inside, the country style works well, and the rustic dark-wood exterior is carried over elegantly into the modern rooms with balconies. The hotel is set in the center of a grassy garden platform, which forms a green belt around the main building and serves as a roof for the ground-floor pool and restaurants. The excellent *Edelweiss* restaurant, with its graceful table settings (candlelit at night), serves regional specialties done with a flair. ✉ *Silvrettastr. 8, A–6780,* ☎ *05556/7141,* FAX *05556/73553. 85 rooms. 4 restaurants,*

bar, indoor pool, sauna, exercise room, dance club, parking. AE, DC, MC, V. Closed mid-Apr.–mid-May and mid-Oct.–mid-Dec.

$$–$$$ ★ ✕ **Alpenhof Messmer.** Set on a lush green hillside slightly out of the center of town, this oversize double chalet welcomes you with fireplaces and comfortable rustic furnishings. Most of the imaginatively decorated rooms have balconies with a view over the town. It is a member of the Silencehotel group. The family management is particularly friendly and helpful, and the same goes for the restaurant staff. ✉ *Grappaweg 6, A–6780,* ☎ *05556/72664–0,* FAX *05556/76156. 35 rooms. Restaurant, bar, indoor pool, sauna, exercise room, parking. No credit cards. Closed mid-Apr.–mid-May and mid-Nov.–mid-Dec.*

$$–$$$ ✕ **Kurhotel Montafon.** This hotel caters to a guest's every need and is well equipped for those seeking the latest beauty treatments. Rooms are light filled and tastefully furnished, and many have balconies where you can savor the view. The restaurant has both traditional Austrian dishes plus low-calorie fare. ✉ *Ausserlitzstr., A–6780,* ☎ *05556–72791,* FAX *05556/72791–70. 50 rooms. Restaurant, indoor pool, sauna, health spa. AE, DC, MC, V.*

Outdoor Activities and Sports

FISHING

The local mountain streams and rivers are full of fish. Licenses are available; ask the regional tourist office for detailed information on seasons and locations.

SKIING

Ski passes are available for three, six, or 13 days, with rates for adults, children, and senior citizens varying according to season. The regional tourist office has details. Rental equipment is available.

Stuben

13 *38 km (23 mi) northeast of Schruns, 29 km (23 mi) east of Bludenz.*

Traveling through the Montafon via Route 316 you'll come to Stuben, hometown of that pioneer of Alpine ski techniques, Hannes Schneider. Appropriately, the magnificent skiing at 4,600 feet from December to the end of April makes Stuben popular among serious skiers who are willing to forgo the stylish resorts, such as Lech, just up the road. It has skiing links with St. Anton, Lech, and Zürs. The town is poised right above the Arlberg Tunnel, so travelers can't—appearance to the contrary on maps—arrive there via rail from Innsbruck or Bregenz. They must detrain at Langen am Arlberg and then take a bus on to Stuben.

Dining and Lodging

$$$ ✕ **Hotel Mondschein.** A traditional Alpine country house, dating back to 1739, is the setting for this hotel. A welcoming exterior, accented with pink geraniums in flower boxes and dark green shutters, greets visitors as they come down the street from the town church. Inside, the greeting is almost as warm as the fires blazing in the hotel's hearths, while the pricey restaurant prides itself on its fish selections. Unlike other Stuben hostelries, this one is right in the center of town. Depending on the season, rates include half board. The hotel is closed May and September 15 through December 15. ✉ *A-6762,* ☎ *05582–511,* FAX *05582–736. 25 rooms with bath. Restaurant, health club, indoor pool, baby sitting. No credit cards.*

En Route Just past Stuben, the Flexen Road (Route 198) over the Arlberg pass begins its descent to the Züs valley. It is protected from avalanches by concrete or timbered roofing; a triumph of engineering, it looks like a giant caterpillar crawling along the face of the cliffs. In summer, the treeless slopes are covered with Alpine flora.

Zürs

14 *13 km (8 mi) north of Stuben, 90 km (56 mi) southeast of Bregenz.*

The chosen resort of royalty and show business on this side of the Arlberg, Zürs is little more than a collection of large hotels. Perched at 5,600 feet, it is strictly a winter-sports community; when the season is over, the hotels close. But Zürs is more exclusive than Lech and certainly more so than Gstaad or St. Moritz in Switzerland—this is the place wealthy emirs bring their private ski instructors. In most hotels, you'll be asked to take full board, so there are relatively few "public" restaurants in town and little chance to dine around. But the hotel dining rooms are elegant; in many, jacket and tie are de rigueur in the evening.

Dining and Lodging

$$$$ ✕🏨 **Alpenhof.** The timber-frame windows here face a great panorama, but who has time to admire the scenery? If you're not on the slopes (the ski school is next door), the house offers dozens of other diversions. The Oriental carpets alone are worthy of a palace. The rooms are elegant yet comfortable. Prices include full board; half board is available by arrangement. ✉ *A-6763,* ☎ *05583/2191,* FAX *05583/3330; out of season,* ☎ *05572/21777. 41 rooms. Restaurant, piano bar, indoor pool, sauna, exercise room. No credit cards. Closed mid-Apr.–Nov.*

$$$$ ✕🏨 **Lorünser.** The hospitable elegance of this hotel draws royalty, including Prince Albert of Monaco and Queen Beatrix of the Netherlands. In the reception area, carved ceiling beams, open fireplaces, and attractive accessories create a welcoming ambience. Rustic wood is used to good effect in the stylish guest rooms. The dining room is open to nonguests with reservations. Prices include full board; half-board by arrangement. ✉ *A-6763,* ☎ *05583/2254–0,* FAX *05583/2254–44. 74 rooms. Restaurant, bar, sauna, exercise room. No credit cards. Closed mid-Apr.–early Dec.*

$$$$ ★ ✕🏨 **Zürserhof.** Once the abode of Gräf Valley Tattenbach and his countess, this world-famous hostelry at the north end of town comprises five chalets—five of the most luxurious and expensive chalets in the world (prices can near $900 a day with board). About a third of the accommodations are elegant, spacious apartments or suites; many have fireplaces, the newer ones have Roman baths. The family-run house has nevertheless managed to preserve the intimate atmosphere. Prices include half board. When celebrities want to be private and exclusive, they come here. ✉ *A-6763,* ☎ *05583/2513–0,* FAX *05583/3165. 97 rooms and suites/apartments with bath. Restaurant, bar, indoor pool, beauty salon, sauna, driving range, tennis court, exercise room, dance club. No credit cards. Closed mid-Apr.–Nov.*

$$$–$$$$ ✕🏨 **Central-Sporthotel Edelweiss.** This 19th-century house has received an agreeable face-lift, giving it a colorful, contemporary interior, including the guest rooms. The Zürserl disco is *the* place in the evening. The restaurant, Chesa Verde, is the best in town, offering fresh fish, game, and regional standards, but be sure to reserve. Prices include half board. ✉ *A-6763,* ☎ *05583/2662,* FAX *05583/3533. 66 rooms, 5 apartments. Restaurant, sauna, exercise room, dance club. No credit cards. Closed mid-Apr.–Nov.*

$$–$$$$ ★ 🏨 **Alpenrose-Post.** This sprawling chalet, with a facade of dark wood, draws a lot of celebrities, in part because of the friendly reception by the family management. The rooms vary from spacious to compact, from elegant (four-posters) to simple but comfortable; some have balconies. Ask for a room on the south side. Prices include half board. ✉ *A-6763,* ☎ *05583/2271–0,* FAX *05583/2271–79. 97 rooms. Restaurant, bar, indoor pool, sauna, exercise room. No credit cards. Closed mid-Apr.–mid-June and mid-Sept.–Nov.*

Outdoor Activities and Sports

SKIING

There are two main chair lifts: east of Zürs, a lift takes you to Hexenboden (7,600 feet) and Trittkopf (7,800 feet), with a restaurant and sun terrace; to the west, a lift takes you to Seekopf (7,000 feet), where there is another restaurant. This is avalanche country, so skiers need to be particularly alert.

Lech

15 *9 km (5 mi) north of Zürs, 90 km (56 mi) southeast of Bregenz.*

Just 3 miles up the road from the Zürs resort, Lech is a full-fledged community—which some argue detracts from its fashionableness. But there are more hotels in Lech, better tourist facilities, bigger ski schools, more shops, more nightlife, and prices nearly as high as those in neighboring Zürs. Zürs has the advantage of altitude, but Lech is a less artificial and very pretty Alpine village. Besides, Princess Diana chose this place to take a winter vacation with Harry and William. Be sure to check with the hotel of your choice about meal arrangements; most hotels require you to take full board. You can't get to Lech via rail; take the train to Langen am Arlberg station stop, then transfer to buses.

Dining and Lodging

$$$$ ★ ✕ **Brunnenhof.** This cozy dinner restaurant in the hotel of the same name, slightly north of the town center, has gotten increasingly better in recent years, justifying the tag "Gourmet-Hotel." The menu has offered such innovative dishes as fillet of perch over a bed of squash, and fillet of beef with artichoke sauce. The wine list includes selections from Austria, France, Italy, Spain, Australia, and California. Be sure to reserve well in advance, for this is one of the best restaurants in town, and it's regularly full. ✉ *A-6764,* ☎ *05583/2349,* FAX *05583/2349–59. Reservations essential. AE, DC, MC, V. Closed Sun. and mid-Apr.–mid-Dec.*

$$$–$$$$ ★ ✕🏨 **Gasthof Post.** A gemütlich atmosphere dominates in this green-shuttered chalet hotel, with murals, flower boxes, and a paneled wood interior. The á la carte restaurant is the best in town; try the medallions of lamb or grilled salmon, but save space for one of the outstanding desserts. ✉ *Dorf-11, A–6764,* ☎ *05583/2206–0,* FAX *05583/2206–23. 40 rooms. Restaurant, bar, indoor pool, sauna. No credit cards. Closed mid-Apr.–June and mid-Sept.–Nov.*

$$$–$$$$ ★ ✕🏨 **Montana.** In Oberlech, in the pedestrian zone just above the town, you'll find this easygoing hotel, run by an outgoing expatriate Alsatian. He has installed a *Vinothek,* or "wine library," where tastings are held and wine is sold by the glass or bottle. The bright interior colors contrast well with the weathered wood; the rooms are friendly and snug. The ski slopes are literally outside the door. The restaurant, *Zur Kanne,* has French overtones and is remarkable for its attention to detail, both in the kitchen and in the table settings. Ingredients are fresh daily, and dishes range from lobster hash to beef fillet gratinée. Prices for hotel include half board. ✉ *A–6764,* ☎ *05583/2460,* FAX *05583/2460–38. 42 rooms. Restaurant, bar, indoor pool, sauna, tennis court, exercise room. No credit cards. Closed May–Nov.*

$$–$$$$ ✕🏨 **Krone.** Directly across the street from two of the main lifts, this family-managed hotel grew out of a 250-year-old house and now belongs to the RomantikHotel group. The adaptations and modernization have not affected the general ambience of comfort and well-being that's reflected in the beamed ceilings, tile stoves, and Oriental carpets. The rooms have tile floors with Oriental rugs. The restaurant, one of

the town's three best, is noted for its game and regional specialties; try the fillet of whitefish on cucumber, or rack of lamb. ✉ *A–6764,* ☎ *05583/2551,* FAX *05583/2551–81. 56 rooms. Restaurant, sauna, exercise room, fishing, dance club. No credit cards. Closed mid-Apr.–mid-June, Oct., and Nov.*

$$ **Solaria.** This hillside chalet, fairly close to the center of town, is not far from the lower station of two of the lifts, one of which runs in summer as well. The hotel is family-run and friendly; the rooms are cheerful and cozy. Half board is mandatory in winter. ✉ *NR 130, A–6764,* ☎ *05583/2214,* FAX *05583/3456. 18 rooms, 4 apartments. Restaurant, bar, children's program. No credit cards. Closed Apr.–Nov.*

Nightlife and the Arts

Lech is known almost as much for après-ski and nightlife as for the snow and the slopes. You can join the crowd as early as 11 AM at the outdoor and famed **Red Umbrella** bar for snacks and drinks at the Petersboden Sport Hotel at Oberlech (☎ 05583/3232). Activity continues at the late afternoon tea dance at the **Tannbergerhof** (☎ 05583/2202). Hot après-ski spots include the bars in the **Goldener Berg** (☎ 05583/2205–0), and **Burg** (☎ 05583/2291–0) hotels in Oberlech, and **Monzabon** (☎ 05583/2104) in Lech. Among the popular places for a mid-evening drink (starting at 9:30) are **Pfefferkörndl** in the Pfefferkörn Hotel (☎ 05583/2224–429), and **Mohnenfluh** in Oberlech (☎ 05583/3311–0). Also check on **Walch's Italiener** (☎ 05583/3734) and the **Klausur** bar (☎ 05583/3500–0) in the Almhof-Schneider hotel in Tannberg. The **Kronen Bar** in the Hotel Krone (☞ Dining and Lodging, *above*) opens at 9 PM and goes on until 2 or 3 AM. Ask at the tourist office about the "in" spots, as the crowd tends to move around. Prices vary from place to place, but in general, you'll pay AS65–AS80 for a mixed drink.

Outdoor Activities and Sports

SKIING

Lech is linked with Oberlech and Zürs with more than 30 ski lifts, all accessed by the regional ski pass, which allows skiers to take in the entire region. You can ski right from Zürs to Lech. In addition, there is a vast network of cross-country trails.

VORARLBERG A TO Z

Arriving and Departing

By Car

From Germany, the autobahn (Route A14/E17) takes you into Bregenz; roads from Switzerland lead to Lustenau and Hohenems; from Liechtenstein, Route 16 (Route 191 in Austria) goes to Feldkirch; and Routes A12/E60 from eastern Austria and 315 from Italy meet at Landeck become Route 316/E60, then head westward through the Arlberg auto tunnel (toll AS150). Alternatively, your car (and you) can get to Vorarlberg on the car train that runs to Feldkirch from Vienna, Graz, or Villach.

By Plane

The closest major airport is Zürich, 120 kilometers (75 miles) away. Munich is 190 kilometers (119 miles) away, and Innsbruck is 200 kilometers (125 miles) away. Several trains a day serve Bregenz from the Zürich Kloten airport. In winter a bus leaves the airport Friday, Saturday, and Sunday at 12:30 PM for resorts in the Arlberg and Montafon regions. You can book through Swissair. On the Austrian side, call

Arlberg Express (✉ Horst Fritz, Klösterle, ☎ 05582/226, FAX 05582/580) for information and bookings.

Rheintalflug flies three times daily weekdays, once a day weekends each way between Vienna and Altenrhein on Lake Constance in Switzerland. A direct bus service takes passengers free of charge to and from the airport to Bregenz, Dornbirn, and Lustenau. *In Vienna,* ☎ *0222/711–10–6911,* FAX *0222/711–10–6915; in Vorarlberg,* ☎ *05574/48800,* FAX *05574/48800–85; in Switzerland,* ☎ *071/435120,* FAX *071/435140.*

By Ship

From May to October, passenger ships of the Austrian railroad's Bodensee **White Fleet** (☎ 05574/42868, FAX 05574/44341–128) connect Bregenz with Lindau, Friedrichshafen, Meersburg, and Konstanz on the German side of the lake. The Eurailpass and Austrian rail passes are valid on these ships. You'll need your passport.

By Train

The main rail line connecting with Vienna and Innsbruck enters Vorarlberg at Langen after coming through the Arlberg tunnel. Both the *Arlberg* and *Orient Express* trains follow this route, which then swings through Bludenz to Feldkirch. There the line splits, with the Arlberg express going south into Liechtenstein and Switzerland, the other branch heading through Dornbirn to Bregenz and on to Lindau in Germany.

Getting Around

By Boat

A *Bodensee-Pass* includes the Swiss and German as well as the Austrian lake steamers, all at half price, plus area trains, buses, and cable car lifts. The pass comes in one-, three-, and seven-day variations; the Vorarlberg information offices in Bregenz and Vienna have details.

By Bus

Post office, railroad, and private bus services connect all the towns and villages not served by the railroad, using tracked vehicles when necessary in winter. Even so, some of the highest roads become impassable, and the only transportation is via helicopter or horse-drawn sleigh.

By Car

A car is the most flexible way of getting about in Vorarlberg, but the roads can be treacherous in winter. You are not allowed on some mountain roads in the Arlberg without chains, which you can rent from a number of service stations.

By Train

The railroads connect the main centers of Vorarlberg remarkably well; besides the lines described above, the Montafoner electric (with occasional steam) rail line runs parallel to the highway from Bludenz southeast to Schruns.

Contacts and Resources

Car Rentals

Avis (✉ Schwefel 53A, A–6850 Dornbirn, ☎ 05572/29780). **Hertz** (✉ Immler Schneeweiss, Am Brand 2, A–6900 Bregenz, ☎ 05574/44995).

Emergencies

In case of an emergency, call 133 for the **police,** 144 for an **ambulance,** and 122 for the **fire department.**

Visitor Information

The headquarters for tourist information about Vorarlberg is based in Bregenz (✉ Römerstr. 7, A–6901 Bregenz, ☎ 05574/42525–0, FAX 05574/42525–5); another regional office is based in Vienna (✉ Singerstr. 12, A–1010 Vienna, ☎ 0222/513–9359, FAX 0222/513–9116–76).

Other regional tourist offices (*Verkehrsamt, Verkehrsverein,* or *Fremdenverkehrsamt*) are located throughout the province at the following addresses.

Bezau (✉ Pl. 39, A–6870, ☎ 05514/2295, FAX 05514/3129). **Bludenz** (✉ Werdenberger Str. 42, A–6700, ☎ 05552/62170, FAX 05552/67597). **Bregenz** (✉ Anton-Schneider-Str. 4a, A–6900, ☎ 05574/43391–0, FAX 05574/43391–10). **Feldkirch** (✉ Herrengasse 12, A–6800, ☎ 05522/73467, FAX 05522/79867). **Lech** (✉ A–6764, ☎ 05583/2161–0, FAX 05583/3155). **Montafon Valley** (✉ Silbertalerstr. 1, A–6780 Schruns, ☎ 05556/72253, FAX 05556/74856). **Zürs** (✉ A–6763, ☎ 05583/2245, FAX 05583/2982).

GERMAN VOCABULARY

To people who have studied only Romance languages in school, the very sight of written German is terrifying—particularly when it's printed in that Gothic script that resembles old English lettering. Take heart, you are not alone. Mark Twain once wrote a funny piece called "The Horrible German Language," expounding on the German habit of tacking pieces of words together until the result fills an entire line. But never mind—you won't be required to speak it, and the section below will help.

Remember that the Austrians sometimes have just as much trouble speaking (and writing) English as you do with German. Witness the sign in a ski-resort hotel:

Not to perambulate the corridors
in the hours of repose
in the boots of ascension

An asterisk (*) denotes common usage in Austria.

Basics

English	German	Pronunciation
Yes/no	Ja/nein	yah/nine
Please	Bitte	**bit**-uh
May I?	Darf ich?	darf isch?
Thank you (very much)	Danke (vielen Dank)	**dahn**-kuh (**fee**-len dahnk)
You're welcome	Bitte, gern geschehen	**bit**-uh, gairn ge**shay**-un
Excuse me	Entschuldigen Sie zee	ent-**shool**-di-gen
What? (What did you say?)	Wie, bitte?	vee, **bit**-uh?
Can you tell me?	Können Sie mir sagen?	kunnen zee meer **sah**-gen?
Do you know ______?	Wissen Sie ______?	**viss**-en zee
I'm sorry	Es tut mir leid.	es toot meer lite
Good day	Guten Tag	**goo**-ten tahk
Goodbye	Auf Wiedersehen	owf **vee**-der-zane
Good morning	Guten Morgen	**goo**-ten **mor**-gen
Good evening	Guten Abend	**goo**-ten **ah**-bend
Good night	Gute Nacht	**goo**-tuh nahkt
Mr./Mrs.	Herr/Frau	hair/frow
Miss	Fräulein	**froy**-line
Pleased to meet you	Sehr erfreut.	zair air-**froyt**
How are you?	Wie geht es Ihnen?	vee **gate** es **ee**-nen?
Very well, thanks.	Sehr gut, danke.	sair goot, **dahn**-kuh
And you?	Und Ihnen?	oont **ee**-nen?
Hi!	*Servus!	**sair**-voos
Hello! (on the telephone)	Hallo!	**hah**-lo

Days of the Week

Sunday	Sonntag	**zohn**-tahk
Monday	Montag	**moan**-tahk
Tuesday	Dienstag	**deens**-tahk
Wednesday	Mittwoch	**mitt**-voak
Thursday	Donnerstag	**doe**-ners-tahk
Friday	Freitag	**fry**-tahk
Saturday	Samstag	**zahm**-stahk

Useful Phrases

Do you speak English?	Sprechen Sie Englisch?	**shprek**-hun zee **eng**-glisch?
I don't speak German.	Ich spreche kein Deutsch.	isch **shprek**-uh kine doych
Please speak slowly.	Bitte sprechen Sie langsam.	**bit**-uh **shprek**-en zee **lahng**-zahm
I don't understand	Ich verstehe nicht nicht	isch fair-**shtay**-uh
I understand	Ich verstehe	isch fair-**shtay**-uh
I don't know	Ich weiss nicht	isch vice nicht
Excuse me/sorry	Entschuldigen Sie	ent-**shool**-di-gen zee
I am American/ British	Ich bin Ameri-kaner(in)/Eng-länder(in)	isch bin a-mer-i-**kahn**-er(in)/**eng**-len-der(in)
What is your name?	Wie heissen Sie?	vee **high**-sen zee
My name is . . .	ich heiße . . .	isch **high**-suh
What time is it?	Wieviel Uhr ist es? *Wie spät ist es?	**vee**-feel oor ist es **vee** shpate ist es
It is one, two, three . . . o'clock.	Es ist ein, zwei, drei . . . Uhr.	es ist ine, tsvy, dry . . . oor
Yes, please/	Ja, bitte/	yah **bi**-tuh/
No, thank you	Nein, danke	**nine** dahng-kuh
How?	Wie?	vee
When?	Wann? (as conjunction, als)	vahn (ahls)
This/next week	Diese/nächste Woche	**dee**-zuh/**nehks**-tuh **vo**-kuh
This/next year	Dieses/nächstes Jahr	**dee**-zuz/ **nehks**-tuhs yahr
Yesterday/today/ tomorrow	Gestern/heute/ morgen	**geh**-stern/ **hoy**-tuh/**mor**-gen
This morning/ afternoon	Heute morgen/ nachmittag	**hoy**-tuh **mor**-gen/ **nahk**-mit-tahk
Tonight	Heute Nacht	**hoy**-tuh nahkt
What?	Was?	vahss
What is it?	Was ist es?	**vahss** ist es
Why?	Warum?	vah-**rum**
Who/whom?	Wer/wen?	vair/vehn
Who is it?	Wer ist da?	vair ist dah

I'd like to have . . .	Ich hätte gerne . . .	isch **het**-uh gairn
a room	ein Zimmer	ine **tsim**-er
the key	den Schlüssel	den **shluh**-sul
a newspaper	eine Zeitung	**i**-nuh **tsy**-toong
a stamp	eine Briefmarke	**i**-nuh **breef**-mark-uh
a map	eine Karte	i-nuh **cart**-uh
a city map	ein Stadtplan	ine **staad**-plahn
I'd like to buy . . .	ich möchte . . . kaufen	isch **merhk**-tuh **cow**-fen
cigarettes	Zigaretten	tzig-ah-**ret**-ten
I'd like to exchange . . .	Ich möchte . . . wechseln	isch **merhk**-tuh . . . **vex**-eln/
dollars to schillings	Dollars in Schillinge	dohl-lars in **shil**-ling-uh
pounds to schillings	Pfunde in Schillinge	pfoonde in **shil**-ling-uh
How much is it?	Wieviel kostet das? dahss?	**vee**-feel **cost**-et
It's expensive/ cheap	Es ist teuer/billig	es ist **toy**-uh/**bill**-ig
A little/a lot	ein wenig/sehr	ine **vay**-nig/zair
More/less	mehr/weniger	mair/**vay**-nig-er
Enough/too much/ too little	genug/zuviel/ zu wenig	geh-**noog**/tsoo-**feel**/ tsoo **vay**-nig
Telegram	Telegramm	tel-eh-**gram**
I am ill/sick	Ich bin krank	isch bin krahnk
I need . . .	Ich brauche . . .	isch **brow**-khuh
a doctor	einen Arzt	I-nen artst
the police	die Polizei	dee po-lee-**tsai**
help	Hilfe	**hilf**-uh
Stop!	Halt!	hahlt
Fire!	Feuer!	**foy**-er
Caution/Look out!	Achtung!/Vorsicht!	**ahk**-tung/**for**-zicht
Is this bus/train/ subway going to . . . ?	Fährt dieser Bus/ dieser Zug/ diese U-Bahn nach . . . ?	fayrt **deez**er buhs/ **deez**-er tsook/ **deez**-uh **oo**-bahn nahk . . .
Where is . . .	Wo ist . . .	**vo** ist
the train station?	der Bahnhof?	dare **bahn**-hof
the subway station?	die U-Bahn-Station?	dee **oo**-bahn-**staht**-sion
the bus stop?	die Bushaltestelle?	dee **booss**-hahlt-uh-**shtel**-uh
the airport?	der Flugplatz? *der Flughafen?	dare **floog**-plats dare **floog**-hafen
the hospital?	das Krankenhaus? house	dahs **krahnk**-en-
the elevator?	der Aufzug?	dare **owf**-tsoog
the telephone?	das Telefon?	dahs te-le-**fone**
the rest room?	die Toilette?	dee twah-**let**-uh

open/closed	offen/geschlossen	**off**-en/ge-**schloss**-en
left/right	links/rechts	links/recktz
straight ahead	geradeaus	geh-**rah**-day-owws
is it near/far?	ist es in der Nähe/ist es weit?	ist es in dare **nay**-uh? ist es

INDEX

T

Fodor's Travel Publications

Available at bookstores everywhere, or call 1-800-533-6478, 24 hours a day.

Gold Guides

U.S.

Alaska
Arizona
Boston
California
Cape Cod, Martha's Vineyard, Nantucket
The Carolinas & the Georgia Coast
Chicago
Colorado
Florida
Hawai'i
Las Vegas, Reno, Tahoe
Los Angeles
Maine, Vermont, New Hampshire
Maui & Lāna'i
Miami & the Keys
New England
New Orleans
New York City
Pacific North Coast
Philadelphia & the Pennsylvania Dutch Country
The Rockies
San Diego
San Francisco
Santa Fe, Taos, Albuquerque
Seattle & Vancouver
The South
U.S. & British Virgin Islands
USA
Virginia & Maryland
Washington, D.C.

Foreign

Australia
Austria
The Bahamas
Belize & Guatemala
Bermuda
Canada
Cancún, Cozumel, Yucatán Peninsula
Caribbean
China
Costa Rica
Cuba
The Czech Republic & Slovakia
Eastern & Central Europe
Europe
Florence, Tuscany & Umbria
France
Germany
Great Britain
Greece
Hong Kong
India
Ireland
Israel
Italy
Japan
London
Madrid & Barcelona
Mexico
Montréal & Québec City
Moscow, St. Petersburg, Kiev
The Netherlands, Belgium & Luxembourg
New Zealand
Norway
Nova Scotia, New Brunswick, Prince Edward Island
Paris
Portugal
Provence & the Riviera
Scandinavia
Scotland
Singapore
South Africa
South America
Southeast Asia
Spain
Sweden
Switzerland
Thailand
Tokyo
Toronto
Turkey
Vienna & the Danube

Fodor's Special-Interest Guides

Caribbean Ports of Call
The Complete Guide to America's National Parks
Family Adventures
Gay Guide to the USA
Halliday's New England Food Explorer
Halliday's New Orleans Food Explorer
Healthy Escapes
Kodak Guide to Shooting Great Travel Pictures
Net Travel
Nights to Imagine
Rock & Roll Traveler USA
Sunday in New York
Sunday in San Francisco
Walt Disney World, Universal Studios and Orlando
Walt Disney World for Adults
Where Should We Take the Kids? California
Where Should We Take the Kids? Northeast
Worldwide Cruises and Ports of Call

Special Series

Affordables

Caribbean

Europe

Florida

France

Germany

Great Britain

Italy

London

Paris

Fodor's Bed & Breakfasts and Country Inns

America

California

The Mid-Atlantic

New England

The Pacific Northwest

The South

The Southwest

The Upper Great Lakes

The Berkeley Guides

California

Central America

Eastern Europe

Europe

France

Germany & Austria

Great Britain & Ireland

Italy

London

Mexico

New York City

Pacific Northwest & Alaska

Paris

San Francisco

Compass American Guides

Arizona

Canada

Chicago

Colorado

Hawaii

Idaho

Hollywood

Las Vegas

Maine

Manhattan

Montana

New Mexico

New Orleans

Oregon

San Francisco

Santa Fe

South Carolina

South Dakota

Southwest

Texas

Utah

Virginia

Washington

Wine Country

Wisconsin

Wyoming

Fodor's Citypacks

Atlanta

Hong Kong

London

New York City

Paris

Rome

San Francisco

Washington, D.C.

Fodor's Español

California

Caribe Occidental

Caribe Oriental

Gran Bretaña

Londres

Mexico

Nueva York

Paris

Fodor's Exploring Guides

Australia

Boston & New England

Britain

California

Caribbean

China

Egypt

Florence & Tuscany

Florida

France

Germany

Ireland

Israel

Italy

Japan

London

Mexico

Moscow & St. Petersburg

New York City

Paris

Prague

Provence

Rome

San Francisco

Scotland

Singapore & Malaysia

Spain

Thailand

Turkey

Venice

Fodor's Flashmaps

Boston

New York

San Francisco

Washington, D.C.

Fodor's Pocket Guides

Acapulco

Atlanta

Barbados

Jamaica

London

New York City

Paris

Prague

Puerto Rico

Rome

San Francisco

Washington, D.C.

Mobil Travel Guides

America's Best Hotels & Restaurants

California & the West

Frequent Traveler's Guide to Major Cities

Great Lakes

Mid-Atlantic

Northeast

Northwest & Great Plains

Southeast

Southwest & South Central

Rivages Guides

Bed and Breakfasts of Character and Charm in France

Hotels and Country Inns of Character and Charm in France

Hotels and Country Inns of Character and Charm in Italy

Hotels and Country Inns of Character and Charm in Paris

Hotels and Country Inns of Character and Charm in Portugal

Hotels and Country Inns of Character and Charm in Spain

Short Escapes

Britain

France

New England

Near New York City

Fodor's Sports

Golf Digest's Best Places to Play

Skiing USA

USA Today The Complete Four Sport Stadium Guide

Fodor's Vacation Planners

Great American Learning Vacations

Great American Sports & Adventure Vacations

Great American Vacations

Great American Vacations for Travelers with Disabilities

National Parks and Seashores of the East

National Parks of the West